Philosophy of Law and Legal Theory

for Dick Hull

Philosophy of Law and Legal Theory

An Anthology

EDITED BY
Dennis Patterson

Blackwell
Publishing

350 Main Street, Malden, MA 02148–5018, USA
108 Cowley Road, Oxford OX4 1JF, UK
550 Swanston Street, Carlton South, Melbourne, Victoria 3053, Australia
Kurfürstendamm 57, 10707 Berlin, Germany

First published 2003 by Blackwell Publishing Ltd

Library of Congress Cataloging-in-Publication Data

Philosophy of law and legal theory: an anthology / edited by Dennis Patterson.
   p.cm.
   Includes bibliographical references and index.
   ISBN 0–631–20287–0 (hb : alk. paper)—ISBN 0–631–20288–9 (pbk.: alk. paper)
   1. Law—Philosophy. I. Patterson, Dennis M. (Dennis Michael), 1955–

K235 .P483 2002
340′.1—dc21

2002074364

A catalogue record for this title is available from the British Library.

Set in 9.5/11.5 Ehrhardt
by Kolam Information Services Pvt Ltd, Pondicherry, India
Printed and bound in the United Kingdom
by TJ International, Padstow, Cornwall

For further information on
Blackwell Publishing, visit our website:
http://www.blackwellpublishing.com

Contents

Acknowledgments

Many of my colleagues have been generous in commenting on proposed lists of articles for this project. I am grateful to them for their time and suggestions. I wish to acknowledge the special contribution of Professor Brian Bix. More than anyone I know, Professor Bix has been selfless in his willingness to discuss this project with me and make suggestions for works to be included in the volume. I am most grateful for his help and collegiality.

The editor and publisher gratefully acknowledge the following for permission to reproduce copyright material:

1   *Harvard Law Review* for O. W. Holmes, "The Path of the Law" from *Harvard Law Review* 10 (1897), pp. 457–78;
2   *Columbia Law Review* for Karl Llewellyn, "A Realistic Jurisprudence – The Next Step" from *Columbia Law Review* 30 (1930), pp. 431–65. Reprinted by permission;
3   *University of Chicago Law Review* for Ronald Dworkin, "The Model of Rules" from *University of Chicago Law Review* 35 (1967), pp. 14–46;
4   *Harvard Law Review* for H. L. A. Hart, "Positivism and the Separation of Law and Morals" from *Harvard Law Review* 71 (1958), pp. 593–629;
5   Lynn D. Fuller for Lon Fuller, "Positivism and Fidelity to Law: A Reply to Professor Hart" from *Harvard Law Review* 71 (1958), pp. 631–72;
6   *The Journal of Legal Studies* for Jules Coleman, "Negative and Positive Positivism" from *The Journal of Legal Studies* 11 (1982), pp. 139–64;
7   *Notre Dame Law Review* for John Finnis, "On the Incoherence of Legal Positivism" from *Notre Dame Law Review* 75:1 (August 2000), pp. 1597–611. © by *Notre Dame Law Review*, University of Notre Dame. Reprinted with permission;
8   Ronald Dworkin and *Harvard Law Review* for Ronald Dworkin, "Hard Cases" from *Harvard Law Review* 88 (1975), pp. 1057–109;
9   *Southern California Law Review* for Richard A. Posner, "What has Pragmatism to Offer Law?" from *Southern California Law Review* 63 (1990), pp. 1653–70. Reprinted with the permission of the *Southern California Law Review*;
10 Duncan Kennedy and *Harvard Law Review* for Duncan Kennedy, "Form and Substance in Private Law Adjudication" from *Harvard Law Review* 89 (1976), pp. 1685–778;
11 Ken Kress for "Legal Indeterminacy" from *California Law Review* 77 (1989), pp. 283–337;
12 The Yale Law Journal Company and William S. Hein Company for Wesley N. Hohfeld, "Some Fundamental Legal Conceptions as Applied in Judicial Reasoning" from *The Yale Law*

Journal 23, pp. 16–59. Reprinted by permission of The Yale Law Journal Company and William S. Hein Company;

13   The Yale Law Journal Company and Fred B. Rothman & Company for Ernest Weinrib, "Legal Formalism: On the Immanent Rationality of Law" from *The Yale Law Journal* 97, pp. 949–1016. Reprinted by permission of the Yale Law Journal Company and Fred B. Rothman & Company;

14   Ronald Dworkin for "Law as Interpretation," *Critical Inquiry* 9 (1982), pp. 179–200;

15   *The Journal of Law and Economics* for Ronald Coase, "The Problem of Social Cost" from *The Journal of Law and Economics* 3 (1960), pp. 1–44. Copyright 1960 by the University of Chicago. All rights reserved.

The publisher apologizes for any errors or omissions in the above list and would be grateful if notified of any corrections that should be incorporated in future reprints or editions of this book.

Introduction

Anthologies – be they about law or any other subject – are deceptive and difficult projects. The deceptive aspect is the apparent ease of putting together a collection of canonical works in a field. In a field as central as law, how challenging could it be to pull together a list of canonical works? With so much to choose from, the only difficulty – if difficulty there be – is paring down the list of possible candidates for inclusion in a single volume.

This surfeit of choices is exacerbated by the fact that in jurisprudence (or "legal theory") there is a lack of widespread agreement on the canonical status of many works. For this reason, any given individual's choices will be more or less controversial. As the editor of this volume, I would like to say why the list of works chosen for this volume makes sense. To do this, I need to address the question of audience: that is, for whom is this volume produced and how can that audience make the highest and best use of its contents?

The works for this volume were selected with two criteria in mind. First, I wanted to include articles that almost every person with a serious interest in jurisprudence would regard as worthy of study by a beginning student. Obviously many articles could have been included and, were it not for limitations of space, might have found their way into the volume. Second, I wanted to give initiates to jurisprudence a sense of current debates in the field. But current debates all proceed against the background of the history of legal theory. Therefore, it was important to select historical works that resonate with contemporary concerns.

With these parameters in mind we come to the first name in American legal theory, that of Christopher Columbus Langdell (1826–1906), the first dean of the Harvard Law School and the author of the first casebook (the subject matter was contracts). Langdell's view of law dominated legal discussion from the end of the nineteenth century into the early twentieth century. Langdell's aspiration was to put law on the same footing as natural science. To this end, he recommended that law students not spend their time reading vast numbers of cases in an effort to compile long lists of legal rules. Instead, Langdell recommended pursuit of the principles which provide the best explanation for the constitution and organization of doctrinal areas of law. Langdell believed that once the few organizing principles of a field were identified, the content of law could be divined. Like nature, law had a hidden order or logic which, once disclosed, revealed an organizing structure of principle which made sense of the play of diverse legal opinions.

Langdell is the figure who comes most readily to mind when legal academics look for an example of "legal formalism." Here history and the contemporary discussion come together for the first time. In the article by Ernest Weinrib (b. 1943), "Legal Formalism: On the Immanent Rationality of Law," Professor Weinrib argues that law does, indeed, exhibit a conceptual architecture. Through his unique synthesis of the work of Aristotle, Aquinas, Kant and Hegel,

Professor Weinrib argues that "law" is not reducible to the discourse of law. In a real sense, "law" is a product of thought or rationality. It is the task of legal theory to identify the fundamental organizing structure of law be it principles or concepts.

In the late nineteenth and early twentieth centuries, formalism was dominant but by no means the only account of the nature of law and legal reasoning. First, there was the "bad man" account of law by Oliver Wendell Holmes (1841–1935). In "The Path of the Law," Holmes asserts that to understand law we need know only what a "bad man" might wish to know, that is, how judges are likely to rule. Thus, prediction is the most important aspect of knowledge of "law." As one might say, "law is what the judges say it is": it is the business of bad men and lawyers alike to predict how judges would rule on questions of the day.

Between Holmes and Langdell we find Wesley Hohfeld (1879–1918). The gravamen of Hohfeld's work is his attempt to articulate fundamental categories of legal thought. Hohfeld believed that legal discourse could be clarified through analysis of what he termed "fundamental legal conceptions." His work is analytic in spirit without being conceptualist in the manner of Langdell. True, Hohfeld's approach to law could be just as abstract as that of Langdell. But unlike Langdell, Hohfeld insisted that jurisprudential analysis be grounded in conventional legal reasoning.

In the early part of the twentieth century, the formalism of Langdell meets its great challenge in the work of the American Legal Realists. The Realists are often seen as a source of great skepticism in legal theory. In a sense, this is true but somewhat misleading. Realists such as the jurist Jerome Frank (1889–1957) took a "psychological" view of legal decision-making. Frank believed that the study of the psychology of individual judges was a clue if not a key to deciphering how cases are "really" decided. Emphasis on the skeptical dimension of Realist thought might give one the impression that the Realists believed that law had no real connection with human reason. The work of the most prominent Realist, Karl Llewellyn (1893–

1962), belies this notion. Llewellyn's greatest contribution to law is his work on the Uniform Commercial Code, which he produced in the 1940s. This statute is in many respects an expression of what is best in realism. True, Llewellyn did reject the Langdellian view of law as grounded in abstract reason. But simply because Llewellyn rejected the formalist account of reason in law, this does not mean that he rejected the idea of reason in law. In fact, it can safely be said that in Llewellyn's hands, reason is not rejected but relocated.

With the Uniform Commercial Code, Llewellyn makes the case that law's "reason" is located not in abstract thought but in the practices of merchants. With concepts like "agreement," "good faith," and "commercial reasonableness," Llewellyn sought to bring the logic of the marketplace into the logic of legal decision-making. In this way, Llewellyn's jurisprudence can rightly be viewed as both skeptical (of formalist methodology) and pragmatic.

In the academic scene beyond the confines of jurisprudence one finds considerable attention given to "pragmatism" of one sort or another. Implicating the work of American pragmatists such as William James (1842–1910) and John Dewey (1859–1952), American philosophers such as Richard Rorty (b. 1931) and Hilary Putnam (b. 1926) have reinvigorated the commonsense tradition in American thought. In "What has Pragmatism to Offer Law?," the distinguished jurist Richard Posner (b. 1939) combines the healthy skepticism of the American Legal Realist tradition with his own application of the insights of law and economics. It might be fair to say that Posner is the Oliver Wendell Holmes of our day. While eschewing any commitment to preordained outcomes, Posner believes deeply in the virtues of efficiency and the practical application of legal norms. Whether this approach is sufficiently broad to characterize pragmatism as a school of thought or "philosophy," the reader must decide. Having written on subjects as diverse as the Bush/Gore election, the impeachment of President Clinton, and the topic of sex, Judge Posner is one of the most interesting figures on the academic legal scene today.

Skepticism about law has its roots in the Legal Realist reaction to formalism (or "mechanical jurisprudence"). The contemporary expression of skepticism about law and "legal reasoning" is best exemplified in the work of the members of the Critical Legal Studies Movement. Professor Duncan Kennedy's (b. 1942) article "Form and Substance in Private Law Adjudication" is rightly regarded as one of the classic works in the field. Together with the work of Roberto Unger (b. 1947), Professor Kennedy presents the most formidable challenge to the idea that legal outcomes are tied – either directly or indirectly – to legal methodology. For clarification and challenge to the central tenets of the indeterminacy thesis, Professor Ken Kress's (b. 1958) article "Legal Indeterminacy" is without equal in the literature. Kress shows that the claim that the indeterminacy of law undermines its legitimacy cannot be sustained.

One long-standing debate in jurisprudence is that between positivism and natural law. Positivists deny any necessary connection between law and morality. More broadly, positivists devote their time to analyzing law as an artifact of human action. In accounting for the nature of law, positivists differ – sometimes starkly – in their respective accounts of what law consists in. In the famous debate between H. L. A. Hart (1907–92) and Lon Fuller (1902–78), the question of the relationship between law and morality is debated at the level of the nature of law, the meaning of legal language, and the question whether evil law can truly be said to be "law." For his part, H. L. A. Hart argues that the moral criticism of law is not possible if there is any deep and abiding connection between law and morality. Fuller counters that there is an internal "morality of order" in any normative system we call "law." No matter which side of the argument one takes, the Hart–Fuller debate remains a central focus of attention within legal theory.

There has been much debate between and among positivists and their critics since the time of the Hart–Fuller debate. The work of Jules Coleman (b. 1947) is both a refinement and development of arguments first articulated by Hart in his famous book *The Concept of Law* (1961). In his essay "Negative and Positive Positivism," Coleman responds to critics of positivism with subtle revisions of central positivist tenets. The most important of these is the "separability thesis" (denying any necessary or constitutive relationship of law to morality) and the relationship of law to morality. Coleman argues that commitment to the separability thesis does not entail denial of a connection between law and morality. The issue, says Coleman, is not whether there is a connection but in what the connection consists. For Coleman, all that positivism need show is the possibility of a convergent practice among judges, one that requires judges to articulate legal decisions in moral terms.

Are Coleman's efforts to recast Hart's positivism successful? In his essay "On the Incoherence of Legal Positivism," John Finnis (b. 1940) applauds the sophistication of modern proponents of positivism but concludes that positivism is an incoherent intellectual enterprise. In addition to arguing that positivists systematically misread the natural law tradition, Professor Finnis asserts that the central question of jurisprudence is not the "nature of law" but the question whether positive law can create moral obligations. To this question, Professor Finnis believes legal positivism has no answer. Thus, the authority of law – its "binding" character – cannot be explained by the positivist account of law.

Perhaps the greatest contemporary critic of legal positivism is Ronald Dworkin (b. 1931). In his early essay "The Model of Rules," Professor Dworkin attacks the ontology of law advanced by H. L. A. Hart. Hart, who argued that law was a matter of rules, is criticized by Dworkin for failing to appreciate the role of principles in adjudication. Through a series of well-developed examples, Dworkin demonstrates rather convincingly the descriptive inadequacies of legal positivism.

The late John Mackie (1917–81) has described Dworkin's theory as a "third theory of law"; that is, a theory that attempts to bridge the divide between positivism and naturalism. Contemporary positivists like to think they can accommodate Dworkin's ontological critique. In this way, contemporary positivists like to acknowledge Dworkin as a "helpful" critic of positivism. The question whether positivism can accommodate the role of principles in law without giving up the separability thesis is a question of deep concern to contemporary positivism.

In addition to his criticism of positivism, Dworkin has advanced some independent and quite controversial theses. In his article "Hard Cases," Dworkin argues that there is always a "right answer" to legal disputes and that law and political morality are connected at the deepest levels of moral and political justification. In "Law as Interpretation," Dworkin advances a thesis that would reach its full expression in his 1986 book *Law's Empire*. In this article, Dworkin borrows a page from continental philosophers, especially Martin Heidegger (1889–1976), with his thesis that law is an interpretive practice. What Dworkin means to say with this provocative assertion is not always clear. What is clear is that Dworkin joins a major academic trend – one could call it "the interpretive turn" – with his claim that the meaning of legal concepts is a function of interpretation. Bold in his presentation, trenchant in argument and always controversial, Dworkin's work is central to any discussion in legal philosophy.

It would be simplistic to see the work of contemporary law and economics scholars as a single-minded focus on the empirical. In fact, law and economics scholarship can usefully be classified along three lines of endeavor. First is the substantive or "positive" evaluation of law. Economists are especially adept at answering the question whether particular laws accomplish the goals and purposes for which they were fashioned. Imagine a regulatory scheme designed to increase the efficiency of business regulation. After defining key terms like "efficiency," economists can employ their sophisticated analytical and measuring tools for evaluation of the success or failure of a legal regime in effecting its avowed purposes.

Normative law and economics does not take the law as we find it. Rather, normative economic theory asks after the ideal point or purpose of law. Over the course of the last two decades there has been a veritable explosion in the volume of normative economic analysis of law, especially in private law areas such as torts and contracts. In tort law, for example, economists have questioned the point or purpose of a regime of tort or accident law and have inquired as to how the rules of tort law may be recast to better effect the ideal purposes of tort law. Much of this work has made its way into the work of legislators and even first-year torts casebooks.

Finally, there is positive law and economics. In many ways, this approach to economics has great affinities with philosophical approaches to law. One of the questions posed by positive law and economics asks why the law is as it is? It might be said that positive law and economics tries to "explain" the law as we find it. For the present volume, I have selected an article from this corner of the economics literature. Ronald Coase (b. 1910) won the Nobel Prize in economics for developing the Coase Theorem. In "The Problem of Social Cost," Coase argues that individuals will value entitlements without regard to their ownership. For example, it matters not whether the law grants water rights to one riparian owner or her neighbor because the parties will themselves ultimately decide who values the entitlement most. In a sense, Coase is arguing that "rights do not matter." Coase's behavioral assumptions have come under scrutiny in recent years, and his central thesis remains controversial. Nevertheless, no understanding of the economic approach to law would be possible without some understanding of the Coase Theorem. For this reason alone, the choice to include "The Problem of Social Cost" was easy.

This anthology is a companion volume to *A Companion to Philosophy of Law and Legal Theory* published in 1996. Since its publication, the *Companion* has enjoyed great success and has proven to be an extremely useful tool for law students interested in having a grasp of the theoretical dimensions of the subjects they study on a daily basis. The anthology is published to provide students with original source material which can be usefully read together with the analytical articles in the *Companion*.

Taken together, these two volumes provide a complete introduction to law and legal theory and provide a solid footing to further study of law and legal theory.

Part I
Nature of Law

1

The Path of the Law

O. W. Holmes

When we study law we are not studying a mystery but a well known profession. We are studying what we shall want in order to appear before judges, or to advise people in such a way as to keep them out of court. The reason why it is a profession, why people will pay lawyers to argue for them or to advise them, is that in societies like ours the command of the public force is intrusted to the judges in certain cases, and the whole power of the state will be put forth, if necessary, to carry out their judgments and decrees. People want to know under what circumstances and how far they will run the risk of coming against what is so much stronger than themselves, and hence it becomes a business to find out when this danger is to be feared. The object of our study, then, is prediction, the prediction of the incidence of the public force through the instrumentality of the courts.

The means of the study are a body of reports, of treatises, and of statutes, in this country and in England, extending back for six hundred years, and now increasing annually by hundreds. In these sibylline leaves are gathered the scattered prophecies of the past upon the cases in which the axe will fall. These are what properly have been called the oracles of the law. Far the most important and pretty nearly the whole meaning of every new effort of legal thought is to make these prophecies more precise, and to generalize them into a thoroughly connected system. The process is one, from a lawyer's statement of a case, eliminating as it does all the dramatic elements with which his client's story has clothed it, and retaining only

the facts of legal import, up to the final analyses and abstract universals of theoretic jurisprudence. The reason why a lawyer does not mention that his client wore a white hat when he made a contract, while Mrs. Quickly would be sure to dwell upon it along with the parcel gilt goblet and the sea-coal fire, is that he forsees that the public force will act in the same way whatever his client had upon his head. It is to make the prophecies easier to be remembered and to be understood that the teachings of the decisions of the past are put into general propositions and gathered into text-books, or that statutes are passed in a general form. The primary rights and duties with which jurisprudence busies itself again are nothing' but prophecies. One of the many evil effects of the confusion between legal and moral ideas, about which I shall have something to say in a moment, is that theory is apt to get the cart before the horse, and to consider the right or the duty as something existing apart from and independent of the consequences of its breach, to which certain sanctions are added afterward. But, as I shall try to show, a legal duty so called is nothing but a prediction that if a man does or omits certain things he will be made to suffer in this or that way by judgment of the court; – and so of a legal right.

The number of our predictions when generalized and reduced to a system is not unmanageably large. They present themselves as a finite body of dogma which may be mastered within a reasonable time. It is a great mistake to be frightened by the ever increasing number of reports. The reports of a given jurisdiction in the course of a generation take up pretty much the whole body of the law, and restate it from the present point of view. We could reconstruct the corpus from them if all that went before were burned. The use of the earlier reports is mainly historical, a use about which I shall have something to say before I have finished.

I wish, if I can, to lay down some first principles for the study of this body of dogma or systematized prediction which we call the law, for men who want to use it as the instrument of their business to enable them to prophesy in their turn, and, as bearing upon the study, I wish to point out an ideal which as yet our law has not attained.

The first thing for a business-like understanding of the matter is to understand its limits, and therefore I think it desirable at once to point out and dispel a confusion between morality and law, which sometimes rises to the height of conscious theory, and more often and indeed constantly is making trouble in detail without reaching the point of consciousness. You can see very plainly that a bad man has as much reason as a good one for wishing to avoid an encounter with the public force, and therefore you can see the practical importance of the distinction between morality and law. A man who cares nothing for an ethical rule which is believed and practised by his neighbors is likely nevertheless to care a good deal to avoid being made to pay money, and will want to keep out of jail if he can.

I take it for granted that no hearer of mine will misinterpret what I have to say as the language of cynicism. The law is the witness and external deposit of our moral life. Its history is the history of the moral development of the race. The practice of it, in spite of popular jests, tends to make good citizens and good men. When I emphasize the difference between law and morals I do so with reference to a single end, that of learning and understanding the law. For that purpose you must definitely master its specific marks, and it is for that that I ask you for the moment to imagine yourselves indifferent to other and greater things.

I do not say that there is not a wider point of view from which the distinction between law and morals becomes of secondary or no import-

ance, as all mathematical distinctions vanish in presence of the infinite. But I do say that that distinction is of the first importance for the object which we are here to consider, — a right study and mastery of the law as a business with well understood limits, a body of dogma enclosed within definite lines. I have just shown the practical reason for saying so. If you want to know the law and nothing else, you must look at it as a bad man, who cares only for the material consequences which such knowledge enables him to predict, not as a good one, who finds his reasons for conduct, whether inside the law or outside of it, in the vaguer sanctions of conscience. The theoretical importance of the distinction is no less, if you would reason on your subject aright. The law is full of phraseology drawn from morals, and by the mere force of language continually invites us to pass from one domain to the other without perceiving it, as we are sure to do unless we have the boundary constantly before our minds. The law talks about rights, and duties, and malice, and intent, and negligence, and so forth, and nothing is easier, or, I may say, more common in legal reasoning, than to take these words in their moral sense, at some stage of the argument, and so to drop into fallacy. For instance, when we speak of the rights of man in a moral sense, we mean to mark the limits of interference with individual freedom which we think are prescribed by conscience, or by our ideal, however reached. Yet it is certain that many laws have been enforced in the past, and it is likely that some are enforced now, which are condemned by the most enlightened opinion of the time, or which at all events pass the limit of interference as many consciences would draw it. Manifestly, therefore, nothing but confusion of thought can result from assuming that the rights of man in a moral sense are equally rights in the sense of the Constitution and the law. No doubt simple and extreme cases can be put of imaginable laws which the statute-making power would not dare to enact, even in the absence of written constitutional prohibitions, because the community would rise in rebellion and fight; and this gives some plausibility to the proposition that the law, if not a part of morality, is limited by it. But this limit of power is not coextensive with any system of morals. For the most part it falls far within the lines of any such system, and in some cases may extend beyond them, for reasons drawn from the habits of a particular people at a particular time. I once heard the late Professor Agassiz say that a German population would rise if you added two cents to the price of a glass of beer. A statute in such a case would be empty words, not because it was wrong, but because it could not be enforced. No one will deny that wrong statutes can be and are enforced, and we should not all agree as to which were the wrong ones.

The confusion with which I am dealing besets confessedly legal conceptions. Take the fundamental question, What constitutes the law? You will find some text writers telling you that it is something different from what is decided by the courts of Massachusetts or England, that it is a system of reason, that it is a deduction from principles of ethics or admitted axioms or what not, which may or may not coincide with the decisions. But if we take the view of our friend the bad man we shall find that he does not care two straws for the axioms or deductions, but that he does want to know what the Massachusetts or English courts are likely to do in fact. I am much of his mind. The prophecies of what the courts will do in fact, and nothing more pretentious, are what I mean by the law.

Take again a notion which as popularly understood is the widest conception which the law contains; – the notion of legal duty, to which already I have referred. We fill the word with all the content which we draw from morals. But what does it mean to a bad man? Mainly, and in the first place, a prophecy that if he does certain things he will be subjected to disagreeable consequences by way of imprisonment or compulsory payment of money. But from his point of view, what is the difference between being fined and being taxed a certain sum for doing a certain thing? That his point of view is the test of legal principles is shown by the many discussions which have arisen in the courts on the very question whether a given statutory liability is a penalty or a tax. On the answer to this question depends the decision whether conduct is legally wrong or right, and

also whether a man is under compulsion or free. Leaving the criminal law on one side, what is the difference between the liability under the mill acts or statutes authorizing a taking by eminent domain and the liability for what we call a wrongful conversion of property where restoration is out of the question? In both cases the party taking another man's property has to pay its fair value as assessed by a jury, and no more. What significance is there in calling one taking right and another wrong from the point of view of the law? It does not matter, so far as the given consequence, the compulsory payment, is concerned, whether the act to which it is attached is described in terms of praise or in terms of blame, or whether the law purports to prohibit it or to allow it. If it matters at all, still speaking from the bad man's point of view, it must be because in one case and not in the other some further disadvantages, or at least some further consequences, are attached to the act by the law. The only other disadvantages thus attached to it which I ever have been able to think of are to be found in two somewhat insignificant legal doctrines, both of which might be abolished without much disturbance. One is, that a contract to do a prohibited act is unlawful, and the other, that, if one of two or more joint wrongdoers has to pay all the damages, he cannot recover contribution from his fellows. And that I believe is all. You see how the vague circumference of the notion of duty shrinks and at the same time grows more precise when we wash it with cynical acid and expel everything except the object of our study, the operations of the law.

Nowhere is the confusion between legal and moral ideas more manifest than in the law of contract. Among other things, here again the so called primary rights and duties are invested with a mystic significance beyond what can be assigned and explained. The duty to keep a contract at common law means a prediction that you must pay damages if you do not keep it, – and nothing else. If you commit a tort, you are liable to pay a compensatory sum. If you commit a contract, you are liable to pay a compensatory sum unless the promised event comes to pass, and that is all the difference. But such a mode of looking at the matter stinks in the nostrils of those who think it advantageous to get as much ethics into the law as they can. It was good enough for Lord Coke, however, and here, as in many other cases, I am content to abide with him. In Bromage v. Genning,[1] a prohibition was sought in the King's Bench against a suit in the marches of Wales for the specific performance of a covenant to grant a lease, and Coke said that it would subvert the intention of the covenantor, since he intends it to be at his election either to lose the damages or to make the lease. Sergeant Harris for the plaintiff confessed that he moved the matter against his conscience, and a prohibition was granted. This goes further than we should go now, but it shows what I venture to say has been the common law point of view from the beginning, although Mr. Harriman, in his very able little book upon Contracts has been misled, as I humbly think, to a different conclusion.

I have spoken only of the common law, because there are some cases in which a logical justification can be found for speaking of civil liabilities as imposing duties in an intelligible sense. These are the relatively few in which equity will grant an injunction, and will enforce it by putting the defendant in prison or otherwise punishing him unless he complies with the order of the court. But I hardly think it advisable to shape general theory from the exception, and I think it would be better to cease troubling ourselves about primary rights and sanctions altogether, than to describe our prophecies concerning the liabilities commonly imposed by the law in those inappropriate terms.

I mentioned, as other examples of the use by the law of words drawn from morals, malice, intent, and negligence. It is enough to take malice as it is used in the law of civil liability for wrongs, – what we lawyers call the law of torts, – to show you that it means something different in law from what it means in morals, and also to show how the difference has been obscured by giving to principles which have little or nothing to do with each other the same name. Three hundred years ago a parson preached a sermon and told a story out of Fox's Book of Martyrs of a man who had assisted at the torture of one of the saints, and afterward died, suffering compensatory inward torment. It happened that Fox was wrong. The man was alive and chanced to hear the sermon, and thereupon he sued the parson. Chief Justice Wray instructed the jury that the defendant was not liable, because the story was told innocently, without malice. He took malice in the moral sense, as importing a malevolent motive. But nowadays no one doubts that a man may be liable, without any malevolent motive at all, for false statements manifestly calculated to inflict temporal damage. In stating the case in pleading, we still should call the defendant's conduct malicious; but, in my opinion at least, the word means nothing about motives, or even about the defendant's attitude toward the future, but only signifies that the tendency of his conduct under the known circumstances was very plainly to cause the plaintiff temporal harm.[2]

In the law of contract the use of moral phraseology has led to equal confusion, as I have shown in part already, but only in part. Morals deal with the actual internal state of the individual's mind, what he actually intends. From the time of the Romans down to now, this mode of dealing has affected the language of the law as to contract, and the language used has reacted upon the thought. We talk about a contract as a meeting of the minds of the parties, and thence it is inferred in various cases that there is no contract because their minds have not met; that is, because they have intended different things or because one party has not known of the assent of the other. Yet nothing is more certain than that parties may be bound by a contract to things which neither of them intended, and when one does not know of the other's assent. Suppose a contract is executed in due form and in writing to deliver a lecture, mentioning no time. One of the parties thinks that the promise will be construed to mean at once, within a week. The other thinks that it means when he is ready. The court says that it means within a reasonable time. The parties are bound by the contract as it is interpreted by the court, yet neither of them meant what the court declares that they have said. In my opinion no one will understand the true theory of contract or be able even to discuss some fundamental questions intelligently until he has understood that all contracts are formal, that the making of a contract depends not on the agreement of two minds in one intention, but on the agreement of two sets of external signs, – not on the parties' having *meant* the same thing but on their having *said* the same thing. Furthermore, as the signs may be addressed to one sense or another, – to sight or to hearing, – on the nature of the sign will depend the moment when the contract is made. If the sign is tangible, for instance, a letter, the contract is made when the letter of acceptance is delivered. If it is necessary that the minds of the parties meet, there will be no contract until the acceptance can be read, – none, for example, if the acceptance be snatched from the hand of the offerer by a third person.

This is not the time to work out a theory in detail, or to answer many obvious doubts and questions which are suggested by these general views. I know of none which are not easy to answer, but what I am trying to do now is only by a series of hints to throw some light on the narrow path of legal doctrine, and upon two pitfalls which, as it seems to me, lie perilously near to it. Of the first of these I have said enough. I hope that my illustrations have shown the danger, both to speculation and to practice, of confounding morality with law, and the trap which legal language lays for us on that side of our way. For my own part, I often doubt whether it would not be a gain if every word of moral significance could be banished from the law altogether, and other words adopted which should convey legal ideas uncolored by anything outside the law. We should lose the fossil records of a good deal of history and the majesty got from ethical associations, but by ridding ourselves of an unnecessary confusion we should gain very much in the clearness of our thought.

So much for the limits of the law. The next thing which I wish to consider is what are the forces which determine its content and its growth. You may assume, with Hobbes and Bentham and Austin, that all law emanates from the sovereign, even when the first human beings to enunciate it are the judges, or you may think that law is the voice of the Zeitgeist, or what you like. It is all one to my present purpose. Even if every decision required the sanction of an emperor with despotic power and a whimsical turn of mind, we should be interested none the less, still with a view to prediction, in discovering some order, some rational explanation, and some principle of growth for the rules which he laid down. In every system there are such explanations and principles to be found. It is with regard to them that a second fallacy comes in, which I think it important to expose.

The fallacy to which I refer is the notion that the only force at work in the development of the law is logic. In the broadest sense, indeed, that notion would be true. The postulate on which we think about the universe is that there is a fixed quantitative relation between every phenomenon and its antecedents and consequents. If there is such a thing as a phenomenon without these fixed quantitative relations, it is a miracle. It is outside the law of cause and effect, and as such transcends our power of thought, or at least is something to or from which we cannot reason. The condition of our thinking about the universe is that it is capable of being thought about rationally, or, in other words, that every part of it is effect and cause in the same sense in which those parts are with which we are most familiar. So in the broadest sense it is true that the law is a logical development, like everything else. The danger of which I speak is not the admission that the principles governing other phenomena also govern the law, but the notion that a given system, ours, for instance, can be worked out like mathematics from some general axioms of conduct. This is the natural error of the schools, but it is not confined to them. I once heard a very eminent judge say that he never let a decision go until he was absolutely sure that it was right. So judicial dissent often is blamed, as if it meant simply that one side or the other were not doing their sums right, and, if they would take more trouble, agreement inevitably would come.

This mode of thinking is entirely natural. The training of lawyers is a training in logic. The processes of analogy, discrimination, and deduction are those in which they are most at home. The language of judicial decision is mainly the language of logic. And the logical method and form flatter that longing for certainty and for repose which is in every human mind. But certainty generally is illusion, and repose is not the destiny of man. Behind the logical form lies a judgment as to the relative worth and importance of competing legislative grounds, often an inarticulate and unconscious judgment, it is true, and yet the very root and nerve of the whole proceeding. You can give any conclusion a logical form. You always can imply a condition in a contract. But why do you imply it? It is because of some belief as to the practice of the community or of a class, or because of some opinion as to policy, or, in short, because of some attitude of yours upon a matter not capable of exact quantitative measurement, and therefore not capable of founding exact logical conclusions. Such matters really are battle grounds where the means do not exist for determinations that shall be good for all time, and where the decision can do no more than embody the preference of a given body in a given time and place. We do not realize how large a part of our law is open to reconsideration upon a slight change in the habit of the public mind. No concrete proposition is self-evident, no matter how ready we may be to accept it, not even Mr. Herbert Spencer's Every man has a right to do what he wills, provided he interferes not with a like right on the part of his neighbors.

Why is a false and injurious statement privileged, if it is made honestly in giving information about a servant? It is because it has been thought more important that information should be given freely, than that a man should be protected from what under other circumstances would be an actionable wrong. Why is a man at liberty to set up a business which he knows will ruin his neighbor? It is because the public good is supposed to be best subserved by free competition. Obviously such judgments of relative importance may vary in different times and places. Why does a judge instruct a jury that an employer is not liable to an employee for an injury received in the course of his employment unless he is negligent, and why do the jury generally find for the plaintiff if the case is allowed to go to them? It is because the traditional policy of our law is to confine liability to cases where a prudent man might have foreseen the injury, or at least the danger, while the inclination of a very large part of the community is to make certain classes of persons insure the safety of those with whom they deal. Since the last words were written, I have seen the requirement of such insurance put forth as part of the programme of one of the best known labor organizations. There is a concealed, half conscious battle on the question of legislative policy, and if any one thinks that it can be settled deductively, or once for all, I only can say that I think he is theoretically wrong, and that I am certain that his conclusion will not be accepted in practice *semper ubique et ab omnibus.*

Indeed, I think that even now our theory upon this matter is open to reconsideration, although I am not prepared to say how I should decide if a reconsideration were proposed. Our law of torts comes from the old days of isolated, ungeneralized wrongs, assaults, slanders, and the like, where the damages might be taken to lie where they fell by legal judgment. But the torts with which our courts are kept busy to-day are mainly the incidents of certain well known businesses. They are injuries to person or property by railroads, factories, and the like. The liability for them is estimated, and sooner or later goes into the price paid by the public. The public really pays the damages, and the question of liability, if pressed far enough, is really the question how far it is desirable that the public should insure the safety of those whose work it uses. It might be said that in such cases the chance of a jury finding for the defendant is merely a chance, once in a while rather arbitrarily interrupting the regular course of recovery, most likely in the case of an unusually conscientious plaintiff, and therefore better done away with. On the other hand, the economic value even of a life to the community can be estimated, and no recovery, it may be said, ought to go beyond that amount. It is conceivable that some day in certain cases we may find ourselves imitating, on a higher plane, the tariff for life and limb which we see in the Leges Barbarorum.

I think that the judges themselves have failed adequately to recognize their duty of weighing considerations of social advantage. The duty is inevitable, and the result of the often proclaimed judicial aversion to deal with such considerations is simply to leave the very ground and foundation of judgments inarticulate, and often unconscious, as I have said. When socialism first began to be talked about, the comfortable classes of the community were a good deal frightened. I suspect that this fear has influenced judicial action both here and in England, yet it is certain that it is not a conscious factor in the decisions to which I refer. I think that something similar has led people who no longer hope to control the legislatures to look to the courts as expounders of the Constitutions, and that in some courts new principles have been discovered outside the bodies of those instruments, which may be generalized into acceptance of the economic doctrines which prevailed about fifty years ago, and a wholesale prohibition of what a tribunal of lawyers does not think about right. I cannot but believe that if the training of lawyers led them habitually to consider more definitely and explicitly the social advantage on which the rule they lay down must be justified, they sometimes would hesitate where now they are confident, and see that really they were taking sides upon debatable and often burning questions.

So much for the fallacy of logical form. Now let us consider the present condition of the law as a subject for study, and the ideal toward which it tends. We still are far from the point of view which I desire to see reached. No one has reached it or can reach it as yet. We are only at the beginning of a philosophical reaction, and of a reconsideration of the worth of doctrines which for the most part still are taken for granted without any deliberate, conscious, and systematic questioning of their grounds. The development of our law has gone on for nearly a thousand years, like the development of a plant, each generation taking the inevitable next step, mind, like matter, simply obeying a law of spontaneous growth. It is perfectly natural and right that it should have been so. Imitation is a necessity of human nature, as has been illustrated by a remarkable French writer, M. Tarde, in an admirable book, "Les Lois de l'Imitation." Most of the things we do, we do for no better reason than that our fathers have done them or that our neighbors do them, and the same is true of a larger part than we suspect of what we think. The reason is a good one, because

our short life gives us no time for a better, but it is not the best. It does not follow, because we all are compelled to take on faith at second hand most of the rules on which we base our action and our thought, that each of us may not try to set some corner of his world in the order of reason, or that all of us collectively should not aspire to carry reason as far as it will go throughout the whole domain. In regard to the law, it is true, no doubt, that an evolutionist will hesitate to affirm universal validity for his social ideals, or for the principles which he thinks should be embodied in legislation. He is content if he can prove them best for here and now. He may be ready to admit that he knows nothing about an absolute best in the cosmos, and even that he knows next to nothing about a permanent best for men. Still it is true that a body of law is more rational and more civilized when every rule it contains is referred articulately and definitely to an end which it subserves, and when the grounds for desiring that end are stated or are ready to be stated in words.

At present, in very many cases, if we want to know why a rule of law has taken its particular shape, and more or less if we want to know why it exists at all, we go to tradition. We follow it into the Year Books, and perhaps beyond them to the customs of the Salian Franks, and somewhere in the past, in the German forests, in the needs of Norman kings, in the assumptions of a dominant class, in the absence of generalized ideas, we find out the practical motive for what now best is justified by the mere fact of its acceptance and that men are accustomed to it. The rational study of law is still to a large extent the study of history. History must be a part of the study, because without it we cannot know the precise scope of rules which it is our business to know. It is a part of the rational study, because it is the first step toward an enlightened scepticism, that is, toward a deliberate reconsideration of the worth of those rules. When you get the dragon out of his cave on to the plain and in the daylight, you can count his teeth and claws, and see just what is his strength. But to get him out is only the first step. The next is either to kill him, or to tame him and make him a useful animal. For the rational study of the law the black-letter man may be the man of the present, but the man of the future is the man of statistics and the master of economics. It is revolting to have no better reason for a rule of law than that so it was laid down in the time of Henry IV. It is still more revolting if the grounds upon which it was laid down have vanished long since, and the rule simply persists from blind imitation of the past. I am thinking of the technical rule as to trespass *ab initio*, as it is called, which I attempted to explain in a recent Massachusetts case.[3]

Let me take an illustration, which can be stated in a few words, to show how the social end which is aimed at by a rule of law is obscured and only partially attained in consequence of the fact that the rule owes its form to a gradual historical development, instead of being re-shaped as a whole, with conscious articulate reference to the end in view. We think it desirable to prevent one man's property being misappropriated by another, and so we make larceny a crime. The evil is the same whether the misappropriation is made by a man into whose hands the owner has put the property, or by one who wrongfully takes it away. But primitive law in its weakness did not get much beyond an effort to prevent violence, and very naturally made a wrongful taking, a trespass, part of its definition of the crime. In modern times the judges enlarged the definition a little by holding that, if the wrong-doer gets possession by a trick or device, the crime is committed. This really was giving up the requirement of a trespass, and it would have been more logical, as well as truer to the present object of the law, to abandon the requirement altogether. That, however, would have seemed too bold, and was left to statute. Statutes were passed making embezzlement a crime. But the force of tradition caused the crime of embezzlement to be regarded as so far distinct from larceny that to this day, in some jurisdictions at least, a slip corner is kept open for thieves to contend, if indicted for larceny, that they should have been indicted for embezzlement, and if indicated for embezzlement, that they should have been indicted for larceny, and to escape on that ground.

Far more fundamental questions still await a better answer than that we do as our fathers have done. What have we better than a blind guess to show that the criminal law in its present form does more good than harm? I do not stop to refer to the effect which it has had in degrading prisoners and in plunging them further into crime, or to the question whether fine and imprisonment do not fall more heavily on a criminal's wife and children than on himself. I have in mind more far-reaching questions. Does punishment deter? Do we deal with criminals on proper principles? A modern school of Continental criminalists plumes itself on the formula, first suggested, it is said, by Gall, that we must consider the criminal rather than the crime. The formula does not carry us very far, but the inquiries which have been started look toward an answer of my questions based on science for the first time. If the typical criminal is a degenerate, bound to swindle or to murder by as deep seated an organic necessity as that which makes the rattlesnake bite, it is idle to talk of deterring him by the classical method of imprisonment. He must be got rid of; he cannot be improved, or frightened out of his structural reaction. If, on the other hand, crime, like normal human conduct, is mainly a matter of imitation, punishment fairly may be expected to help to keep it out of fashion. The study of criminals has been thought by some well known men of science to sustain the former hypothesis. The statistics of the relative increase of crime in crowded places like large cities, where example has the greatest chance to work, and in less populated parts, where the contagion spreads more slowly, have been used with great force in favor of the latter view. But there is weighty authority for the belief that, however this may be, "not the nature of the crime, but the dangerousness of the criminal, constitutes the only reasonable legal criterion to guide the inevitable social reaction against the criminal."[4]

The impediments to rational generalization, which I illustrated from the law of larceny, are shown in the other branches of the law, as well as in that of crime. Take the law of tort or civil liability for damages apart from contract and the like. Is there any general theory of such liability, or are the cases in which it exists simply to be enumerated, and to be explained each on its special ground, as is easy to believe from the fact that the right of action for certain well known classes of wrongs like trespass or slander has its special history for each class? I think that there is a general theory to be discovered, although resting in tendency rather than established and accepted. I think that the law regards the infliction of temporal damage by a responsible person as actionable, if under the circumstances known to him the danger of his act is manifest according to common experience, or according to his own experience if it is more than common, except in cases where upon special grounds of policy the law refuses to protect the plaintiff or grants a privilege to the defendant.[5] I think that commonly malice, intent, and negligence mean only that the danger was manifest to a greater or less degree, under the circumstances known to the actor, although in some cases of privilege malice may mean an actual malevolent motive, and such a motive may take away a permission knowingly to inflict harm, which otherwise would be granted on this or that ground of dominant public good. But when I stated my view to a very eminent English judge the other day, he said: "You are discussing what the law ought to be; as the law is, you must show a right. A man is not liable for negligence unless he is subject to a duty." If our difference was more than a difference in words, or with regard to the proportion between the exceptions and the rule, then, in his opinion, liability for an act cannot be referred to the manifest tendency of the act to cause temporal damage in general as a sufficient explanation, but must be referred to the special nature of the damage, or must be derived from some special circumstances outside of the tendency of the act, for which no generalized explanation exists. I think that such a view is wrong, but it is familiar, and I dare say generally is accepted in England.

Everywhere the basis of principle is tradition, to such an extent that we even are in danger of making the rôle of history more important than it is. The other day Professor Ames wrote a learned article to show, among other things, that the common law did not recognize the defence of fraud in actions upon specialties, and the moral might seem to be that the personal character of that defence is due to its equitable origin.

But if, as I have said, all contracts are formal, the difference is not merely historical, but theoretic, between defects of form which prevent a contract from being made, and mistaken motives which manifestly could not be considered in any system that we should call rational except against one who was privy to those motives. It is not confined to specialties, but is of universal application. I ought to add that I do not suppose that Mr. Ames would disagree with what I suggest.

However, if we consider the law of contract, we find it full of history. The distinctions between debt, covenant, and assumpsit are merely historical. The classification of certain obligations to pay money, imposed by the law irrespective of any bargain as quasi contracts, is merely historical. The doctrine of consideration is merely historical. The effect given to a seal is to be explained by history alone. – Consideration is a mere form. Is it a useful form? If so, why should it not be required in all contracts? A seal is a mere form, and is vanishing in the scroll and in enactments that a consideration must be given, seal or no seal. – Why should any merely historical distinction be allowed to affect the rights and obligations of business men?

Since I wrote this discourse I have come on a very good example of the way in which tradition not only overrides rational policy, but overrides it after first having been misunderstood and having been given a new and broader scope than it had when it had a meaning. It is the settled law of England that a material alteration of a written contract by a party avoids it as against him. The doctrine is contrary to the general tendency of the law. We do not tell a jury that if a man ever has lied in one particular he is to be presumed to lie in all. Even if a man has tried to defraud, it seems no sufficient reason for preventing him from proving the truth. Objections of like nature in general go to the weight, not to the admissibility, of evidence. Moreover, this rule is irrespective of fraud, and is not confined to evidence. It is not merely that you cannot use the writing, but that the contract is at an end. What does this mean? The existence of a written contract depends on the fact that the offerer and offeree have interchanged their written expressions, not on the continued existence of those expressions. But in the case of a bond the primitive notion was different. The contract was inseparable from the parchment. If a stranger destroyed it, or tore off the seal, or altered it, the obligee could not recover, however free from fault, because the defendant's contract, that is, the actual tangible bond which he had sealed, could not be produced in the form in which it bound him. About a hundred years ago Lord Kenyon undertook to use his reason on this tradition, as he sometimes did to the detriment of the law, and, not understanding it, said he could see no reason why what was true of a bond should not be true of other contracts. His decision happened to be right, as it concerned a promissory note, where again the common law regarded the contract as inseparable from the paper on which it was written, but the reasoning was general, and soon was extended to other written contracts, and various absurd and unreal grounds of policy were invented to account for the enlarged rule.

I trust that no one will understand me to be speaking with disrespect of the law, because I criticise it so freely. I venerate the law, and especially our system of law, as one of the vastest products of the human mind. No one knows better than I do the countless number of great intellects that have spent themselves in making some addition or improvement, the greatest of which is trifling when compared with the mighty whole. It has the final title to respect that it exists, that it is not a Hegelian dream, but a part of the lives of men. But one may criticise even what one reveres. Law is the business to which my life is devoted, and I should show less than devotion if I did not do what in me lies to improve it, and, when I perceive what seems to me the ideal of its future, if I hesitated to point it out and to press toward it with all my heart.

Perhaps I have said enough to show the part which the study of history necessarily plays in the intelligent study of the law as it is to-day. In the teaching of this school and at Cambridge it is in no danger of being undervalued. Mr. Bigelow here and Mr. Ames and Mr. Thayer there have made important contributions which will not be forgotten, and in England the recent history of early English law by Sir Frederick

Pollock and Mr. Maitland has lent the subject an almost deceptive charm. We must beware of the pitfall of antiquarianism, and must remember that for our purposes our only interest in the past is for the light it throws upon the present. I look forward to a time when the part played by history in the explanation of dogma shall be very small, and instead of ingenious research we shall spend our energy on a study of the ends sought to be attained and the reasons for desiring them. As a step toward that ideal it seems to me that every lawyer ought to seek an understanding of economics. The present divorce between the schools of political economy and law seems to me an evidence of how much progress in philosophical study still remains to be made. In the present state of political economy, indeed, we come again upon history on a larger scale, but there we are called on to consider and weigh the ends of legislation, the means of attaining them, and the cost. We learn that for everything we have to give up something else, and we are taught to set the advantage we gain against the other advantage we lose, and to know what we are doing when we elect.

There is another study which sometimes is undervalued by the practical minded, for which I wish to say a good word, although I think a good deal of pretty poor stuff goes under that name. I mean the study of what is called jurisprudence. Jurisprudence, as I look at it, is simply law in its most generalized part. Every effort to reduce a case to a rule is an effort of jurisprudence, although the name as used in English is confined to the broadest rules and most fundamental conceptions. One mark of a great lawyer is that he sees the application of the broadest rules. There is a story of a Vermont justice of the peace before whom a suit was brought by one farmer against another for breaking a churn. The justice took time to consider, and then said that he had looked through the statutes and could find nothing about churns, and gave judgment for the defendant. The same state of mind is shown in all our common digests and text-books. Applications of rudimentary rules of contract or tort are tucked away under the head of Railroads or Telegraphs or go to swell treatises on historical subdivisions, such as Shipping or Equity, or are gathered under an arbitrary title which is thought likely to appeal to the practical mind, such as Mercantile Law. If a man goes into law it pays to be a master of it, and to be a master of it means to look straight through all the dramatic incidents and to discern the true basis for prophecy. Therefore, it is well to have an accurate notion of what you mean by law, by a right, by a duty, by malice, intent, and negligence, by ownership, by possession, and so forth. I have in my mind cases in which the highest courts seem to me to have floundered because they had no clear ideas on some of these themes. I have illustrated their importance already. If a further illustration is wished, it may be found by reading the Appendix to Sir James Stephen's Criminal Law on the subject of possession, and then turning to Pollock and Wright's enlightened book. Sir James Stephen is not the only writer whose attempts to analyze legal ideas have been confused by striving for a useless quintessence of all systems, instead of an accurate anatomy of one. The trouble with Austin was that he did not know enough English law. But still it is a practical advantage to master Austin, and his predecessors, Hobbes and Bentham, and his worthy successors, Holland and Pollock. Sir Frederick Pollock's recent little book is touched with the felicity which marks all his works, and is wholly free from the perverting influence of Roman models.

The advice of the elders to young men is very apt to be as unreal as a list of the hundred best books. At least in my day I had my share of such counsels, and high among the unrealities I place the recommendation to study the Roman law. I assume that such advice means more than collecting a few Latin maxims with which to ornament the discourse, – the purpose for which Lord Coke recommended Bracton. If that is all that is wanted, the title "De Regulis Juris Antiqui" can be read in an hour. I assume that, if it is well to study the Roman law, it is well to study it as a working system. That means mastering a set of technicalities more difficult and less understood than our own, and studying another course of history by which even more than our own the Roman law must be explained. If any one doubts me, let him read Keller's "Der Römische Civil Process und die Actionen," a treatise on the prætor's edict, Muirhead's most interesting "Historical Introduction to the Private Law of Rome," and, to give him the best chance possible, Sohm's admirable Institutes. No. The way to gain a liberal view of your subject is not to read something else, but to get to the bottom of the subject itself. The means of doing that are, in the first place, to follow the existing body of dogma into its highest generalizations by the help of jurisprudence; next, to discover from history how it has come to be what it is; and, finally, so far as you can, to consider the ends which the several rules seek to accomplish, the reasons why those ends are desired, what is given up to gain them, and whether they are worth the price.

We have too little theory in the law rather than too much, especially on this final branch of study. When I was speaking of history, I mentioned larceny as an example to show how the law suffered from not having embodied in a clear form a rule which will accomplish its manifest purpose. In that case the trouble was due to the survival of forms coming from a time when a more limited purpose was entertained. Let me now give an example to show the practical importance, for the decision of actual cases, of understanding the reasons of the law, by taking an example from rules which, so far as I know, never have been explained or theorized about in any adequate way. I refer to statutes of limitation and the law of prescription. The end of such rules is obvious, but what is the justification for depriving a man of his rights, a pure evil as far as it goes, in consequence of the lapse of time? Sometimes the loss of evidence is referred to, but that is a secondary matter. Sometimes the desirability of peace, but why is peace more desirable after twenty years than before? It is increasingly likely to come without the aid of legislation. Sometimes it is said that, if a man neglects to enforce his rights, he cannot complain if, after a while, the law follows his example. Now if this is all that can be said about it, you probably will decide a case I am going to put, for the plaintiff; if you take the view which I shall suggest, you possibly will decide it for the defendant. A man is sued for trespass upon land, and justifies under a right of way. He proves that he has used the way openly and adversely for twenty years, but it turns out that the plaintiff had granted a license to a person whom he reasonably supposed to be the defendant's agent, although not so in fact, and therefore had assumed that the use of the way was permissive, in which case no right would be gained. Has the defendant gained a right or not? If his gaining it stands on the fault and neglect of the landowner in the ordinary sense, as seems commonly to be supposed, there has been no such neglect, and the right of way has not been acquired. But if I were the defendant's counsel, I should suggest that the foundation of the acquisition of rights by lapse of time is to be looked for in the position of the person who gains them, not in that of the loser. Sir Henry Maine has made it fashionable to connect the archaic notion of property with prescription. But the connection is further back than the first recorded history. It is in the nature of man's mind. A thing which you have enjoyed and used as your own for a long time, whether property or an opinion, takes root in your being and cannot be torn away without your resenting the act and trying to defend yourself, however you came by it. The law can ask no better justification than the deepest instincts of man. It is only by way of reply to the suggestion that you are disappointing the former owner, that you refer to his neglect having allowed the gradual dissociation between himself and what he claims, and the gradual association of it with another. If he knows that another is doing acts which on their face show that he is on the way toward establishing such an association, I should argue that in justice to that other he was bound at his peril to find out whether the other was acting under his permission, to see that he was warned, and, if necessary, stopped.

I have been speaking about the study of the law, and I have said next to nothing of what commonly is talked about in that connection, — text-books and the case system, and all the machinery with which a student comes most immediately in contact. Nor shall I say anything about them. Theory is my subject, not practical details. The modes of teaching have been improved since my time, no doubt, but ability

and industry will master the raw material with any mode. Theory is the most important part of the dogma of the law, as the architect is the most important man who takes part in the building of a house. The most important improvements of the last twenty-five years are improvements in theory. It is not to be feared as unpractical, for, to the competent, it simply means going to the bottom of the subject. For the incompetent, it sometimes is true, as has been said, that an interest in general ideas means an absence of particular knowledge. I remember in army days reading of a youth who, being examined for the lowest grade and being asked a question about squadron drill, answered that he never had considered the evolutions of less than ten thousand men. But the weak and foolish must be left to their folly. The danger is that the able and practical minded should look with indifference or distrust upon ideas the connection of which with their business is remote. I heard a story, the other day, of a man who had a valet to whom he paid high wages, subject to deduction for faults. One of his deductions was, "For lack of imagination, five dollars." The lack is not confined to valets. The object of ambition, power, generally presents itself nowadays in the form of money alone. Money is the most immediate form, and is a proper object of desire. "The fortune," said Rachel, "is the measure of the intelligence." That is a good text to waken people out of a fool's paradise. But, as Hegel says,[6] "It is in the end not the appetite, but the opinion, which has to be satisfied." To an imagination of any scope the most far-reaching form of power is not money, it is the command of ideas. If you want great examples read Mr. Leslie Stephen's "History of English Thought in the Eighteenth Century," and see how a hundred years after his death the abstract speculations of Descartes had become a practical force controlling the conduct of men. Read the works of the great German jurists, and see how much more the world is governed to-day by Kant than by Bonaparte. We cannot all be Descartes or Kant, but we all want happiness. And happiness, I am sure from having known many successful men, cannot be won simply by being counsel for great corporations and having an income of fifty thousand dollars. An intellect great enough to win the prize needs other food beside success. The remoter and more general aspects of the law are those which give it universal interest. It is through them that you not only become a great master in your calling, but connect your subject with the universe and catch an echo of the infinite, a glimpse of its unfathomable process, a hint of the universal law.

Notes

1   I Roll. Rep. 368.

2   See Hanson *v.* Globe Newspaper Co., 159 Mass. 293, 302.

3   Commonwealth *v.* Rubin, 165 Mass. 453.

4   Havelock Ellis, "The Criminal," 41, citing Garofalo. See also Ferri, "Sociologie Criminelle," *passim.* Compare Tarde, "La Philosophie Pénale."

5   An example of the law's refusing to protect the plaintiff is when he is interrupted by a stranger in the use of a valuable way, which he has travelled adversely for a week less than the period of prescription. A week later he will have gained a right, but now he is only a trespasser. Examples of privilege I have given already. One of the best is competition in business.

6   Phil. des Rechts, § 190.

2

A Realistic Jurisprudence – The Next Step

Karl Llewellyn

The Problem of Defining Law; Focus versus Confines

The difficulty in framing any concept of "law" is that there are so many things to be included, and the things to be included are so unbelievably different from each other. Perhaps it is possible to get them all under one verbal roof. But I do not see what you have accomplished if you do. For a concept, as I understand it, is built for a purpose. It is a thinking tool. It is to make your data more manageable in doing something, in getting somewhere with them. And I have not yet met the job, or heard of it, to which all the data that associate themselves with this loosest of suggestive symbols, "law," are relevant at once. We do and have too many disparate things and thinkings to which we like to attach that name. For instance, legislators pass "a law," by which we mean that they officially put a new form of words on the statute books. That calls up associations with regard to attorneys and judges, and to suits being brought "under the statute." But it also calls up associations with regard to those sets of practices and expectations and people which we call political parties and machines and lobbies. The former we should want, in some way, to include under the head "law," I suspect. If we did not, we ought to stop defining and think a little further. The latter – the parties and lobbies – we might have more doubt about, even if we did stop and think. Again, it seems fairly clear that there has been something we could not well

dissociate from our symbol "law" in places and times when there was no legislature and even no state – indeed when there was no organization we can call "political" that was distinct from any other organization. You cannot study the simpler forms of society nor "the law" of such forms without looking into the mechanisms of organized control at such times and places; but today you will be likely to distinguish such types of control as *non-legal*. Of course, you would not disregard them, if you wanted to know anything about "law" that was worth knowing. But you would regard them as background, or foreground, or underground, to your center of interest. They would be something that you would compare and contrast with "law," I suspect, in the present order of society. And yet I also suspect you would have your hands full if you set about to draw the line between "the two." Or again, there are gentlemen who spend a good deal of time discussing "the ends of law," or "what law ought to be." Are they talking about "law"? Certainly their postulates and conclusions, in gross and in detail, have no need to look like anything any judge ever did; and at times some of those gentlemen seem to avail themselves of that freedom; but it would be a case-hardened person who denied that what they are dealing with is closely connected with this same loose suggestive symbol. What interests me about that is when a judge is working in a "well-settled field" he is likely to pay no attention to what such gentlemen say, and to call it irrelevant speculation; whereas when he is working in an "unsettled field" he seems to pay a lot of attention to their ideas, or to ideas of much the same order. This I take to mean that *for some purposes* they are talking something very close to "law," under any definition; and for *other* purposes, they are talking something whose connection with "law" as just used is fairly remote. And this problem of the word calling up wide-scattered and disparate references, *according to the circumstance*, seems to me vital.

So that I am not going to attempt a definition of law. Not anybody's definition; much less my own. A definition both excludes and includes. It marks out a field. It makes some matters fall inside the field; it makes some fall outside. And the exclusion is almost always rather arbitrary. I have no desire to exclude anything from matters legal. In one aspect law is as broad as life, and for some purposes one will have to follow life pretty far to get the bearings of the legal matters one is examining. I say again, therefore, that I shall not attempt a definition. I shall not describe a periphery, a stopping place, a barrier. I shall instead devote my attention to the *focus* of matters legal. I shall try to discuss a *point of reference*; a point of reference to which I believe all matters legal can most usefully be referred, if they are to be seen with intelligence and with appreciation of their bearings. A focus, a core, a center – with the bearings and boundaries outward unlimited. Pardon my saying it so often; but I find it very hard to make people understand that I am not talking about putting or pushing anything *out of* the field or concept of law. People are so much used to definitions – although definitions have not always been of so much use to people. I am, therefore, going to talk about substituting a somewhat unfamiliar, but more exciting and more useful focus, for the focus that most thinking about law in the past has had.

Two references to the course that thought has taken will help to set the perspective: one, to the tenets of the nineteenth century schools of jurisprudence; one, to the development of the concepts of rights and of interests.

For the nineteenth century schools I am content to accept one of Pound's summaries.[1] It fits with what reading in the field I have done; it is based upon vastly more reading in the field than

I shall ever do. With regard to the analytical jurists, Pound stresses their interest in a body of established precepts whereby a definite legal result is supposed to be fitted to a definite set of facts; he stresses the centering of their definition upon the "aggregate of authoritative legal precepts applied by tribunals as such in a given time and place," and their presupposition of a state to make precepts and tribunals authoritative. The historical jurists, on the other hand, he finds making little distinction between law and other forms of social control; with them customary precepts, irrespective of whether they originate in the organs of politically organized societies, come in for heavy attention; central in their picture of law are the traditional techniques of decision and the traditional or customary notions of rightness. (All this, it may be added, without any too close analysis as to what is meant by "custom.") For the philosophical jurists, finally, Pound finds that "philosophical, political and ethical ideas as to the end of law and as to what legal precepts should be in view thereof" occupy the center of the stage.

I have no wish to put the tenets of these schools to the test, nor to pursue them further. Their value here is limited, but great within its limits: taken together, they hammer home the complexity of law. Each school was reaching for a single definition of all that was significant about law. Each school wound up with a definition which stressed some phases and either overlooked or greatly understressed others. Each had a definition with which, for its purposes, and especially in the hands of its creative thinkers, it made striking headway. But too close attention to any one of the definitions – in its exclusion aspects – for too long, would have meant ultimate barrenness. And I gather that one lesson Pound has drawn from his study of these and other schools has been to insist rather on what goes into the idea of law than on what is to be kept out of it.

Precepts as the Heart and Core of Most Thinking About Law

Moreover, you will have noted running through his summary of their views the word "precepts." This is traditional. When men talk or think about law, they talk and think about *rules*. "Precepts" as used by Pound, for instance, I take to be roughly synonymous with rules and principles, the principles being wider in scope and proportionately vaguer in connotation, with a tendency toward idealization of some portion of the *status quo* at any given time. And I think you will find as you read Pound that the precepts are *central* to his thinking about law. Along with rules and principles – along with precepts proper, may I say? – he stresses for instance "standards" as a part of the subject matter of law. These standards seem to be those vague but useful pictures with which one approaches a wide and varied field of conduct to measure the rights of a particular situation: a conception of what a reasonable man would do in the circumstances, or of what good faith requires, and similar pictures. They differ from rules, though not from principles, partly in their vagueness; they differ from both in being not propositions in themselves, but normative approaches to working out the application of some one *term* in a major proposition. The principle, let us say, would read: a man must answer for what good faith requires. But a standard (like a concept; like any class-term, loose or sharp) functions chiefly or exclusively as *part* of a precept. Consequently, it belongs in much the same world. It, too, *centers* on precepts. But Pound mentions more as law than precepts and standards. Along with the standards he stresses also ideals as to "the end" of law. These I take to be in substance standards on a peculiarly vague and majestic scale; standards, perhaps, to be applied to rules rather than to individual transactions.[2] Finally, he stresses – and we meet here a very different order of phenomena – "the traditional techniques of developing and applying" precepts. Only a man gifted with insight would have added to the verbal formulae and verbalized (though vague) conceptual pictures thus far catalogued, such an element *of practices*, of habits and techniques of action, of *behavior*. But only a man partially caught in the traditional precept-thinking of an age that is passing would have focussed that behavior on, have given it a major reference to, have belittled its importance by dealing with it as

a phase of, those merely verbal formulae: precepts. I have no wish to argue the point. It will appeal, or it will not, and argument will be of little service. But not only this particular bit of phrasing (which might be accidental), but the use made in Pound's writings of the idea, brings out vigorously the limitations of rules, of precepts, of *words*, when made the focus, the *center of reference*, in thinking about law.[3]

Remedies, Rights and Interests: A Developing Insight

Indeed, those limitations appear throughout the current analysis of law in terms of interests, rights and remedies. The growth of that analysis requires a short digression, but one that I believe worth making. It has to do with the *subject matter* of the rules and precepts of which men regarded the legal system as made up. Both with us and in the Roman system that subject matter has in the course of time undergone striking changes.

In the earlier stages the rules were thought of almost exclusively as rules of remedies.[4] Remedies were few and specific. There were a few certain ways to lug a man into court and a few certain things that you or the court could do with him when you got him there. We are concerned here not with why that was (why "can" a court of law give no injunctive relief today?) but only with *that* it was. The question for the man of that day took this shape: on what facts could one man make use of any specific one of the specific ways of making the court bother another man? And the rules of law were rules about that. They clustered around each remedy. In those terms people thought.[5] They thought about what they could see and do. Their crude minds dealt only with what they could observe. What they observed, they described.

To later writers this seemed primitive. The later thinkers find a different kind of order in the field of law. Remedies seem to them to have a *purpose*, to be protections of something else. They could imagine these somethings and give them a name: *rights*, substantive rights. Thus the important, the substantive rules of law become rules defining rights. Remedies are relegated to the periphery of attention. They are "adjective law" merely – devices more or less imperfect for giving effect to the important things, the substantive rights which make up the substance of the law. The relation of rights to rules is fairly clear: the two are aspects of the same thing. When a rule runs in favor of a person, he has a right, as measured by the rule. Or, if he has a right, that can be phrased by setting out a rule ascribing to him and persons in like situation with him the benefits connoted by the rights. Rights are thus precise counterparts of rules, when the rights are ascribed generally to all persons in a class in given circumstances; and this is the typical postmortemizer's line of discourse. Or rights, when ascribed to particular individuals in specific circumstances, are deductions which presuppose the rule; the major premise is the general rule on rights; the minor is the proposition hooking up this individual and these circumstances with that general rule. Rights and rules are therefore for present purposes pretty much interchangeable; the right is a shorthand symbol for the rule.[6]

Substantive rights and rules are spoken of as prevailing between people, laymen: one has, *e.g.*, a right to the performance of a contract. It is a heresy when Coke or Holmes speaks of a man having liberty under the law to perform his contract, or pay damages, at his option. It would likewise be a heresy to argue that the vital real evidence of this supposed "right" lies in an action for damages, and that the right could rather more accurately be phrased somewhat as follows: if the other party does not perform as agreed, you can sue, and *if* you have a fair lawyer, and nothing goes wrong with your witnesses or the jury, *and* you give up four or five days of time and some ten to thirty percent of the proceeds, and wait two to twenty months, you will *probably* get a judgment for a sum considerably less than what the performance would have been worth – which, if the other party is solvent and has not secreted his assets, you can in further due course collect with six percent interest for delay. To argue thus would be to confuse the remedy (which you can see) with the substantive right (which you cannot see, but which you know is there – somewhere; people tell you so). The substantive right in this body of thought has a shape and scope inde-

pendent of the accidents of remedies. And herein lies the scientific advance involved in the concept. You are freed of any necessity of observing what courts do, and of limiting your discussion to that. You get back into the ultimate realities behind their doing. Obviously you can think more clearly among those ultimate realities. They are not so much obscured by inconsistency and divergence of detail. They are not answerable to fact.

Most lay thinking, it may be noted in passing, is on this level today. Typical is the current acceptance of a paper rule or statute as meaning something simply because it has paper authority – indeed, as meaning all it says, or all it is supposed to have been intended to say, simply because it has paper authority.

Far be it from me to dispute that the concepts of substantive rights and of rules of substantive law have had great value.[7] They moved definitely and sharply toward fixing the attention of thinkers on the idea that procedure, remedies, existed not merely because they existed, nor because they had value in themselves, but because they had a purpose. From which follows immediate inquiry into what the purpose is, and criticism, if the means to its accomplishment be poor. They moved, moreover, to some extent, toward sizing up the law by situations, instead of under the categories of historically conditioned, often archaic remedy-law: a new base for a new synthesis; a base for law reform.

The Ambiguities in the Concepts of Rules and Rights

But that should not obscure the price that was paid for the advance. A price first, as already described, of moving discussion away from the checkup of fact. To a legal reformer in his campaigning, in his getting of new views across, this may have value, if "the fact" in question be existing positive law. He may move more comfortably if he can keep people from observing that his moves mean change. To a scientist, observing, or to a reformer engaged not in selling his reform, in propaganding, in putting ideas over, but in inquiring what is before him, where he wants to get, and how to get there, this obfuscation of the facts is another matter.

Secondly, a price was paid, of ambiguity – indeed of multiguity. "Rules" is a term sufficiently ambiguous. A rule may be prescriptive: "this is what *ought* to be; what the judges *ought* to do in such cases." Or it may be descriptive: "this is what *is*; what the judges *actually* do in such cases." Or it may be both at once: "this is *both* what they do *and* what they ought to do."[7a] And when theorists discuss, they will move from one of these meanings into another without notice, and with all and any gradations of connotations. In the particular case of rules "of law" a further ambiguity affects the word "rule": whether descriptive or prescriptive, there is little effort to make out *whose* action and *what* action is prescribed or described. The statement "this is the rule" typically means: "I find this formula of words in authoritative books."[8] Does this connote: "*Courts are actually proceeding* according to this formula"; or "*Courts* always *rehearse* this formula in this connection?" Does it connote: "*People* are conducting themselves in the light of this formula"; or even "People are conducting themselves as this formula suggests that they ought to." The theorist will rarely trouble to tell you how many (if any) of these connotations are implicit in his statement: "this is the rule." But he will reason, on the next page, from some one of such implications. Which means: confusion, profuse and inevitable.[9]

The confusion is stirred blacker with the concept "right" poured in. "Right" adds nothing to descriptive power. But it gives a specious appearance of substance to prescriptive rules. They seem to be *about* some *thing*. So that to clothe one's statement about what rules of law are in terms of rights, is to double the tendency to disregard the limitations actually put on rules or rights by practice and by remedies. At the vital core of thought about law, at the very place where one thought impinges on another, or where one part of law impinges on another, one sees the impingement in terms of idealized somethings which may not, which mostly *do* not, reflect men's actions. In terms of words, and not in terms of conduct; in terms of what *apparently* is understandable *without* checking up in life. So that one makes the assumption –

without the urge to inquiry – that one is dealing with reality when he talks of rights, and proceeds to use these unchecked words for further building.

There is another confusion, found in dealing with rules, and strengthened by the associated idea of rights, within the field of doctrine itself. Having come to regard words as sound bases for further thinking, the tendency is well nigh inevitable to simplify the formulations more and more: to rub out of the formulations even the discrepancies in paper doctrine which any growing system of law contains in heaping measure; doubly so because the word "rights" introduces *sub rosa* at this point the additional notion of "rightness" (in the sense of what ought to be) – before which unwanted discrepancies must fall. I am speaking here of the effects of the idea of rightness on the rejection of some of the existent purely doctrinal materials in favor of other equally doctrinal materials, the case of conflicts in and within legal doctrine – a matter of vast concern to a lawyer, though perhaps of no great moment to a political scientist.

But the same tendency carries over quite as well into the confusion of legal with non-legal materials, where it concerns political scientist and lawyer in common; and here the idea of "rights" seems to be the heavy tool of confusion, with no help at all from the idea of "rules." "Right" eternally suggests its connotation of inherent "rightness" – social, political, economic, and especially moral. It takes more careful self-analysis than most have been interested in giving to keep the *non-legal* "right" (which was a reason for claiming or striving toward or awarding a legal right) distinguished from the "legal right" which was conceived, I take it, as something not quite a mere description of an available remedy, but at least an official recognition that some kind of remedy could be had. The threat of ambiguous middle is obvious.[9a] The natural rights theorists did little to make it less.

Interests

This third confusion (but, be it noted, neither the second nor the first) was cleared up by the controversy that centered about Ihering. Since that controversy we take some care to limit our term "rights" to legal rights ("substantive," if nothing more be said), and are thereby aided in keeping the legal separate from the social factors at work in a situation. The term *interests*, on the other hand, comes in to focus attention on the presence of social factors, and to urge that substantive rights themselves, like remedies, exist only for a purpose. Their purpose is now perceived to be the protection of the interests. To be sure, we do not know what interests are. Hence, behind substantive rights (which we need not check against anything courts *do*) we now have interests (which we need not check against anything at all, and about whose presence, extent, nature and importance, whether the interests be taken absolutely or taken relatively one to another, no two of us seem to be able to agree). The scientific advance should again be obvious. Complete subjectivity has been achieved.

At this stage of the development, then, one arrives at a double chain of purposes. One starts with the interest. That is a social fact or factor of some kind, existing dependent of the law.[9b] And it has value independent of the law. Indeed, its protection is the purpose of substantive legal rights, of legal rules, of precepts of substantive law. "Security of transactions" is such an interest. The rules and rights of contract law exist to protect and effectuate it. The rules and rights are not ends, but means. But they are means which in another aspect (like most means) themselves become ends: remedies exist as means to effectuate the substantive rights, to realize the substantive rules. Obviously the means may be inadequate, badly chosen, wasteful, even self-defeating, at either stage. They may be so, cumulatively, at both stages. The rule that consideration is necessary to make an offer irrevocable for three days, even when the offer is fully intended, business like, signed, in writing, and expressed to be irrevocable for three days, may be thought not adapted to further security of transactions. The rule that certain oral and essential terms of an agreement are without force, if the balance of the agreement has been committed to writing, and looks on its face to be complete, raises considerable doubts as

to its furtherance of security of transactions – sufficiently so as to have made our rules on the subject rather intricate and uncertain, and our judicial practices at times highly uncertain. The rules standardizing the remedies in contracts for the sale of goods, limiting the remedy to a suit before a jury, and for damages, and measuring the damages in the great body of cases by arbitrary standards which presuppose a frictionless market, may be thought to give inadequate remedy, even if the basis of supposed substantive rules and rights be thought wholly adequate to *its* purposes. The means, I say, may be inadequate; but the analysis invites discovery of the inadequacy. Hence, whatever one thinks of the sufficiency in the large of the analysis in the three-fold terms of interests, substantive rights and rules, and remedies, one can but pay homage to the sureness with which it forces law on the attention as something man-made, something capable of criticism, of change, of reform – and capable of criticism, change, and reform not only according to standards found inside law itself (inner harmony, logical consistence of rules, parts and tendencies, *elegantia juris*) but also according to standards vastly more vital found *outside* law itself, in the society law purports both to govern *and to serve*.

On the other hand, the set-up in these terms has carried over its full measure of confusion, as I have tried to indicate above. And the confusion thus carried over is not – like the virtues of the analysis – familiar, well understood, and regularly taken account of. Which brings me again to the suggestion made above, that the use of precepts, or rules, or of rights which are logical counterparts of rules – of *words*, in a word – as the *center* of reference in thinking about law, is a block to clear thinking about matters legal. I want again to make sure that I am not misunderstood. (1) I am not arguing that "rules of substantive law" are without importance. (2) I am not arguing that it is not humanly *possible* to use the interests-rights and rules-remedies analysis and still think clearly and usefully about law. (3) Least of all, am I attempting to urge the exclusion of substantive rights and rules from the field of "law." Instead of these things, I am arguing (1) that rules of substantive law are of far less importance than most legal theorizers have assumed in most of their thinking and writing, and that they are *not* the most useful center of reference for discussion of law; (2) that the presence of the term "rights and rules" in the interest set-up (a) has persistent tendency to misfocus attention on that term; (b) that the avoidance of that tendency is a great gain in clarity; and (c) that to both attempt such avoidance and retain the term is to cumber all discussion with embarrassing and quite unnecessary baggage; (3) that substantive rights and rules should be removed from their present position at the *focal point* of legal discussion, in favor of the *area of contact* between judicial (or official) *behavior* and the *behavior* of laymen; that the substantive rights and rules should be studied not as self-existent, nor as a major point of reference, but themselves with constant reference to that area of behavior-contacts. Let me take up the second and third of these positions together, and turn then to the first.

The Interests-Rights-Remedies Analysis: Words v. Practice

I see no value to be gained from the interests-rights and rules-remedies set up except to bring out, to underscore, that law is not all, nor yet the major part of, society; and to force attention to the relations and interactions of law and the rest of society; and as a matter of method, to provide words which keep legal and non-legal aspects of the situation and the interactions distinct. And it would seem to go without demonstration that *the most significant* (I do *not* say the *only* significant) aspects of the relations of law and society lie in the field of behavior, and that words take on importance either because and insofar as they are behavior, or because and insofar as they demonstrably reflect or influence other behavior. This statement seems not worth making. Its truth is absurdly apparent. For all that, it reverses, it upsets, the whole traditional approach to law. It turns accepted theory on its head. The traditional approach is in terms of words; it centers on words; it has the utmost difficulty in getting beyond words. If nothing be said about behavior, the *tacit* assumption is that

the words do reflect behavior, and if they be the words of rules of law, do influence behavior, even influence behavior effectively and precisely to conform completely to those words. Here lies the key to the muddle. The "rules" are laid down; in the typecase they are "ought" rules, prescriptive rules: the writer's prescriptions, the writer's oughts, individually proclaimed oughts – the true rule is that judges should give judgment for the plaintiff on these facts.[10] From this we jump without necessary notice into equivalent oughts as *accepted* in the legal system under discussion: prevailing oughts – the authorities agree that judges should give judgment for the plaintiff on these facts. Here, again without notice and without inquiry, we *assume* that *practice* of the judges conforms to the accepted oughts on the books; that the verbal formulations of oughts *describe* precisely the is-es of practice; that they *do* give such judgment on such facts. A toothed bird of a situation, in law or any other walk of life. Where is men's ideology about their doing, about what is good practice – where is that ideology or has it ever been an adequate description of their *working* practice?

This is the first tacit imputation of factuality to the rules of ought. A second such imputation follows forthwith – again without explicitness, again without inquiry, again (save in odd instances) without challenge or suggestion or doubt. The paper rule of ought which has now been *assumed* to *describe* the judges' *working* rule of ought (*i.e.*, to correspond with the judges' practice of decision) is now further assumed to *control* the practice of the interested laymen, to *govern* people's conduct. Pray for the storm-tossed mariner on a night like this! What hope is there for clarity of reasoning with such a waste of billowing to build on?

Do I suggest that (to cut in at one crucial point) the "accepted rules," the rules the judges say that they apply, are without influence upon their actual behavior? I do not. I do not even say that, *sometimes*, these "accepted rules" may not be a very accurate description of the judges' actual behavior. What I say is that such accuracy of description is rare. The question is how, and how much, and in what direction, do the accepted rule and the practice of decision diverge? More: how, and how much, *in each case?* You cannot generalize on this, *without investigation.* Your guesses may be worth something, in the large. *They are worth nothing at all, in the particular.* The one thing we know now for certain is, that different rules have totally different relations to the behavior of judges, of other officials, and of the particular persons "governed" (optimistic word!) by those different rules. The approach here argued for admits, then, out of hand, *some* relation between *any* accepted rule and judicial behavior; and then proceeds to deny that that admission involves anything but a problem for investigation in the case in hand; and to argue that the significance of the particular rule will appear only *after* the investigation of the vital, focal, phenomenon: the behavior. And if an empirical *science* of law is to have any realistic basis, any responsibility to the facts, I see no escape from moving to this position. Thus, and only thus, is the real gain sought by the interests-rights and rules-remedies analysis to be made tangible. I do not deny, be it noted, that those who have cast their thinking in that set-up are from time to time aware of the importance of what is here urged. "Law-in-books and law-in-action." Indeed, whenever challenged on the point, any one of them will proceed to remodel his emphasis *ad hoc*; he will, for a moment, fix his stress on the remedy, even on the effects of the remedy, as used, in life. *But* it is an *ad hoc* remodelling. It is forgotten when the immediate issue is passed. It is no part of the standard equipment of investigation, discussion, synthesis; it is a part only of the equipment of defense. When used apart from combat, as a result of a worker's own curiosity or of some sudden fact-stimulus from outside, it flares like a shooting star, and disappears. Always the night of words will close again in beauty over the wild, streaked disturbance.

Interests: What Are They?

This emphasis on behavior, on the observable, on *attempts* at objective cross-check on the data under discussion, on *attempts* to find words which describe and do not misdescribe those data, ought to bear fruit in the discussion of interests, as well. The attribution of "interest" quality to anything of necessity involves a value-judgment over and above those value-judgments inherent in any scientific inquiry.[11] At that point the behavior approach ceases to promise objective agreement, except in this – that isolation of the value-judgment, in presentation, from the observed phenomena on which it in part rests, would clarify much discussion. Above all, such an approach to interests would move in terms of *demonstrating the existence of groupings* of behavior claimed to be significant, as the part of scientific decency when any "interest" is set up for discussion. The present approach tends instead to set up the broadest of formulae about interests, and to attribute them to situations in magisterial unconcern for the specific facts. I have paid my respects briefly above to some aspects of "security of transactions." I would not be understood thereby to deny that those three words are highly useful, or that they refer to very significant aspects of our life. But I am very eager to be understood as questioning how much is accomplished, for any given specific problem, by resting merely on the magic of those words. I think my friend Patterson has wisely described the interest-concept, in its present stage of development, as merely a red flag to *challenge investigation* in certain general directions – as leaving in any concrete situation most of the fact gathering and most of the fact weighing still to be done. "Security of transactions," in the contract cases I have put above would, to him, mean the most useful raising of a query: what kind of transactions is involved? Better, what *kinds* of transactions are involved? How many? What results, at present? What disappointments? What effects would any proposed change have? What possible undesired effects, in the hands of interested parties? And so on. "Security of transactions" would settle nothing. It would, as facts become clear, suggest one line of policy which has come in many phases of the law to be regarded as important; but it would leave the importance of that line of policy in any case to be illumined by the facts relevant to the situation in that instant case. No elimination of the subjective value-judgment, then; but an illumination by objective data of the basis and bearings of a subjective value-judgment. Insofar, a comparison of *facts* with *facts*, and not of *words* with *words*. Not a comparison of a mere formula of words about an interest with a formula of words said to be a "rule of law," a precept with no man knows what unexamined meaning in life. Nay, rather the objective data, the *specific* data, *claimed* to represent an interest, compared with the *actual doings* of the judges and the *actual effects* of their doings *on the data claimed to represent an interest.* If the judges' *sayings* have *demonstrable* effects, add those to the comparison. What else is relevant? Better: is anything else anything like *so* relevant?

I have said above that this can be done under the more cumbersome three-fold analytical set-up.[12] I have said that it semi-occasionally has been done. I have said that it is rarely done, and that the definite tendency of that set-up is to block off the doing of it. I venture to predict that without the shift of emphasis, of focus, to behavior, that tendency will continue cheerfully in evidence.

Meaning of Rules and Rights Under the Behavior Analysis

What now, is the place of rules and rights, under such an approach? To attempt their excision from the field of law would be to fly in the face of fact. I should like to begin by distinguishing real "rules" and rights from paper rules and rights. The former are conceived in terms of behavior; they are but other names, convenient shorthand symbols, for the remedies, the actions of the courts. They are descriptive, not prescriptive, except insofar as there may occasionally be implied that courts *ought to* continue in their practices.[13] "Real rules," then, if I had my way with words, would by legal scientists be called the practices of the courts, and not "rules" at all. And statements of "rights" would be statements of likelihood that in a given situation a certain type of court action loomed in the offing. Factual terms. No more. This use of "rights," at least, has already considerable standing among the followers of Hohfeld. This concept of "real rule" has been gaining favor since it was first put into clarity by Holmes. "Paper rules" are what have

been treated, traditionally, as rules of law: the accepted *doctrine* of the time and place – what the books there say "the law" is. The "real rules" and rights – "what the courts will do in a given case, and nothing more pretentious" – are then predictions. They are, I repeat, on the level of isness and not of oughtness; they seek earnestly to go no whit, in their suggestion, beyond the remedy actually available. Like all shorthand symbols, they are dangerous in connotation, when applied to situations which are not all quite alike. But their intent and effort is to describe. And one can borrow for them Max Weber's magnificent formulation in terms of probability: a right (or practice, or "real rule") exists *to the extent that* a likelihood exists that A can induce a court to squeeze, out of B, A's damages; more: *to the extent that* the likely collections will cover A's damage. In this aspect *substantive* rights and "rules," as distinct from adjective, simply disappear – on the descriptive level. The measure of a "rule," the measure of a right, becomes what can be done about the situation. *Accurate* statement of a "real rule" or of a right includes all procedural limitations on what can be done about the situation. What are left, in the realm of *description*, are at the one end the facts, the groupings of conduct (and demonstrable expectations) which may be claimed to constitute an interest; and on the other the practices of courts in their effects upon the conduct and expectations of the laymen in question. Facts, in the world of isness, to be compared directly with other facts, also in the world of isness.

A reversion, do you say, to the crude and outmoded thinking of rules in terms of remedies only, to confining legal thinking to the vagaries of tradition-bound procedure? Not quite. It is a reversion to the realism of that primitive point of view. But a sophisticated reversion to a sophisticated realism. Gone is the ancient assumption that law is because law is; there has come since, and remains, the inquiry into the purpose of what courts are doing, the criticism in terms of searching out purposes and criticizing means. Here value-judgments reenter the picture, and should. Observing particular, concrete facts of conduct and of expectation which suggest the presence of "an interest," one arrives at his value conclusion that something in those facts calls for protection at the hands of state officials. What protection is called for, and called for in terms of what *action* of the state officials? Again a matter of judgment – but a matter of judgment which at least foots on reality and comes to results in terms of action. With that hypothetical action, the actual conduct of those officials can be directly compared. Room for error, in plenty, in diagnosing interests, and in imagining the forms of official conduct suited to their protection. But realism in discussion; realism at each end of the comparison; a narrowing as far as the present state of knowledge will permit, of the field for obstructing eyes with words that masquerade as things without a check-up.

The Place and Treatment of Paper Rules

Are "rules of law" in the accepted sense eliminated in such a course of thought? Somewhat obviously not. Whether they be pure paper rules, or are the accepted patter of the law officials, they remain present, and their presence remains an actuality – an actuality of importance – but an actuality whose *precise* importance, whose bearing and influence become clear. First of all they appear as what they are: rules of authoritative ought, addressed *to* officials, telling *officials* what the *officials* ought to do.[14] To which telling the officials either pay no heed at all (the pure paper rule; the dead-letter statute; the obsolete case) or listen partly (the rule "construed" out of recognition; the rule to which lip-service only is paid, while practice runs another course) or listen with all care (the rule with which the official practice pretty accurately coincides). I think that every such official precept-on-the-books (statute, doctrine laid down in the decision of a court, administrative regulation) tacitly contains an element of pseudo-description along with its statement of what officials ought to do; a tacit statement that officials do act according to the tenor of the rule; a tacit prediction that officials will act according to its tenor. Neither statement nor prediction is often true *in toto*. And the first point of the approach here made is skepticism as to the truth of either in the case in hand. Yet it is an accepted convention to act and talk as if this statement and prediction were most solemn truth: a tradition marked peculiarly among the legal profession when engaged officially. It is indeed of first importance to remember that such a tradition contains a tendency to verify itself.[15] But no more so than to remember that such a tendency is no more powerful than its opposite: that other tendency to move quietly into falsifying the prediction in fact, while laying on an ointment of conventional words to soothe such as wish to believe the prediction has worked out.

Thus the problem of official formulations of rules and rights becomes complex. First, as to formulations already present, already existent: the accepted doctrine. There, I repeat, one lifts an eye canny and skeptical as to whether judicial behavior is in fact what the paper rule purports (implicitly) to state. One seeks the real practice on the subject, by study of how the cases do in fact eventuate. One seeks to determine how far the paper rule is real, how far *merely* paper.[16] One seeks an understanding of *actual* judicial behavior, in that comparison of rule with practice; one follows also the use made of the paper rule in argument by judges and by counsel, and the apparent influence of its official presence on decisions. One seeks to determine when it is stated, but ignored; when it is stated and followed; when and why it is *expressly* narrowed or extended or modified, so that a new paper rule is created. One observes the level of *silent* application or modification or escape, in the "interpretation" of the facts of a case, in contrast to that other and quite distinct level of express wrestling with the language of the paper rule. One observes how strongly ingrained is the tradition of requiring a good paper justification, in terms of officially accepted paper rules, before any decision, however appealing on the facts, can be regarded as likely of acceptance. And by the same token, one observes the importance of the official formulae as tools of argument and persuasion; one observes both the stimuli to be derived from, and the limitations set by, their language. Very rapidly, too, one perceives that neither are all official formulae alike in these regards, nor are all courts, nor are all times and circumstances for the same formula in the same court. The *handling* of the official formulae to influence court behavior then comes to appear as an art, capable only to a limited extent of routinization or (to date) of accurate and satisfying description. And the discrepancy, great or small, between the official formula and what actually results, obtains the limelight attention it deserves.

Paper Rules and New Control

I am tempted, however, to regard the *new* formulation of official rules as even more vitally affected by the approach here suggested than is the dealing with existing formulations. For such new formulation is always with a purpose.[17] The effectuation of this purpose (one recalls "the protection of an interest," *supra*) *must be sought by means of verbal formulation.* In part the need is based on our legal tradition: our officials move to a great extent on the stimulus of and in the light of verbally formulated rules.[18] In part, moreover, verbal formulations, and especially those in regard to *new, planned* change in action, are an inherently essential tool of communication in a complex society; they are peculiarly important in a society which depends in good part upon written records to maintain continuity of practice between successive incumbents of an office, and between successive generations. But since the ultimate effectuation of a purpose is in terms of action, of behavior, the verbal formulation, to be an efficient tool, must be such as will produce the behavior[19] desired. *This turns on the relevant prevailing practices and attitudes of the relevant persons.* In one familiar doctrinal illustration, language used in a statute "will be read" in the light both of the existing common law, and of prior judicial construction of that language. But that is a matter of the top, the most superficial, level. Below that are the more vital practices prevalent as to *handling* official rules, described roughly above; practices, *i.e.*, of courts and of lawyers.

But in regard to the new (and especially the statutory) formulation, the behavior problem goes much deeper than such practices of the legal elect. The ways of appellate courts in handling existing official rules presuppose the cracking of the toughest nut the statutory draftsman has to crack: the case is already in court; someone is already making an appeal to the official formula. Whereas one of the statutory draftsman's major problems is to look into existent behavior beforehand, to make sure that his formula, when it becomes an official rule, will not merely bask in the sun upon the books. He must so shape it as to *induce its application* (with all the discrepancies that may entail) or else (for any purpose save that of pacifying clamorous constituents content with words) his blow is spent in air.[20]

Only as a second job does he have to wrestle with making his formula so impinge upon judicial tradition that the results in action will be those desired *if* a case gets into court. Again there is little to be gained by laboring the point. It seems patent that only a gain in realism and effectiveness of thinking can come from consistently (not occasionally) regarding the official formulation as a tool, not as a thing of value in itself; as a means without meaning save in terms of its workings, and of meaning in its workings only when these last are compared with the results desired. In the terms used above: as *prima facie* pure paper until the contrary is demonstrated; and as at best a new piece of an established but moving environment, one single element in a complex of practices, ideas and institutions without whose study the one element means nothing. Hence: not the elimination of rules, but the setting of words and paper in perspective.

The Place and Treatment of Concepts

Like rules, concepts are not to be eliminated; it cannot be done. Behavior is too heterogeneous to be dealt with except after some artificial ordering. The sense impressions which make up what we call observation are useless unless gathered into some arrangement. Nor can thought go on without categories.

A realistic approach would, however, put forward two suggestions on the making of such categories. The first of them rests primarily upon the knowledge that to classify is to disturb. It is to build emphases, to create stresses, which obscure some of the data under observation and give fictitious value to others – a process which can be excused only insofar as it is necessary to the accomplishing of a purpose. The data to be singled out in reference to that purpose are obviously those which appear most relevant. But true relevancy can be determined only as the inquiry advances. For this reason a realistic approach to any new problem would begin by skepticism as to the adequacy of the *received* categories for ordering the phenomena effectively toward a solution of the new problem. It is quite possible that the received categories as they already stand are perfect for the purpose. It is, however, altogether unlikely. The suggestion then comes to this: that with the new purpose in mind one approach the data afresh, taking them in as raw a condition as possible, and discovering how far and how well the available traditional categories really cover the most relevant of the raw data. And that before proceeding one undertake such modifications in the categories as may be necessary or look promising. In view of the tendency toward overgeneralization in the past this is likely to mean the making of smaller categories – which may be either sub-groupings inside the received categories, or may cut across them.

The other suggestion of a realistic approach rests on the observation that categories and concepts, once formulated and once they have entered into thought processes, tend to take on an appearance of solidity, reality and inherent value which has no foundation in experience. More than this: although orginally formulated on the model of at least some observed data, they tend, once they have entered into the organization of thinking, both to suggest the presence of corresponding data when these data are not in fact present, and to twist any fresh observation of data into conformity with the terms of the categories. This has been discussed above in its application to rules; it holds true, however, of any concept. It is peculiarly troublesome in regard to legal concepts, because of the tendency of the crystallized legal concept to persist after the fact model from which the concept was once derived has disappeared or changed out of recognition. A simple but striking in-

stance is the resistance opposed by the "master – servant" concept to each readjustment along the lines of a new industrial labor situation. The counsel of the realistic approach here, then, would be the constant back-checking of the category against the data, to see whether the data are still present *in the form suggested by the category-name*. This slows up thinking. But it makes for results which means something when one gets them.

Background of the Behavior Approach

All this is nothing new in social science. It is of a piece with the work of the modern ethnographer. He substitutes painstaking objective description of practice, for local *report* of what the practice is, or for (what is worse) a report either of local practice or of local ideology pleasantly distorted by the observer's own home-grown conventions. It is of a piece with the development of objective method in psychology. It fits into the pragmatic and instrumental developments in logic.[21] It seeks to capitalize the methodological worries that have been working through in these latter years to new approaches in sociology, economics, political science. The only novel feature is the application to that most conventionalized and fiction-ridden of disciplines, the law. In essence the historical school of jurists from the one side, and Bentham and later Ihering from the other, were approaching the lines of theorizing here put forth. Holmes' mind had travelled most of the road two generations back. What has been done in the last decades that has some touch of novelty, is for theorizers to go beyond theorizing, to move, along such lines as these, into the gathering and interpretation of facts about legal behavior: Ehrlich, Nussbaum, Hedemann, Brandeis, Frankfurter, Moore, Clark, Douglas, Moley, Yntema, Klaus, Handler, Lambert[22] – I name only enough to show that neither a single country nor a single school is involved, and to make clear that the point of view has moved beyond the stage of chatter and has proved itself in operation. That out of the way, I should like to glance at a few further implications of the approach.

Administrative Action as Law

Three of them appear together. First, to focus on the area of contact between judicial behavior and the behavior of the "governed" is to stress *interactions*. Second, central as are the judges' actions in disputed cases, there is a vast body of other officials whose actions are of no less importance; quantitatively their actions are of vastly greater importance, though it may well be that the judge's position gives him a leverage of peculiar power. In what has preceded I have somewhat lightly argued as if judge and court were the be-all and end-all of the legal focus. It is time to reformulate, to grow at once more accurate and more inclusive.[23] The actions of these other officials touch the interested layman more often than do those of the judge; increasingly so, and apparently increasing at a rising rate of increase as the administrative machine gains in force and function. More often than not, administrative action is, *to the layman affected*, the last expression of the law on the case. In such a situation, I think it highly useful to regard it as the law of the case. I see no gain whatever, and much loss, from setting up a fictitious unity in the law, when some officials do one thing, some another, and the courts now and again a third. Realistically, the law is then not one, but at least three, and by no means three-in-one. If what the courts do ultimately prevails *and is translated into* administrative practice, that is that. If such an event is predictable in advance, I find it vastly more useful to think of that event as the emerging unity of the law, which until it happens may be an ought, and is already an opportunity (at a price) for him with gumption and money to reach for it, but is not *yet* the probable law for the ordinary case. What – more than one law, on a single point, in a single jurisdiction, according to the whim or practice of an official, or according to the funds or temperament or political complexion of the layman affected? Just that. What else expresses the facts? Why blink and squint because the paper tradition is annoyed? As long as there are words to describe the court rule which will ultimately prevail (in a case where it will!), and to describe the situation differently before

and after the victory, what is gained in a *science of observation* by using the same words to describe both conditions – except a sure confusion?[24]

Hence I argue that the focus, the center of law, is not merely what the judge does, in the impact of that doing on the interested layman, but what *any* state official does, officially.[25] Lawyers are curious. As to a *court* of first instance, though it be a justice's court, they would have no difficulty seeing this. They could even see that a wrong decision below, appealed from and reversed, would be part of the troubles of a litigant, would reduce his effective rights – how often do they jockey the case to bring about a settlement, by trading on just such friction-factors! But to say that the decision of the eighteen hundred dollar clerk in Bureau *B* that certain expenses are not deductible from my income tax return *is* the law in my case, gives a lawyer's ideology the same shock that it gives to a political scientist to urge that for purposes of that decision, that official *is* the State. One needs again to wash the matter down with Holmes' "cynical acid" and see what is left. In the same manner, if the official's decision is adverse and erroneous, I should include as a subtraction from my effective rights, if I proceeded to get a reversal, the ill-will and subsequent trouble I might incur at the hands of that official; as a part of the law, if I won; and its predictability as a determining part of the law, if I decided not to fight.

Laymen's Behavior as a Part of Law

Interactions between official behavior and laymen's behavior, first; and second, the recognition of official behavior of all officials as part of the core of law. Third, and an immediate part of both, the recognition of what Nicholas Spykman so strongly and properly stresses: that the word "official" tacitly presupposes, connotes, reaches out to include, all those patterns of action (ordering, initiative) and obedience (including passivity) on the part both of the official and of all laymen affected which *make up* the official's position and authority as such. Something of this sort is the idea underlying "consent of the governed," "ultimate dependence upon public opinion," and the like; but these older phrasings have no neatness of outline; they do not even suggest the need of sharp-edged drawing, which I take to be the reason why they act as a soporific, while the Spykman formulation acts as a stimulant to the curiosity and imagination. In a passing it is well to note that here, too, Max Weber's method of formulation becomes classic: the official exists as such precisely *insofar as* such patterns of action and obedience prevail.[26] I agree whole-heartedly that these patterns are an essential part of any phenomena we call law. The more whole-heartedly because Spykman's formulation brings out with fresh emphasis the difference between paper rules and resultant behavior, and the extent to which the behavior which results (if any) from the official formulation of a rule depends on the patterns of thought and action of the persons whose behavior is in question.

The Need for Narrower, More Concrete Study

How far these patterns can be presupposed, how far they require specific examination, depends on the individual case. Here as throughout we run into the need for reexamining the majestic categories of the romantic period of jurisprudence. The old categories are imposing in their purple, but they are all too big to handle. They hold too many heterogeneous items to be of any use. What is true of some law simply will not hold of other law. What is true of some persons as to some law will not hold of other persons, even as to the same or similar law.[27] I care not how reclassification be made, so long as it is in terms of observation and of organizing the data usably, *and* with back-check to the facts. But reclassification is called for. From another angle, what we need is patience to look and see what is there; and to do that we must become less ambitious as to how much we are going to look at all at once.

An illustration may make the point clearer. Some "rules" are aimed at controlling and affecting the behavior of persons whose whole set and interest is opposed to making the adjust-

ment desired; others are aimed at affecting behavior of persons who are not only willing to adjust, but have an existing effective machinery for accomplishing the adjustment. A type of the first is almost any phase of professional crime; a type of the second, perhaps, would be some change in the law affecting city real estate transactions which happens to be desired by the dealers. Most cases are compounded of both elements. If city real estate alone is involved, much might be said at first blush for law reform being peculiarly easy and quick, because the practice is firmly entrenched of never entering a real estate deal without consulting a lawyer. But other practices are also entrenched, such as relying upon first mortgage finance from a particular type of concern which in turn insists upon a title policy which in turn is under control of companies whose interest runs counter to certain types of law reform. The troubles of Torrens titles in New York City are an instance. They are substantially unmarketable; no mortgage company will loan on them because no title company will insure them.[28] That is, however, an instance of attempted "helpful-device" legal innovation. It is a different problem from the "ordering-and-forbidding" legal innovation. Barring questions of constitutionality, and barring the political question of how far legislation running counter to the desires of a well organized and powerful group can be achieved at all, it is obvious that enforcement of a new prescribed style of doing business upon New York City title companies would be *prima facie* a promising problem of legal engineering, precisely because their business is localized, well organized, and run by relatively few business units. Unlike the professional criminal, they could not dive underground and survive. The problem of detection would therefore be one of detecting not persons, but infractions by known units; and their deals could almost certainly be forced into the open. The major policing problem would therefore in all likelihood become one of anticipating and barring out in advance "evasions" undertaken by changing the methods of business under advice of counsel: *i.e.*, a problem of initially or subsequently so framing the official formulae of ordering and forbidding that transactions could not be accomplished (at a profit, after deducting fines, etc.) except along lines of the general purposes of the legislation. True, unless the engineering were so successful that a somewhat comparably profitable new turn to the business developed, the legislator would have to reckon not only with initial, but with persistent and highly skilled resistance – which might even take the line it once did with the railroads, of seeking to capture the governmental machine. And it is of course this type of resistance which would in fact (contrary to our hypothesis) keep the constitutional issue in the forefront of the fight. The parallels and the divergencies from regulation or prohibition of liquor traffic would be instructive. As one moves to bank robberies or jewelry thefts the parallels begin to fade out and the divergencies to sharpen. I have purposely chosen an illustration from a field in which I am blankly ignorant, in order to bring out the lines of thought and inquiry which open, under the approach, *even before the gathering of data is begun*. It is obvious that the set or attitude of those affected or sought to be affected by any piece of "law" is at the heart of the problem of control; it should be equally obvious that the style of organization of those persons, their group ways of action – whether among themselves or with regard to society at large – is equally vital. Behavior effects depend upon present behavior conditions.

The Narrow Application of Most Rules – and Its Implications

This leads directly into the next point: most pieces of law affect only a *relatively* small number of persons ever or at all, with any directness – or are intended to. Where that is the case, the *organization, attitude, present and probable behavior of the persons sought to be affected* is what needs major consideration, from the angle of getting results (or of understanding results). Indeed, the very *identification* of those persons may be a precondition calling for much study. Which is a somewhat absurdly roundabout way of saying that unless those matters are studied, the rules drawn, and the administrative behavior adapted to the persons in question, results will be an

accident. "*To the persons in question*," and, indeed, "to those persons *under the conditions in question*." It cannot be too strongly insisted that our attitude toward "rules" of law, treating them as universal in *application*, involves a persistent twisting of observation. "Rules" in the realm of action *mean* what rules *do*; "rules" in the realm of action *are* what they do. The *possible* application and applicability are not without importance, but the *actual* application and applicability are of controlling importance. To think of rules as universals – especially, to think of them as being applicable to "all persons who bring themselves within their terms" – is to muffle one's eyes in a constitutional fiction before beginning a survey of the scene. To be sure, constitutions purport to require rules of law to be "equal and general."[29] But most rules, however general as to the few they cover, are highly special, when viewed from the angle of how many citizens there are. And most rules "applying" to "all who come within their terms" (all those who set up barber shops, or are tempted to commit murder, or to bribe officials, or to embezzle from banks or certify checks without the drawer having funds, or to adopt a child, or run a manufacturing establishment employing five or more persons) do not and will not, realistically considered, ever be "applicable" in any meaningful sense of the term, to *most* people in the community. Such rules are indeed open. Persons do move in and out of the sphere of their applicability. But that sphere is much more clearly seen, when viewed (as compared with the community) as narrow, as special, as peculiar. Obviously even more special is the sphere of *real* application: of official *behavior* with reference to application. (And is it not clear that this most special sphere is the one of greatest consequence to the persons on whose behavior any results depend: the objects of the "regulation?")[30]

I know of no consequence of the approach here contended for – the approach in terms of organized behavior interacting with organized behavior – no consequence more illuminating than this immediate opening up for study of the sub-group and institutional structure both of "governors" and of "governed." Its opening up for study as a first essential to any understanding at all, as making the study of law a study in first instance of particularized situations and what happens in or can be done about them.[31]

Realism as to "Society"

"What can be done," and by whom? I have spoken of law as a means: *whose* means, to *whose* end? Discussions of law, like discussions of "social control," tend a little lightly to assume "*a* society" and to assume the antecedent discovery of "social" objectives. Either is hard to find in any sense which corresponds with the facts of control. Where is the unity, the single coherent group? Where is the demonstrable objective which is social, and not opposed by groups well nigh as important as those which support it? And law in particular presents over most, if not all of its bulk, the phenomenon of clashing interests; of antagonistic persons or groups, with officials stepping in to favor some as against some others. Either to line up the dissenter in the interests of his own group; that is one broad phase. Or to regulate the relations between two groups, or to alter the terms of the struggle (competitive or other) between them. Hence the eternal fight for the control of the machinery of law, and of law making, whereby the highly interested *A*s can hope partially to force their will upon the equally but adversely interested *B*s, and to put behind that control the passive approval and support of the great body of *C*s – who happen to be disinterested, or, what is equally to the point, uninterested. To the truth of this observation it makes little difference whether the ends of the *A*s are material or idealistic whether wholly selfish, or dedicated most altruistically to some concept of the welfare of the whole. And while this welter with regard to change in law may, if you will, be thought of as political, the presence of the welter raises problems in defining "interests." One must also recur to the fact that it is on the same welter that official behavior is expected to be brought to bear when the new "rule" has been proclaimed.[32] Thus raising all the problems raised above, with this addition: the possibility, not there mentioned, of a group of laymen pushing to help the official program through.

One matter does need mention here, however: the eternal dilemma of the law, indeed of society; and of the law because the law purports peculiarly among our institutions to "represent" the whole. There is, amid the welter of self-serving groups, clamoring and struggling over this machine that will give power over others, the recurrent emergence of some wholeness, some sense of responsibility which outruns enlightened self-interest, and results in action apparently headed (often purposefully) for the common good. To affirm this is to confess no Hegelian mysticism of the State. It leaves quite open any question of the existence of some "life principle" in a society. It merely notes that, lacking such a self-sanation in terms of the whole, the whole would not indefinitely continue as a whole. And to deny that would be folly. It would be to carry emancipation from the idle ideology of "representation of the whole" into blindness to the half-truth around which that once-precious ideology was built. But to deny the emancipation, to worship the half-truth without dire and specific concern for the details of the welter, would be a folly quite as great.[33]

What Law is Thought to Be: Folk-Law

In all the emphasis placed upon behavior I may have created the impression that a "realistic" approach would make itself unrealistic by disregarding what people *think* law is. Not so. But a realistic approach would cut at once into analysis and subdivision of the terms "people," "think," and "law" in such a phrase. For the great mass of persons not particularly concerned, I suspect that "law" in this aspect, *so far as* it concerns themselves, means "what I ought to do" and is not much distinguished from those selective slight idealizations of current practice we think of as morals. At times the issue certainly gets closer: "I want this contract to stick" – and doubtless I will then think of putting it in writing, and will meditate on reciting a formula I saw somewhere (in a deed, was it?): "for one dollar and other good and valuable considerations"; I may get a witness to the signing, too. In the field of private law we know singularly little of this folk-law-in-action. In that of criminal law we can suspect a very rough coincidence of folk-law-in-action with folk-morality-in-action,[34] except that here and there the thought of cop and jail will work deterrently when plain external and internal non-official social sanctions might not wholly click; we can suspect further that over considerable fields criminal law is too new and too specialized to have much background or counterpart in folk-morality; and, finally, that some fairly wide bodies of non-moral (or not yet moral) criminal law aspects will have percolated into folk-law: I think of traffic law (as known to the traffickers) as distinctly in advance in most places of traffic morality, and of similar discrepancies in regard to liquor, gambling, and sex matters, as to some portions of a population with variant morals. Now clearly what people think law to be, as regards themselves, has some effect at times upon their action. My guess is, however, the effect on the side of forbidding is much slighter than the lawyer is likely to imagine, whenever any important pressure of self-interest is present, except for a relatively small minority, or over relatively small areas of action for any particular person. On the other hand, my guess is that in the field in which law provides "helpful devices" – the attempt to use which presupposes concurrent self-interest – folk-law has very considerable influence in shaping conduct. The problem calls for exploration, from the realist's angle, by cautious study of detail. Even more important, I suspect, is the problem of what law is supposed to be with regard to others than the supposer. But important in accounting less for action than for inaction. For it seems likely that in this aspect law is mainly conceived simply as being all right, without concern for detail; and that this aspect of folk-law is close to the heart of the grand-scale passive cooperation of the uninterested which makes control of the political machinery a prize.

Ideals as to What Law Ought to Be

No less important than what people think law is, is what people conceive that law should be. Any change in law is in good part a reflection of someone's desire to produce a difference. And just as attitudes and expectations must be taken into account along with overt behavior, so must purposes and the ideal pictures toward which purposes drive. Thus far, even from the angle of a purely descriptive science.

Into another aspect of ideals as to what law ought to be this paper does not attempt to go. I make no effort here to indicate either the proper rule, or the proper action on any legal subject. I do, however, argue, and with some vigor, that as soon as one turns from the *formulation* of ideals to their *realization*, the approach here indicated is vital to his making headway. It is only in terms of a sound descriptive science of law (or of what is roughly equivalent, a soundly built working art, which takes equal account of conditions) that ideals move beyond the stage of dreams. Moreover, as has so often been pointed out, both the feasibility of accomplishing a policy and the cost of its accomplishment are in a world of limited possibilities vital elements in arriving at a judgment of the worthwhileness of the policy itself.

Conclusion

In conclusion, then, may I repeat that I have been concerned not at all with marking a periphery of law, with defining "it," with *excluding* anything at all from its field. I have argued that the trend of the most fruitful thinking about law has run steadily toward regarding law as an engine (a heterogenous multitude of engines) having purposes, not values in itself; and that the clearer visualization of the problems involved moves toward ever-decreasing emphasis on words, and ever-increasing emphasis on observable behavior (in which any demonstrably probable attitudes and thought-patterns should be included). Indeed that the focus of study, the point of reference for all things legal has been shifting, and should now be consciously shifted to the area of contact, of interaction, between official regulatory behavior and the behavior of those affecting or affected by official regulatory behavior; and that the rules and precepts and principles which have hitherto tended to keep the limelight should be displaced, and treated with severe reference to their bearing upon that area of contact – in order that paper rules may be revealed for what they are, and rules with real behavior correspondences come into due importance. That the complex phenomena which are lumped under the term "law" have been too broadly treated in the past, and that a realistic understanding, possible only in terms of observable behavior, is again possible only in terms of study of the way in which persons and institutions are organized in our society, and of the cross-bearings of any particular *part* of law and of any particular *part* of the social organization.

Included in the field of law under such an approach is everything currently included, and a vast deal more. At the very heart, I suspect, is the behavior of judges, peculiarly, that part of their behavior which marks them as judges – those practices which establish the continuity of their office with their predecessors and successors, and which make their official contacts with other persons; but that suspicion on my part may be a relic of the case law tradition in which we American lawyers have been raised. Close around it on the one hand lies the behavior of other government officials. On the other, the sets of accepted formulae which judges recite, seek light from, try to follow. Distinguishing here the formulae with close behavior-correspondences from others; those of frequent application from those of infrequent. Close around these again, lie various persons' ideas of what the law is; and especially their views of what it or some part of it ought to accomplish. At first hand contact with officials' behavior, from another angle, lies the social set-up where the official's acts impinge directly on it; and behind that the social set-up which resists or furthers or reflects the impingement of his acts. Farther from the center lies legal and social philosophy – approaching that center more directly in proportion as the materials with which it deals are taken directly from the center. Part of law, in many aspects, is all of society, and all of man in society. But that is a question of periphery and not of center, of the reach of a specific problem in hand, not of a general discussion. As to the overlapping of the field as thus sketched with that of other social sciences,

I should be sorry if no overlapping were observable. The social sciences are not staked out like real estate. Even in law the sanctions for harmless trespass are not heavy.

Notes

1　LAW AND MORALS (1924), 25 *et seq.*

2　Not only ideals, but standards, not only standards, but concepts, not only concepts, but rules, involve of course generalized mental pictures which play a part in shaping both rules and the actions of courts. But as traditionally dealt with, this ideal element, even where observed, is promptly related in the first instance to rules.

3　Pound's work in this aspect is as striking in its values as in its limitations. It is full to bursting of magnificient insight. It is to Pound we owe the suggestion of "the limits of effective legal action" (worked out in terms of *court* decisions). It is to Pound we owe the contrast of law-in-books and law-in-action (the latter limited again, in his working out of it, to what *courts* do; though in other places he insists upon *administrative* organs as the present center of legal growth). It is to Pound we owe the formulation "individualization of treatment of an offender," and the reference to the proceedings of the Conference on Charities and Corrections to see what the criminal law is really doing. And so it goes. I am not concerned here with whether prior writers may have contributed to, or anticipated, some or all of these ideas. Pound saw them, he formulated them, he drove them home. But these brilliant buddings have in the main not come to fruition. No one thinks them through in their relation either to each other or to the bulk of received jurisprudence. "Balancing of interests" remains with no indication of how to tell an interest when you see one, much less with any study of how they are or should be balanced. "Sociological jurisprudence" remains bare of most that is significant in sociology. "Law-in-action" is left as a suggestion, while further discussion of "the law" centers on "precept." "The limits of effective legal action" – a formulation that fairly shrieks for study of the habit and control set-up of society (that *complex*, industrialized, [partially] urban, indirect-cooperation society he has given us words for) – is left without study of the society to which law is supposed to have relation. The more one learns, the more one studies, the more light and stimulus Pound's writings give. But always peculiarly on a fringe of insight which fails to penetrate at all to the more systematic set-up of the material. One is tempted to see in the thinking of the one man and of the American school of sociological jurisprudence a parallel to the development of case law as a whole: accepting in the main what has been handed down; systematizing compartment-wise; innovating where need shows, powerfully and surely – but *ad hoc* only, with little drive toward or interest in incorporating the innovation into or aligning it with the mass of the material as received.

Critical reading of Pound's work, it may be noted in passing, and especially the phrasing of any concrete criticism, are embarrassed by the constant indeterminacy of the level of his discourse. At times the work purports clearly to travel on the level of considered and buttressed scholarly discussion; at times on the level of bedtime stories for the tired bar; at times on an intermediate level, that of the thoughtful but unproved essay. Most often, it is impossible to tell the intended level of any chapter or passage, and the writing seems to pass without notice from one to another. Now it is obvious that three successive, mutually inconsistent generalizations, though no one of them sustainable as the deliberate propositions of a scholar, may all be illuminating and indeed all true at once – on the level of the after-dinner speech, or even of the thought-provoking essay. All of which gags the critic at the same time that it perhaps stimulates his critical faculties. There is value in this. There is value, even, in the legal bed-time story. But there is greater value to be had. What would one not give for the actual appearance of the long-awaited *Sociological Jurisprudence*, if its author would integrate it in terms of those pioneering thoughts of his which thus far have been waiting to be called together in a Constituent Assembly?

4   I am presupposing the presence of "rules of law," *i.e.*, at least assuming law as a semi-specialized activity of control distinguished from other mechanisms of control; and also presupposing generalization to have set in. Just how far this first assumption reaches I am sure I do not know; I should be inclined to regard any special assembly held for the purpose of adjusting disputes, by say village elders otherwise without official position or authority (*cf.* Gutman, Das Recht der Dschagga, Der Spruchrasen), as one instance of its presence. The second assumption presupposes that prior decision has begun to be dealt with as precedent; that *Themis* is not merely an oracle, but marks a norm. But I am insisting that it be a norm *of law*. Vinogradoff cogently points out that Maine's *Themis* is not a pure creation of the judgment maker; before the *Themis* was a societal life in which norms were both explicit and implicit. I hesitate, however, to call the *im*plicit norms either "rules" or "legal," and see nothing but confusion to be had from so doing. I see only *practices*, more or less definite, more or less conscious, plus a generalized attitude that whatever is practice is right, and whatever varies widely enough is wrong. Certainly the process of making the implicit norm express calls for difficult creative work (two pieces of gold as the reward, on the shield of Achilles!) though any man can *recognize* the result once arrived at *as* right, if it is right (the crowd will award the gold!). Certainly also the "explicit making" permits a twisting. Finally, once the judgment is made, it is both clearer to see, firmer in outline, more rigid, and perhaps more authoritative than it was before. If authoritative at all *because of who made it*, or the circumstances of its making, moreover, it has certainly begun the differentiation out of the general social matrix into the specific character of legality. (Malinowski's analysis in *Crime and Custom in Savage Society* (1926) is somewhat similar; but it moves in terms of dominant authoritativeness of the norm, not of the functionary. If, *when appealed to*, a norm will prevail over an inconsistent norm of common practice, he thinks of it as legal. An illuminating discrimination.)

5   Here and in the following I am talking about the thinking of what my friend T. R. Powell calls the "postmortemizers," those who hash over events that are past, and write books about them, or build taught law. Such persons typically show a wider range of thought than the practical man of similar ability, but a greater naiveté. The practical man seems to think in two water-tight compartments. One half of his mind grinds out the ideology of the day, as gospel, over pippins and cheese or from the rostrum; that half belongs to the postmortemizers. The other half deals cannily with existing institutions, of whatever holiness, to shape (at times it verges on twisting) them to the needs of the practical man or of his client. This side of the practical man's mind must have been at work in every legal system from the days of the most formal rigidity. (Compare the whole preparation and sequence of the lawsuit in Dasent's *Njals-Saga*.) And some persons – conscious creators – must have taken thought of the

relation of interest and remedy since there has been law. (Compare the protection of the Church in the old English laws.) But the tone and ideas of the postmortemizers have changed from age to age, and while not altering the basic attitudes of the practical man, have changed his words and his stock of ideas, his tools, seemingly with powerful effects on his results.

6   For present purposes the dubious distinction taken by the German thinkers: "objective *Recht*" (rather "law" than "right") and "subjective *Recht*" (close to our pre-Hohfeldian "right") can be disregarded. It fits the discussion in that the subjective *Recht* is viewed first of all as a deduction from the rule of law, and then as an independent something.

7   Neither would I be understood to deny practical consequences to this mode of thinking, in our case results, in constitutional law, limitation of actions, etc., or to urge that describing the remedy describes the whole situation, today. It *does* describe the most important, and a much neglected aspect of the situation.

7a   Put another way, prescriptive rules are rules *for* doing something; descriptive rules are so-called rules *of* doing something – statements of observed regularity. But "rules *of*" in common speech includes both aspects at once, and "rules *for*" as often as not connotes the presence of a corresponding practice. I shall limit my term "rules" to "rules for," and shall not *imply* any such connotation.

8   I omit from discussion here one other troublesome confusion: whenever rules are discussed in their prescriptive aspect, it is frequently difficult to tell whether a writer is giving *his own view* of what ought to be, or, on the other hand, a view sanctioned by authority – the prevailingly accepted prescriptive rules. In this last case the *prevalence* of a given prescriptive rule is a fact capable of description (or misdescription); but it always remains to be noted whether that prevailing prescriptive rule has any counterpart in *practice*, or remains in the paper or lip-service stage.

9   Refinement of terms goes some distance to avoid this confusion. "Rule" is well confined to the *pre*scriptive sphere. "Paper rule" is a fair name for a rule to which no counterpart in practice is ascribed. "Working rule" indicates a rule with counterpart in practice, or else a practice *consciously* normatized. *Cf. supra* note 4. "Practice" indicates an observable course of action, with no necessary ascription of conscious normatizing about it. In an earlier paper (15 AM. EC. REV.

671) I failed to make this last distinction; it seems obvious, however, that it refines one's descriptive and reasoning technique in an important detail. Consider, *e.g.*, the double value Ehrlich's work would have had, if his stock of terms had served to keep such distinctions clear, and to let his magnificent thinking work itself out free of confusion.

9a   Wherever the plaintiff has a [legal] right to recover, he can recover at law. This plaintiff has a [social, moral, economic] right to recover. Therefore this plaintiff can recover in this action at law. This may improve the law. It has. It is not, for that, any the better thinking for a scientist *to use*.

9b   This is an overstatement. Past law may have contributed much to the present existence of an interest, and to its shape and extent.

10   How joyously sharp, under this addressing of the rule to the judge becomes the distinction between a rule telling him what to *do*, himself, and one telling him how to instruct a jury!

11   As, *e.g.*, that it is worth while finding out; that it is worth while checking conclusions constantly by facts; and striving to state conclusions which stay within the observed facts; probably also that it is worth while to publish such conclusions for discussion irrespective of what prejudices they may affront, or what accepted values they may disturb.

12   Throughout this paper I am speaking primarily from the viewpoint of the postmortemizer, the observer, the orderer, the scientist. But in passing let me pay my respects to four other lines of legal thinking in which the utility of the suggested approach seems equally striking. (a) That of the practicing lawyer. In his moments of action, in his actual handling of a case or situation, the measure of his success is the measure in which he actually uses this approach. (The question of how far he uses it consciously, how far intuitively, is immaterial.) His job is either to guide a specific client through the difficulties of action in a concrete situation, or to bring the personnel of a specific tribunal to a specific result. The desired results, and not formulae, are his focus, and he uses formulae as he uses his knowledge of both judicial tradition and individual peculiarity: as tools to reach his desired result. He can be more effective, as any other practical man or artist can, if his technique be consciously studied. This is not to say that all that goes to make up his technique can be laid down or be consciously imparted. Still less is it

to urge that he is himself a trustworthy reporter of his own technique.

(b) That of the legislator. Here is a man who wants results. How can one doubt the added utility to be derived from his wrestling with the observable facts of official action and lay action as those facts exist? Indeed, the successful practitioner and the successful politician are precisely the men whose grasp of the realities of law puts the word-beclouded theorist to shame.

(c) That of the philosopher of law – on the side of the "ends of law" and social values. He takes his data for philosophizing from somewhere. The worthwhileness of his philosophy is to a considerable degree conditioned on those data. If they be data of life, his problems become more real, his check-up easier, his basis of thinking more actual. This means at least, when he comes to the application of his chosen values to the criticism of "positive law," that he would bridge to the law-in-action of his day, not merely to the books. If he be a pure mystic, this may be immaterial; otherwise the gain seems inevitable.

For the devotee of formal logic in the law the picture is somewhat different. He will be concerned with words, with propositions. Probably almost wholly with propositions which move within the realm of ought – of doctrine – presumably the accepted doctrine of the system. Once he has his propositions, he runs free of the approach here discussed. He meets that approach in two places: the first, when he puts concrete content into his symbols, to start with. He will be no more accurate a logician, but a more useful one, if he reaches into observed fact, not merely into paper words, for that life content. And again, when the logical process is over, and he wishes to compare his results with something, to see whether he would not prefer another line of systematizing, he can use the behavior-area effectively for his comparison.

But what I have said of the logician suggests the making express of a matter implicit throughout the paper. To say that the area of behavior contact is the most useful point of reference for all matters legal is *not* to say that a specialist may not do the most useful of work, conceivably, without even reaching to that point of reference. A careful study of the formal logic of judicial opinions would be a useful study. But I would urge that even its usefulness would be hugely increased by an equally careful study of the instrumentalism, the pragmatic and socio-psychological decision elements in the same cases. And that an equally geometric increase in illumination would follow a further careful study of the effects on the society concerned of the same cases. Under the present "words" and "rules" approach, all the tendency would be to stop with, or slightly modify, the first of these hypothetical studies. Under the behavior-contact approach each would be welcome, but the insistent drive would be toward completing the last before the significance of the others would be thought even measurably understood.

(d) That of the judge. His approach as one member of a bench to his colleagues does not seem to me to differ significantly for the present purpose from that of the practicing lawyer. His approach *for himself* involves (as does the approach of the philosopher) his forming a value-judgment on the case in hand, in addition to observation and prediction. How his value-judgment can fail of higher utility if he sees his problem not as the mere making of an abstract paper formula, but as the devising of a *way of working* in court *which will in due course affect people* is hard for me to see. The latter approach will certainly force him toward using all facilities he has available to *visualize* in advance the effects of the decision. Such visualization has been thought – and, I conceive, rightly – to be the essence of case-law wisdom-in-action. The approach described should make this wisdom-in-action a reality in a higher percentage of cases. I have developed elsewhere that whereas the net effect is undoubtedly an expansion of the traditional field of discretion and judicial law-making, yet this should give even a conservative no cause for alarm: first, because even when expanded, that field remains amazingly narrow, taken in relation to law as a whole, or to the movement of law – only cumulative changes over decades being in the main of much note; second, because it involves the introduction of no technique of change not already hallowed by conservative tradition, but only a reorganization, for conscious utilization, of techniques accepted for centuries as good; third (this an article of faith, not a matter capable as yet of proof) because the type of change produced under these circumstances is change which moves official action more into keeping with current needs; and another type of change, now constantly occurring, though hidden, tends to be eliminated: change by way of over-simplification of verbal formulae and over "application" of such formulae to cases they never had before been applied to, and do not fit. DAS AMERIKANISCHE PRÄ-JUDIZIENRECHT (published as Karl N. Llewellyn, *The Case Law System in America* (Paul Gewirth, ed; and Michael Ansald, trans, 1989).

13 Eliminating such an implication would to my mind be pure gain. The question of desirability of continuing a given practice, when it comes up for discussion at all, is better made express.

14 This I think holds true of *all* official ought-rules, irrespective of their form. I speak of their effects, not of their purposes. And the rights of laymen result through the screen of the official's practice, by a kind of social reflex. Ehrlich described the phenomenon cogently, so far as concerned the rules governing the set-up of the state governmental machine. A legal philosopher or a normatizer, with his mind fixed on the purpose of rules to ultimately affect the conduct of the "governed," will quarrel with this. A sociologist is content to see and describe what happens — and *compare* that with what is purposed.

15 Ehrlich, again, brings this out beautifully.

16 And on moving into the further fields of contact between judicial or official behavior and lay behavior, one gets into much deeper water: how does the paper rule work out (*i.e.*, have a reflection or a counterpart in behavior) in lower court cases, unappealed? How often does it have any influence? What influence on administrative officials? On transactions between laymen which never reach any officials? All signs point to this being vastly more important than the set-up of doctrine, or even than the actual practices of higher courts. What is documented takes on a specious appearance of value, as against the unexplored.

17 This hopelessly over-simplifies. There may be as many divergent purposes as there are participants. Almost regularly the formulator's purpose and the purpose he publicly assigns are in part disparate.

18 This factor has by no means the exclusive importance the devotees of paper rules tend to attribute to it. The keener observers constantly stress this: what other meaning has the emphasis on the traditional techniques "for developing and applying precepts"; the *practice* of the office, or of the Constitution, which shift emphases, and often create or abrogate whole institutions; the "interpreting away" of a rule; the importance of experience in the office, of the "trained" incumbent. And so forth.

On the other hand the factor of verbally formulated rules has enough importance to explain why they have so long been considered the core of even the substance of law. They are not the sole machinery for *producing* regularity. Habit, practice, unverbalized experience and tradition, are vital to regularity. But they are *a* factor in *producing* it — to the extent that officials react to words, and read words, alike. They are, moreover, the main device for *checking* regularity, for letting outsiders get an idea that officials are staying within the due limits of discretion. And they are, as indicated, a most vital element in introducing change in regularity. Where official behavior occurs *without* regularity, the older views tend to deny it the character of law (the assumed irregularity or caprice of cadijustice, and the like). On this I differ. I should of course stress as the more perfect illustration of the concept *regular* official behavior; but I regard the behavior as more vital than the regularity, and the mere paper expression of desired regularity — save so far as it expresses an ideal — well, as paper.

19 I have not attempted in this paper to define conduct, action, behavior. I have no desire to exclude such things as the arousing and disappointment of expectations, the creation of hopes and fears, etc. The approach advocated would, however, go vigorously to inquiring into the grounds for claiming the arousing or disappointment of expectations in any given case, — as also to inquiring into what expectations, and whose. So, too, for example, with the thought processes of judges, the influence of ideology on judges and laymen, etc. *Cf.* 15 AM. Ec. REV. 670, n. 17, 675, n. 32.

20 Other aspects are developed in PROCEEDINGS OF CONFERENCE OF SOCIAL WORK (1928), at 129 *et seq.*

21 Mortimer Adler suggests to me that the operational approach to modern physics is a classic analogue and precursor.

22 The work of the different men moves in somewhat different fields, and is uneven in value. The same holds often of different work of the same man. And an exhaustive bibliography of all that has been done along the lines discussed would be long. Probably most titles would fall in the useful but less advanced field of discovering the appellate courts' real practice as distinct from the paper pattern of courts or writers. The names listed were chosen with reference to work at the next stage beyond: facts as to lower court operations, and the beginnings of inquiry into the contact-area between official and layman's conduct.

EHRLICH (Czernowitz), GRUNDLEGUNG EINER SOZIOLOGIE DES RECHTS, and see PAGE, PRO. ASSN. AM. L. S. (1914), 46. Unfortunately most of the findings of his investigations into "living law" are inaccessible. NUSSBAUM (Berlin), in his RECHTSTATSACHEN-FORSCHUNG; HEDEMANN (Jena), REICHSGERICHT UND WIRTSCHAFSRECHT; Brandeis, the brief in *Muller v. Oregon*, and his opinions, repeatedly; FRANKFURTER AND LANDIS (Harvard), THE BUSINESS OF THE SUPREME COURT (1928); FRANKFURTER AND GREEN, THE LABOR INJUNCTION (1930); Underhill Moore (Yale), mimeographed and MS. materials on banking in relation to the law of banking; Moore and Shamos, *Interest on the Balances of Checking Accounts* (1927) 27 COLUMBIA LAW REV. 633; C. E. Clark (Yale), MS. materials on the actual practice of litigation in Connecticut and New York; partial results appear in the CONN. BAR J. for July, 1928, April and July, 1929, and the W. VA. L. J. for Dec. 1929; Wm. Douglas (Yale), study in bankruptcy and insolvency practice, still under way; Moley (Columbia), the crime surveys, generally; Yntema and Theo. Hope (Johns Hopkins), pending investigations into the use of federal jurisdiction and into the actual course of litigation in state courts; Klaus (Columbia), *Sale, Agency and Price Maintenance* (1928) 28 COLUMBIA LAW REV. 312, 441; Handler (Columbia), *False and Misleading Advertising* (1929) 39 YALE L. J. 22; IHIGAHI, LE DROIT CORPORATIF INTERNATIONAL DE LA VENTE DE SOILS (1928); and Klaus' excellent review (1928) 28 COLUMBIA LAW REV. 991.

23   The reformulation would complicate the preceding argument, but would not essentially change it. Except insofar as the argument would thereby gain cogency.

24   On the *normative* side of law no confusion or doubt would exist in this case. The "right rule" would be the same all along. But that is no reason for obscuring the divergence in the results, on the level of description and prediction. We need, precisely for such purposes, to sever the normative from the descriptive aspects of law. Moreover, results affect norms, quite as much as norms affect results. If the outcome were going to be the overthrow of the judicial by the administrative practice, in the case put, the norm would pending outcome be in considerable doubt. And one of the (quite incidental) advantages of the approach contended for is to make explicit, understandable, *and non-shocking* the fact and realm of occurrence of such doubts as to norm.

25   If we were dealing with a society which lacked political organization, this obviously would be a bad terminology. But another of the futilities of overgeneralization in the law has been the attempt to find *one* set of terms to cover the institutions of disparate societies. Before political organization we find control, and often specialized or semi-specialized control institutions. But in describing a politically organized society it is exceedingly convenient to limit the term to the official Big Stick. A convenient term for the closely similar "law" of the subgroup in such a society is "by-law." Sociologically the two are often more similar than dissimilar. *Cf.* MAX WEBER, WIRTSCHAFT U. GESELLSCHAFT, 16, 17, 27 etc.; and 15 AM. EC. REV. 672 *et seq.*

26   In the same way (borrowing Spykman again) *to the extent that* the official's behavior plays into these interlocking patterns of action it becomes "official" rather than personal behavior, and so of direct interest here. "Purely" personal behavior of an official approaches inconceivability; but substantially personal behavior may take up a great bulk of a given official's time.

27   *Cf.* PRO. CONF. SOCIAL WORK (1928), 129, 131, *et seq.*

28   Thus one Torrens title to one lot in a block makes the block unavailable for large scale improvement. R. R. B. Powell tells me that Torrens titles have even on occasion been deregistered, in order to gain access to mortgage money.

29   In practice this comes to: "*equable* in the choice of the very limited class to be affected." *Equality* of rule is impossible in a specialized society. It is true that some few of the lines of discrimination which are under our system excluded from consideration, are suggested by the word "equality." But it is not particularly significant, save historically.

30   I have stressed elsewhere that the vital problem in such cases is that of creating in the conduct of the relevant persons new *practices* (folkways) which conform to the purposes sought *via* the new legal rules. PROC. CONF. SOC. WORK (1928), at 132 *et seq.* And that the effectiveness of legal rules, old or new, is not to be measured simply by how often officials act in accordance with them. *Ibid.*, and 15 AM. EC. REV. 682. Indeed the ideal effectiveness is not achieved until officials do not have to act at all. But if

the rules are of the kind which coincide roughly with ancient, established lay practice (*mores*) it becomes a serious problem how far we have in such cases effectiveness of the *legal rule*, or of the occasional official behavior with reference to the rule. Contrast the extreme opposite case: an entire organized line of activity all units of which are prepared to move or not to move along lines newly prescribed, according to the outcome in court of a deliberately chosen test case. It is behavior of officials *alone*, but behavior of officials in its *interaction* with that of the relevant laymen.

31   What is wanted in the way of generalization must come from a resynthesis of such particularized studies, when we have them. Meantime, we have our common sense and tradition-given understanding of *some* of the regularities of official behavior, and sufficient traditional skills in predicting, influencing, managing official or other behavior to get on after a fashion, in practice, while we learn more.

32   Not quite the same. The fight and victory may have somewhat changed the picture. And the enactment of a new formula has some consequences in itself: among others, that the formula chosen imposes temporary (though sometimes wide) limits upon what the officials can do, whereas the prior struggle is typically in terms of policies, not measures.

33   It is along the same line that I feel strongly the unwisdom, when turning the spotlight on behavior, of throwing overboard emphasis on rules, concepts, ideology, and ideological stereotypes or patterns. These last are, by themselves, confusing, misleading, inadequate to describe or explain. But a jurisprudence which was practically workable could not have been built in terms of them, if they had not contained a goodly core of truth and sense. To be sure, it was not the precept-ideology of jurisprudence, but the practice that jurisprudence only partly mirrored, which actually worked. But one thing sociological study ought to do for the advance of science is to school the advocates of new insight no longer to junk wholesale the old insight against which they are rebelling. The rebelling indicates inadequacy in the old. It does not indicate that the old did not have much solid basis. The bare fact that the old exists, could come into existence and persist, evidences that it had. If we can examine it for what it has, and carry that with us into a new alignment, we shall do much to reduce the well-known pendulum swing from exaggeration to exaggeration. This is of less moment in the early stages of a new movement. The innovator carries over willy-nilly the virtues of the same training against which he is in intellectual revolt. But those newly trained in the new school will be half-trained unsound exaggerators, if the original innovators fail to incorporate *in their doctrine as in their practice* the life-power of the older school, even while attacking the latter's false emphases and implications.

34   May I insist again at this point that "folk morality" really means at least as many important varieties in specific details as there are subgroups within the main group.

3

The Model of Rules

Ronald Dworkin

I Embarrassing Questions

Lawyers lean heavily on the connected concepts of legal right and legal obligation. We say that someone has a legal right or duty, and we take that statement as a sound basis for making claims and demands, and for criticizing the acts of public officials. But our understanding of these concepts is remarkably fragile, and we fall into trouble when we try to say what legal rights and obligations are. We say glibly that whether someone has a legal obligation is determined by applying "the law" to the particular facts of his case, but this is not a helpful answer, because we have the same difficulties with the concept of law.

We are used to summing up our troubles in the classic questions of jurisprudence: What is "the law"? When two sides disagree, as often happens, about a proposition "of law," what are they disagreeing about, and how shall we decide which side is right? Why do we call what "the law" says a matter of legal "obligation"? Is "obligation" here just a term of art, meaning only "what the law says"? Or does legal obligation have something to do with moral obligation? Can we say that we have, in principle at least, the same reasons for meeting our legal obligations that we have for meeting our moral obligations?

These are not puzzles for the cupboard, to be taken down on rainy days for fun. They are sources of continuing embarrassment, and they nag at our attention. They embarrass us in dealing with particular problems that we must solve, one way or another. Suppose a novel right-of-

privacy case comes to court, and there is no statute or precedent either granting or denying the particular right of anonymity claimed by the plaintiff. What role in the court's decision should be played by the fact that most people in the community think that private individuals are "morally" entitled to that particular privacy? Suppose the Supreme Court orders some prisoner freed because the police used procedures that the Court now says are constitutionally forbidden, although the Court's earlier decisions upheld these procedures. Must the Court, to be consistent, free all other prisoners previously convicted through these same procedures?[1] Conceptual puzzles about "the law" and "legal obligation" become acute when a court is confronted with a problem like this.

These eruptions signal a chronic disease. Day in and day out we send people to jail, or take money away from them, or make them do things they do not want to do, under coercion of force, and we justify all of this by speaking of such persons as having broken the law or having failed to meet their legal obligations, or having interfered with other people's legal rights. Even in clear cases (a bank robber or a willful breach of contract), when we are confident that someone had a legal obligation and broke it, we are not able to give a satisfactory account of what that means, or why that entitles the state to punish or coerce him. We may feel confident that what we are doing is proper, but until we can identify the principles we are following we cannot be sure that they are sufficient, or whether we are applying them consistently. In less clear cases, when the issue of whether an obligation has been broken is for some reason controversial, the pitch of these nagging questions rises, and our responsibility to find answers deepens.

Certain lawyers (we may call them "nominalists") urge that we solve these problems by ignoring them. In their view the concepts of "legal obligation" and "the law" are myths, invented and sustained by lawyers for a dismal mix of conscious and subconscious motives. The puzzles we find in these concepts are merely symptoms that they are myths. They are unsolvable because unreal, and our concern with them is just one feature of our enslavement. We would do better to flush away the puzzles and the concepts altogether, and pursue our important social objectives without this excess baggage.

This is a tempting suggestion, but it has fatal drawbacks. Before we can decide that our concepts of law and of legal obligation are myths, we must decide what they are. We must be able to state, at least roughly, what it is we all believe that is wrong. But the nerve of our problem is that we have great difficulty in doing just that. Indeed, when we ask what law is and what legal obligations are, we are asking for a theory of how we use those concepts and of the conceptual commitments our use entails. We cannot conclude, before we have such a general theory, that our practices are stupid or superstitious.

Of course, the nominalists think they know how the rest of us use these concepts. They think that when we speak of "the law," we mean a set of timeless rules stocked in some conceptual warehouse awaiting discovery by judges, and that when we speak of legal obligation we mean the invisible chains these mysterious rules somehow drape around us. The theory that there are such rules and chains they call "mechanical jurisprudence," and they are right in ridiculing its practitioners. Their difficulty, however, lies in finding practitioners to ridicule. So far they have had little luck in caging and exhibiting mechanical jurisprudents (all specimens captured – even Blackstone and Joseph Beale – have had to be released after careful reading of their texts).

In any event, it is clear that most lawyers have nothing like this in mind when they speak of the law and of legal obligation. A superficial examination of our practices is enough to show this, for we speak of laws changing and evolving, and of legal obligation sometimes being problematical. In these and other ways we show that we are not addicted to mechanical jurisprudence.

Nevertheless, we do use the concepts of law and legal obligation, and we do suppose that society's warrant to punish and coerce is written in that currency. It may be that when the details of this practice are laid bare, the concepts we do use will be shown to be as silly and as thick with illusion as those the nominalists invented. If so, then we shall have to find other ways to describe what we do, and either provide other justifications or change our practices. But until we have discovered this and made these adjustments, we cannot accept the nominalists' premature invitation to turn our backs on the problems our present concepts provide.

Of course the suggestion that we stop talking about "the law" and "legal obligation" is mostly bluff. These concepts are too deeply cemented into the structure of our political practices – they cannot be given up like cigarettes or hats. Some of the nominalists have half-admitted this and said that the myths they condemn should be thought of as Platonic myths and retained to seduce the masses into order. This is perhaps not so cynical a suggestion as it seems; perhaps it is a covert hedging of a dubious bet.

If we boil away the bluff, the nominalist attack reduces to an attack on mechanical jurisprudence. Through the lines of the attack, and in spite of the heroic calls for the death of law, the nominalists themselves have offered an analysis of how the terms "law" and "legal obligation" should be used which is not very different from that of more classical philosophers. Nominalists present their analysis as a model of how legal institutions (particularly courts) "really operate." But their model differs mainly in emphasis from the theory first made popular by the nineteenth century philosopher John Austin, and now accepted in one form or another by most working and academic lawyers who hold views on jurisprudence. I shall call this theory, with some historical looseness, "positivism." I want to examine the soundness of positivism, particularly in the powerful form that Professor H. L. A. Hart of Oxford has given to it. I choose to focus on his position, not only because of its clarity and elegance, but because here, as almost everywhere else in legal philosophy, constructive thought must start with a consideration of his views.

II Positivism

Positivism has a few central and organizing propositions as its skeleton, and though not every philosopher who is called a positivist would subscribe to these in the way I present them, they do define the general position I want to examine. These key tenets may be stated as follows:

(a) The law of a community is a set of special rules used by the community directly or indirectly for the purpose of determining which behavior will be punished or coerced by the public power. These special rules can be identified and distinguished by specific criteria, by tests having to do not with their content but with their *pedigree* or the manner in which they were adopted or developed. These tests of pedigree can be used to distinguish valid legal rules from spurious legal rules (rules which lawyers and litigants wrongly argue are rules of law) and also from other sorts of social rules (generally lumped together as "moral rules") that the community follows but does not enforce through public power.

(b) The set of these valid legal rules is exhaustive of "the law," so that if someone's case is not clearly covered by such a rule (because there is none that seems appropriate, or those that seem appropriate are vague, or for some other reason) then that case cannot be decided by "applying the law." It must be decided by some official, like a judge, "exercising his discretion," which means reaching beyond the law for some other sort of standard to guide him in manufacturing a fresh legal rule or supplementing an old one.

(c) To say that someone has a "legal obligation" is to say that his case falls under a valid legal rule that requires him to do or to forbear from doing something. (To say he has a legal right, or has a legal power of some sort, or a legal privilege or immunity, is to assert, in a

shorthand way, that others have actual or hypothetical legal obligations to act or not to act in certain ways touching him.) In the absence of such a valid legal rule there is no legal obligation; it follows that when the judge decides an issue by exercising his discretion, he is not enforcing a legal obligation as to that issue.

This is only the skeleton of positivism. The flesh is arranged differently by different positivists, and some even tinker with the bones. Different versions differ chiefly in their description of the fundamental test of pedigree a rule must meet to count as a rule of law.

Austin, for example, framed his version of the fundamental test as a series of interlocking definitions and distinctions.[2] He defined having an obligation as lying under a rule, a rule as a general command, and a command as an expression of desire that others behave in a particular way, backed by the power and will to enforce that expression in the event of disobedience. He distinguished classes of rules (legal, moral or religious) according to which person or group is the author of the general command the rule represents. In each political community, he thought, one will find a sovereign – a person or a determinate group whom the rest obey habitually, but who is not in the habit of obeying anyone else. The legal rules of a community are the general commands its sovereign has deployed. Austin's definition of legal obligation followed from this definition of law. One has a legal obligation, he thought, if one is among the addressees of some general order of the sovereign, and is in danger of suffering a sanction unless he obeys that order.

Of course, the sovereign cannot provide for all contingencies through any scheme of orders, and some of his orders will inevitably be vague or have furry edges. Therefore (according to Austin) the sovereign grants those who enforce the law (judges) discretion to make fresh orders when novel or troublesome cases are presented. The judges then make new rules or adapt old rules, and the sovereign either overturns their creations, or tacitly confirms them by failing to do so.

Austin's model is quite beautiful in its simplicity. It asserts the first tenet of positivism, that the law is a set of rules specially selected to govern public order, and offers a simple factual test – what has the sovereign commanded? – as the sole criterion for identifying those special rules. In time, however, those who studied and tried to apply Austin's model found it too simple. Many objections were raised, among which were two that seemed fundamental. First, Austin's key assumption that in each community a determinate group or institution can be found, which is in ultimate control of all other groups, seemed not to hold in a complex society. Political control in a modern nation is pluralistic and shifting, a matter of more or less, of compromise and cooperation and alliance, so that it is often impossible to say that any person or group has that dramatic control necessary to qualify as an Austinian sovereign. One wants to say, in the United States for example, that the "people" are sovereign. But this means almost nothing, and in itself provides no test for determining what the "people" have commanded, or distinguishing their legal from their social or moral commands.

Second, critics began to realize that Austin's analysis fails entirely to account for, even to recognize, certain striking facts about the attitudes we take toward "the law." We make an important distinction between law and even the general orders of a gangster. We feel that the law's strictures – and its sanctions – are different in that they are obligatory in a way that the outlaw's commands are not. Austin's analysis has no place for any such distinction, because it defines an obligation as subjection to the threat of force, and so founds the authority of law entirely on the sovereign's ability and will to harm those who disobey. Perhaps the distinction we make is illusory – perhaps our feelings of some special authority attaching to the law is based on religious hangover or another sort of mass self-deception. But Austin does not demonstrate this, and we are entitled to insist that an analysis of our concept of law either acknowledge and explain our attitudes, or show why they are mistaken.

H. L. A. Hart's version of positivism is more complex than Austin's, in two ways. First, he recognizes, as Austin did not, that rules are of different logical kinds (Hart distinguishes two kinds, which he calls "primary" and "secondary" rules). Second, he rejects Austin's theory that a rule is a kind of command, and substitutes a more elaborate general analysis of what rules are. We must pause over each of these points, and then note how they merge in Hart's concept of law.

Hart's distinction between primary and secondary rules is of great importance.[3] Primary rules are those that grant rights or impose obligations upon members of the community. The rules of the criminal law that forbid us to rob, murder or drive too fast are good examples of primary rules. Secondary rules are those that stipulate how, and by whom, such primary rules may be formed, recognized, modified or extinguished. The rules that stipulate how Congress is composed, and how it enacts legislation, are examples of secondary rules. Rules about forming contracts and executing wills are also secondary rules because they stipulate how very particular rules governing particular legal obligations (*i.e.*, the terms of a contract or the provisions of a will) come into existence and are changed.

His general analysis of rules is also of great importance.[4] Austin had said that every rule is a general command, and that a person is obligated under a rule if he is liable to be hurt should he disobey it. Hart points out that this obliterates the distinction between being *obliged* to do something and being *obligated* to do it. If one is bound by a rule he is obligated, not merely obliged, to do what it provides, and therefore being bound by a rule must be different from being subject to an injury if one disobeys an order. A rule differs from an order, among other ways, by being *normative*, by setting a standard of behavior that has a call on its subject beyond the threat that may enforce it. A rule can never be binding just because some person with physical power wants it to be so. He must have *authority* to issue the rule or it is no rule, and such authority can only come from another rule which is already binding on those to whom he speaks. That is the difference between a valid law and the orders of a gunman.

So Hart offers a general theory of rules that does not make their authority depend upon the physical power of their authors. If we examine the way different rules come into being, he tells us, and attend to the distinction between primary and secondary rules, we see that there are two possible sources of a rule's authority.[5]

(a) A rule may become binding upon a group of people because that group through its practices *accepts* the rule as a standard for its conduct. It is not enough that the group simply conforms to a pattern of behavior: even though most Englishmen may go to the movies on Saturday evening, they have not accepted a rule requiring that they do so. A practice constitutes the acceptance of a rule only when those who follow the practice regard the rule as binding, and recognize the rule as a reason or justification for their own behavior and as a reason for criticizing the behavior of others who do not obey it.

(b) A rule may also become binding in quite a different way, namely by being enacted in conformity with some *secondary* rule that stipulates that rules so enacted shall be binding. If the constitution of a club stipulates, for example, that by-laws may be adopted by a majority of the members, then particular by-laws so voted are binding upon all the members, not because of any practice of acceptance of these particular by-laws, but because the constitution says so. We use the concept of *validity* in this connection: rules binding because they have been created in a manner stipulated by some secondary rule are called "valid" rules. Thus we can record Hart's fundamental distinction this way: a rule may be binding (a) because it is accepted or (b) because it is valid.

Hart's concept of law is a construction of these various distinctions.[6] Primitive communities have only primary rules, and these are binding entirely because of practices of acceptance. Such communities cannot be said to have "law," because there is no way to distinguish a set of legal rules from amongst other social rules, as the first tenet of positivism requires. But when a particular community has developed a fundamental secondary rule that stipulates how legal rules are to be identified, the idea of a distinct set of legal rules, and thus of law, is born.

Hart calls such a fundamental secondary rule a "rule of recognition." The rule of recognition of a given community may be relatively simple ("What the king enacts is law") or it may be very complex (the United States Constitution, with all its difficulties of interpretation, may be considered a single rule of recognition). The demonstration that a particular rule is valid may therefore require tracing a complicated chain of validity back from that particular rule ultimately to the fundamental rule. Thus a parking ordinance of the city of New Haven is valid because it is adopted by a city council, pursuant to the procedures and within the competence specified by the municipal law adopted by the state of Connecticut, in conformity with the procedures and within the competence specified by the constitution of the state of Connecticut, which was in turn adopted consistently with the requirements of the United States Constitution.

Of course, a rule of recognition cannot itself be valid, because by hypothesis it is ultimate, and so cannot meet tests stipulated by a more fundamental rule. The rule of recognition is the sole rule in a legal system whose binding force depends upon its acceptance. If we wish to know what rule of recognition a particular community has adopted or follows, we must observe how its citizens, and particularly its officials, behave. We must observe what ultimate arguments they accept as showing the validity of a particular rule, and what ultimate arguments they use to criticize other officials or institutions. We can apply no mechanical test, but there is no danger of our confusing the rule of recognition of a community with its rules of morality. The rule of recognition is identified by the fact that its province is the operation of the governmental apparatus of legislatures, courts, agencies, policemen, and the rest.

In this way Hart rescues the fundamentals of positivism from Austin's mistakes. Hart agrees with Austin that valid rules of law may be created through the acts of officials and public institutions. But Austin thought that the authority of these institutions lay only in their monopoly of power. Hart finds their authority in the background of constitutional standards against which they act, constitutional standards that have been accepted, in the form of a fundamental rule of recognition, by the community which they govern. This background legitimates the decisions of government and gives them the cast and call of obligation that the naked commands of Austin's sovereign lacked. Hart's theory differs from Austin's also, in recognizing that different communities use different ultimate tests of law, and that some allow other means of creating law than the deliberate act of a legislative institution. Hart mentions "long customary practice" and "the relation [of a rule] to judicial decisions" as other criteria that are often used, though generally along with and subordinate to the test of legislation.

So Hart's version of positivism is more complex than Austin's, and his test for valid rules of law is more sophisticated. In one respect, however, the two models are very similar. Hart, like Austin, recognizes that legal rules have furry edges (he speaks of them as having "open texture") and, again like Austin, he accounts for troublesome cases by saying that judges have and exercise discretion to decide these cases by fresh legislation.[7] (I shall later try to show why one who thinks of law as a special set of rules is almost inevitably drawn to account for difficult cases in terms of someone's exercise of discretion.)

III   Rules, Principles, and Policies

I want to make a general attack on positivism, and I shall use H. L. A. Hart's version as a target, when a particular target is needed. My strategy will be organized around the fact that when lawyers reason or dispute about legal rights and obligations, particularly in those hard cases when our problems with these concepts seem most acute, they make use of standards that do not function as rules, but operate differently as principles, policies, and other sorts of standards. Positivism, I shall argue, is a model of and for a system of rules, and its central notion of a single fundamental test for law forces us to miss the important roles of these standards that are not rules.

I just spoke of "principles, policies, and other sorts of standards." Most often I shall use the term "principle" generically, to refer to the whole set of these standards other than rules; occasionally, however, I shall be more precise, and distinguish between principles and policies. Although nothing in the present argument will turn on the distinction, I should state how I draw it. I call a "policy" that kind of standard that sets out a goal to be reached, generally an improvement in some economic, political, or social feature of the community (though some goals are negative, in that they stipulate that some present feature is to be protected from adverse change). I call a "principle" a standard that is to be observed, not because it will advance or secure an economic, political, or social situation deemed desirable, but because it is a requirement of justice or fairness or some other dimension of morality. Thus the standard that automobile accidents are to be decreased is a policy, and the standard that no man may profit by his own wrong a principle. The distinction can be collapsed by construing a principle as stating a social goal (*i.e.*, the goal of a society in which no man profits by his own wrong), or by construing a policy as stating a principle (*i.e.*, the principle that the goal the policy embraces is a worthy one) or by adopting the utilitarian thesis that principles of justice are disguised statements of goals (securing the greatest happiness of the greatest number). In some contexts the distinction has uses which are lost if it is thus collapsed.[8]

My immediate purpose, however, is to distinguish principles in the generic sense from rules, and I shall start by collecting some examples of the former. The examples I offer are chosen haphazardly; almost any case in a law school casebook would provide examples that would serve as well. In 1889 a New York court, in the famous case of *Riggs v. Palmer*,[9] had to decide whether an heir named in the will of his grandfather could inherit under that will, even though he had murdered his grandfather to do so. The court began its reasoning with this admission: "It is quite true that statutes regulating the making, proof and effect of wills, and the devolution of property, if literally construed, and if their force and effect can in no way and under no circumstances be controlled or modified, give this property to the murderer."[10] But the court continued to note that "all laws as well as all contracts may be controlled in their operation and effect by general, fundamental maxims of the common law. No one shall be permitted to profit by his own fraud, or to take advantage of his own wrong, or to found any claim upon his own iniquity, or to acquire property by his own crime."[11] The murderer did not receive his inheritance.

In 1960, a New Jersey court was faced, in *Henningsen v. Bloomfield Motors, Inc.,*[12] with the important question of whether (or how much) an automobile manufacturer may limit his liability in case the automobile is defective. Henningsen had bought a car, and signed a contract which said that the manufacturer's liability for defects was limited to "making good" defective parts – "this warranty being expressly in lieu of all other warranties, obligations or liabilities." Henningsen argued that, at least in the circumstances of his case, the manufacturer ought not to be protected by this limitation, and ought to be liable for the medical and other expenses of persons injured in a crash. He was not able to point to any statute, or to any established rule of law, that prevented the manufacturer from standing on the contract. The court nevertheless agreed with Henningsen. At various points in the court's argument the following appeals to standards are made: (a) "[W]e must keep in mind the general principle that, in the absence of fraud, one who does not choose to read a contract before signing it cannot later relieve himself of its burdens."[13] (b) "In applying that principle, the basic tenet of freedom of competent parties to contract is a factor of importance."[14] (c) "Freedom of contract is not such an immutable doctrine as to admit of no qualification in the area in which we are concerned."[15] (d) "In a society such as ours, where the automobile is a common and necessary adjunct of daily life, and where its use is so fraught with danger to the driver, passengers and the public, the manufacturer is under a special obligation in connection with the construction, promotion and sale of his cars. Consequently, the courts must examine purchase agreements closely to see if consumer and public interests are treated fairly."[16] (e) " '[I]s there any principle which is more familiar or more firmly embedded in the history of Anglo–American law than the basic doctrine that the courts will not permit themselves to be used as instruments of inequity and injustice?' "[17] (f) " 'More specif-

ically, the courts generally refuse to lend themselves to the enforcement of a "bargain" in which one party has unjustly taken advantage of the economic necessities of other. . . .' "[18]

The standards set out in these quotations are not the sort we think of as legal rules. They seem very different from propositions like "The maximum legal speed on the turnpike is sixty miles an hour" or "A will is invalid unless signed by three witnesses." They are different because they are legal principles rather than legal rules.

The difference between legal principles and legal rules is a logical distinction. Both sets of standards point to particular decisions about legal obligation in particular circumstances, but they differ in the character of the direction they give. Rules are applicable in an all-or-nothing fashion. If the facts a rule stipulates are given, then either the rule is valid, in which case the answer it supplies must be accepted, or it is not, in which case it contributes nothing to the decision.

This all-or-nothing is seen most plainly if we look at the way rules operate, not in law, but in some enterprise they dominate – a game, for example. In baseball a rule provides that if the batter has had three strikes, he is out. An official cannot consistently acknowledge that this is an accurate statement of a baseball rule, and decide that a batter who has had three strikes is not out. Of course, a rule may have exceptions (the batter who has taken three strikes is not out if the catcher drops the third strike). However, an accurate statement of the rule would take this exception into account, and any that did not would be incomplete. If the list of exceptions is very large, it would be too clumsy to repeat them each time the rule is cited; there is, however, no reason in theory why they could not all be added on, and the more that are, the more accurate is the statement of the rule.

If we take baseball rules as a model, we find that rules of law, like the rule that a will is invalid unless signed by three witnesses, fit the model well. If the requirement of three witnesses is a valid legal rule, then it cannot be that a will has been signed by only two witnesses and is valid. The rule might have exceptions, but if it does then it is inaccurate and incomplete to state the rule so simply, without enumerating the exceptions. In theory, at least, the exceptions could all be listed, and the more of them that are, the more complete is the statement of the rule.

But this is not the way the sample principles in the quotations operate. Even those which look most like rules do not set out legal consequences that follow automatically when the conditions provided are met. We say that our law respects the principle that no man may profit from his own wrong, but we do not mean that the law never permits a man to profit from wrongs he commits. In fact, people often profit, perfectly legally, from their legal wrongs. The most notorious case is adverse possession – if I trespass on your land long enough, some day I will gain a right to cross your land whenever I please. There are many less dramatic examples. If a man leaves one job, breaking a contract, to take a much higher paying job, he may have to pay damages to his first employer, but he is usually entitled to keep his new salary. If a man jumps bail and crosses state lines to make a brilliant investment in another state, he may be sent back to jail, but he will keep his profits.

We do not treat these – and countless other counter-instances that can easily be imagined – as showing that the principle about profiting from one's wrongs is not a principle of our legal system, or that it is incomplete and needs qualifying exceptions. We do not treat counter-instances as exceptions (at least not exceptions in the way in which a catcher's dropping the third strike is an exception) because we could not hope to capture these counter-instances simply by a more extended statement of the principle. They are not, even in theory, subject to enumeration, because we would have to include not only these cases (like adverse possession) in which some institution has already provided that profit can be gained through a wrong, but also those numberless imaginary cases in which we know in advance that the principle would not hold. Listing some of these might sharpen our sense of the principle's weight (I shall mention that dimension in a moment), but it would not make for a more accurate or complete statement of the principle.

A principle like "No man may profit from his own wrong" does not even purport to set out conditions that make its application necessary. Rather, it states a reason that argues in one direction, but does not necessitate a particular decision. If a man has or is about to receive something, as a direct result of something illegal he did to get it, then that is a reason which the law will take into account in deciding whether he should keep it. There may be other principles or policies arguing in the other direction – a policy of securing title, for example, or a principle limiting punishment to what the legislature has stipulated. If so, our principle may not prevail, but that does not mean that it is not a principle of our legal system, because in the next case, when these contravening considerations are absent or less weighty, the principle may be decisive. All that is meant, when we say that a particular principle is a principle of our law, is that the principle is one which officials must take into account, if it is relevant, as a consideration inclining in one direction or another.

The logical distinction between rules and principles appears more clearly when we consider principles that do not even look like rules. Consider the proposition, set out under "(d)" in the excerpts from the *Henningsen* opinion, that "the manufacturer is under a special obligation in connection with the construction, promotion and sale of his cars." This does not even purport to define the specific duties such a special obligation entails, or to tell us what rights automobile consumers acquire as a result. It merely states – and this is an essential link in the *Henningsen* argument – that automobile manufacturers must be held to higher standards than other manufacturers, and are less entitled to rely on the competing principle of freedom of contract. It does not mean that they may never rely on that principle, or that courts may rewrite automobile purchase contracts at will; it means only that if a particular clause seems unfair or burdensome, courts have less reason to enforce the clause than if it were for the purchase of neckties. The "special obligation" counts in favor, but does not in itself necessitate, a decision refusing to enforce the terms of an automobile purchase contract.

This first difference between rules and principles entails another. Principles have a dimension that rules do not – the dimension of weight or importance. When principles intersect (the policy of protecting automobile consumers intersecting with principles of freedom of contract, for example), one who must resolve the conflict has to take into account the relative weight of each. This cannot be, of course, an exact measurement, and the judgment that a particular principle or policy is more important than another will often be a controversial one. Nevertheless, it is an integral part of the concept of a principle that it has this dimension, that it makes sense to ask how important or how weighty it is.

Rules do not have this dimension. We can speak of rules as being *functionally* important or unimportant (the baseball rule that three strikes are out is more important than the rule that runners may advance on a balk, because the game would be much more changed with the first rule altered than the second). In this sense, one legal rule may be more important than another because it has a greater or more important role in regulating behavior. But we cannot say that one rule is more important than another within the system of rules, so that when two rules conflict one supercedes the other by virtue of its greater weight. If two rules conflict, one of them cannot be a valid rule. The decision as to which is valid, and which must be abandoned or recast, must be made by appealing to considerations beyond the rules themselves. A legal system might regulate such conflicts by other rules, which prefer the rule enacted by the higher authority, or the rule enacted later, or the more specific rule, or something of that sort. A legal system may also prefer the rule supported by the more important principles. (Our own legal system uses both of these techniques.)

It is not always clear from the form of a standard whether it is a rule or a principle. "A will is invalid unless signed by three witnesses" is not very different in form from "A man may not profit from his own wrong," but one who knows something of American law knows that he must take the first as stating a rule and the second as stating a principle. In many cases the distinction is difficult to make – it may not have

been settled how the standard should operate, and this issue may itself be a focus of controversy. The first amendment to the United States Constitution contains the provision that Congress shall not abridge freedom of speech. Is this a rule, so that if a particular law does abridge freedom of speech, it follows that it is unconstitutional? Those who claim that the first amendment is "an absolute" say that it must be taken in this way, that is, as a rule. Or does it merely state a principle, so that when an abridgement of speech is discovered, it is unconstitutional unless the context presents some other policy or principle which in the circumstances is weighty enough to permit the abridgement? That is the position of those who argue for what is called the "clear and present danger" test or some other form of "balancing."

Sometimes a rule and a principle can play much the same role, and the difference between them is almost a matter of form alone. The first section of the Sherman Act states that every contract in restraint of trade shall be void. The Supreme Court had to make the decision whether this provision should be treated as a rule in its own terms (striking down every contract "which restrains trade," which almost any contract does) or as a principle, providing a reason for striking down a contract in the absence of effective contrary policies. The Court construed the provision as a rule, but treated that rule as containing the word "unreasonable," and as prohibiting only "unreasonable" restraints of trade.[19] This allowed the provision to function logically as a rule (whenever a court finds that the restraint is "unreasonable" it is bound to hold the contract invalid) and substantially as a principle (a court must take into account a variety of other principles and policies in determining whether a particular restraint in particular economic circumstances is "unreasonable").

Words like "reasonable," "negligent," "unjust," and "significant" often perform just this function. Each of these terms makes the application of the rule which contains it depend to some extent upon principles or policies lying beyond the rule, and in this way makes that rule itself more like a principle. But they do not quite turn the rule into a principle, because even the least confining of these terms restricts the *kind* of other principles and policies on which the rule depends. If we are bound by a rule that says that "unreasonable" contracts are void, or that grossly "unfair" contracts will not be enforced, much more judgment is required than if the quoted terms were omitted. But suppose a case in which some consideration of policy or principle suggests that a contract should be enforced even though its restraint is not reasonable, or even though it is grossly unfair. Enforcing these contracts would be forbidden by our rules, and thus permitted only if these rules were abandoned or modified. If we were dealing, however, not with a rule but with a policy against enforcing unreasonable contracts, or a principle that unfair contracts ought not to be enforced, the contracts could be enforced without alteration of the law.

IV   Principles and the Concept of Law

Once we identify legal principles as separate sorts of standards, different from legal rules, we are suddenly aware of them all around us. Law teachers teach them, lawbooks cite them, legal historians celebrate them. But they seem most energetically at work, carrying most weight, in difficult lawsuits like *Riggs* and *Henningsen*. In cases like these, principles play an essential part in arguments supporting judgments about particular legal rights and obligations. After the case is decided, we may say that the case stands for a particular rule (*e.g.*, the rule that one who murders is not eligible to take under the will of his victim). But the rule does not exist before the case is decided; the court cites principles as its justification for adopting and applying a new rule. In *Riggs*, the court cited the principle that no man may profit from his own wrong as a background standard against which to read the statute of wills and in this way justified a new interpretation of that statute. In *Henningsen*, the court cited a variety of intersecting principles and policies as authority for a new rule respecting manufacturer's liability for automobile defects.

An analysis of the concept of legal obligation must therefore account for the important role of principles in reaching particular decisions of

law. There are two very different tacks we might take.

(a) We might treat legal principles the way we treat legal rules and say that some principles are binding as law and must be taken into account by judges and lawyers who make decisions of legal obligation. If we took this tack, we should say that in the United States, at least, the "law" includes principles as well as rules.

(b) We might, on the other hand, deny that principles can be binding the way some rules are. We would say, instead, that in cases like *Riggs* or *Henningsen* the judge reaches beyond the rules that he is bound to apply (reaches, that is, beyond the "law") for extra-legal principles he is free to follow if he wishes.

One might think that there is not much difference between these two lines of attack, that it is only a verbal question of how one wants to use the word "law." But that is a mistake, because the choice between these two accounts has the greatest consequences for an analysis of legal obligation. It is a choice between two *concepts* of a legal principle, a choice we can clarify by comparing it to a choice we might make between two concepts of a legal rule. We sometimes say of someone that he "makes it a rule" to do something, when we mean that he has chosen to follow a certain practice. We might say that someone has made it a rule, for example, to run a mile before breakfast because he wants to be healthy and believes in a regimen. We do not mean, when we say this, that he is *bound* by the rule that he must run a mile before breakfast, or even that he regards it as binding upon him. Accepting a rule as binding is something different from making it a rule to do something. If we use Hart's example again, there is a difference between saying that Englishmen make it a rule to see a movie once a week, and saying that the English have a rule that one must see a movie once a week. The second implies that if an Englishman does not follow the rule, he is subject to criticism or censure, but the first does not. The first does not exclude the possibility of a *sort* of criticism — we may say that one who does not see movies is neglecting his education — but we do not suggest that he is doing something wrong *just* in not following the rule.[20]

If we think of the judges of a community as a group, we could describe the rules of law they follow in these two different ways. We could say, for instance, that in a certain state the judges make it a rule not to enforce wills unless there are three witnesses. This would not imply that the rare judge who enforces such a rule is doing anything wrong just for that reason. On the other hand we can say that in that state a rule of law requires judges not to enforce such wills; this does imply that a judge who enforces them is doing something wrong. Hart, Austin and other positivists, of course, would insist on this latter account of legal rules; they would not at all be satisfied with the "make it a rule" account. It is not a verbal question of which account is right. It is a question of which describes the social situation more accurately. Other important issues turn on which description we accept. If judges simply "make it a rule" not to enforce certain contracts, for example, then we cannot say, before the decision, that anyone is "entitled" to that result, and that proposition cannot enter into any justification we might offer for the decision.

The two lines of attack on principles parallel these two accounts of rules. The first tack treats principles as binding upon judges, so that they are wrong not to apply the principles when they are pertinent. The second tack treats principles as summaries of what most judges "make it a principle" to do when forced to go beyond the standards that bind them. The choice between these approaches will affect, perhaps even determine, the answer we can give to the question whether the judge in a hard case like *Riggs* or *Henningsen* is attempting to enforce pre-existing legal rights and obligations. If we take the first tack, we are still free to argue that because such judges are applying binding legal standards they are enforcing legal rights and obligations. But if we take the second, we are out of court on that issue, and we must acknowledge that the murderer's family in *Riggs* and the manufacturer in *Henningsen* were deprived of their property by an act of judicial discretion applied *ex post facto*. This may not shock many readers – the notion of judicial discretion has percolated through the legal community – but it does illustrate one of the most nettlesome of the puzzles that drive

philosophers to worry about legal obligation. If taking property away in cases like these cannot be justified by appealing to an established obligation, another justification must be found, and nothing satisfactory has yet been supplied.

In my skeleton diagram of positivism, previously set out, I listed the doctrine of judicial discretion as the second tenet. Positivists hold that when a case is not covered by a clear rule, a judge must exercise his discretion to decide that case by what amounts to a fresh piece of legislation. There may be an important connection between this doctrine and the question of which of the two approaches to legal principles we must take. We shall therefore want to ask whether the doctrine is correct, and whether it implies the second approach, as it seems on its face to do. En route to these issues, however, we shall have to polish our understanding of the concept of discretion. I shall try to show how certain confusions about that concept, and in particular a failure to discriminate different senses in which it is used, account for the popularity of the doctrine of discretion. I shall argue that in the sense in which the doctrine does have a bearing on our treatment of principles, it is entirely unsupported by the arguments the positivists use to defend it.

V   Discretion

The concept of discretion was lifted by the positivists from ordinary language, and to understand it we must put it back *in habitat* for a moment. What does it mean, in ordinary life, to say that someone "has discretion"? The first thing to notice is that the concept is out of place in all but very special contexts. For example, you would not say that I either do or do not have discretion to choose a house for my family. It is not true that I have "no discretion" in making that choice, and yet it would be almost equally misleading to say that I do have discretion. The concept of discretion is at home in only one sort of context: when someone is in general charged with making decisions subject to standards set by a particular authority. It makes sense to speak of the discretion of a sergeant who is subject to orders of superiors, or the discretion of a sports official or contest judge who is governed by a rule book or the terms of the contest. Discretion, like the hole in a doughnut, does not exist except as an area left open by a surrounding belt of restriction. It is therefore a relative concept. It always makes sense to ask, "Discretion under which standards?" or "Discretion as to which authority?" Generally the context will make the answer to this plain, but in some cases the official may have discretion from one standpoint though not from another.

Like almost all terms, the precise meaning of "discretion" is affected by features of the context. The term is always colored by the background of understood information against which it is used. Although the shadings are many, it will be helpful for us to recognize some gross distinctions.

Sometimes we use "discretion" in a weak sense, simply to say that for some reason the standards an official must apply cannot be applied mechanically but demand the use of judgment. We use this weak sense when the context does not already make that clear, when the background our audience assumes does not contain that piece of information. Thus we might say, "The sergeant's orders left him a great deal of discretion," to those who do not know what the sergeant's orders were or who do not know something that made those orders vague or hard to carry out. It would make perfect sense to add, by way of amplification, that the lieutenant had ordered the sergeant to take his five most experienced men on patrol but that it was hard to determine which were the most experienced.

Sometimes we use the term in a different weak sense, to say only that some official has final authority to make a decision and cannot be reviewed and reversed by any other official. We speak this way when the official is part of a hierarchy of officials structured so that some have higher authority but in which the patterns of authority are different for different classes of decision. Thus we might say that in baseball certain decisions, like the decision whether the ball or the runner reached second base first, are left to the discretion of the second base umpire, if we mean that on this issue the head umpire has no power to substitute his own judgment if he disagrees.

I call both of these senses weak to distinguish them from a stronger sense. We use "discretion" sometimes not merely to say that an official must use judgment in applying the standards set him by authority, or that no one will review that exercise of judgment, but to say that on some issue he is simply not bound by standards set by the authority in question. In this sense we say that a sergeant has discretion who has been told to pick any five men for patrol he chooses or that a judge in a dog show has discretion to judge airedales before boxers if the rules do not stipulate an order of events. We use this sense not to comment on the vagueness or difficulty of the standards, or on who has the final word in applying them, but on their range and the decisions they purport to control. If the sergeant is told to take the five most experienced men, he does not have discretion in this strong sense because that order purports to govern his decision. The boxing referee who must decide which fighter has been the more aggressive does not have discretion, in the strong sense, for the same reason.[21]

If anyone said that the sergeant or the referee had discretion in these cases, we should have to understand him, if the context permitted, as using the term in one of the weak senses. Suppose, for example, the lieutenant ordered the sergeant to select the five men he deemed most experienced, and then added that the sergeant had discretion to choose them. Or the rules provided that the referee should award the round to the more aggressive fighter, with discretion in selecting him. We should have to understand these statements in the second weak sense, as speaking to the question of review of the decision. The first weak sense – that the decisions take judgment – would be otiose, and the third, strong sense is excluded by the statements themselves.

We must avoid one tempting confusion. The strong sense of discretion is not tantamount to license, and does not exclude criticism. Almost any situation in which a person acts (including those in which there is no question of decision under special authority, and so no question of discretion) makes relevant certain standards of rationality, fairness, and effectiveness. We criticize each other's acts in terms of these standards, and there is no reason not to do so when the acts are within the center rather than beyond the perimeter of the doughnut of special authority. So we can say that the sergeant who was given discretion (in the strong sense) to pick a patrol did so stupidly or maliciously or carelessly, or that the judge who had discretion in the order of viewing dogs made a mistake because he took boxers first although there were only three airedales and many more boxers. An official's discretion means not that he is free to decide without recourse to standards of sense and fairness, but only that his decision is not controlled by a standard furnished by the particular authority we have in mind when we raise the question of discretion. Of course this latter sort of freedom is important; that is why we have the strong sense of discretion. Someone who has discretion in this third sense can be criticized, but not for being disobedient, as in the case of the soldier. He can be said to have made a mistake, but not to have deprived a participant of a decision to which he was entitled, as in the case of a sports official or contest judge.

We may now return, with these observations in hand, to the positivists' doctrine of judicial discretion. That doctrine argues that if a case is not controlled by an established rule, the judge must decide it by exercising discretion. We want to examine this doctrine and to test its bearing on our treatment of principles; but first we must ask in which sense of discretion we are to understand it.

Some nominalists argue that judges always have discretion, even when a clear rule is in point, because judges are ultimately the final arbiters of the law. This doctrine of discretion uses the second weak sense of that term, because it makes the point that no higher authority reviews the decisions of the highest court. It therefore has no bearing on the issue of how we account for principles, any more than it bears on how we account for rules.

The positivists do not mean their doctrine this way, because they say that a judge has no discretion when a clear and established rule is available. If we attend to the positivists' arguments for the doctrine we may suspect that they use discretion in the first weak sense to mean only that judges must sometimes exercise judgment in applying legal standards. Their arguments call attention to the fact that some rules of law are vague (Professor Hart, for example, says that all rules of law have "open texture"), and that some cases arise (like *Henningsen*) in which no established rule seems to be suitable. They emphasize that judges must sometimes agonize over points of law, and that two equally trained and intelligent judges will often disagree.

These points are easily made; they are commonplace to anyone who has any familiarity with law. Indeed, that is the difficulty with assuming that positivists mean to use "discretion" in this weak sense. The proposition that when no clear rule is available discretion in the sense of judgment must be used is a tautology. It has no bearing, moreover, on the problem of how to account for legal principles. It is perfectly consistent to say that the judge in *Riggs*, for example, had to use judgment, and that he was bound to follow the principle that no man may profit from his own wrong. The positivists speak as if their doctrine of judicial discretion is an insight rather than a tautology, and as if it does have a bearing on the treatment of principles. Hart, for example, says that when the judge's discretion is in play, we can no longer speak of his being bound by standards, but must speak rather of what standards he "characteristically uses."[22] Hart thinks that when judges have discretion, the principles they cite must be treated on our second approach, as what courts "make it a principle" to do.

It therefore seems that positivists, at least sometimes, take their doctrine in the third, strong sense of discretion. In that sense it does bear on the treatment of principles; indeed, in that sense it is nothing less than a restatement of our second approach. It is the same thing to say that when a judge runs out of rules he has discretion, in the sense that he is not bound by any standards from the authority of law, as to say that the legal standards judges cite other than rules are not binding on them.

So we must examine the doctrine of judicial discretion in the strong sense. (I shall henceforth use the term "discretion" in that sense.)

Do the principles judges cite in cases like *Riggs* or *Henningsen* control their decisions, as the sergeant's orders to take the most experienced men or the referee's duty to choose the more aggressive fighter control the decisions of these officials? What arguments could a positivist supply to show that they do not?

(1) A positivist might argue that principles cannot be binding or obligatory. That would be a mistake. It is always a question, of course, whether any particular principle is *in fact* binding upon some legal official. But there is nothing in the logical character of a principle that renders it incapable of binding him. Suppose that the judge in *Henningsen* had failed to take any account of the principle that automobile manufacturers have a special obligation to their consumers, or the principle that the courts seek to protect those whose bargaining position is weak, but had simply decided for the defendant by citing the principle of freedom of contract without more. His critics would not have been content to point out that he had not taken account of considerations that other judges have been attending to for some time. Most would have said that it was his duty to take the measure of these principles and that the plaintiff was entitled to have him do so. We mean no more, when we say that a *rule* is binding upon a judge, than that he must follow it if it applies, and that if he does not he will on that account have made a mistake.

It will not do to say that in a case like *Henningsen* the court is only "morally" obligated to take particular principles into account, or that it is "institutionally" obligated, or obligated as a matter of judicial "craft," or something of that sort. The question will still remain why this type of obligation (whatever we call it) is different from the obligation that rules impose upon judges, and why it entitles us to say that principles and policies are not part of the law but are merely extra-legal standards "courts characteristically use."

(2) A positivist might argue that even though some principles are binding, in the sense that the judge must take them into account, they cannot determine a particular result. This is a harder argument to assess because it is not clear what it means for a standard to "determine" a

result. Perhaps it means that the standard *dictates* the result whenever it applies so that nothing else counts. If so, then it is certainly true that individual principles do not determine results, but that is only another way of saying that principles are not rules. Only rules dictate results, come what may. When a contrary result has been reached, the rule has been abandoned or changed. Principles do not work that way; they incline a decision one way, though not conclusively, and they survive intact when they do not prevail. This seems no reason for concluding that judges who must reckon with principles have discretion because a set of principles *can* dictate a result. If a judge believes that principles he is bound to recognize point in one direction and that principles pointing in the other direction, if any, are not of equal weight, then he must decide accordingly, just as he must follow what he believes to be a binding rule. He may, of course, be wrong in his assessment of the principles, but he may also be wrong in his judgment that the rule is binding. The sergeant and the referee, we might add, are often in the same boat. No one factor dictates which soldiers are the most experienced or which fighter the more aggressive. These officials must make judgments of the relative weights of these various factors; they do not on that account have discretion.

(3) A positivist might argue that principles cannot count as law because their authority, and even more so their weight, are congenitally *controversial*. It is true that generally we cannot *demonstrate* the authority or weight of a particular principle as we can sometimes demonstrate the validity of a rule by locating it in an act of Congress or in the opinion of an authoritative court. Instead, we make a case for a principle, and for its weight, by appealing to an amalgam of practice and other principles in which the implications of legislative and judicial history figure along with appeals to community practices and understandings. There is no litmus paper for testing the soundness of such a case – it is a matter of judgment, and reasonable men may disagree. But again this does not distinguish the judge from other officials who do not have discretion. The sergeant has no litmus paper for experience, the referee none for

aggressiveness. Neither of these has discretion, because he is bound to reach an understanding, controversial or not, of what his orders or the rules require, and to act on that understanding. That is the judge's duty as well.

Of course, if the positivists are right in another of their doctrines – the theory that in each legal system there is an ultimate *test* for binding law like Professor Hart's rule of recognition – it follows that principles are not binding law. But the incompatibility of principles with the positivists' theory can hardly be taken as an argument that principles must be treated any particular way. That begs the question; we are interested in the status of principles because we want to evaluate the positivists' model. The positivist cannot defend his theory of a rule of recognition by fiat; if principles are not amenable to a test he must show some other reason why they cannot count as law. Since principles seem to play a role in arguments about legal obligation (witness, again, *Riggs* and *Henningsen*), a model that provides for that role has some initial advantage over one that excludes it, and the latter cannot properly be inveighed in its own support.

These are the most obvious of the arguments a positivist might use for the doctrine of discretion in the strong sense, and for the second approach to principles. I shall mention one strong counter-argument against that doctrine and in favor of the first approach. Unless at least some principles are acknowledged to be binding upon judges, requiring them as a set to reach particular decisions, then no rules, or very few rules, can be said to be binding upon them either.

In most American jurisdictions, and now in England also, the higher courts not infrequently reject established rules. Common law rules – those developed by earlier court decisions – are sometimes overruled directly, and sometimes radically altered by further development. Statutory rules are subjected to interpretation and reinterpretation, sometimes even when the result is not to carry out what is called the "legislative intent."[23] If courts had discretion to change established rules, then these rules would of course not be binding upon them, and so would not be law on the positivists' model. The positivist must therefore argue

that there are standards, themselves binding upon judges, that determine when a judge may overrule or alter an established rule, and when he may not.

When, then, is a judge permitted to change an existing rule of law? Principles figure in the answer in two ways. First, it is necessary, though not sufficient, that the judge find that the change would advance some policy or serve some principle, which policy or principle thus justifies the change. In *Riggs* the change (a new interpretation of the statute of wills) was justified by the principle that no man should profit from his own wrong; in *Henningsen* certain rules about automobile manufacturer's liability were altered on the basis of the principles and policies I quoted from the opinion of the court.

But not any principle will do to justify a change, or no rule would ever be safe. There must be some principles that count and others that do not, and there must be some principles that count for more than others. It could not depend on the judge's own preferences amongst a sea of respectable extra-legal standards, any one in principle eligible, because if that were the case we could not say that any rules were binding. We could always imagine a judge whose preferences amongst extra-legal standards were such as would justify a shift or radical reinterpretation of even the most entrenched rule.

Second, any judge who proposes to change existing doctrine must take account of some important standards that argue against departures from established doctrine, and these standards are also for the most part principles. They include the doctrine of "legislative supremacy," a set of principles and policies that require the courts to pay a qualified deference to the acts of the legislature. They also include the doctrine of precedent, another set of principles and policies reflecting the equities and efficiencies of consistency. The doctrines of legislative supremacy and precedent incline toward the *status quo*, each within its sphere, but they do not command it. Judges are not free, however, to pick and choose amongst the principles and policies that make up these doctrines – if they were, again, no rule could be said to be binding.

Consider, therefore, what someone implies who says that a particular rule is binding. He may imply that the rule is affirmatively supported by principles the court is not free to disregard, and which are collectively more weighty than other principles that argue for a change. If not, he implies that any change would be condemned by a combination of conservative principles of legislative supremacy and precedent that the court is not free to ignore. Very often, he will imply both, for the conservative principles, being principles and not rules, are usually not powerful enough to save a common law rule or an aging statute that is entirely unsupported by substantive principles the court is bound to respect. Either of these implications, of course, treats a body of principles and policies as law in the sense that rules are; it treats them as standards binding upon the officials of a community, controlling their decisions of legal right and obligation.

We are left with this issue. If the positivists' theory of judicial discretion is either trivial because it uses "discretion" in a weak sense, or unsupported because the various arguments we can supply in its defense fall short, why have so many careful and intelligent lawyers embraced it? We can have no confidence in our treatment of that theory unless we can deal with that question. It is not enough to note (although perhaps it contributes to the explanation) that "discretion" has different senses that may be confused. We do not confuse these senses when we are not thinking about law.

Part of the explanation, at least, lies in a lawyer's natural tendency to associate laws and rules, and to think of "the law" as a collection or system of rules. Roscoe Pound, who diagnosed this tendency long ago, thought that English speaking lawyers were tricked into it by the fact that English uses the same word, changing only the article, for "a law" and "the law."[24] (Other languages, on the contrary, use two words: "loi" and "droit," for example, and "Gesetz" and "Recht.") This may have had its effect, with the English speaking positivists, because the expression "a law" certainly does suggest a rule. But the principal reason for associating law with rules runs deeper, and lies, I think, in the fact that legal education has for a long time consisted of teaching and examining those established rules that form the cutting edge of law.

In any event, if a lawyer thinks of law as a system of rules, and yet recognizes, as he must, that judges change old rules and introduce new ones, he will come naturally to the theory of judicial discretion in the strong sense. In those other systems of rules with which he has experience (like games), the rules are the only special authority that govern official decisions, so that if an umpire could change a rule, he would have discretion as to the subject matter of that rule. Any principles umpires might mention when changing the rules would represent only their "characteristic" preferences. Positivists treat law like baseball revised in this way.

There is another, more subtle consequence of this initial assumption that law is a system of rules. When the positivists do attend to principles and policies, they treat them as rules *manqué*. They assume that *if* they are standards of law they must be rules, and so they read them as standards that are trying to be rules. When a positivist hears someone argue that legal principles are part of the law, he understands this to be an argument for what he calls the "higher law" theory, that these principles are the rules of a law above the law.[25] He refutes this theory by pointing out that these "rules" are sometimes followed and sometimes not, that for every "rule" like "no man shall profit from his own wrong" there is another competing "rule" like "the law favors security of title," and that there is no way to test the validity of "rules" like these. He concludes that these principles and policies are not valid rules of a law above the law, which is true, because they are not rules at all. He also concludes that they are extra-legal standards which each judge selects according to his own lights in the exercise of his discretion, which is false. It is as if a zoologist had proved that fish are not mammals, and then concluded that they are really only plants.

VI The Rule of Recognition

This discussion was provoked by our two competing accounts of legal principles. We have been exploring the second account, which the positivists seem to adopt through their doctrine of judicial discretion, and we have discovered grave difficulties. It is time to return to the fork in the road. What if we adopt the first approach? What would the consequences of this be for the skeletal structure of positivism? Of course we should have to drop the second tenet, the doctrine of judicial discretion (or, in the alternative, to make plain that the doctrine is to be read merely to say that judges must often exercise judgment). Would we also have to abandon or modify the first tenet, the proposition that law is distinguished by tests of the sort that can be set out in a master rule like Professor Hart's rule of recognition? If principles of the *Riggs* and *Henningsen* sort are to count as law, and we are nevertheless to preserve the notion of a master rule for law, then we must be able to deploy some test that all (and only) the principles that do count as law meet. Let us begin with the test Hart suggests for identifying valid *rules* of law, to see whether these can be made to work for principles as well.

Most rules of law, according to Hart, are valid because some competent institution enacted them. Some were created by a legislature, in the form of statutory enactments. Others were created by judges who formulated them to decide particular cases, and thus established them as precedents for the future. But this test of pedigree will not work for the *Riggs* and *Henningsen* principles. The origin of these as legal principles lies not in a particular decision of some legislature or court, but in a sense of appropriateness developed in the profession and the public over time. Their continued power depends upon this sense of appropriateness being sustained. If it no longer seemed unfair to allow people to profit by their wrongs, or fair to place special burdens upon oligopolies that manufacture potentially dangerous machines, these principles would no longer play much of a role in new cases, even if they had never been overruled or repealed. (Indeed, it hardly makes sense to speak of principles like these as being "overruled" or "repealed." When they decline they are eroded, not torpedoed.)

True, if we were challenged to back up our claim that some principle is a principle of law, we would mention any prior cases in which that principle was cited, or figured in the argument. We would also mention any statute that seemed

to exemplify that principle (even better if the principle was cited in the preamble of the statute, or in the committee reports or other legislative documents that accompanied it). Unless we could find some such institutional support, we would probably fail to make out our case, and the more support we found, the more weight we could claim for the principle.

Yet we could not devise any formula for testing how much and what kind of institutional support is necessary to make a principle a legal principle, still less to fix its weight at a particular order of magnitude. We argue for a particular principle by grappling with a whole set of shifting, developing and interacting standards (themselves principles rather than rules) about institutional responsibility, statutory interpretation, the persuasive force of various sorts of precedent, the relation of all these to contemporary moral practices, and hosts of other such standards. We could not bolt all of these together into a single "rule," even a complex one, and if we could the result would bear little relation to Hart's picture of a rule of recognition, which is the picture of a fairly stable master rule specifying "some feature or features possession of which by a suggested rule is taken as a conclusive affirmative indication that it is a rule...."[26]

Moreover, the techniques we apply in arguing for another principle do not stand (as Hart's rule of recognition is designed to) on an entirely different level from the principles they support. Hart's sharp distinction between acceptance and validity does not hold. If we are arguing for the principle that a man should not profit from his own wrong, we could cite the acts of courts and legislatures that exemplify it, but this speaks as much to the principle's acceptance as its validity. (It seems odd to speak of a principle as being valid at all, perhaps because validity is an all-or-nothing concept, appropriate for rules, but inconsistent with a principle's dimension of weight.) If we are asked (as we might well be) to defend the particular doctrine of precedent, or the particular technique of statutory interpretation, that we used in this argument, we should certainly cite the practice of others in using that doctrine or technique. But we should also cite other general principles that we believe support that practice, and this introduces a note of validity into the chord of acceptance. We might argue, for example, that the use we make of earlier cases and statutes is supported by a particular analysis of the point of the practice of legislation or the doctrine of precedent, or by the principles of democratic theory, or by a particular position on the proper division of authority between national and local institutions, or something else of that sort. Nor is this path of support a one-way street leading to some ultimate principle resting on acceptance alone. Our principles of legislation, precedent, democracy, or federalism might be challenged too; and if they were we should argue for them, not only in terms of practice, but in terms of each other and in terms of the implications of trends of judicial and legislative decisions, even though this last would involve appealing to those same doctrines of interpretation we justified through the principles we are now trying to support. At this level of abstraction, in other words, principles rather hang together than link together.

So even though principles draw support from the official acts of legal institutions, they do not have a simple or direct enough connection with these acts to frame that connection in terms of criteria specified by some ultimate master rule of recognition. Is there any other route by which principles might be brought under such a rule?

Hart does say that a master rule might designate as law not only rules enacted by particular legal institutions, but rules established by *custom* as well. He has in mind a problem that bothered other positivists, including Austin. Many of our most ancient legal rules were never explicitly created by a legislature or a court. When they made their first appearance in legal opinions and texts, they were treated as already being part of the law because they represented the customary practice of the community, or some specialized part of it, like the business community. (The examples ordinarily given are rules of mercantile practice, like the rules governing what rights arise under a standard form of commercial paper.)[27] Since Austin thought that all law was the command of a determinate sovereign, he held that these customary practices

were not law until the courts (as agents of the sovereign) recognized them, and that the courts were indulging in a fiction in pretending otherwise. But that seemed arbitrary. If everyone thought custom might in itself be law, the fact that Austin's theory said otherwise was not persuasive.

Hart reversed Austin on this point. The master rule, he says, might stipulate that some custom counts as law even before the courts recognize it. But he does not face the difficulty this raises for his general theory because he does not attempt to set out the criteria a master rule might use for this purpose. It cannot use, as its only criterion, the provision that the community regard the practice as *morally* binding, for this would not distinguish legal customary rules from moral customary rules, and of course not all of the community's long-standing customary moral obligations are enforced at law. If, on the other hand, the test is whether the community regards the customary practice as *legally* binding, the whole point of the master rule is undercut, at least for this class of legal rules. The master rule, says Hart, marks the transformation from a primitive society to one with law, because it provides a test for determining social rules of law other than by measuring their acceptance. But if the master rule says merely that whatever other rules the community accepts as legally binding are legally binding, then it provides no such test at all, beyond the test we should use were there no master rule. The master rule becomes (for these cases) a non-rule of recognition; we might as well say that every primitive society has a secondary rule of recognition, namely the rule that whatever is accepted as binding is binding. Hart himself, in discussing international law, ridicules the idea that such a rule could be a rule of recognition, by describing the proposed rule as "an empty repetition of the mere fact that the society concerned . . . observes certain standards of conduct as obligatory rules."[28]

Hart's treatment of custom amounts, indeed, to a confession that there are at least some rules of law that are not binding because they are valid under standards laid down by a master rule but are binding – like the master rule – because they are accepted as binding by the community. This chips at the neat pyramidal architecture we admired in Hart's theory: we can no longer say that only the master rule is binding because of its acceptance, all other rules being valid under its terms.

This is perhaps only a chip, because the customary rules Hart has in mind are no longer a very significant part of the law. But it does suggest that Hart would be reluctant to widen the damage by bringing under the head of "custom" all those crucial principles and policies we have been discussing. If he were to call these part of the law and yet admit that the only test of their force lies in the degree to which they are accepted as law by the community or some part thereof, he would very sharply reduce that area of the law over which his master rule held any dominion. It is not just that all the principles and policies would escape its sway, though that would be bad enough. Once these principles and policies are accepted as law, and thus as standards judges must follow in determining legal obligations, it would follow that *rules* like those announced for the first time in *Riggs* and *Henningsen* owe their force at least in part to the authority of principles and policies, and so not entirely to the master rule of recognition.

So we cannot adapt Hart's version of positivism by modifying his rule of recognition to embrace principles. No tests of pedigree, relating principles to acts of legislation, can be formulated, nor can his concept of customary law, itself an exception to the first tenet of positivism, be made to serve without abandoning that tenet altogether. One more possibility must be considered, however. If no rule of recognition can provide a test for identifying principles, why not say that principles are ultimate, and *form* the rule of recognition of our law? The answer to the general question "What is valid law in an American jurisdiction?" would then require us to state all the principles (as well as ultimate constitutional rules) in force in that jurisdiction at the time, together with appropriate assignments of weight. A positivist might then regard the complete set of these standards as the rule of recognition of the jurisdiction. This solution has the attraction of paradox, but of course it is an unconditional surrender.

If we simply designate our rule of recognition by the phrase "the complete set of principles in force," we achieve only the tautology that law is law. If, instead, we tried actually to list all the principles in force we would fail. They are controversial, their weight is all important, they are numberless, and they shift and change so fast that the start of our list would be obsolete before we reached the middle. Even if we succeeded, we would not have a key for law because there would be nothing left for our key to unlock.

I conclude that if we treat principles as law we must reject the positivists' first tenet, that the law of a community is distinguished from other social standards by some test in the form of a master rule. We have already decided that we must then abandon the second tenet – the doctrine of judicial discretion – or clarify it into triviality. What of the third tenet, the positivists' theory of legal obligation?

This theory holds that a legal obligation exists when (and only when) an established rule of law imposes such an obligation. It follows from this that in a hard case – when no such established rule can be found – there is no legal obligation until the judge creates a new rule for the future. The judge may apply that new rule to the parties in the case, but this is *ex post facto* legislation, not the enforcement of an existing obligation.

The positivists' doctrine of discretion (in the strong sense) required this view of legal obligation, because if a judge has discretion there can be no legal right or obligation – no entitlement – that he must enforce. Once we abandon that doctrine, however, and treat principles as law, we raise the possibility that a legal obligation might be imposed by a constellation of principles as well as by an established rule. We might want to say that a legal obligation exists whenever the case supporting such an obligation, in terms of binding legal principles of different sorts, is stronger than the case against it.

Of course, many questions would have to be answered before we could accept that view of legal obligation. If there is no rule of recognition, no test for law in that sense, how do we decide which principles are to count, and how much, in making such a case? How do we decide whether one case is better than another? If legal obligation rests on an undemonstrable judgment of that sort, how can it provide a justification for a judicial decision that one party had a legal obligation? Does this view of obligation square with the way lawyers, judges and laymen speak, and is it consistent with our attitudes about moral obligation? Does this analysis help us to deal with the classical jurisprudential puzzles about the nature of law?

These questions must be faced, but even the questions promise more than positivism provides. Positivism, on its own thesis, stops short of just those puzzling, hard cases that send us to look for theories of law. When we reach these cases, the positivist remits us to a doctrine of discretion that leads nowhere and tells nothing. His picture of law as a system of rules has exercised a tenacious hold on our imagination, perhaps through its very simplicity. If we shake ourselves loose from this model of rules, we may be able to build a model truer to the complexity and sophistication of our own practices.

Notes

1 *See* Linkletter v. Walker, 381 U.S. 618 (1965).
2 J. Austin, The Province of Jurisprudence Determined (1832).
3 *See* H. L. A. Hart, The Concept of Law 89–96 (1961).
4 *Id.* at 79–88.
5 *Id.* at 97–107.
6 *Id. passim*, particularly ch. VI.
7 *Id.* ch. VII.
8 *See* Dworkin, *Wasserstrom: The Judicial Decision*, 75 Ethics 47 (1964), reprinted as *Does Law Have a Function?*, 74 Yale L.J. 640 (1965).
9 115 N.Y. 506, 22 N.E. 188 (1889).
10 *Id.* at 509, 22 N.E. at 189.
11 *Id.* at 511, 22 N.E. at 190.
12 32 N.J. 358, 161 A.2d 69 (1960).
13 *Id.* at 386, 161 A.2d at 84.
14 *Id.*
15 *Id.* at 388, 161 A.2d at 86.
16 *Id.* at 387, 161 A.2d at 85.
17 *Id.* at 389, 161 A.2d at 86 (quoting Frankfurter, J., in United States v. Bethlehem Steel, 315 U.S. 289, 326 (1942)).
18 *Id.*
19 Standard Oil v. United States, 221 U.S. 1, 60 (1911); United States v. American Tobacco Co., 221 U.S. 106, 180 (1911).
20 The distinction is in substance the same as that made by Rawls, *Two Concepts of Rules*, 64 Philosophical Rev. 3 (1955).
21 I have not spoken of that jurisprudential favorite, "limited" discretion, because that concept presents no special difficulties if we remember the relativity of discretion. Suppose the sergeant is told to choose from "amongst" experienced men, or to "take experience into account." We might say either that he has (limited) discretion in picking his patrol, or (full) discretion to either pick amongst experienced men or decide what else to take into account.
22 H. L. A. Hart, The Concept of Law 144 (1961).
23 *See* Wellington & Albert, *Statutory Interpretation and the Political Process: A Comment on Sinclair v. Atkinson*, 72 Yale L. J. 1547 (1963).
24 R. Pound, An Introduction to the Philosophy of Law 56 (rev. ed. 1954).
25 *See, e.g.,* Dickinson, *The Law Behind Law* (pts. 1 & 2), 29 Colum. L. Rev. 112, 254 (1929).
26 H. L. A. Hart, The Concept of Law 92 (1961).
27 *See* Note, *Custom and Trade Usage: Its Application to Commercial Dealings and the Common Law*, 55 Colum. L. Rev. 1192 (1955), and materials cited therein at 1193 n.1. As that note makes plain, the actual practices of courts in recognizing trade customs follow the pattern of applying a set of general principles and policies rather than a test that could be captured as part of a rule of recognition.
28 H. L. A. Hart, The Concept of Law 230 (1961).

Part II

Relation of Law and Morality

4

Positivism and the Separation of Law and Morals

H. L. A. Hart

In this article I shall discuss and attempt to defend a view which Mr. Justice Holmes, among others, held and for which he and they have been much criticized. But I wish first to say why I think that Holmes, whatever the vicissitudes of his American reputation may be, will always remain for Englishmen a heroic figure in jurisprudence. This will be so because he magically combined two qualities: one of them is imaginative power, which English legal thinking has often lacked; the other is clarity, which English legal thinking usually possesses. The English lawyer who turns to read Holmes is made to see that what he had taken to be settled and stable is really always on the move. To make this discovery with Holmes is to be with a guide whose words may leave you unconvinced, sometimes even repelled, but never mystified. Like our own Austin, with whom Holmes shared many ideals and thoughts, Holmes was sometimes clearly wrong; but again like Austin, when this was so he was always wrong clearly. This surely is a sovereign virtue in jurisprudence. Clarity I know is said not to be enough; this may be true, but there are still questions in jurisprudence where the issues are confused because they are discussed in a style which Holmes would have spurned for its obscurity. Perhaps this is inevitable: jurisprudence trembles so uncertainly on the margin of many subjects that there will

always be need for someone, in Bentham's phrase, "to pluck the mask of Mystery" from its face.[1] This is true, to a pre-eminent degree, of the subject of this article. Contemporary voices tell us we must recognize something obscured by the legal "positivists" whose day is now over: that there is a "point of intersection between law and morals,"[2] or that what *is* and what *ought* to be are somehow indissolubly fused or inseparable,[3] though the positivists denied it. What do these phrases mean? Or rather which of the many things that they *could* mean, *do* they mean? Which of them do "positivists" deny and why is it wrong to do so?

I

I shall present the subject as part of the history of an idea. At the close of the eighteenth century and the beginning of the nineteenth the most earnest thinkers in England about legal and social problems and the architects of great reforms were the great Utilitarians. Two of them, Bentham and Austin, constantly insisted on the need to distinguish, firmly and with the maximum of clarity, law as it is from law as it ought to be. This theme haunts their work, and they condemned the natural-law thinkers precisely because they had blurred this apparently simple but vital distinction. By contrast, at the present time in this country and to a lesser extent in England, this separation between law and morals is held to be superficial and wrong. Some critics have thought that it blinds men to the true nature of law and its roots in social life.[4] Others have thought it not only intellectually misleading but corrupting in practice, at its worst apt to weaken resistance to state tyranny or absolutism,[5] and at its best apt to bring law into disrespect. The nonpejorative name "Legal Positivism," like most terms which are used as missiles in intellectual battles, has come to stand for a baffling multitude of different sins. One of them is the sin, real or alleged, of insisting, as Austin and Bentham did, on the separation of law as it is and law as it ought to be.

How then has this reversal of the wheel come about? What are the theoretical errors in this distinction? Have the practical consequences of stressing the distinction as Bentham and Austin did been bad? Should we now reject it or keep it? In considering these questions we should recall the social philosophy which went along with the Utilitarians' insistence on this distinction. They stood firmly but on their own utilitarian ground for all the principles of liberalism in law and government. No one has ever combined, with such even-minded sanity as the Utilitarians, the passion for reform with respect for law together with a due recognition of the need to control the abuse of power even when power is in the hands of reformers. One by one in Bentham's works you can identify the elements of the *Rechtstaat* and all the principles for the defense of which the terminology of natural law has in our day been revived. Here are liberty of speech, and of press, the right of association,[6] the need that laws should be published and made widely known before they are enforced,[7] the need to control administrative agencies,[8] the insistence that there should be no criminal liability without fault,[9] and the importance of the principle of legality, *nulla poena sine lege*.[10] Some, I know, find the political and moral insight of the Utilitarians a very simple one, but we should not mistake this simplicity for superficiality nor forget how favorably their simplicities compare with the profundities of other thinkers. Take only one example: Ben-

tham on slavery. He says the question at issue is not whether those who are held as slaves can reason, but simply whether they suffer.[11] Does this not compare well with the discussion of the question in terms of whether or not there are some men whom Nature has fitted only to be the living instruments of others? We owe it to Bentham more than anyone else that we have stopped discussing this and similar questions of social policy in that form.

So Bentham and Austin were not dry analysts fiddling with verbal distinctions while cities burned, but were the vanguard of a movement which laboured with passionate intensity and much success to bring about a better society and better laws. Why then did they insist on the separation of law as it is and law as it ought to be? What did they mean? Let us first see what they said. Austin formulated the doctrine:

> The existence of law is one thing; its merit or demerit is another. Whether it be or be not is one enquiry; whether it be or be not conformable to an assumed standard, is a different enquiry. A law, which actually exists, is a law, though we happen to dislike it, or though it vary from the text, by which we regulate our approbation and disapprobation. This truth, when formally announced as an abstract proposition, is so simple and glaring that it seems idle to insist upon it. But simple and glaring as it is, when enunciated in abstract expressions the enumeration of the instances in which it has been forgotten would fill a volume.
>
> Sir William Blackstone, for example, says in his "Commentaries," that the laws of God are superior in obligation to all other laws; that no human laws should be suffered to contradict them; that human laws are of no validity if contrary to them; and that all valid laws derive their force from that Divine original.
>
> Now, he *may* mean that all human laws ought to conform to the Divine laws. If this be his meaning, I assent to it without hesitation.... Perhaps, again, he means that human lawgivers are themselves obliged by the Divine laws to fashion the laws which they impose by that ultimate standard, because if they do not, God will punish them. To this also I entirely assent....
>
> But the meaning of this passage of Blackstone, if it has a meaning, seems rather to be this: that no human law which conflicts with the Divine law is obligatory or binding; in other words, that no

human law which conflicts with the Divine law *is a law....*[12]

Austin's protest against blurring the distinction between what law is and what it ought to be is quite general: it is a mistake, whatever our standard of what ought to be, whatever "the text by which we regulate our approbation or disapprobation." His examples, however, are always a confusion between law as it is and law as morality would require it to be. For him, it must be remembered, the fundamental principles of morality were God's commands, to which utility was an "index": besides this there was the actual accepted morality of a social group or "positive" morality.

Bentham insisted on this distinction without characterizing morality by reference to God but only, of course, by reference to the principles of utility. Both thinkers' prime reason for this insistence was to enable men to see steadily the precise issues posed by the existence of morally bad laws, and to understand the specific character of the authority of a legal order. Bentham's general recipe for life under the government of laws was simple: it was "*to obey punctually; to censure freely.*"[13] But Bentham was especially aware, as an anxious spectator of the French revolution, that this was not enough: the time might come in any society when the law's commands were so evil that the question of resistance had to be faced, and it was then essential that the issues at stake at this point should neither be oversimplified nor obscured.[14] Yet, this was precisely what the confusion between law and morals had done and Bentham found that the confusion had spread symmetrically in two different directions. On the one hand Bentham had in mind the anarchist who argues thus: "This ought not to be the law, therefore it is not and I am free not merely to censure but to disregard it." On the other hand he thought of the reactionary who argues: "This is the law, therefore it is what it ought to be," and thus stifles criticism at its birth. Both errors, Bentham thought, were to be found in Blackstone: there was his incautious statement that human laws were invalid if contrary to the law of God,[15] and "that spirit of obsequious *quietism* that seems constitutional in our

Author" which "will scarce ever let him recognise a difference" between what is and what ought to be.[16] This indeed was for Bentham the occupational disease of lawyers: "[I]n the eyes of lawyers – not to speak of their dupes – that is to say, as yet, the generality of non-lawyers – the *is* and *ought to be*...were one and indivisible."[17] There are therefore two dangers between which insistence on this distinction will help us to steer: the danger that law and its authority may be dissolved in man's conceptions of what law ought to be and the danger that the existing law may supplant morality as a final test of conduct and so escape criticism.

In view of later criticisms it is also important to distinguish several things that the Utilitarians did not mean by insisting on their separation of law and morals. They certainly accepted many of the things that might be called "the intersection of law and morals." First, they never denied that, as a matter of historical fact, the development of legal systems had been powerfully influenced by moral opinion, and, conversely, that moral standards had been profoundly influenced by law, so that the content of many legal rules mirrored moral rules or principles. It is not in fact always easy to trace this historical causal connection, but Bentham was certainly ready to admit its existence; so too Austin spoke of the "frequent coincidence"[18] of positive law and morality and attributed the confusion of what law is with what law ought to be to this very fact.

Secondly, neither Bentham nor his followers denied that by explicit legal provisions moral principles might at different points be brought into a legal system and form part of its rules, or that courts might be legally bound to decide in accordance with what they thought just or best. Bentham indeed recognized, as Austin did not, that even the supreme legislative power might be subjected to legal restraints by a constitution[19] and would not have denied that moral principles, like those of the fifth amendment, might form the content of such legal constitutional restraints. Austin differed in thinking that restraints on the supreme legislative power could not have the force of law, but would remain merely political or moral checks;[20] but of course he would have recognized that a statute, for example, might confer a delegated legislative power and restrict the area of its exercise by reference to moral principles.

What both Bentham and Austin were anxious to assert were the following two simple things: first, in the absence of an expressed constitutional or legal provision, it could not follow from the mere fact that a rule violated standards of morality that it was not a rule of law; and, conversely, it could not follow from the mere fact that a rule was morally desirable that it was a rule of law.

The history of this simple doctrine in the nineteenth century is too long and too intricate to trace here. Let me summarize it by saying that after it was propounded to the world by Austin it dominated English jurisprudence and constitutes part of the framework of most of those curiously English and perhaps unsatisfactory productions – the omnibus surveys of the whole field of jurisprudence. A succession of these were published after a full text of Austin's lectures finally appeared in 1863. In each of them the utilitarian separation of law and morals is treated as something that enables lawyers to attain a new clarity. Austin was said by one of his English successors, Amos, "to have delivered the law from the dead body of morality that still clung to it";[21] and even Maine, who was critical of Austin at many points, did not question this part of his doctrine. In the United States men like N. St. John Green,[22] Gray, and Holmes considered that insistence on this distinction had enabled the understanding of law as a means of social control to get off to a fruitful new start; they welcomed it both as self-evident and as illuminating – as a revealing tautology. This distinction is, of course, one of the main themes of Holmes' most famous essay "The Path of the Law,"[23] but the place it had in the estimation of these American writers is best seen in what Gray wrote at the turn of the century in *The Nature and Sources of the Law*. He said:

> The great gain in its fundamental conceptions which Jurisprudence made during the last century was the recognition of the truth that the Law of a State ... is not an ideal, but something which actually exists. ... [I]t is not that which ought to be, but that which is. To fix this definitely in the

Jurisprudence of the Common Law, is the feat that Austin accomplished.[24]

II

So much for the doctrine in the heyday of its success. Let us turn now to some of the criticisms. Undoubtedly, when Bentham and Austin insisted on the distinction between law as it is and as it ought to be, they had in mind *particular* laws the meanings of which were clear and so not in dispute, and they were concerned to argue that such laws, even if morally outrageous, were still laws. It is, however, necessary, in considering the criticisms which later developed, to consider more than those criticisms which were directed to this particular point if we are to get at the root of the dissatisfaction felt; we must also take account of the objection that, even if what the Utilitarians said on this particular point were true, their insistence on it, in a terminology suggesting a general cleavage between what is and ought to be law, obscured the fact that at other points there is an essential point of contact between the two. So in what follows I shall consider not only criticisms of the particular point which the Utilitarians had in mind, but also the claim that an essential connection between law and morals emerges if we examine how laws, the meanings of which are in dispute, are interpreted and applied in concrete cases; and that this connection emerges again if we widen our point of view and ask, not whether every particular rule of law must satisfy a moral minimum in order to be a law, but whether a system of rules which altogether failed to do this could be a legal system.

There is, however, one major initial complexity by which criticism has been much confused. We must remember that the Utilitarians combined with their insistence on the separation of law and morals two other equally famous but distinct doctrines. One was the important truth that a purely analytical study of legal concepts, a study of the meaning of the distinctive vocabulary of the law, was as vital to our understanding of the nature of law as historical or sociological studies, though of course it could not supplant them. The other doctrine was the famous imperative theory of law – that law is essentially a command.

These three doctrines constitute the utilitarian tradition in jurisprudence; yet they are distinct doctrines. It is possible to endorse the separation between law and morals and to value analytical inquiries into the meaning of legal concepts and yet think it wrong to conceive of law as essentially a command. One source of great confusion in the criticism of the separation of law and morals was the belief that the falsity of any one of these three doctrines in the utilitarian tradition showed the other two to be false; what was worse was the failure to see that there were three quite separate doctrines in this tradition. The indiscriminate use of the label "positivism" to designate ambiguously each one of these three separate doctrines (together with some others which the Utilitarians never professed) has perhaps confused the issue more than any other single factor.[25] Some of the early American critics of the Austinian doctrine were, however, admirably clear on just this matter. Gray, for example, added at the end of the tribute to Austin, which I have already quoted, the words, "He may have been wrong in treating the Law of the State as being the command of the sovereign"[26] and he touched shrewdly on many points where the command theory is defective. But other critics have been less clear-headed and have thought that the inadequacies of the command theory which gradually came to light were sufficient to demonstrate the falsity of the separation of law and morals.

This was a mistake, but a natural one. To see how natural it was we must look a little more closely at the command idea. The famous theory that law is a command was a part of a wider and more ambitious claim. Austin said that the notion of a command was "the *key* to the sciences of jurisprudence and morals,"[27] and contemporary attempts to elucidate moral judgments in terms of "imperative" or "prescriptive" utterances echo this ambitious claim. But the command theory, viewed as an effort to identify even the quintessence of law, let alone the quintessence of morals, seems breathtaking in its simplicity and quite inadequate. There is much, even in the simplest legal system, that

is distorted if presented as a command. Yet the Utilitarians thought that the essence of a legal system could be conveyed if the notion of a command were supplemented by that of a habit of obedience. The simple scheme was this: What is a command? It is simply an expression by one person of the desire that another person should do or abstain from some action, accompanied by a threat of punishment which is likely to follow disobedience. Commands are laws if two conditions are satisfied: first, they must be general; second, they must be commanded by what (as both Bentham and Austin claimed) exists in every political society whatever its constitutional form, namely, a person or a group of persons who are in receipt of habitual obedience from most of the society but pay no such obedience to others. These persons are its sovereign. Thus law is the command of the uncommanded commanders of society – the creation of the legally untrammelled will of the sovereign who is by definition outside the law.

It is easy to see that this account of a legal system is threadbare. One can also see why it might seem that its inadequacy is due to the omission of some essential connection with morality. The situation which the simple trilogy of command, sanction, and sovereign avails to describe, if you take these notions at all precisely, is like that of a gunman saying to his victim, "Give me your money or your life." The only difference is that in the case of a legal system the gunman says it to a large number of people who are accustomed to the racket and habitually surrender to it. Law surely is not the gunman situation writ large, and legal order is surely not to be thus simply identified with compulsion.

This scheme, despite the points of obvious analogy between a statute and a command, omits some of the most characteristic elements of law. Let me cite a few. It is wrong to think of a legislature (and a fortiori an electorate) with a changing membership, as a group of persons habitually obeyed: this simple idea is suited only to a monarch sufficiently long-lived for a "habit" to grow up. Even if we waive this point, nothing which legislators do makes law unless they comply with fundamental accepted rules specifying the essential lawmaking procedures. This is true even in a system having a simple unitary constitution like the British. These fundamental accepted rules specifying what the legislature must do to legislate are not commands habitually obeyed, nor can they be expressed as habits of obedience to persons. They lie at the root of a legal system, and what is most missing in the utilitarian scheme is an analysis of what it is for a social group and its officials to accept such rules. This notion, not that of a command as Austin claimed, is the "key to the science of jurisprudence," or at least one of the keys.

Again, Austin, in the case of a democracy, looked past the legislators to the electorate as "the sovereign" (or in England as part of it). He thought that in the United States the mass of the electors to the state and federal legislatures were the sovereign whose commands, given by their "agents" in the legislatures, were law. But on this footing the whole notion of the sovereign outside the law being "habitually obeyed" by the "bulk" of the population must go: for in this case the "bulk" obeys the bulk, that is, it obeys itself. Plainly the general acceptance of the authority of a lawmaking procedure, irrespective of the changing individuals who operate it from time to time, can be only distorted by an analysis in terms of mass habitual obedience to certain persons who are by definition outside the law, just as the cognate but much simpler phenomenon of the general social acceptance of a rule, say of taking off the hat when entering a church, would be distorted if represented as habitual obedience by the mass to specific persons.

Other critics dimly sensed a further and more important defect in the command theory, yet blurred the edge of an important criticism by assuming that the defect was due to the failure to insist upon some important connection between law and morals. This more radical defect is as follows. The picture that the command theory draws of life under law is essentially a simple relationship of the commander to the commanded, of superior to inferior, of top to bottom; the relationship is vertical between the commanders or authors of the law conceived of as essentially outside the law and those who are commanded and subject to the law. In this picture no place, or only an accidental or subordinate place, is afforded for a distinction between types of legal rules which are in fact radically different. Some laws require men to act in certain ways or to abstain from acting whether they wish to or not. The criminal law consists largely of rules of this sort: like commands they are simply "obeyed" or "disobeyed." But other legal rules are presented to society in quite different ways and have quite different functions. They provide facilities more or less elaborate for individuals to create structures of rights and duties for the conduct of life within the coercive framework of the law. Such are the rules enabling individuals to make contracts, wills, and trusts, and generally to mould their legal relations with others. Such rules, unlike the criminal law, are not factors designed to obstruct wishes and choices of an antisocial sort. On the contrary, these rules provide facilities for the realization of wishes and choices. They do not say (like commands) "do this whether you wish it or not," but rather "if you wish to do this, here is the way to do it." Under these rules we exercise powers, make claims, and assert rights. These phrases mark off characteristic features of laws that confer rights and powers; they are laws which are, so to speak, put at the disposition of individuals in a way in which the criminal law is not. Much ingenuity has gone into the task of "reducing" laws of this second sort to some complex variant of laws of the first sort. The effort to show that laws conferring rights are "really" only conditional stipulations of sanctions to be exacted from the person ultimately under a legal duty characterizes much of Kelsen's work.[28] Yet to urge this is really just to exhibit dogmatic determination to suppress one aspect of the legal system in order to maintain the theory that the stipulation of a sanction, like Austin's command, represents the quintessence of law. One might as well urge that the rules of baseball were "really" only complex conditional directions to the scorer and that this showed their real or "essential" nature.

One of the first jurists in England to break with the Austinian tradition, Salmond, complained that the analysis in terms of commands left the notion of a right unprovided with a place.[29] But he confused the point. He argued first, and correctly, that if laws are merely commands it is inexplicable that we should have come to speak of legal rights and powers as conferred or arising under them, but then wrongly concluded that the rules of a legal system must necessarily be connected with moral rules or principles of justice and that only on this footing could the phenomenon of legal rights be explained. Otherwise, Salmond thought, we would have to say that a mere "verbal coincidence" connects the concepts of legal and moral right. Similarly, continental critics of the Utilitarians, always alive to the complexity of the notion of a subjective right, insisted that the command theory gave it no place. Hägerström insisted that if laws were merely commands the notion of an individual's right was really inexplicable, for commands are, as he said, something which we either obey or we do not obey; they do not confer rights.[30] But he, too, concluded that moral, or, as he put it, common-sense, notions of justice must therefore be necessarily involved in the analysis of any legal structure elaborate enough to confer rights.[31]

Yet, surely these arguments are confused. Rules that confer rights, though distinct from commands, need not be moral rules or coincide with them. Rights, after all, exist under the rules of ceremonies, games, and in many other spheres regulated by rules which are irrelevant to the question of justice or what the law ought to be. Nor need rules which confer rights be just or morally good rules. The rights of a master over his slaves show us that. "Their merit or demerit," as Austin termed it, depends on how rights are distributed in society and over whom or what they are exercised. These critics indeed revealed the inadequacy of the simple notions of command and habit for the analysis of law; at many points it is apparent that the social acceptance of a rule or standard of authority (even if it is motivated only by fear or superstition or rests on inertia) must be brought into the analysis and cannot itself be reduced to the two simple terms. Yet nothing in this showed the utilitarian insistence on the distinction between the existence of law and its "merits" to be wrong.

III

I now turn to a distinctively American criticism of the separation of the law that is from the law that ought to be. It emerged from the critical study of the judicial process with which American jurisprudence has been on the whole so beneficially occupied. The most skeptical of these critics – the loosely named "Realists" of the 1930's – perhaps too naïvely accepted the conceptual framework of the natural sciences as adequate for the characterization of law and for the analysis of rule-guided action of which a living system of law at least partly consists. But they opened men's eyes to what actually goes on when courts decide cases, and the contrast they drew between the actual facts of judicial decision and the traditional terminology for describing it as if it were a wholly logical operation was usually illuminating; for in spite of some exaggeration the "Realists" made us acutely conscious of one cardinal feature of human language and human thought, emphasis on which is vital not only for the understanding of law but in areas of philosophy far beyond the confines of jurisprudence. The insight of this school may be presented in the following example. A legal rule forbids you to take a vehicle into the public park. Plainly this forbids an automobile, but what about bicycles, roller skates, toy automobiles? What about airplanes? Are these, as we say, to be called "vehicles" for the purpose of the rule or not? If we are to communicate with each other at all, and if, as in the most elementary form of law, we are to express our intentions that a certain type of behavior be regulated by rules, then the general words we use – like "vehicle" in the case I consider – must have some standard instance in which no doubts are felt about its application. There must be a core of settled meaning, but there will be, as well, a penumbra of debatable cases in which words are neither obviously applicable nor obviously ruled out. These cases will each have some features in common with the standard case; they will lack others or be accompanied by features not present in the standard case. Human invention and natural processes continually throw up such variants on the familiar, and if we are to say that these ranges of facts do or do not fall under existing rules, then the classifier must make a decision which is not dictated to him, for the facts and phenomena to which we fit our words and apply our rules are as it were *dumb*. The toy automobile cannot speak up and say, "I am a vehicle for the purpose of this legal rule," nor can the roller skates chorus, "We are not a vehicle." Fact situations do not await us neatly labeled, creased, and folded, nor is their legal classification written on them to be simply read off by the judge. Instead, in applying legal rules, someone must take the responsibility of deciding that words do or do not cover some case in hand with all the practical consequences involved in this decision.

We may call the problems which arise outside the hard core of standard instances or settled meaning "problems of the penumbra"; they are always with us whether in relation to such trivial things as the regulation of the use of the public park or in relation to the multidimensional generalities of a constitution. If a penumbra of uncertainty must surround all legal rules, then their application to specific cases in the penumbral area cannot be a matter of logical deduction, and so deductive reasoning, which for generations has been cherished as the very perfection of human reasoning, cannot serve as a model for what judges, or indeed anyone, should do in bringing particular cases under general rules. In this area men cannot live by deduction alone. And it follows that if legal arguments and legal decisions of penumbral questions are to be rational, their rationality must lie in something other than a logical relation to premises. So if it is rational or "sound" to argue and to decide that for the purposes of this rule an airplane is not a vehicle, this argument must be sound or rational without being logically conclusive. What is it then that makes such decisions correct or at least better than alternative decisions? Again, it seems true to say that the criterion which makes a decision sound in such cases is some concept of what the law ought to be; it is easy to slide from that into saying that it must be a moral judgment about what law ought to be. So here we touch upon a point of necessary "intersection between law and morals" which demonstrates the falsity

or, at any rate, the misleading character of the Utilitarians' emphatic insistence on the separation of law as it is and ought to be. Surely, Bentham and Austin could only have written as they did because they misunderstood or neglected this aspect of the judicial process, because they ignored the problems of the penumbra.

The misconception of the judicial process which ignores the problems of the penumbra and which views the process as consisting preeminently in deductive reasoning is often stigmatized as the error of "formalism" or "literalism." My question now is, how and to what extent does the demonstration of this error show the utilitarian distinction to be wrong or misleading? Here there are many issues which have been confused, but I can only disentangle some. The charge of formalism has been leveled both at the "positivist" legal theorist and at the courts, but of course it must be a very different charge in each case. Leveled at the legal theorist, the charge means that he has made a theoretical mistake about the character of legal decision; he has thought of the reasoning involved as consisting in deduction from premises in which the judges' practical choices or decisions play no part. It would be easy to show that Austin was guiltless of this error; only an entire misconception of what analytical jurisprudence is and why he thought it important has led to the view that he, or any other analyst, believed that the law was a closed logical system in which judges deduced their decisions from premises.[32] On the contrary, he was very much alive to the character of language, to its vagueness or open character;[33] he thought that in the penumbral situation judges must necessarily legislate,[34] and, in accents that sometimes recall those of the late Judge Jerome Frank, he berated the common-law judges for legislating feebly and timidly and for blindly relying on real or fancied analogies with past cases instead of adapting their decisions to the growing needs of society as revealed by the moral standard of utility.[35] The villains of this piece, responsible for the conception of the judge as an automaton, are not the Utilitarian thinkers. The responsibility, if it is to be laid at the door of any theorist, is with thinkers like Blackstone and, at an earlier stage,

Montesquieu. The root of this evil is preoccupation with the separation of powers and Blackstone's "childish fiction" (as Austin termed it) that judges only "find," never "make," law.

But we are concerned with "formalism" as a vice not of jurists but of judges. What precisely is it for a judge to commit this error, to be a "formalist," "automatic," a "slot machine"? Curiously enough the literature which is full of the denunciation of these vices never makes this clear in concrete terms; instead we have only descriptions which cannot mean what they appear to say: it is said that in the formalist error courts make an excessive use of logic, take a thing to "a dryly logical extreme,"[36] or make an excessive use of analytical methods. But just how in being a formalist does a judge make an excessive use of logic? It is clear that the essence of his error is to give some general term an interpretation which is blind to social values and consequences (or which is in some other way stupid or perhaps merely disliked by critics). But logic does not prescribe interpretation of terms; it dictates neither the stupid nor intelligent interpretation of any expression. Logic only tells you hypothetically that *if* you give a certain term a certain interpretation then a certain conclusion follows. Logic is silent on how to classify particulars – and this is the heart of a judicial decision. So this reference to logic and to logical extremes is a misnomer for something else, which must be this. A judge has to apply a rule to a concrete case – perhaps the rule that one may not take a stolen "vehicle" across state lines, and in this case an airplane has been taken.[37] He either does not see or pretends not to see that the general terms of this rule are susceptible of different interpretations and that he has a choice left open uncontrolled by linguistic conventions. He ignores, or is blind to, the fact that he is in the area of the penumbra and is not dealing with a standard case. Instead of choosing in the light of social aims, the judge fixes the meaning in a different way. He either takes the meaning that the word most obviously suggests in its ordinary nonlegal context to ordinary men, or one which the word has been given in some other legal context, or, still worse, he thinks of a standard case and then arbitrarily identifies certain features in it – for example, in the case of a vehicle, (1) normally used on land, (2) capable of carrying a human person, (3) capable of being self-propelled – and treats these three as always necessary and always sufficient conditions for the use in all contexts of the word "vehicle," irrespective of the social consequences of giving it this interpretation. This choice, not "logic," would force the judge to include a toy motor car (if electrically propelled) and to exclude bicycles and the airplane. In all this there is possibly great stupidity but no more "logic," and no less, than in cases in which the interpretation given to a general term and the consequent application of some general rule to a particular case is consciously controlled by some identified social aim.

Decisions made in a fashion as blind as this would scarcely deserve the name of decisions; we might as well toss a penny in applying a rule of law. But it is at least doubtful whether any judicial decisions (even in England) have been quite as automatic as this. Rather, either the interpretations stigmatized as automatic have resulted from the conviction that it is fairer in a criminal statute to take a meaning which would jump to the mind of the ordinary man at the cost even of defeating other values, and this itself is a social policy (though possibly a bad one); or much more frequently, what is stigmatized as "mechanical" and "automatic" is a determined choice made indeed in the light of a social aim but of a conservative social aim. Certainly many of the Supreme Court decisions at the turn of the century which have been so stigmatized[38] represent clear choices in the penumbral area to give effect to a policy of a conservative type. This is peculiarly true of Mr. Justice Peckham's opinions defining the spheres of police power and due process.[39]

But how does the wrongness of deciding cases in an automatic and mechanical way and the rightness of deciding cases by reference to social purposes show that the utilitarian insistence on the distinction between what the law is and what it ought to be is wrong? I take it that no one who wished to use these vices of formalism as proof that the distinction between what is and what ought to be is mistaken would deny that the decisions stigmatized as automatic are law; nor would he deny that the system in which such automatic decisions are made is a legal system. Surely he would say that they are law, but they are bad law, they ought not to be law. But this would be to use the distinction, not to refute it; and of course both Bentham and Austin used it to attack judges for failing to decide penumbral cases in accordance with the growing needs of society.

Clearly, if the demonstration of the errors of formalism is to show the utilitarian distinction to be wrong, the point must be drastically re-stated. The point must be not merely that a judicial decision to be rational must be made in the light of some conception of what ought to be, but that the aims, the social policies and purposes to which judges should appeal if their decisions are to be rational, are themselves to be considered as part of the law in some suitably wide sense of "law" which is held to be more illuminating than that used by the Utilitarians. This restatement of the point would have the following consequence: instead of saying that the recurrence of penumbral questions shows us that legal rules are essentially incomplete, and that, when they fail to determine decisions, judges must legislate and so exercise a creative choice between alterna-tives, we shall say that the social policies which guide the judges' choice are in a sense there for them to discover; the judges are only "drawing out" of the rule what, if it is properly understood, is "latent" within it. To call this judicial legislation is to obscure some essential continuity between the clear cases of the rule's application and the penumbral decisions. I shall question later whether this way of talking is salutary, but I wish at this time to point out something obvious, but likely, if not stated, to tangle the issues. It does not follow that, be-cause the opposite of a decision reached blindly in the formalist or literalist manner is a decision intelligently reached by reference to some con-ception of what ought to be, we have a junction of law and morals. We must, I think, beware of thinking in a too simple-minded fashion about the word "ought." This is not because there is no distinction to be made between law as it is and ought to be. Far from it. It is because the distinction should be between what is and what from many different points of view ought to be.

The word "ought" merely reflects the presence of some standard of criticism; one of these standards is a moral standard but not all stan-dards are moral. We say to our neighbour, "You ought not to lie," and that may certainly be a moral judgment, but we should remember that the baffled poisoner may say, "I ought to have given her a second dose." The point here is that intelligent decisions which we oppose to mech-anical or formal decisions are not necessarily identical with decisions defensible on moral grounds. We may say of many a decision: "Yes, that is right; that is as it ought to be," and we may mean only that some accepted purpose or policy has been thereby advanced; we may not mean to endorse the moral propri-ety of the policy or the decision. So the contrast between the mechanical decision and the intelli-gent one can be reproduced inside a system dedicated to the pursuit of the most evil aims. It does not exist as a contrast to be found only in legal systems which, like our own, widely rec-ognize principles of justice and moral claims of individuals.

An example may make this point plainer. With us the task of sentencing in criminal cases is the one that seems most obviously to demand from the judge the exercise of moral judgment. Here the factors to be weighed seem clearly to be moral factors: society must not be exposed to wanton attack; too much misery must not be inflicted on either the victim or his dependents; efforts must be made to enable him to lead a better life and regain a position in the society whose laws he has violated. To a judge striking the balance among these claims, with all the discretion and perplexities involved, his task seems as plain an example of the exer-cise of moral judgment as could be; and it seems to be the polar opposite of some mechanical application of a tariff of penalties fixing a sen-tence careless of the moral claims which in our system have to be weighed. So here intelligent and rational decision is guided however uncer-tainly by moral aims. But we have only to vary the example to see that this need not necessarily be so and surely, if it need not necessarily be so, the Utilitarian point remains unshaken. Under the Nazi regime men were sentenced by courts for criticism of the regime. Here the choice of sentence might be guided exclusively by consideration of what was needed to maintain the state's tyranny effectively. What sentence would both terrorize the public at large and keep the friends and family of the prisoner in suspense so that both hope and fear would cooperate as factors making for subservience? The prisoner of such a system would be regarded simply as an object to be used in pursuit of these aims. Yet, in contrast with a mechanical decision, decision on these grounds would be intelligent and purposive, and from one point of view the decision would be as it ought to be. Of course, I am not unaware that a whole philosophical tradition has sought to demonstrate the fact that we cannot correctly call decisions or behavior truly rational unless they are in conformity with moral aims and principles. But the example I have used seems to me to serve at least as a warning that we cannot use the errors of formalism as something which per se demonstrates the falsity of the utilitarian insistence on the distinction between law as it is and law as *morally* it ought to be.

We can now return to the main point. If it is true that the intelligent decision of penumbral questions is one made not mechanically but in the light of aims, purposes, and policies, though not necessarily in the light of anything we would call moral principles, is it wise to express this important fact by saying that the firm utilitarian distinction between what the law is and what it ought to be should be dropped? Perhaps the claim that it is wise cannot be theoretically refuted for it is, in effect, an *invitation* to revise our conception of what a legal rule is. We are invited to include in the "rule" the various aims and policies in the light of which its penumbral cases are decided on the ground that these aims have, because of their importance, as much right to be called law as the core of legal rules whose meaning is settled. But though an invitation cannot be refuted, it may be refused and I would proffer two reasons for refusing this invitation. First, everything we have learned about the judicial process can be expressed in other less mysterious ways. We can say laws are incurably incomplete and we must decide the penumbral cases rationally by reference to social aims. I think Holmes, who had such a vivid

appreciation of the fact that "general propositions do not decide concrete cases," would have put it that way. Second, to insist on the utilitarian distinction is to emphasize that the hard core of settled meaning is law in some centrally important sense and that even if there are borderlines, there must first be lines. If this were not so the notion of rules controlling courts' decisions would be senseless as some of the "Realists" – in their most extreme moods, and, I think, on bad grounds – claimed.[40]

By contrast, to soften the distinction, to assert mysteriously that there is some fused identity between law as it is and as it ought to be, is to suggest that all legal questions are fundamentally like those of the penumbra. It is to assert that there is no central element of actual law to be seen in the core of central meaning which rules have, that there is nothing in the nature of a legal rule inconsistent with *all* questions being open to reconsideration in the light of social policy. Of course, it is good to be occupied with the penumbra. Its problems are rightly the daily diet of the law schools. But to be occupied with the penumbra is one thing, to be preoccupied with it another. And preoccupation with the penumbra is, if I may say so, as rich a source of confusion in the American legal tradition as formalism in the English. Of course we might abandon the notion that rules have authority; we might cease to attach force or even meaning to an argument that a case falls clearly within a rule and the scope of a precedent. We might call all such reasoning "automatic" or "mechanical," which is already the routine invective of the courts. But until we decide that this *is* what we want, we should not encourage it by obliterating the Utilitarian distinction.

IV

The third criticism of the separation of law and morals is of a very different character; it certainly is less an intellectual argument against the Utilitarian distinction than a passionate appeal supported not by detailed reasoning but by reminders of a terrible experience. For it consists of the testimony of those who have descended into Hell, and, like Ulysses or Dante, brought back a message for human beings. Only in this case the Hell was not beneath or beyond earth, but on it; it was a Hell created on earth by men for other men.

This appeal comes from those German thinkers who lived through the Nazi regime and reflected upon its evil manifestations in the legal system. One of these thinkers, Gustav Radbruch, had himself shared the "positivist" doctrine until the Nazi tyranny, but he was converted by this experience and so his appeal to other men to discard the doctrine of the separation of law and morals has the special poignancy of a recantation. What is important about this criticism is that it really does confront the particular point which Bentham and Austin had in mind in urging the separation of law as it is and as it ought to be. These German thinkers put their insistence on the need to join together what the Utilitarians separated just where this separation was of most importance in the eyes of the Utilitarians; for they were concerned with the problem posed by the existence of morally evil laws.

Before his conversion Radbruch held that resistance to law was a matter for the personal conscience, to be thought out by the individual as a moral problem, and the validity of a law could not be disproved by showing that its requirements were morally evil or even by showing that the effect of compliance with the law would be more evil than the effect of disobedience. Austin, it may be recalled, was emphatic in condemning those who said that if human laws conflicted with the fundamental principles of morality then they cease to be laws, as talking "stark nonsense."

> The most pernicious laws, and therefore those which are most opposed to the will of God, have been and are continually enforced as laws by judicial tribunals. Suppose an act innocuous, or positively beneficial, be prohibited by the sovereign under the penalty of death; if I commit this act, I shall be tried and condemned, and if I object to the sentence, that it is contrary to the law of God . . . the court of justice will demonstrate the inconclusiveness of my reasoning by hanging me up, in pursuance of the law of which I have impugned the validity. An exception, demurrer, or plea, founded on the law of God was never

heard in a Court of Justice, from the creation of the world down to the present moment.[41]

These are strong, indeed brutal words, but we must remember that they went along – in the case of Austin and, of course, Bentham – with the conviction that if laws reached a certain degree of iniquity then there would be a plain moral obligation to resist them and to withhold obedience. We shall see, when we consider the alternatives, that this simple presentation of the human dilemma which may arise has much to be said for it.

Radbruch, however, had concluded from the ease with which the Nazi regime had exploited subservience to mere law – or expressed, as he thought, in the "positivist" slogan "law as law" (*Gesetz als Gesetz*) – and from the failure of the German legal profession to protest against the enormities which they were required to perpetrate in the name of law, that "positivism" (meaning here the insistence on the separation of law as it is from law as it ought to be) had powerfully contributed to the horrors. His considered reflections led him to the doctrine that the fundamental principles of humanitarian morality were part of the very concept of *Recht* or Legality and that no positive enactment or statute, however clearly it was expressed and however clearly it conformed with the formal criteria of validity of a given legal system, could be valid if it contravened basic principles of morality. This doctrine can be appreciated fully only if the nuances imported by the German word *Recht* are grasped. But it is clear that the doctrine meant that every lawyer and judge should denounce statutes that transgressed the fundamental principles not as merely immoral or wrong but as having no legal character, and enactments which on this ground lack the quality of law should not be taken into account in working out the legal position of any given individual in particular circumstances. The striking recantation of his previous doctrine is unfortunately omitted from the translation of his works, but it should be read by all who wish to think afresh on the question of the interconnection of law and morals.[42]

It is impossible to read without sympathy Radbruch's passionate demand that the German legal conscience should be open to the demands of morality and his complaint that this has been too little the case in the German tradition. On the other hand there is an extraordinary naïveté in the view that insensitiveness to the demands of morality and subservience to state power in a people like the Germans should have arisen from the belief that law might be law though it failed to conform with the minimum requirements of morality. Rather this terrible history prompts inquiry into why emphasis on the slogan "law is law," and the distinction between law and morals, acquired a sinister character in Germany, but elsewhere, as with the Utilitarians themselves, went along with the most enlightened liberal attitudes. But something more disturbing than naïveté is latent in Radbruch's whole presentation of the issues to which the existence of morally iniquitous laws give rise. It is not, I think, uncharitable to say that we can see in his argument that he has only half digested the spiritual message of liberalism which he is seeking to convey to the legal profession. For everything that he says is really dependent upon an enormous overvaluation of the importance of the bare fact that a rule may be said to be a valid rule of law, as if this, once declared, was conclusive of the final moral question: "Ought this rule of law to be obeyed?" Surely the truly liberal answer to any sinister use of the slogan "law is law" or of the distinction between law and morals is, "Very well, but that does not conclude the question. Law is not morality; do not let it supplant morality."

However, we are not left to a mere academic discussion in order to evaluate the plea which Radbruch made for the revision of the distinction between law and morals. After the war Radbruch's conception of law as containing in itself the essential moral principle of humanitarianism was applied in practice by German courts in certain cases in which local war criminals, spies, and informers under the Nazi regime were punished. The special importance of these cases is that the persons accused of these crimes claimed that what they had done was not illegal under the laws of the regime in force at the time these actions were performed. This plea was met with the reply that the laws upon which they relied were invalid as contra-

vening the fundamental principles of morality. Let me cite briefly one of these cases.[43]

In 1944 a woman, wishing to be rid of her husband, denounced him to the authorities for insulting remarks he had made about Hitler while home on leave from the German army. The wife was under no legal duty to report his acts, though what he had said was apparently in violation of statutes making it illegal to make statements detrimental to the government of the Third Reich or to impair by any means the military defense of the German people. The husband was arrested and sentenced to death, apparently pursuant to these statutes, though he was not executed but was sent to the front. In 1949 the wife was prosecuted in a West German court for an offense which we would describe as illegally depriving a person of his freedom (*rechtswidrige Freiheitsberaubung*). This was punishable as a crime under the German Criminal Code of 1871 which had remained in force continuously since its enactment. The wife pleaded that her husband's imprisonment was pursuant to the Nazi statutes and hence that she had committed no crime. The court of appeal to which the case ultimately came held that the wife was guilty of procuring the deprivation of her husband's liberty by denouncing him to the German courts, even though he had been sentenced by a court for having violated a statute, since, to quote the words of the court, the statute "was contrary to the sound conscience and sense of justice of all decent human beings." This reasoning was followed in many cases which have been hailed as a triumph of the doctrines of natural law and as signaling the overthrow of positivism. The unqualified satisfaction with this result seems to me to be hysteria. Many of us might applaud the objective – that of punishing a woman for an outrageously immoral act – but this was secured only by declaring a statute established since 1934 not to have the force of law, and at least the wisdom of this course must be doubted. There were, of course, two other choices. One was to let the woman go unpunished; one can sympathize with and endorse the view that this might have been a bad thing to do. The other was to face the fact that if the woman were to be punished it must be pursuant to the introduction of a frankly retrospective law and with a full consciousness of what was sacrificed in securing her punishment in this way. Odious as retrospective criminal legislation and punishment may be, to have pursued it openly in this case would at least have had the merits of candour. It would have made plain that in punishing the woman a choice had to be made between two evils, that of leaving her unpunished and that of sacrificing a very precious principle of morality endorsed by most legal systems. Surely if we have learned anything from the history of morals it is that the thing to do with a moral quandary is not to hide it. Like nettles, the occasions when life forces us to choose between the lesser of two evils must be grasped with the consciousness that they are what they are. The vice of this use of the principle that, at certain limiting points, what is utterly immoral cannot be law or lawful is that it will serve to cloak the true nature of the problems with which we are faced and will encourage the romantic optimism that all the values we cherish ultimately will fit into a single system, that no one of them has to be sacrificed or compromised to accommodate another.

> "All Discord Harmony not understood
> All Partial Evil Universal Good"

This is surely untrue and there is an insincerity in any formulation of our problem which allows us to describe the treatment of the dilemma as if it were the disposition of the ordinary case.

It may seem perhaps to make too much of forms, even perhaps of words, to emphasize one way of disposing of this difficult case as compared with another which might have led, so far as the woman was concerned, to exactly the same result. Why should we dramatize the difference between them? We might punish the woman under a new retrospective law and declare overtly that we were doing something inconsistent with our principles as the lesser of two evils; or we might allow the case to pass as one in which we do not point out precisely where we sacrifice such a principle. But candour is not just one among many minor virtues of the administration of law, just as it is not merely a minor virtue of morality. For if we adopt Radbruch's view, and with him and the German courts make

our protest against evil law in the form of an assertion that certain rules cannot be law because of their moral iniquity, we confuse one of the most powerful, because it is the simplest, forms of moral criticism. If with the Utilitarians we speak plainly, we say that laws may be law but too evil to be obeyed. This is a moral condemnation which everyone can understand and it makes an immediate and obvious claim to moral attention. If, on the other hand, we formulate our objection as an assertion that these evil things are not law, here is an assertion which many people do not believe, and if they are disposed to consider it at all, it would seem to raise a whole host of philosophical issues before it can be accepted. So perhaps the most important single lesson to be learned from this form of the denial of the Utilitarian distinction is the one that the Utilitarians were most concerned to teach: when we have the ample resources of plain speech we must not present the moral criticism of institutions as propositions of a disputable philosophy.

V

I have endeavored to show that, in spite of all that has been learned and experienced since the Utilitarians wrote, and in spite of the defects of other parts of their doctrine, their protest against the confusion of what is and what ought to be law has a moral as well as an intellectual value. Yet it may well be said that, though this distinction is valid and important if applied to any particular law of a system, it is at least misleading if we attempt to apply it to "law," that is, to the notion of a legal system, and that if we insist, as I have, on the narrower truth (or truism), we obscure a wider (or deeper) truth. After all, it may be urged, we have learned that there are many things which are untrue of laws taken separately, but which are true and important in a legal system considered as a whole. For example, the connection between law and sanctions and between the existence of law and its "efficacy" must be understood in this more general way. It is surely not arguable (without some desperate extension of the word "sanction" or artificial narrowing of the word "law") that every law in a municipal legal system must have a sanction, yet it is at least plausible to argue that a legal system must, to be a legal system, provide sanctions for certain of its rules. So too, a rule of law may be said to exist though enforced or obeyed in only a minority of cases, but this could not be said of a legal system as a whole. Perhaps the differences with respect to laws taken separately and a legal system as a whole are also true of the connection between moral (or some other) conceptions of what law ought to be and law in this wider sense.

This line of argument, found (at least in embryo form) in Austin, where he draws attention to the fact that every developed legal system contains certain fundamental notions which are "necessary" and "bottomed in the common nature of man,"[44] is worth pursuing – up to a point – and I shall say briefly why and how far this is so.

We must avoid, if we can, the arid wastes of inappropriate definition, for, in relation to a concept as many-sided and vague as that of a legal system, disputes about the "essential" character, or necessity to the whole, of any single element soon begin to look like disputes about whether chess could be "chess" if played without pawns. There is a wish, which may be understandable, to cut straight through the question whether a legal system, to be a legal system, must measure up to some moral or other standard with simple statements of fact: for example, that no system which utterly failed in this respect has ever existed or could endure; that the normally fulfilled assumption that a legal system aims at some form of justice colours the whole way in which we interpret specific rules in particular cases, and if this normally fulfilled assumption were not fulfilled no one would have any reason to obey except fear (and probably not that) and still less, of course, any moral obligation to obey. The connection between law and moral standards and principles of justice is therefore as little arbitrary and as "necessary" as the connection between law and sanctions, and the pursuit of the question whether this necessity is logical (part of the "meaning" of law) or merely factual or causal can safely be left as an innocent pastime for philosophers.

Yet in two respects I should wish to go further (even though this involves the use of a philosophical fantasy) and show what could intelligibly be meant by the claim that certain provisions in a legal system are "necessary." The world in which we live, and we who live in it, may one day change in many different ways; and if this change were radical enough not only would certain statements of fact now true be false and vice versa, but whole ways of thinking and talking which constitute our present conceptual apparatus, through which we see the world and each other, would lapse. We have only to consider how the whole of our social, moral, and legal life, as we understand it now, depends on the contingent fact that though our bodies do change in shape, size, and other physical properties they do not do this so drastically nor with such quicksilver rapidity and irregularity that we cannot identify each other as the same persistent individual over considerable spans of time. Though this is but a contingent fact which may one day be different, on it at present rest huge structures of our thought and principles of action and social life. Similarly, consider the following possibility (not because it is more than a possibility but because it reveals why we think certain things necessary in a legal system and what we mean by this): suppose that men were to become invulnerable to attack by each other, were clad perhaps like giant land crabs with an impenetrable carapace, and could extract the food they needed from the air by some internal chemical process. In such circumstances (the details of which can be left to science fiction) rules forbidding the free use of violence and rules constituting the minimum form of property – with its rights and duties sufficient to enable food to grow and be retained until eaten – would not have the necessary nonarbitrary status which they have for us, constituted as we are in a world like ours. At present, and until such radical changes supervene, such rules are so fundamental that if a legal system did not have them there would be no point in having any other rules at all. Such rules overlap with basic moral principles vetoing murder, violence, and theft; and so we can add to the factual statement that all legal systems in fact coincide with morality at such vital points, the statement that this is, in this sense, necessarily so. And why not call it a "natural" necessity?

Of course even this much depends on the fact that in asking what content a legal system must have we take this question to be worth asking only if we who consider it cherish the humble aim of survival in close proximity to our fellows. Natural-law theory, however, in all its protean guises, attempts to push the argument much further and to assert that human beings are equally devoted to and united in their conception of aims (the pursuit of knowledge, justice to their fellow men) other than that of survival, and these dictate a further necessary content to a legal system (over and above my humble minimum) without which it would be pointless. Of course we must be careful not to exaggerate the differences among human beings, but it seems to me that above this minimum the purposes men have for living in society are too conflicting and varying to make possible much extension of the argument that some fuller overlap of legal rules and moral standards is "necessary" in this sense.

Another aspect of the matter deserves attention. If we attach to a legal system the minimum meaning that it must consist of general rules – general both in the sense that they refer to courses of action, not single actions, and to multiplicities of men, not single individuals – this meaning connotes the principle of treating like cases alike, though the criteria of when cases are alike will be, so far, only the general elements specified in the rules. It is, however, true that *one* essential element of the concept of justice is the principle of treating like cases alike. This is justice in the administration of the law, not justice of the law. So there is, in the very notion of law consisting of general rules, something which prevents us from treating it as if morally it is utterly neutral, without any necessary contact with moral principles. Natural procedural justice consists therefore of those principles of objectivity and impartiality in the administration of the law which implement just this aspect of law and which are designed to ensure that rules are applied only to what are genuinely cases of the rule or at least to minimize the risks of inequalities in this sense.

These two reasons (or excuses) for talking of a certain overlap between legal and moral standards as necessary and natural, of course, should not satisfy anyone who is really disturbed by the Utilitarian or "positivist" insistence that law and morality are distinct. This is so because a legal system that satisfied these minimum requirements might apply, with the most pedantic impartiality as between the persons affected, laws which were hideously oppressive, and might deny to a vast rightless slave population the minimum benefits of protection from violence and theft. The stink of such societies is, after all, still in our nostrils and to argue that they have (or had) no legal system would only involve the repetition of the argument. Only if the rules failed to provide these essential benefits and protection for anyone – even for a slave-owning group – would the minimum be unsatisfied and the system sink to the status of a set of meaningless taboos. Of course no one denied those benefits would have any reason to obey except fear and people would have every moral reason to revolt.

VI

I should be less than candid if I did not, in conclusion, consider something which, I suspect, most troubles those who react strongly against "legal positivism." Emphasis on the distinction between law as it is and law as it ought to be may be taken to depend upon and to entail what are called "subjectivist" and "relativist" or "noncognitive" theories concerning the very nature of moral judgments, moral distinctions, or "values." Of course the Utilitarians themselves (as distinct from later positivists like Kelsen) did not countenance any such theories, however unsatisfactory their moral philosophy may appear to us now. Austin thought ultimate moral principles were the commands of God, known to us by revelation or through the "index" of utility, and Bentham thought they were verifiable propositions about utility. Nonetheless I think (though I cannot prove) that insistence upon the distinction between law as it is and ought to be has been, under the general head of "positivism," confused with a moral theory according to which statements of what is the case ("statements of fact") belong to a category or type radically different from statements of what ought to be ("value statements"). It may therefore be well to dispel this source of confusion.

There are many contemporary variants of this type of moral theory: according to some, judgments of what ought to be, or ought to be done, either are or include as essential elements expressions of "feeling," "emotion," or "attitudes" or "subjective preferences"; in others such judgments both express feelings or emotions or attitudes and enjoin others to share them. In other variants such judgments indicate that a particular case falls under a general principle or policy of action which the speaker has "chosen" or to which he is "committed" and which is itself not a recognition of what is the case but analogous to a general "imperative" or command addressed to all including the speaker himself. Common to all these variants is the insistence that judgments of what ought to be done, because they contain such "non-cognitive" elements, cannot be argued for or established by rational methods as statements of fact can be, and cannot be shown to follow from any statement of fact but only from other judgments of what ought to be done in conjunction with some statement of fact. We cannot, on such a theory, demonstrate, *e.g.*, that an action was wrong, ought not to have been done, merely by showing that it consisted of the deliberate infliction of pain solely for the gratification of the agent. We only show it to be wrong if we add to those verifiable "cognitive" statements of fact a general principle not itself verifiable or "cognitive" that the infliction of pain in such circumstances is wrong, ought not to be done. Together with this general distinction between statements of what is and what ought to be go sharp parallel distinctions between statements about means and statements of moral ends. We can rationally discover and debate what are appropriate means to given ends, but ends are not rationally discoverable or debatable; they are "fiats of the will," expressions of "emotions," "preferences," or "attitudes."

Against all such views (which are of course far subtler than this crude survey can convey) others urge that all these sharp distinctions between is and ought, fact and value, means and ends, cognitive and noncognitive, are wrong. In acknowledging ultimate ends or moral values we are recognizing something as much imposed upon us by the character of the world in which we live, as little a matter of choice, attitude, feeling, emotion as the truth of factual judgments about what is the case. The characteristic moral argument is not one in which the parties are reduced to expressing or kindling feelings or emotions or issuing exhortations or commands to each other but one by which parties come to acknowledge after closer examination and reflection that an initially disputed case falls within the ambit of a vaguely apprehended principle (itself no more "subjective," no more a "fiat of our will" than any other principle of classification) and this has as much title to be called "cognitive" or "rational" as any other initially disputed classification of particulars.

Let us now suppose that we accept this rejection of "noncognitive" theories of morality and this denial of the drastic distinction in type between statements of what is and what ought to be, and that moral judgments are as rationally defensible as any other kind of judgments. What would follow from this as to the nature of the connection between law as it is and law as it ought to be? Surely, from this alone, nothing. Laws, however morally iniquitous, would still (so far as this point is concerned) be laws. The only difference which the acceptance of this view of the nature of moral judgments would make would be that the moral iniquity of such laws would be something that could be demonstrated; it would surely follow merely from a statement of what the rule required to be done that the rule was morally wrong and so ought not to be law or conversely that it was morally desirable and ought to be law. But the demonstration of this would not show the rule not to be (or to be) law. Proof that the principles by which we evaluate or condemn laws are rationally discoverable, and not mere "fiats of the will," leaves untouched the fact that there are laws which may have any degree of iniquity or stupidity and still be laws. And conversely there are rules that have every moral qualification to be laws and yet are not laws.

Surely something further or more specific must be said if disproof of "noncognitivism" or kindred theories in ethics is to be relevant to the distinction between law as it is and law as it ought to be, and to lead to the abandonment at some point or some softening of this distinction. No one has done more than Professor Lon Fuller of the Harvard Law School in his various writings to make clear such a line of argument and I will end by criticizing what I take to be its central point. It is a point which again emerges when we consider not those legal rules or parts of legal rules the meanings of which are clear and excite no debate but the interpretation of rules in concrete cases where doubts are initially felt and argument develops about their meaning. In no legal system is the scope of legal rules restricted to the range of concrete instances which were present or are believed to have been present in the minds of legislators; this indeed is one of the important differences between a legal rule and a command. Yet, when rules are recognized as applying to instances beyond any that legislators did or could have considered, their extension to such new cases often presents itself not as a deliberate choice or fiat on the part of those who so interpret the rule. It appears neither as a decision to give the rule a new or extended meaning nor as a guess as to what legislators, dead perhaps in the eighteenth century, would have said had they been alive in the twentieth century. Rather, the inclusion of the new case under the rule takes its place as a natural elaboration of the rule, as something implementing a "purpose" which it seems natural to attribute (in some sense) to the rule itself rather than to any particular person dead or alive. The Utilitarian description of such interpretative extension of old rules to new cases as judicial legislation fails to do justice to this phenomenon; it gives no hint of the differences between a deliberate fiat or decision to treat the new case in the same way as past cases and a recognition (in which there is little that is deliberate or even voluntary) that inclusion of the new case under the rule will implement or articulate a continuing and identical purpose, hitherto less specifically apprehended.

Perhaps many lawyers and judges will see in this language something that precisely fits their experience; others may think it a romantic gloss on facts better stated in the Utilitarian language of judicial "legislation" or in the modern American terminology of "creative choice."

To make the point clear Professor Fuller uses a nonlegal example from the philosopher Wittgenstein which is, I think, illuminating.

> Someone says to me: "Show the children a game."
> I teach them gaming with dice and the other says
> "I did not mean that sort of game." Must the
> exclusion of the game with dice have come before
> his mind when he gave me the order?[45]

Something important does seem to me to be touched on in this example. Perhaps there are the following (distinguishable) points. First, we normally do interpret not only what people are trying to do but what they say in the light of assumed common human objectives so that unless the contrary were expressly indicated we would not interpret an instruction to show a young child a game as a mandate to introduce him to gambling even though in other contexts the word "game" would be naturally so interpreted. Second, very often, the speaker whose words are thus interpreted might say: "Yes, that's what I mean [or "that's what I meant all along"] though I never thought of it until you put this particular case to me." Third, when we thus recognize, perhaps after argument or consultation with others, a particular case not specifically envisaged beforehand as falling within the ambit of some vaguely expressed instruction, we may find this experience falsified by description of it as a mere decision on our part so to treat the particular case, and that we can only describe this faithfully as coming to realize and to articulate what we "really" want or our "true purpose" – phrases which Professor Fuller uses later in the same article.[46]

I am sure that many philosophical discussions of the character of moral argument would benefit from attention to cases of the sort instanced by Professor Fuller. Such attention would help to provide a corrective to the view that there is a sharp separation between "ends" and "means" and that in debating "ends" we can only work on each other nonrationally, and that rational argument is reserved for discussion of "means."

But I think the relevance of his point to the issue whether it is correct or wise to insist on the distinction between law as it is and law as it ought to be is very small indeed. Its net effect is that in interpreting legal rules there are some cases which we find after reflection to be so natural an elaboration or articulation of the rule that to think of and refer to this as "legislation," "making law," or a "fiat" on our part would be misleading. So, the argument must be, it would be misleading to distinguish in such cases between what the rule is and what it ought to be – at least in some sense of ought. We think it ought to include the new case and come to see after reflection that it really does. But even if this way of presenting a recognizable experience as an example of a fusion between is and ought to be is admitted, two caveats must be borne in mind. The first is that "ought" in this case need have nothing to do with morals for the reasons explained already in section III: there may be just the same sense that a new case will implement and articulate the purpose of a rule in interpreting the rules of a game or some hideously immoral code of oppression whose immorality is appreciated by those called in to interpret it. They too can see what the "spirit" of the game they are playing requires in previously unenvisaged cases. More important is this: after all is said and done we must remember how rare in the law is the phenomenon held to justify this way of talking, how exceptional is this feeling that one way of deciding a case is imposed upon us as the only natural or rational elaboration of some rule. Surely it cannot be doubted that, for most cases of interpretation, the language of choice between alternatives, "judicial legislation" or even "fiat" (though not arbitrary fiat), better conveys the realities of the situation.

Within the framework of relatively well-settled law there jostle too many alternatives too nearly equal in attraction between which judge and lawyer must uncertainly pick their way to make appropriate here language which may well describe those experiences which we have in interpreting our own or others' principles of conduct, intention, or wishes, when we are not conscious of exercising a deliberate choice, but rather of recognizing something awaiting recognition. To use in the description of the interpretation of laws the suggested terminology of a fusion or inability to separate what is law and ought to be will serve (like earlier stories that judges only find, never make, law) only to conceal the facts, that here if anywhere we live among uncertainties between which we have to choose, and that the existing law imposes only limits on our choice and not the choice itself.

Notes

1 BENTHAM, *A Fragment on Government*, in 1 WORKS 221, 235 (Bowring ed. 1859) (preface, 41st para.).

2 D'ENTRÈVES, NATURAL LAW 116 (2d ed. 1952).

3 FULLER, THE LAW IN QUEST OF ITSELF 12 (1940); Brecht, *The Myth of Is and Ought*, 54 HARV. L. REV. 811 (1941); Fuller, *Human Purpose and Natural Law*, 53 J. PHILOS 697 (1953).

4 See FRIEDMANN, LEGAL THEORY 154, 294–5 (3d ed. 1953). Friedmann also says of Austin that "by his sharp distinction between the science of legislation and the science of law," he "inaugurated an era of legal positivism and self-sufficiency which enabled the rising national State to assert its authority undisturbed by juristic doubts." *Id.* at 416. Yet, "the existence of a highly organised State which claimed sovereignty and unconditional obedience of the citizen" is said to be "the political condition which makes analytical positivism possible." *Id.* at 163. There is therefore some difficulty in determining which, in this account, is to be hen and which egg (analytical positivism or political condition). Apart from this, there seems to be little evidence that any national State rising in or after 1832 (when the *Province of Jurisprudence Determined* was first published) was enabled to assert its authority by Austin's work or "the era of legal positivism" which he "inaugurated."

5 See Radbruch, *Die Erneuerung des Rechts*, 2 DIE WANDLUNG 8 (Germany 1947); Radbruch, *Gesetzliches Unrecht und Übergesetzliches Recht*, 1 SÜDDEUTSCHE JURISTEN-ZEITUNG 105 (Germany 1946) (reprinted in RADBRUCH, RECHTSPHILOSOPHIE 347 (4th ed. 1950)).

6 BENTHAM, *A Fragment on Government*, in 1 WORKS 221, 230 (Bowring ed. 1859) (preface,

16th para.); BENTHAM, *Principles of Penal Law*, in 1 WORKS 365, 574–75, 576–78 (Bowring ed. 1859) (pt. III, c. XXI, 8th para., 12th para.).

7   BENTHAM, *Of Promulgation of the Laws*, in 1 WORKS 155 (Bowring ed. 1859); BENTHAM, *Principles of the Civil Code*, in 1 WORKS 297, 323 (Bowring ed. 1859) (pt. I, c. XVII, 2d para.); BENTHAM, *A Fragment on Government*, in 1 WORKS 221, 233 n.[*m*] (Bowring ed. 1859) (preface, 35th para.).

8   BENTHAM, *Principles of Penal Law*, in 1 WORKS 365, 576 (Bowring ed. 1859) (pt. III, c. XXI, 10th para., 11th para.).

9   BENTHAM, *Principles of Morals and Legislation*, in 1 WORKS 1, 84 (Bowring ed. 1859) (c. XIII).

10 BENTHAM, *Anarchical Fallacies*, in 2 WORKS 489, 511–12 (Bowring ed. 1859) (art. VIII); BENTHAM, *Principles of Morals and Legislation*, in 1 WORKS 1, 144 (Bowring ed. 1859) (c. XIX, 11th para.).

11 *Id.* at 142 n.§ (c. XIX, 4th para. n.§).

12 AUSTIN, THE PROVINCE OF JURISPRUDENCE DETERMINED 184–85 (Library of Ideas ed. 1954).

13 BENTHAM, *A Fragment on Government*, in 1 WORKS 221, 230 (Bowring ed. 1859) (preface, 16th para.).

14 See BENTHAM, *Principles of Legislation*, in THE THEORY OF LEGISLATION 1, 65 n.* (Ogden ed. 1931) (c. XII, 2d para. n.*):

Here we touch upon the most difficult of questions. If the law is not what it ought to be; if it openly combats the principle of utility; ought we to obey it? Ought we to violate it? Ought we to remain neuter between the law which commands an evil, and morality which forbids it?

See also BENTHAM, *A Fragment on Government*, in 1 WORKS 221, 287–88 (Bowring ed. 1859) (c. IV, 20th–25th paras.).

15 I BLACKSTONE, COMMENTARIES *41. Bentham criticized "this dangerous maxim," saying "the natural tendency of such a doctrine is to impel a man, by the force of conscience, to rise up in arms against any law whatever that he happens not to like." BENTHAM, *A Fragment on Government*, in 1 WORKS 221, 287 (Bowring ed. 1859) (c. IV, 19th para.). See also BENTHAM, A COMMENT ON THE COMMENTARIES 49 (1928) (c. III). For an expression of a fear lest anarchy result from such a doctrine, combined with a recognition that resistance may be

justified on grounds of utility, see AUSTIN, *op. cit. supra* note 12, at 186.

16 BENTHAM, *A Fragment on Government*, in 1 WORKS 221, 294 (Bowring ed. 1859) (c. V, 10th para.).

17 BENTHAM, *A Commentary on Humphreys' Real Property Code*, in 5 WORKS 389 (Bowring ed. 1843).

18 AUSTIN, *op. cit. supra* note 12, at 162.

19 BENTHAM, *A Fragment on Government*, in 1 WORKS 221, 289–90 (Bowring ed. 1859) (c. IV, 33d–34th paras.).

20 See AUSTIN, *op. cit. supra* note 12, at 231.

21 AMOS, THE SCIENCE OF LAW 4 (5th ed. 1881). See also MARKBY, ELEMENTS OF LAW 4–5 (5th ed. 1896):

Austin, by establishing the distinction between positive law and morals, not only laid the foundation for a science of law, but cleared the conception of law … of a number of pernicious consequences to which … it had been supposed to lead. Positive laws, as Austin has shown, must be legally binding, and yet a law may be unjust. … He has admitted that law itself may be immoral, in which case it may be our moral duty to disobey it. …

Cf. HOLLAND, JURISPRUDENCE 1–20 (1880).

22 See Green, Book Review, 6 AM. L. REV. 57, 61 (1871) (reprinted in GREEN, ESSAYS AND NOTES ON THE LAW OF TORT AND CRIME 31, 35 (1933)).

23 10 HARV. L. REV. 457 (1897).

24 GRAY, THE NATURE AND SOURCES OF THE LAW 94 (1st ed. 1909) (§ 213).

25 It may help to identify five (there may be more) meanings of "positivism" bandied about in contemporary jurisprudence:

(1) the contention that laws are commands of human beings,

(2) the contention that there is no necessary connection between law and morals or law as it is and ought to be,

(3) the contention that the analysis (or study of the meaning) of legal concepts is (a) worth pursuing and (b) to be distinguished from historical inquiries into the causes or origins of laws, from sociological inquiries into the relation of law and other social phenomena, and from the criticism or appraisal of law whether in terms of morals, social aims, "functions," or otherwise,

(4) the contention that a legal system is a "closed logical system" in which correct legal decisions can be deduced by logical

means from predetermined legal rules without reference to social aims, policies, moral standards, and

(5) the contention that moral judgments cannot be established or defended, as statements of facts can, by rational argument, evidence, or proof ("noncognitivism" in ethics).

Bentham and Austin held the views described in (1), (2), and (3) but not those in (4) and (5). Opinion (4) is often ascribed to analytical jurists, but I know of no "analyst" who held this view.

26   GRAY, THE NATURE AND SOURCES OF THE LAW 94–5 (2d ed. 1921).

27   AUSTIN, *op. cit. supra* note 12, at 13.

28   See, *e.g.*, KELSEN, GENERAL THEORY OF LAW AND STATE 58–61, 143–44 (1945). According to Kelsen, all laws, not only those conferring rights and powers, are reducible to such "primary norms" conditionally stipulating sanctions.

29   SALMOND, THE FIRST PRINCIPLES OF JURISPRUDENCE 97–98 (1893). He protested against "the creed of what is termed the English school of jurisprudence," because it "attempted to deprive the idea of law of that ethical significance which is one of its most essential elements." *Id.* at 9, 10.

30   HÄGERSTRÖM, INQUIRIES INTO THE NATURE OF LAW AND MORALS 217 (Olivecrona ed. 1953): "[T]he whole theory of the subjective rights of private individuals . . . is incompatible with the imperative theory." See also *id.* at 221:

> The description of them [claims to legal protection] as rights is wholly derived from the idea that the law which is concerned with them is a true expression of rights and duties in the sense in which the popular notion of justice understands these terms.

31   *Id.* at 218.

32   This misunderstanding of analytical jurisprudence is to be found in, among others, STONE, THE PROVINCE AND FUNCTION OF LAW 141 (1950):

> In short, rejecting the implied assumption that all propositions of all parts of the law must be logically consistent with each other and proceed on a single set of definitions . . . he [Cardozo, J.,] denied that the law is actually what the analytical jurist, *for his limited purposes,* assumes it to be.

See also *id.* at 49, 52, 138, 140; FRIEDMANN, LEGAL THEORY 209 (3d ed. 1953). This mis-

understanding seems to depend on the unexamined and false belief that analytical studies of the meaning of legal terms would be impossible or absurd if, to reach sound decisions in particular cases, more than a capacity for formal logical reasoning from unambiguous and clear predetermined premises is required.

33   See the discussion of vagueness and uncertainty in law, in AUSTIN, *op. cit. supra* note 12, at 202–05, 207, in which Austin recognized that, in consequence of this vagueness, often only "fallible tests" can be provided for determining whether particular cases fall under general expressions.

34   See AUSTIN, *op. cit. supra* note 12, at 191: "I cannot understand how any person who has considered the subject can suppose that society could possibly have gone on if judges had not legislated. . . ." As a corrective to the belief that the analytical jurist must take a "slot machine" or "mechanical" view of the judicial process it is worth noting the following observations made by Austin:

(1) Whenever law has to be applied, the " 'competition of opposite analogies' " may arise, for the case "may resemble in some of its points" cases to which the rule has been applied in the past and in other points "cases from which the application of the law has been withheld." 2 AUSTIN, LECTURES ON JURISPRUDENCE 633 (5th ed. 1885).

(2) Judges have commonly decided cases and so derived new rules by "building" on a variety of grounds including sometimes (in Austin's opinion too rarely) their views of what law ought to be. Most commonly they have derived law from preexisting law by "consequence founded on analogy," *i.e.*, they have made a new rule "in *consequence* of the existence of a similar rule applying to subjects which are *analogous*. . . ." 2 *id.* at 638–39.

(3) "[I]f every rule in a system of law were perfectly definite or precise," these difficulties incident to the application of law would not arise. "But the ideal completeness and correctness I now have imagined is not attainable in fact. . . . though the system had been built and ordered with matchless solicitude and skill." 2 *id.* at 997–98. Of course he thought that much could and should be done by codification to eliminate uncertainty. See 2 *id.* at 662–81.

35   2 *id*. at 641:

> Nothing, indeed, can be more natural, than that legis-
> lators, direct or judicial (especially if they be narrow-
> minded, timid and unskillful), should lean as much as
> they can on the examples set by their predecessors.

See also 2 *id*. at 647:

> But it is much to be regretted that Judges of capacity,
> experience and weight, have not seized every oppor-
> tunity of introducing a new rule (a rule beneficial for
> the future).... This is the reproach I should be in-
> clined to make against Lord Eldon.... [T]he Judges
> of the Common Law Courts would not do what they
> ought to have done, namely to model their rules of law
> and of procedure to the growing exigencies of society,
> instead of stupidly and sulkily adhering to the old and
> barbarous usages.

36   Hynes v. New York Cent. R.R., 231 N.Y. 229,
     235, 131 N.E. 898, 900 (1921); see POUND,
     INTERPRETATIONS OF LEGAL HISTORY 123
     (2d ed. 1930); STONE, *op. cit. supra* note 32, at
     140–41.

37   See McBoyle v. United States, 283 U.S. 25
     (1931).

38   See, *e.g.*, Pound, *Mechanical Jurisprudence*, 8
     COLUM. L. REV. 605, 615–16 (1908).

39   See, *e.g.*, Lochner v. New York, 198 U.S. 45
     (1905). Justice Peckham's opinion that there
     were no reasonable grounds for interfering with
     the right of free contract by determining the
     hours of labour in the occupation of a baker may
     indeed be a wrongheaded piece of conservatism
     but there is nothing automatic or mechanical
     about it.

40   One recantation of this extreme position is worth
     mention in the present context. In the first edi-
     tion of *The Bramble Bush*, Professor Llewellyn
     committed himself wholeheartedly to the view
     that "what these officials do about disputes is, to
     my mind, the law itself" and that "*rules* ... are
     important so far as they help you ... predict
     what judges will do.... That is all their import-
     ance, except as pretty playthings." LLEWEL-
     LYN, THE BRAMBLE BUSH 3, 5 (1st ed.
     1930). In the second edition he said that these
     were "unhappy words when not more fully de-
     veloped, and they are plainly at best a very
     partial statement of the whole truth.... [O]ne
     office of law is to control officials in some part,
     and to guide them even ... where no thorough-
     going control is possible, or is desired.... [T]he
     words fail to take proper account ... of the office
     of the institution of law as an instrument of
     conscious shaping...." LLEWELLYN, THE
     BRAMBLE BUSH 9 (2d ed. 1951).

41   AUSTIN, THE PROVINCE OF JURISPRU-
     DENCE DETERMINED 185 (Library of Ideas
     ed. 1954).

42   See Radbruch, *Gesetzliches Unrecht und Überge-
     setzliches Recht*, I SÜDDEUTSCHE JURISTEN-
     ZEITUNG 105 (Germany 1946) (reprinted in
     RADBRUCH, RECHTSPHILOSOPHIE 347 (4th
     ed. 1950)). I have used the translation of part
     of this essay and of Radbruch, *Die Erneuerung des
     Rechts*, 2 DIE WANDLUNG 8 (Germany 1947),
     prepared by Professor Lon Fuller of the Harvard
     Law School as a mimeographed supplement to
     the readings in jurisprudence used in his course
     at Harvard.

43   Judgment of July 27, 1949, Oberlandesgericht,
     Bamberg, 5 SÜDDEUTSCHE JURISTEN-ZEI-
     TUNG 207 (Germany 1950), 64 HARV. L. REV.
     1005 (1951); see FRIEDMANN, LEGAL THEORY
     457 (3d ed. 1953).

44   AUSTIN, *Uses of the Study of Jurisprudence*, in
     THE PROVINCE OF JURISPRUDENCE DETER-
     MINED 365, 373, 367–69 (Library of Ideas ed.
     1954).

45   Fuller, *Human Purpose and Natural Law*, 53 J.
     PHILOS. 697, 700 (1956).

46   *Id*. at 701, 702.

5

Positivism and Fidelity to Law: A Reply to Professor Hart

Lon L. Fuller

Professor Hart has made an enduring contribution to the literature of legal philosophy. I doubt if the issues he discusses will ever again assume quite the form they had before being touched by his analytical powers. His argument is no mere restatement of Bentham, Austin, Gray, and Holmes. Their views receive in his exposition a new clarity and a new depth that are uniquely his own.

I must confess that when I first encountered the thoughts of Professor Hart's essay, his argument seemed to me to suffer from a deep inner contradiction. On the one hand, he rejects emphatically any confusion of "what is" with "what ought to be." He will tolerate no "merger" of law and conceptions of what law ought to be, but at the most an antiseptic "intersection." Intelligible communication on any subject, he seems to imply, becomes impossible if we leave it uncertain whether we are talking about "what is" or "what ought to be." Yet it was precisely this uncertainty about Professor Hart's own argument which made it difficult for me at first to follow the thread of his thought. At times he seemed to be saying that the distinction between law and morality is something that exists, and will continue to exist, however we may talk about it. It expresses a reality which, whether we like it or not, we must accept if we are to avoid talking nonsense. At other times, he seemed to be warning us that the reality of the distinction is itself in danger and that if we do not mend our ways of thinking and talking we may lose a "precious moral ideal," that of fidelity to law. It is not clear, in other words, whether in Professor Hart's own thinking the distinction between law and morality simply "is," or is something that "ought to be" and that we should join with him in helping to create and maintain.

These were the perplexities I had about Professor Hart's argument when I first encountered it. But on reflection I am sure any criticism of his essay as being self-contradictory would be both unfair and unprofitable. There is no reason why the argument for a strict separation of law and morality cannot be rested on the double ground that this separation serves both intellectual clarity and moral integrity. If there are certain difficulties in bringing these two lines of reasoning into proper relation to one another, these difficulties affect also the position of those who reject the views of Austin, Gray, and Holmes. For those of us who find the "positivist" position unacceptable do ourselves rest our argument on the double ground that its intellectual clarity is specious and that its effects are, or may be, harmful. On the one hand, we assert that Austin's definition of law, for example, violates the reality it purports to describe. Being false in fact, it cannot serve effectively what Kelsen calls "an interest of cognition." On the other hand, we assert that under some conditions the same conception of law may become dangerous, since in human affairs what men mistakenly accept as real tends, by the very act of their acceptance, to become real.

It is a cardinal virtue of Professor Hart's argument that for the first time it opens the way for a truly profitable exchange of views between those whose differences center on the distinction between law and morality. Hitherto there has been no real joinder of issue between the opposing camps. On the one side, we encounter a series of definitional fiats. A rule of law is – that is to say, it really and simply and always is – the command of a sovereign, a rule laid down by a judge, a prediction of the future incidence of state force, a pattern of official behavior, etc. When we ask what purpose these definitions serve, we receive the answer, "Why, no purpose, except to describe accurately the social reality that corresponds to the word 'law.'" When we reply, "But it doesn't look like that to me," the answer comes back, "Well, it does to me." There the matter has to rest.

This state of affairs has been most unsatisfactory for those of us who are convinced that "positivistic" theories have had a distorting effect on the aims of legal philosophy. Our dissatisfaction arose not merely from the impasse we confronted, but because this impasse seemed to us so unnecessary. All that was needed to surmount it was an acknowledgment on the other side that its definitions of "what law really is" are not mere images of some datum of experience, but direction posts for the application of human energies. Since this acknowledgment was not forthcoming, the impasse and its frustrations continued. There is indeed no frustration greater than to be confronted by a theory which purports merely to describe, when it not only plainly prescribes, but owes its special prescriptive powers precisely to the fact that it disclaims prescriptive intentions. Into this murky debate, some shafts of light did occasionally break through, as in Kelsen's casual admission, apparently never repeated, that his whole system might well rest on an emotional preference for the ideal of order over that of justice.[1] But I have to confess that in general the dispute that has been conducted during the last twenty years has not been very profitable.

Now, with Professor Hart's paper, the discussion takes a new and promising turn. It is now explicitly acknowledged on both sides that one of the chief issues is how we can best define and serve the ideal of fidelity to law. Law, as something deserving loyalty, must represent a human achievement; it cannot be a simple fiat of power or a repetitive pattern discernible in the behavior of state officials. The respect we owe to human laws must surely be something different from the respect we accord to the law of gravitation. If laws, even bad laws, have a claim to our respect, then law must represent some general direction of human effort that we can understand and describe, and that we can approve in principle even at the moment when it seems to us to miss its mark.

If, as I believe, it is a cardinal virtue of Professor Hart's argument that it brings into the dispute the issue of fidelity to law, its chief defect, if I may say so, lies in a failure to perceive and accept the implications that this enlargement of the frame of argument necessarily entails. This defect seems to me more or less to permeate the whole essay, but it comes most prominently to the fore in his discussion of Gustav Radbruch and the Nazi regime.[2] Without any inquiry into the actual workings of whatever remained of a legal system under the Nazis, Professor Hart assumes that something must have persisted that still deserved the name of law in a sense that would make meaningful the ideal of fidelity to law. Not that Professor Hart believes the Nazis' laws should have been obeyed. Rather he considers that a decision to disobey them presented not a mere question of prudence or courage, but a genuine moral dilemma in which the ideal of fidelity to law had to be sacrificed in favor of more fundamental goals. I should have thought it unwise to pass such a judgment without first inquiring with more particularity what "law" itself meant under the Nazi regime.

I shall present later my reasons for thinking that Professor Hart is profoundly mistaken in his estimate of the Nazi situation and that he gravely misinterprets the thought of Professor

Radbruch. But first I shall turn to some preliminary definitional problems in which what I regard as the central defect in Professor Hart's thesis seems immediately apparent.

I   The Definition of Law

Throughout his essay Professor Hart aligns himself with a general position which he associates with the names of Bentham, Austin, Gray, and Holmes. He recognizes, of course, that the conceptions of these men as to "what law is" vary considerably, but this diversity he apparently considers irrelevant in his defense of their general school of thought.

If the only issue were that of stipulating a meaning for the word "law" that would be conducive to intellectual clarity, there might be much justification for treating all of these men as working in the same direction. Austin, for example, defines law as the command of the highest legislative power, called the sovereign. For Gray, on the other hand, law consists in the rules laid down by judges. A statute is, for Gray, not a law, but only a source of law, which becomes law only after it has been interpreted and applied by a court. Now if our only object were to obtain that clarity which comes from making our definitions explicit and then adhering strictly to those definitions, one could argue plausibly that either conception of the meaning of "law" will do. Both conceptions appear to avoid a confusion of morals and law, and both writers let the reader know what meaning they propose to attribute to the word "law."

The matter assumes a very different aspect, however, if our interest lies in the ideal of fidelity to law, for then it may become a matter of capital importance what position is assigned to the judiciary in the general frame of government. Confirmation for this observation may be found in the slight rumbling of constitutional crisis to be heard in this country today. During the past year readers of newspapers have been writing to their editors urging solemnly, and even apparently with sincerity, that we should abolish the Supreme Court as a first step toward a restoration of the rule of law. It is unlikely that this remedy for our governmental ills derives

from any deep study of Austin or Gray, but surely those who propose it could hardly be expected to view with indifference the divergent definitions of law offered by those two jurists. If it be said that it is a perversion of Gray's meaning to extract from his writings any moral for present controversies about the role of the Supreme Court, then it seems to me there is equal reason for treating what he wrote as irrelevant to the issue of fidelity to law generally.

Another difference of opinion among the writers defended by Professor Hart concerns Bentham and Austin and their views on constitutional limitations on the power of the sovereign. Bentham considered that a constitution might preclude the highest legislative power from issuing certain kinds of laws. For Austin, on the other hand, any legal limit on the highest lawmaking power was an absurdity and an impossibility. What guide to conscience would be offered by these two writers in a crisis that might some day arise out of the provision of our constitution to the effect that the amending power can never be used to deprive any state without its consent of its equal representation in the Senate?[3] Surely it is not only in the affairs of everyday life that we need clarity about the obligation of fidelity to law, but most particularly and urgently in times of trouble. If all the positivist school has to offer in such times is the observation that, however you may choose to define law, it is always something different from morals, its teachings are not of much use to us.

I suggest, then, that Professor Hart's thesis as it now stands is essentially incomplete and that before he can attain the goals he seeks he will have to concern himself more closely with a definition of law that will make meaningful the obligation of fidelity to law.

II   The Definition of Morality

It is characteristic of those sharing the point of view of Professor Hart that their primary concern is to preserve the integrity of the concept of law. Accordingly, they have generally sought a precise definition of law, but have not been at pains to state just what it is they mean to exclude by their definitions. They are like men building a wall for the defense of a village, who must know what it is they wish to protect, but who need not, and indeed cannot, know what invading forces those walls may have to turn back.

When Austin and Gray distinguish law from morality, the word "morality" stands indiscriminately for almost every conceivable standard by which human conduct may be judged that is not itself law. The inner voice of conscience, notions of right and wrong based on religious belief, common conceptions of decency and fair play, culturally conditioned prejudices – all of these are grouped together under the heading of "morality" and are excluded from the domain of law. For the most part Professor Hart follows in the tradition of his predecessors. When he speaks of morality he seems generally to have in mind all sorts of extralegal notions about "what ought to be," regardless of their sources, pretensions, or intrinsic worth. This is particularly apparent in his treatment of the problem of interpretation, where uncodified notions of what ought to be are viewed as affecting only the penumbra of law, leaving its hard core untouched.

Toward the end of the essay, however, Professor Hart's argument takes a turn that seems to depart from the prevailing tenor of his thought. This consists in reminding us that there is such a thing as an immoral morality and that there are many standards of "what ought to be" that can hardly be called moral.[4] Let us grant, he says, that the judge may properly and inevitably legislate in the penumbra of a legal enactment, and that this legislation (in default of any other standard) must be guided by the judge's notions of what ought to be. Still, this would be true even in a society devoted to the most evil ends, where the judge would supply the insufficiencies of the statute with the iniquity that seemed to him most apt for the occasion. Let us also grant, says Professor Hart toward the end of his essay, that there is at times even something that looks like discovery in the judicial process, when a judge by restating a principle seems to bring more clearly to light what was really sought from the beginning. Again, he reminds us, this could happen in a society devoted to the highest refinements of sin, where the implicit demands of an evil rule might be a matter for discovery when the rule was applied to a situation not consciously considered when it was formulated.

I take it that this is to be a warning addressed to those who wish "to infuse more morality into the law." Professor Hart is reminding them that if their program is adopted the morality that actually gets infused may not be to their liking. If this is his point it is certainly a valid one, though one wishes it had been made more explicitly, for it raises much the most fundamental issue of his whole argument. Since the point is made obliquely, and I may have misinterpreted it, in commenting I shall have to content myself with a few summary observations and questions.

First, Professor Hart seems to assume that evil aims may have as much coherence and inner logic as good ones. I, for one, refuse to accept that assumption. I realize that I am here raising, or perhaps dodging, questions that lead into the most difficult problems of the epistemology of ethics. Even if I were competent to undertake an excursus in that direction, this is not the place for it. I shall have to rest on the assertion of a belief that may seem naïve, namely, that coherence and goodness have more affinity than coherence and evil. Accepting this belief, I also believe that when men are compelled to explain and justify their decisions, the effect will generally be to pull those decisions toward goodness, by whatever standards of ultimate goodness there are. Accepting these beliefs, I find a considerable incongruity in any conception that envisages a possible future in which the common law would "work itself pure from case to case" toward a more perfect realization of iniquity.

Second, if there is a serious danger in our society that a weakening of the partition between law and morality would permit an infusion of "immoral morality," the question remains, what is the most effective protection against this danger? I cannot myself believe it is to be found in the positivist position espoused by Austin, Gray, Holmes, and Hart. For those writers seem to me to falsify the problem into a specious simplicity which leaves untouched the difficult issues where real dangers lie.

Third, let us suppose a judge bent on realizing through his decisions an objective that most ordinary citizens would regard as mistaken or evil. Would such a judge be likely to suspend the letter of the statute by openly invoking a "higher law"? Or would he be more likely to take refuge behind the maxim that "law is law" and explain his decision in such a way that it would appear to be demanded by the law itself?

Fourth, neither Professor Hart nor I belong to anything that could be said in a significant sense to be a "minority group" in our respective countries. This has its advantages and disadvantages to one aspiring to a philosophic view of law and government. But suppose we were both transported to a country where our beliefs were anathemas, and where we, in turn, regarded the prevailing morality as thoroughly evil. No doubt in this situation we would have reason to fear that the law might be covertly manipulated to our disadvantage: I doubt if either of us would be apprehensive that its injunctions would be set aside by an appeal to a morality higher than law. If we felt that the law itself was our safest refuge, would it not be because even in the most perverted regimes there is a certain hesitancy about writing cruelties, intolerances, and inhumanities into law? And is it not clear that this hesitancy itself derives, not from a separation of law and morals, but precisely from an identification of law with those demands of morality that are the most urgent and the most obviously justifiable, which no man need be ashamed to profess?

Fifth, over great areas where the judicial process functions, the danger of an infusion of immoral, or at least unwelcome, morality does not, I suggest, present a real issue. Here the danger is precisely the opposite. For example, in the field of commercial law the British courts in recent years have, if I may say so, fallen into a "law-is-law" formalism that constitutes a kind of belated counter-revolution against all that was accomplished by Mansfield.[5] The matter has reached a stage approaching crisis as commercial cases are increasingly being taken to arbitration. The chief reason for this development is that arbitrators are willing to take into account the needs of commerce and ordinary standards of commercial fairness. I realize that Professor Hart repudiates "formalism," but I shall try to show later why I think his theory necessarily leads in that direction.[6]

Sixth, in the thinking of many there is one question that predominates in any discussion of the relation of law and morals, to the point of coloring everything that is said or heard on the subject. I refer to the kind of question raised by the Pope's pronouncement concerning the duty of Catholic judges in divorce actions.[7] This pronouncement does indeed raise grave issues. But it does not present a problem of the relation between law, on the one hand, and, on the other, generally shared views of right conduct that have grown spontaneously through experience and discussion. The issue is rather that of a conflict between two pronouncements, both of which claim to be authoritative: if you will, it is one kind of law against another. When this kind of issue is taken as the key to the whole problem of law and morality, the discussion is so denatured and distorted that profitable exchange becomes impossible. In mentioning this last aspect of the dispute about "positivism." I do not mean to intimate that Professor Hart's own discussion is dominated by any *arrière-pensée*; I know it is not. At the same time I am quite sure that I have indicated accurately the issue that will be uppermost in the minds of many as they read his essay.

In resting content with these scant remarks, I do not want to seem to simplify the problem in a direction opposite to that taken by Professor Hart. The questions raised by "immoral morality" deserve a more careful exploration than either Professor Hart or I have offered in these pages.

III   The Moral Foundations of a Legal Order

Professor Hart emphatically rejects "the command theory of law," according to which law is simply a command backed by a force sufficient to make it effective. He observes that such a command can be given by a man with a loaded gun, and "law surely is not the gunman situation writ large."[8] There is no need to dwell here on the inadequacies of the command theory, since Professor Hart has already revealed its defects more clearly and succinctly than I could. His conclusion is that the foundation of a legal system is not coercive power, but certain "fundamental accepted rules specifying the essential lawmaking procedures."[9]

When I reached this point in his essay, I felt certain that Professor Hart was about to acknowledge an important qualification on his thesis. I confidently expected that he would go on to say something like this: I have insisted throughout on the importance of keeping sharp the distinction between law and morality. The question may now be raised, therefore, as to the nature of these fundamental rules that furnish the framework within which the making of law takes place. On the one hand, they seem to be rules, not of law, but of morality. They derive their efficacy from a general acceptance, which in turn rests ultimately on a perception that they are right and necessary. They can hardly be said to be law in the sense of an authoritative pronouncement, since their function is to state when a pronouncement is authoritative. On the other hand, in the daily functioning of the legal system they are often treated and applied much as ordinary rules of law are. Here, then, we must confess there is something that can be called a "merger" of law and morality, and to which the term "intersection" is scarcely appropriate.

Instead of pursuing some such course of thought, to my surprise I found Professor Hart leaving completely untouched the nature of the fundamental rules that make law itself possible, and turning his attention instead to what he considers a confusion of thought on the part of the critics of positivism. Leaving out of account his discussion of analytical jurisprudence, his argument runs something as follows: Two views are associated with the names of Bentham and Austin. One is the command theory of law, the other is an insistence on the separation of law and morality. Critics of these writers came in time to perceive – "dimly" Professor Hart says – that the command theory is untenable. By a loose association of ideas they wrongly supposed that in advancing reasons for rejecting the command theory they had also refuted the view that law and morality must be sharply separated. This was a "natural mistake," but plainly a mistake just the same.

I do not think any mistake is committed in believing that Bentham and Austin's error in formulating improperly and too simply the problem of the relation of law and morals was part of a larger error that led to the command theory of law. I think the connection between these two errors can be made clear if we ask ourselves what would have happened to Austin's system of thought if he had abandoned the command theory.

One who reads Austin's Lectures V and VI[10] cannot help being impressed by the way he hangs doggedly to the command theory, in spite of the fact that every pull of his own keen mind was toward abandoning it. In the case of a sovereign monarch, law is what the monarch commands. But what shall we say of the "laws" of succession which tell who the "lawful" monarch is? It is of the essence of a command that it be addressed by a superior to an inferior, yet in the case of a "sovereign many," say, a parliament, the sovereign seems to command itself since a member of parliament may be convicted under a law he himself drafted and voted for. The sovereign must be unlimited in legal power, for who could adjudicate the legal bounds of a supreme lawmaking power? Yet a "sovereign many" must accept the limitation of rules before it can make law at all. Such a body can gain the power to issue commands only by acting in a "corporate capacity"; this it can do only by proceeding "agreeably to the modes and forms" established and accepted for the making of law. Judges exercise a power delegated to them by the supreme lawmaking power, and are commissioned to carry out its "direct or circuitous commands." Yet in a federal system it is the courts which must resolve conflicts of competence between the federation and its components.

All of these problems Austin sees with varying degrees of explicitness, and he struggles mightily with them. Over and over again he teeters on the edge of an abandonment of the command theory in favor of what Professor

Hart has described as a view that discerns the foundations of a legal order in "certain fundamental accepted rules specifying the essential lawmaking procedures." Yet he never takes the plunge. He does not take it because he had a sure insight that it would forfeit the black-and-white distinction between law and morality that was the whole object of his Lectures – indeed, one may say, the enduring object of a dedicated life. For if law is made possible by "fundamental accepted rules" – which for Austin must be rules, not of law, but of positive morality – what are we to say of the rules that the lawmaking power enacts to regulate its own lawmaking? We have election laws, laws allocating legislative representation to specific geographic areas, rules of parliamentary procedure, rules for the qualification of voters, and many other laws and rules of similar nature. These do not remain fixed, and all of them shape in varying degrees the lawmaking process. Yet how are we to distinguish between those basic rules that owe their validity to acceptance, and those which are properly rules of law, valid even when men generally consider them to be evil or ill-advised? In other words, how are we to define the words "fundamental" and "essential" in Professor Hart's own formulation: "certain fundamental accepted rules specifying the essential lawmaking procedure"?

The solution for this problem in Kelsen's theory is instructive. Kelsen does in fact take the plunge over which Austin hesitated too long. Kelsen realizes that before we can distinguish between what is law and what is not there must be an acceptance of some basic procedure by which law is made. In any legal system there must be some fundamental rule that points unambiguously to the source from which laws must come in order to be laws. This rule Kelsen called "the basic norm." In his own words,

> The basic norm is not valid because it has been created in a certain way, but its validity is assumed by virtue of its content. It is valid, then, like a norm of natural law.... The idea of a pure positive law, like that of natural law, has its limitations.[11]

It will be noted that Kelsen speaks, not as Professor Hart does, of "fundamental rules" that regulate the making of law, but of a single rule or norm. Of course, there is no such single rule in any modern society. The notion of the basic norm is admittedly a symbol, not a fact. It is a symbol that embodies the positivist quest for some clear and unambiguous test of law, for some clean, sharp line that will divide the rules which owe their validity to their source and those which owe their validity to acceptance and intrinsic appeal. The difficulties Austin avoided by sticking with the command theory, Kelsen avoids by a fiction which simplifies reality into a form that can be absorbed by positivism.

A full exploration of all the problems that result when we recognize that law becomes possible only by virtue of rules that are not law, would require drawing into consideration the effect of the presence or absence of a written constitution. Such a constitution in some ways simplifies the problems I have been discussing, and in some ways complicates them. In so far as a written constitution defines basic lawmaking procedure, it may remove the perplexities that arise when a parliament in effect defines itself. At the same time, a legislature operating under a written constitution may enact statutes that profoundly affect the lawmaking procedure and its predictable outcome. If these statutes are drafted with sufficient cunning, they may remain within the frame of the constitution and yet undermine the institutions it was intended to establish. If the "court-packing" proposal of the 'thirties does not illustrate this danger unequivocally, it at least suggests that the fear of it is not fanciful. No written constitution can be self-executing. To be effective it requires not merely the respectful deference we show for ordinary legal enactments, but that willing convergence of effort we give to moral principles in which we have an active belief. One may properly work to amend a constitution, but so long as it remains unamended one must work with it, not against it or around it. All this amounts to saying that to be effective a written constitution must be accepted, at least provisionally, not just as law, but as good law.

What have these considerations to do with the ideal of fidelity to law? I think they have a great deal to do with it, and that they reveal the essential incapacity of the positivistic view to serve that ideal effectively. For I believe that a realization of this ideal is something for which we must plan, and that is precisely what positivism refuses to do.

Let me illustrate what I mean by planning for a realization of the ideal of fidelity to law. Suppose we are drafting a written constitution for a country just emerging from a period of violence and disorder in which any thread of legal continuity with previous governments has been broken. Obviously such a constitution cannot lift itself unaided into legality; it cannot be law simply because it says it is. We should keep in mind that the efficacy of our work will depend upon general acceptance and that to make this acceptance secure there must be a general belief that the constitution itself is necessary, right, and good. The provisions of the constitution should, therefore, be kept simple and understandable, not only in language, but also in purpose. Preambles and other explanations of what is being sought, which would be objectionable in an ordinary statute, may find an appropriate place in our constitution. We should think of our constitution as establishing a basic procedural framework for future governmental action in the enactment and administration of laws. Substantive limitations on the power of government should be kept to a minimum and should generally be confined to those for which a need can be generally appreciated. In so far as possible, substantive aims should be achieved procedurally, on the principle that if men are compelled to act in the right way, they will generally do the right things.

These considerations seem to have been widely ignored in the constitutions that have come into existence since World War II. Not uncommonly these constitutions incorporate a host of economic and political measures of the type one would ordinarily associate with statutory law. It is hardly likely that these measures have been written into the constitution because they represent aims that are generally shared. One suspects that the reason for their inclusion is precisely the opposite, namely, a fear that they would not be able to survive the vicissitudes of an ordinary exercise of parliamentary power. Thus, the divisions of opinion that are a normal accompaniment of lawmaking are written into the document that makes law itself possible. This is obviously a procedure that contains serious dangers for a future realization of the ideal of fidelity to law.

I have ventured these remarks on the making of constitutions not because I think they can claim any special profundity, but because I wished to illustrate what I mean by planning the conditions that will make it possible to realize the ideal of fidelity to law. Even within the limits of my modest purpose, what I have said may be clearly wrong. If so, it would not be for me to say whether I am also wrong clearly. I will, however, venture to assert that if I am wrong, I am wrong significantly. What disturbs me about the school of legal positivism is that it not only refuses to deal with problems of the sort I have just discussed, but bans them on principle from the province of legal philosophy. In its concern to assign the right labels to the things men do, this school seems to lose all interest in asking whether men are doing the right things.

IV   The Morality of Law Itself

Most of the issues raised by Professor Hart's essay can be restated in terms of the distinction between order and good order. Law may be said to represent order *simpliciter*. Good order is law that corresponds to the demands of justice, or morality, or men's notions of what ought to be. This rephrasing of the issue is useful in bringing to light the ambitious nature of Professor Hart's undertaking, for surely we would all agree that it is no easy thing to distinguish order from good order. When it is said, for example, that law simply represents that public order which obtains under all governments – democratic, Fascist, or Communist[12] – the order intended is certainly not that of a morgue or cemetery. We must mean a functioning order, and such an order has to be at least good enough to be considered as functioning by some standard or other. A reminder that workable order usually requires some play in the joints, and therefore cannot be too orderly, is enough to suggest some of the complexities that would be involved in any attempt to draw a sharp distinction between order and good order.

For the time being, however, let us suppose we can in fact clearly separate the concept of order from that of good order. Even in this unreal and abstract form the notion of order itself contains what may be called a moral element. Let me illustrate this "morality of order" in its crudest and most elementary form. Let us suppose an absolute monarch, whose word is the only law known to his subjects. We may further suppose him to be utterly selfish and to seek in his relations with his subjects solely his own advantage. This monarch from time to time issues commands, promising rewards for compliance and threatening punishment for disobedience. He is, however, a dissolute and forgetful fellow, who never makes the slightest attempt to ascertain who have in fact followed his directions and who have not. As a result he habitually punishes loyalty and rewards disobedience. It is apparent that this monarch will never achieve even his own selfish aims until he is ready to accept that minimum self-restraint that will create a meaningful connection between his words and his actions.

Let us now suppose that our monarch undergoes a change of heart and begins to pay some attention to what he said yesterday when, today, he has occasion to distribute bounty or to order the chopping off of heads. Under the strain of this new responsibility, however, our monarch relaxes his attention in other directions and becomes hopelessly slothful in the phrasing of his commands. His orders become so ambiguous and are uttered in so inaudible a tone that his subjects never have any clear idea what he wants them to do. Here, again, it is apparent that if our monarch for his own selfish advantage wants to create in his realm anything like a system of law he will have to pull himself together and assume still another responsibility.

Law, considered merely as order, contains, then, its own implicit morality. This morality of order must be respected if we are to create anything that can be called law, even bad law. Law by itself is powerless to bring this morality into existence. Until our monarch is really ready to face the responsibilities of his position, it will

do no good for him to issue still another futile command, this time self-addressed and threatening himself with punishment if he does not mend his ways.

There is a twofold sense in which it is true that law cannot be built on law. First of all, the authority to make law must be supported by moral attitudes that accord to it the competency it claims. Here we are dealing with a morality external to law, which makes law possible. But this alone is not enough. We may stipulate that in our monarchy the accepted "basic norm" designates the monarch himself as the only possible source of law. We still cannot have law until our monarch is ready to accept the internal morality of law itself.

In the life of a nation these external and internal moralities of law reciprocally influence one another; a deterioration of the one will almost inevitably produce a deterioration in the other. So closely related are they that when the anthropologist Lowie speaks of "the generally accepted ethical postulates underlying our ... legal institutions as their ultimate sanction and guaranteeing their smooth functioning,"[13] he may be presumed to have both of them in mind.

What I have called "the internal morality of law" seems to be almost completely neglected by Professor Hart. He does make brief mention of "justice in the administration of the law," which consists in the like treatment of like cases, by whatever elevated or perverted standards the word "like" may be defined.[14] But he quickly dismisses this aspect of law as having no special relevance to his main enterprise.

In this I believe he is profoundly mistaken. It is his neglect to analyze the demands of a morality of order that leads him throughout his essay to treat law as a datum projecting itself into human experience and not as an object of human striving. When we realize that order itself is something that must be worked for, it becomes apparent that the existence of a legal system, even a bad or evil legal system, is always a matter of degree. When we recognize this simple fact of everyday legal experience, it becomes impossible to dismiss the problems presented by the Nazi regime with a simple assertion: "Under the Nazis there was law, even if it was bad law." We have instead to inquire how much of a legal system survived the general debasement and perversion of all forms of social order that occurred under the Nazi rule, and what moral implications this mutilated system had for the conscientious citizen forced to live under it.

It is not necessary, however, to dwell on such moral upheavals as the Nazi regime to see how completely incapable the positivistic philosophy is of serving the one high moral ideal it professes, that of fidelity to law. Its default in serving this ideal actually becomes most apparent, I believe, in the everyday problems that confront those who are earnestly desirous of meeting the moral demands of a legal order, but who have responsible functions to discharge in the very order toward which loyalty is due.

Let us suppose the case of a trial judge who has had an extensive experience in commercial matters and before whom a great many commercial disputes are tried. As a subordinate in a judicial hierarchy, our judge has of course the duty to follow the law laid down by his supreme court. Our imaginary Scrutton has the misfortune, however, to live under a supreme court which he considers woefully ignorant of the ways and needs of commerce. To his mind, many of this court's decisions in the field of commercial law simply do not make sense. If a conscientious judge caught in this dilemma were to turn to the positivistic philosophy what succor could he expect? It will certainly do no good to remind him that he has an obligation of fidelity to law. He is aware of this already and painfully so, since it is the source of his predicament. Nor will it help to say that if he legislates, it must be "interstitially," or that his contributions must be "confined from molar to molecular motions."[15] This mode of statement may be congenial to those who like to think of law, not as a purposive thing, but as an expression of the dimensions and directions of state power. But I cannot believe that the essentially trite idea behind this advice can be lifted by literary eloquence to the point where it will offer any real help to our judge; for one thing, it may be impossible for him to know whether his supreme court would regard any

particular contribution of his as being wide or narrow.

Nor is it likely that a distinction between core and penumbra would be helpful. The predicament of our judge may well derive, not from particular precedents, but from a mistaken conception of the nature of commerce which extends over many decisions and penetrates them in varying degrees. So far as his problem arises from the use of particular words, he may well find that the supreme court often uses the ordinary terms of commerce in senses foreign to actual business dealings. If he interprets those words as a business executive or accountant would, he may well reduce the precedents he is bound to apply to a logical shambles. On the other hand, he may find great difficulty in discerning the exact sense in which the supreme court used those words, since in his mind that sense is itself the product of a confusion.

Is it not clear that it is precisely positivism's insistence on a rigid separation of law as it is from law as it ought to be that renders the positivistic philosophy incapable of aiding our judge? Is it not also clear that our judge can never achieve a satisfactory resolution of his dilemma unless he views his duty of fidelity to law in a context which also embraces his responsibility for making law what it ought to be?

The case I have supposed may seem extreme, but the problem it suggests pervades our whole legal system. If the divergence of views between our judge and his supreme court were less drastic, it would be more difficult to present his predicament graphically, but the perplexity of his position might actually increase. Perplexities of this sort are a normal accompaniment of the discharge of any adjudicative function; they perhaps reach their most poignant intensity in the field of administrative law.

One can imagine a case – surely not likely in Professor Hart's country or mine – where a judge might hold profound moral convictions that were exactly the opposite of those held, with equal attachment, by his supreme court. He might also be convinced that the precedents he was bound to apply were the direct product of a morality he considered abhorrent. If such a judge did not find the solution for his dilemma in surrendering his office, he might well be driven to a wooden and literal application of precedents which he could not otherwise apply because he was incapable of understanding the philosophy that animated them. But I doubt that a judge in this situation would need the help of legal positivism to find these melancholy escapes from his predicament. Nor do I think that such a predicament is likely to arise within a nation where both law and good law are regarded as collaborative human achievements in need of constant renewal, and where lawyers are still at least as interested in asking "What is good law?" as they are in asking "What is law?"

V The Problem of Restoring Respect for Law and Justice After the Collapse of a Regime That Respected Neither

After the collapse of the Nazi regime the German courts were faced with a truly frightful predicament. It was impossible for them to declare the whole dictatorship illegal or to treat as void every decision and legal enactment that had emanated from Hitler's government. Intolerable dislocations would have resulted from any such wholesale outlawing of all that occurred over a span of twelve years. On the other hand, it was equally impossible to carry forward into the new government the effects of every Nazi perversity that had been committed in the name of law; any such course would have tainted an indefinite future with the poisons of Nazism.

This predicament – which was, indeed, a pervasive one, affecting all branches of law – came to a dramatic head in a series of cases involving informers who had taken advantage of the Nazi terror to get rid of personal enemies or unwanted spouses. If all Nazi statutes and judicial decisions were indiscriminately "law," then these despicable creatures were guiltless, since they had turned their victims over to processes which the Nazis themselves knew by the name of law. Yet it was intolerable, especially for the surviving relatives and friends of the victims, that these people should go about unpunished, while the objects of their spite were dead, or were just being released after

years of imprisonment, or, more painful still, simply remained unaccounted for.

The urgency of this situation does not by any means escape Professor Hart. Indeed, he is moved to recommend an expedient that is surely not lacking itself in a certain air of desperation. He suggests that a retroactive criminal statute would have been the least objectionable solution to the problem. This statute would have punished the informer, and branded him as a criminal, for an act which Professor Hart regards as having been perfectly legal when he committed it.[16]

On the other hand, Professor Hart condemns without qualification those judicial decisions in which the courts themselves undertook to declare void certain of the Nazi statutes under which the informer's victims had been convicted. One cannot help raising at this point the question whether the issue as presented by Professor Hart himself is truly that of fidelity to law. Surely it would be a necessary implication of a retroactive criminal statute against informers that, for purposes of that statute at least, the Nazi laws as applied to the informers or their victims were to be regarded as void. With this turn the question seems no longer to be whether what was once law can now be declared not to have been law, but rather who should do the dirty work, the courts or the legislature.

But, as Professor Hart himself suggests, the issues at stake are much too serious to risk losing them in a semantic tangle. Even if the whole question were one of words, we should remind ourselves that we are in an area where words have a powerful effect on human attitudes. I should like, therefore, to undertake a defense of the German courts, and to advance reasons why, in my opinion, their decisions do not represent the abandonment of legal principle that Professor Hart sees in them. In order to understand the background of those decisions we shall have to move a little closer within smelling distance of the witches' caldron than we have been brought so far by Professor Hart. We shall have also to consider an aspect of the problem ignored in his essay, namely, the degree to which the Nazis observed what I have called the inner morality of law itself.

Throughout his discussion Professor Hart seems to assume that the only difference between Nazi law and, say, English law is that the Nazis used their laws to achieve ends that are odious to an Englishman. This assumption is, I think, seriously mistaken, and Professor Hart's acceptance of it seems to me to render his discussion unresponsive to the problem it purports to address.

Throughout their period of control the Nazis took generous advantage of a device not wholly unknown to American legislatures, the retroactive statute curing past legal irregularities. The most dramatic use of the curative powers of such a statute occurred on July 3, 1934, after the "Roehm purge." When this intraparty shooting affair was over and more than seventy Nazis had been – one can hardly avoid saying – "rubbed out," Hitler returned to Berlin and procured from his cabinet a law ratifying and confirming the measures taken between June 30, and July 1, 1934, without mentioning the names of those who were now considered to have been lawfully executed.[17] Some time later Hitler declared that during the Roehm purge "the supreme court of the German people... consisted of myself,"[18] surely not an overstatement of the capacity in which he acted if one takes seriously the enactment conferring retroactive legality on "the measures taken."

Now in England and America it would never occur to anyone to say that "it is in the nature of law that it cannot be retroactive," although, of course, constitutional inhibitions may prohibit certain kinds of retroactivity. We would say it is normal for a law to operate prospectively, and that it may be arguable that it ought never operate otherwise, but there would be a certain occult unpersuasiveness in any assertion that retroactivity violates the very nature of law itself. Yet we have only to imagine a country in which *all* laws are retroactive in order to see that retroactivity presents a real problem for the internal morality of law. If we suppose an absolute monarch who allows his realm to exist in a constant state of anarchy, we would hardly say that he could create a regime of law simply by enacting a curative statute conferring legality on everything that had happened up to its date and

by announcing an intention to enact similar statutes every six months in the future.

A general increase in the resort to statutes curative of past legal irregularities represents a deterioration in that form of legal morality without which law itself cannot exist. The threat of such statutes hangs over the whole legal system, and robs every law on the books of some of its significance. And surely a general threat of this sort is implied when a government is willing to use such a statute to transform into lawful execution what was simple murder when it happened.

During the Nazi regime there were repeated rumors of "secret laws." In the article criticized by Professor Hart, Radbruch mentions a report that the wholesale killings in concentration camps were made "lawful" by a secret enactment.[19] Now surely there can be no greater legal monstrosity than a secret statute. Would anyone seriously recommend that following the war the German courts should have searched for unpublished laws among the files left by Hitler's government so that citizens' rights could be determined by a reference to these laws?

The extent of the legislator's obligation to make his laws known to his subjects is, of course, a problem of legal morality that has been under active discussion at least since the Secession of the Plebs. There is probably no modern state that has not been plagued by this problem in one form or another. It is most likely to arise in modern societies with respect to unpublished administrative directions. Often these are regarded in quite good faith by those who issue them as affecting only matters of internal organization. But since the procedures followed by an administrative agency, even in its "internal" actions, may seriously affect the rights and interests of the citizen, these unpublished, or "secret," regulations are often a subject for complaint.

But as with retroactivity, what in most societies is kept under control by the tacit restraints of legal decency broke out in monstrous form under Hitler. Indeed, so loose was the whole Nazi morality of law that it is not easy to know just what should be regarded as an unpublished or secret law. Since unpublished instructions to those administering the law could destroy the letter of any published law by imposing on it an outrageous interpretation, there was a sense in which the meaning of every law was "secret." Even a verbal order from Hitler that a thousand prisoners in concentration camps be put to death was at once an administrative direction and a validation of everything done under it as being "lawful."

But the most important affronts to the morality of law by Hitler's government took no such subtle forms as those exemplified in the bizarre outcroppings I have just discussed. In the first place, when legal forms became inconvenient, it was always possible for the Nazis to bypass them entirely and "to act through the party in the streets." There was no one who dared bring them to account for whatever outrages might thus be committed. In the second place, the Nazi-dominated courts were always ready to disregard any statute, even those enacted by the Nazis themselves, if this suited their convenience or if they feared that a lawyer-like interpretation might incur displeasure "above."

This complete willingness of the Nazis to disregard even their own enactments was an important factor leading Radbruch to take the position he did in the articles so severely criticized by Professor Hart. I do not believe that any fair appraisal of the action of the postwar German courts is possible unless we take this factor into account, as Professor Hart fails completely to do.

These remarks may seem inconclusive in their generality and to rest more on assertion than evidentiary fact. Let us turn at once, then, to the actual case discussed by Professor Hart.[20]

In 1944 a German soldier paid a short visit to his wife while under travel orders on a reassignment. During the single day he was home, he conveyed privately to his wife something of his opinion of the Hitler government. He expressed disapproval of (*sich abfällig geäussert über*) Hitler and other leading personalities of the Nazi party. He also said it was too bad Hitler had not met his end in the assassination attempt that had occurred on July 20th of that year. Shortly after his departure, his wife, who during his long absence on military duty "had turned to

other men" and who wished to get rid of him, reported his remarks to the local leader of the Nazi party, observing that "a man who would say a thing like that does not deserve to live." The result was a trial of the husband by a military tribunal and a sentence of death. After a short period of imprisonment, instead of being executed, he was sent to the front again. After the collapse of the Nazi regime, the wife was brought to trial for having procured the imprisonment of her husband. Her defense rested on the ground that her husband's statements to her about Hitler and the Nazis constituted a crime under the laws then in force. Accordingly, when she informed on her husband she was simply bringing a criminal to justice.

This defense rested on two statutes, one passed in 1934, the other in 1938. Let us first consider the second of these enactments, which was part of a more comprehensive legislation creating a whole series of special wartime criminal offenses. I reproduce below a translation of the only pertinent section:

> The following persons are guilty of destroying the national power of resistance and shall be punished by death: Whoever publicly solicits or incites a refusal to fulfill the obligations of service in the armed forces of Germany, or in armed forces allied with Germany, or who otherwise publicly seeks to injure or destroy the will of the German people or an allied people to assert themselves stalwartly against their enemies.[21]

It is almost inconceivable that a court of present-day Germany would hold the husband's remarks to his wife, who was barred from military duty by her sex, to be a violation of the final catch-all provision of this statute, particularly when it is recalled that the text reproduced above was part of a more comprehensive enactment dealing with such things as harboring deserters, escaping military duty by self-inflicted injuries, and the like. The question arises, then, as to the extent to which the interpretive principles applied by the courts of Hitler's government should be accepted in determining whether the husband's remarks were indeed unlawful.

This question becomes acute when we note that the act applies only to *public* acts or utterances, whereas the husband's remarks were in the privacy of his own home. Now it appears that the Nazi courts (and it should be noted we are dealing with a special military court) quite generally disregarded this limitation and extended the act to all utterances, private or public.[22] Is Professor Hart prepared to say that the legal meaning of this statute is to be determined in the light of this apparently uniform principle of judicial interpretation?

Let us turn now to the other statute upon which Professor Hart relies in assuming that the husband's utterance was unlawful. This is the act of 1934, the relevant portions of which are translated below:

(1) Whoever publicly makes spiteful or provocative statements directed against, or statements which disclose a base disposition toward, the leading personalities of the nation or of the National Socialist German Workers' Party, or toward measures taken or institutions established by them, and of such a nature as to undermine the people's confidence in their political leadership, shall be punished by imprisonment.

(2) Malicious utterances not made in public shall be treated in the same manner as public utterances when the person making them realized or should have realized they would reach the public.

(3) Prosecution for such utterances shall be only on the order of the National Minister of Justice; in case the utterance was directed against a leading personality of the National Socialist German Workers' Party, the Minister of Justice shall order prosecution only with the advice and consent of the Representative of the Leader.

(4) The National Minister of Justice shall, with the advice and consent of the Representative of the Leader, determine who shall belong to the class of leading personalities for purposes of Section I above.[23]

Extended comment on this legislative monstrosity is scarcely called for, overlarded and undermined as it is by uncontrolled adminis-
trative discretion. We may note only: first, that it offers no justification whatever for the death penalty actually imposed on the husband, though never carried out; second, that if the wife's act in informing on her husband made his remarks "public," there is no such thing as a private utterance under this statute. I should like to ask the reader whether he can actually share Professor Hart's indignation that, in the perplexities of the postwar reconstruction, the German courts saw fit to declare this thing not a law. Can it be argued seriously that it would have been more beseeming to the judicial process if the postwar courts had undertaken a study of "the interpretative principles" in force during Hitler's rule and had then solemnly applied those "principles" to ascertain the meaning of this statute? On the other hand, would the courts really have been showing respect for Nazi law if they had construed the Nazi statutes by their own, quite different, standards of interpretation?

Professor Hart castigates the German courts and Radbruch, not so much for what they believed had to be done, but because they failed to see that they were confronted by a moral dilemma of a sort that would have been immediately apparent to Bentham and Austin. By the simple dodge of saying, "When a statute is sufficiently evil it ceases to be law," they ran away from the problem they should have faced.

This criticism is, I believe, without justification. So far as the courts are concerned, matters certainly would not have been helped if, instead of saying, "This is not law," they had said, "This is law but it is so evil we will refuse to apply it." Surely moral confusion reaches its height when a court refuses to apply something it admits to be law, and Professor Hart does not recommend any such "facing of the true issue" by the courts themselves. He would have preferred a retroactive statute. Curiously, this was also the preference of Radbruch.[24] But unlike Professor Hart, the German courts and Gustav Radbruch were living participants in a situation of drastic emergency. The informer problem was a pressing one, and if legal institutions were to be rehabilitated in Germany it would not do to allow the people to begin taking the law into their own hands, as might have occurred while the courts were waiting for a statute.

As for Gustav Radbruch, it is, I believe, wholly unjust to say that he did not know he was faced with a moral dilemma. His postwar writings repeatedly stress the antinomies confronted in the effort to rebuild decent and orderly government in Germany. As for the ideal of fidelity to law, I shall let Radbruch's own words state his position:

> We must not conceal from ourselves – especially not in the light of our experiences during the twelve-year dictatorship – what frightful dangers for the rule of law can be contained in the notion of "statutory lawlessness" and in refusing the quality of law to duly enacted statutes.[25]

The situation is not that legal positivism enables a man to know when he faces a difficult problem of choice, while Radbruch's beliefs deceive him into thinking there is no problem to face. The real issue dividing Professors Hart and Radbruch is: How shall we state the problem? What is the nature of the dilemma in which we are caught?

I hope I am not being unjust to Professor Hart when I say that I can find no way of describing the dilemma as he sees it but to use some such words as the following: On the one hand, we have an amoral datum called law, which has the peculiar quality of creating a moral duty to obey it. On the other hand, we have a moral duty to do what we think is right and decent. When we are confronted by a statute we believe to be thoroughly evil, we have to choose between those two duties.

If this is the positivist position, then I have no hesitancy in rejecting it. The "dilemma" it states has the verbal formulation of a problem, but the problem it states makes no sense. It is like saying I have to choose between giving food to a starving man and being mimsy with the borogoves. I do not think it is unfair to the positivistic philosophy to say that it never gives any coherent meaning to the moral obligation of fidelity to law. This obligation seems to be conceived as sui generis, wholly unrelated to any of the ordinary, extralegal ends of human life. The fundamental postulate of positivism –

that law must be strictly severed from morality – seems to deny the possibility of any bridge between the obligation to obey law and other moral obligations. No mediating principle can measure their respective demands on conscience, for they exist in wholly separate worlds.

While I would not subscribe to all of Radbruch's postwar views – especially those relating to "higher law" – I think he saw, much more clearly than does Professor Hart, the true nature of the dilemma confronted by Germany in seeking to rebuild her shattered legal institutions. Germany had to restore both respect for law and respect for justice. Though neither of these could be restored without the other, painful antinomies were encountered in attempting to restore both at once, as Radbruch saw all too clearly. Essentially Radbruch saw the dilemma as that of meeting the demands of order, on the one hand, and those of good order, on the other. Of course no pat formula can be derived from this phrasing of the problem. But, unlike legal positivism, it does not present us with opposing demands that have no living contact with one another, that simply shout their contradictions across a vacuum. As we seek order, we can meaningfully remind ourselves that order itself will do us no good unless it is good for something. As we seek to make our order good, we can remind ourselves that justice itself is impossible without order, and that we must not lose order itself in the attempt to make it good.

VI The Moral Implications of Legal Positivism

We now reach the question whether there is any ground for Gustav Radbruch's belief that a general acceptance of the positivistic philosophy in pre-Nazi Germany made smoother the route to dictatorship. Understandably, Professor Hart regards this as the most outrageous of all charges against positivism.

Here indeed we enter upon a hazardous area of controversy, where ugly words and ugly charges have become commonplace. During the last half century in this country no issue of legal philosophy has caused more spilling of ink and adrenalin than the assertion that there are "totalitarian" implications in the views of Oliver Wendell Holmes, Jr. Even the most cautiously phrased criticisms of that grand old figure from the age of Darwin, Huxley, and Haeckel seem to stir the reader's mind with the memory of past acerbities.[26] It does no good to suggest that perhaps Holmes did not perceive all the implications of his own philosophy, for this is merely to substitute one insult for another. Nor does it help much to recall the dictum of one of the closest companions of Holmes' youth – surely no imperceptive observer – that Holmes was "composed of at least two and a half different people rolled into one, and the way he keeps them together in one tight skin, without quarreling any more than they do, is remarkable."[27]

In venturing upon these roughest of all jurisprudential waters, one is not reassured to see even so moderate a man as Professor Hart indulging in some pretty broad strokes of the oar. Radbruch disclosed "an extraordinary naïveté" in assessing the temper of his own profession in Germany and in supposing that its adherence to positivism helped the Nazis to power.[28] His judgment on this and other matters shows that he had "only half digested the spiritual message of liberalism" he mistakenly thought he was conveying to his countrymen.[29] A state of "hysteria"[30] is revealed by those who see a wholesome reorientation of German legal thinking in such judicial decisions as were rendered in the informer cases.

Let us put aside at least the blunter tools of invective and address ourselves as calmly as we can to the question whether legal positivism, as practiced and preached in Germany, had, or could have had, any causal connection with Hitler's ascent to power. It should be recalled that in the seventy-five years before the Nazi regime the positivistic philosophy had achieved in Germany a standing such as it enjoyed in no other country. Austin praised a German scholar for bringing international law within the clarity-producing restraints of positivism.[31] Gray reported with pleasure that the "abler" German jurists of his time were "abjuring all '*nicht positivisches Recht*,' " and cited Bergbohm as an example.[32] This is an illuminating example, for Bergbohm was a scholar whose ambition was to make German positivism live up to its own pretensions. He was distressed to encounter vestigial traces of natural-law thinking in writings claiming to be positivistic. In particular, he was disturbed by the frequent recurrence of such notions as that law owes its efficacy to a perceived moral need for order, or that it is in the nature of man that he requires a legal order, etc. Bergbohm announced a program, never realized, to drive from positivistic thinking these last miasmas from the swamp of natural law.[33] German jurists generally tended to regard the Anglo-American common law as a messy and unprincipled conglomerate of law and morals.[34] Positivism was the only theory of law that could claim to be "scientific" in an Age of Science. Dissenters from this view were characterized by positivists with that epithet modern man fears above all others: "naïve." The result was that it could be reported by 1927 that "to be found guilty of adherence to natural law theories is a kind of social disgrace."[35]

To this background we must add the observation that the Germans seem never to have achieved that curious ability possessed by the British, and to some extent by the Americans, of holding their logic on short leash. When a German defines law, he means his definition to be taken seriously. If a German writer had hit upon the slogan of American legal realism, "Law is simply the behavior patterns of judges and other state officials," he would not have regarded this as an interesting little conversation-starter. He would have believed it and acted on it.

German legal positivism not only banned from legal science any consideration of the moral ends of law, but it was also indifferent to what I have called the inner morality of law itself. The German lawyer was therefore peculiarly prepared to accept as "law" anything that called itself by that name, was printed at government expense, and seemed to come "*von oben herab*."

In the light of these considerations I cannot see either absurdity or perversity in the suggestion that the attitudes prevailing in the German legal profession were helpful to the Nazis. Hitler did not come to power by a violent revolution. He was Chancellor before he became the

Leader. The exploitation of legal forms started cautiously and became bolder as power was consolidated. The first attacks on the established order were on ramparts which, if they were manned by anyone, were manned by lawyers and judges. These ramparts fell almost without a struggle.

Professor Hart and others have been understandably distressed by references to a "higher law" in some of the decisions concerning informers and in Radbruch's postwar writings. I suggest that if German jurisprudence had concerned itself more with the inner morality of law, it would not have been necessary to invoke any notion of this sort in declaring void the more outrageous Nazi statutes.

To me there is nothing shocking in saying that a dictatorship which clothes itself with a tinsel of legal form can so far depart from the morality of order, from the inner morality of law itself, that it ceases to be a legal system. When a system calling itself law is predicated upon a general disregard by judges of the terms of the laws they purport to enforce, when this system habitually cures its legal irregularities, even the grossest, by retroactive statutes, when it has only to resort to forays of terror in the streets, which no one dares challenge, in order to escape even those scant restraints imposed by the pretence of legality – when all these things have become true of a dictatorship, it is not hard for me, at least, to deny to it the name of law.

I believe that the invalidity of the statutes involved in the informer cases could have been grounded on considerations such as I have just outlined. But if you were raised with a generation that said "law is law" and meant it, you may feel the only way you can escape one law is to set another off against it, and this perforce must be a "higher law." Hence these notions of "higher law," which are a justifiable cause for alarm, may themselves be a belated fruit of German legal positivism.

It should be remarked at this point that it is chiefly in Roman Catholic writings that the theory of natural law is considered, not simply as a search for those principles that will enable men to live together successfully, but as a quest for something that can be called "a higher law." This identification of natural law with a law that is above human laws seems in fact to be demanded by any doctrine that asserts the possibility of an authoritative pronouncement of the demands of natural law. In those areas affected by such pronouncements as have so far been issued, the conflict between Roman Catholic doctrine and opposing views seems to me to be a conflict between two forms of positivism. Fortunately, over most of the area with which lawyers are concerned, no such pronouncements exist. In these areas I think those of us who are not adherents of its faith can be grateful to the Catholic Church for having kept alive the rationalistic tradition in ethics.

I do not assert that the solution I have suggested for the informer cases would not have entailed its own difficulties, particularly the familiar one of knowing where to stop. But I think it demonstrable that the most serious deterioration in legal morality under Hitler took place in branches of the law like those involved in the informer cases; no comparable deterioration was to be observed in the ordinary branches of private law. It was in those areas where the ends of law were most odious by ordinary standards of decency that the morality of law itself was most flagrantly disregarded. In other words, where one would have been most tempted to say, "This is so evil it cannot be a law," one could usually have said instead, "This thing is the product of a system so oblivious to the morality of law that it is not entitled to be called a law." I think there is something more than accident here, for the overlapping suggests that legal morality cannot live when it is severed from a striving toward justice and decency.

But as an actual solution for the informer cases, I, like Professors Hart and Radbruch, would have preferred a retroactive statute. My reason for this preference is not that this is the most nearly lawful way of making unlawful what was once law. Rather I would see such a statute as a way of symbolizing a sharp break with the past, as a means of isolating a kind of cleanup operation from the normal functioning of the judicial process. By this isolation it would become possible for the judiciary to return more rapidly to a condition in which the demands of legal morality could be given proper respect. In other words, it would make it possible to plan more effectively to regain for the ideal of fidelity to law its normal meaning.

VII   The Problem of Interpretation: The Core and the Penumbra

It is essential that we be just as clear as we can be about the meaning of Professor Hart's doctrine of "the core and the penumbra,"[36] because I believe the casual reader is likely to misinterpret what he has to say. Such a reader is apt to suppose that Professor Hart is merely describing something that is a matter of everyday experience for the lawyer, namely, that in the interpretation of legal rules it is typically the case (though not universally so) that there are some situations which will seem to fall rather clearly within the rule, while others will be more doubtful. Professor Hart's thesis takes no such jejune form. His extended discussion of the core and the penumbra is not just a complicated way of recognizing that some cases are hard, while others are easy. Instead, on the basis of a theory about language meaning generally, he is proposing a theory of judicial interpretation which is, I believe, wholly novel. Certainly it has never been put forward in so uncompromising a form before.

As I understand Professor Hart's thesis (if we add some tacit assumptions implied by it, as well as some qualifications he would no doubt wish his readers to supply) a full statement would run something as follows: The task of interpretation is commonly that of determining the meaning of the individual words of a legal rule, like "vehicle" in a rule excluding vehicles from a park. More particularly, the task of interpretation is to determine the range of reference of such a word, or the aggregate of things to which it points. Communication is possible only because words have a "standard instance," or a "core of meaning" that remains relatively constant, whatever the context in which the word may appear. Except in unusual circumstances, it will always be proper to regard a word like "vehicle" as embracing its "standard instance," that is, that aggregate of things it would include in all ordinary contexts, within or without the law. This meaning the word will

have in any legal rule, whatever its purpose. In applying the word to its "standard instance," no creative role is assumed by the judge. He is simply applying the law "as it is."

In addition to a constant core, however, words also have a penumbra of meaning which, unlike the core, will vary from context to context. When the object in question (say, a tricycle) falls within this penumbral area, the judge is forced to assume a more creative role. He must now undertake, for the first time, an interpretation of the rule in the light of its purpose or aim. Having in mind what was sought by the regulation concerning parks, ought it to be considered as barring tricycles? When questions of this sort are decided there is at least an "intersection" of "is" and "ought," since the judge, in deciding what the rule "is," does so in the light of his notions of what "it ought to be" in order to carry out its purpose.

If I have properly interpreted Professor Hart's theory as it affects the "hard core," then I think it is quite untenable. The most obvious defect of his theory lies in its assumption that problems of interpretation typically turn on the meaning of individual words. Surely no judge applying a rule of the common law ever followed any such procedure as that described (and, I take it, prescribed) by Professor Hart; indeed, we do not normally even think of his problem as being one of "interpretation." Even in the case of statutes, we commonly have to assign meaning, not to a single word, but to a sentence, a paragraph, or a whole page or more of text. Surely a paragraph does not have a "standard instance" that remains constant whatever the context in which it appears. If a statute seems to have a kind of "core meaning" that we can apply without a too precise inquiry into its exact purpose, this is because we can see that, however one might formulate the precise objective of the statute, *this* case would still come within it.

Even in situations where our interpretive difficulties seem to head up in a single word, Professor Hart's analysis seems to me to give no real account of what does or should happen. In his illustration of the "vehicle," although he tells us this word has a core of meaning that in all contexts defines unequivocally a range of objects embraced by it, he never tells us what these objects might be. If the rule excluding vehicles from parks seems easy to apply in some cases, I submit this is because we can see clearly enough what the rule "is aiming at in general" so that we know there is no need to worry about the difference between Fords and Cadillacs. If in some cases we seem to be able to apply the rule without asking what its purpose is, this is not because we can treat a directive arrangement as if it had no purpose. It is rather because, for example, whether the rule be intended to preserve quiet in the park, or to save carefree strollers from injury, we know, "without thinking," that a noisy automobile must be excluded.

What would Professor Hart say if some local patriots wanted to mount on a pedestal in the park a truck used in World War II, while other citizens, regarding the proposed memorial as an eyesore, support their stand by the "no vehicle" rule? Does this truck, in perfect working order, fall within the core or the penumbra?

Professor Hart seems to assert that unless words have "standard instances" that remain constant regardless of context, effective communication would break down and it would become impossible to construct a system of "rules which have authority."[37] If in every context words took on a unique meaning, peculiar to that context, the whole process of interpretation would become so uncertain and subjective that the ideal of a rule of law would lose its meaning. In other words, Professor Hart seems to be saying that unless we are prepared to accept his analysis of interpretation, we must surrender all hope of giving an effective meaning to the ideal of fidelity to law. This presents a very dark prospect indeed, if one believes, as I do, that we cannot accept his theory of interpretation. I do not take so gloomy a view of the future of the ideal of fidelity to law.

An illustration will help to test, not only Professor Hart's theory of the core and the penumbra, but its relevance to the ideal of fidelity to law as well. Let us suppose that in leafing through the statutes, we come upon the following enactment: "It shall be a misdemeanor, punishable by a fine of five dollars, to sleep in any railway station." We have no trouble in perceiving the general nature of the target toward which this statute is aimed. Indeed, we are likely at once to call to mind the picture of a disheveled tramp, spread out in an ungainly fashion on one of the benches of the station, keeping weary passengers on their feet and filling their ears with raucous and alcoholic snores. This vision may fairly be said to represent the "obvious instance" contemplated by the statute, though certainly it is far from being the "standard instance" of the physiological state called "sleep."

Now let us see how this example bears on the ideal of fidelity to law. Suppose I am a judge, and that two men are brought before me for violating this statute. The first is a passenger who was waiting at 3 A.M. for a delayed train. When he was arrested he was sitting upright in an orderly fashion, but was heard by the arresting officer to be gently snoring. The second is a man who had brought a blanket and pillow to the station and had obviously settled himself down for the night. He was arrested, however, before he had a chance to go to sleep. Which of these cases presents the "standard instance" of the word "sleep"? If I disregard that question, and decide to fine the second man and set free the first, have I violated a duty of fidelity to law? Have I violated that duty if I interpret the word "sleep" as used in this statute to mean something like "to spread oneself out on a bench or floor to spend the night, or as if to spend the night"?

Testing another aspect of Professor Hart's theory, is it really ever possible to interpret a word in a statute without knowing the aim of the statute? Suppose we encounter the following incomplete sentence: "All improvements must be promptly reported to . . ." Professor Hart's theory seems to assert that even if we have only this fragment before us we can safely construe the word "improvement" to apply to its "standard instance," though we would have to know the rest of the sentence before we could deal intelligently with "problems of the penumbra." Yet surely in the truncated sentence I have quoted, the word "improvement" is almost as devoid of meaning as the symbol "X."

The word "improvement" will immediately take on meaning if we fill out the sentence with the words, "the head nurse," or, "the Town Planning Authority," though the two meanings that come to mind are radically dissimilar. It can hardly be said that these two meanings represent some kind of penumbral accretion to the word's "standard instance." And one wonders, parenthetically, how helpful the theory of the core and the penumbra would be in deciding whether, when the report is to be made to the planning authorities, the word "improvement" includes an unmortgageable monstrosity of a house that lowers the market value of the land on which it is built.

It will be instructive, I think, to consider the effect of other ways of filling out the sentence. Suppose we add to, "All improvements must be promptly reported to . . ." the words, "the Dean of the Graduate Division." Here we no longer seem, as we once did, to be groping in the dark; rather, we seem now to be reaching into an empty box. We achieve a little better orientation if the final clause reads, "to the Principal of the School," and we feel completely at ease if it becomes, "to the Chairman of the Committee on Relations with the Parents of Children in the Primary Division."

It should be noted that in deciding what the word "improvement" means in all these cases, we do not proceed simply by placing the word in some general context, such as hospital practice, town planning, or education. If this were so, the "improvement" in the last instance might just as well be that of the teacher as that of the pupil. Rather, we ask ourselves, What can this rule be for? What evil does it seek to avert? What good is it intended to promote? When it is "the head nurse" who receives the report, we are apt to find ourselves asking, "Is there, perhaps, a shortage of hospital space, so that patients who improve sufficiently are sent home or are assigned to a ward where they will receive less attention?" If "Principal" offers more orientation than "Dean of the Graduate Division," this must be because we know something about the differences between primary education and education on the postgraduate university level. We must have some minimum acquaintance with the ways in which these two educational enterprises are conducted, and with the problems encountered in both of them, before any

distinction between "Principal" and "Dean of the Graduate Division" would affect our interpretation of "improvement." We must, in other words, be sufficiently capable of putting ourselves in the position of those who drafted the rule to know what they thought "ought to be." It is in the light of this "ought" that we must decide what the rule "is."

Turning now to the phenomenon Professor Hart calls "preoccupation with the penumbra," we have to ask ourselves what is actually contributed to the process of interpretation by the common practice of supposing various "borderline" situations. Professor Hart seems to say, "Why, nothing at all, unless we are working with problems of the penumbra." If this is what he means, I find his view a puzzling one, for it still leaves unexplained why, under his theory, if one is dealing with a penumbral problem, it could be useful to think about other penumbral problems.

Throughout his whole discussion of interpretation, Professor Hart seems to assume that it is a kind of cataloguing procedure. A judge faced with a novel situation is like a library clerk who has to decide where to shelve a new book. There are easy cases: the *Bible* belongs under Religion, *The Wealth of Nations* under Economics, etc. Then there are hard cases, when the librarian has to exercise a kind of creative choice, as in deciding whether *Das Kapital* belongs under Politics or Economics, *Gulliver's Travels* under Fantasy or Philosophy. But whether the decision where to shelve is easy or hard, once it is made all the librarian has to do is to put the book away. And so it is with judges, Professor Hart seems to say, in all essential particulars. Surely the judicial process is something more than a cataloguing procedure. The judge does not discharge his responsibility when he pins an apt diagnostic label on the case. He has to do something about it, to treat it, if you will. It is this larger responsibility which explains why interpretative problems almost never turn on a single word, and also why lawyers for generations have found the putting of imaginary borderline cases useful, not only "on the penumbra," but in order to know where the penumbra begins.

These points can be made clear, I believe, by drawing again on our example of the statutory fragment which reads, "All improvements must be promptly reported to...." Whatever the concluding phrase may be, the judge has not solved his problems simply by deciding what kind of improvement is meant. Almost all of the words in the sentence may require interpretation, but most obviously this is so of "promptly" and "reported." What kind of "report" is contemplated: a written note, a call at the office, entry in a hospital record? How specific must it be? Will it be enough to say "a lot better," or "a big house with a bay window"?

Now it should be apparent to any lawyer that in interpreting words like "improvement," "prompt," and "report," no real help is obtained by asking how some extralegal "standard instance" would define these words. But, much more important, when these words are all parts of a single structure of thought, they are in interaction with one another during the process of interpretation. "What is an 'improvement'? Well, it must be something that can be made the subject of a report. So, for purposes of this statute 'improvement' really means 'reportable improvement.' What kind of 'report' must be made? Well, that depends upon the sort of 'improvement' about which information is desired and the reasons for desiring the information."

When we look beyond individual words to the statute as a whole, it becomes apparent how the putting of hypothetical cases assists the interpretative process generally. By pulling our minds first in one direction, then in another, these cases help us to understand the fabric of thought before us. This fabric is something we seek to discern, so that we may know truly what it is, but it is also something that we inevitably help to create as we strive (in accordance with our obligation of fidelity to law) to make the statute a coherent, workable whole.

I should have considered all these remarks much too trite to put down here if they did not seem to be demanded in an answer to the theory of interpretation proposed by Professor Hart, a theory by which he puts such store that he implies we cannot have fidelity to law in any meaningful sense unless we are prepared to accept it. Can it be possible that the positivistic philosophy demands that we abandon a view of

interpretation which sees as its central concern, not words, but purpose and structure? If so, then the stakes in this battle of schools are indeed high.

I am puzzled by the novelty Professor Hart attributes to the lessons I once tried to draw from Wittgenstein's example about teaching a game to children.[38] I was simply trying to show the role reflection plays in deciding what ought to be done. I was trying to make such simple points as that decisions about what ought to be done are improved by reflection, by an exchange of views with others sharing the same problems, and by imagining various situations that might be presented. I was assuming that all of these innocent and familiar measures might serve to sharpen our perception of what we were trying to do, and that the product of the whole process might be, not merely a more apt choice of means for the end sought, but a clarification of the end itself. I had thought that a famous judge of the English bench had something like this in mind when he spoke of the common law as working "itself pure."[39] If this view of the judicial process is no longer entertained in the country of its origin, I can only say that, whatever the vicissitudes of Lord Mansfield's British reputation may be, he will always remain for us in this country a heroic figure of jurisprudence.

I have stressed here the deficiencies of Professor Hart's theory as that theory affects judicial interpretation. I believe, however, that its defects go deeper and result ultimately from a mistaken theory about the meaning of language generally. Professor Hart seems to subscribe to what may be called "the pointer theory of meaning,"[40] a theory which ignores or minimizes the effect on the meaning of words of the speaker's purpose and the structure of language. Characteristically, this school of thought embraces the notion of "common usage." The reason is, of course, that it is only with the aid of this notion that it can seem to attain the inert datum of meaning it seeks, a meaning isolated from the effects of purpose and structure.

It would not do to attempt here an extended excursus into linguistic theory. I shall have to content myself with remarking that the theory of meaning implied in Professor Hart's essay seems to me to have been rejected by three men who stand at the very head of modern developments in logical analysis: Wittgenstein, Russell, and Whitehead. Wittgenstein's posthumous *Philosophical Investigations* constitutes a sort of running commentary on the way words shift and transform their meanings as they move from context to context. Russell repudiates the cult of "common usage," and asks what "instance" of the word "word" itself can be given that does not imply some specific intention in the use of it.[41] Whitehead explains the appeal that "the deceptive identity of the repeated word" has for modern philosophers: only by assuming some linguistic constant (such as the "core of meaning") can validity be claimed for procedures of logic which of necessity move the word from one context to another.[42]

VIII   The Moral and Emotional Foundations of Positivism

If we ignore the specific theories of law associated with the positivistic philosophy, I believe we can say that the dominant tone of positivism is set by a fear of a purposive interpretation of law and legal institutions, or at least by a fear that such an interpretation may be pushed too far. I think one can find confirmatory traces of this fear in all of those classified as "positivists" by Professor Hart, with the outstanding exception of Bentham, who is in all things a case apart and who was worlds removed from anything that could be called *ethical* positivism.

Now the belief that many of us hold, that this fear of purpose takes a morbid turn in positivism, should not mislead us into thinking that the fear is wholly without justification, or that it reflects no significant problem in the organization of society.

Fidelity to law *can* become impossible if we do not accept the broader responsibilities (themselves purposive, as all responsibilities are and must be) that go with a purposive interpretation of law. One can imagine a course of reasoning that might run as follows: This statute says absinthe shall not be sold. What is its purpose? To promote health. Now, as everyone knows, absinthe is a sound, wholesome, and beneficial beverage. Therefore, interpreting the statute in the light of its purpose, I construe it to direct a general sale and consumption of that most healthful of beverages, absinthe.

If the risk of this sort of thing is implicit in a purposive interpretation, what measures can we take to eliminate it, or to reduce it to bearable proportions? One is tempted to say, "Why, just use ordinary common sense." But this would be an evasion, and would amount to saying that although we know the answer, we cannot say what it is. To give a better answer, I fear I shall have to depart from those high standards of clarity Professor Hart so rightly prizes and so generally exemplifies. I shall have to say that the answer lies in the concept of *structure*. A statute or a rule of common law has, either explicitly, or by virtue of its relation with other rules, something that may be called a structural integrity. This is what we have in mind when we speak of "the intent of the statute," though we know it is men who have intentions and not words on paper. Within the limits of that structure, fidelity to law not only permits but demands a creative role from the judge, but beyond that structure it does not permit him to go. Of course, the structure of which I speak presents its own "problems of the penumbra." But the penumbra in this case surrounds something real, something that has a meaning and integrity of its own. It is not a purposeless collocation of words that gets its meaning on loan from lay usage.

It is one of the great virtues of Professor Hart's essay that it makes explicit positivism's concern for the ideal of fidelity to law. Yet I believe, though I cannot prove, that the basic reason why positivism fears a purposive interpretation is not that it may lead to anarchy, but that it may push us too far in the opposite direction. It sees in a purposive interpretation, carried too far, a threat to human freedom and human dignity.

Let me illustrate what I mean by supposing that I am a man without religious beliefs living in a community of ardent Protestant Christian faith. A statute in this community makes it unlawful for me to play golf on Sunday. I find this statute an annoyance and accept its restraints reluctantly. But the annoyance I feel is not greatly different from that I might experience if, though it were lawful to play on Sunday, a power failure prevented me from taking the streetcar I would normally use in reaching the course. In the vernacular, "it is just one of those things."

What a different complexion the whole matter assumes if a statute compels me to attend church, or, worse still, to kneel and recite prayers! Here I may feel a direct affront to my integrity as a human being. Yet the purpose of both statutes may well be to increase church attendance. The difference may even seem to be that the first statute seeks its end slyly and by indirection, the second, honestly and openly. Yet surely this is a case in which indirection has its virtues and honesty its heavy price in human dignity.

Now I believe that positivism fears that a too explicit and uninhibited interpretation in terms of purpose may well push the first kind of statute in the direction of the second. If this is a basic concern underlying the positivistic philosophy, that philosophy is dealing with a real problem, however inept its response to the problem may seem to be. For this problem of the impressed purpose is a crucial one in our society. One thinks of the obligation to bargain "in good faith" imposed by the National Labor Relations Act.[43] One recalls the remark that to punish a criminal is less of an affront to his dignity than to reform and improve him. The statutory preamble comes to mind: the increasing use made of it, its legislative wisdom, the significance that should be accorded to it in judicial interpretation. The flag salute cases[44] will, of course, occur to everyone. I myself recall the splendid analysis by Professor von Hippel of the things that were fundamentally wrong about Nazism, and his conclusion that the grossest of all Nazi perversities was that of coercing acts, like the putting out of flags and saying, "Heil Hitler!" that have meaning only when done voluntarily, or, more accurately, have a meaning when coerced that is wholly parasitic on an association of them with past voluntary expressions.[45]

Questions of this sort are undoubtedly becoming more acute as the state assumes a more active role with respect to economic activity. No significant economic activity can be organized

exclusively by "don'ts." By its nature economic production requires a co-operative effort. In the economic field there is special reason, therefore, to fear that "This you may not do" will be transformed into "This you must do – but willingly." As we all know, the most tempting opportunity for effecting this transformation is presented by what is called in administrative practice "the prehearing conference," in which the negative threat of a statute's sanctions may be used by its administrators to induce what they regard, in all good conscience, as "the proper attitude."

I look forward to the day when legal philosophy can address itself earnestly to issues of this sort, and not simply exploit them to score points in favor of a position already taken. Professor Hart's essay seems to me to open the way for such a discussion, for it eliminates from the positivistic philosophy a pretense that has hitherto obscured every issue touched by it. I mean, of course, the pretense of the ethical neutrality of positivism. That is why I can say in all sincerity that, despite my almost paragraph-by-paragraph disagreement with the views expressed in his essay, I believe Professor Hart has made an enduring contribution to legal philosophy.

Notes

1 Kelsen, *Die Idee des Naturrechtes*, 7 ZEITSCHRIFT FÜR ÖFFENTLICHES RECHT 221, 248 (AUSTRIA 1927).

2 Hart, *Positivism and the Separation of Law and Morals*, 71 HARV. L. REV. 593, 615–21 (1958).

3 U.S. CONST, art. V.

4 Hart, *supra* note 2, at 624.

5 For an outstanding example, see G. Scammell and Nephew, Ltd. v. Ouston, [1941] A.C. 251 (1940). I personally would be inclined to put under the same head Victoria Laundry, Ltd. v. Newman Industries, Ltd., [1949] 2 K.B. 528 (C.A.).

6 See Hart, *supra* note 2, at 608–12.

7 See N.Y. Times, Nov. 8, 1949, p. 1. col. 4 (late city ed.) (report of a speech made on November 7, 1949 to the Central Committee of the Union of Catholic Italian Lawyers).

8 Hart, *supra* note 2, at 603.

9 *Ibid*.

10 AUSTIN, LECTURES ON JURISPRUDENCE 167–341 (5th ed. 1885).

11 KELSEN, GENERAL THEORY OF LAW AND STATE 401 (3d ed. 1949).

12 *E.g.*, Friedmann, *The Planned State and the Rule of Law*, 22 AUSTR. L. J. 162, 207 (1948).

13 LOWIE, THE ORIGIN OF THE STATE 113 (1927).

14 Hart, *supra* note 2, at 623–24.

15 Southern Pac. Co. v. Jensen, 244 U.S. 205, 221 (1917) (Holmes, J., dissenting), paraphrasing Storti v. Commonwealth, 178 Mass. 549, 554, 60 N.E. 210, 211 (1901) (Holmes, C. J.), in which it was held that a statute providing for electrocution as a means of inflicting the punishment of death was not cruel or unusual punishment within the Massachusetts Declaration of Rights, MASS. CONST. pt. First, art. XXVI, simply because it accomplished its object by molecular, rather than molar, motions.

16 See Hart, *supra* note 2, at 619–20.

17 N.Y. Times, July 4, 1934, p. 3, col. 3 (late city ed.).

18 See N.Y. Times, July 14, 1934, p. 5, col. 2 (late city ed.).

19 Radbruch, *Die Erneuerung des Rechts*, 2 DIE WANDLUNG 8, 9 (Germany 1947). A useful discussion of the Nazi practice with reference to the publicity given laws will be found in Giese, *Verkündung und Gesetzeskraft*, 76 ARCHIV DES ÖFFENTLICHEN RECHTS 464, 471–72 (Germany 1951). I rely on this article for the remarks that follow in the text.

20 Judgment of July 27, 1949, Oberlandesgericht, Bamberg, 5 SÜDDEUTSCHE JURISTEN-ZEITUNG 207 (Germany 1950), 64 HARV. L. REV. 1005 (1951).

21 The passage translated is § 5 of a statute creating a Kriegssonderstrafrecht. Law of Aug. 17, 1938, [1939] 2 REICHSGESETZBLATT pt. 1, at 1456. The translation is mine.

22 See 5 SÜDDEUTSCHE JURISTEN-ZEITUNG 207, 210 (Germany 1950).

23 The translated passage is article II of A Law Against Malicious Attacks on the State and the Party and for the Protection of the Party Uniform, Law of Dec. 20, 1934, [1934] I REICHSGESETZBLATT 1269. The translation is mine.

24 See Radbruch, *Die Erneuerung des Rechts*, 2 DIE WANDLUNG 8, 10 (Germany 1947).

25 Radbruch, *Gesetzliches Unrecht und Übergesetzliches Recht*, I SÜDDEUTSCHE JURISTEN-ZEITUNG 105, 107 (Germany 1946) (reprinted in RADBRUCH, RECHTSPHILOSOPHIE 347, 354 (4th ed. 1950)). The translation is mine.

26 See, *e.g.*, Howe, *The Positivism of Mr. Justice Holmes*, 64 HARV. L. REV. 529 (1951).

27 See I PERRY, THE THOUGHT AND CHARACTER OF WILLIAM JAMES 297 (1935) (quoting a letter written by William James in 1869).

28 Hart, *supra* note 2, at 617–18.

29 *Id.* at 618.

30 *Id.* at 619.

31 I AUSTIN, LECTURES ON JURISPRUDENCE 173 (5th ed. 1885) (Lecture V).

32 GRAY, THE NATURE AND SOURCES OF THE LAW 96 (2d ed. 1921).

33 I BERGBOHM, JURISPRUDENZ UND RECHTSPHILOSOPHIE 355–552 (1892).

34 See, *e.g.*, Heller, *Die Krisis der Staatslehre*, 55 ARCHIV FÜR SOZIALWISSENSCHAFT UND SOZIALPOLITIK 289, 309 (Germany 1926).

35 Voegelin, *Kelsen's Pure Theory of Law*, 42 POL. SCI. Q. 268, 269 (1927).

36 Hart, *supra* note 2, at 606–08.

37 See *id.* at 607.

38 Fuller, *Human Purpose and Natural Law*, 53 J. PHILOS, 607, 700 (1956).

39 Omychund v. Barker, I Atk. 21, 33, 26 Eng. Rep. 15, 22–23 (Ch. 1744) (argument of Solicitor-General Murray, later Lord Mansfield):

> All occasions do not arise at once; . . . a statute very seldom can take in all cases, therefore the common law, *that works itself pure* by rules drawn from the fountain of justice, is for this reason superior to an act of parliament.

40 I am speaking of the linguistic theory that seems to be implied in the essay under discussion here. In Professor Hart's brilliant inaugural address, *Definition and Theory in Jurisprudence*, 70 L.Q. REV. 37 (1954), the most important point made is that terms like "rule," "right," and "legal person" cannot be defined by pointing to correspondent things or actions in the external world, but can only be understood in terms of the function performed by them in the larger system, just as one cannot understand the umpire's ruling, "Y're out!" without having at least a general familiarity with the rules of baseball. Even in the analysis presented in the inaugural address, however, Professor Hart seems to think that the dependence of meaning on function and context is a peculiarity of formal and explicit systems, like those of a game or a legal system. He seems not to recognize that what he has to say about explicit systems is also true of the countless informal and overlapping systems that run through language as a whole. These implicit systematic or structural elements in lan-

guage often enable us to understand at once the meaning of a word used in a wholly novel sense, as in the statement, "Experts regard the English Channel as the most difficult swim in the world." In the essay now being discussed, Professor Hart seems nowhere to recognize that a rule or statute has a structural or systematic quality that reflects itself in some measure into the meaning of every principal term in it.

41 Russell, *The Cult of "Common Usage,"* in Portraits From Memory and Other Essays 166, 170–71 (1956).

42 Whitehead, *Analysis of Meaning*, in Essays in Science and Philosophy 122.

43 § 8(d), added by 61 Stat. 142 (1947), 29 U.S.C. § 158(d) (1952); see NLRA §§ 8(a) (5), (b) (3), as amended, 61 Stat. 141 (1947), 29 U.S.C. §§ 158(a) (5), (b) (3) (1952).

44 Minersville School Dist. v. Gobitis, 310 U.S. 586 (1940), *overruled*, West Virginia State Bd. of Educ. v. Barnette, 319 U.S. 624 (1943).

45 Von Hippel, Die Nationalsozialistische Herrschaftsordnung als Warnung und Lehre 6–7 (1946).

6

Negative and Positive Positivism

Jules L. Coleman

Every theory about the nature or essence of law purports to provide a standard, usually in the form of a statement of necessary and sufficient conditions, for determining which of a community's norms constitute its law. For example, the naive version of legal realism maintains that the law of a community is constituted by the official pronouncements of judges. For the early positivists like Austin, law consists in the commands of a sovereign, properly so-called. For substantive natural law theory, in every conceivable legal system, being a true principle of morality is a necessary condition of legality for at least some norms. Legal positivism of the sort associated with H. L. A. Hart maintains that, in every community where law exists, there exists a standard that determines which of the community's norms are legal ones. Following Hart, this standard is usually referred to as a rule of recognition. If all that positivism meant by a rule of recognition were "the standard in every community by which a community's legal norms were made determinate," every theory of law would be reducible to one or another version of positivism. Which form of positivism each would take would depend on the particular substantive conditions of legality that each theory set out. Legal positivism would be true analytically, since it would be impossible to conceive of a theory of law that did not satisfy the minimal conditions for a rule of recognition. Unfortunately, the sort of truth legal positivism would then reveal would be an uninteresting one.

In order to distinguish a rule of recognition in the positivist sense from other statements of the conditions of legality, and therefore to distinguish positivism from alternative jurisprudential theses, additional constraints must be placed on the rule of recognition. Candidates for these constraints fall into two categories: restrictions on the conditions of legality set out in a rule of recognition; and constraints on the possible sources of authority (or normativity) of the rule of recognition.

An example of the first sort of constraint is expressed by the requirement that in every community the conditions of legality must be ones of pedigree or form, not substance or content. Accordingly, for a rule specifying the conditions of legality in any society to constitute a rule of recognition in the positivist sense, legal normativity under it must be determined, for example, by a norm's being enacted in the requisite fashion by a proper authority.

The claim that the authority of the rule of recognition is a matter of its acceptance by officials, rather than its truth as a normative principle, and the related claim that judicial duty under a rule of recognition is one of conventional practice rather than critical morality, express constraints of the second sort.

Ronald Dworkin expresses this second constraint as the claim that a rule of recognition in the positivist sense must be a social, rather than a normative, rule. A social rule is one whose authority is a matter of convention; the nature and scope of the duty it imposes is specified or constituted by an existing, convergent social practice. In contrast, a normative rule may impose an obligation or confer a right in the absence of the relevant practice or in the face of a contrary one. If a normative rule imposes an obligation, it does so because it is a correct principle of morality, not, *ex hypothesi*, because it corresponds to an accepted practice.

Dworkin, for one, conceives of the rule of recognition as subject to constraints of both sorts. His view is that only pedigree standards of legality can constitute rules of recognition, and that a rule of recognition must be a social rule.[1] Is legal positivism committed to either or both of these constraints on the rule of recognition?

I Negative Positivism

Candidates for constraints on the rule of recognition are motivated by the need to distinguish legal positivism from other jurisprudential theses: in particular, natural law theory. Positivism denies what natural law theory asserts: namely, a necessary connection between law and morality. I refer to the denial of a necessary or constitutive relationship between law and morality as the separability thesis. One way of asking whether positivism is committed to any particular kind of constraint on the rule of recognition is simply to ask whether any constraints on the rule are required by commitment to the separability thesis.

To answer this question we have to make some preliminary remarks concerning how we are to understand both the rule of recognition and the separability thesis. The notion of a rule of recognition is ambiguous; it has both an epistemic and a semantic sense. In one sense, the rule of recognition is a standard which one can use to identify, validate, or discover a community's law. In another sense, the rule of recognition specifies the conditions a norm must satisfy to constitute part of a community's law. The same rule may or may not be a rule of recognition in both senses, since the rule one employs to determine the law need not be the same rule as the one that makes law determin-

ate. This ambiguity between the epistemic and semantic interpretations of the rule of recognition pervades the literature and is responsible for a good deal of confusion about the essential claims of legal positivism. In my view, legal positivism is committed to the rule of recognition in the semantic sense at least; whether it is committed to the rule of recognition as a standard for identifying law (epistemic sense) is a question to which we shall return later.[2]

In the language that is fashionable in formal semantics, to say that the rule of recognition is a semantic rule is to say that it specifies the truth conditions for singular propositions of law of the form, "it is the law in *C* that *P*," where *C* is a particular community and *P* a putative statement of law. The question whether the separability thesis imposes substantive constraints on the rule of recognition is just the question whether the separability thesis restricts the conditions of legality for norms or the truth conditions for propositions of law.

The separability thesis is the claim that there exists at least one conceivable rule of recognition (and therefore one possible legal system) that does not specify truth as a moral principle among the truth conditions for any proposition of law.[3] Consequently, a particular rule of recognition may specify truth as a moral principle as a truth condition for some or all propositions of law without violating the separability thesis, since it does not follow from the fact that, in one community in order to be law a norm must be a principle of morality, being a true principle of morality is a necessary condition of legality in all possible legal systems.

It is tempting to confuse the separability thesis with the very different claim that the law of a community is one thing and its morality another. This last claim is seriously ambiguous. In one sense, the claim that the law of a community is one thing and its morality another may amount to the very strong assertion that there exists no convergence between the norms that constitute a community's law and those that constitute its morality. Put this way, the thesis is an empirical one whose inadequacies are demonstrated by the shared legal and moral prohibitions against murder, theft, battery, and the like.

Instead, the claim may be that one can identify or discover a community's law without having recourse to discovering its morality. This is an epistemic claim about how, in a particular community, one might go about learning the law. It may well be that in some communities – even those in which every legal norm is a moral principle as well – one can learn which norms are law without regard to their status as principles of morality. Whether in every community this is the case depends on the available sources of legal knowledge, not on the existence of a conceptual relationship, if any, between law and morality.

A third interpretation of the thesis that a community's law is one thing and its morality another, the one Dworkin is anxious to ascribe to positivism, is that being a moral principle is not a truth condition for any proposition of law (in any community). Put this way the claim would be false, just in case "it is the law in *C* that *P*" (for any community, *C*, and any proposition of law, *P*) were true only if *P* stated a (true) principle of morality. Were the separability thesis understood this way, it would require particular substantive constraints on each rule of recognition, that is, no rule of recognition could specify truth as a moral principle among its conditions of legality. Were legal positivism committed to both the rule of recognition and to this interpretation of the claim that the law and morality of a community are distinct, Dworkin's arguments in Model of Rules I (MOR-I) would suffice to put it to rest.

However, were the claim that the law of a community is one thing and its morality another understood, not as the claim that in every community law and morality are distinct, but as the assertion that they are conceptually distinguishable, it would be reducible to the separability thesis, for it would assert no more than the denial of a constitutive relationship between law and morality.

In sum, "the law of a community is one thing and its morality another," makes either a false factual claim, an epistemic claim about the sources of legal knowledge, or else it is reducible to the separability thesis. In no case does it warrant substantive constraints on particular rules of recognition.

Properly understood and adequately distinguished from the claim that the law and morality of a community are distinct, the separability thesis does not warrant substantive constraints on any particular rule of recognition. It does not follow, however, that the separability thesis imposes no constraints at all on any rule of recognition. The separability thesis commits positivism to the proposition that there exists at least one conceivable legal system in which the rule of recognition does not specify being a principle of morality among the truth conditions for any proposition of law. Positivism is true, then, just in case we can imagine a legal system in which being a principle of morality is not a condition of legality for any norm: that is, just as long as the idea of a legal system in which moral truth is not a necessary condition of legal validity is not self-contradictory.

The form of positivism generated by commitment to the rule of recognition as constrained by the separability thesis I call negative positivism to draw attention both to the character and the weakness of the claim it makes.[4] Because negative positivism is essentially a negative thesis, it cannot be undermined by counterexamples, any one of which will show only that, in some community or other, morality is a condition of legality at least for some norms.

II   Positive Positivism: Law as Hard Facts

In MOR-I, Dworkin persuasively argues that in some communities moral principles have the force of law, though what makes them law is their truth or their acceptance as appropriate to the resolution of controversial disputes rather than their having been enacted in the appropriate way by the relevant authorities. These arguments would suffice to undermine positivism were it committed to the claim that truth as a moral principle could never constitute a truth condition for a proposition of law under any rule of recognition. The arguments are inadequate to undermine the separability thesis, which makes no claim about the truth conditions of any particular proposition of law in any particular community. The arguments in MOR-I, therefore, are inadequate to undermine negative positivism.

However, Dworkin's target in MOR-I is not really negative positivism; it is that version of positivism one would get by conjoining the rule of recognition with the requirement that the truth conditions for any proposition of law could not include reference to the morality of a norm. Moreover, in fairness to Dworkin, one has to evaluate his arguments in a broader context. In MOR-I Dworkin is anxious to demonstrate, not only the inadequacy of the separability thesis, but that of other essential tenets of positivism – or at least what Dworkin takes to be essential features of positivism – as well.

The fact that moral principles have the force of law, because they are appropriate, true, or accepted even though they are not formally enacted, establishes for Dworkin that: (1) the positivist's conception of law as rules must be abandoned; as must (2) the claim that judges exercise discretion – the authority to extend beyond the law to appeal to moral principles – to resolve controversial cases; and (3) the view that the law of every community can be identified by use of a noncontroversial or pedigree test of legality.

The first claim of positivism must be abandoned because principles, as well as rules, constitute legal norms; the second because, while positivists conceive of judges as exercising discretion by appealing to moral principles, Dworkin rightly characterizes them as appealing to moral principles, which, though they are not rules, nevertheless may be binding legal standards. The third tenet of positivism must be abandoned because the rule of recognition in Dworkin's view must be one of pedigree, that is, it cannot make reference to the content or truth of a norm as a condition of its legality; and any legal system that includes moral principles among its legal standards cannot have as its standard of authority a pedigree criterion.[5]

The question, of course, is whether positivism is committed to either judicial discretion, the model of rules, or to a pedigree or uncontroversial standard of legality. We know at least that it is committed to the separability thesis from which only negative positivism appears to follow. Negative positivism is committed to none of these claims. Is there another form of positivism that is so committed?

Much of the debate between the positivists and Dworkin appears rather foolish, unless there is a version of positivism that makes Dworkin's criticisms, if not compelling, at least relevant. That version of positivism, whatever it is, cannot be motivated by the separability thesis alone. The question then is whether anything other than its denial of the central tenet of natural law theory motivates positivism?

One easy, but ultimately unsatisfying, response is to maintain that Dworkin's objections are to Hart's version of positivism. While this is no doubt true, such a remark gives no indication of what it is in Hart's version of positivism that is essential to positivism generally. Dworkin, after all, takes his criticisms of Hart to be criticisms of positivism generally, and the question remains whether positivism is committed to the essentials of Hart's version of it.

A more promising line of argument is the following. No doubt positivism is committed to the separability thesis. Still, one can ask whether commitment to the separability thesis is basic or derivative from some other, perhaps programmatic, commitments of legal positivism. That is, one can look at the separability thesis in isolation or as a component, perhaps even a derivative element, of a network of commitments of legal positivism.[6] We are led to negative positivism when we pursue the former route. Perhaps there is a more interesting form of positivism in the cards if we pursue the latter.

Certainly one reason some positivists have insisted upon the distinction between law and morality is the following: While both law and morality provide standards by which the affairs of people are to be regulated, morality is inherently controversial. People disagree about what morality prescribes, and uncertainty exists concerning the limits of permissible conduct and the nature and scope of one's moral obligations to others. In contrast, for these positivists at least, law is apparently concrete and uncontroversial. Moreover, when a dispute arises over whether or not something is law, there exists a decision procedure that, in the bulk of cases, settles the issue. Law is knowable and ascertainable; so that, while a person may not know the range of his moral obligations, he is aware of (or can find out) what the law expects of him. Commitment to the traditional legal values associated with the rule of law requires that law consist in knowable, largely uncontroversial fact; and it is this feature of law that positivism draws attention to and which underlies it.

One can reach the same characterization of law as consisting in uncontroversial, hard facts by ascribing to legal positivism the epistemological and semantic constraints of logical positivism on legal facts. For the logical positivists, moral judgments were meaningless because they could not be verified by a reliable and essentially uncontroversial test. In order for statements of law to be meaningful, they must be verifiable by such a test (the epistemic conception of the rule of recognition). To be meaningful, therefore, law cannot be essentially controversial.

Once positivism is characterized as the view of law as consisting in hard facts, Dworkin's ascription of certain basic tenets to it is plausible, and his objections to them are compelling. First, law for positivism consists in rules rather than principles, because the legality of a rule depends on its formal characteristics – the manner and form of its enactment – whereas the legality of a moral principle will depend on its content. The legality of rules, therefore, will be essentially uncontroversial; the legal normativity of principles will be essentially controversial. Second, adjudication takes place in both hard and simple cases. Paradigm or simple cases are uncontroversial. The answer to them as a matter of law is clear, and the judge is obligated to provide it. Cases falling within the penumbra of a general rule, however, are uncertain. There is no uncontroversial answer as a matter of law to them, and judges must go beyond the law to exercise their discretion in order to resolve them. Controversy implies the absence of legal duty and, to the extent to which legal rules have controversial instances, positivism is committed to a theory of discretion in the resolution of disputes involving them. Third, positivism must be committed to a rule of recognition in both the epistemic and the semantic

senses, for the rule of recognition not only sets out the conditions of legality, it provides the mechanism by which one settles disputes about what, on a particular matter, the law is. The rule of recognition for the positivist is the principle by which particular propositions of law are verified. Relatedly, the conditions of legality set forth in the rule of recognition must be ones of pedigree or form, otherwise the norm will fail to provide a reliable principle for verifying and adjudicating competing claims about the law. Finally, law and morality are distinct (the separability thesis) because law consists in hard facts, while morality does not.

Unfortunately for positivism, if the distinction between law and morality is motivated by commitment to law as uncontroversial, hard facts, it must be abandoned because, as Dworkin rightly argues, law is controversial, and even where it is, law may involve matters of obligation and right rather than discretion.

There is no more plausible way of understanding Dworkin's conception of positivism and of rendering his arguments against it (at least those in MOR-I) persuasive. The result is a form of positive positivism that makes an interesting claim about the essence of law – that by and large law consists in hard, concrete facts – a claim that Dworkin neatly shows is mistaken. The entire line of argument rests, however, on ascribing to legal positivism either a programmatic or metaphysical thesis about law. It is the thesis of law as hard facts – whether motivated by semantic, epistemic, or normative arguments – that explains not only positivism's commitment to the separability thesis, but its adherence to other claims about law, that is, discretion, the model of rules, and the noncontentful standard of legality.

The argument for law as hard facts that relies on the positivist program of knowable, ascertainable law is straightforwardly problematic. Legal positivism makes a conceptual or analytic claim about law, and that claim should not be confused with programmatic or normative interests certain positivists, especially Bentham, might have had. Ironically, to hold otherwise is to build into the conceptual account of law a particular normative theory of law; it is to infuse morality, or the way law ought to be, into the concept of law (or the account of the way law is). In other words, the argument for ascribing certain tenets to positivism in virtue of the positivist's normative ideal of law is to commit the very mistake positivism is so intent on drawing attention to and rectifying.

The argument for law as hard facts that relies, not on the programmatic interests of some positivists, but on the semantics and epistemology of logical positivism is both more plausible and interesting. Hart's characterization of his inquiry as an analysis both of the concept of law and of how one determines if a norm constitutes valid law as if these were one and the same thing suggests a conflation of semantic and epistemic inquiries of the sort one associates with logical positivism. Recall, in this regard, Hart's discussion of the move from the "prelegal" to the "legal." The move from the prelegal to the legal is accomplished by the addition of secondary rules to the set of primary social rules of obligation: in particular, by the addition of a rule of recognition that solves the problem of uncertainty, that is, the epistemic problem of determining which norms are law. Moreover Hart's discussion of judicial discretion – that is, the absence of legal duty – as arising whenever the application of a general term in a rule of law is controversial further suggests the identification, for Hart at least, of law with fact ascertainable by the use of a reliable method of verification. Still, in order to justify the ascription to positivism of the view that law consists in hard facts, we need an argument to the effect that part of what it means to be a legal positivist is to be committed to some form of verificationism.

The problem with any such argument is that the separability thesis can stand on its own as a fundamental tenet of positivism without further motivation. After all, verificationism may be wrong and the separability thesis right; without fear of contradiction one can assert both a (metaphysical) realist position about legal facts and the separability thesis. (As an aside, this fact alone should suffice to warrant caution in ascribing logical positivism to legal positivism on the grounds that they are both forms of positivism; otherwise one might be tempted to ascribe metaphysical or scientific realism to legal realism on similar grounds, which, to say the least, would be preposterous.)[7] In short, one alleging to be a positivist can abandon the metaphysics of verificationism, hang on to the separability thesis, and advance the rather plausible position that the motive for the separability thesis – if indeed there is one – is simply that the distinction it insists on between law and morality is a valid one; and, just in case that is not enough, the positivist can point out that there is a school of jurisprudence that denies the existence of the distinction. In effect, the positivist can retreat to negative positivism and justify his doing so by pointing out that the separability thesis needs no further motivation, certainly none that winds up committing the advocate of a sound jurisprudential thesis to a series of dubious metaphysical ones.

While I am sympathetic to this response, it is not going to satisfy Dworkin. There is something unsatisfactory about a theory of law that does not make an affirmative claim about law. Indeed, one might propose as an adequacy condition that any theory of law must have a point about law. Negative positivism fails to satisfy this adequacy condition. Natural law theory satisfies this adequacy condition by asserting that in every conceivable legal system moral truth is a necessary condition of legality – at least for some norms. Since it consists in the denial of this claim, negative positivism makes no assertion about what is true of law in every conceivable legal system. The view Dworkin rightly ascribes to Hart, but wrongly to positivism generally, that the point of positivism is that law consists in hard facts, meets the adequacy condition and makes the kind of claim, mistaken though it may be, that one can sink one's teeth into.

I want to offer an alternative version of positivism, which, like the "law-as-hard-facts" conception, is a form of positive positivism. The form of positive positivism I want to characterize and defend has, as its point, not that law is largely uncontroversial – it need not be – but that law is ultimately conventional: That the authority of law is a matter of its acceptance by officials.

III Positive Positivism: Law as Social Convention

It is well known that one can meet the objections to positivism Dworkin advances in MOR-I by constructing a rule of recognition (in the semantic sense) that permits moral principles as well as rules to be binding legal standards.[8] Briefly the argument is this: Even if some moral principles are legally binding, not every moral principle is a legal one. Therefore, a test must exist for distinguishing moral principles that are legally binding from those that are not. The characteristic of legally binding moral principles that distinguishes them from nonbinding moral principles can be captured in a clause in the relevant rule of recognition. In other words, a rule is a legal rule if it possesses characteristic C; and a moral principle is a legal principle if it possesses characteristic C_1. The rule of recognition then states that a norm is a legal one if and only if it possesses either C or C_1. Once this rule of recognition is formulated, everything Dworkin ascribes to positivism, other than the model of rules, survives. The (semantic) rule of recognition survives, since whether a norm is a legal one does not depend on whether it is a rule or a principle, but on whether it satisfies the conditions of legality set forth in a rule of recognition. The separability thesis survives just so long as not every conceivable legal system has in its rule of recognition a C_1 clause; that is, a clause that sets out conditions of legality for some moral principles, or if it has such a clause, there exists at least one conceivable legal system in which no principle satisfies that clause. Finally, one argument for judicial discretion – the one that relies not on controversy but on the exhaustibility of legal standards – survives. That is, only a determinate number of standards possess either C or C_1, so that a case may arise in which no legal standard under the rule of recognition is suitable or adequate to its resolution. In such cases, judges must appeal to nonlegal standards to resolve disputes.[9]

Given Dworkin's view of positivism as law consisting in hard facts, he might simply object to this line of defense by noting that the "rule of recognition" formed by the conjunction of the conditions of legality for both principles and rules could not be a rule of recognition in the positivist's sense because its reference to morality would make it inherently controversial. Put another way, a controversial rule of recognition could not be a rule of recognition in the epistemic sense; it could not provide a reliable verification principle. For that reason, it could not be a rule of recognition in the positivist sense. Interestingly, that is not quite the argument Dworkin advances. To be sure, he argues that a rule of recognition of this sort could not constitute a rule of recognition in the positivist's sense. Moreover, he argues that such a rule would be inherently controversial. But the argument does not end with the allegation that such a rule would be controversial. The controversial character of the rule is important for Dworkin, not because it is incompatible with law as hard fact or because a controversial rule cannot be a reliable verification principle, but because a controversial rule of recognition cannot be a social rule. A controversial rule of recognition cannot be a conventional one, or one whose authority depends on its acceptance.

At the outset of the essay I distinguished between two kinds of constraints that might be imposed on the rule of recognition: those having to do with substantive conditions of legality and those having to do with the authority of the rule of recognition itself. The difference between Dworkin's arguments against positivism in MOR-I and MOR-II is that, in the former essay, the version of positivism he objects to is constrained in the first way – legality must be determined by a non-contentful (or pedigree) test – whereas the version of positivism he objects to in MOR-II is constrained in the second way – the rule-of-recognition's authority must be a matter of convention.

Against the law-as-convention version of positivism, Dworkin actually advances four related arguments, none of which, I want to argue, is ultimately convincing. These are what I will refer to as: (1) the social rule argument; (2) the pedigree argument; (3) the controversy argument; and (4) the moral argument.[10]

A. *The Social Rule Argument*

Legal obligations are imposed by valid legal norms. A rule or principle is a valid one provided it satisfies the conditions of legality set forth in the rule of recognition. The question Dworkin raises in MOR-II concerns the nature of duties under rule of recognition itself. Does the rule of recognition impose duties on judges because they accept it or because the rule is defensible within a more comprehensive moral theory of law? For Dworkin this is the question of whether the rule of recognition is a social or a normative rule.

Dworkin's first argument in MOR-II against law-as-convention positivism is that the social rule theory provides an inadequate general theory of duty. The argument is this: According to the social rule theory an individual has an obligation to act in a particular way only if (1) there is a general practice of acting in that way; and (2) the rule that is constructed or built up from the practice is accepted from an internal point of view. To accept a rule from an internal point of view is to use it normatively as providing reasons both for acting in accordance with it and for criticizing departures from it. But, as Dworkin rightly notes, there may be duties even where no social practice exists, or where a contrary practice prevails. This is just another way of saying that not every duty is one of conventional morality.

If the positivist's thesis is that the social rule theory provides an adequate account of the source of all noninstitutional duties or of the meaning of all claims about such duties, it is surely mistaken. Not all duties imposed by rules are imposed by conventional rules. Fortunately, the law-as-convention version of positivism makes no such claim. The question is not whether the social rule theory is adequate to account for duties generally; it is whether the theory accounts for the duty of judges under a rule of recognition. An inadequate general theory of obligation may be an adequate theory of judicial duty. Were one to take the social rule argument seriously, it would amount to the odd claim that the rule of recognition cannot be a social rule and, therefore, that obligations under

it could not be ones of conventional morality, simply because not every duty-imposing rule is a social rule.

B. *The Pedigree Argument*

The first serious argument Dworkin makes against the social rule theory of judicial obligation relies, in part, on the arguments in MOR-I. In meeting the objection to MOR-I, I constructed a rule of recognition that set out distinct conditions of legality for both rules (C) and moral principles (C_1). Let us abbreviate this rule as "C and C_1." Dworkin's claim is that such a rule cannot be a social rule.

The argument is this: The truth conditions in "$C + C_1$" make reference to moral principles as well as to legal rules. Unlike legal rules, moral principles cannot be identified by their pedigree. Because to determine which of a community's moral principles are legal ones will rely on the content of the principles, it will be a matter of some controversy. But if there is substantial controversy, then there cannot be convergence of behavior sufficient to specify a social rule. The social rule theory requires convergence of behavior, that is, a social practice. A nonpedigree standard implies controversy; controversy implies the absence of a social practice; the absence of the requisite social practice means that the rule cannot be a social rule. A rule of recognition that made reference to morality – the kind of rule of recognition we constructed to overcome Dworkin's objections in MOR-I – could not be a social rule and, therefore, could not be a rule of recognition in the positivist's sense.

The argument moves too quickly. Not every reference that a rule of recognition might make to morality would be inherently controversial. It does not follow from the fact that $C + C_1$ refers to moral principles that this rule cannot determine legality in virtue of some noncontent characteristic of moral principles. For example, C_1 could be an "entrenchment" requirement of the sort Rolf Sartorius has proposed, so that whether a moral principle is a legal principle will depend on whether it is mentioned in preambles to legislation and in other authoritative documents: The more mentions, the more weight the principle receives.[11] Or C_1 could state that a moral principle is a legal principle only if it is widely shared by members of the community. In short, the legality of a moral principle could be determined by some of its noncontentful characteristics. In such cases, to determine which moral principles are legally binding would be no more troublesome or controversial than to determine which rules are legal ones.

Though not every reference to morality will render a rule of recognition controversial, some ways of identifying which of a community's moral principles are law will. Suppose C_1 makes moral truth a condition of legality, so that a moral principle could not be part of a community's law unless it were true. Whereas its entrenchment is not a controversial characteristic of a moral principle, its truth is. Any rule of recognition that made moral truth a condition of legality would be controversial. A controversial rule of recognition results in divergence of behavior sufficient to undermine its claim to being a social rule. If a rule of recognition is not a social rule, it cannot be a rule of recognition in the positivist's sense.

Not every possible rule of recognition, therefore, would be a social rule. For example, "the law is whatever is morally right" could never be a rule of recognition in the positivist's sense. Because positivism of the sort I want to defend holds that law is everywhere conventional – that (in the language of this discussion) the rule of recognition in every community is a social rule – it must be mistaken.

C. *The Controversy Argument*

Dworkin's view is that the rule of recognition in any jurisdiction is either a social rule or a normative rule; it imposes a duty, in other words, either because it is accepted or because it is true. Law-as-convention positivism is the view that, in every community, the rule of recognition is a social rule. At this level, negative positivism is the view that, in at least one conceivable community, the rule of recognition is a social rule. Natural law theory would then be the view that, in every conceivable legal system, the rule of recognition is a normative rule. Dworkin's claim is that the rule of recognition is a normative rule, and therein lies the justification for placing him within the natural law tradition.

The argument in the previous section is compatible with some rules of recognition being normative rules and others being social rules. For example, a rule of recognition that made no reference to morality or, if it did, referred only to noncontentful features of moral principles, might, for all that the previous argument shows, still be a social rule. If it were, Dworkin's arguments, based on the controversial nature of rules of recognition that refer to morality, would be inadequate to establish the normative theory of law.

What Dworkin needs is an argument that no rule of recognition can be a social rule: That regardless of the conditions of legality it sets forth, no rule of recognition can account for certain features of law unless it is a normative rule. Dworkin has such an argument and it appears to be this: Regardless of the specific conditions of legality it sets forth, every rule of recognition will give rise to controversy at some point. For example, a rule that made no reference to morality could still give rise to controversy concerning either the weight to be given to precedent, or the question of whether – and if so, to what extent – the present legislature could bind a future one. Though the rule itself would not be controversial, particular instances of it would be. Were the rule of recognition a social rule, it could not impose duties on judges in such controversial cases. The existence of judicial duties in controversial cases can only be explained by interpreting the rule of recognition as a normative rule.

This argument relies on the fact that even rules of recognition which are by and large uncontroversial will have controversial applications. In those controversial cases, the social rule interpretation of the rule of recognition could not account for the rule's imposing an obligation on judges. That is because, in the social rule theory, obligations derive from convergent practice; and in both the controversial, as well as the as yet unresolved, cases there exists no convergent practice or opinion from which an obligation might derive.

The rule of recognition is either a social rule or a normative rule. If it imposes obligations in controversial cases, it cannot be a social rule. Therefore, if the rule of recognition imposes a duty upon judges in controversial cases, it must be a normative rule. Because the rule of recognition in every community is a normative rule, the obligations of judges under it are ones of critical rather than conventional morality; and the ultimate authority of law is a matter of morality, not convention.

The argument from controversy presupposes that judges are bound by duty, even in controversial cases, under the rule of recognition. Positivism, it appears, is committed to judicial discretion in such cases and is, therefore, unable to explain either the source or nature of the duty. Because the social rule theory of judicial obligation is unable to explain the fact of judicial obligation in controversial cases, it must be false and, therefore, its alternative, the normative rule theory, true.

One response a positivist might make to Dworkin's argument is to deny that in such cases judges are bound by duty, in which case the failure of the social rule theory to account for judicial duty would not be troublesome. Dworkin quickly dismisses the plausibility of this response with the offhand remark that such a view likens law to a game in which the participants agree in advance that there are no right answers and no duties where sufficient controversy or doubt exists regarding the requirements of a rule. The analogy to a game is supposed to embarrass positivism, but it need not. Anyone even superficially familiar with Hart's work knows that the bulk of examples he draws upon to illustrate his claims about rules, law, and the nature of adjudication are drawn from games like baseball and chess. So the positivist might welcome, rather than eschew, the analogy to games.

Whether it is advanced to support or to criticize positivism, the alleged analogy to games is unsatisfying. The more interesting tack is to suppose along with Dworkin that judges may be obligated by a rule of recognition, even in its controversial applications, and then ask whether, in spite of Dworkin's arguments to the contrary, the social rule theory can explain this feature of law.

D. The Moral Argument

That Dworkin takes judicial obligations in cases involving controversial applications of the rule of recognition to be ones of critical morality rather than conventional practice is illustrated by the moral argument. Unlike the previous arguments I have outlined, the moral argument is direct and affirmative in the sense that, instead of trying to establish the inadequacies of the social rule theory, its purpose is to provide direct support for the normative interpretation of the rule of recognition. The argument is simply this: In resolving hard or controversial cases that arise under the rule of recognition, judges do not typically cite the practice or opinions of other judges. Because these cases are controversial, there exists no convergent practice among judges to cite. Instead, in order to resolve these disputes, judges typically appeal to principles of political morality. For example, in determining how much weight to give precedent, judges may apply alternative conceptions of fairness. If, as the social rule theory claims, the source of a judge's duty depends on the rule or principle he cites as its basis, the sources of judicial obligation in these controversial cases are the principles of political morality judges cite as essential to the resolution of the dispute. The duty of judges in controversial cases can only be explained if the rule of recognition is a normative one whose authority depends on its moral merits; whose normativity, in other words, depends on moral argument of precisely the sort judges appear to engage in.

E. Summary

Dworkin has three distinct, powerful arguments against law-as-convention positivism. Each argument has a slightly different character and force. The point of the pedigree argument is that a rule of recognition that makes reference to the content of moral principles as a condition of their legality will spur controversy and, because it will, it cannot be a social rule, or, therefore, a rule of recognition in the positivist's sense. The argument is weak in the sense that, even if sound, it would be inadequate to establish the normative account of the rule of recognition. Only controversial rules of recognition fail to be social rules; for all the argument shows, uncontroversial rules of recognition may be social rules.

The more general argument from controversy appears to fill the gap left by the pedigree argument. Here the argument is not that every rule of recognition will be systematically controversial. Instead, the argument relies on the plain fact that even basically uncontroversial rules of recognition will have controversial instances. The social rule theory cannot account for judicial obligation in the face of controversy. If the rule of recognition imposes an obligation on judges in controversial cases, as Dworkin presumes it does, the obligation can be accounted for only if the rule is a normative one whose capacity to impose a duty does not depend on widespread convergence of conduct or opinion. The point of the argument can be put in weaker or stronger terms. One can say simply that obligations in controversial cases exist and positivism cannot account for them; or one can put the point in terms of natural law theory as the claim that the duties that exist are ones of critical morality, rather than conventional practice.

The point of the moral argument is that, in resolving hard cases, judges appear to rely on principles of political morality rather than on convergent social practice. Judges apparently believe that they are bound to resolve these controversies and, more important, that their duty to resolve them in one way rather than another depends on the principles of morality to which they appeal.

IV   Convention and Controversy

Each of the objections to the social rule theory can be met.[12] Consider the pedigree argument first, that is, the claim that a rule of recognition which refers to morality – which has a C_1 clause satisfied by some norm – will be controversial and, therefore, cannot be a social rule of recognition. Suppose the clause in the rule of recognition states: The law is whatever is morally correct. The controversy among judges does not arise over the content of the rule of recognition itself. It arises over which norms satisfy the standards set forth in it. The divergence in behavior among officials as exemplified in their identifying different standards as legal ones does not establish their failure to accept the same rule of recognition. On the contrary, judges accept the same truth conditions for propositions of law, that is, that law consists in moral truth. They disagree about which propositions satisfy those conditions. While there may be no agreement whatsoever regarding which standards are legal ones – since there is no agreed upon standard for determining the truth of a moral principle – there is complete agreement among judges concerning the standard of legality. That judges reach different conclusions regarding the law of a community does not mean that they are employing different standards of legality. Since disagreement concerning which principles satisfy the rule of recognition presupposes that judges accept the same rule of recognition, the sort of controversy envisaged by the pedigree argument is compatible with the conventionalist account of the authority of the rule of recognition.

Notice, however, that were we to understand the rule of recognition epistemically, as providing a reliable test for identifying law, rather than as specifying truth conditions for statements of law, the sort of controversy generated by a rule of recognition like the law is whatever is morally right would be problematic, since the proposed rule of recognition would be incapable of providing a reliable test for identifying legal norms. This just draws our attention once again both to the importance of distinguishing between the epistemic and semantic interpretations of the rule of recognition, and to the necessity of insisting upon the semantic interpretation of it.

Even on the semantic interpretation, the phrase "controversy in the rule of recognition" is ambiguous. Controversy may arise, as it does in the previous case, over which norms satisfy the conditions of legality set forth in the rule of recognition; or it can arise over the conditions of legality set out in the rule of recognition. Cases of the first sort are the ones Dworkin envisions arising from a rule of recognition that includes a clause specifying legality conditions for moral principles. These cases are not problematic because controversy presupposes agreement about and acceptance of the rule of recognition. In contrast, the claim that every rule of recognition will be controversial in some of its details is precisely the claim that, in some cases, controversy will arise over the content or proper formulation of the rule of recognition itself. The question that these cases pose is not whether judges agree about which norms satisfy the same rule of recognition; rather, it is whether judges can be said to be applying the same rule. Since the social rule theory requires of the rule of recognition that its formulation be specified by convergence of behavior or belief, the controversy concerning the proper formulation of the rule means that the rule cannot be a social rule and, therefore, not a rule of recognition in the positivist's sense.

One way of interpreting Dworkin's claim is that, wherever controversy exists in the proper formulation of a rule, the rule cannot be a conventional or social rule. This is counterintuitive, since all rules – those of conventional as well as critical morality – are vague at points and, therefore, their application in some contexts will be controversial. If we take Dworkin to be making the argument that the existence of controversy is straightforwardly incompatible with the idea of a social rule, then no rule could ever be a social rule. Certainly, in spite of the controversial nature of all rules governing behavior, we are able to distinguish (at least in broad terms) the conventional rules from those whose authority depends on their truth.

A more sympathetic and plausible reading of Dworkin is that he does not mean to contest the existence of social rules. Instead his claim is that social rules cannot account for duties beyond the range of convergent practice. Social rules cannot explain duties in controversial cases. With respect to the rule of recognition, the social rule theory cannot account for the obligation of judges to give the correct formulation of the rule of recognition in its controversial instances. On the assumption that judges have such an obligation, the social rule theory fails. Only a normative interpretation of the rule of recognition can explain the duty in cases of divergent opinions or conduct, since the duty,

according to the normative theory, does not derive from convergent practice but from sound moral argument.

Schematically, Dworkin's argument is as follows.

1. Every rule of recognition will be controversial with respect to its scope and, therefore, with respect to the nature and scope of the obligations it imposes.
2. Nevertheless, in resolving disputes involving controversial aspects of the rule, judges are under an obligation, as they are in the uncontroversial cases, to give the right answer.
3. The social rule theory which requires convergence of behavior as a condition of an obligation cannot account for the obligation of judges in 2.
4. Therefore, positivism cannot account for judicial obligation in 2.
5. Therefore, only a normative theory of law in which the duty of judges depends on moral argument rather than convergent practice can account for judicial duty in 2.

As I suggested earlier, a positivist might respond by denying the truth of 2, that is, that judges are obligated in controversial cases in which behavior and opinion diverge. Hart, for one, denies 2, and he appears to do so because he accepts 3. That he denies 2 is made evident by his characterizing these kinds of cases as involving "uncertainty in the rule of recognition" in which "all that succeeds is success." If a positivist were to deny 2 to meet Dworkin's objections on the grounds that he (the positivist) accepts 3, it would be fair to accuse him of begging the question. He would be denying the existence of judicial obligation simply because his theory cannot account for it. Moreover, from a strategic point of view, it would be better to leave open the question of whether such duties exist, rather than to preclude the very possibility of their existence as a consequence of the theory; otherwise any argument that made the existence of such duties conceivable would have the effect of completely undermining the theory. Notice, however, that Dworkin is led to an analogous position, since his argument for the normative theory of law (i.e., 5) requires that judges are under obligations in every conceivable controversial case (i.e., 2). The social rule theory logically precludes judicial obligation in such cases; the normative theory requires it. Both theories of law will fail, just in case the existence of judicial duty in controversial cases involving the rule of recognition is a contingent feature of law. In other words, if it turns out that in some legal systems judges have an obligation to provide a particular formulation of the rule of recognition when controversy arises over its proper formulation, whereas in other legal systems no such duty exists and judges are free to exercise discretion – at least until one or another formulation takes hold – both the theory that logically precludes judicial duties in all controversial cases, and that which logically entails such duties, will fail.

Denying the existence of the duties to which Dworkin draws attention is a strategy that will not serve the positivist well. One alternative would be to admit the existence of the duty in some cases, but to give up the social rule theory according to which the nature and scope of a duty are completely specified by convergent practice in favor of some other theory concerning the way in which conventional or social rules give rise to duties. This is a promising line of argument I am not prepared to discuss here. However, it seems to me that the discussion of conventions in David Lewis's brilliant book, *Convention*,[13] might provide the theoretical foundations for an alternative to the standard social rule theory. Briefly, the idea is that the duties imposed by social rules or conventions are the results of expectations that arise from efforts to coordinate behavior. Vested, warranted expectations may extend beyond the area of convergent practice, in which case the obligations to which a social rule gives rise might cover controversial, as well as uncontroversial, cases.[14]

Another alternative strategy, the one I have been trying to develop, follows the social rule theory in restricting the duty imposed by a conventional rule to the area of convergent practice. In this view, if controversy arises in the rule of recognition itself, it does not follow that the judges are free to exercise discretion in

providing a formulation of the rule. What counts is not whether controversy exists, but whether there exists a practice among judges of resolving the controversy in a particular way. And to answer the question of whether such a practice exists, we do not look to the rule of recognition – whose conditions of legality are presumably in dispute – but to the social rule constituted by the behavior of judges in applying the rule of recognition. Whether a duty exists will depend, in part, on whether the judges have developed an accepted social practice of resolving these controversies in a particular way.

Suppose that, in applying the rule of recognition, judges have developed a practice of resolving controversial instances of it. Suppose further that in some jurisdictions, for example, the United States and England, judges, by and large, resolve such disputes, as Dworkin believes they do, by providing arguments of principle; so that in determining, for example, whether and to what extent the Supreme Court can review the constitutionality of federal legislation, judges argue from principles of political morality, for example, the separation of powers and so on. According to Dworkin, we would have a controversy in the rule of recognition itself that judges would be required to resolve in the appropriate way; and the obligation of judges would derive from principles of morality that constitute the best argument. This is the essence of what I referred to as the "moral argument," and it would show that the rule of recognition is a normative, not a social, rule.

For the traditional positivist, we would have a case in which no obligation existed, where all that succeeded was success: A case in which the judges' recourse to the principles of political morality necessarily involved an exercise of discretion.

Both of these positions are mistaken. If, as Dworkin supposes, judges as a general rule look to moral principles in resolving controversial features of the rule of recognition, then there exists a practice among them of resolving controversial aspects of the rule of recognition in that way; that is, as the moral argument suggests judges in the United States and Britain do. If this is, in fact, the practice of judges in constitutional democracies like ours – as it must be if Dworkin's arguments are to be taken seriously – and if the practice is critically accepted by judges, then there is a legal duty even in controversial cases: A duty that does not derive from the principles judges cite (as in Dworkin) but from their acceptance of the practice of resolving these disputes by offering substantive moral arguments. All Dworkin's arguments really show is that judges have adopted critically the practice that the best moral argument wins, which explains both their appeal to substantive moral principles and, contrary to the traditional positivist, their duty to do so.

What, in Dworkin's view, is evidence for the normative theory of the rule of recognition – that is, general and widespread appeal to moral principle to resolve controversies in it – is, in my view, evidence of the existence of a social practice among judges of resolving such disputes in a particular way; a practice that specifies part of the social rule regarding judicial behavior. The appeal to substantive moral argument is, then, perfectly compatible with the conventionalist account of law.

To argue that the appeal to moral argument is compatible with the conventionalist account is not to establish that account, since the appeal to moral argument as a vehicle of dispute resolution is also consistent with the normative theory of law. One could argue that, at most, my argument shows only that Dworkin's arguments, which rely on both the controversial nature of law and the appeal to moral principle to resolve controversy, are inadequate to undermine positivism. We need some further reason to choose between the normative and conventional theories of law.

Dworkin has taken the "acid test" for positivism to be whether it can account for judicial behavior in jurisdictions, such as the United States and England, in which both prospective litigants and judges believe that disputes which arise because of controversy in the rule of recognition are to be resolved, not by discretion, but by principled argument. His arguments are all to the effect that positivism cannot account for either the expectations of litigants or the behavior of judges, because positivism is committed to discretion whenever controversy arises. If controversy arises in a rule subordinate to the rule of recognition, positivism is committed to discretion in virtue of the theory of language it adopts that makes so much of the difference between "core" and "penumbra" instances of general terms. If controversy arises in the rule of recognition itself, positivism is committed to discretion because the rule of recognition is a social rule specified by the behavior of judges; and a social rule can impose an obligation only to the extent behavior converges, that is, only in the absence of controversy. I have argued that, contrary to Dworkin, positivism can, in fact, account for the obligations of judges in controversial instances of the rule of recognition, since the existence of controversy does not preclude the existence of conformity of practice in resolving it. If I am correct, neither the existence of controversy nor the appeal to moral argument in certain jurisdictions as necessary to its resolution are incompatible with law-as-convention positivism. What then is the acid test?

For the normative theory of law to be correct, judges must be under a legal obligation to resolve controversies arising in every conceivable rule of recognition by reliance on substantive moral argument. That is because Dworkin's version of the normative theory entails the existence of judicial duty in all cases, and because the resolution of the dispute must involve moral argument. After all, if the rule of recognition is, as Dworkin claims, a normative rule, then its authority rests on sound moral argument and the resolution of disputes concerning its scope must call for moral argument. Were judges to rely on anything else, the authority of the rule of recognition will not be a matter of its moral merits; or if they appeal to nothing at all, then in such jurisdictions we would have reason to believe that judges are under no particular obligation to resolve a controversy in the rule of recognition.

The real acid test seems to be not whether positivism of the sort I am developing can account for judicial obligations in the kinds of cases we are discussing, but whether these obligations constitute a necessary feature of law which, in every jurisdiction, is imposed by moral principle. As long as the existence of such duties is a contingent feature of law, as is the duty to resolve disputes by appealing to moral argument, the normative theory of law is a less plausible account than is the conventionalist theory. Indeed, it seems straightforwardly false, since we can imagine immature legal systems (which are legal systems nonetheless) in which no practice for resolving disputes in the rule of recognition has as yet developed – where all that succeeds is success. Or we could imagine the development of considerably less attractive practices for resolving such disputes, for example, the flip of a coin: heads, defendant wins; tails, plaintiff does. In the first sort of legal system, it would seem odd to say judges were legally bound to resolve such disputes (though they might always be morally bound to do so), since no practice had as yet developed. Eventually, such a practice is likely to develop, and the range of judicial discretion will narrow as the practice becomes widespread and critically accepted. As the second example shows, the practice that finally develops need not conform to judicial practice in the United States and England. Though judicial discretion narrows as the range of judicial obligation expands, it may do so in a way that is considerably less attractive than the moral argument envisions; in a way that is, in fact, less attractive than a system in which all that succeeded was success.

Unlike traditional positivism, which has trouble explaining judicial behavior in mature legal systems, and the normative theory of law, which has difficulty explaining developing and immature legal systems (for the reasons that the first precludes obligations in controversial cases, while the second requires them), law-as-convention positivism understands such duties to be a contingent feature of law that can be explained as arising from the critical acceptance of a practice of dispute resolution, rather than from the principles of morality which judges under one kind of practice might cite.

V   Conclusion

Dworkin makes three correct observations about the controversial nature of some legal standards.

1. A legal system can (and does in the United States and Britain) recognize certain standards as part of the law even though they are "essentially controversial" in the sense that there may be disagreements among judges as to which these are, and there is no decision procedure which, even in principle, can demonstrate what they are, and so settle disagreements.

2. Among such essentially controversial legal standards are moral principles owing their status as law to their being "true" moral principles, though their "truth" cannot be demonstrated by any agreed upon test.

3. The availability of such controversial principles fills the "gaps" left by ordinary sources of law, which may be partially indeterminate, vague, or conflicting. So that, at least with respect to the resolution of disputes involving standards subordinate to the rule of recognition, a judge never has to exercise law-making power or "discretion" to fill the gaps or remove the indeterminacy if such moral principles are a part of the law.

In this essay, I have drawn distinctions among three versions of positivism and have discussed their relationship to Dworkin's claims: (1) "Negative positivism," the view that the legal system need not recognize as law "controversial" moral standards; (2) "positive, hard-facts positivism," the view that controversial standards cannot be regarded as law and, hence, rejects Dworkin's three points; (3) "positive, social rule positivism," which insists only on the conventional status of the rule of recognition but accepts Dworkin's three points.

Since the inclusion of controversial moral principles is not a necessary feature of the concept of law, Dworkin's arguments to the effect that such principles figure in judicial practice in the United States and in Britain, are inadequate to undermine the very weak claim of negative positivism. On the other hand, if Dworkin is right – and I am inclined to think that he is – in thinking that controversial moral principles sometimes figure in legal argument, then any form of positivism that is committed to the essentially noncontroversial nature of law is mistaken. Finally, what I have tried to do is to develop a form of positivism which accepts the controversial nature of some legal reasoning, while denying that this is incompatible with the essential, affirmative claim of the theory that law is everywhere conventional in nature. If I am correct, there is a form of positivism which can do justice to Dworkin's insights while rendering his objections harmless.[15]

Notes

1 Dworkin's claim that positivism is committed to a pedigree standard of legality is too narrow. What he means to argue, I believe, is that positivism is committed to some form of "noncontentful" criterion of legality, of which a pedigree standard would be one. For ease of exposition, I will use "pedigree test" broadly to mean any sort of non-contentful criterion of legality.

2 See pp. 119–21 *infra*.

3 The phrase "truth as a moral principle as a condition of legality" does seem a bit awkward. However, any other phrase, such as "morality as a condition of legality," or "moral content as a condition of legality" would be ambiguous, since it would be unclear whether the separability thesis were a claim about the relationship between law and critical morality or between law and conventional morality. My understanding of the separability thesis is as a denial of a constitutive relationship between law and critical morality. For another interpretation of the separability thesis see p. 124 *infra*.

4 This seems to be in the form of positivism David Lyons advances to meet Dworkin's objections to positivism. Cf. David Lyons, Review: Principles, Positivism, and Legal Theory, 87 Yale L. J. 415 (1977).

5 But see Rolf Sartorius, Social Policy and Judicial Legislation, 8 Am. Philosophical Q. 151 (1971); Jules Coleman, Review, Taking Rights Seriously, 66 Calif. L. Rev. 885 (1978).

6 The following characterization of positivism in virtue of motivations for the separability thesis was developed after numerous discussions with Professor Dworkin. I am particularly grateful to him for remarks, but it is likely that I have not put the characterizations as well as he would have.

7 That is because legal realism is skeptical about the existence of legal facts. Legal facts are "created" by official action; they are not "out there" to be discovered by judges. Scientific or metaphysical realism maintains exactly the opposite view of facts.

8 See note 5 *supra*.

9 Often overlooked is the fact that there are two distinct arguments for discretion: One relies on the controversial nature of penumbra cases involving general terms; the other relies on the finiteness of legal standards. The first argument is actually rooted in a theory of language; the second, which would survive a rejection of that theory, relies on gaps in the law. See Coleman, *supra* note 5.

10 Dworkin does not explicitly distinguish among these various arguments, nor does he label any of them. The labels and distinctions are mine.

11 Sartorius, *supra* note 5; Dworkin himself discusses, but wrongly rejects this possibility; see Model of Rules I, in Taking Rights Seriously 977 (1977). See also C. L. Ten's useful discussion, The Soundest Theory of Law, 88 Mind 522 (1979).

12 There are two ways in which we might understand the notion of a social rule. Under one interpretation, not every rule of recognition would be a social rule; under the other, each would be. As both Hart and Dworkin use the term, a social rule is specified by behavior. It cannot be formulated in the absence of a practice, and the nature of the practice determines the scope of the rule and the extent of the duties it imposes. The rule that men must doff their hats upon entering church is a social rule in this sense. Not every rule of recognition, however, is a social rule in this sense for two reasons. First, at least in some jurisdictions, the content of the rule may be specified prior to the existence of an appropriate practice. For example, the formulation of the Constitution of the United States did not require the existence of the relevant judicial practice; it preceded the practice. No doubt ambiguities and other uncertainties in the rule are resolved through judicial practice; nevertheless, the general form and nature of the rule had been specified without regard to practice. Second, whereas Dworkin's contrast between social rule and normative rule theories of law turns on the manner in which legal rules give rise to duties, the rule of recognition is not itself a duty-imposing rule. We might construct a broader notion of a social rule. In this sense a rule will be a social rule if its existence or authority depends, in part, on the existence of a social practice. Here the requirement is not that the rule's proper formulation be specified by practice. Instead, the claim is that the authority of the rule depends on the existence of a practice. The rule itself may be specifiable, at least in

general terms and at some points in time, without regard to the practice. However, in the absence of the practice, the rule is empty in that it is incapable of providing justifications for action. In short, its normativity depends on the practice, though its content need not be specified by it. Every rule of recognition for the positivist is a social rule in this sense.

13   David Lewis, Convention: A Philosophical Study (1969).

14   Gerald Postema has been trying to develop an alternative to the social rule theory that relies heavily on Lewis's theory of conventions. See Gerald J. Postema, Coordination and Convention at the Foundations of Law, 11 J. Legal Stud.

15   I have refrained from discussing the arguments against positivism that Dworkin advances in his brilliant essay "Hard Cases" because in that essay Dworkin reveals himself to be much more of a conventionalist than he would have us believe. The main purpose of that essay is to provide a theory of adjudication that makes plain the sense in which right answers and judicial obligations exist in controversial cases. If Dworkin makes his case for right answers, positivism – at least versions of it that deny judicial duty in the face of controversy – must be mistaken. Moreover, Dworkin attempts to show that the theory of adjudication which provides right answers necessarily makes morality part of the concept of law. Some comments regarding at least this latter claim are in order. Dworkin's general theory of adjudication may be explicated as follows. A case, A, comes before an appellate judge. The judge must decide whether to give a decision in favor of the defendant (decision D), or in favor of the plaintiff, $\bar{D}$. In making his decision, the judge notes that there exists a large body of settled law, S, that is suitably purged of its "mistakes." (Dworkin has a theory of the way in which judges identify mistaken decisions). Once S has been purged of mistakes, it can be systematized. The judge is required then to construct a theory of law that best explains and justifies S by subsuming S under a set of general principles that constitute the best explanation of S. These principles constitute the soundest theory of the existing law (STL). Dworkin employs the standard philosophic notion of explanation so that if STL explains S, then S follows logically or theoretically from STL. Once STL is constructed, the judge must ask whether either D or $\bar{D}$ follows from it. If either statement follows logically from STL, the case presents no problem for the positivist. In the event that neither D nor $\bar{D}$ follows logically from STL, the case is one that, for the positivists at least, calls for discretion, since both conclusions are equally inadequately warranted by the existing law. Dworkin's theory of adjudication here departs from positivism. For while neither D nor $\bar{D}$ is entailed by STL, either D or $\bar{D}$, but not both, "coheres" or "fits" best with it. While neither a decision in favor of the plaintiff nor the defendant is a logical consequence of the soundest theory of law, one, but not the other, is a coherence consequence of it. Whichever is the coherence consequence is the "right" answer, the one the judge is obligated to provide. More important, in determining the right answer the judge is required to invoke considerations of morality, since the soundest theory of law not only explains the settled law but justifies it as well. While I have other systematic objections to the argument for right answers, I doubt that the theory of adjudication Dworkin outlines accurately describes judicial practice everywhere, or that it is a necessary feature of legal practice. More important for our present purposes, the claim that determining right answers necessarily involves a moral theory of law which is incompatible with the conventionalist account of law is simply mistaken. On the contrary, Dworkin's argument is thoroughly conventionalist in nature. First, Dworkin must be committed to some standard version of a rule of recognition, since he is committed to a judge's being able to identify the existing body of settled law. Like the positivists he criticizes, Dworkin is, therefore, committed to an epistemic rule of recognition – at least for determining settled law. In Dworkin's view, the judge must construct a theory of law that explains the settled law once it is discovered. The theory of law consists in a set of principles which explain and justify S. The argument for the claim that the soundest theory of law is a moral theory rests either on the requirement that the principles justify the law, or on the claim that the principles which constitute the theory are moral principles. In neither case can the argument be sustained. Dworkin's argument for the justification requirement relies on a deeper principle of political responsibility; the judge must be able to give reasons in support of his decisions by showing a consistency between this, and previous, similar cases. The notion of justification, however, is ambiguous.

There are both weaker and stronger notions of justification. On the other hand, there is the notion of justification that is part of critical morality according to which if a principle or decision is justified it is morally defensible. In this sense, bad law can never be morally justified. But Dworkin (rightly) believes that bad law can be law nonetheless, so he cannot mean that the best theory of law justifies the existing law in the sense that it shows the law to be morally defensible. It is clear, then, that the principle of political responsibility requires the weaker notion of justification. This notion is institutional in nature and is akin to the requirement of consistency or formal justice, the requirement that like cases be treated alike. But then this notion of justification does not establish the link between law and critical morality necessary to undermine positivism. The argument that the best theory of law is a moral theory because it consists in a set of moral principles fails primarily because the principles which constitute the best theory do not do so because they are true, but because they best systemize the existing law.

7

On the Incoherence of Legal Positivism

John Finnis

Legal positivism is an incoherent intellectual enterprise. It sets itself an explanatory task which it makes itself incapable of carrying through. In the result it offers its students purported and invalid derivations of *ought* from *is*.

In this brief Essay I note various features of legal positivism and its history, before trying to identify this incoherence at its heart. I do not mean to renege on my belief that reflections on law and legal theory are best carried forward without reference to unstable and parasitic academic categories, or labels, such as "positivism" (or "liberalism" or "conservatism," etc.). I use the term for convenience, to pick out a loose family of theories and theorists who are part of our contemporary conversation and who have used the term to describe their own theories, or the legal theories of writers they wish us to admire.

I

The notion that there are no standards of action save those created – put in place, posited – by conventions, commands, or other such social facts was well known to Plato[1] and Aristotle.[2] Developing a sustained critique of any such notion was a primary objective of these philosophers, and to some extent of successors of theirs such as Cicero.[3] Today the promoters of this radical kind of "exclusive positivism" are the followers, conscious or unconscious, of

Nietzsche or of others who like him reduce ethics and normative political or legal theory to a search for the "genealogy," the historical (perhaps partly or wholly physiological) sources of ethical, political, or legal standards. These sources, they assume or assert, can only consist in exercises of the will of charismatic individuals or power-seeking groups, or in the supposedly will-like sub-rational drives and compulsions of domination, submission, and so forth.

Legal positivism is in principle a more modest proposal: that state law is, or should systematically be studied as if it were, a set of standards originated exclusively by conventions, commands, or other such social facts. As developed by Bentham, Austin, and Kelsen, legal positivism was officially neutral on the question whether, outside the law, there are moral standards whose directiveness (normativity, authority, obligatoriness) in deliberation is not to be explained entirely by any social fact. Bentham and Austin certainly did not think that the utilitarian morality they promoted depended for its obligatoriness upon the say-so of any person or group, even though Austin held that the whole content of utilitarian moral requirements is also commanded by God. Kelsen's official theory, until near the end of his life, was – at least when he was doing legal philosophy – that there may be moral truths, but if so they are completely outside the field of vision of legal science or legal philosophy. His final position, however, was one of either complete moral scepticism[4] or undiluted moral voluntarism: moral norms could not be other than commands of God, if God there were. These final positions of Kelsen are the consummation not only of the seam of voluntarism running through all his theorising about positive law, but also of every earlier theory which took for granted that law and its obligatoriness are and must be a product of the will and coercive power of a superior.

What is often called "modern natural law theory" exemplifies, in large part, such a theory. This tradition emerges clearly by 1660, when Samuel Pufendorf published in The Hague his *Elements of Universal Jurisprudence*.[5] Characteristic features of this kind of natural law theory can be studied there, or in John Locke's long-unpublished *Questions Concerning the Law of Nature*[6] (c. 1660–1664). Both writers are clearly derivative in some ways from Hugo Grotius and in other ways from Thomas Hobbes. Very tellingly, Pufendorf describes Hobbes's *De Cive* (1642) (On Being a Citisen), a work announcing the main moral and jurisprudential theses of Hobbes's more famous *Leviathan* (1651), as "for the most part extremely acute and sound."[7]

From Grotius's massively influential *On the Law of War and Peace* (1625), Locke and Pufendorf take the well-sounding but quite opaque idea that morality and the law's basic principles are a matter of "conformity with rational nature."[8] The questions how this nature is known, and why it is normative for anyone, these writers never seriously tackle. Such fundamental questions are confronted and answered by Hobbes. But his answers treat our practical reasoning as all in the service of motivating sub-rational passions such as fear of death and desire to surpass others – motivations of the very kind identified by the classical tradition as in need of direction by our reason's grasp of more ultimate and better ends, of true and intrinsic goods, of really intelligent reasons for action.

"[N]o law without a legislator."[9] No obligation without subjection to the "will of a superior power."[10] "Law's formal definition is: the declaration of a superior will."[11] "The rule of our actions is the will of a superior power."[12] Law is

in vain without (the prospect of) punishment.[13] These definitions and axioms (Locke's) are meant by the founders of modern natural law theory to be as applicable to natural law, the very principles of morality, as to the positive law of states.[14] So obligation is being openly "deduced" from fact, the fact that such and such has been willed by one who has power to harm. To be sure, when natural law (morality) is in issue, the superior, God, is assumed to be wise. But the idea of divine wisdom is given no positive role in explaining why God's commands create obligations for a rational conscience. God's *right* to legislate is explained instead by the analogy of sheer power: "Who, indeed, will say that clay is not subject to the potter's will and that the pot cannot be destroyed by the same hand that shaped it?"[15]

Locke, like Hobbes, is uneasily though dimly aware that "ought" cannot be inferred from "is" without some further "ought." That is to say, he is uneasily aware that the fact that conduct *was* willed by a superior, or indeed by a party to a contract, does not explain why that conduct is *now* obligatory. So he sometimes thinks of supplementing his naked voluntarism (oughts are explained by acts of *will*) by the rationality of logical coherence: fundamental moral principles are tautologies, norms which it would be *self-contradictory* to deny.[16] Hobbes had ventured a similar account of the obligatoriness of contracts (such as his fundamental social contract, of subjection to the sovereign). Still, his official and prominent explanation was of the form, "clubs are trumps" (will backed by superior force, i.e. capacity to harm).[17] Such an appeal to coercion tacitly admits that the fact that someone else has *willed* or *ordered* me to do something provides of itself no reason for me to act, no normativity or directiveness for my deliberations.

Moreover, as Kelsen argues, reliance upon the will of a superior to explain law and its normativity leaves, in the end, no room for a requirement of logical consistency in the law, or for any attempt to reason from a general rule ("murder is to be punished") to a normative conclusion ("Smith, having murdered Jones, is to be punished").[18] Hence Kelsen's final position, distressing to many of those who wish to be positivists: the only source of normativity, and therefore of the normativity of a particular norm, is positivity, that is, the actual willing of that norm by a superior. On this assumption, even the rationality of logic and uncontroversial legal reasoning can never yield normativity: nothing but a will-act can do that.[19]

Kelsen's final positions cannot be written off as eccentricities, of merely biographical interest. Still, the legal positivism – sometimes called "exclusive legal positivism" – defended today by legal philosophers such as Joseph Raz, is very different. While affirming that all *law* is based upon and validated by social-fact sources – the affirmation which makes it exclusive legal positivism – it accepts also that judges can and not rarely do have a legal and moral obligation to include in their judicial reasoning principles and norms which are applicable because, although not legally valid (because not hitherto posited by any social-fact source), they are, or are taken by the judge in question to be, *morally true*.[20]

II

Classical natural law theory does not reject the theses that what has been posited is positive and what has not been posited is not positive. (Indeed, the very term "positive law" is one imported into philosophy by Aquinas, who was also the first to propose that the whole law of a political community may be considered philosophically as *positive* law.[21]) But the theses need much clarification. What does it mean to say that a rule, principle, or other standard "has been posited by a social-fact source?" Does it mean what Kelsen finally took it to mean, that nothing short of express articulation of the very norm in all its specificity – and no kind of mere derivation (inference) or derivability – will suffice? Virtually no other positivist can be found to follow Kelsen here. But if not, which kinds of consistency-with-what-has-been-specifically-articulated by a social-fact source are necessary and sufficient to entitle a standard to be counted as "posited"? By what criteria is one to answer that last theoretical question?

Clearly, then, legal theorists have little reason to be content with any notion that legal theory should merely report the social facts about what has and has not been expressly posited, by actual acts of deliberate articulation, in this or that community. Raz himself goes well beyond so confined a project when he affirms that courts characteristically have the legal and/or moral duty to apply non-legal standards.

Now consider the judicial or juristic process of identifying a moral standard as one which anyone adjudicating a given case has the duty to apply even though it has not (yet) been posited by the social facts of custom, enactment, or prior adjudication. This specific moral standard will usually be a specification of some very general principle such as fairness, of rejecting favourable or unfavourable treatment which is arbitrary when measured by the principles that like cases are to be treated alike, unlike cases differently, and that one should do for others what one would have them do for oneself or for those one already favours. But such a specification – a making more specific – of a general moral principle cannot proceed without close attention to the way classes of persons, things, and activities are already treated by the indubitably posited law. Without such attention one cannot settle what cases are alike and what different, and cannot know what classes of persons, acts, or things are already favoured, or disfavoured, by the existing positive law. The selection of the morally right standard, the morally right resolution of the case in hand, can therefore be done properly only by those who know the relevant body of posited laws well enough to know what new dispute-resolving standard really fits them better than any alternative standard. This selection, when thus made judicially, is in a sense making new law. But this judicial responsibility, as judges regularly remind themselves (and counsel, and their readers), is significantly different from the authority of legislatures to enact wide measures of repeal, make novel classifications of persons, things, and acts, and draw bright lines of distinction which could reasonably have been drawn in other ways. This significant difference can reasonably be signalled by saying that the "new" judicially adopted standard, being so narrowly controlled by the contingencies of the existing posited law, was in an important sense *already part* of the law.[22] Exclusive legal positivism's refusal to countenance such a way of speaking is unwarranted and inadequately motivated.

III

For a judge, and for a lawyer trying to track judicial reasoning, the law has a double life.

One of its lives (so to speak) is (i) its existence as the sheer fact that certain people have done such and such in the past, and that certain people here and now have such and such dispositions to decide and act. These facts provide "exclusive legal positivism" with its account of a community's law. (But note that legal positivists rightly begin to leave behind the view that legal theory should attend only to what is posited in social-fact sources when they affirm that law is systemic: the content of what counts as "expressly posited" is settled by the content of *other* norms and principles of the system, with the result that, even if these other standards are each posited by social facts, no law-makers, judicial or otherwise, do or can settle by themselves the legal content and effect of their act – the social fact – of positing.)

The other life of the law is (ii) its existence as standards directive for the conscientious deliberations of those whose responsibility is to decide (do justice) according to law. From this "internal" viewpoint, the social facts of positing yield both too little and too much. Too little, because in cases of legal *development* of the kind I have sketched, those facts, while never irrelevant, must be supplemented by moral standards to be applied because true. And too much, because sometimes the social-fact sources yield standards so morally flawed that even judges sworn to follow the law should set them aside in favour of alternative norms more consistent both with moral principle (full practical reasonableness) and with all those other parts of the posited law which are consistent with moral principle.

"Inclusive legal positivists" are unwilling to sever the question "What is the law governing this case?" from the question "What, according to our law, is my duty as judge in this case?" If the community's law, taken as a whole, expli-

citly or implicitly requires or even authorises the judges, in certain kinds of cases, to ask themselves what morality requires in circumstances of this kind, then the moral standard(s) answering that question – or at least the moral conclusions applicable in such circumstances – have legal as well as moral authority. The moral standard(s) are so far forth, and for that reason, to be counted as part of our law. They are, as some people say, "included" within or "incorporated" into the community's law. The exclusive legal positivist (to recall) insists that such standards, even if controlling the judges' duty in such a case, remain outside the law, excluded from it by their lack (at least hitherto) of social-fact pedigree.

The disputes between exclusive and inclusive legal positivists are, I suggest, a fruitless demarcation dispute, little more than a squabble about the words "law" or "legal system." One may indeed consider law in general, and the law of a particular community past or present, as (i) a complex fact about the opinions and practices of a set of persons at some time. Those who consider the law in precisely this way not unreasonably tend to prioritise the beliefs and practices of those members of the community who are professionally concerned with law as judges, legal advisers, bailiffs, police, and so forth. In describing this complex fact, they (like Hart) may well treat law as a reason for action, and describe the law as a set of reasons (some authorising, some obligating, some both) which are systematised by interrelationships of derivation, interpretative constraint, or other kinds of interdependence, and which purport to give coherent guidance. Still, since theorists of this kind are concerned with the facts about a set of people's belief and practice, they need make no judgments about whether the system's standards are indeed coherent, or whether its most basic rules of validation, authorisation, origination, or recognition satisfyingly account for the system's other standards or give anyone a truly reasonable, rationally sufficient reason for acting in a specific way, whether as judge, citizen, or otherwise.

One may, however, consider law and the law of a particular community precisely as (ii) good reasons for action. But, when deliberation runs its course, the really good and only truly suffi-cient *reasons* we have for action (and forbearance from action) are moral reasons: that is what it is for a reason to be moral, in the eyes of anyone who intends to think and act with the auton-omy, the self-determination and conscientious-ness, that the classical tradition makes central.[23] And it is obvious that, *for the purposes of this kind of consideration*, nothing will count as law unless it is in line with morality's requirements, both positive and negative. A sound morality cer-tainly requires that we concern ourselves with making, executing, complying with, and main-taining positive, social-fact source-based and pedigreed laws, and that we keep them coherent with each other. Such positive laws add some-thing, indeed much, to morality's inherent di-rectives. That something added is specific to the community, time, and place in question, even if it is, as it doubtless often should be, the same in content as other specific communities' positive-law standards on the relevant matters.

Classical natural law theory is primarily con-cerned with this second kind of enquiry. But it has every respect for descriptive, historical, "sociological" considerations of the first kind, and seeks to benefit from them. Classical nat-ural law theory also offers reasons[24] for judging that *general* descriptions of law will be fruitful only if their basic conceptual structure is, self-consciously and critically, derived from the understanding of *good reasons* which enquiries of the second kind seek to reach by open debate and critical assessment.

Anyone who makes and adheres steadily to this basic distinction between (i) enquiries about what *is* (or *was*, or *is likely*) and (ii) enquiries about what *ought* to be will notice that much of the debate among legal positivists arises from, or at least involves, an inattention to the distinc-tion. Indeed, much of the contemporary juris-prudential literature seems to swing helplessly back and forth between the rigorously descrip-tive ("external" to conscience) and the rigor-ously normative ("internal" to conscience), offering various but always incoherent mixes of the two. What entitles "exclusive" legal posi-tivists to assert, or even to concede, that the judge sometimes has a duty to *go outside the law* and apply moral standards? How can a

"positivism" devoted to (as they say) *the facts* include propositions about moral duty?

A rigorously descriptive understanding of Ruritania's law can do no more than report the more or less wide *acceptance* in Ruritania that in certain circumstances the judges should settle cases by applying standards which they judge morally true even though unpedigreed – i.e., not hitherto certified by any social-fact source of law. Now suppose that the rule of recognition so reported includes in its own terms the state-ment that any unpedigreed standard which the judges are required or authorised by this rule of recognition to apply (because considered by them to be morally true) shall be taken and declared by the judges to be *an integral part of the community's law*. What reason have exclusive positivists to say that such a rule of recognition is somehow false to the nature of law?

Suppose, on the other hand, that the Rurita-nian rule of recognition stipulates that, where judges are required or authorised to apply an unpedigreed standard because they consider it morally true, they shall in doing so treat that standard *not* as part of Ruritanian law, but rather as analogous to those rules of foreign states which are applicable in Ruritanian courts by virtue of the choice-of-law rules in Rurita-nia's law of Conflicts of Laws. (This stipulation could well have legal consequences, e.g. in cases concerning the retrospective applicability of the standard, or its use in assessing whether there has been a "mistake of law" for the purposes of rules of limitation of action, or restitution.) What reason have "inclusive legal positivists" to assert that such a rule of recognition is somehow false to the nature of law? But if they concede that it is not somehow false to the nature of law, what is "positivist" about their position? And can a dispute between rival "isms" in legal philosophy have serious theoretical content if it could be affected by what a particular com-munity declares to be its law?

No truth about law, I suggest, is systematic-ally at stake in contemporary disputes between exclusive and inclusive legal positivists. The central dispute is not worth pursuing. Provided one makes oneself clear and unambiguous to one's readers, it matters not at all whether one defines positive law as (all and only) the *pedi-*

greed standards or instead as (all and only) the standards *applicable by judges* acting as such.[25] Either definition has its advantages and inconveniences. Counting as law only what has been pedigreed has the inconveniences already mentioned: (a) the relationship between legal duty and the duty of courts seems to fall outside the "science" or "philosophy" *of law*, and (b) there seems no way of specifying precisely what counts as "pedigreed" ("derived," "derivable," etc.) short of the late-Kelsenian amputation of most of juristic thought and method – all reasoning from one standard to another, or from systematic consistency – by virtue of the demand that there be a specific act of will to pedigree each and every proposition of law. Counting as law whatever standards the courts have a judicial duty to enforce has the inconvenience that it cannot be done well – critically and sufficiently – without undertaking precisely the task, and following substantially the route, of classical natural law theory.

IV

Law's "positivity" was first articulated, embraced, and explained, as I have noted, by the classical natural law theorists. Legal positiv*ism* identifies itself as a challenge to natural law theories. It has had, say, 225 years[26] to make its challenge intelligible. The best its contemporary exponents can offer to state its challenge is, "there is no necessary connection between law and morality."[27] But classic law theory has always enthusiastically affirmed that statement. Some laws are utterly unjust, utterly immoral; the fact that something is declared or enacted as law by the social sources authorised or recognised as sources of valid law in no way entails that it is (or is even regarded by anyone as) morally acceptable or is even relevant to a consideration of someone's moral responsibilities (whether in truth, or according to some conventional or idiosyncratic understanding). Thus there is no necessary connection between law and morality or moral responsibility. The claim that natural law theories overlook some of the social facts relevant to law is simply, and demonstrably, false.

So the statement meant to define legal positivism is badly in need of clarification.[28] More fundamentally still, no genuine clarification is possible without considering *both* terms of the alleged disjunction: law *and* morality. That there is *no* necessary connection, in any relevant sense of "connection" and "necessity," cannot be rationally affirmed without steady, critical attention to *what morality has to say* about law, either in general or as the law of particular communities. What basis is there for asserting, or implying, or allowing it to be thought, that lawyers, judges, and other citisens or subjects of the law should not, or need not, be concerned – precisely when considering how the law bears on their responsibilities as lawyers, etc. – with the question what *morality* has to say about law, and about what is *entitled* to count as law? And where is a student of law going to find such a steady, critical attention to morality as it bears on law, and on the very idea of law, and on particular laws, other than in an enquiry which, whatever its label, extends as ambitiously far as classical natural law theory does?

Consider the following argument offered recently by Jules Coleman and Brian Leiter:

> Now we can see the problem with the natural lawyer's account of authority. For in order to be law, a norm must be required by morality. Morality has authority, in the sense that the fact that a norm is a requirement of morality gives agents a (perhaps overriding) reason to comply with it. If morality has authority, and legal norms are necessarily moral, then law has authority too.
>
> This argument for the authority of law, however, is actually fatal to it, because it makes law's authority redundant on morality's . . . if all legal requirements are also moral requirements (as the natural lawyer would have it) then the fact that a norm is a norm of law does not provide citisens with an additional reason for acting. Natural law theory, then, fails to account for the authority of law.[29]

The criticism here launched by Coleman and Leiter entirely fails. No natural law theory of law has ever claimed that "in order to be law, a norm must be required by morality," or that "all legal requirements are also" – independently of being validly posited as law – "moral requirements." Natural law theorists hold that the contents of a just and validly enacted rule of law such as "do not exceed thirty-five m.p.h. in city streets" are NOT required by morality until validly posited by the legal authority with jurisdiction (legal authority) to make such a rule. The centrepiece of natural law theory of law is its explanation of how the making of "purely positive" law can create moral obligations which did NOT exist until the moment of enactment.

Unfortunately, Coleman and Leiter's error, thoroughgoing as it is, has many precedents. Kelsen, particularly, used to claim that, according to natural law theory, positive law is a mere "copy" of natural law and "merely reproduces the true law which is already somehow in existence";[30] the claim has been shown to be mere travesty.[31] Like Coleman and Leiter, Kelsen cited no text to support his claims about what natural law theory says, because (as he had every opportunity to know) none could be cited.

As the fifty-five years of Kelsen's jurisprudence abundantly illustrate, positivism's efforts to explain the law's authority are doomed to fail. For, as Coleman and Leiter rightly say, "a practical authority is a person or institution whose directives provide individuals with *a reason for* acting (in compliance with those dictates),"[32] and they might have added, a reason that is not merely a replica, for each individual, of that individual's self-interested "prudential" reasons for so acting. But, as they ought (but fail) to acknowledge, no fact or set of facts, however complex, can by itself provide a *reason for* acting, let alone an "ought" of the kind that could speak with authority against an individual's self-interest. (To repeat, "authority" that does no more than track the "I want" of self-interest is redundant for the individual addressed and futile for the community.) No *ought* from a mere *is*. So, since positivism prides itself on dealing only in facts, it can offer an adequate understanding neither of reasons for action (oughts), nor of their only conceivable *source*, namely true and intrinsic values (basic human goods, and the propositional first principles of practical reason that direct us to those goods as to-be-pursued, and point to what damages them as to-be-shunned).

V

The incoherence of positivism – its inherent and self-imposed incapacity to succeed in the explanatory task it sets itself – is nicely illustrated by Coleman and Leiter's effort to explain "the authority of the rule of recognition."[33] Since they preface this explanation with the remark that "we all recognise cases of binding laws that are morally reprehensible (for example, the laws that supported apartheid in South Africa),"[34] we can conveniently test their explanations of this bindingness, this authoritativeness, by asking how such explanations could figure in the deliberations of an official (say Nelson Mandela in the 1950s) in South Africa in those days. Young Mandela (let us imagine) asks Coleman and Leiter why the South African rule of recognition, which he knows is the propositional content of the attitudes accompanying and supporting the massive fact of convergent official behaviour in South Africa, gives him a reason for action of a kind that he could reasonably judge authoritative. How does this fact of convergent official behaviour, he asks, make the law not merely *accepted as* legally authoritative but actually *authoritative as law* for him or anyone else who recognises its injustice?

Coleman and Leiter's explanation goes like this: (1) Often your self-interest requires you to co-ordinate your behaviour with that of these officials or of other people who are in fact acting in line with those officials. (But Mandela is enquiring about authoritative directions, not guides to self-interest. Self-interest requires co-operation with local gangsters, but their directions are not authoritative.) (2) Moreover, if you think that those officials are trying to do what morality requires, you have reason to follow their lead. (Mandela will not think so, and will be right.) (3) You may "believe that the rule of recognition provides something like the right standards for evaluating the validity of norms subordinate to it."[35] (He rightly does not.) (4) "[Q]uite apart from [your] views about the substantive merits of the rule of recognition itself, the avoidance of confusion and mayhem, as well as the conditions of liberal stability[,] require co-ordination among officials."[36]

Here at last, in (4), Coleman and Leiter offer a reason of the relevant kind, a reason which could be rationally debated by being confronted with reasons of the same kind. The requirement asserted in the quoted sentence goes far beyond the "fact of convergent behaviour"; it acknowledges strong evaluations of order, peace, and justice ("liberalism"); it is indeed nothing if not a moral requirement. It is *available* to explain the law's authoritativeness only if the "separability thesis" is recognised as an equivocation between defensible and indefensible theses, and if Coleman and Leiter's favoured "positivist" interpretation or version is abandoned as the mistake it is. In jurisprudence, there is a name for a theory of law that undertakes to identify and debate, openly and critically, the moral principles and requirements which respond to *deliberating persons'* requests to be shown why a legal rule, validly enacted, is binding and authoritative *for them*, precisely as law: That name (for good and ill) is "natural law theory."

Coleman and Leiter might reply that I am confusing legal with moral authority. But this kind of reply depends upon their mistaken view, already discussed, that positive law, as understood in natural law theory, adds nothing to pre-existing moral requirements. Once we acknowledge that very many (not all!) legal requirements would not be moral requirements unless legally created in accordance with the law's own criteria of legal validity, we can readily see the sense in saying that the law's authoritativeness, in the focal sense of "authoritative," is nothing other than its moral authoritativeness. To repeat, most of our laws would have no moral authority unless they were legally valid, positive laws. So their moral authority is also truly *legal* authority. Laws that, because of their injustice, are without moral authoritativeness, are not legally authoritative in the focal sense of "authoritative." Their "authority" is in the end no more than the "authority" of the Syndicate, of powerful people who can *oblige* you to comply with their will on pain of unpleasant consequences, but who cannot create what any self-respecting person would count as a genuine obligation.

Natural law theory's central strategy for explaining the law's authority points to the under-

determinacy (far short of sheer indeterminacy) of most if not all of practical reason's requirements in the field of open-ended (not merely technological) self-determination by individuals and societies. Indeed, the more benevolent and intelligent people are, the more they will come up with good but incompatible (non-compossible) schemes of social co-ordination (including always the "negative" co-ordination of mutual forbearances) at the political level – property, currency, defence, legal procedure, etc., etc. Unanimity on the merits of particular schemes being thus practically unavailable, but co-ordination around *some* scheme(s) being required for common good (justice, peace, welfare), these good people have sufficient reason to acknowledge authority, that is, an accepted and acceptable procedure for selecting particular schemes of co-ordination with which, once they are so selected, each reasonable member of the community is morally obligated to co-operate *precisely because they have been selected* – that is, precisely as *legally* obligatory for the morally decent conscience.

This is the source of the content-independence and peremptoriness that Hart, in his late work, rightly acknowledged as characteristic of legal reasons for action, and as the essence of their authoritativeness.[37] And as the explanation shows, this content-independence and peremptoriness is neither unconditional nor exceptionless. A sufficient degree of injustice in content will negate the peremptoriness-for-conscience. *Pace* Coleman and Leiter, the laws of South Africa, or some of them, were not binding, albeit widely *regarded and treated and enforced as* binding.

Positivism never coherently reaches beyond reporting attitudes and convergent behaviour (perhaps the sophisticated and articulate attitudes that constitute a set of rules of recognition, change, and adjudication). It has nothing to say to officials or private citisens who want to judge whether, when, and why the authority and obligatoriness *claimed* and *enforced* by those who are *acting as* officials of a legal system, and by their directives, are indeed *authoritative reasons* for their own conscientious action. Positivism does no more than repeat (1) what any competent lawyer – including every legally competent adherent of natural law theory – would say are (or are not) intra-systemically valid laws, imposing "legal requirements," and (2) what any street-wise observer would warn are the likely consequences of non-compliance. It cannot explain the authoritativeness, for an official's or a private citisen's conscience (ultimate rational judgment), of these alleged and imposed requirements, nor their lack of such authority when radically unjust. Positivism is in the last analysis redundant.

For all its sophistication, contemporary positivism cannot get beyond the position adopted by Austin in his brutal account of the authoritativeness of wicked laws: if I say that laws gravely contrary to morality are not binding, "the Court of Justice will demonstrate the inconclusiveness of my reasoning by hanging me up, in pursuance of the law of which I have impugned the validity."[38] What it is most important to understand is that Austin's account is farcically *irrelevant*, unresponsive, to any of the genuine questions that might be asked about the law's authority.

Notes

1 *See* PLATO, LAWS IV.
2 *See* ARISTOTLE, NICOMACHEAN ETHICS bk. I, § 13.
3 *See* CICERO, DE FINIBUS 1.7, 3.20.
4 *See, e.g.,* HANS KELSEN, GENERAL THEORY OF NORMS 226 (Michael Hartney trans., Oxford Univ. Press 1990).
5 2 SAMUEL PUFENDORF, ELEMENTORUM JURISPRUDENTIAE UNIVERSALIS LIBRI DUO (William Abbott Oldfather trans., Clarendon Press 1931) (1672).
6 JOHN LOCKE, QUESTIONS CONCERNING THE LAW OF NATURE (Robert Horwitz et al. trans., Cornell Univ. Press 1990) (1664).
7 2 PUFENDORF, *supra* note 5, at xxx.
8 HUGO GROTIUS, ON THE LAW OF WAR AND PEACE bk. I, at 38 (Francis W. Kelsey trans., William S. Hein & Co. 1995) (1625).
9 LOCKE, *supra* note 6, at 193.
10 *Id.* at 167; *see also id.* at 159.
11 *Id.* at 103.
12 *Id.* at 205.
13 *See id.* at 193.
14 *See, e.g.,* 2 PUFENDORF, *supra* note 5, at 89.

For, if you have removed God from the function of administering justice, all the efficacy of . . . pacts, to the observance of which one of the contracting parties is not able to compel the other by force, will immediately expire, and everyone will measure justice by his own particular advantage. And assuredly, if we are willing to confess the truth, once the fear of divine vengeance has been removed, there appears no sufficient reason why I should be at all obligated, after the conditions governing my advantage have once changed, to furnish that thing, for the furnishing of which to the second party I had bound myself while my interests led in that direction; that is, of course, if I have to fear no real evil, at least from any man, in consequence of that act.

Id.

15 LOCKE, *supra* note 6, at 167; *see also id.* at 164–66 ("[P]atet . . . posse homines a rebus sensibilibus *colligere superiorem esse aliquem potentem sapientemque* qui in homines ipsos *jus habet et imperium.* Quis enim negabit lutum figuli *voluntati esse subjectum,* testamque eadem manu qua formata est.") (emphasis added).
16 *See id.* at 178–79 (This passage was deleted by Locke in 1664).
17 *See* JOHN FINNIS, NATURAL LAW AND NATURAL RIGHTS 348–49 (1980).
18 *See* KELSEN, *supra* note 4, at 189–93, 211–51.
19 *See id.* at 6 ("In general terms: No Ought without a will (even if it is only fictitious).").
20 *See, e.g.,* JOSEPH RAZ, ETHICS IN THE PUBLIC DOMAIN 190–91 (1994).
21 *See* John Finnis, *The Truth in Legal Positivism, in* THE AUTONOMY OF LAW 195–214 (Robert P. George ed., 1996).
22 *See* John Finnis, *The Fairy Tale's Moral,* 115 LAW Q. REV. 170, 174–75 (1999).
23 *See* PLATO, GORGIAS; THOMAS AQUINAS, SUMMA THEOLOGIAE I–II Prologue; JOHN FINNIS, AQUINAS 20, 124–25 (1998).
24 *See* FINNIS, *supra* note 17, at 3–22.
25 For an example of a dispute about which of these alternatives is right, see Ronald Dworkin, *A Reply by Ronald Dworkin, in* RONALD DWORKIN AND CONTEMPORARY JURISPRUDENCE 261 (Marshall Cohen ed., 1984), and Joseph Raz, *Legal Principles and the Limits of the Law, in* RONALD DWORKIN AND CONTEMPORARY JURISPRUDENCE 84–85.
26 That is, since Jeremy Bentham. *See* JEREMY BENTHAM, A COMMENT ON THE COMMENTARIES AND A FRAGMENT ON GOVERN-

MENT (J. H. Burns & H. L. A. Hart eds., Humanities Press 1977) (1776).

27 Jules L. Coleman & Brian Leiter, *Legal Positivism, in* A COMPANION TO PHILOSOPHY OF LAW AND LEGAL THEORY 241, 241 (Dennis Patterson ed., 1996). They add one other "central belief" and one further "commitment": (i) "what counts as law in any particular society is fundamentally a matter of social fact or convention ('the social thesis')." *Id.* The classical natural law theorist will comment that this is equivocal between (a) the tautologous proposition that what is counted as law, in a particular society, is counted as law in that society and (b) the false proposition that what counts as law for fully reasonable persons (e.g., fully reasonable judges) deliberating about their responsibilities is all and only what is counted as law by others in that society – false because *ought* (e.g., the ought of reasonable responsibility) is not entailed by *is*; (ii) "a commitment to the idea that the phenomena comprising the domain at issue (for example, law . . .) must be accessible to the human mind"; classical natural law theory fully shares this com-mitment, since it defines natural law as principles accessible to the human mind, and positive law as rules devised by human minds.

28 *See* Finnis, *supra* note 21, at 203–04.

29 Coleman & Leiter, *supra* note 27, at 244.

30 HANS KELSEN, GENERAL THEORY OF LAW AND STATE 416–17 (Anders Wedberg trans., Harvard Univ. Press 1945).

31 *See* FINNIS, *supra* note 17, at 28.

32 Coleman & Leiter, *supra* note 27, at 243 (emphasis added). For "dictates" read directive or prescription (enactment, judicial judgement, etc.). *See* FINNIS, *supra* note 23, at 256 n.4.

33 Coleman & Leiter, *supra* note 27, at 248.

34 *Id.* at 243.

35 *Id.* at 248.

36 *Id.*

37 *See* H. L. A. HART, ESSAYS ON BENTHAM: STUDIES IN JURISPRUDENCE AND POLITICAL THEORY 243–68 (1982).

38 JOHN AUSTIN, THE PROVINCE OF JURISPRUDENCE DETERMINED 185 (H. L. A. Hart ed., Noonday Press 1954) (1832); *see also* FINNIS, *supra* note 23, at 355.

Part III

Theories of Adjudication

8

Hard Cases

Ronald Dworkin

This essay is a revised form of an inaugural lecture given at Oxford in June of 1971. I should like to repeat what I said then about my predecessor in the Chair of Jurisprudence. The philosophers of science have developed a theory of the growth of science; it argues that from time to time the achievement of a single man is so powerful and so original as to form a new paradigm, that is, to change a discipline's sense of what its problems are and what counts as success in solving them. Professor H. L. A. Hart's work is a paradigm for jurisprudence, not just in his country and not just in mine, but throughout the world. The province of jurisprudence is now the province he has travelled; it extends from the modal logic of legal concepts to the details of the law of criminal responsibility, and in each corner his is the view that others must take as their point of departure. It is difficult to think of any serious writing in jurisprudence in recent years, certainly in Great Britain and America, that has not either claimed his support or taken him as a principal antagonist. This essay is no exception.

His influence has extended, I might add, to form as well as substance. His clarity is famous and his diction contagious: other legal philosophers, for example, once made arguments, but now we only deploy them, and there has been a perfect epidemic of absent-mindedness in imitation of the master. How shall we account for this extraordinary influence? In him reason and passion do not contend, but combine in intelligence, the faculty of making clear what was dark without making it dull. In his hands clarity

enhances rather than dissipates the power of an idea. That is magic, and it is the magic that jurisprudence needs to work.

I   Introduction

A.   *The Rights Thesis*

Theories of adjudication have become more sophisticated, but the most popular theories still put judging in the shade of legislation. The main outlines of this story are familiar. Judges should apply the law that other institutions have made; they should not make new law. That is the ideal, but for different reasons it cannot be realized fully in practice. Statutes and common law rules are often vague and must be interpreted before they can be applied to novel cases. Some cases, moreover, raise issues so novel that they cannot be decided even by stretching or reinterpreting existing rules. So judges must sometimes make new law, either covertly or explicitly. But when they do, they should act as deputy to the appropriate legislature, enacting the law that they suppose the legislature would enact if seized of the problem.

That is perfectly familiar, but there is buried in this common story a further level of subordination not always noticed. When judges make law, so the expectation runs, they will act not only as deputy to the legislature but as a deputy legislature. They will make law in response to evidence and arguments of the same character as would move the superior institution if it were acting on its own. This is a deeper level of subordination because it makes any understanding of what judges do in hard cases parasitic on a prior understanding of what legislators do all the time. This deeper subordination is therefore conceptual as well as political.

In fact, however, judges neither should be nor are deputy legislators, and the familiar assumption, that when they go beyond political decisions already made by someone else they are legislating, is misleading. It misses the importance of a fundamental distinction within political theory, which I shall now introduce in a crude form. This is the distinction between arguments of principle on the one hand and arguments of policy on the other.[1]

Arguments of policy justify a political decision by showing that the decision advances or protects some collective goal of the community as a whole. The argument in favor of a subsidy for aircraft manufacturers, that the subsidy will protect national defense, is an argument of policy. Arguments of principle justify a political decision by showing that the decision respects or secures some individual or group right. The argument in favor of anti-discrimination statutes, that a minority has a right to equal respect and concern, is an argument of principle. These two sorts of argument do not exhaust political argument. Sometimes, for example, a political decision, like the decision to allow extra income tax exemptions for the blind, may be defended as an act of public generosity or virtue rather than on grounds of either policy or principle. But principle and policy are the major grounds of political justification.

The justification of a legislative program of any complexity will ordinarily require both sorts of argument. Even a program that is chiefly a matter of policy, like a subsidy program for important industries, may require strands of principle to justify its particular design. It may be, for example, that the program provides equal subsidies for manufacturers of different capabilities, on the assumption that weaker aircraft manufacturers have some right not to be driven out of business by government intervention, even though the industry would be more efficient without them. On the other hand, a program that depends chiefly on principle, like

an antidiscrimination program, may reflect a sense that rights are not absolute and do not hold when the consequences for policy are very serious. The program may provide, for example, that fair employment practice rules do not apply when they might prove especially disruptive or dangerous. In the subsidy case we might say that the rights conferred are generated by policy and qualified by principle; in the antidiscrimination case they are generated by principle and qualified by policy.

It is plainly competent for the legislature to pursue arguments of policy and to adopt programs that are generated by such arguments. If courts are deputy legislatures, then it must be competent for them to do the same. Of course, unoriginal judicial decisions that merely enforce the clear terms of some plainly valid statute are always justified on arguments of principle, even if the statute itself was generated by policy. Suppose an aircraft manufacturer sues to recover the subsidy that the statute provides. He argues his right to the subsidy; his argument is an argument of principle. He does not argue that the national defense would be improved by subsidizing him; he might even concede that the statute was wrong on policy grounds when it was adopted, or that it should have been repealed, on policy grounds, long ago. His right to a subsidy no longer depends on any argument of policy because the statute made it a matter of principle.

But if the case at hand is a hard case, when no settled rule dictates a decision either way, then it might seem that a proper decision could be generated by either policy or principle. Consider, for example, the problem of the recent *Spartan Steel* case.[2] The defendant's employees had broken an electrical cable belonging to a power company that supplied power to the plaintiff, and the plaintiff's factory was shut down while the cable was repaired. The court had to decide whether to allow the plaintiff recovery for economic loss following negligent damage to someone else's property. It might have proceeded to its decision by asking either whether a firm in the position of the plaintiff had a right to a recovery, which is a matter of principle, or whether it would be economically wise to distribute liability for accidents in the way the plaintiff suggested, which is a matter of policy.

If judges are deputy legislators, then the court should be prepared to follow the latter argument as well as the former, and decide in favor of the plaintiff if that argument recommends. That is, I suppose, what is meant by the popular idea that a court must be free to decide a novel case like *Spartan Steel* on policy grounds; and indeed Lord Denning described his own opinion in that case in just that way.[3] I do not suppose he meant to distinguish an argument of principle from an argument of policy in the technical way I have, but he in any event did not mean to rule out an argument of policy in that technical sense.

I propose, nevertheless, the thesis that judicial decisions in civil cases, even in hard cases like *Spartan Steel*, characteristically are and should be generated by principle not policy. That thesis plainly needs much elaboration, but we may notice that certain arguments of political theory and jurisprudence support the thesis even in its abstract form. These arguments are not decisive, but they are sufficiently powerful to suggest the importance of the thesis, and to justify the attention that will be needed for a more careful formulation.

B.   *Principles and Democracy*

The familiar story, that adjudication must be subordinated to legislation, is supported by two objections to judicial originality. The first argues that a community should be governed by men and women who are elected by and responsible to the majority. Since judges are, for the most part, not elected, and since they are not, in practice, responsible to the electorate in the way legislators are, it seems to compromise that proposition when judges make law. The second argues that if a judge makes new law and applies it retroactively in the case before him, then the losing party will be punished, not because he violated some duty he had, but rather a new duty created after the event.

These two arguments combine to support the traditional ideal that adjudication should be as unoriginal as possible. But they offer much more powerful objections to judicial deci-

sions generated by policy than to those generated by principle. The first objection, that law should be made by elected and responsible officials, seems unexceptionable when we think of law as policy; that is, as a compromise among individual goals and purposes in search of the welfare of the community as a whole. It is far from clear that interpersonal comparisons of utility or preference, through which such compromises might be made objectively, make sense even in theory; but in any case no proper calculus is available in practice. Policy decisions must therefore be made through the operation of some political process designed to produce an accurate expression of the different interests that should be taken into account. The political system of representative democracy may work only indifferently in this respect, but it works better than a system that allows nonelected judges, who have no mail bag or lobbyists or pressure groups, to compromise competing interests in their chambers.

The second objection is also persuasive against a decision generated by policy. We all agree that it would be wrong to sacrifice the rights of an innocent man in the name of some new duty created after the event; it does, therefore, seem wrong to take property from one individual and hand it to another in order just to improve overall economic efficiency. But that is the form of the policy argument that would be necessary to justify a decision in *Spartan Steel*. If the plaintiff had no right to the recovery and the defendant no duty to offer it, the court could be justified in taking the defendant's property for the plaintiff only in the interest of wise economic policy.

But suppose, on the other hand, that a judge successfully justifies a decision in a hard case, like *Spartan Steel*, on grounds not of policy but of principle. Suppose, that is, that he is able to show that the plaintiff has a *right* to recover its damages. The two arguments just described would offer much less of an objection to the decision. The first is less relevant when a court judges principle, because an argument of principle does not often rest on assumptions about the nature and intensity of the different demands and concerns distributed throughout the community. On the contrary, an argument of principle fixes on some interest presented by the proponent of the right it describes, an interest alleged to be of such a character as to make irrelevant the fine discriminations of any argument of policy that might oppose it. A judge who is insulated from the demands of the political majority whose interests the right would trump is, therefore, in a better position to evaluate the argument.

The second objection to judicial originality has no force against an argument of principle. If the plaintiff has a right against the defendant, then the defendant has a corresponding duty, and it is that duty, not some new duty created in court, that justifies the award against him. Even if the duty has not been imposed upon him by explicit prior legislation, there is, but for one difference, no more injustice in enforcing the duty than if it had been.

The difference is, of course, that if the duty had been created by statute the defendant would have been put on much more explicit notice of that duty, and might more reasonably have been expected to arrange his affairs so as to provide for its consequences. But an argument of principle makes us look upon the defendant's claim, that it is unjust to take him by surprise, in a new light. If the plaintiff does indeed have a right to a judicial decision in his favor, then he is entitled to rely upon that right. If it is obvious and uncontroversial that he has the right, the defendant is in no position to claim unfair surprise just because the right arose in some way other than by publication in a statute. If, on the other hand, the plaintiff's claim is doubtful, then the court must, to some extent, surprise one or another of the parties; and if the court decides that on balance the plaintiff's argument is stronger, then it will also decide that the plaintiff was, on balance, more justified in his expectations. The court may, of course, be mistaken in this conclusion; but that possibility is not a consequence of the originality of its argument, for there is no reason to suppose that a court hampered by the requirement that its decisions be unoriginal will make fewer mistakes of principle than a court that is not.

C. *Jurisprudence*

We have, therefore, in these political considerations, a strong reason to consider more carefully whether judicial arguments cannot be understood, even in hard cases, as arguments generated by principle. We have an additional reason in a familiar problem of jurisprudence. Lawyers believe that when judges make new law their decisions are constrained by legal traditions but are nevertheless personal and original. Novel decisions, it is said, reflect a judge's own political morality, but also reflect the morality that is embedded in the traditions of the common law, which might well be different. This is, of course, only law school rhetoric, but it nevertheless poses the problem of explaining how these different contributions to the decision of a hard case are to be identified and reconciled.

One popular solution relies on a spatial image; it says that the traditions of the common law contract the area of a judge's discretion to rely upon his personal morality, but do not entirely eliminate that area. But this answer is unsatisfactory on two grounds. First, it does not elucidate what is at best a provocative metaphor, which is that some morality is embedded in a mass of particular decisions other judges have reached in the past. Second, it suggests a plainly inadequate phenomenological account of the judicial decision. Judges do not decide hard cases in two stages, first checking to see where the institutional constraints end, and then setting the books aside to stride off on their own. The institutional constraints they sense are pervasive and endure to the decision itself. We therefore need an account of the interaction of personal and institutional morality that is less metaphorical and explains more successfully that pervasive interaction.

The rights thesis, that judicial decisions enforce existing political rights, suggests an explanation that is more successful on both counts. If the thesis holds, then institutional history acts not as a constraint on the political judgment of judges but as an ingredient of that judgment, because institutional history is part of the background that any plausible judgment about the rights of an individual must accommodate. Political rights are creatures of both history and morality: what an individual is entitled to have, in civil society, depends upon both the practice and the justice of its political institutions. So the supposed tension between judicial originality and institutional history is dissolved: judges must make fresh judgments about the rights of the parties who come before them, but these political rights reflect, rather than oppose, political decisions of the past. When a judge chooses between the rule established in precedent and some new rule thought to be fairer, he does not choose between history and justice. He rather makes a judgment that requires some compromise between considerations that ordinarily combine in any calculation of political right, but here compete.

The rights thesis therefore provides a more satisfactory explanation of how judges use precedent in hard cases than the explanation provided by any theory that gives a more prominent place to policy. Judges, like all political officials, are subject to the doctrine of political responsibility. This doctrine states, in its most general form, that political officials must make only such political decisions as they can justify within a political theory that also justifies the other decisions they propose to make. The doctrine seems innocuous in this general form; but it does, even in this form, condemn a style of political administration that might be called, following Rawls, intuitionistic.[4] It condemns the practice of making decisions that seem right in isolation, but cannot be brought within some comprehensive theory of general principles and policies that is consistent with other decisions also thought right. Suppose a Congressman votes to prohibit abortion, on the ground that human life in any form is sacred, but then votes to permit the parents of babies born deformed to withhold medical treatment that will keep such babies alive. He might say that he feels that there is some difference, but the principle of responsibility, strictly applied, will not allow him these two votes unless he can incorporate the difference within some general political theory he sincerely holds.

The doctrine demands, we might say, articulate consistency. But this demand is relatively weak when policies are in play. Policies are aggregative in their influence on political decisions and it need not be part of a responsible strategy for reaching a collective goal that individuals be treated alike. It does not follow from the doctrine of responsibility, therefore, that if the legislature awards a subsidy to one aircraft manufacturer one month it must award a subsidy to another manufacturer the next. In the case of principles, however, the doctrine insists on distributional consistency from one case to the next, because it does not allow for the idea of a strategy that may be better served by unequal distribution of the benefit in question. If an official believes, for example, that sexual liberty of some sort is a right of individuals, then he must protect that liberty in a way that distributes the benefit reasonably equally over the class of those whom he supposes to have the right. If he allows one couple to use contraceptives on the ground that this right would otherwise be invaded, then he must, so long as he does not recant that earlier decision, allow the next couple the same liberty. He cannot say that the first decision gave the community just the amount of sexual liberty it needed, so that no more is required at the time of the second.

Judicial decisions are political decisions, at least in the broad sense that attracts the doctrine of political responsibility. If the rights thesis holds, then the distinction just made would account, at least in a very general way, for the special concern that judges show for both precedents and hypothetical examples. An argument of principle can supply a justification for a particular decision, under the doctrine of responsibility, only if the principle cited can be shown to be consistent with earlier decisions not recanted, and with decisions that the institution is prepared to make in the hypothetical circumstances. That is hardly surprising, but the argument would not hold if judges based their decisions on arguments of policy. They would be free to say that some policy might be adequately served by serving it in the case at bar, providing, for example, just the right subsidy to some troubled industry, so that neither earlier decisions nor hypothetical future decisions need be understood as serving the same policy.

Consistency here, of course, means consistency in the application of the principle relied upon, not merely in the application of the particular rule announced in the name of that principle. If, for example, the principle that no one has the duty to make good remote or unexpected losses flowing from his negligence is relied upon to justify a decision for the defendant in *Spartan Steel*, then it must be shown that the rule laid down in other cases, which allows recovery for negligent misstatements, is consistent with that principle; not merely that the rule about negligent misstatements is a different rule from the rule in *Spartan Steel*.

D.   *Three Problems*

We therefore find, in these arguments of political theory and jurisprudence, some support for the rights thesis in its abstract form. Any further defense, however, must await a more precise statement. The thesis requires development in three directions. It relies, first, on a general distinction between individual rights and social goals, and that distinction must be stated with more clarity than is provided simply by examples. The distinction must be stated, moreover, so as to respond to the following problem. When politicians appeal to individual rights, they have in mind grand propositions about very abstract and fundamental interests, like the right to freedom or equality or respect. These grand rights do not seem apposite to the decision of hard cases at law, except, perhaps, constitutional law; and even when they are apposite they seem too abstract to have much argumentative power. If the rights thesis is to succeed, it must demonstrate how the general distinction between arguments of principle and policy can be maintained between arguments of the character and detail that do figure in legal argument. In Part II of this essay I shall try to show that the distinction between abstract and concrete rights, suitably elaborated, is sufficient for that purpose.

The thesis provides, second, a theory of the role of precedent and institutional history in the decision of hard cases. I summarized that theory in the last section, but it must be expanded and illustrated before it can be tested against our experience of how judges actually decide cases. It must be expanded, moreover, with an eye to

the following problem. No one thinks that the law as it stands is perfectly just. Suppose that some line of precedents is in fact unjust, because it refuses to enforce, as a legal right, some political right of the citizens. Even though a judge deciding some hard case disapproves of these precedents for that reason, the doctrine of articulate consistency nevertheless requires that he allow his argument to be affected by them. It might seem that his argument cannot be an argument of principle, that is, an argument designed to establish the political rights of the parties, because the argument is corrupted, through its attention to precedent, by a false opinion about what these rights are. If the thesis is to be defended, it must be shown why this first appearance is wrong. It is not enough to say that the argument may be an argument of principle because it establishes the legal, as distinguished from the political, rights of the litigants. The rights thesis supposes that the right to win a law suit is a genuine political right, and though that right is plainly different from other forms of political rights, like the right of all citizens to be treated as equals, just noticing that difference does not explain why the former right may be altered by misguided earlier decisions. It is necessary, in order to understand that feature of legal argument, to consider the special qualities of institutional rights in general, which I consider in Part III, and the particular qualities of legal rights, as a species of institutional rights, which I consider in Part IV.

But the explanation I give of institutional and legal rights exposes a third and different problem for the rights thesis. This explanation makes plain that judges must sometimes make judgments of political morality in order to decide what the legal rights of litigants are. The thesis may therefore be thought open, on that ground, to the first challenge to judicial originality that I mentioned earlier. It might be said that the thesis is indefensible because it cheats the majority of its right to decide questions of political morality for itself. I shall consider that challenge in Part V.

These, then, are three problems that any full statement of the rights thesis must face. If that full statement shows these objections to the thesis misconceived, then it will show the thesis to be less radical than it might first have seemed. The thesis presents, not some novel information about what judges do, but a new way of describing what we all know they do; and the virtues of this new description are not empirical but political and philosophical.

II   Rights and Goals

A.   *Types of Rights*

Arguments of principle are arguments intended to establish an individual right; arguments of policy are arguments intended to establish a collective goal. Principles are propositions that describe rights; policies are propositions that describe goals. But what are rights and goals and what is the difference? It is hard to supply any definition that does not beg the question. It seems natural to say, for example, that freedom of speech is a right, not a goal, because citizens are entitled to that freedom as a matter of political morality, and that increased munitions manufacture is a goal, not a right, because it contributes to collective welfare, but no particular manufacturer is entitled to a government contract. This does not improve our understanding, however, because the concept of entitlement uses rather than explains the concept of a right.

In this essay I shall distinguish rights from goals by fixing on the distributional character of claims about rights, and on the force of these claims, in political argument, against competing claims of a different distributional character. I shall make, that is, a formal distinction that does not attempt to show which rights men and women actually have, or indeed that they have any at all. It rather provides a guide for discovering which rights a particular political theory supposes men and women to have. The formal distinction does suggest, of course, an approach to the more fundamental question: it suggests that we discover what rights people actually have by looking for arguments that would justify claims having the appropriate distributional character. But the distinction does not itself supply any such arguments.

I begin with the idea of a political aim as a generic political justification. A political theory takes a certain state of affairs as a political aim if, for that theory, it counts in favor of any political decision that the decision is likely to advance, or to protect, that state of affairs, and counts against the decision that it will retard or endanger it. A political right is an individuated political aim. An individual has a right to some opportunity or resource or liberty if it counts in favor of a political decision that the decision is likely to advance or protect the state of affairs in which he enjoys the right, even when no other political aim is served and some political aim is disserved thereby, and counts against that decision that it will retard or endanger that state of affairs, even when some other political aim is thereby served.[5] A goal is a nonindividuated political aim, that is, a state of affairs whose specification does not in this way call for any particular opportunity or resource or liberty for particular individuals.

Collective goals encourage trade-offs of benefits and burdens within a community in order to produce some overall benefit for the community as a whole. Economic efficiency is a collective goal: it calls for such distribution of opportunities and liabilities as will produce the greatest aggregate economic benefit defined in some way. Some conception of equality may also be taken as a collective goal; a community may aim at a distribution such that maximum wealth is no more than double minimum wealth, or, under a different conception, so that no racial or ethnic group is much worse off than other groups. Of course, any collective goal will suggest a particular distribution, given particular facts. Economic efficiency as a goal will suggest that a particular industry be subsidized in some circumstances, but taxed punitively in others. Equality as a goal will suggest immediate and complete redistribution in some circumstances, but partial and discriminatory redistribution in others. In each case distributional principles are subordinate to some conception of aggregate collective good, so that offering less of some benefit to one man can be justified simply by showing that this will lead to a greater benefit overall.

Collective goals may, but need not, be absolute. The community may pursue different goals at the same time, and it may compromise one goal for the sake of another. It may, for example, pursue economic efficiency, but also military strength. The suggested distribution will then be determined by the sum of the two policies, and this will increase the permutations and combinations of possible trade-offs. In any case, these permutations and combinations will offer a number of competing strategies for serving each goal and both goals in combination. Economic efficiency may be well served by offering subsidies to all farmers, and to no manufacturers, and better served by offering double the subsidy to some farmers and none to others. There will be alternate strategies of pursuing any set of collective goals, and, particularly as the number of goals increases, it will be impossible to determine in a piecemeal or case-by-case way the distribution that best serves any set of goals. Whether it is good policy to give double subsidies to some farmers and none to others will depend upon a great number of other political decisions that have been or will be made in pursuit of very general strategies into which this particular decision must fit.

Rights also may be absolute: a political theory which holds a right to freedom of speech as absolute will recognize no reason for not securing the liberty it requires for every individual; no reason, that is, short of impossibility. Rights may also be less than absolute; one principle might have to yield to another, or even to an urgent policy with which it competes on particular facts. We may define the weight of a right, assuming it is not absolute, as its power to withstand such competition. It follows from the definition of a right that it cannot be outweighed by all social goals. We might, for simplicity, stipulate not to call any political aim a right unless it has a certain threshold weight against collective goals in general; unless, for example, it cannot be defeated by appeal to any of the ordinary, routine goals of political administration, but only by a goal of special urgency. Suppose, for example, some man says he recognizes the right of free speech, but adds that free speech must yield whenever its exercise would inconvenience the public. He means, I take it, that he recognizes the pervasive goal of collective welfare, and only such distribution of liberty of speech as that collective goal recommends in particular circumstances. His political position is exhausted by the collective goal; the putative right adds nothing and there is no point to recognizing it as a right at all.

These definitions and distinctions make plain that the character of a political aim – its standing as a right or goal – depends upon its place and function within a single political theory. The same phrase might describe a right within one theory and a goal within another, or a right that is absolute or powerful within one theory but relatively weak within another. If a public official has anything like a coherent political theory that he uses, even intuitively, to justify the particular decisions he reaches, then this theory will recognize a wide variety of different types of rights, arranged in some way that assigns rough relative weight to each.

Any adequate theory will distinguish, for example, between background rights, which are rights that provide a justification for political decisions by society in the abstract, and institutional rights, that provide a justification for a decision by some particular and specified political institution. Suppose that my political theory provides that every man has a right to the property of another if he needs it more. I might yet concede that he does not have a legislative right to the same effect; I might concede, that is, that he has no institutional right that the present legislature enact legislation that would violate the Constitution, as such a statute presumably would. I might also concede that he has no institutional right to a judicial decision condoning theft. Even if I did make these concessions, I could preserve my initial background claim by arguing that the people as a whole would be justified in amending the Constitution to abolish property, or perhaps in rebelling and overthrowing the present form of government entirely. I would claim that each man has a residual background right that would justify or require these acts, even though I concede that he does not have the right to specific institutional decisions as these institutions are now constituted.

Any adequate theory will also make use of a distinction between abstract and concrete rights, and therefore between abstract and concrete principles. This is a distinction of degree, but I shall discuss relatively clear examples at two poles of the scale it contemplates, and therefore treat it as a distinction in kind. An abstract right is a general political aim the statement of which does not indicate how that general aim is to be weighed or compromised in particular circumstances against other political aims. The grand rights of political rhetoric are in this way abstract. Politicians speak of a right to free speech or dignity or equality, with no suggestion that these rights are absolute, but with no attempt to suggest their impact on particular complex social situations.

Concrete rights, on the other hand, are political aims that are more precisely defined so as to express more definitely the weight they have against other political aims on particular occasions. Suppose I say, not simply that citizens have a right to free speech, but that a newspaper has a right to publish defense plans classified as secret provided this publication will not create an immediate physical danger to troops. My principle declares for a particular resolution of the conflict it acknowledges between the abstract right of free speech, on the one hand, and competing rights of soldiers to security or the urgent needs of defense on the other. Abstract rights in this way provide arguments for concrete rights, but the claim of a concrete right is more definitive than any claim of abstract right that supports it.[6]

B. *Principles and Utility*

The distinction between rights and goals does not deny a thesis that is part of popular moral anthropology. It may be entirely reasonable to think, as this thesis provides, that the principles the members of a particular community find persuasive will be causally determined by the collective goals of that community. If many people in a community believe that each individual has a right to some minimal concern on the part of others, then this fact may be explained, as a matter of cultural history, by the further fact that their collective welfare is advanced by that belief. If some novel arrangement of rights would serve their collective welfare better, then we should expect, according to

this thesis, that in due time their moral convictions will alter in favor of that new arrangement.

I do not know how far this anthropological theory holds in our own society, or any society. It is certainly untestable in anything like the simple form in which I have put it, and I do not see why its claim, that rights are psychologically or culturally determined by goals, is a priori more plausible than the contrary claim. Perhaps men and women choose collective goals to accommodate some prior sense of individual rights, rather than delineating rights according to collective goals. In either case, however, there must be an important time lag, so that at any given time most people will recognize the conflict between rights and goals, at least in particular cases, that the general distinction between these two kinds of political aims presupposes.

The distinction presupposes, that is, a further distinction between the force of a particular right within a political theory and the causal explanation of why the theory provides that right. This is a formal way of putting the point, and it is appropriate only when, as I am now supposing, we can identify a particular political theory and so distinguish the analytical question of what it provides from the historical question of how it came to provide it. The distinction is therefore obscured when we speak of the morality of a *community* without specifying which of the many different conceptions of a community morality we have in mind. Without some further specification we cannot construct even a vague or abstract political theory as the theory of the community at any particular time, and so we cannot make the distinction between reasons and force that is analytically necessary to understand the concepts of principle and policy. We are therefore prey to the argument that the anthropological thesis destroys the distinction between the two; we speak as if we had some coherent theory in mind, as the community's morality, but we deny that it distinguishes principle from policy on the basis of an argument that seems plausible just because we do not have any particular theory in mind. Once we do make plain what we intend by some reference to the morality of a community, and proceed to identify, even crudely, what we take the principles of that morality to be, the anthropological argument is tamed.

There are political theories, however, that unite rights and goals not causally but by making the force of a right contingent upon its power, as a right, to promote some collective goal. I have in mind various forms of the ethical theory called rule utilitarianism. One popular form of that theory, for example, holds that an act is right if the general acceptance of a rule requiring that act would improve the average welfare of members of the community.[7] A political theory might provide for a right to free speech, for example, on the hypothesis that the general acceptance of that right by courts and other political institutions would promote the highest average utility of the community in the long run.

But we may nevertheless distinguish institutional rights, at least, from collective goals within such a theory. If the theory provides that an official of a particular institution is justified in making a political decision, and not justified in refusing to make it, whenever that decision is necessary to protect the freedom to speak of any individual, without regard to the impact of the decision on collective goals, the theory provides free speech as a right. It does not matter that the theory stipulates this right on the hypothesis that if all political institutions do enforce the right in that way an important collective goal will in fact be promoted. What is important is the commitment to a scheme of government that makes an appeal to the right decisive in particular cases.

So neither the anthropological thesis nor rule utilitarianism offers any objection to the distinction between arguments of principle and arguments of policy. I should mention, out of an abundance of caution, one further possible challenge to that distinction. Different arguments of principle and policy can often be made in support of the same political decision. Suppose that an official wishes to argue in favor of racial segregation in public places. He may offer the policy argument that mixing races causes more overall discomfort than satisfaction. Or he may offer an argument of principle appealing to the rights of those who might be killed or maimed in riots that desegregation would produce. It might be thought that the substitutibility of these arguments defeats the distinction between arguments of principle and policy, or in any case makes the distinction less useful, for the following reason. Suppose it is conceded that the right to equality between races is sufficiently strong that it must prevail over all but the most pressing argument of policy, and be compromised only as required by competing arguments of principle. That would be an empty concession if arguments of principle could always be found to substitute for an argument of policy that might otherwise be made.

But it is a fallacy to suppose that because some argument of principle can always be found to substitute for an argument of policy, it will be as cogent or as powerful as the appropriate argument of policy would have been. If some minority's claim to an antidiscrimination statute were itself based on policy, and could therefore be defeated by an appeal to overall general welfare or utility, then the argument that cites the majority's discomfort or annoyance might well be powerful enough. But if the claim cites a right to equality that must prevail unless matched by a competing argument of principle, the only such argument available may be, as here, simply too weak. Except in extraordinary cases, the danger to any particular man's life that flows from desegregation adequately managed and policed will be very small. We might therefore concede that the competing right to life offers some argument countervailing against the right to equality here, and yet maintain that that argument is of negligible weight; strong enough, perhaps, to slow the pace of desegregation but not strong enough even to slow it very much.

C. *Economics and Principle*

The rights thesis, in its descriptive aspect, holds that judicial decisions in hard cases are characteristically generated by principle not policy. Recent research into the connections between economic theory and the common law might be thought to suggest the contrary: that judges almost always decide on grounds of policy rather than principle. We must, however, be careful to distinguish between two propositions said to be established by that research. It is argued, first, that almost every rule developed by judges in such disparate fields as tort, contract and property can be shown to serve the collective goal of making resource allocation more efficient.[8] It is argued, second, that in certain cases judges explicitly base their decisions on economic policy.[9] Neither of these claims subverts the rights thesis.

The first claim makes no reference to the intentions of the judges who decided the cases establishing rules that improve economic efficiency. It does not suppose that these judges were aware of the economic value of their rules, or even that they would have acknowledged that value as an argument in favor of their decisions. The evidence, for the most part, suggests the contrary. The courts that nourished the unfortunate fellow-servant doctrine, for example, thought that the rule was required by fairness, not utility, and when the rule was abolished it was because the argument from fairness, not the argument from utility, was found wanting by a different generation of lawyers.[10]

If this first claim is sound, it might seem to some an important piece of evidence for the anthropological thesis described in the last section. They will think that it suggests that judges and lawyers, reflecting the general moral attitudes of their time, thought that corporations and individuals had just those rights that an explicit rule utilitarian would legislate to serve the general welfare. But the first claim might equally well suggest the contrary conclusion I mentioned, that our present ideas of general welfare reflect our ideas of individual right. Professor Posner, for example, argues for that claim by presupposing a particular conception of efficient resource allocation. He says that the value of some scarce resource to a particular individual is measured by the amount of money he is willing to pay for it, so that community welfare is maximized when each resource is in the hands of someone who would pay more than anyone else to have it.[11] But that is hardly a self-evident or neutral conception of value. It is congenial to a political theory that celebrates competition, but far less congenial to a more

egalitarian theory, because it demotes the claims of the poor who are willing to spend less because they have less to spend. Posner's conception of value, therefore, seems as much the consequence as the cause of a theory of individual rights. In any case, however, the anthropological thesis of the first claim offers no threat to the rights thesis. Even if we concede that a judge's theory of rights is determined by some instinctive sense of economic value, rather than the other way about, we may still argue that he relies on that theory, and not economic analysis, to justify decisions in hard cases.

The second claim we distinguished, however, may seem to present a more serious challenge. If judges explicitly refer to economic policy in some cases, then these cases cannot be understood simply as evidence for the anthropological thesis. Learned Hand's theory of negligence is the most familiar example of this explicit reference to economics. He said, roughly, that the test of whether the defendant's act was unreasonable, and therefore actionable, is the economic test which asks whether the defendant could have avoided the accident at less cost to himself than the plaintiff was likely to suffer if the accident occurred, discounted by the improbability of the accident.[12] It may be said that this economic test provides an argument of policy rather than principle, because it makes the decision turn on whether the collective welfare would have been advanced more by allowing the accident to take place or by spending what was necessary to avoid it. If so, then cases in which some test like Hand's is explicitly used, however few they might be, would stand as counterexamples to the rights thesis.

But the assumption that an economic calculation of any sort must be an argument of policy overlooks the distinction between abstract and concrete rights. Abstract rights, like the right to speak on political matters, take no account of competing rights; concrete rights, on the other hand, reflect the impact of such competition. In certain kinds of cases the argument from competing abstract principles to a concrete right can be made in the language of economics. Consider the principle that each member of a community has a right that each other member treat him with the minimal respect due a fellow human being.[13] That is a very abstract principle: it demands some balance, in particular cases, between the interests of those to be protected and the liberty of those from whom the principle demands an unstated level of concern and respect. It is natural, particularly when economic vocabulary is in fashion, to define the proper balance by comparing the sum of the utilities of these two parties under different conditions. If one man acts in a way that he can foresee will injure another so that the collective utility of the pair will be sharply reduced by his act, he does not show the requisite care and concern. If he can guard or insure against the injury much more cheaply or effectively than the other can, for example, then he does not show care and concern unless he takes these precautions or arranges that insurance.

That character of argument is by no means novel, though perhaps its economic dress is. Philosophers have for a long time debated hypothetical cases testing the level of concern that one member of a community owes to another. If one man is drowning, and another may save him at minimal risk to himself, for example, then the first has a moral right to be saved by the second. That proposition might easily be put in economic form: if the collective utility of the pair is very sharply improved by a rescue, then the drowning man has a right to that rescue and the rescuer a duty to make it. The parallel legal proposition may, of course, be much more complex than that. It may specify special circumstances in which the crucial question is not whether the collective utility of the pair will be sharply advanced, but only whether it will be marginally advanced. It might put the latter question, for example, when one man's positive act, as distinct from a failure to act, creates a risk of direct and foreseeable physical injury to the person or property of another. If the rights thesis is sound, of course, then no judge may appeal to that legal proposition unless he believes that the principle of minimal respect states an abstract legal right; but if he does, then he may cast his argument in economic form without thereby changing its character from principle to policy.

Since Hand's test, and the parallel argument about rescuing a drowning man, are methods of compromising competing rights, they consider only the welfare of those whose abstract rights are at stake. They do not provide room for costs or benefits to the community at large, except as these are reflected in the welfare of those whose rights are in question. We can easily imagine an argument that does not concede these restrictions. Suppose someone argued that the principle requiring rescue at minimal risk should be amended so as to make the decision turn, not on some function of the collective utilities of the victim and rescuer, but on marginal utility to the community as a whole, so that the rescuer must take into account not only the relative risks to himself and the victim, but the relative social importance of the two. It might follow that an insignificant man must risk his life to save a bank president, but that a bank president need not even tire himself to save a nobody. The argument is no longer an argument of principle, because it supposes the victim to have a right to nothing but his expectations under general utility. Hand's formula, and more sophisticated variations, are not arguments of that character; they do not subordinate an individual right to some collective goal, but provide a mechanism for compromising competing claims of abstract right.

Negligence cases are not the only cases in which judges compromise abstract rights in defining concrete ones. If a judge appeals to public safety or the scarcity of some vital resource, for example, as a ground for limiting some abstract right, then his appeal might be understood as an appeal to the competing rights of those whose security will be sacrificed, or whose just share of that resource will be threatened if the abstract right is made concrete. His argument is an argument of principle if it respects the distributional requirements of such arguments, and if it observes the restriction mentioned in the last section: that the weight of a competing principle may be less than the weight of the appropriate parallel policy. We find a different sort of example in the familiar argument that certain sorts of law suits should not be allowed because to do so would "swamp" the courts with litigation. The court supposes that if it were to allow that type of suit it would lack the time to consider promptly enough other law suits aiming to vindicate rights that are, taken together, more important than the rights it therefore proposes to bar.

This is an appropriate point to notice a certain limitation of the rights thesis. It holds in standard civil cases, when the ruling assumption is that one of the parties has a right to win; but it holds only asymmetrically when that assumption cannot be made. The accused in a criminal case has a right to a decision in his favor if he is innocent, but the state has no parallel right to a conviction if he is guilty. The court may therefore find in favor of the accused, in some hard case testing rules of evidence, for example, on an argument of policy that does not suppose that the accused has any right to be acquitted. The Supreme Court in *Linkletter v. Walker*[14] said that its earlier decision in *Mapp v. Ohio*[15] was such a decision. The Court said it had changed the rules permitting the introduction of illegally obtained evidence, not because Miss Mapp had any right that such evidence not be used if otherwise admissible, but in order to deter policemen from collecting such evidence in the future. I do not mean that a constitutional decision on such grounds is proper, or even that the Court's later description of its earlier decision was accurate. I mean only to point out how the geometry of a criminal prosecution, which does not set opposing rights in a case against one another, differs from the standard civil case in which the rights thesis holds symmetrically.

III Institutional Rights

The rights thesis provides that judges decide hard cases by confirming or denying concrete rights. But the concrete rights upon which judges rely must have two other characteristics. They must be institutional rather than background rights, and they must be legal rather than some other form of institutional rights. We cannot appreciate or test the thesis, therefore, without further elaboration of these distinctions.

Institutional rights may be found in institutions of very different character. A chess player has a "chess" right to be awarded a point in a tournament if he checkmates an opponent.

A citizen in a democracy has a legislative right to the enactment of statutes necessary to protect his free speech. In the case of chess, institutional rights are fixed by constitutive and regulative rules that belong distinctly to the game, or to a particular tournament. Chess is, in this sense, an autonomous institution; I mean that it is understood, among its participants, that no one may claim an institutional right by direct appeal to general morality. No one may argue, for example, that he has earned the right to be declared the winner by his general virtue. But legislation is only partly autonomous in that sense. There are special constitutive and regulative rules that define what a legislature is, and who belongs to it, and how it votes, and that it may not establish a religion. But these rules belonging distinctly to legislation are rarely sufficient to determine whether a citizen has an institutional right to have a certain statute enacted; they do not decide, for example, whether he has a right to minimum wage legislation. Citizens are expected to repair to general considerations of political morality when they argue for such rights.

The fact that some institutions are fully and others partly autonomous has the consequence mentioned earlier, that the institutional rights a political theory acknowledges may diverge from the background rights it provides. Institutional rights are nevertheless genuine rights. Even if we suppose that the poor have an abstract background right to money taken from the rich, it would be wrong, not merely unexpected, for the referees of a chess tournament to award the prize money to the poorest contestant rather than the contestant with the most points. It would provide no excuse to say that since tournament rights merely describe the conditions necessary for calling the tournament a chess tournament, the referee's act is justified so long as he does not use the word "chess" when he hands out the award. The participants entered the tournament with the understanding that chess rules would apply; they have genuine rights to the enforcement of these rules and no others.

Institutional autonomy insulates an official's institutional duty from the greater part of background political morality. But how far does the force of this insulation extend? Even in the case of a fully insulated institution like chess some rules will require interpretation or elaboration before an official may enforce them in certain circumstances. Suppose some rule of a chess tournament provides that the referee shall declare a game forfeit if one player "unreasonably" annoys the other in the course of play. The language of the rule does not define what counts as "unreasonable" annoyance; it does not decide whether, for example, a player who continually smiles at his opponent in such a way as to unnerve him, as the Russian grandmaster Tal once smiled at Fischer, annoys him unreasonably.

The referee is not free to give effect to his background convictions in deciding this hard case. He might hold, as a matter of political theory, that individuals have a right to equal welfare without regard to intellectual abilities. It would nevertheless be wrong for him to rely upon that conviction in deciding difficult cases under the forfeiture rule. He could not say, for example, that annoying behavior is reasonable so long as it has the effect of reducing the importance of intellectual ability in deciding who will win the game. The participants, and the general community that is interested, will say that his duty is just the contrary. Since chess is an intellectual game, he must apply the forfeiture rule in such a way as to protect, rather than jeopardize, the role of intellect in the contest.

We have, then, in the case of the chess referee, an example of an official whose decisions about institutional rights are understood to be governed by institutional constraints even when the force of these constraints is not clear. We do not think that he is free to legislate interstitially within the "open texture" of imprecise rules.[16] If one interpretation of the forfeiture rule will protect the character of the game, and another will not, then the participants have a right to the first interpretation. We may hope to find, in this relatively simple case, some general feature of institutional rights in hard cases that will bear on the decision of a judge in a hard case at law.

I said that the game of chess has a character that the referee's decisions must respect. What does that mean? How does a referee know that chess is an intellectual game rather than a game of chance or an exhibition of digital ballet? He may well start with what everyone knows. Every institution is placed by its participants in some very rough category of institution; it is taken to be a game rather than a religious ceremony or a form of exercise or a political process. It is, for that reason, definitional of chess that it is a game rather than an exercise in digital skill. These conventions, exhibited in attitudes and manners and in history, are decisive. If everyone takes chess to be a game of chance, so that they curse their luck and nothing else when a piece *en prise* happens to be taken, then chess is a game of chance, though a very bad one.

But these conventions will run out, and they may run out before the referee finds enough to decide the case of Tal's smile. It is important to see, however, that the conventions run out in a particular way. They are not incomplete, like a book whose last page is missing, but abstract, so that their full force can be captured in a concept that admits of different conceptions; that is, in a *contested* concept.[17] The referee must select one or another of these conceptions, not to supplement the convention, but to enforce it. He must *construct* the game's character by putting to himself different sets of questions. Given that chess is an intellectual game, is it, like poker, intellectual in some sense that includes ability at psychological intimidation? Or is it, like mathematics, intellectual in some sense that does not include that ability? This first set of questions asks him to look more closely at the game, to determine whether its features support one rather than the other of these conceptions of intellect. But he must also ask a different set of questions. Given that chess is an intellectual game of some sort, what follows about reasonable behavior in a chess game? Is ability at psychological intimidation, or ability to resist such intimidation, really an intellectual quality? These questions ask him to look more closely at the concept of intellect itself.

The referee's calculations, if they are self-conscious, will oscillate between these two sets of questions, progressively narrowing the questions to be asked at the next stage. He might first identify, by reflecting on the concept, different conceptions of intellect. He might suppose at this first stage, for example, that physical grace of the sort achieved in ballet is one form of intelligence. But he must then test these different conceptions against the rules and practices of the game. That test will rule out any physical conception of intelligence. But it may not discriminate between a conception that includes or a conception that rejects psychological intimidation, because either of these conceptions would provide an account of the rules and practices that is not plainly superior, according to any general canons of explanation, to the account provided by the other. He must then ask himself which of these two accounts offers a deeper or more successful account of what intellect really is. His calculations, so conceived, oscillate between philosophy of mind and the facts of the institution whose character he must elucidate.

This is, of course, only a fanciful reconstruction of a calculation that will never take place; any official's sense of the game will have developed over a career, and he will employ rather than expose that sense in his judgments. But the reconstruction enables us to see how the concept of the game's character is tailored to a special institutional problem. Once an autonomous institution is established, such that participants have institutional rights under distinct rules belonging to that institution, then hard cases may arise that must, in the nature of the case, be supposed to have an answer. If Tal does not have a right that the game be continued, it must be because the forfeiture rule, properly understood, justifies the referee's intervention; if it does, then Fischer has a right to win at once. It is not useful to speak of the referee's "discretion" in such a case. If some weak sense of discretion is meant, then the remark is unhelpful; if some strong sense is meant, such that Tal no longer has a right to win, then this must be, again, because the rule properly understood destroys the right he would otherwise have.[18] Suppose we say that in such a case all the parties have a right to expect is that the referee will use his best judgment. That is, in a sense, perfectly true, because they can have no more, by way of the referee's judgment, than his best judgment. But they are nevertheless entitled to his best judgment about which behavior is, in the circumstances of the game,

unreasonable; they are entitled, that is, to his best judgment about what their rights are. The proposition that there is some "right" answer to that question does not mean that the rules of chess are exhaustive and unambiguous; rather it is a complex statement about the responsibilities of its officials and participants.

But if the decision in a hard case must be a decision about the rights of the parties, then an official's reason for that judgment must be the sort of reason that justifies recognizing or denying a right. He must bring to his decision a general theory of why, in the case of his institution, the rules create or destroy any rights at all, and he must show what decision that general theory requires in the hard case. In chess the general ground of institutional rights must be the tacit consent or understanding of the parties. They consent, in entering a chess tournament, to the enforcement of certain and only those rules, and it is hard to imagine any other general ground for supposing that they have any institutional rights. But if that is so, and if the decision in a hard case is a decision about which rights they actually have, then the argument for the decision must apply that general ground to the hard case.

The hard case puts, we might say, a question of political theory. It asks what it is fair to suppose that the players have done in consenting to the forfeiture rule. The concept of a game's character is a conceptual device for framing that question. It is a contested concept that internalizes the general justification of the institution so as to make it available for discriminations within the institution itself. It supposes that a player consents not simply to a set of rules, but to an enterprise that may be said to have a character of its own; so that when the question is put – To what did he consent in consenting to that? – the answer may study the enterprise as a whole and not just the rules.

IV   LEGAL RIGHTS

A.   *Legislation*

Legal argument, in hard cases, turns on contested concepts whose nature and function are very much like the concept of the character of a game. These include several of the substantive concepts through which the law is stated, like the concept of a contract and of property. But they also include two concepts of much greater relevance to the present argument. The first is the idea of the "intention" or "purpose" of a particular statute or statutory clause. This concept provides a bridge between the political justification of the general idea that statutes create rights and those hard cases that ask what rights a particular statute has created. The second is the concept of principles that "underlie" or are "embedded in" the positive rules of law. This concept provides a bridge between the political justification of the doctrine that like cases should be decided alike and those hard cases in which it is unclear what that general doctrine requires. These concepts together define legal rights as a function, though a very special function, of political rights. If a judge accepts the settled practices of his legal system – if he accepts, that is, the autonomy provided by its distinct constitutive and regulative rules – then he must, according to the doctrine of political responsibility, accept some general political theory that justifies these practices. The concepts of legislative purpose and common law principles are devices for applying that general political theory to controversial issues about legal rights.

We might therefore do well to consider how a philosophical judge might develop, in appropriate cases, theories of what legislative purpose and legal principles require. We shall find that he would construct these theories in the same manner as a philosophical referee would construct the character of a game. I have invented, for this purpose, a lawyer of superhuman skill, learning, patience and acumen, whom I shall call Hercules. I suppose that Hercules is a judge in some representative American jurisdiction. I assume that he accepts the main uncontroversial constitutive and regulative rules of the law in his jurisdiction. He accepts, that is, that statutes have the general power to create and extinguish legal rights, and that judges have the general duty to follow earlier decisions of their court or higher courts whose rationale, as lawyers say, extends to the case at bar.

1. *The Constitution.*—Suppose there is a written constitution in Hercules' jurisdiction which provides that no law shall be valid if it establishes a religion. The legislature passes a law purporting to grant free busing to children in parochial schools. Does the grant establish a religion?[19] The words of the constitutional provision might support either view. Hercules must nevertheless decide whether the child who appears before him has a right to her bus ride.

He might begin by asking why the constitution has any power at all to create or destroy rights. If citizens have a background right to salvation through an established church, as many believe they do, then this must be an important right. Why does the fact that a group of men voted otherwise several centuries ago prevent this background right from being made a legal right as well? His answer must take some form such as this. The constitution sets out a general political scheme that is sufficiently just to be taken as settled for reasons of fairness. Citizens take the benefit of living in a society whose institutions are arranged and governed in accordance with that scheme, and they must take the burdens as well, at least until a new scheme is put into force either by discrete amendment or general revolution. But Hercules must then ask just what scheme of principles has been settled. He must construct, that is, a constitutional theory; since he is Hercules we may suppose that he can develop a full political theory that justifies the constitution as a whole. It must be a scheme that fits the particular rules of this constitution, of course. It cannot include a powerful background right to an established church. But more than one fully specified theory may fit the specific provision about religion sufficiently well. One theory might provide, for example, that it is wrong for the government to enact any legislation that will cause great social tension or disorder; so that, since the establishment of a church will have that effect, it is wrong to empower the legislature to establish one. Another theory will provide a background right to religious liberty, and therefore argue that an established church is wrong, not because it will be socially disruptive, but because it violates that background right. In that case Hercules must turn to the remaining constitutional rules and settled practices under these rules to see which of these two theories provides a smoother fit with the constitutional scheme as a whole.

But the theory that is superior under this test will nevertheless be insufficiently concrete to decide some cases. Suppose Hercules decides that the establishment provision is justified by a right to religious liberty rather than any goal of social order. It remains to ask what, more precisely, religious liberty is. Does a right to religious liberty include the right not to have one's taxes used for any purpose that helps a religion to survive? Or simply not to have one's taxes used to benefit one religion at the expense of another? If the former, then the free transportation legislation violates that right, but if the latter it does not. The institutional structure of rules and practice may not be sufficiently detailed to rule out either of these two conceptions of religious liberty, or to make one a plainly superior justification of that structure. At some point in his career Hercules must therefore consider the question not just as an issue of fit between a theory and the rules of the institution, but as an issue of political philosophy as well. He must decide which conception is a more satisfactory elaboration of the general idea of religious liberty. He must decide that question because he cannot otherwise carry far enough the project he began. He cannot answer in sufficient detail the question of what political scheme the constitution establishes.

So Hercules is driven, by this project, to a process of reasoning that is much like the process of the self-conscious chess referee. He must develop a theory of the constitution, in the shape of a complex set of principles and policies that justify that scheme of government, just as the chess referee is driven to develop a theory about the character of his game. He must develop that theory by referring alternately to political philosophy and institutional detail. He must generate possible theories justifying different aspects of the scheme and test the theories against the broader institution. When the discriminating power of that test is exhausted, he must elaborate the contested concepts that the successful theory employs.

2. *Statutes.*—A statute in Hercules' jurisdiction provides that it is a federal crime for someone knowingly to transport in interstate commerce "any person who shall have been unlawfully seized, confined, inveigled, decoyed, kidnapped, abducted, or carried away by any means whatsoever...." Hercules is asked to decide whether this statute makes a federal criminal of a man who persuaded a young girl that it was her religious duty to run away with him, in violation of a court order, to consummate what he called a celestial marriage.[20] The statute had been passed after a famous kidnapping case, in order to enable federal authorities to join in the pursuit of kidnappers. But its words are sufficiently broad to apply to this case, and there is nothing in the legislative record or accompanying committee reports that says they do not.

Do they apply? Hercules might himself despise celestial marriage, or abhor the corruption of minors, or celebrate the obedience of children to their parents. The groom nevertheless has a right to his liberty, unless the statute properly understood deprives him of that right; it is inconsistent with any plausible theory of the constitution that judges have the power retroactively to make conduct criminal. Does the statute deprive him of that right? Hercules must begin by asking why any statute has the power to alter legal rights. He will find the answer in his constitutional theory: this might provide, for example, that a democratically elected legislature is the appropriate body to make collective decisions about the conduct that shall be criminal. But that same constitutional theory will impose on the legislature certain responsibilities: it will impose not only constraints reflecting individual rights, but also some general duty to pursue collective goals defining the public welfare. That fact provides a useful test for Hercules in this hard case. He might ask which interpretation more satisfactorily ties the language the legislature used to its constitutional responsibilities. That is like the referee's question about the character of a game. It calls for the construction, not of some hypotheses about the mental state of particular legislators, but of a special political theory that justifies this statute, in the light of the legislature's more general responsibilities, better than any alternative theory.[21]

Which arguments of principle and policy might properly have persuaded the legislature to enact just that statute? It should not have pursued a policy designed to replace state criminal enforcement by federal enforcement whenever constitutionally possible. That would represent an unnecessary interference with the principle of federalism that must be part of Hercules' constitutional theory. It might, however, responsibly have followed a policy of selecting for federal enforcement all crimes with such an interstate character that state enforcement was hampered. Or it could responsibly have selected just specially dangerous or widespread crimes of that character. Which of these two responsible policies offers a better justification of the statute actually drafted? If the penalties provided by the statute are large, and therefore appropriate to the latter but not the former policy, the latter policy must be preferred. Which of the different interpretations of the statute permitted by the language serves that policy better? Plainly a decision that inveiglement of the sort presented by the case is not made a federal crime by the statute.

I have described a simple and perhaps unrepresentative problem of statutory interpretation, because I cannot now develop a theory of statutory interpretation in any detail. I want only to suggest how the general claim, that calculations judges make about the purposes of statutes are calculations about political rights, might be defended. There are, however, two points that must be noticed about even this simple example. It would be inaccurate, first, to say that Hercules supplemented what the legislature did in enacting the statute, or that he tried to determine what it would have done if it had been aware of the problem presented by the case. The act of a legislature is not, as these descriptions suggest, an event whose force we can in some way measure so as to say it has run out at a particular point; it is rather an event whose content is contested in the way in which the content of an agreement to play a game is contested. Hercules constructs his political theory as an argument about what the legislature has, on this occasion, done. The contrary

argument, that it did not actually do what he said, is not a realistic piece of common sense, but a competitive claim about the true content of that contested event.

Second, it is important to notice how great a role the canonical terms of the actual statute play in the process described. They provide a limit to what must otherwise be, in the nature of the case, unlimited. The political theory Hercules developed to interpret the statute, which featured a policy of providing federal enforcement for dangerous crimes, would justify a great many decisions that the legislature did not, on any interpretation of the language, actually make. It would justify, for example, a statute making it a federal crime for a murderer to leave the state of his crime. The legislature has no general duty to follow out the lines of any particular policy, and it would plainly be wrong for Hercules to suppose that the legislature had in some sense enacted that further statute. The statutory language they did enact enables this process of interpretation to operate without absurdity; it permits Hercules to say that the legislature pushed some policy to the limits of the language it used, without also supposing that it pushed that policy to some indeterminate further point.

B.   The Common Law

1. Precedent.—One day lawyers will present a hard case to Hercules that does not turn upon any statute; they will argue whether earlier common law decisions of Hercules' court, properly understood, provide some party with a right to a decision in his favor. *Spartan Steel* was such a case. The plaintiff did not argue that any statute provided it a right to recover its economic damages; it pointed instead to certain earlier judicial decisions that awarded recovery for other sorts of damage, and argued that the principle behind these cases required a decision for it as well.

Hercules must begin by asking why arguments of that form are ever, even in principle, sound. He will find that he has available no quick or obvious answer. When he asked himself the parallel question about legislation he found, in general democratic theory, a ready reply. But the details of the practices of precedent he must now justify resist any comparably simple theory.

He might, however, be tempted by this answer. Judges, when they decide particular cases at common law, lay down general rules that are intended to benefit the community in some way. Other judges, deciding later cases, must therefore enforce these rules so that the benefit may be achieved. If this account of the matter were a sufficient justification of the practices of precedent, then Hercules could decide these hard common law cases as if earlier decisions were statutes, using the techniques he worked out for statutory interpretation. But he will encounter fatal difficulties if he pursues that theory very far. It will repay us to consider why, in some detail, because the errors in the theory will be guides to a more successful theory.

Statutory interpretation, as we just noticed, depends upon the availability of a canonical form of words, however vague or unspecific, that set limits to the political decisions that the statute may be taken to have made. Hercules will discover that many of the opinions that litigants cite as precedents do not contain any special propositions taken to be a canonical form of the rule that the case lays down. It is true that it was part of Anglo-American judicial style, during the last part of the nineteenth century and the first part of this century, to attempt to compose such canonical statements, so that one could thereafter refer, for example, to the rule in *Rylands v. Fletcher*.[22] But even in this period, lawyers and textbook writers disagreed about which parts of famous opinions should be taken to have that character. Today, in any case, even important opinions rarely attempt that legislative sort of draftsmanship. They cite reasons, in the form of precedents and principles, to justify a decision, but it is the decision, not some new and stated rule of law, that these precedents and principles are taken to justify. Sometimes a judge will acknowledge openly that it lies to later cases to determine the full effect of the case he has decided.

Of course, Hercules might well decide that when he does find, in an earlier case, a canonical form of words, he will use his techniques of statutory interpretation to decide whether the rule composed of these words embraces a novel case.[23] He might well acknowledge what could be called an enactment force of precedent. He will nevertheless find that when a precedent does have enactment force, its influence on later cases is not taken to be limited to that force. Judges and lawyers do not think that the force of precedents is exhausted, as a statute would be, by the linguistic limits of some particular phrase. If *Spartan Steel* were a New York case, counsel for the plaintiff would suppose that Cardozo's earlier decision in *MacPherson v. Buick*,[24] in which a woman recovered damages for injuries from a negligently manufactured automobile, counted in favor of his client's right to recover, in spite of the fact that the earlier decision contained no language that could plausibly be interpreted to enact that right. He would urge that the earlier decision exerts a gravitational force on later decisions even when these later decisions lie outside its particular orbit.

This gravitational force is part of the practice Hercules' general theory of precedent must capture. In this important respect, judicial practice differs from the practice of officials in other institutions. In chess, officials conform to established rules in a way that assumes full institutional autonomy. They exercise originality only to the extent required by the fact that an occasional rule, like the rule about forfeiture, demands that originality. Each decision of a chess referee, therefore, can be said to be directly required and justified by an established rule of chess, even though some of these decisions must be based on an interpretation, rather than on simply the plain and unavoidable meaning, of that rule.

Some legal philosophers write about common law adjudication as if it were in this way like chess, except that legal rules are much more likely than chess rules to require interpretation. That is the spirit, for example, of Professor Hart's argument that hard cases arise only because legal rules have what he calls "open texture."[25] In fact, judges often disagree not simply about how some rule or principle should be interpreted, but whether the rule or principle one judge cites should be acknowledged to be a rule or principle at all. In some cases both the majority and the dissenting opinions recognize the same earlier cases as relevant, but disagree about what rule or principle these precedents should be understood to have established. In adjudication, unlike chess, the argument *for* a particular rule may be more important than the argument *from* that rule to the particular case; and while the chess referee who decides a case by appeal to a rule no one has ever heard of before is likely to be dismissed or certified, the judge who does so is likely to be celebrated in law school lectures.

Nevertheless, judges seem agreed that earlier decisions do contribute to the formulation of new and controversial rules in some way other than by interpretation; they are agreed that earlier decisions have gravitational force even when they disagree about what that force is. The legislator may very often concern himself only with issues of background morality or policy in deciding how to cast his vote on some issue. He need not show that his vote is consistent with the votes of his colleagues in the legislature, or with those of past legislatures. But the judge very rarely assumes that character of independence. He will always try to connect the justification he provides for an original decision with decisions that other judges or officials have taken in the past.

In fact, when good judges try to explain in some general way how they work, they search for figures of speech to describe the constraints they feel even when they suppose that they are making new law, constraints that would not be appropriate if they were legislators. They say, for example, that they find new rules imminent in the law as a whole, or that they are enforcing an internal logic of the law through some method that belongs more to philosophy than to politics, or that they are the agents through which the law works itself pure, or that the law has some life of its own even though this belongs to experience rather than to logic. Hercules must not rest content with these famous metaphors and personifications, but he must also not be content with any description of the judicial process that ignores their appeal to the best lawyers.

The gravitational force of precedent cannot be captured by any theory that takes the full force of precedent to be its enactment force as a piece of legislation. But the inadequacy of that approach suggests a superior theory. The gravitational force of a precedent may be explained by appeal, not to the wisdom of enforcing enactments, but to the fairness of treating like cases alike. A precedent is the report of an earlier political decision; the very fact of that decision, as a piece of political history, provides some reason for deciding other cases in a similar way in the future. This general explanation of the gravitational force of precedent accounts for the feature that defeated the enactment theory, which is that the force of a precedent escapes the language of its opinion. If the government of a community has forced the manufacturer of defective motor cars to pay damages to a woman who was injured because of the defect, then that historical fact must offer some reason, at least, why the same government should require a contractor who has caused economic damage through the defective work of his employees to make good that loss. We may test the weight of that reason, not by asking whether the language of the earlier decision, suitably interpreted, requires the contractor to pay damages, but by asking the different question whether it is fair for the government, having intervened in the way it did in the first case, to refuse its aid in the second.

Hercules will conclude that this doctrine of fairness offers the only adequate account of the full practice of precedent. He will draw certain further conclusions about his own responsibilities when deciding hard cases. The most important of these is that he must limit the gravitational force of earlier decisions to the extension of the arguments of principle necessary to justify those decisions. If an earlier decision were taken to be entirely justified by some argument of policy, it would have no gravitational force. Its value as a precedent would be limited to its enactment force, that is, to further cases captured by some particular words of the opinion. The distributional force of a collective goal, as we noticed earlier, is a matter of contingent fact and general legislative strategy. If the government intervened on behalf of Mrs. Mac-Pherson, not because she had any right to its intervention, but only because wise strategy suggested that means of pursuing some collective goal like economic efficiency, there can be no effective argument of fairness that it therefore ought to intervene for the plaintiff in *Spartan Steel*.

We must remind ourselves, in order to see why this is so, of the slight demands we make upon legislatures in the name of consistency when their decisions are generated by arguments of policy.[26] Suppose the legislature wishes to stimulate the economy and might do so, with roughly the same efficiency, either by subsidizing housing or by increasing direct government spending for new roads. Road construction companies have no right that the legislature choose road construction; if it does, then home construction firms have no right, on any principle of consistency, that the legislature subsidize housing as well. The legislature may decide that the road construction program has stimulated the economy just enough, and that no further programs are needed. It may decide this even if it now concedes that subsidized housing would have been the more efficient decision in the first place. Or it might concede even that more stimulation of the economy is needed, but decide that it wishes to wait for more evidence – perhaps evidence about the success of the road program – to see whether subsidies provide an effective stimulation. It might even say that it does not now wish to commit more of its time and energy to economic policy. There is, perhaps, some limit to the arbitrariness of the distinctions the legislature may make in its pursuit of collective goals. Even if it is efficient to build all shipyards in southern California, it might be thought unfair, as well as politically unwise, to do so. But these weak requirements, which prohibit grossly unfair distributions, are plainly compatible with providing sizeable incremental benefits to one group that are withheld from others.

There can be, therefore, no general argument of fairness that a government which serves a collective goal in one way on one occasion must serve it that way, or even serve the same goal, whenever a parallel opportunity arises. I do not mean simply that the government may change its mind, and regret either the goal or the means of its earlier decision. I mean that a responsible government may serve different goals in a piecemeal and occasional fashion, so that even though it does not regret, but continues to enforce, one rule designed to serve a particular goal, it may reject other rules that would serve that same goal just as well. It might legislate the rule that manufacturers are responsible for damages flowing from defects in their cars, for example, and yet properly refuse to legislate the same rule for manufacturers of washing machines, let alone contractors who cause economic damage like the damage of *Spartan Steel*. Government must, of course, be rational and fair; it must make decisions that overall serve a justifiable mix of collective goals and nevertheless respect whatever rights citizens have. But that general requirement would not support anything like the gravitational force that the judicial decision in favor of Mrs. MacPherson was in fact taken to have.

So Hercules, when he defines the gravitational force of a particular precedent, must take into account only the arguments of principle that justify that precedent. If the decision in favor of Mrs. MacPherson supposes that she has a right to damages, and not simply that a rule in her favor supports some collective goal, then the argument of fairness, on which the practice of precedent relies, takes hold. It does not follow, of course, that anyone injured in any way by the negligence of another must have the same concrete right to recover that she has. It may be that competing rights require a compromise in the later case that they did not require in hers. But it might well follow that the plaintiff in the later case has the same abstract right, and if that is so then some special argument citing the competing rights will be required to show that a contrary decision in the later case would be fair.

2. The Seamless Web.—Hercules' first conclusion, that the gravitational force of a precedent is defined by the arguments of principle that support the precedent, suggests a second. Since judicial practice in his community assumes that earlier cases have a *general* gravitational force, then he can justify that judicial practice only by supposing that the rights thesis holds in his community. It is never taken to be a satisfactory argument against the gravitational force of some precedent that the goal that precedent served has now been served sufficiently, or that the courts would now be better occupied in serving some other goal that has been relatively neglected, possibly returning to the goal the precedent served on some other occasion. The practices of precedent do not suppose that the *rationales* that recommend judicial decisions can be served piecemeal in that way. If it is acknowledged that a particular precedent is justified for a particular reason; if that reason would also recommend a particular result in the case at bar; if the earlier decision has not been recanted or in some other way taken as a matter of institutional regret; then that decision must be reached in the later case.

Hercules must suppose that it is understood in his community, though perhaps not explicitly recognized, that judicial decisions must be taken to be justified by arguments of principle rather than arguments of policy. He now sees that the familiar concept used by judges to explain their reasoning from precedent, the concept of certain principles that underlie or are embedded in the common law, is itself only a metaphorical statement of the rights thesis. He may henceforth use that concept in his decisions of hard common law cases. It provides a general test for deciding such cases that is like the chess referee's concept of the character of a game, and like his own concept of a legislative purpose. It provides a question – What set of principles best justifies the precedents? – that builds a bridge between the general justification of the practice of precedent, which is fairness, and his own decision about what that general justification requires in some particular hard case.

Hercules must now develop his concept of principles that underlie the common law by assigning to each of the relevant precedents some scheme of principle that justifies the decision of that precedent. He will now discover a further important difference between this concept and the concept of statutory purpose that he used in statutory interpretation. In the case of statutes, he found it necessary to choose some theory about the purpose of the particular statute in question, looking to other acts of the legislature only insofar as these might help to select between theories that fit the statute about

equally well. But if the gravitational force of precedent rests on the idea that fairness requires the consistent enforcement of rights, then Hercules must discover principles that fit, not only the particular precedent to which some litigant directs his attention, but all other judicial decisions within his general jurisdiction and, indeed, statutes as well, so far as these must be seen to be generated by principle rather than policy. He does not satisfy his duty to show that his decision is consistent with established principles, and therefore fair, if the principles he cites as established are themselves inconsistent with other decisions that his court also proposes to uphold.

Suppose, for example, that he can justify Cardozo's decision in favor of Mrs. MacPherson by citing some abstract principle of equality, which argues that whenever an accident occurs then the richest of the various persons whose acts might have contributed to the accident must bear the loss. He nevertheless cannot show that that principle has been respected in other accident cases, or, even if he could, that it has been respected in other branches of the law, like contract, in which it would also have great impact if it were recognized at all. If he decides against a future accident plaintiff who is richer than the defendant, by appealing to this alleged right of equality, that plaintiff may properly complain that the decision is just as inconsistent with the government's behavior in other cases as if *MacPherson* itself had been ignored. The law may not be a seamless web; but the plaintiff is entitled to ask Hercules to treat it as if it were.

You will now see why I called our judge Hercules. He must construct a scheme of abstract and concrete principles that provides a coherent justification for all common law precedents and, so far as these are to be justified on principle, constitutional and statutory provisions as well. We may grasp the magnitude of this enterprise by distinguishing, within the vast material of legal decisions that Hercules must justify, a vertical and a horizontal ordering. The vertical ordering is provided by distinguishing layers of authority; that is, layers at which official decisions might be taken to be controlling over decisions made at lower levels. In the United States the rough character of the vertical ordering is apparent. The constitutional struc-ture occupies the highest level, the decisions of the Supreme Court and perhaps other courts interpreting that structure the next, enactments of the various legislatures the next and decisions of the various courts developing the common law different levels below that. Hercules must arrange justification of principle at each of these levels so that the justification is consistent with principles taken to provide the justification of higher levels. The horizontal ordering simply requires that the principles taken to justify a decision at one level must also be consistent with the justification offered for other decisions at that level.

Suppose Hercules, taking advantage of his unusual skills, proposed to work out this entire scheme in advance, so that he would be ready to confront litigants with an entire theory of law should this be necessary to justify any particular decision. He would begin, deferring to vertical ordering, by setting out and refining the constitutional theory he has already used. That constitutional theory would be more or less different from the theory that a different judge would develop, because a constitutional theory requires judgments about complex issues of institutional fit, as well as judgments about political and moral philosophy, and Her-cules' judgments will inevitably differ from those other judges would make. These differ-ences at a high level of vertical ordering will exercise considerable force on the scheme each judge would propose at lower levels. Hercules might think, for example, that certain substan-tive constitutional constraints on legislative power are best justified by postulating an ab-stract right to privacy against the state, because he believes that such a right is a consequence of the even more abstract right to liberty that the constitution guarantees. If so, he would regard the failure of the law of tort to recognize a parallel abstract right to privacy against fellow citizens, in some concrete form, as an inconsistency. If another judge did not share his beliefs about the connection between privacy and liberty, and so did not accept his consti-tutional interpretation as persuasive, that judge would also disagree about the proper develop-ment of tort.

So the impact of Hercules' own judgments will be pervasive, even though some of these will be controversial. But they will not enter his calculations in such a way that different parts of the theory he constructs can be attributed to his independent convictions rather than to the body of law that he must justify. He will not follow those classical theories of adjudication I mentioned earlier, which suppose that a judge follows statutes or precedent until the clear direction of these runs out, after which he is free to strike out on his own. His theory is rather a theory about what the statute or the precedent itself requires, and though he will, of course, reflect his own intellectual and philo-sophical convictions in making that judgment, that is a very different matter from supposing that those convictions have some independent force in his argument just because they are his.[27]

3. Mistakes.—I shall not now try to develop, in further detail, Hercules' theory of law. I shall mention, however, two problems he will face. He must decide, first, how much weight he must give, in constructing a scheme of justi-fication for a set of precedents, to the arguments that the judges who decided these cases attached to their decisions. He will not always find in these opinions any proposition precise enough to serve as a statute he might then interpret. But the opinions will almost always contain argument, in the form of propositions that the judge takes to recommend his decision. Hercules will decide to assign these only an initial or prima facie place in his scheme of justification. The purpose of that scheme is to satisfy the requirement that the government must extend to all the rights it supposes some to have. The fact that one officer of the government offers a certain principle as the ground of his decision may be taken to establish prima facie that the government does rely that far upon that principle.

But the main force of the underlying argu-ment of fairness is forward-looking, not backward-looking. The gravitational force of Mrs. MacPherson's case depends not simply on the fact that she recovered for her Buick, but also on the fact that the government proposes to allow others in just her position to recover in the future. If the courts proposed to overrule the decision, no substantial argument of fairness, fixing on the actual decision in the case, survives in favor of the plaintiff in *Spartan Steel*. If, therefore, a principle other than the principle Cardozo cited can be found to justify *MacPherson*, and if this other principle also justifies a great deal of precedent that Cardozo's does not, or if it provides a smoother fit with arguments taken to justify decisions of a higher rank in vertical order, then this new principle is a more satisfactory basis for further decisions. Of course, this argument for not copying Cardozo's principle is unnecessary if the new principle is more abstract, and if Cardozo's principle can be seen as only a concrete form of that more abstract principle. In that case Hercules incorporates, rather than rejects, Cardozo's account of his decision. Cardozo, in fact, used the opinion in the earlier case of *Thomas v. Winchester*,[28] on which case he relied, in just that fashion. It may be, however, that the new principle strikes out on a different line, so that it justifies a precedent or a series of precedents on grounds very different from what their opinions propose. Brandeis' and Warren's famous argument about the right to privacy[29] is a dramatic illustration: they argued that this right was not unknown to the law but was, on the contrary, demonstrated by a wide variety of decisions, in spite of the fact that the judges who decided these cases mentioned no such right. It may be that their argument, so conceived, was unsuccessful, and that Hercules in their place, would have reached a different result. Hercules' theory nevertheless shows why their argument, sometimes taken to be a kind of brilliant fraud, was at least sound in its ambition.

Hercules must also face a different and greater problem. If the history of his court is at all complex, he will find, in practice, that the requirement of total consistency he has accepted will prove too strong, unless he develops it further to include the idea that he may, in applying this requirement, disregard some part of institutional history as a mistake. For he will be unable, even with his superb imagination, to find any set of principles that reconciles all standing statutes and precedents. This is hardly surprising: the legislators and judges of the past

did not all have Hercules' ability or insight, nor were they men and women who were all of the same mind and opinion. Of course, any set of statutes and decisions can be explained historically, or psychologically, or sociologically, but consistency requires justification, not explanation, and the justification must be plausible and not sham. If the justification he constructs makes distinctions that are arbitrary and deploys principles that are unappealing, then it cannot count as a justification at all.

Suppose the law of negligence and accidents in Hercules' jurisdiction has developed in the following simplified and imaginary way. It begins with specific common law decisions recognizing a right to damages for bodily injury caused by very dangerous instruments that are defectively manufactured. These cases are then reinterpreted in some landmark decision, as they were in *MacPherson*, as justified by the very abstract right of each person to the reasonable care of others whose actions might injure his person or property. This principle is then both broadened and pinched in different ways. The courts, for example, decide that no concrete right lies against an accountant who has been negligent in the preparation of financial statements. They also decide that the right cannot be waived in certain cases; for example, in a standard form contract of automobile purchase. The legislature adds a statute providing that in certain cases of industrial accident, recovery will be allowed unless the defendant affirmatively establishes that the plaintiff was entirely to blame. But it also provides that in other cases, for example, in airplane accidents, recovery will be limited to a stipulated amount, which might be much less than the actual loss; and it later adds that the guest in an automobile cannot sue his host even if the host drives negligently and the guest is injured. Suppose now, against this background, that Hercules is called upon to decide *Spartan Steel*.

Can he find a coherent set of principles that justifies this history in the way that fairness requires? He might try the proposition that individuals have no right to recover for damages unless inflicted intentionally. He would argue that they are allowed to recover damages in negligence only for policy reasons, not in recognition of any abstract right to such damages, and he would cite the statutes limiting liability to protect airlines and insurance companies, and the cases excluding liability against accountants, as evidence that recovery is denied when policy argues the other way. But he must concede that this analysis of institutional history is incompatible with the common law decisions, particularly the landmark decision recognizing a general right to recovery in negligence. He cannot say, compatibly with the rest of his theory, that these decisions may themselves be justified on policy grounds, if he holds, by virtue of the rights thesis, that courts may extend liability only in response to arguments of principle and not policy. So he must set these decisions aside as mistakes.

He might try another strategy. He might propose some principle according to which individuals have rights to damages in just the circumstances of the particular cases that decided they did, but have no general right to such damages. He might concede, for example, a legal principle granting a right to recover for damages incurred within an automobile owned by the plaintiff, but deny a principle that would extend to other damage. But though he could in this way tailor his justification of institutional history to fit that history exactly, he would realize that this justification rests on distinctions that are arbitrary. He can find no room in his political theory for a distinction that concedes an abstract right if someone is injured driving his own automobile but denies it if he is a guest or if he is injured in an airplane. He has provided a set of arguments that cannot stand as a coherent justification of anything.

He might therefore concede that he can make no sense of institutional history except by supposing some general abstract right to recover for negligence: but he might argue that it is a relatively weak right and so will yield to policy considerations of relatively minor force. He will cite the limiting statutes and cases in support of his view that the right is a weak one. But he will then face a difficulty if, though the statute limiting liability in airplane accidents has never been repealed, the airlines have become sufficiently secure, and the mechanisms of insurance available to airlines so efficient and

inexpensive, that a failure to repeal the statute can only be justified by taking the abstract right to be so weak that relatively thin arguments of policy are sufficient to defeat it. If Hercules takes the right to be that weak then he cannot justify the various common law decisions that support the right, as a concrete right, against arguments of policy much stronger than the airlines are now able to press. So he must choose either to take the failure to repeal the airline accident limitation statute, or the common law decisions that value the right much higher, as mistakes.

In any case, therefore, Hercules must expand his theory to include the idea that a justification of institutional history may display some part of that history as mistaken. But he cannot make impudent use of this device, because if he were free to take any incompatible piece of institutional history as a mistake, with no further consequences for his general theory, then the requirement of consistency would be no genuine requirement at all. He must develop some theory of institutional mistakes, and this theory of mistakes must have two parts. It must show the consequences for further arguments of taking some institutional event to be mistaken; and it must limit the number and character of the events that can be disposed of in that way.

He will construct the first part of this theory of mistakes by means of two sets of distinctions. He will first distinguish between the specific authority of any institutional event, which is its power as an institutional act to effect just the specific institutional consequences it describes, and its gravitational force. If he classifies some event as a mistake, then he does not deny its specific authority, but he does deny its gravitational force, and he cannot consistently appeal to that force in other arguments. He will also distinguish between embedded and corrigible mistakes; embedded mistakes are those whose specific authority is fixed so that it survives their loss of gravitational force; corrigible mistakes are those whose specific authority depends on gravitational force in such a way that it cannot survive this loss.

The constitutional level of his theory will determine which mistakes are embedded. His theory of legislative supremacy, for example, will insure that any statutes he treats as mistakes will lose their gravitational force but not their specific authority. If he denies the gravitational force of the aircraft liability limitation statute, the statute is not thereby repealed; the mistake is embedded so that the specific authority survives. He must continue to respect the limitations the statute imposes upon liability, but he will not use it to argue in some other case for a weaker right. If he accepts some strict doctrine of precedent, and designates some judicial decision, like the decision denying a right in negligence against an accountant, a mistake, then the strict doctrine may preserve the specific authority of that decision, which might be limited to its enactment force, but the decision will lose its gravitational force; it will become, in Justice Frankfurter's phrase, a piece of legal flotsam or jetsam. It will not be necessary to decide which.

That is fairly straightforward, but Hercules must take more pains with the second part of his theory of mistakes. He is required, by the justification he has fixed to the general practice of precedent, to compose a more detailed justification, in the form of a scheme of principle, for the entire body of statutes and common law decisions. But a justification that designates part of what is to be justified as mistaken is prima facie weaker than one that does not. The second part of his theory of mistakes must show that it is nevertheless a stronger justification than any alternative that does not recognize any mistakes, or that recognizes a different set of mistakes. That demonstration cannot be a deduction from simple rules of theory construction, but if Hercules bears in mind the connection he earlier established between precedent and fairness, this connection will suggest two guidelines for his theory of mistakes. In the first place, fairness fixes on institutional history, not just as history but as a political program that the government proposed to continue into the future; it seizes, that is, on forward-looking, not the backward-looking implications of precedent. If Hercules discovers that some previous decision, whether a statute or a judicial decision, is now widely regretted within the pertinent branch of the profession, that fact in itself distinguishes that decision as vulnerable. He must remember,

second, that the argument from fairness that demands consistency is not the only argument from fairness to which government in general, or judges in particular, must respond. If he believes, quite apart from any argument of consistency, that a particular statute or decision was wrong because unfair, within the community's own concept of fairness, then that belief is sufficient to distinguish the decision, and make it vulnerable. Of course, he must apply the guidelines with a sense of the vertical structure of his overall justification, so that decisions at a lower level are more vulnerable than decisions at a higher.

Hercules will therefore apply at least two maxims in the second part of his theory of mistakes. If he can show, by arguments of history or by appeal to some sense of the legal community, that a particular principle, though it once had sufficient appeal to persuade a legislature or court to a legal decision, has now so little force that it is unlikely to generate any further such decisions, then the argument from fairness that supports that principle is undercut. If he can show by arguments of political morality that such a principle, apart from its popularity, is unjust, then the argument from fairness that supports that principle is overridden. Hercules will be delighted to find that these discriminations are familiar in the practice of other judges. The jurisprudential importance of his career does not lie in the novelty, but just in the familiarity, of the theory of hard cases that he has now created.

V Political Objections

The rights thesis has two aspects. Its descriptive aspect explains the present structure of the institution of adjudication. Its normative aspect offers a political justification for that structure. The story of Hercules shows how familiar judicial practice might have developed from a general acceptance of the thesis. This at once clarifies the thesis by showing its implications in some detail, and offers powerful, if special, argument for its descriptive aspect. But the story also provides a further political argument in favor of its normative aspect. Hercules began his calculations with the intention, not simply to replicate what other judges do, but to enforce the genuine institutional rights of those who came to his court. If he is able to reach decisions that satisfy our sense of justice, then that argues in favor of the political value of the thesis.

It may now be said, however, by way of rebuttal, that certain features of Hercules' story count against the normative aspect of the thesis. In the introductory part of this essay I mentioned a familiar objection to judicial originality: this is the argument from democracy that elected legislators have superior qualifications to make political decisions. I said that this argument is weak in the case of decisions of principle, but Hercules' story may give rise to fresh doubts on that score. The story makes plain that many of Hercules' decisions about legal rights depend upon judgments of political theory that might be made differently by different judges or by the public at large. It does not matter, to this objection, that the decision is one of principle rather than policy. It matters only that the decision is one of political conviction about which reasonable men disagree. If Hercules decides cases on the basis of such judgments, then he decides on the basis of his own convictions and preferences, which seems unfair, contrary to democracy, and offensive to the rule of law.

That is the general form of the objection I shall consider in this final Part. It must first be clarified in one important respect. The objection charges Hercules with relying upon his own convictions in matters of political morality. That charge is ambiguous, because there are two ways in which an official might rely upon his own opinions in making such a decision. One of these, in a judge, is offensive, but the other is inevitable.

Sometimes an official offers, as a reason for his decision, the fact that some person or group holds a particular belief or opinion. A legislator might offer, as a reason for voting for an anti-abortion statute, the fact that his constituents believe that abortion is wrong. That is a form of appeal to authority: the official who makes that appeal does not himself warrant the substance of the belief to which he appeals, nor does he count the soundness of the belief as part of his

argument. We might imagine a judge appealing, in just this way, to the fact that he *himself* has a particular political preference. He might be a philosophical skeptic in matters of political morality. He might say that one man's opinion in such matters is worth no more than another's, because neither has any objective standing, but that, since he himself happens to favor abortion, he will hold anti-abortion statutes unconstitutional.

That judge relies upon the naked fact that he holds a particular political view as itself a justification for his decision. But a judge may rely upon his own belief in the different sense of relying upon the truth or soundness of that belief. Suppose he believes, for example, that the due process clause of the Constitution, as a matter of law, makes invalid any constraint of a fundamental liberty, and that anti-abortion statutes constrain a fundamental liberty. He might rely upon the soundness of those convictions, not the fact that he, as opposed to others, happens to hold them. A judge need not rely upon the soundness of any *particular* belief in this way. Suppose the majority of his colleagues, or the editors of a prominent law journal, or the majority of the community voting in some referendum, holds a contrary view about abortion. He may decide that it is his duty to defer to their judgment of what the Constitution requires, in spite of the fact that their view is, as he thinks, unsound. But in that case he relies upon the soundness of his own conviction that his institutional duty is to defer to the judgment of others in this matter. He must, that is, rely upon the substance of his own judgment at some point, in order to make any judgment at all.

Hercules does not rely upon his own convictions in the first of these two ways. He does not count the fact that he himself happens to favor a particular conception of religious liberty, for example, as providing an argument in favor of a decision that advances that conception. If the objection we are considering is pertinent, therefore, it must be an objection to his relying upon his own convictions in the second way. But in that case the objection cannot be a blanket objection to his relying upon any of his convictions, because he must, inevitably, rely on some.

It is rather an objection to his relying on the soundness of certain of his own convictions; it argues that he ought to defer to others in certain judgments even though their judgments are, as he thinks, wrong.

It is difficult, however, to see *which* of his judgments the objection supposes he should remand to others. We would not have any such problem if Hercules had accepted, rather than rejected, a familiar theory of adjudication. Classical jurisprudence supposes, as I said earlier, that judges decide cases in two steps: they find the limit of what the explicit law requires, and they then exercise an independent discretion to legislate on issues which the law does not reach. In the recent abortion cases,[30] according to this theory, the Supreme Court justices first determined that the language of the due process clause and of prior Supreme Court decisions did not dictate a decision either way. They then set aside the Constitution and the cases to decide whether, in their opinion, it is fundamentally unfair for a state to outlaw abortion in the first trimester.

Let us imagine another judge, called Herbert, who accepts this theory of adjudication and proposes to follow it in his decisions. Herbert might believe both that women have a background right to abort fetuses they carry, and that the majority of citizens think otherwise. The present objection argues that he must resolve that conflict in favor of democracy, so that, when he exercises his discretion to decide the abortion cases, he must decide in favor of the prohibitive statutes. Herbert might agree, in which case we should say that he has set aside his morality in favor of the people's morality. That is, in fact, a slightly misleading way to put the point. His own morality made the fact that the people held a particular view decisive; it did not withdraw in favor of the substance of that view. On the other hand, Herbert might disagree. He might believe that background rights in general, or this right in particular, must prevail against popular opinion even in the legislature, so that he has a duty, when exercising a legislative discretion, to declare the statutes unconstitutional. In that case, the present objection argues that he is mistaken, because he insufficiently weighs the principle of democracy in his political theory.

In any case, however, these arguments that seem tailor-made for Herbert are puzzling as arguments against Hercules. Hercules does not first find the limits of law and then deploy his own political convictions to supplement what the law requires. He uses his own judgment to determine what legal rights the parties before him have, and when that judgment is made nothing remains to submit to either his own or the public's convictions. The difference is not simply a difference in ways of describing the same thing: we saw in Part III that a judgment of institutional right, like the chess referee's judgment about the forfeiture rule, is very different from an independent judgment of political morality made in the interstices provided by the open texture of rules.

Herbert did not consider whether to consult popular morality until he had fixed the legal rights of the parties. But when Hercules fixes legal rights he has already taken the community's moral traditions into account, at least as these are captured in the whole institutional record that it is his office to interpret. Suppose two coherent justifications can be given for earlier Supreme Court decisions enforcing the due process clause. One justification contains some principle of extreme liberality that cannot be reconciled with the criminal law of most of the states, but the other contains no such principle. Hercules cannot seize upon the former justification as license for deciding the abortion cases in favor of abortion, even if he is himself an extreme liberal. His own political convictions, which favor the more liberal justification of the earlier cases, must fall, because they are inconsistent with the popular traditions that have shaped the criminal law that his justification must also explain.

Of course, Hercules' techniques may sometimes require a decision that opposes popular morality on some issue. Suppose no justification of the earlier constitutional cases can be given that does not contain a liberal principle sufficiently strong to require a decision in favor of abortion. Hercules must then reach that decision, no matter how strongly popular morality condemns abortion. He does not, in this case, enforce his own convictions against the community's. He rather judges that the community's morality is inconsistent on this issue: its constitutional morality, which is the justification that must be given for its constitution as interpreted by its judges, condemns its discrete judgment on the particular issue of abortion. Such conflicts are familiar within individual morality; if we wish to use the concept of a community morality in political theory, we must acknowledge conflicts within that morality as well. There is no question, of course, as to how such a conflict must be resolved. Individuals have a right to the consistent enforcement of the principles upon which their institutions rely. It is this institutional right, as defined by the community's constitutional morality, that Hercules must defend against any inconsistent opinion however popular.

These hypothetical cases show that the objection designed for Herbert is poorly cast as an objection against Hercules. Hercules' theory of adjudication at no point provides for any choice between his own political convictions and those he takes to be the political convictions of the community at large. On the contrary, his theory identifies a particular conception of community morality as decisive of legal issues; that conception holds that community morality is the political morality presupposed by the laws and institutions of the community. He must, of course, rely on his own judgment as to what the principles of that morality are, but this form of reliance is the second form we distinguished, which at some level is inevitable.

It is perfectly true that in some cases Hercules' decision about the content of this community morality, and thus his decision about legal rights, will be controversial. This will be so whenever institutional history must be justified by appeal to some contested political concept, like fairness or liberty or equality, but it is not sufficiently detailed so that it can be justified by only one among different conceptions of that concept. I offered, earlier, Hercules' decision of the free busing case as an example of such a decision; we may now take a more topical example. Suppose the earlier due process cases can be justified only by supposing some important right to human dignity, but do not themselves force a decision one way or the other on the issue of whether dignity requires complete

control over the use of one's uterus. If Hercules sits in the abortion cases, he must decide that issue and must employ his own understanding of dignity to do so.

It would be silly to deny that this is a political decision, or that different judges, from different subcultures, would make it differently. Even so, it is nevertheless a very different decision from the decision whether women have, all things considered, a background right to abort their fetuses. Hercules might think dignity an unimportant concept; if he were to attend a new constitutional convention he might vote to repeal the due process clause, or at least to amend it so as to remove any idea of dignity from its scope. He is nevertheless able to decide whether that concept, properly understood, embraces the case of abortion. He is in the shoes of the chess referee who hates meritocracy, but is nevertheless able to consider whether intelligence includes psychological intimidation.

It is, of course, necessary that Hercules have some understanding of the concept of dignity, even if he denigrates that concept; and he will gain that understanding by noticing how the concept is used by those to whom it is important. If the concept figures in the justification of a series of constitutional decisions, then it must be a concept that is prominent in the political rhetoric and debates of the time. Hercules will collect his sense of the concept from its life in these contexts. He will do the best he can to understand the appeal of the idea to those to whom it does appeal. He will devise, so far as he can, a conception that explains that appeal to them.

This is a process that can usefully be seen as occupying two stages. Hercules will notice, simply as a matter of understanding his language, which are the clear, settled cases in which the concept holds. He will notice, for example, that if one man is thought to treat another as his servant, though he is not in fact that man's employer, then he will be thought to have invaded his dignity. He will next try to put himself, so far as he can, within the more general scheme of beliefs and attitudes of those who value the concept, to look at these clear cases through their eyes. Suppose, for example, that they believe in some Aristotelian doctrine of the urgency of self-fulfillment, or they take self-reliance to be a very great virtue. Hercules must construct some general theory of the concept that explains why those who hold that belief, or accept that virtue, will also prize dignity; if his theory also explains why he, who does not accept the belief or the virtue, does not prize dignity, then the theory will be all the more successful for that feature.

Hercules will then use his theory of dignity to answer questions that institutional history leaves open. His theory of dignity may connect dignity with independence, so that someone's dignity is compromised whenever he is forced, against his will, to devote an important part of his activity to the concerns of others. In that case, he may well endorse the claim that women have a constitutional liberty of abortion, as an aspect of their conceded constitutional right to dignity.

That is how Hercules might interpret a concept he does not value, to reach a decision that, as a matter of background morality, he would reject. It is very unlikely, however, that Hercules will often find himself in that position; he is likely to value most of the concepts that figure in the justification of the institutions of his own community. In that case his analysis of these concepts will not display the same self-conscious air of sociological inquiry. He will begin within, rather than outside, the scheme of values that approves the concept, and he will be able to put to himself, rather than to some hypothetical self, questions about the deep morality that gives the concept value. The sharp distinction between background and institutional morality will fade, not because institutional morality is displaced by personal convictions, but because personal convictions have become the most reliable guide he has to institutional morality.

It does not follow, of course, that Hercules will even then reach exactly the same conclusions that any other judge would reach about disputed cases of the concept in question. On the contrary, he will then become like any reflective member of the community willing to debate about what fairness or equality or liberty requires on some occasion. But we now see that it is wrong to suppose that reflective citizens, in such debates, are simply setting their personal convictions against the convictions of others. They too are contesting different conceptions of a concept they suppose they hold in common; they are debating which of different theories of that concept best explains the settled or clear cases that fix the concept. That character of their debate is obscured by the fact that they do value the concepts they contest, and therefore reason intuitively or introspectively rather than in the more sociological mode that an outsider might use; but, so long as they put their claims as claims about concepts held in common, these claims will have the same structure as the outsider's. We may summarize these important points this way: the community's morality, on these issues at least, is not some sum or combination or function of the competing claims of its members; it is rather what each of the competing claims claims to be. When Hercules relies upon his own conception of dignity, in the second sense of reliance we distinguished, he is still relying on his own sense of what the community's morality provides.

It is plain, therefore, that the present objection must be recast if it is to be a weapon against Hercules. But it cannot be recast to fit Hercules better without losing its appeal. Suppose we say that Hercules must defer, not to his own judgment of the institutional morality of his community, but to the judgment of most members of that community about what that is. There are two apparent objections to that recommendation. It is unclear, in the first place, how he could discover what that popular judgment is. It does not follow from the fact that the man in the street disapproves of abortion, or supports legislation making it criminal, that he has considered whether the concept of dignity presupposed by the Constitution, consistently applied, supports his political position. That is a sophisticated question requiring some dialectical skill, and though that skill may be displayed by the ordinary man when he self-consciously defends his position, it is not to be taken for granted that his political preferences, expressed casually or in the ballot, have been subjected to that form of examination.

But even if Hercules is satisfied that the ordinary man has decided that dignity does not require the right to abortion, the question remains why Hercules should take the ordinary man's opinion on that issue as decisive. Suppose Hercules thinks that the ordinary man is wrong; that he is wrong, that is, in his philosophical opinions about what the community's concepts require. If Herbert were in that position, he would have good reason to defer to the ordinary man's judgments. Herbert thinks that when the positive rules of law are vague or indeterminate, the litigants have no institutional right at all, so that any decision he might reach is a piece of fresh legislation. Since nothing he decides will cheat the parties of what they have a right to have at his hands, the argument is plausible, at least, that when he legislates he should regard himself as the agent of the majority. But Hercules cannot take that view of the matter. He knows that the question he must decide is the question of the parties' institutional rights. He knows that if he decides wrongly, as he would do if he followed the ordinary man's lead, he cheats the parties of what they are entitled to have. Neither Hercules nor Herbert would submit an ordinary legal question to popular opinion; since Hercules thinks that parties have rights in hard cases as well as in easy ones, he will not submit to popular opinion in hard cases either.

Of course, any judge's judgment about the rights of parties in hard cases may be wrong, and the objection may try, in one final effort, to capitalize on that fact. It might concede, *arguendo*, that Hercules' technique is appropriate to Hercules, who by hypothesis has great moral insight. But it would deny that the same technique is appropriate for judges generally, who do not. We must be careful, however, in assessing this challenge, to consider the alternatives. It is a matter of injustice when judges make mistakes about legal rights, whether these mistakes are in favor of the plaintiff or defendant. The objection points out that they will sometimes make such mistakes, because they are fallible and in any event disagree. But of course, though we, as social critics, know that mistakes will be made, we do not know when because we are not Hercules either. We must commend techniques of adjudication that might be expected to reduce the number of mistakes

overall based on some judgment of the relative capacities of men and women who might occupy different roles.

Hercules' technique encourages a judge to make his own judgments about institutional rights. The argument from judicial fallibility might be thought to suggest two alternatives. The first argues that since judges are fallible they should make no effort at all to determine the institutional rights of the parties before them, but should decide hard cases only on grounds of policy, or not at all. But that is perverse; it argues that because judges will often, by misadventure, produce unjust decisions they should make no effort to produce just ones. The second alternative argues that since judges are fallible they should submit questions of institutional right raised by hard cases to someone else. But to whom? There is no reason to credit any other particular group with better facilities of moral argument; or, if there is, then it is the process of selecting judges, not the techniques of judging that they are asked to use, that must be changed. So this form of skepticism does not in itself argue against Hercules' technique of adjudication, though of course it serves as a useful reminder to any judge that he might well be wrong in his political judgments, and that he should therefore decide hard cases with humility.

Notes

1 I discussed the distinction between principles and policies in an earlier article. *See* Dworkin, *The Model of Rules*, 35 U. Chi. L. Rev. 14, 22–29 (1967). The more elaborate formulation in Part II of this essay is an improvement; among other virtues it prevents the collapse of the distinction under the (artificial) assumptions described in the earlier article.

2 Spartan Steel & Alley Ltd. v. Martin & Co., [1973] 1 Q.B. 27.

3 *Id.* at 36.

4 *See generally* Dworkin, *The Original Position*, 40 U. Chi. L. Rev. 500 (1973).

5 I count legal persons as individuals, so that corporations may have rights; a political theory that counts special groups, like racial groups, as having some corporate standing within the community may therefore speak of group rights.

6   A complete political theory must also recognize two other distinctions that I use implicitly in this essay. The first is the distinction between rights against the state and rights against fellow citizens. The former justify a political decision that requires some agency of the government to act; the latter justify a decision to coerce particular individuals. The right to minimum housing, if accepted at all, is accepted as a right against the state. The right to recover damages for a breach of contract, or to be saved from great danger at minimum risk of a rescuer, is a right against fellow citizens. The right to free speech is, ordinarily, both. It seems strange to define the rights that citizens have against one another as political rights at all; but we are now concerned with such rights only insofar as they justify political decisions of different sorts. The present distinction cuts across the distinction between background and institutional rights; the latter distinguishes among persons or institutions that must make a political decision, the former between persons or institutions whom that decision directs to act or forbear. Ordinary civil cases at law, which are the principal subject of this essay, involve rights against fellow citizens; but I also discuss certain issues of constitutional and criminal law and so touch on rights against the state as well.

The second distinction is between universal and special rights; that is, between rights that a political theory provides for all individuals in the community, with exceptions only for phenomena like incapacity or punishment, and rights it provides for only one section of the community, or possibly only one member. I shall assume, in this essay, that all political rights are universal.

7   *See* Brandt, *Toward a Credible Form of Utilitarianism*, in MORALITY AND THE LANGUAGE OF CONDUCT 107 (H. Castenada and G. Nakhnikian, eds. 1963).

8   *See, e.g.*, R. POSNER, ECONOMIC ANALYSIS OF LAW 10–104 (1972).

9   *See, e.g.*, Coase, *The Problem of Social Cost*, 3 J. LAW & ECON. 1, 19–28 (1960).

10 *See* Posner, *A Theory of Negligence*, 1 J. LEGAL STUD. 29, 71 (1972).

11 R. POSNER, *supra* note 8, at 4.

12 *United States v. Carroll Towing Co.*, 159 F. 2d 169, 173 (2d Cir. 1947). Coase, *supra* note 9, at 22–23, gives other examples, mostly of nuisance cases interpreting the doctrine that a "reasonable" interference with the plaintiff's use of his property is not a nuisance.

13 A more elaborate argument of principle might provide a better justification for Hand's test than does this simple principle. I described a more elaborate argument in a set of Rosenthal Lectures delivered at Northwestern University Law School in March, 1975. The simple principle, however, provides a sufficiently good justification for the present point.

14 381 U.S. 618 (1965).

15 367 U.S. 643 (1961).

16 *See generally* H. L. A. HART, THE CONCEPT OF LAW 121–32 (1961).

17 *See* Gallie, *Essentially Contested Concepts*, 56 PROCEEDINGS OF THE ARISTOTELIAN SOCIETY 167, 167–68 (1955–56). *See also* Dworkin, *The Jurisprudence of Richard Nixon*, NEW YORK REVIEW OF BOOKS, May 4, 1972, at 27.

18 *See* Dworkin, *The Model of Rules*, 35 U. CHI L. REV. 14, 32–40 (1967).

19 *See* Everson v. Board of Educ., 330 U.S. 1 (1947).

20 *See* Chatwin v. United States, 326 U.S. 455 (1946).

21 One previous example of the use of policy in statutory interpretations illustrates this form of construction. In Charles River Bridge v. Warren Bridge, 24 Mass. (7 Pick.) 344 (1830), *aff'd*, 36 U.S. (II Pet.) 420 (1837), the court had to decide whether a charter to construct a bridge across the Charles River was to be taken to be exclusive, so that no further charters could be granted. Justice Morton of the Supreme Judicial Court held that the grant was not to be taken as exclusive, and argued, in support of that interpretation, that:

> [I]f consequences so inconsistent with the improvement and prosperity of the state result from the liberal and extended construction of the charters which have been granted, we ought, if the terms used will admit of it, rather to adopt a more limited and restricted one, than to impute such improvidence to the legislature.

> ... [Construing the grant as exclusive] would amount substantially to a covenant, that during the plaintiffs' charter an important portion of our commonwealth, as to facilities for travel and transportation, should remain *in statu quo*. I am on the whole irresistibly brought to the conclusion, that this construction is neither consonant with sound reason, with judicial authorities, with the course of legislation, nor with the principles of our free institutions.

Id. at 460.

22 L.R. 1 Ex. 265 (1866), *aff'd*, L.R. 3 H.L. 330 (1868).

23 But since Hercules will be led to accept the rights thesis, *see* pp. 1091–93 *infra*, his "interpretation" of judicial enactments will be different from his interpretation of statutes in one important respect. When he interprets statutes he fixes to some statutory language, as we saw, arguments of principle or policy that provide the best justification of that language in the light of the legislature's responsibilities. His argument remains an argument of principle; he uses policy to determine what rights the legislature has already created. But when he "interprets" judicial enactments he will fix to the relevant language only arguments of principle, because the rights thesis argues that only such arguments acquit the responsibility of the "enacting" court.

24 MacPherson v. Buick Motor Co., 217 N.Y. 382, III N.E. 1050 (1916).

25 H. L. A. HART, *supra* note 18, at 121–32.

26 In Williamson v. Lee Optical Co., 348 U.S. 483 (1955), Justice Douglas suggested that legislation generated by policy need not be uniform or consistent:

> The problem of legislative classification is a perennial one, admitting of no doctrinaire definition. Evils in the same field may be of different dimensions and proportions, requiring different remedies. Or so the legislature may think. Or the reform may take one step at a time, addressing itself to the phase of the problem which seems most acute to the legislative mind. The legislature may select one phase of one field and apply a remedy there, neglecting the others. The prohibition of the Equal Protection Clause goes no further than the invidious discrimination.

Id. at 489 (citations omitted).

Of course the point of the argument here, that the demands of consistency are different in the cases of principle and policy, is of great importance in understanding the recent history of the equal protection clause. It is the point behind attempts to distinguish "old" from "new" equal protection, or to establish "suspect" classifications, and it provides a more accurate and intelligible distinction than these attempts have furnished.

27 *See* pp. 1101–09 [of original text].

28 6 N.Y. 397 (1852).

29 Warren & Brandeis, *The Right of Privacy*, 4 HARV. L. REV. 193 (1890).

30 Roe v. Wade, 410 U.S. 113 (1973); Doe v. Bolton, 410 U.S. 179 (1973).

9

What has Pragmatism to Offer Law?

Richard A. Posner

[T]he great weakness of Pragmatism is that it ends by being of no use to anybody.

T. S. Eliot[1]

I

The pragmatic movement gave legal realism such intellectual shape and content as it had. Then pragmatism died (or merged into other philosophical movements and lost its separate identity), and legal realism died (or was similarly absorbed and transcended). Lately pragmatism has revived, and the question I address in this Article is whether this revival has produced or is likely to produce a new jurisprudence that will bear the same relation to the new pragmatism as legal realism bore to the old. My answer is no on both counts. The new pragmatism, like the old, is not a distinct philosophical movement but an umbrella term for diverse tendencies in philosophical thought. What is more, it is a term for the same tendencies; the new pragmatism is not new. Some of the tendencies that go to make up the pragmatic tradition were fruitfully absorbed into legal realism, particularly in the forms articulated by Holmes and Cardozo; others led, and still lead, nowhere. The tendencies that many years ago were fruitfully absorbed into legal realism can indeed help in the formulation of a new jurisprudence, but it will be new largely in jettisoning the naive politics and other immaturities and excesses of legal realism.[2] This refurbished, modernized realism will owe little or nothing, however, to the new pragmatism – if indeed there is such a thing, as I doubt.

Histories of pragmatism[3] usually begin with Charles Sanders Peirce, although he himself gave credit for the idea to a lawyer friend, Nicholas St. John Green, and anticipations can be found much earlier – in Epicurus, for example.[4] From Peirce the baton is (in conventional accounts) handed to William James, then to John Dewey, George Mead, and (in England) F. S. C. Schiller. Parallel to and influenced by the pragmatists, legal realism comes on the scene, inspired by the work of Oliver Wendell Holmes, John Chipman Grey, and Benjamin Cardozo and realized in the work of the self-described realists, such as Jerome Frank, William Douglas, Karl Llewellyn, Felix Cohen, and Max Radin. Pragmatism and legal realism join in Dewey's essays on law.[5] But by the end of World War II both philosophical pragmatism and legal realism have expired, the first superseded by logical positivism and other "hard" analytic philosophy, the other absorbed into the legal mainstream and particularly into the "legal process" school that reaches its apogee in 1958 with Hart and Sacks's *The Legal Process*. Then, beginning in the 1960s with the waning of logical positivism, pragmatism comes charging back in the person of Richard Rorty, followed in the 1970s by critical legal studies – the radical son of legal realism – and in the 1980s by a school of legal neopragmatists that includes Martha Minow, Thomas Grey, Daniel Farber, Philip Frickey, and others. The others include myself, and perhaps also, as suggested by Professor Rorty in his comment on this paper, Ronald Dworkin – despite Dworkin's overt hostility to pragmatism[6] – and even Roberto Unger. The ideological diversity of this group is noteworthy.

In the account I am offering (not endorsing), pragmatism, whether of the paleo or neo varieties, stands for a progressively more emphatic rejection of Enlightenment dualisms such as subject and object, mind and body, perception and reality, form and substance; these dualisms being regarded as the props of a conservative social, political, and legal order.

This picture is too simple. The triumphs of science, particularly Newtonian physics, in the seventeenth and eighteenth centuries persuaded most thinking people that the physical universe had a uniform structure accessible to human reason. It began to seem that human nature and human social systems might have a similarly mechanical structure. This emerging world view cast humankind in an observing mold. Through perception, measurement, and mathematics, the human mind would uncover the secrets of nature (including those of the mind itself, a part of nature) and the laws (natural, not positive) of social interaction – including laws decreeing balanced government, economic behavior in accordance with the principles of supply and demand, and moral and legal principles based on immutable principles of psychology and human behavior. The mind was a camera, recording activities both natural and social and alike determined by natural laws, and an adding machine.

This view, broadly scientific but flavored with a Platonic sense of a world of order behind the chaos of sense impressions, was challenged by the Romantic poets (such as Blake and Wordsworth) and Romantic philosophers. They emphasized the plasticity of the world and especially the esemplastic power of the human imagination. Institutional constraints they despised along with all other limits on human aspiration, as merely contingent; science they found dreary; they celebrated potency and the sense of community – the sense of unlimited potential and of oneness with humankind and with nature – that an infant feels. They were Prometheans. The principal American representative of this school was Emerson, and he left traces of his thought on Peirce and Holmes alike. Emerson's European counterpart (and admirer) was Nietzsche. It is not that Peirce or Holmes or Nietzsche was a "Romantic" in a precise sense, if there is such a sense. It is that they wished to shift attention from a passive, contemplative relation between an observing subject and an objective reality, whether natural or social, to an active, creative relation between striving human beings and the problems that beset them and that they seek to overcome. For these thinkers, thought was an exertion of will instrumental to some human desire (and we see here the link between pragmatism and utilitarianism). Social institutions – whether science, law, or religion – were the product of shifting human desires rather than of a reality external to those desires. Human beings had not only eyes but hands as well.

Without going any further, we can see that "truth" is going to be a problematic concept for the pragmatist. The essential meaning of the word is observer independence, which is just what the pragmatist is inclined to deny. It is no surprise, therefore, that the pragmatists' stabs at defining truth – truth is what is fated to be believed in the long run (Peirce), truth is what is good to believe (James), or truth is what survives in the competition among ideas (Holmes) – are riven by paradox. The pragmatist's real interest is not in truth at all, but in belief justified by social need.

This change in direction does not necessarily make the pragmatist unfriendly to science (there is a deep division within pragmatism over what attitude to take toward science).[7] But it shifts the emphasis in philosophy of science from the discovery of nature's laws by observation to the formulation of theories about nature that are motivated by the desire of human beings to predict and control their environment. The implication, later made explicit by Thomas Kuhn, is that scientific theories are a function of human need and desire rather than of the way things are in nature, so that the succession of theories on a given topic need not bring us closer to "ultimate reality" (which is not to deny that scientific *knowledge* may be growing steadily). But this is to get ahead of the story, because I want to pause in 1921 and examine the formulation of legal pragmatism that Benjamin Cardozo offered in his book published that year, *The Nature of the Judicial Process*.[8] Most of what Cardozo has to say in this book (and elsewhere) is latent in Holmes's voluminous but scattered and often cryptic academic, judicial, and occasional writings. But the book is worthwhile and important as a clear, concise, and sensible manifesto of legal pragmatism and harbinger of the realist movement.

"The final cause of law," writes Cardozo, "is the welfare of society."[9] So much for the formalist idea, whose scientistic provenance and pretensions are evident, of law as a body of immutable principles. Cardozo does not mean, however, that judges "are free to substitute their own ideas of reason and justice for those of the men and women whom they serve. Their standard must be an objective one" – but objective in a pragmatic sense, which is not the sense of correspondence with an external reality. "In such matters, the thing that counts is not what I believe to be right. It is what I may reasonably believe that some other man of normal intellect and conscience might reasonably look upon as right."[10]

The thing that counts the most is that legal rules be understood in instrumental terms, implying contestability, revisability, and mutability.

> Few rules in our time are so well established that they may not be called upon any day to justify their existence as means adapted to an end. If they do not function, they are diseased. If they are diseased, they need not propagate their kind. Sometimes they are cut out and extirpated altogether. Sometimes they are left with the shadow of continued life, but sterilized, truncated, impotent for harm.[11]

A related point is that law is forward-looking. This point is implicit in an instrumental concept of law – which is the pragmatic concept of

law, law as the servant of human needs, and is in sharp contrast to Aristotle's influential theory of corrective justice. That theory is quintessentially backward-looking. The function of law as corrective justice is to restore a preexisting equilibrium of rights, while in Cardozo's account "[n]ot the origin, but the goal, is the main thing. There can be no wisdom in the choice of a path unless we know where it will lead. . . . The rule that functions well produces a title deed to recognition. . . . [T]he final principle of selection for judges . . . is one of fitness to an end."[12] The "title deed" sentence is particularly noteworthy; it is a rebuke to formalist theories that require that for a law to be valid it must be "pedigreed" by being shown to derive from some authoritative source.

Where does the judge turn for the knowledge that is needed to weigh the social interests that shape the law? "I can only answer that he must get his knowledge . . . from experience and study and reflection; in brief, from life itself."[13] The judge is not a finder, but a maker, of law. John Marshall "gave to the constitution of the United States the impress of his own mind; and the form of our constitutional law is what it is, because he moulded it while it was still plastic and malleable in the fire of his own intense convictions."[14]

The focus of *The Nature of the Judicial Process* is on the common law, but in the last quoted passage we can see that Cardozo did not think the creative powers of the judicial imagination bound to wither when confronted by the challenge of textual interpretation. Although the self-described legal realists (from whom Cardozo, conscious of their excesses, carefully distanced himself)[15] added little to what had been said by Cardozo and before him by Holmes, a notable essay by Max Radin[16] clarifies and in so doing emphasizes the parity of statutes and the common law. Judges, it is true, are not to revise a statute, as they are free to do with a common law doctrine. But interpretation is a creative rather than contemplative task – indeed judges have as much freedom in deciding difficult statutory (and of course constitutional) cases as they have in deciding difficult common law cases.

Yet, despite Radin's notable essay and the realists' salutary effort to refocus legal scholarship from the common law to the emergent world of statute-dominated law, legislation proved a challenge to which the realist tradition, from Holmes to the petering out of legal realism in the 1940s and its replacement by the legal process school in the 1950s, was unable to rise. The trouble started with Holmes's well-known description of the judge as an interstitial legislator, a description that Cardozo echoes in *The Nature of the Judicial Process*. The implication is that judges and legislators are officials of the same stripe – guided and controlled by the same goals, values, incentives, and constraints. If this were true, the judicial role would be greatly simplified; it would be primarily a matter of helping the legislature forge sound policy. It is not true. The legislative process is buffeted by interest-group pressures to an extent rare in the judicial process. The result is a body of laws far less informed by sound policy judgments than the realists in the heyday and aftermath of the New Deal believed. It is no longer possible to imagine the good pragmatist judge as one who acts merely as the faithful agent of the legislature. Indeed, the faithful-agent conception has become a hallmark of modern formalism – judges as faithful agents *despite* the perversity of so many of the statutes that they are interpreting.

A closely related failing of legal realism was its naive enthusiasm for government, an enthusiasm that marked legal realism as a "liberal" movement (in the modern, not nineteenth-century, sense) and is part of the legacy of legal realism to today's neopragmatism. As strikingly shown by the other papers and the comments and floor discussion at the Symposium for which this Article was prepared, today's legal pragmatism is so dominated by persons of liberal or radical persuasion as to make the movement itself seem (not least in their eyes) a school of left-wing thought. Yet not only has pragmatism no inherent political valence, but those pragmatists who attack the pieties of the Right while exhibiting a wholly uncritical devotion to the pieties of the Left (such as racial and sexual equality, the desirability of a more equal distribution of income and wealth, and the pervasiveness of oppression and injustice in modern Western society) are not genuine pragmatists; they are dogmatists in pragmatists' clothing.

Another great weakness of legal realism was the lack of method. The realists knew what to do – think things not words, trace the actual consequences of legal doctrines, balance competing policies – but they didn't have a clue as to how to do any of these things. It was not their fault. The tools of economics, statistics, and other pertinent sciences were insufficiently developed to enable a social-engineering approach to be taken to law.

I want to go back and pick up the thread of philosophical pragmatism. When *The Nature of the Judicial Process* appeared, John Dewey was the leading philosopher of pragmatism, and it is his version of pragmatism that is most in evidence in Cardozo's book and other extrajudicial writings.[17] Dewey continued to be productive for many years, but until the 1960s there was little that was new in pragmatism. Yet much that was happening in philosophy during this interval supported the pragmatic outlook. Logical positivism itself, with its emphasis on verifiability and its consequent hostility to metaphysics, is pragmatic in demanding that theory make a difference in the world of fact, the empirical world. Popper's falsificationist philosophy of science is close to Peirce's philosophy of science; in both, doubt is the engine of progress and truth an ever-receding goal, rather than an attainment. The antifoundationalism, anti-metaphysicality, and rejection of certitude that are leitmotifs of the later Wittgenstein and of Quine can be thought of as extensions of the ideas of James and Dewey. By the 1970s and 1980s, the streams have merged and we have a mature pragmatism represented by such figures as Davidson, Putnam, and Rorty in analytical philosophy, Habermas in political philosophy, Geertz in anthropology, Fish in literary criticism, and the academic lawyers whom I mentioned at the outset.[18]

There is little to be gained, however, from calling this recrudescence of pragmatism the "new" pragmatism. That would imply that there were (at least) two schools of pragmatism, each of which could be described and then compared. Neither the old nor the new pragmatism is a school. The differences between a

Peirce and a James, or between a James and a Dewey, are profound. The differences among current advocates of pragmatism are even more profound, making it possible to find greater affinities across than within the "schools" – Peirce has more in common with Putnam than Putnam with Rorty, and I have more in common (I think) with Peirce, James, and Dewey than I have with Cornel West or Stanley Fish. What is more useful than to attempt to descry and compare old and new schools of pragmatism is to observe simply that the strengths of pragmatism are better appreciated today than they were thirty years ago and that this is due in part to the apparent failure of alternative philosophies such as logical positivism, but more to a growing recognition that the strengths of such alternatives lie in features shared with pragmatism, such as hostility to metaphysics and sympathy with the *methods* of science as distinct from faith in the power of science to deliver final truths.

If both the old and the new pragmatisms are as heterogeneous as I have suggested, the question arises whether pragmatism has any common core, and, if not, what use the term is. To speak in nonpragmatic terms, pragmatism has three "essential" elements. (To speak in pragmatic, nonessentialist terms, there is nothing practical to be gained from attaching the pragmatist label to any philosophy that does not have all three elements.) The first is a distrust of metaphysical entities ("reality," "truth," "nature," etc.) viewed as warrants for certitude whether in epistemology, ethics, or politics. The second is an insistence that propositions be tested by their consequences, by the difference they make – and if they make none, set aside. The third is an insistence on judging our projects, whether scientific, ethical, political, or legal, by their conformity to social or other human needs rather than to "objective," "impersonal" criteria. These elements in turn imply an outlook that is progressive (in the sense of forward-looking), secular, and experimental, and that is commonsensical without making a fetish of common sense – for common sense is a repository of prejudice and ignorance as well as a fount of wisdom. R. W. Sleeper has helpfully summarized the pragmatic outlook in

describing Dewey's philosophy as "a philosophy rooted in common sense and dedicated to the transformation of culture, to the resolution of the conflicts that divide us."[19] Also apt is Cornel West's description of the "common denominator" of pragmatism as "a future-oriented instrumentalism that tries to deploy thought as a weapon to enable more effective action."[20]

II

It should be apparent that what I am calling the core of pragmatism or the pragmatic temper or outlook is vague enough to embrace a multitude of philosophies that are profoundly inconsistent at the operating level (anyone who still doubts this after the examples I gave earlier would do well to recall that Sidney Hook and Jürgen Habermas are both distinguished figures in pragmatic philosophy), including a multitude of inconsistent jurisprudences. Indeed there is a serious question – the question raised by the quotation from T. S. Eliot that is the epigraph of this Article – whether pragmatism is specific enough to have any use, specifically in law. To that question I devote the balance of the Article. I shall be brief and summary; the reader is referred to my forthcoming book[21] for elucidation of the points that follow and for necessary references.

1.   There is at least one specific legal question to which pragmatism is directly applicable and that is the question of the basis and extent of the legal protection of free speech. If pragmatists are right and objective truth is just not in the cards, this may seem to weaken the case for providing special legal protections for free inquiry, viewed as the only dependable path to truth. Actually the case is strengthened. If truth is unattainable, the censor cannot appeal to a higher truth as the ground for foreclosing further inquiry on a subject; but the libertarian, in resisting censorship, can appeal to the demonstrated efficacy of free inquiry in enlarging knowledge. One can doubt that we shall ever attain "truth," but not that our knowledge is growing steadily. Even if every scientific truth

that we accept today is destined someday to be overthrown, our ability to cure tuberculosis and generate electrical power and build airplanes that fly will be unimpaired. The succession of scientific theories not only coexists with, but in fact contributes greatly to, the growth of scientific knowledge.

The pragmatist is apt also to be sympathetic to the argument that art and other nondiscursive modes of communication, and the "hot" rhetoric of the demagogue, and even of the flag or draft-card burner, ought to be protected. The pragmatist doubts that there are ascertainable, "objective" standards for establishing the proprieties of expression and therefore prefers to allow the market to be the arbiter. It is a plausible extension of Holmes's marketplace-of-ideas approach – an approach that rests on a pragmatist rejection of the proposition that there are objective criteria of truth.

2. The pragmatic outlook can help us maintain a properly critical stance toward mysterious entities that seem to play a large role in many areas of law, particularly tort and criminal law. Such entities as mind, intent, free will, and causation are constantly invoked in debates over civil and criminal liability. Tested by the pragmatic criterion of practical consequence, these entities are remarkably elusive. Even if they exist, law has no practical means of locating them and in fact ignores them on any but the most superficial verbal level. Judges and juries do not, as a precondition to finding that a killing was intentional, peer into the defendant's mind in quest of the required intent. They look at the evidence of what the defendant did and try to infer from it whether the deed involved advance planning or other indicia of high probability of success, whether there was concealment of evidence or other indicia of likely escape, and whether the circumstances of the crime argue a likelihood of repetition – all considerations that go to dangerousness rather than to intent or free will. The legal factfinder follows this approach because the social concern behind criminal punishment is a concern with dangerousness rather than with mental states (evil or otherwise), and because the methods of litigation do not enable the factfinder to probe beneath dangerousness into

mental or spiritual strata so elusive they may not even exist.

Similarly, while interested in consequences and therefore implicitly in causality, the law does not make a fetish of "causation." It does not commit itself to any side of the age-old philosophical controversy over causation, but instead elides the issue by basing judgments of liability on social, rather than philosophical, considerations. People who have caused no harm at all because their plans were interrupted are regularly punished for attempt and conspiracy; persons may be held liable in tort law when their acts were neither a necessary nor a sufficient condition of the harm that ensued (as where two defendants, acting independently, simultaneously inflict the harm, and only one is sued); and persons whose acts "caused" injury in an uncontroversial sense may be excused from liability because the harm was an unforeseeable consequence of the act. The principle of legal liability can be redescribed without reference to metaphysical entities such as mind and causation. This redescription is an important part of the project of a pragmatic jurisprudence, although it will not please those for whom law's semantic level is its most interesting and important.

There is nothing new about endeavoring to puncture the law's metaphysical balloons. It was a favorite pursuit of the legal realists. But they did it with a left-wing slant. They were derisive of the proposition that a corporation had natural rights, since a corporation is just the name of a set of contracts. But they were not derisive of the idea of corporate taxation, though, since the corporation is not a person, it cannot bear the burden of taxation. The ultimate payors of the corporate income tax are flesh-and-blood persons, by no means all wealthy, for among them are employees as well as shareholders.

3. Pragmatism remains a powerful antidote to formalism, which is enjoying a resurgence in the Supreme Court. Legal formalism is the idea that legal questions can be answered by inquiry into the relation between concepts and hence without need for more than a superficial examination of their relation to the world of fact. It is, therefore, anti-pragmatic as well as anti-empirical. It asks not, What works?, but instead,

What rules and outcomes have a proper pedigree in the form of a chain of logical links to an indisputably authoritative source of law, such as the text of the United States Constitution? Those rules and outcomes are correct and the rest incorrect. Formalism is the domain of the logician, the casuist, the Thomist, the Talmudist.

The desire to sever knowledge from observation is persistent and, to some extent, fruitful. Armed with the rules of arithmetic, one can drop a succession of balls into an urn and, if one has counted carefully, one will *know* how many balls there are in the urn without looking into it. Similarly, if the rule of the common law that there are no nonpossessory rights in wild animals can be thought somehow to generalize automatically to the rule that there are no such rights in *any* fugitive natural resource, then we can obtain the "correct" rule for property rights in oil and gas without having to delve into the economics of developing these resources. The pragmatic approach reverses the sequence. It asks, What is the right rule – the sensible, the socially apt, the efficient, the fair rule – for oil and gas? In the course of investigating this question, the pragmatist will consult the wild animal law for what (little) light it may throw on the question, but the emphasis will be empirical from the start. There will be no inclination to allow existing rules to expand to their semantic limits, engrossing ever greater areas of experience by a process of analogy or of verbal similitude. The tendency of formalism is to force the practices of business and lay persons into the mold of existing legal concepts, viewed as immutable, such as "contract." The pragmatist thinks that concepts should be subservient to human need and therefore wants law to adjust its categories to fit the practices of the nonlegal community.

4.   The current bulwark of legal formalism, however, is not the common law, but statutory and constitutional interpretation. It is here that we find the most influential modern attempts to derive legal outcomes by methods superficially akin to deduction. The attempts are unlikely to succeed. The interpretation of texts is not a logical exercise and the bounds of "interpretation" are so expansive (when we consider that

among the verbal and other objects that are interpreted are dreams, texts in foreign languages, and musical compositions) as to cast the utility of the concept into doubt. Pragmatists will emphasize the role of consequences in "interpretation," viewed humbly as the use of a text in aid of an outcome. They will point out, for example, that one reason we interpret the sentence "I'll eat my hat" as facetious is that the consequences of attempting to eat one's hat are so untoward.

In approaching an issue that has been posed as one of statutory "interpretation," pragmatists will ask which of the possible resolutions has the best consequences, all things (that lawyers are or should be interested in) considered, including the importance of preserving language as a medium of effective communication and of preserving the separation of powers. Except as may be implied by the last clause, pragmatists are not interested in the authenticity of a suggested interpretation as an expression of the intent of legislators or of the framers of constitutions. They are interested in using the legislative or constitutional text as a resource in the fashioning of a pragmatically attractive result. They agree with Cardozo that what works carries with it the best of title deeds; they prefer the sturdy mongrel to the sickly pedigreed purebred.

Take the old jurisprudential chestnut, discussed briefly in *The Nature of the Judicial Process*,[22] whether a "murdering heir" shall be allowed to inherit. The wills statute allows testators who comply with certain formalities to leave their property to whomever they please. There is no exception for the eventuality in which the beneficiary named in the will murders the testator. Should such an exception be interpolated by the courts? The answer, to the pragmatist, depends on the consequences. On the one hand, it can be objected that by interpolating an exception the courts will relax the pressure on legislators to draft statutes carefully and will violate the principle that legislatures rather than courts prescribe the penalties for criminal behavior. On the other hand, there is a natural concern that allowing the murderer to inherit will encourage murder; a reluctance to pile more work on already overburdened legislatures; and recognition that disinheriting the murderer is apt to fulfill, rather than to defeat, the testator's intentions, which is the ultimate purpose of the wills statute. A testator who foresaw the murder would not have made the murderer a beneficiary under the will; so if no exception to the wills statute is recognized, farseeing testators may decide to insert express provisions in their wills disinheriting murdering beneficiaries. The courts can save them the trouble by interpolating such a provision by interpretation. All these consequences have somehow to be analyzed and compared if the courts are to interpret the wills statute pragmatically.

Further complicating the interpretive picture in general is our current understanding of the legislative process, a more critical understanding than reigned when Cardozo, the legal realists, and the realists' successors in the legal process school wrote. We no longer think of statutes as typically, let alone invariably, the product of well-meaning efforts to maximize the public interest by legislators who are devoted to the public interest and who are the faithful representatives of constituents who share the same devotion. The wills statute can probably be viewed in faithful-agent terms, but many other statutes cannot be. The theory of social choice has instructed us about the difficulties of aggregating preferences by the method of voting, while the interest-group theory of politics in the version revived by economists has taught us that the legislative process often caters to the redistributive desires of narrow coalitions and, in so doing, disserves the public interest, plausibly construed. Under pressure of the insights of both theories it becomes unclear where to locate statutory meaning, problematic to speak of judges discerning legislative intent, and uncertain why judges should seek to perfect through interpretation the decrees of the special-interest state. The main choices in "interpretive" theory that the new learning allows are either some version of strict construction or a pragmatic approach in which, recognizing the difficult and problematic nature of statutory interpretation, judges use consequences to guide their decisions, always bearing in mind that the relevant consequences

include systemic ones such as debasing the currency of statutory language by straying too far from it.

Mention of systemic concerns should help demolish the canard that legal pragmatism implies the suppression of such concerns in favor of doing shortsighted substantive justice between the parties to the particular case.[23] The relevant consequences to the pragmatist are long run as well as short run, systemic as well as individual, the importance of stability and predictability as well as the importance of justice to the individual parties, and the importance of maintaining language as a reliable method of communication as well as the importance of interpreting statutes and constitutional provisions freely in order to make them speak intelligently to circumstances not envisaged by their drafters.

5.   Pragmatism has implications, some already sketched under the rubrics of formalism and interpretation, for the theory of adjudication – of what judges do and should do. Although professional discourse has always been predominantly formalist, most American judges have been practicing pragmatists, in part because the materials for decision in American law have always been so various and conflicting that formalism was an unworkable ideal.[24] But after a bout of conspicuous judicial activism that lasted several decades, there is renewed interest in approaches that favor continuity with the past over social engineering of the future – approaches embraced by many quondam judicial activists eager to conserve the work of the past decades against inroads by conservative judges, and by many conservatives who believe that the judiciary remains committed to liberal policies. There is renewed talk of tradition, of embodied but inarticulate wisdom (embodied in precedent, in professional training, in law's customary language), of the limitedness of individual reason and the danger of precipitate social change. The cautionary stance implicit in these approaches is congenial to the pragmatist, for whom the historical record of reform efforts is full of sobering lessons. But pragmatists are not content with a vague neotraditionalism. They know it will not do to tell judges to resolve all doubts against change and freeze law as it is, let

alone to return to some past epoch in legal revolution (1950? 1850?). As society changes, judges, within the broad limits set by the legislators and by the makers of the Constitution, must adapt the law to its altered environment. No version of traditionalism will tell them how to do this. For this they need ends and an awareness of how social change affects the appropriate means – how, for example, the coming of the telegraph and the telephone altered the conditions for regulating contracts. They need, in short, the instrumental sense that is basic to pragmatism.

6. This brings me to the question of the relation between pragmatism and our most highly developed instrumental concept of law, the economic. Among the recurrent criticisms of efforts to defend the economic approach as a worthwhile guide for legal reform is that the defenders have failed to ground the approach securely in one of the great traditions of ethical insight, such as the Kantian or the utilitarian. The criticism is sound as observation, but not as criticism. The economic approach to law that I defend – the idea that law should strive to support competitive markets and to simulate their results in situations in which market-transaction costs are prohibitive – has affinities with both Kantian and utilitarian ethics: with the former, because the approach protects the autonomy of people who are productive or at least potentially so (granted, this isn't everyone); with the latter, because of the empirical relation between free markets and human welfare. Although it is easily shown that the economic approach is neither deducible from nor completely consistent with either system of ethics, this is not a decisive objection from a pragmatic standpoint. Pragmatists are unperturbed by a lack of foundations. We ask not whether the economic approach to law is adequately grounded in the ethics of Kant or Rawls or Bentham or Mill or Hayek or Nozick – and not whether any of those ethics is adequately grounded – but whether it is the best approach for the contemporary American legal system to follow, given what we know about markets (and we are learning more about them every day from the economic and political changes in Communist and Third World coun-

tries), about American legislatures, about American judges, and about the values of the American people.

The economic approach cannot be the whole content of legal pragmatism. Because it works well only where there is at least moderate agreement on ends, it cannot answer the question whether abortion should be restricted, although it can tell us something, maybe much, about the efficacy and consequences of the restrictions. One value of pragmatism is its recognition that there are areas of discourse where lack of common ends precludes rational resolution; and here the pragmatic counsel (or one pragmatic counsel) to the legal system is to muddle through, preserve avenues of change, do not roil needlessly the political waters. On a pragmatic view, the error of *Roe v. Wade*[25] is not that it read the Constitution wrong – for there are plenty of well-regarded decisions that reflect an equally freewheeling approach to constitutional interpretation – but that it prematurely nationalized an issue best left to simmer longer at the state and local level until a consensus based on experience with a variety of approaches to abortion emerged.

7. To those who equate economics with scientism and who consider pragmatism the rejection of the scientistic approach to philosophy,[26] my attempt to relate the economic approach to pragmatism will seem perverse. But scientistic philosophy – the attempt to construct a metaphysics, a theory of action, an ethical theory, a political theory or what have you that has the rigor and generality that we associate with the natural sciences – is not at all the same thing as social science, which is the application of scientific method to social behavior. Most pragmatists have not disbelieved in the utility of scientific method. Quite the contrary, pragmatism in the style of Peirce and Dewey can be viewed as a generalization of the ethic of scientific inquiry – open-minded, forward-looking, respectful of fact, willing to experiment, disrespectful of sacred cows, anti-metaphysical. And this is an ethic of which law needs more. I am not saying that the economic approach to law is rooted in or inspired by pragmatism, for in truth it is rooted in and inspired by a belief in the intellectual power and pertinence of

economics. But economic analysis and pragmatism are thoroughly, and I think fruitfully, compatible.

8. There is renewed interest in the rhetoric of law.[27] This may appear to have nothing to do with pragmatism, but the appearance is misleading. By making the concept of "objective truth" problematic, the pragmatic distrust of foundations expands the range in which metaphor and other forms of emotive argument may legitimately upset belief. In Holmes's pragmatic metaphor of the marketplace of ideas, competing theorists, ideologues, and reformers hawk their intellectual wares. Knowing how important persuasion is in the market for goods and services, we should not be surprised to find it playing a big role in the market in ideas as well. We should expect change in law to be related not only to politics and economics and not only to the correction of error, but also to new slogans, metaphors, imagery, and other means of bringing about changes in perspective.

III

With muddling through offered as one method of pragmatic jurisprudence (see point 6), one may wonder whether that jurisprudence has progressed an inch beyond *The Nature of the Judicial Process*. Certainly the essence of that jurisprudence is in Cardozo's book and indeed can be found much earlier, though in a more elliptical form, in Holmes's writings, especially "The Path of the Law."[28] But there has been some progress since 1921. Reviewing my eight items, we can see that Cardozo had a solid pragmatic grasp of the weakness of formalism (point 3) and a good pragmatic theory of adjudication (point 6), but free speech was not an issue about which he was much concerned (point 1); the critique of intention and causation (point 2) was less developed than it is today and certainly less salient in Cardozo's thinking; he was uninterested in interpretation and unrealistic about the legislative process (point 3); and he was innocent of the economic approach to law as a self-conscious methodology (point 6) – it did not exist in 1921, or indeed until half a century later – but like most good common law judges

he had intuitions of it.[29] A closely related point is that the application of scientific method to law lay in the future (point 7). Cardozo in his judicial opinions was very much the rhetorician (point 8), but his essay on judicial rhetoric[30] is a disappointment – cute, civilized, but unanalytic.

Although pragmatic jurisprudence embraces a richer set of ideas than can be found in *The Nature of the Judicial Process* or "The Path of the Law," one can hardly say that there has been much progress, and perhaps in the nature of pragmatism there cannot be. All that a pragmatic jurisprudence really connotes – and it connoted it in 1897 or 1921 as much as it does today – is a rejection of a concept of law as grounded in permanent principles and realized in logical manipulations of those principles, and a determination to use law as an instrument for social ends. It signals an attitude, an orientation, at times a change in direction. It clears the underbrush; it does not plant the forest.

Notes

1 T. S. Eliot, *Francis Herbert Bradley*, in SELECTED PROSE OF T. S. ELIOT 196, 204 (F. Kermode ed. 1975) (essay first published in 1927).

2 I present my full argument for this new jurisprudence in my book, THE PROBLEMS OF JURISPRUDENCE (1990).

3 Illustrated by D. HOLLINGER, IN THE AMERICAN PROVINCE: STUDIES IN THE HISTORY AND HISTORIOGRAPHY OF IDEAS 23–32 (1985); J. SMITH, PURPOSE AND THOUGHT: THE MEANING OF PRAGMATISM (1978); H. S. THAYER, MEANING AND ACTION: A CRITICAL HISTORY OF PRAGMATISM (1968).

4 *See* Nussbaum, *Therapeutic Arguments: Epicurus and Aristotle*, in THE NORMS OF NATURE 31 (M. Schofield & G. Striker eds. 1986); *see also id.* at 41, 71–72.

5 Notably his essay *Logical Method and Law*, 10 CORNELL L.Q. 17 (1924).

6 *See infra* note 23.

7 *See, e.g.*, Levi, *Escape From Boredom: Edification According to Rorty*, 11 CAN. J. PHIL. 589 (1981).

8 B. CARDOZO, THE NATURE OF THE JUDICIAL PROCESS (1921).

9 *Id.* at 66.

10 *Id.* at 88–89.

11 *Id.* at 98–99.

12   *Id.* at 102–03.

13   *Id.* at 113.

14   *Id.* at 169–70.

15   *See* B. CARDOZO, *Jurisprudence*, in SELECTED WRITINGS OF BENJAMIN NATHAN CARDOZO: THE CHOICE OF TYCHO BRAHE 7 (M. Hall ed. 1947).

16   *See* Radin, *Statutory Interpretation*, 43 HARV. L. REV. 863, 884 (1930).

17   I discuss the matter of Cardozo's pragmatism at greater length in my Cooley Lectures, CARDOZO: A STUDY IN REPUTATION, to be published in the fall of 1990 by the University of Chicago Press.

18   For good recent discussions of pragmatism from a variety of perspectives, see ANTI-FOUNDATIONALISM AND PRACTICAL REASONING: CONVERSATIONS BETWEEN HERMENEUTICS AND ANALYSIS (E. Simpson ed. 1987); J. MARGOLIS, PRAGMATISM WITHOUT FOUNDATIONS: RECONCILING REALISM AND RELATIVISM, in 1 THE PERSISTENCE OF REALITY (1961); R. RORTY, CONTINGENCY, IRONY, AND SOLIDARITY (1989); C. WEST, THE AMERICAN EVASION OF PHILOSOPHY: A GENEALOGY OF PRAGMATISM (1989); Levi, *supra* note 7; PRAGMATISM: ITS SOURCES AND PROSPECTS (R. Mulvaney & P. Zeltner eds. 1981); Putnam & Putnam, *William James's Ideas*, 8 RARITAN 27 (Winter 1989); RORTY, CONSEQUENCES OF PRAGMATISM (ESSAYS 1972–1980) 160–66 (1982); Rorty, *The Priority of Democracy*, in THE VIRGINIA STATUTE FOR RELIGIOUS FREEDOM: ITS EVOLUTION AND CONSEQUENCES IN AMERICAN HISTORY 257 (M. Peterson & R. Vaughan eds. 1988). The work of the new legal pragmatists is illustrated by Farber, *Legal Pragmatism and the Constitution*, 72 MINN. L. REV. 1331 (1988); Grey, *Holmes and Legal Pragmatism*, 41 STAN. L. REV. 787 (1989); Minow, *The Supreme Court 1986 Term – Foreword: Justice Engendered*, 101 HARV. L. REV. 10 (1987).

19   R. SLEEPER, THE NECESSITY OF PRAGMATISM: JOHN DEWEY'S CONCEPTION OF PHILOSOPHY 8–9 (1986).

20   C. WEST, *supra* note 18, at 5.

21   *See supra* note 2.

22   The case is Riggs v. Palmer, 115 N.Y. 506, 22 N.E. 188 (1889), and the discussion is in B. CARDOZO, *supra* note 8, at 41–43.

23   An implication readers might draw from Dworkin's statement in *Law's Empire* that "the pragmatist thinks judges should always do the best they can for the future, in the circumstances, unchecked by any need to respect or secure consistency in principle with what other officials have done or will do." R. DWORKIN, LAW'S EMPIRE 161 (1986). This is an impoverished conception of pragmatism, one that merges pragmatism with act utilitarianism.

24   Against the suggestion that "pragmatism provides the best explanations of how judges actually decide cases," Dworkin argues that it "leaves unexplained one prominent feature of judicial practice – the attitude judges take toward statutes and precedents in hard cases – except on the awkward hypothesis that this practice is designed to deceive the public, in which case the public has not consented to it." *Id.* Dworkin is inferring judges' attitude from the rhetoric of judicial opinions, and this is perilous, because judges are not always candid and also because they often are not self-aware. Even if judges are consistently and deliberately deceptive, this would not impair the soundness of the pragmatic *explanation* of judicial behavior. Similarly, a lack of public consent would have nothing to do with the explanatory power of the pragmatic explanation. The issue of consent is in any event artificial, since judicial opinions are with rare exceptions written to be read by lawyers, not by lay people, and have in fact virtually no lay readership. Since Dworkin knows all these things as well as I do, I infer that his discussion of judicial behavior and legitimacy, like so much discussion in law, is itself highly rhetorical.

25   410 U.S. 113 (1973).

26   For a clear statement of this rejection, see Rorty, *Philosophy as Science, as Metaphor, and as Politics*, in THE INSTITUTION OF PHILOSOPHY: A DISCIPLINE IN CRISIS? 13 (A. Cohen & M. Dascal eds. 1989).

27   *See* R. POSNER, LAW AND LITERATURE: A MISUNDERSTOOD RELATION 269–316 (1988), and references therein.

28   Holmes, *The Path of the Law*, 10 HARV. L. REV. 457 (1897).

29   Professor Landes and I discuss an example – Cardozo's decision in Adams v. Bullock, 227 N.Y. 208, 125 N.E. 93 (1919) – in W. LANDES & R. POSNER, THE ECONOMIC STRUCTURE OF TORT LAW 97–98 (1987).

30   B. CARDOZO, *Law and Literature*, in SELECTED WRITINGS OF BENJAMIN NATHAN CARDOZO: THE CHOICE OF TYCHO BRAHE 339 (M. Hall ed. 1947).

Part IV

Legal Indeterminacy

10

Form and Substance in Private Law Adjudication

Duncan Kennedy

This article is an inquiry into the nature and interconnection of the different rhetorical modes found in American private law opinions, articles and treatises. I argue that there are two opposed rhetorical modes for dealing with substantive issues, which I will call individualism and altruism. There are also two opposed modes for dealing with questions of the form in which legal solutions to the substantive problems should be cast. One formal mode favors the use of clearly defined, highly administrable, general rules; the other supports the use of equitable standards producing ad hoc decisions with relatively little precedential value.

My purpose is the rational vindication of two common intuitions about these arguments as they apply to private law disputes in which the validity of legislation is not in question. The first is that altruist views on substantive private law issues lead to willingness to resort to standards in administration, while individualism seems to harmonize with an insistence on rigid rules rigidly applied. The second is that substantive and formal conflict in private law cannot be reduced to disagreement about how to apply some neutral calculus that will "maximize the total satisfactions of valid human wants."[1] The opposed rhetorical modes lawyers use reflect a deeper level of contradiction. At this deeper level, we are divided, among ourselves and also within ourselves, between irreconcilable visions of humanity and society, and between radically different aspirations for our common future.

The discussion proceeds as follows. Sections I and II address the problem of the choice between rules and standards as the form for legal directives, collecting and organizing the wide variety of arguments that have been found persuasive in different areas of legal study. Sections III and IV develop the dichotomy of individualism and altruism, with the hope of bringing a measure of order to the chaotic mass of "policies" lawyers use in justifying particular legal rules. Sections V, VI and VII argue that the formal and substantive dichotomies are in fact aspects of a single conflict, whose history is briefly traced through a hundred and fifty years of moral, economic and political dispute. Section VIII outlines the contradictory sets of fundamental premises that underlie this conflict. Section IX is a conclusion.

I will use the law of contracts as a primary source of illustrations, for two reasons. I know it better than other private law subjects, and it is blessed with an extraordinary scholarly literature full of insights that seem to beg for application beyond the narrow compass within which their authors developed them. For example, much of this article simply abstracts to the level of "private law" the argument of an article by Stewart Macaulay on credit cards.[2] It may be useful to take, as a beginning text, the following passage from the Kessler and Gilmore *Contracts* casebook:[3]

> The eventual triumph of the third party beneficiary idea may be looked on as still another instance of the progressive liberalization or erosion of the rigid rules of the late nineteenth century theory of contractual obligation. That such a process has been going on throughout this century is so clear as to be beyond argument. The movement on all fronts has been in the direction of expanding the range and the quantum of obligation and liability. We have seen the development of theories of quasi-contractual liability, of the doctrines of promissory estoppel and culpa in contrahendo, of the perhaps revolutionary idea that the law imposes on the parties to a contract an affirmative duty to act in good faith. During the same period the sanctions for breach of contract have been notably expanded. Recovery of "special" or "consequential" damages has become routinely available in situations in which the recovery would have been as routinely denied fifty years ago. The once "exceptional" remedy of specific performance is rapidly becoming the order of the day. On the other hand the party who has failed to perform his contractual duty but who, in the light of the circumstances, is nevertheless felt to be without fault has been protected by a notable expansion of theories of excuse, such as the overlapping ideas of mistake and frustration. To the nineteenth century legal mind the propositions that no man was his brother's keeper, that the race was to the swift and that the devil should take the hindmost seemed not only obvious but morally right. The most striking feature of nineteenth century contract theory is the narrow scope of social duty which it implicitly assumed. In our own century we have witnessed what it does not seem to fanciful to describe as a socialization of our theory of contract.

My purpose is to examine the relationship between the first and last sentences of the quoted passage. What is the connection between the "*erosion of the rigid rules* of the late nineteenth century theory of contractual obligation" and the "*socialization* of our theory of contract?" I will begin by investigating the formal concept of a rigid rule.

I   The Jurisprudence of Rules

The jurisprudence of rules is the body of legal thought that deals explicitly with the question of legal form. It is premised on the notion that the choice between standards and rules of different degrees of generality is significant, and can be analyzed in isolation from the substantive issues that the rules or standards respond to.[4]

A.   Dimensions of Form

1. Formal Realizability.—The first dimension of rules is that of formal realizability. I will use this term, borrowed from Rudolph von Ihering's classic *Spirit of Roman Law*, to describe the degree to which a legal directive has the quality of "ruleness." The extreme of formal realizability is a directive to an official that requires him to respond to the presence together of each of a list of easily distinguishable factual aspects of a situation by intervening in a determinate way. Ihering used the determination of legal capacity by sole reference to age as a prime example of a formally realizable definition of liability; on the remedial side, he used the fixing of money fines of definite amounts as a tariff of damages for particular offenses.[5]

At the opposite pole from a formally realizable rule is a standard or principle or policy. A standard refers directly to one of the substantive objectives of the legal order. Some examples are good faith, due care, fairness, unconscionability, unjust enrichment, and reasonableness. The application of a standard requires the judge both to discover the facts of a particular situation and to assess them in terms of the purposes or social values embodied in the standard.[6]

It has been common ground, at least since Ihering, that the two great social virtues of formally realizable rules, as opposed to standards or principles, are the restraint of official arbitrariness and certainty. The two are distinct but overlapping. Official arbitrariness means the sub rosa use of criteria of decision that are inappropriate in view of the underlying purposes of the rule.

These range from corruption to political bias. Their use is seen as an evil in itself, quite apart from their impact on private activity.

Certainty, on the other hand, is valued for its effect on the citizenry: if private actors can know in advance the incidence of official intervention, they will adjust their activities in advance to take account of them. From the point of view of the state, this increases the likelihood that private activity will follow a desired pattern. From the point of view of the citizenry, it removes the inhibiting effect on action that occurs when one's gains are subject to sporadic legal catastrophe.[7]

It has also been common ground, at least since Ihering,[8] that the virtues of formal realizability have a cost. The choice of rules as the mode of intervention involves the sacrifice of precision in the achievement of the objectives lying behind the rules. Suppose that the reason for creating a class of persons who lack capacity is the belief that immature people lack the faculty of free will. Setting the age of majority at 21 years will incapacitate many but *not all* of those who lack this faculty. And it will incapacitate some who actually possess it. From the point of view of the purpose of the rules, this combined over- and underinclusiveness amounts not just to licensing but to requiring official arbitrariness. If we adopt the rule, it is because of a judgment that this kind of arbitrariness is less serious than the arbitrariness and uncertainty that would result from empowering the official to apply the standard of "free will" directly to the facts of each case.

2. Generality.—The second dimension that we commonly use in describing legal directives is that of generality vs. particularity. A rule setting the age of legal majority at 21 is more general than a rule setting the age of capacity to contract at 21. A standard of reasonable care in the use of firearms is more particular than a standard of reasonable care in the use of "any dangerous instrumentality." Generality means that the framer of the legal directive is attempting to kill many birds with one stone. The wide scope of the rule or standard is an attempt to deal with as many as possible of the different imaginable fact situations in which a substantive issue may arise.[9]

The dimensions of generality and formal realizability are logically independent: we can have general or particular standards, and general or particular rules. But there are relationships between the dimensions that commonly emerge in practice. First, a general rule will be more over- and underinclusive than a particular rule. Every rule involves a measure of imprecision vis-à-vis its purpose (this is definitional), but the wider the scope of the rule, the more serious the imprecision becomes.

Second, the multiplication of particular rules undermines their formal realizability by increasing the number of "jurisdictional" questions. Even where the scope of each particular rule is defined in terms of formally realizable criteria, if we have a different age of capacity for voting, drinking, driving, contracting, marrying and tortfeasing, there are likely to be contradictions and uncertainty in borderline cases. One general rule of legal capacity at age 18 eliminates all these at a blow, and to that extent makes the system more formally realizable.[10]

Third, a regime of general rules should reduce to a minimum the occasions of judicial lawmaking. Generality in statement guarantees that individual decisions will have far reaching effects. There will be fewer cases of first impression, and because there are fewer rules altogether, there will be fewer occasions on which a judge is free to choose between conflicting lines of authority. At the same time, formal realizability eliminates the sub rosa lawmaking that is possible under a regime of standards. It will be clear what the rule is, and everyone will know whether the judge is applying it. In such a situation, the judge is forced to confront the extent of his power, and this alone should make him more wary of using it than he would otherwise be.[11]

Finally, the application of a standard to a particular fact situation will often generate a particular rule much narrower in scope than that standard. One characteristic mode of ordering a subject matter area including a vast number of possible situations is through the combination of a standard with an ever increasing group of particular rules of this kind. The generality of the standard means that there are no gaps: it is possible to find out something about how judges will dispose of cases that have not yet arisen. But no attempt is made to formulate a formally realizable general rule. Rather, case law gradually fills in the area with rules so closely bound to particular facts that they have little or no precedential value.[12]

3. Formalities vs. Rules Designed to Deter Wrongful Behavior.—There is a third dimension for the description of legal directives that is as important as formal realizability and generality. In this dimension, we place at one pole legal institutions whose purpose is to prevent people from engaging in particular activities because those activities are morally wrong or otherwise flatly undesirable. Most of the law of crimes fits this pattern: laws against murder aim to eliminate murder. At the other pole are legal institutions whose stated object is to facilitate private ordering. Legal institutions at this pole, sometimes called formalities,[13] are supposed to help parties in communicating clearly to the judge which of various alternatives they want him to follow in dealing with disputes that may arise later in their relationship. The law of conveyancing is the paradigm here.

Formalities are premised on the lawmaker's indifference as to which of a number of alternative relationships the parties decide to enter. Their purpose is to make sure, first, that the parties know what they are doing, and, second, that the judge will know what they did. These are often referred to as the cautionary and evidentiary functions of formalities.[14] Thus the statute of frauds is supposed both to make people take notice of the legal consequences of a writing and to reduce the occasions on which judges enforce non-existent contracts because of perjured evidence.

Although the premise of formalities is that the law has no preference as between alternative private courses of action, they operate through the contradiction of private intentions. This is true whether we are talking about the statute of frauds,[15] the parol evidence rule,[16] the requirement of an offer and acceptance,[17] of definiteness,[18] or whatever. In every case, the formality means that unless the parties adopt the prescribed mode of manifesting their wishes, they will be ignored. The reason for ignoring them, for applying the sanction of nullity, is to force them to be self conscious and to express themselves clearly, not to influence the substantive choice about whether or not to contract, or what to contract for.

By contrast, legal institutions aimed at wrongdoing attach sanctions to courses of conduct in order to discourage them. There is a wide gamut of possibilities, ranging from outright criminalization to the mere refusal to enforce contracts to perform acts "contrary to public policy" (*e.g.*, contracts not to marry). In this area, the sanction of nullity is adopted not to force the parties to adopt a prescribed form, but to discourage them by making it more difficult to achieve a particular objective.

While the two poles are quite clear in theory, it is often extremely difficult to decide how the concepts involved apply in practice. One reason for this is that, whatever its purpose, the requirement of a formality imposes some cost on those who must use it, and it is often unclear whether the lawmaker intended this cost to have a deterrent effect along with its cautionary and evidentiary functions. Thus the requirement that promises of bequests be in writing may have been aimed to discourage the descent of property outside of the normal family channel, as well as to decrease the probability of perjurious claims.[19]

Another source of difficulty is that there exists an intermediate category of legal institutions that partakes simultaneously of the nature of formalities and of rules designed to deter wrongdoing.[20] In this category fall a vast number of directives applied in situations where one party has injured another, but has not done something that the legal system treats as intrinsically immoral or antisocial. It is generally the case that the parties could have, but have not made an agreement that would have determined the outcome under the circumstances. In the absence of prior agreement, it is up to the court to decide what to do. The following are examples of rules of this kind:

(a)   Rules defining nonconsensual duties of care to another, imposed by the law of torts, property, quasi-contract, or fiduciary relations, or through the "good faith" requirement in the performance of contractual obligations.

(b) Rules defining the circumstances in which violations of legal duty will be excused (*e.g.*, for mistake, impossibility, assumption of risk, contributory negligence, laches).

(c) Rules for the interpretation of contracts and other legal instruments, insomuch as those rules go beyond attempting to determine the actual intent of the parties (*e.g.*, interpretation of form contracts against the drafting party).

(d) The law of damages.

The ambiguity of the legal directives in this category is easiest to grasp in the cases of interpretation and excuses. For example, the law of impossibility allocates risks that the parties might have allocated themselves. Doctrines of this kind, which I will call suppletive, can be interpreted as merely facilitative. In other words, we can treat them *not* as indicating a preference for particular conduct (sharing of losses when unexpected events occur within a contractual context), but as cheapening the contracting process by making it known in advance that particular terms need not be explicitly worked out and written in. The parties remain free to specify to the contrary whenever the suppletive term does not meet their purposes.

On the other hand, it may be clear that the terms in question *are* designed to induce people to act in particular ways, and that the lawmaker is not indifferent as to whether the parties adopt them. This approach may be signalled by a requirement of "clear and unambiguous statement" of contrary intent, or by other rules of interpretation, like that in favor of bilateral rather than unilateral contracts. But it is only when the courts refuse to allow even an explicit disclaimer or modification of the term that we know that we are altogether out of the realm of formalities.[21]

The same kind of obscurity of purpose is present in the legal rules defining liability and fixing damages in tort, property and contract. *Sometimes* it is quite clear that the legal purpose is to eradicate a particular kind of behavior. By granting punitive damages or specific performance, for example, the lawmaker indicates that he is not indifferent as between

the courses of action open to the parties. But where damages are merely compensatory, and perhaps even then not *fully* compensatory, there is a problem. The problem is aggravated when these damages are exacted both for breaches or torts involving some element of fault and for those that are innocent (nonnegligent injury; involuntary breach).

It is nonetheless possible to take a determinedly moralistic view of tort and breach of contract. The limitation of damages to compensation may be seen not as condoning the conduct involved, but as recognizing the deterrent effect that higher damages would have on activity in general, including innocent and desirable activity. It may also reflect qualms about windfall gains to the victims. Liability for involuntary breach and for some nonnegligent injuries are overinclusive from the moralistic point of view, but may be justified by the need to avoid hopelessly difficult factual issues.

The contrary view is that contract and tort liability reflect a decision that, so long as compensation is paid, the lawmaker is indifferent as between "wrongful" and "innocent" behavior.[22] Legal directives defining breach of contract and tortious activity, and fixing damage measures, are then in a special class situated midway between formalities and rules punishing crimes that are *mala in se*. Unlike the rules of offer and acceptance, for example, they reflect a moral objective: that private actors should internalize particular costs of their activities, and have some security that they will not have to bear the costs of the activities of others. But the moral objective is a limited one, implying no judgment about the qualities of tort or breach of contract in themselves. The wrong involved is the failure to compensate, not the infliction of damage.

Along with a limited substantive content, these legal doctrines have limited cautionary and evidentiary functions. They define in advance a tariff that the private actor must pay if he wishes to behave in a particular way. The lawmaker does not care what choice the actor makes within this structure, but has an interest in the choice being made knowingly and deliberately, and in the accuracy of the judicial processes that will assess liability to pay the tariff and determine its amount. Since he is not trying to discourage torts or breaches of contract, it is important to define liability and its consequences in such a way as to facilitate private choice.[23]

B.   *Relationship of the Formal Dimensions To One Another*

The categorization of rules as formalities or as designed to deter wrongdoing is logically independent of the issues of formal realizability and generality. In other words, legal directives designed to deter immoral or antisocial conduct can be couched in terms of general or particular rules, general or particular standards, or some combination. This is equally true, though less obvious in the case of formalities. While it is easy to imagine formalities cast as rules (general or particular) and difficult to see them as standards, there is nothing to prevent a judge from nullifying a transaction in which the parties have failed to use a prescribed mode of communication by applying a standard. For example, Williston favored a general rule that contracts must be definite as to price and quantity, or they were not legally binding.[24] But the UCC takes the general position that an agreement is not void for indefiniteness if the parties intended a contract *and* there is an adequate basis for the provision of a remedy for breach.[25] The judge can still disregard the will of the parties, sanctioning them for failure to observe the formality, but he does so according to criteria patently lacking in formal realizability.[26]

In spite of logical independence, there are conventional arguments pro and con the use of general rules both in the design of formalities and in the design of directives that deter immoral or antisocial conduct. The argument about laws designed to deter wrongdoing focuses on the "chilling" effect of standards on those parties who will come as close to the forbidden behavior as they can without getting caught. That about formalities identifies as the crucial issue the impact of general rules on the parties' willingness to master the language of form.

1. Directives Designed to Deter Wrongdoing.[27]—The use of rules, as opposed to standards, to deter immoral or antisocial conduct

means that sometimes perfectly innocent behavior will be punished, and that sometimes plainly guilty behavior will escape sanction. These costs of mechanical over- and underinclusion are the price of avoiding the potential arbitrariness and uncertainty of a standard.

As between the mechanical arbitrariness of rules and the biased arbitrariness of standards, there is an argument that bias is preferable, because it will "chill" behavior on the borderline of substantive obnoxiousness. For example, a measure of uncertainty about when a judge will find a representation, or a failure to disclose, to be fraudulent may encourage openness and honesty. Rules, on the other hand, allow the proverbial "bad man" to "walk the line," that is, to take conscious advantage of underinclusion to perpetrate fraud with impunity.

There are three familiar counterarguments in favor of rules. First, a standard will deter desirable as well as undesirable conduct.[28] Second, *in terrorem* general standards are likely to be paper tigers in practice. Uncertainty about whether the sanction will in fact materialize may lead to a lower level of actual social control than would occur if there were a well defined area within which there was a high probability of even a mild punishment. Death is likely to be an ineffective penalty for theft.[29]

Third, where the substantively undesirable conduct can be deterred effectively by *private* vigilance, rules alert, or should alert the potential victims to the danger. For example, a formally realizable general rule of caveat emptor should stimulate buyers to take all kinds of precautions against the uncommunicative seller. It is true that the rule will also allow many successful frauds. But these may be *less* numerous in the end than those that would occur if buyers knew that there was the possibility, however uncertain, of a legal remedy to save them from their sloppiness in inspecting the goods. Likewise, the rigid rule that twenty-one year olds are adult for purposes of contractual capacity makes their change of status more conspicuous; it puts them on notice in a way that a standard (*e.g.*, undue influence) would not.[30]

These arguments apply to suppletive terms and to the rules defining civil liability and damage measures, at least in so far as we regard those institutions as designed to deter wrong-doing. For example, expectation damages should discourage breach of contract more effectively than would a reliance recovery. Reliance is difficult to measure and to prove, whereas in many situations the expectancy can be determined almost mechanically. While our real concern may be with the promisee's out-of-pocket loss from breach, the occasional imprecision of expectation damages may be justified at least in commercial situations, on the grounds of superior deterrent power.[31]

2. Formalities.—Here, as in the area of immoral or antisocial conduct, the main disadvantage of general rules is their over- and underinclusiveness from the point of view of the lawmaker's purposes. In the context of formalities the problem is that general rules will lead to many instances in which the judge is obliged to disregard the real intent of the parties choosing between alternative legal relationships. For example, he will refuse to enforce contracts intended to be binding (underinclusion), and he will enforce terms in agreements contrary to the intent of one or even both parties (overinclusion).[32] Since we are dealing with formalities, this is an evil: the lawmaker has no substantive preferences about the parties' choice, and he would like to follow their wishes.

(*a*) *The Argument for Casting Formalities as Rules.*—The response is that the problem of over- and underinclusiveness has a special aspect in the case of formalities because the lawmaker can enlist the energies of the parties in reducing the seriousness of the imprecision of rules. The parties have an interest in communicating their exact intentions to the judge, an interest that is absent when they are engaged in activity the legal system condemns as immoral or antisocial. But this communication has a cost and involves risks of miscarriage. The lower the cost, and the greater the probability that the judge will respond as expected, the more the parties will invest in getting the message across.

The lawmaker can take this private calculus into account in designing the formalities. He can reduce the cost of learning the language of form by making his directives as general as possible. A "technical" system composed of many different rules or standards applying to

closely related situations will be difficult to master and confusing in practice. For example, Williston's formulation of the parol evidence rule involves a rule of "plain meaning of the writing on its face" to determine whether a given integration embodies the total agreement of the parties. But this is subject to exceptions for fraud and duress. Another rule applies in determining whether the integration was intended to be "final," and yet another to the problem of agreements whose enforceability was meant to be conditional on the occurence of events not mentioned in the document. It is hard to imagine a layperson setting out to master this doctrinal tangle.[33]

If generality can reduce the cost of formal proficiency, formal realizability should reduce the risk that the exercise of judicial discretion will bring formal proficiency to naught. Standards discourage investment in two ways. The uncertainty of the outcome if the judge is at large in finding intent, rather than bound to respond mechanically to ritual acts like sealing, will reduce the payoff that can be expected from being careful. Second, the dangers of imprecision are reduced because the judge may bail you out if you blunder. The result *may* be a slippery slope of increasing informality that ends with the legal system treating disputes about wills as though they were automobile accidents litigated under a fault standard.

If general rules lead people to invest in formal proficiency, at least as compared to standards, the result should be the reduction of their over- and underinclusiveness. In other words, the application of the rule should only very rarely lead to the nullification of the intent of the parties. The rare cases that do occur can then be written off as a small cost to pay for the reinforcement of the sanction of nullity. People will miss fewer trains, the argument goes, if they know the engineer will leave without them rather than delay even a few seconds. Standards, by contrast, are dynamically unstable. Rather than evoking private action that compensates their inadequacies, they stimulate responses that aggravate their defects.

Finally, rules encourage transaction in general. If an actor knows that the use of a formality guarantees the execution of his intentions, he will do things that he would not do if there were a risk that the intention would be defeated. In particular, actors will rely on enforcement of contracts, trusts, and so forth, in making investments. Since we are dealing with formalities, it is a matter of definition that the legal system is anxious to encourage this kind of activity so long as private parties desire to engage in it.[34]

Suppletive rules and the general principles of tort and contract liability can be treated, as we have seen already, either as primarily aimed to suppress breach of contract and tortious injury or to structure private choice between injury *cum* compensation and no injury. If we choose to analogize the tortfeasor to a testator or a bond indenture lawyer, it is easy to argue that formally realizable general rules are as important in torts as they are in the area of pure formalities.

If the rules are clear, people will invest time and energy in finding out what they are. They will then adjust their behavior so that they commit torts only up to the point at which what they gain is equal to what they have to pay in compensation. A regime of standards, on the other hand will "chill" private activity by making its consequences less certain. At the same time uncertainty reduces the incentive to find out the nature of one's duties and then choose rationally between performing them and paying damages.

(*b*) *The Critique of the Argument for Rules.*— The argument for casting formalities as rules rests on two sets of assumptions, each of which is often challenged in discussions of actual legal institutions. The first set of assumptions concerns the impact on real participants in a real legal system of the demand for formal proficiency. If the argument for rules is to work, we must anticipate that private parties will in fact respond to the threat of the sanction of nullity by learning to operate the system. But real as opposed to hypothetical legal actors may be unwilling or unable to do this.[35]

The contracts of dealers on produce exchanges are likely to use the most exquisite and most precisely manipulable formal language. Poor consumers, by contrast, are likely to be formally illiterate. Somewhere in between lie the businessmen who have a highly developed understanding of the mechanics of their deals, yet persistently — and perfectly rationally, given the money cost of lawyers and the social and business cost of legalism — fail to master legal technicalities that return to plague them when things go wrong. We must take all the particular variations into account. In the end, we may decide that a particular formal system works so smoothly that a refusal to fill the gaps with general rules would be a wanton sacrifice of the parties to a judicial prima donna. But others work so badly that little is lost by riddling them with loopholes.

This problem of differing degrees of responsiveness to the sanction of nullity can be generalized to the intermediate category of rules defining tort and contract liability in the absence of party specification. It can be argued that private activity is only rarely and sporadically undertaken with a view to legal consequences. The law intervenes only when things have gone so far astray that all the private mechanisms for adjusting disputes have been tried and failed. It is therefore unwise to treat the judicial decision process as though it could or should legislate effectively for all or even most contract or tort disputes, let alone all contracts or torts. The parties have an immediate interest in a resolution that will be neither under- nor over-inclusive from the point of view of the lawmaker's purposes. The countervailing interest in telling others clearly what will happen in their hypothetical future lawsuits is weak, because it is so unlikely that "others" will listen.[36]

In those situations in which some parties *are* responsive to the legal system, a regime of formally realizable general rules may intensify the disparity in bargaining power in transactions between legally skilled actors who use the legal system constantly, and unskilled actors without lawyers or prior experience.[37] At one extreme there is a kind of fraud that is extremely difficult to police effectively: one party knows that the other party does *not* know that the contract must be in writing if it is to be legally binding. At the other is the bargaining confrontation in which the party with the greater skills legitimately relies on them to obtain a result more favorable than would have occurred if everyone knew that the issue *had* to be left to the judge's discretion.

The second set of assumptions under-lying the argument for rules concerns the practical possibility of maintaining a highly formal regime. A great deal of legal scholarship between the First and Second World Wars went into showing that legal directives that looked general and formally realizable were in fact indeterminate.[38] Take, for example, the "rule" that a contract will be rescinded for mutual mistake going to the "substance" or "essence" of the transaction, but not for mistakes as to a "mere quality or accident," even though the quality or accident in question was the whole reason for the transaction. We have come to see legal directives of this kind as invitations to sub rosa balancing of the equities. Such covert standards may generate more uncertainty than would a frank avowal that the judge is allocating a loss by reference to an open textured notion of good faith and fair dealing.[39]

In other situations, a "rule" that appears to dispose cleanly of a fact situation is nullified by a counterrule whose scope of application seems to be almost identical. Agreements that gratuit-ously increase the obligations of one contractual partner are unenforceable for want of consider-ation. *But*, such agreements may be binding if the judge can find an implied recission of the old contract and the formation of a new one incorporating the unilaterally onerous terms. The realists taught us to see this arrangement as a smokescreen hiding the skillful judge's decision as to duress in the process of renegoti-ation, and as a source of confusion and bad law when skill was lacking.[40]

The critic of the argument for rules can often use this sort of analysis to show that what looks like a rule is really a covert standard. It is also often possible to make a plausible claim that the reason for the "corruption" of what was sup-posed to be a formal regime was that the judges were simply unwilling to bite the bullet, shoot the hostages, break the eggs to make the omelette and leave the passengers on the plat-form. The more general and the more formally realizable the rule, the greater the equitable pull of extreme cases of over- or underinclusion. The result may be a dynamic instability as pernicious as that of standards. There will be exceptions that are only initially innocuous,

playing with the facts, the invention of counter-rules (*e.g.*, waiver and estoppel), the manipula-tion of manifestations of intent, and so forth. Each successful evasion makes it seem more unjust to apply the rule rigidly in the next case; what was once clear comes to be sur-rounded by a technical and uncertain penumbra that is more demoralizing to investment in form than an outright standard would be.[41]

II   Types of Relationship Between Form and Substance

The jurisprudence of form presented in the last section is common to legal thinkers of many times and places. There seems no basis for disputing that the notions of rule and standard, and the idea that the choice between them will have wide-ranging practical consequences, are useful in understanding and designing legal institutions. But there is more to the matter than that.

The discussion presented a pro-rules position and a pro-standards position, but there was nothing to suggest that these were truly incompatible. A hypothetical lawmaker with undefined purposes could approach the prob-lem of form with no bias one way or another. He could use the analysis to identify the likely benefits of using rules by applying the pro-rules position to the particular circumstances that concerned him. He could then review the opposed position to get an idea of the costs of using rules and the advantages of standards. He might make up his mind to adopt one form, or the other, or one of the infinite number of intermediate positions, by assessing the net balance of advantage in terms of his underlying legislative objective.

From this starting point of "value neutral" description of the likely consequences of adopting rules or standards, there are two quite different directions in which one might press the analysis of legal form. One alternative is to attempt to enrich the initial schema by contextualizing it. This approach involves being more specific both about the particular situations in which lawmakers operate and about the different objectives that they try to achieve in those situations. The first part of this section provides some illustrations of this line of investigation.

The second, and I think more important, approach ignores both the question of how rules and standards work in realistic settings and the question of how we can best solve the problem of fitting form to particular objectives. The purpose of the second line of investigation is to relate the pro-rules and pro-standards positions to other ideas about the proper ordering of society, and particularly to ideas about the proper substantive content of legal rules. The second part of this section describes this approach, as a preliminary to its pursuit in Section III.

A.   Contextualization

There are two primary modes of contextualization, which might be called the social engineering and the social science approaches, respectively. The first aims to develop principles that will guide the legislator in deciding when to use rules and when standards. The second eschews normative judgments, preferring simply to describe the various effects, legitimate and illegitimate, that follow from the choice of form.

1. Social Engineering.—It seems that the first self-conscious general statement of principles for the choice of form, at least by an American, is Pound's *Theory of Judicial Decision*, published in 1923. The thesis of the article is simple: "rules of law ... which are applied mechanically are more adapted to property and to business transactions; standards where application proceeds upon intuition are more adapted to human conduct and to the conduct of enterprises."[42]

If we ask the criterion of "adaptedness," Pound had a ready but from today's perspective vacuous answer: "for the purposes of today our picture should be one, not ... of a body of unchallengeable deductions from ultimate metaphysically-given data at which men arrived a century ago in seeking to rationalize the social phenomena of that time, ... but rather a picture of a process of social engineering. Such a pic-

ture, I venture to think, would represent the social order as an organized human endeavor to satisfy a maximum of human wants with a minimum of sacrifice of other wants."[43]

Pound was explicit that "individualization" of law through the use of standards was inappropriate where "security of transaction" was the paramount value. At the same time, he made free use of the argument that the certainty of rules was often illusory. Where he favored standards, he claimed that the special nature of the circumstances made "the sacrifice of certainty ... more theoretical than actual."[44]

There are few areas of law in which there has not been, since Pound's article, an attempt to generalize about what form best suits the peculiar nature of the subject matter. In family[45] and labor law,[46] in antitrust[47] and tax law,[48] in juvenile delinquency[49] and sentencing of criminals,[50] there have been fluctuations from one model to the other and back again. The same is true of administrative law,[51] civil procedure,[52] and the law of contracts.[53]

The social engineering approach has not produced convincing results beyond the confines of particular fields. Generalizations that at first seem highly plausible turn out on further examination to be false, or at least no more convincing than diametrically opposed counterprinciples. For example, Larry Tribe has recently argued, as a matter of constitutional right, that the treatment of unwed motherhood is "an area in which the need to reflect rapidly changing norms affecting important interests in liberty compels an individualized determination, one not bound by any pre-existing rule of thumb within the zone of moral change."[54] But a recent article by Heymann and Holtz takes the position that the existence of moral flux makes it overwhelmingly important that we use rigid per se rules in defining "personhood" for purposes of decisions about the treatment of severely defective newborn infants.[55] Perhaps the positions can be reconciled in terms of a more abstract principle, but none comes to mind.

The difficulty of arriving at a consensus about the optimal social role of rules is best illustrated by the case of Article 2 of the Uniform Commerical Code, which governs commercial contracts. According to a persistent line of theorizing associated with Max Weber,[56] this should be an area prototypically adapted to rules. The "social function of maintaining the market" supposedly requires a formal approach here, if anywhere. Yet the drafters of Article 2 proceeded on the conviction that general commercial law was prototypically adapted to standards. This choice was explicitly based on the claim that ideas like "reasonableness" and "good faith" provide greater predictability in practice than the intricate and technical rule system they have replaced.[57]

2. The Social Science Approach.—Efforts like those of Pound have a legislative focus and are therefore concerned with the impact of rules on generalized "social interests" or "functions" assertedly important regardless of the "partisan" or "political" objectives of particular groups. The social science approach is not restricted in this way. The "scientist" as opposed to the "engineer" can ask how the choice of form will favor the interests of some participants in a conflict and disfavor others. My aim here is simply to illustrate this perspective rather than to investigate it fully or develop it. For this purpose, it may be useful to make the following subdivision among types of conflict to which the choice of form is relevant:

(a) Conflict between lawmakers within a single institution, particularly that between "reform" and the status quo, however those may be defined.

(b) Conflict between lawmakers and a group that is supposed to execute the law (*e.g.*, the police) or to obey it (the citizenry).

(c) Conflict between lawmakers within one institution (*e.g.*, the courts) and those in other institutions (*e.g.*, the legislature, the jury) which have a parallel or overlapping jurisdiction.

(*a*) *Standards as Instruments of Change.*—Imagine a court with a rule that legislative interference with freedom of contract is unconstitutional. Some newly appointed judges disapprove of this policy. They *might* come up with a new rule: the question of whether or not to interfere with freedom of contract is inherently legislative, and not open to judicial review. But they might find it preferable to argue for a rule that only "unreasonable" interference is forbidden. Some reasons for such a posture have to do with the relationship between court and legislature as competing institutions, but others might be internal to the court.

First, the standard might represent a substantive compromise between all and nothing. The reformers might support it because they lacked the power to impose their ideal solution. Second, the standard could be adopted without overruling any earlier cases. Previous invalidations of statutes could simply be reinterpreted as findings of unreasonableness. Third, the reformers might themselves be unsure of how far they wanted to go. Experience under a standard might lead with time to the emergence of the knowledge necessary to formulate a more precise rule than that of blanket deference to the legislature.

Of course, the reformers might adopt other tactics, such as undermining the formal realizability of the existing rule, proposing exceptions or counterrules, or developing jurisdictional limitations on effective legal challenges to legislation. All one can say is that standards *may* be advocated because they fit a political strategy for dealing with conflict rather than for reasons intrinsic to the social situation in which they will be applied, or to the substantive content of the law in question.[58]

(*b*) *Rules as a Means to Control Action.*—A court charged with laying down rules for police behavior in investigating crimes may be convinced that the police have a tendency to place an impermissibly low value on the rights of suspects to be secure against unreasonable searches and seizures and to refrain from testifying against themselves. This difference in valuation arises, let us suppose, both from a substantive disagreement about the content of constitutional guarantees and from inherent tendencies of large bureaucratic organizations.

In this situation, a court might believe that formally realizable general rules (notification of legal rights prior to interrogation) would function much better than standards to force the executive agency to put the court's view of the issue into practice. A standard might be much preferable to a rule if the court could itself apply it in every case, but the necessity of delegation of the application function creates an excessive danger of de facto nullification.[59]

Similar dilemmas arise in the relation of courts to juries, to legislatures, to inferior tribunals, and to private parties. In each of these relationships, there may be an unquestioned consensus that the court is the legitimate lawmaker, and that the other party has no other duty than to carry out judicial directives. But given a standard of "fair compensation" juries may habitually award punitive damages, leading judges to impose detailed rules about how damage *must* be measured in typical fact situations.[60] "One man, one vote" may seem the only feasible mechanism for policing reapportionment although the judges believe strongly that a standard of "fair representation" would better reflect their own and the nation's political philosophy. A court with no desire to punish innocent employers may nonetheless hesitate to read a "good faith" defense against back pay awards into an equal employment opportunity statute.[61]

But it will not always be true that the best way for the lawmaking institution to control the subordinate is through rules. The very widespread acceptance of the proposition appears to be based on implicit assumptions about the bureaucratic costs of direct control through the application of standards. Where these costs are low or non-existent, it is common to argue that the superior will prefer the ad hoc approach because it maximizes his discretion. By refusing to enunciate anything but a standard, the superior with powers of review can induce the inferior to follow its wishes with an attentiveness and submissiveness born of insecurity. If the executive agency experiences "reversal" as a serious sanction, and will try to avoid it by sensitivity to all the subtle overtones and cues provided by the reviewing institution's applications of the standard, the use of rules may be counterproductive. Indeed, rules may foster a sense of bureaucratic (or private) autonomy and provide a basis of independent executive power that would be absent under a regime of standards.[62]

(c) *Rules and the Legitimacy of Judicial Action.*—In many situations that arise in our legal system, it is open to argument whether substantive norms of conduct ought to be laid down by the courts or by some other, more "democratically legitimate" institution, such as the legislature, the jury, or private parties pursuing their own objectives through institutions like contract or corporate law. Judges making law in these situations have to worry not only about conflict within the judiciary and about effectively controlling subordinate agencies but also about the question of whether they will be seen as "usurping" the jurisdiction of other institutions. In short, there may be conflict about who is the superior and who the inferior legal actor in the premises.

In disputes about the judicial role, the parties appeal to stereotyped images of what courts, legislators, juries, and private right holders "ought" to do. A very deepseated idea of the judicial function is that judges apply rules. It follows that there will often be a great tactical advantage, for a court which wants to expand its power at the expense of another institution, in casting the norms it wants to impose in the rule form. The object is to draw on the popular lay notion that "discretion" and "value judgments" are the province of legislatures, juries, and private parties, while judges are concerned with techniques of legal reasoning that are neutral and ineluctable, however incomprehensible.

There are two different ways in which the rule form shores up the legitimacy of judicial action. First, the discretionary elements in the choice of a norm to impose are obscured by the process of justification that pops a rule out of the hat of policy, precedent, the text of the Constitution, or some other source of law. Second, once the norm has been chosen, the rule form disguises the discretionary element involved in applying it to cases. A standard is often a tactically inferior weapon in jurisdictional struggle, both because it seems less plausible that it is the only valid outcome of the reasoning process and because it is often clear that its application will require or permit resort to "political" or at least non-neutral aspects of the situation.[63] For example, the Supreme Court in the 1950's adopted a "balancing test" for the interpretation of the first amendment to the Constitution. The issue was typically whether or not the Court should nullify a statute that the legislature claimed was necessary to protect "national security." The proponents of the balancing test attempted to "weigh the interest in free speech against the interest in national security" as a means to deciding whether the statute was constitutional.

The Justices who favored this procedure were quite explicitly concerned to prevent the Court from encroaching on legislative power. They argued that the use of a standard would enhance both judicial and legislative awareness of the inherently discretionary nature of the Court's jurisdiction.[64] The opposed position was that the first amendment was an "absolute," meaning that it was a rigid rule. The absolutists bottomed their claim on the very nature of legal as opposed to discretionary justice.[65] They also admitted on occasion that the trouble with balancing was that "it will be almost impossible at this late date to rid the formula of the elements of political surrender with which it has long been associated. The very phrase, balancing of interests, has such a legislative ring about it that it undermines judicial self-confidence unduly."[66]

Nonetheless, there are limits to the usefulness of the rule form as a tactical weapon, as the Supreme Court has discovered in the controversies both about the one-man-one-vote decision[67] and about its specific time limits for different aspects of the regulation of abortion.[68] It seems to be the case that while judges are expected to deal in rules, the rules are not expected to be *quantitatively* precise. Like "value judgments," the choice between 30 days and 31 days is thought of as political or administrative. The reason, presumably, is that quantitatively precise rules are obviously compromises: the cases close to the line on either side have been disposed of arbitrarily in order to *have* a line. This makes it implausible that precedent or "legal reasoning" were the only elements entering into the decision.[69]

We might contextualize indefinitely. The problem of form, in this perspective, is never more than one of political tactics, analogous to the reformer's problem of choosing between gradualist and confrontational lines of attack, or between centralized and decentralized emphases in organization. Tactics are rigidly subordinate to the choice among goals, form follows function, and the main lesson to be drawn is that one should have no a priori biases in choosing among the possibilities. In assessing a proposal to change a regime of rules to standards, or vice versa, we should ignore all claims about the intrinsic merits of formal positions and demand an accounting of effects. What is the substantive objective? How does the choice of form affect the likelihood of embodying the objective in law? Who will implement the rule or standard? How can it be evaded? How will the choice of form affect the lawmaker's claim to institutional legitimacy?

B.   *Form as Substance*

The main problem with contextualization as I have presented it thus far is that it leaves out of account the common sense that the choice of form is seldom purely instrumental or tactical. As they appear in real life, the arguments pro and con the use of rules have powerful overtones of substantive debates about what values and what visions of the universe we should adopt. In picking a form through which to achieve some goal, we are almost always making a statement that is independent or at least distinguishable from the statement we make in choosing the goal itself. What we need is a way to relate the values intrinsic *to* form to the values we try to achieve *through* form.

The different values that people commonly associate with the formal modes of rule and standard are conveyed by the emotive or judgmental words that the advocates of the two positions use in the course of debate about a particular issue. Here is a suggestive list drawn from the vast data bank of casual conversation. Imagine, for the items in each row, an exchange: "Rules are A." "No, they are B." "But standards are C." "On the contrary, they are D."

RULES		STANDARDS	
Good	*Bad*	*Bad*	*Good*
Neutrality	Rigidity	Bias	Flexibility
Uniformity	Conformity	Favoritism	Individualization
Precision	Anality	Sloppiness	Creativity
Certainty	Compulsiveness	Uncertainty	Spontaneity
Autonomy	Alienation	Totalitarianism	Participation
Rights	Vested Interests	Tyranny	Community
Privacy	Isolation	Intrusiveness	Concern
Efficiency	Indifference	Sentimentality	Equity
Order	Reaction	Chaos	Evolution
Exactingness	Punitiveness	Permissiveness	Tolerance
Self-reliance	Stinginess	Romanticism	Generosity
Boundaries	Walls	Invasion	Empathy
Stability	Sclerosis	Disintegration	Progress
Security	Threatenedness	Dependence	Trust

This list suggests something that we all know: that the preference for rules or standards is an aspect of opposed substantive positions in family life, art, psychotherapy, education, ethics, politics and economics. It is also true that everyone is to some degree ambivalent in his feelings about these substantive conflicts.

There are only a few who are confident either that one side is right or that they have a set of metacategories that allow one to choose the right side for any particular situation. Indeed, most of the ideas that might serve to dissolve the conflict and make rational choice possible are claimed vociferously by both sides:

RULES		STANDARDS	
Good	*Bad*	*Bad*	*Good*
Morality (playing by the rules)	Moralism (self-righteous strictness)	Moralism (self-righteousness about own intuitions)	Morality (openness to the situation)
Freedom			Freedom
Fairness	Mechanical arbitrariness	Arbitrariness of subjectivity	Fairness
Equality (of opportunity)	of right to sleep under the bridges of Paris	of subjection to other people's value judgments	Equality (in fact)
Realism	Cynicism	Romanticism	Realism

So long as we regard the debate about form as a debate only about means, it is a debate about facts, and reality can be conceived as an ultimate arbiter to whose final decision we must submit if we are rational.[70] But if the question is whether "real" equality is equality of opportunity or equality of enjoyment of the good things

of life, then the situation is different. Likewise if the question is whether human nature "is" good or bad, or whether people "do" act as rational maximizers of their interests. For this kind of question, whether phrased in terms of what is or what ought to be, we accept that there is no arbiter (or that he is silent, or that the arbiter is history, which will have nothing to say until we are all long dead).[71] Thus the pro-rules and pro-standards positions are more than an invitation to a positivist investigation of reality. They are also an invitation to choose between sets of values and visions of the universe.

The great limitation of the method of contextualization is that it is useless in trying to understand the character of such a choice. The contextualizer takes values and visions of the universe as given, and investigates their implications in particular situations. Yet it is not impossible or futile to talk about the choice of goals, or about their nature and interrelationship. We do this constantly, we change in consequence, and these changes are neither random nor ineffable. The rest of this essay is an example of this sort of discussion. Its premise is that we will have a better understanding of issues of form if we can relate them meaningfully to substantive questions about what we should want and about the nature of humanity and society.[72] There are two steps to the argument. The first is to set up the substantive dichotomy of individualism and altruism, and to show that the issue of form is one of its aspects. The second is to trace historically and analytically the course of the conflict between the two larger positions.

The method I have adopted in place of contextualization might be called, in a loose sense, dialectical or structuralist or historicist or the method of contradictions.[73] One of its premises is that the experience of unresolvable conflict among our *own* values and ways of understanding the world is here to stay. In this sense it is pessimistic, one might even say defeatist. But another of its premises is that there is order and meaning to be discovered even within the sense of contradiction. Further, the process of discovering this order and this meaning is both good in itself and enormously useful. In this sense, the method of contradiction represents an attitude that is optimistic and even utopian. None of which is to say that any particular attempt will be worth the paper it is printed on.

III   Altruism and Individualism

This section introduces the substantive dichotomy of individualism and altruism. These are two opposed attitudes that manifest themselves in debates about the content of private law rules. My assertion is that the arguments lawyers use are relatively few in number and highly stereotyped, although they are applied in an infinite diversity of factual situations. What I have done is to abstract these typical forms or rhetorical set pieces and attempt to analyze them. I believe that they are helpful in the general task of understanding why judges and legislators have chosen to enact or establish particular private law doctrines. For that reason this section and the next should be useful independently of their immediate purpose, which is to establish a substantive legal correlate for the dichotomy of rules and standards. Later sections attempt to link attitudes in the formal dimension to those in the substantive, and then to identify the contradictory sets of premises that underlie both kinds of conflict.

A.   The Content of the Ideal of Individualism

The essence of individualism is the making of a sharp distinction between one's interests and those of others, combined with the belief that a preference in conduct for one's own interests is legitimate, but that one should be willing to respect the rules that make it possible to coexist with others similarly self-interested. The form of conduct associated with individualism is self-reliance. This means an insistence on defining and achieving objectives without help from others (*i.e.*, without being dependent on them or asking sacrifices of them). It means accepting that they will neither share their gains nor one's own losses. And it means a firm conviction that I am entitled to enjoy the benefits of my efforts without an obligation to share or sacrifice them to the interests of others.[74]

It is important to be clear from the outset that individualism is sharply distinct from pure egotism, or the view that it is impossible and undesirable to set any limits at all to the pursuit of self-interest. The notion of self-reliance has a strong affirmative moral content, the demand for respect for the rights of others. This means that the individualist ethic is as demanding in its way as the counterethic of altruism. It involves the renunciation of the use of both private and public force in the struggle for satisfaction, and acquiescence in the refusal of others to behave in a communal fashion.

Individualism provides a justification for the fundamental legal institutions of criminal law, property, tort, and contract. The function of law is the definition and enforcement of rights, of those limits on the pursuit of self-interest that distinguish an individualist from a purely egotistical regime. The great preoccupation of individualist legal philosophy is to justify these restrictions, in the face of appetites that are both boundless and postulated to be legitimate.[75]

A pure egotist defends the laws against force on the sole ground that they are necessary to prevent civil war.[76] For the individualist, the rules against the use of force have intrinsic rightness, because they are identified with the ideal of self-reliance, the economic objective of security for individual effort, and the political rhetoric of free will, autonomy, and natural rights.[77] Rules against violence provide a space within which to realize this program, rather than a mere bulwark against chaos.

Some level of protection of person and property against non-violent interference (theft, fraud, negligence) is also desirable from the point of view of self-reliance. First, the thief is violating the injunction to rely on his own efforts in pursuing his goals. Second, the self-reliant man will be discouraged if he must devote all his energies to protecting the fruits of his labor. The rationale for contract is derivative from that of property. The law creates a property in expectations. One who breaches deprives the promisee in a sense no less real than the thief.

Beyond these fundamental legal institutions, the individualist program is much less clear.

Moreover, it has varied greatly even within the two hundred year history of individualism as an organizing element in American public discourse. The next section presents a synopsis of these historical variations that should give both this concept and that of altruism more concreteness.

Just as there are a multitude of implications that legal thinkers of different periods have drawn from individualism, there are a number of more abstract ideas that are possible bases for adopting it as an attitude and as a guide in formulating legal rules. What this means is that the idea of the "legitimacy" of the pursuit of self-interest within a framework of rights is ambiguous, and different thinkers have given it different contents.

The simplest explanation of the legitimacy of self-interestedness is that it is a moral good in itself. When the law refuses to interfere with its pursuit, it does so because it approves of it, and disapproves of people's attempts at altruism. Since this approach seems to flatly contradict the basic precepts of the Judaeo-Christian ethic, even in its most secularized form, it is not surprising that it is more common to find social thinkers justifying individualism in more circuitous, if sometimes less convincing ways.

The first of these is the notion of the invisible hand transforming apparent selfishness into public benefit. In this view, the moral problem presented by the law's failure to interfere with unsavory instances of individualism is apparent rather than real. If we are concerned with the ultimate good of the citizenry, then individualists are pursuing it *and will achieve it*, even when they are most convinced that they care only about themselves.

A much more common justification for individualism in law might be called the "clenched teeth" idea. It is that the refusal to consult the interests of others is an evil, and an evil not redeemed by any long-term good effects. But for the *state* to attempt to suppress this evil would lead to a greater one. As soon as the state attempts to legislate an ethic more demanding than that of individualism, it runs up against two insuperable problems: the relative inability of the legal system to alter human nature, and the tendency of officials to impose tyranny behind a smokescreen of morality. The immorality of law is therefore the necessary price for avoiding the greater immoralities that would result from trying to make law moral.

A third view is that there is a viable distinction to be made between the "right" (law) and the "good" (morals). Since the criterion for the legitimacy of state intervention is radically different from that for moral judgment, one can favor an individualist legal system while remaining opposed to the behavior that such a system permits or even encourages. This view is often associated with the claim that individuals have inalienable rights whose content can be derived from fundamental concepts like freedom or human personality. The individual can set these up in his defense when the state claims the power to make him act in the interests of others.[78]

B. The Content of the Ideal of Altruism

The rhetoric of individualism so thoroughly dominates legal discourse at present that it is difficult even to identify a counterethic. Nonetheless, I think there is a coherent, pervasive notion that constantly competes with individualism, and I will call it altruism. The essence of altruism is the belief that one ought *not* to indulge a sharp preference for one's own interest over those of others. Altruism enjoins us to make sacrifices, to share, and to be merciful. It has roots in culture, in religion, ethics and art, that are as deep as those of individualism. (Love thy neighbor as thyself.)

The simplest of the practices that represent altruism are sharing and sacrifice. Sharing is a static concept, suggesting an existing distribution of goods which the sharers rearrange. It means giving up to another gains or wealth that one has produced oneself or that have come to one through some good fortune. It is motivated by a sense of duty or by a sense that the other's satisfaction is a reward at least comparable to the satisfaction one might have derived from consuming the thing oneself. Sharing may also involve participation in another's losses: a spontaneous decision to shift to oneself a part of the ill fortune, deserved

or fortuitous, that has befallen someone else. Sacrifice is the dynamic notion of taking action that will change an ongoing course of events, at some expense to oneself, to minimize another's loss or maximize his gain.[79]

The polar opposite concept for sharing and sacrifice is exchange (a crucial individualist notion). The difference is that sharing and sacrifice involve a vulnerability to non-reciprocity. Further, this vulnerability is undergone out of a sense of solidarity: with the hope of a return but with a willingness to accept the possibility that there will be none. Exchange, on the contrary, signifies a transfer of resources in which equivalents are defined, and the structure of the situation, legal or social, is designed in order to make it unlikely that either party will disappoint the other. If there is some chance of disappointment, then this is experienced as a risk one must run, a cost that is unavoidable if one is to obtain what one wants from the other. The difference is one of degree, and it is easy to imagine arrangements that are such a thorough mixture, or so ambiguous, that they defy characterization one way or the other.[80]

Individualism is to pure egotism as altruism is to total selflessness or saintliness. Thus the altruist is unwilling to carry his premise of solidarity to the extreme of making everyone responsible for the welfare of everyone else. The altruist believes in the necessity and desirability of a sphere of autonomy or liberty or freedom or privacy within which one is free to ignore both the plights of others and the consequences of one's own acts for their welfare.

Just as the individualist must find a justification for those minimal restraints on self-interest that distinguish him from the pure egotist, the altruist must justify stopping short of saintliness. The basic notion is that altruistic duties are the product of the interaction of three main aspects of a situation. First, there is the degree of communal involvement or solidarity or intimacy that has grown up between the parties. Second, there is the issue of moral fault or moral virtue in the conduct by A and B that gives rise to the duty. Third, there is the intensity of the deprivation that can be averted, or of the benefit that can be secured in relation to the size of the sacrifice demanded by altruism.

Thus we can define a continuum. At one extreme, there is the duty to make a small effort to save a best friend from a terrible disaster that is no fault of his own. At the other, there are remote strangers suffering small injuries induced by their own folly and remediable only at great expense.

At first glance the usefulness of the concept of altruism in describing the legal system is highly problematic. A very common view alike in the lay world and within the legal profession is that law is unequivocally the domain of individualism, and that this is true most clearly of the private law of property, torts, and contract. Private legal justice supposedly consists in the respect for rights, never in the performance of altruistic duty. The state acts through private law only to protect rights, not to enforce morality.

Of course, there are institutions, like the progressive income tax, that seem to have an unmistakable altruistic basis. But these are exceptional. They are after-the-fact adjustments to a preexisting legal structure that has its own, individualist, logical coherence. Likewise, social security or the minimum wage or pure food and drug laws are often seen as designed to force people with power to have a due regard for the interests of others. Many lay people see the employer's share of social security payments as designed to redistribute income from bosses to workers. But all of this takes place against a background of private law rules whose altruistic content is invisible if it exists at all.

Nonetheless, it is easy enough to fit fundamental legal institutions into the altruist mold. The rules against violence, for example, have the *effect* of changing the balance of power that would exist in the state of nature into that of civil society. The strong, who would supposedly dominate everyone if there were no state, are deprived of their advantages and forced to respect the "rights" of the weak. If altruism is the sharing or sacrifice of advantages that one might have kept for oneself, then the state forces the strong to behave altruistically. Further, the argument that the prohibition of theft is based on the ethic of self-reliance is weak at best. The thief is a very paragon of self-reliance, and the property owning victim

has failed to act effectively in his own defense. The point for the altruist is not that the thief is a slacker, but that he is oblivious to any interest but his own. The law, as the expression goes, "provides him a conscience."

The rules of tort law can likewise be seen as enforcing some degree of altruism. Compensation for injuries means that the interests of the injured party must be taken into account by the tortfeasor. In deciding what to do, he is no longer free to consult only his own gains and losses, since these are no longer the only gains and losses for which he is legally responsible. Likewise in contract, when I want to breach because I have found a better deal with a new partner, the law makes me incorporate into my calculation the losses I will cause to the promisee. If my breach is without fault because wholly involuntary, I may be excused for mistake or impossibility.

There are two intuitively appealing objections to this way of looking at the legal order. The first is that "rights" and "justice" are much more plausible explanations of the rules than altruism. But as we will see, in this century at least, individualists have had a hard time showing that "rights" are anything more than after-the-fact rationalizations of the actual rules. Contemporary legal thinkers tend to agree that we decide whether I have a right to performance of a contract by examining the rules, rather than deciding what rules to have by first defining and then "protecting" the right. The distinction between justice and morality has proved no less problematic.[81]

The second objection is that the rules fall so far short of imposing the outcomes required by our moral sense that there must be some other way to account for them. If the solution is not "rights" in the abstract, then perhaps it is "the social function of maintaining a market economy." Or perhaps the rules simply carry into effect the objectives of the dominant political or economic groups within society.[82]

Each of these propositions has a great deal of truth to it, but neither is a valid objection to the point of view I am suggesting. First, it is important to distinguish the use of the concept of altruism as a direction in an altruism-individualism continuum from its use as an absolute standard for judging a situation. The way I am using the term, we can say that even a very minimal legal regime, one that permitted outcomes extremely shocking to our moral sense, would impose more altruistic duty than a regime still closer to the state of nature. In this near tautological sense, virtually *all* the rules of our own legal regime impose altruistic duty, because they make us show greater regard for the interests of others than we would if there were no laws. Only rules *prohibiting* sacrifice and sharing are truly anti-altruistic, and of these there are very few.

Second, to describe a given legal regime as more altruistic than another should suggest nothing about the motives of those who impose the regime. Every change in legal rules produces a pattern of changes in benefits to different affected parties. It is often a good inference that those who seemed likely to gain were influential in bringing the change about. It may nonetheless be useful to describe the change as one increasing or decreasing the degree of legally enforced altruistic duty.

Third, the "social function of maintaining the market" or the interests of dominant groups are, as tools, simply too crude to explain the detailed content of, say, the law of contracts. The vast majority of issues that arouse sharp conflict within contract law are either irrelevant to these larger considerations or of totally problematic import. Take the question of the "good faith" duties of a buyer in a requirements contract when there is a sudden price increase. The buyer may be able to bankrupt the seller and make a large profit by sharply increasing his requirements, supposing that the item in question accounts for much of his own cost of manufacture, or that he can resell it without using it at all.

The buyers and sellers in these situations do not seem to line up in terms of any familiar categories of political or economic power, and the effects on "the market" of deciding one way or another are highly problematic. Yet there is clearly something important at stake. The possible solutions range from a minimal buyer's duty not to "speculate" against the seller's interests to a good faith duty to absorb some loss in order to avoid a larger loss to one's

contractual partner.[83] The notion of altruism captures the court's dilemma far better than either class struggle or the needs of a market economy.[84] There are hundreds of such problems in private law.

Finally, it is a familiar fact that for about a century there has been a movement of "reform" of private law. It began with the imposition of statutory strict liability on railroads for damage to cattle and crops, and has persisted through the current redefinition of property law in the interests of the environment. In the battles and skirmishes of reform, across an enormous variety of particular issues, it has been common for conservatives to argue that liberals are consciously or unconsciously out to destroy the market system. Liberals respond that the conservative program is a cloak for the interests of big business.

Yet it is perfectly clear that all the changes of 100 years have not "destroyed the market," nor would further vast changes throughout property, torts, and contracts. It is equally clear that the nineteenth century rules the liberals have been attacking form a complex intellectual system whose vitality even in the last quarter of the twentieth century is as much or more the product of its ideological power as of the direct material dominance of particular economic or political interests. If the concepts of individualism and altruism turn out to be useful, it is because they capture something of this struggle of contradictory utopian visions. It is this dimension that the ideas of class domination and of social function cannot easily grasp. The approaches should therefore be complementary rather than conflicting.

The last objection I will consider is that to characterize fundamental legal institutions like tort or contract in terms of altruism is wrong because it is nonsense to speak of forcing someone to behave altruistically. True, the notion requires the *experience* of solidarity and the voluntary undertaking of vulnerability in consequence. It therefore implies duties that transcend those imposed by the legal order. It is precisely the refusal to take all the advantage to which one is legally, but not morally entitled that is most often offered as an example of altruism. It follows that when the law "enforces" such conduct, it can do no more than make people behave "as if" they had really experienced altruistic motives. Yet nothing could be clearer than that, in many circumstances, this is exactly what we want the law to do. One idea of justice is the organization of society so that the outcomes of interaction are equivalent to those that would occur *if* everyone behaved altruistically. I take this as a given in the rest of the discussion.[85]

C. *Methodological Problems*

There are many problems with the use of concepts like individualism and altruism. Both positions have been assembled from diverse legal, moral, economic, and political writings, and I can give no plausible description of the principle of selection at work. As a result, it is impossible to "prove" or "disprove" the validity of the two constructs. They are neither falsifiable empirical statements about a determinate mass of data, nor logically pure "models" totally abstracted from reality.

Nonetheless, I hope that the reader will find that the bits and pieces fit together into two intuitively familiar, easily recognizable wholes. Not being a systematic nominalist, I believe that there really *is* an altruist and an individualist mode of argument. More, I believe that the rhetorical modes are responsive to real issues in the real world. They are opposed concepts like Romanticism *vs.* Classicism, Gothic *vs.* Renaissance, toughminded *vs.* tenderminded, shame culture *vs.* guilt culture, or *Gemeinschaft vs. Gesellschaft*. As with Romanticism, we can believe in the usefulness of the notion of altruism without being able to demonstrate its existence experimentally, or show the inevitability of the association of the elements that compose it.

Methodological difficulties of this kind color all of the analysis that follows. One must keep constantly in mind that the individualist arguments are drawn from the same basic sources as the altruist ones. The same judge may, in a single opinion, provide examples of each mode. Over time, a single judge may provide complete statements of both positions. In other words, a person can use the arguments that compose the individualist set without being an

"individualist character." When I speak of "altruist judges" or "altruist legislators," I mean only the proponents of particular arguments that fall within one set or the other. I have no intention of characterizing these proponents as *personalities*.

When we set out to analyze an action, and especially a judicial opinion, it is only rarely possible to make a direct inference from the rhetoric employed to the real motives or ideals that animate the judge. And it is even harder to characterize outcomes than it is personalities or opinions. It will almost always be possible to argue that, if we look hard at its actual effects on significant aspects of the real world, a particular decision will further both altruist and individualist values, or neither. I will therefore avoid talking about "altruist outcomes" as much as possible.

Given that individualism and altruism are sets of stereotyped pro and con arguments, it is hard to see how either of them can ever be "responsible" for a decision. First, each argument is applied, in almost identical form, to hundreds or thousands of fact situations. When the shoe fits, it is obviously not because it was designed for the wearer. Second, for each pro argument there is a con twin. Like Llewellyn's famous set of contradictory "canons on statutes," the opposing positions seem to cancel each other out.[86] Yet somehow this is not *always* the case in practice. Although each argument has an absolutist, imperialist ring to it, we find that we are able to distinguish particular fact situations in which one side is much more plausible than the other. The difficulty, the mystery, is that there are no available metaprinciples to explain just what it is about these particular situations that make them ripe for resolution. And there are many, many cases in which confidence in intuition turns out to be misplaced.

These are problems of a kind familiar in some other fields.[87] Lawyers don't usually confront them, because lawyers usually believe that their analytic skills can produce explanations of legal rules and decisions more convincing than any that employ such vague, "value laden" concepts. The typical legal argument at least pretends that it is possible to get from some universally agreed or positively enacted premise (which may be the importance of protecting a "social interest") to some particular desirable outcome through a combination of logic and "fact finding" (or, more likely, "fact asserting").

Yet most contemporary students of legal thought seem to agree that an account of adjudication limited to the three dimensions of authoritative premises, facts and analysis is incomplete.[88] One way to express this is to say that "policy" plays a large though generally unacknowledged part in decisionmaking. The problem is to find a way to describe this part. My hope is that the substantive and formal categories I describe can help in rendering the contribution of "policy" intelligible. Although individualism and altruism can be reduced neither to facts nor to logic, although they cannot be used with any degree of consistency to characterize personalities or opinions or the outcomes of lawsuits, they may nonetheless be helpful in this enterprise.

The ultimate goal is to break down the sense that legal argument is autonomous from moral, economic, and political discourse in general. There is nothing innovative about this. Indeed, it has been a premise of legal scholars for several generations that it is impossible to construct an autonomous logic of legal rules. What is new in this piece is the attempt to show an orderliness to the debates about "policy" with which we are left after abandonment of the claim of neutrality.

IV   Three Phases of the Conflict of Individualism and Altruism

Eighteenth century common law thinking does not seem to have been afflicted with a sense of conflict between two legal ideals. Positive law was of a piece with God's moral law as understood through reason and revelation. In Blackstone, for example, there is no suggestion of recurrent conflicts either about the nature of legal morality or about which of two general utilitarian strategies the legislator had best pursue.[89] The sense of a conflict between systems of thought emerged only at the begin-

ning of the nineteenth century. It has had three overlapping phases, corresponding roughly to the periods 1800–1870, 1850–1940, and 1900 to the present.[90]

A.   The Antebellum Period (1800–1870): Morality vs. Policy

Individualism was at first not an *ethic* in conflict with the ethic of altruism, but a set of pragmatic arguments perceived as in conflict with ethics in general. Antebellum judges and commentators referred to these pragmatic arguments by the generic name of "policy," and contrasted it to "morality." A crucial fact about the legal order was that it stopped short of the full enforcement of morality. Counsel in an 1817 Supreme Court case defended his client's failure to reveal crucial information to a buyer as follows:[91]

> Even admitting that his conduct was unlawful, in foro conscientiae, does that prove that it was so in the civil forum? Human laws are imperfect in this respect, and the sphere of morality is more extensive than the limits of civil jurisdiction. The maxim of caveat emptor could never have crept into the law, if the province of ethics had been co-extensive with it.

The explanation for the distinction between laws of perfect and imperfect obligation was that imposing high standards of conduct in contract and tort, and then granting large damage judgments for violating those standards, would discourage economic development.[92] This is a prototypically individualist position. The "morality" that opposed this program of limited liability was the first systematic version of common law altruism. The idea was that the purpose of law and the source of its legitimacy was that it forced people to behave toward one another in a substantively equitable fashion. The contraction of liability amounted to permitting or encouraging people to disregard the impact of their actions on those around them, and was therefore unjustifiable.

The antebellum conception of the conflict is perhaps most perfectly expressed by Parsons (1855) in his discussion of the law of fraud. He distinguished between:[93]

that kind and measure of craft and cunning which the law deems it impossible or inexpedient to detect and punish, and therefore leaves unrecognized, and that worse kind and higher degree of craft and cunning which the law prohibits, and of which it takes away all the advantage from him by whom it is practised.

The law of morality, which is the law of God, acknowledges but one principle, and that is the duty of doing to others as we would that others should do to us, and this principle absolutely excludes and prohibits all cunning; if we mean by this word any astuteness practised by any one for his own exclusive benefit. But this would be perfection; and the law of God requires it because it requires perfection; that is, it sets up a perfect standard, and requires a constant and continual effort to approach it. But human law, or municipal law, is the rule which men require each other to obey; and it is of its essence that it should have an effectual sanction, by itself providing that a certain punishment should be administered by men, or certain adverse consequences take place, as the direct effect of a breach of this law. If therefore the municipal law were identical with the law of God, or adopted all its requirements, one of three consequences must flow therefrom; either the law would become confessedly, and by a common understanding, powerless and dead as to a part of it; or society would be constantly employed in visiting all its members with punishment; or, if the law annulled whatever violated its principles, a very great part of human transactions would be rendered void. Therefore the municipal law leaves a vast proportion of unquestionable duty to motives, sanctions, and requirements very different from those which it supplies. And no man has any right to say, that whatever human law does not prohibit, that he has a right to do; for that only is right which violates no law, and there is another law besides human law. Nor, on the other hand, can any one reasonably insist, that whatever one should do or should abstain from doing, this may properly be made a part of the municipal law, for this law must necessarily fail to do all the great good that it can do and therefore should, if it attempts to do that which, while society and human nature remain what they are it cannot possibly accomplish.

In this early nineteenth century view, the law aimed at and usually achieved the imposition of a high level of altruistic duty, but had an occa-

sion to make concessions to individualism. Here are a few examples:

Negotiability: It was common to argue that it was immoral to force the maker of a note to pay a holder in due course after failure of the consideration: the law was requiring the maker to pay for something he never got. But the policy of encouraging transactions dictated the cutting off of defenses.[94]

Incorporation: It was a Jacksonian objection to limited corporate liability that it allowed stockholders to escape their share of the debts of the corporation. The law obliged partners to live up to their moral obligations, but allowed stockholders to behave dishonorably. The answer was the policy in favor of the pooling of resources.[95]

Consideration: The common law refused to enforce promises whose performance was dictated by the most solemn moral obligation when they lacked consideration. The reason was the policy against the multiplication of lawsuits and the legalization of family life.[96]

Breaching Plaintiff's Suit for Restitution: Most courts refused to honor the breaching plaintiff's claim for restitution even when the result was a windfall unjust enrichment of the defendant. To allow recovery would have created a dangerous incentive to lax performance.[97]

Bankruptcy: Bankruptcy laws sanctioned and even encouraged the dishonorable conduct of refusing to pay one's debts. The reason was the policy against demoralizing economic actors by eliminating the incentive of self-enrichment.[98]

Still, there was no question which of the ethics was primary: we would achieve a social order according to the law of God if we could. We can't, because the ideal is too demanding. We therefore validate a certain amount of conduct inconsistent with altruism but consistent with individualism, hoping that by accepting to this extent the imperfections of human nature we will at least forestall pure egotism, while at the same time promoting economic growth.

B. Classical Individualism (1850–1940): Free Will

Modern legal thought is preoccupied with "competing policies," conflicting "value judgments" and the idea of a purposive legal order, and to that extent has much in common with pre-Civil War thinking. One major difference is the total disappearance of religious arguments, and the fading of overtly moralistic discussion. More important for our purposes, the modern situation has been conditioned by the post-Civil War triumph of what I will call Classical individualism,[99] which represented not just a rhetorical shift away from the earlier emphasis on altruism, but the denial that altruism had anything at all to do with basic legal doctrines.

The reasons for this conceptual revolution will not concern us here. It is enough to say that they were complex, involving the triumph of particular economic interests, the desire to establish an apolitical scientific justification for the power of judges and lawyers, and autonomous movements in all the different areas of late nineteenth century thought. What does concern us is the structure of the Classical individualist position, since this structure forms the backdrop for the modern discussion.

Classical individualism rejected the idea that particular rules represented an ad hoc compromise between policy and altruist morality. Rather, the rules represented a fully principled and consistent solution *both* to the ethical and to the practical dilemmas of legal order. The contraction of liability that occurred over the course of the nineteenth century was thereby rationalized, and shielded from the charge that it represented the sacrifice of equity to expediency.

The Classical position can be reduced to three propositions concerning the proper definition of liability. First, the fundamental theory of our political and economic institutions is that there should exist an area of individual autonomy or freedom or liberty within which there is no responsibility at all for effects on others.[100] Second, the meaning of this political and economic theory for private law is that there are only two legitimate sources of liability: fault, meaning intentional or negligent interference with the property or personal rights of another, and contract. As between strangers, there are no duties of mutual assistance; there are only duties to abstain from violence and negligence. Contract adds new duties, and these are enforced as

a matter of right, rather than of judicial discretion.[101] The content of contractual duty is strictly limited by the intent of the parties. The third proposition is that the concepts of fault and free will to contract can generate, through a process of deduction, determinate legal rules defining the boundaries and content of tort and contract duties.[102]

The important thing about the Classical position, from our point of view, is that it presented the choice between individualism and altruism as one of all-or-nothing commitment to a complete system. One might accept or reject the individualist claim that our institutions are based on liberty, private property and bodily security. But if one once subscribed to these ideas, a whole legal order followed inescapably. To reject the particular applications was a sign either of error or of bad faith, since they were no more than the logical implications of the abstract premises.

If one believed in the first principles and in the possibility of deducing rules from them, then it was easy to believe that the Classical regime was both morally and practically far superior to the state of nature. The restrictions on pure egotism imposed by that regime did not represent a concession to the utopian ideal of altruism. They embodied the individualist morality of self-reliance, the individualist economic theory of free competition, and the individualist political philosophy of natural rights, which set well-defined boundaries to the demand that people treat the interests of others as of equal importance with their own.

For example, the contract law of 1825 was full of protective doctrines, such as the incapacity of married women, infants, lunatics and seamen. The consideration doctrine often functioned to enforce an altruist contractual morality, as did the doctrines of fraud, mistake, duress, undue influence and unconscionability. Jury discretion in setting damages provided a further vehicle for importing community standards of fair conduct. For antebellum legal thought, there was not much difficulty in explaining all of this: the doctrines represented the legal enforcement of straightforward moral norms, but raised questions of policy in so much as an insistence on policing bargains might be harmful to the goal of economic development.[103]

During the latter part of the century, some of these doctrines were cut back, and others expanded somewhat. But *all* of the doctrines were recast as implications of the fundamental idea that private law rules protect individual free will. The basis of restrictions on capacity is that infants and those like them lack free will; duress is the overbearing of the will, undue influence its subversion; fraud leads to a consent that is only apparent; mistake meant that the wills of the parties had miscarried; the measure of damages was defined by the will of the parties with respect to the extent of liability.[104]

Recast in terms of will, the rules of contract law still represented a moral as well as a practical vision, but that vision was no longer perceptibly altruist. The new premise was that people were responsible for themselves unless they could produce evidence that they lacked free will in the particular circumstances. If no such evidence was available, then they were bound to look to their own resources in performing what they had undertaken. In place of a situational calculus of altruistic duty and an equally situational calculus of economic effects, there was a single individualist moral-political-economic premise from which everything else followed.

We could trace a similar process of development in torts or property or corporate law. In each case, there was a central individualist concept representing a substantial limitation on the total freedom of the state of nature. In each case, the concept defined an area of autonomy, of "absolute right," and also provided the basis for limiting the right. Since the basis of tort law, for example, was the enforcement of compensation for wrongful injury, it followed that there could be no tort liability without fault. Existing instances, such as strict liability in trespass or respondeat superior, must either be rationalized in terms of the will theory or rejected as anachronistic.[105]

It is common to equate late nineteenth century thought with conceptualism, that is with my third proposition about the possibility of a *deductive* process of defining

the boundaries and content of liability. This is misleading to the extent that it suggests that the concepts were just "there," as arbitrary starting points for judicial reasoning. They were, on the contrary, crucial components in the larger individualist argument designed to link the very general proposition, that the American system is based on freedom, with the very concrete rules and doctrines of the legal order. "Free will" in law followed from, indeed was simply the practical application of, the freedom of individualist political, moral and economic theory.[106]

C. Modern Legal Thought (1900 to the present): The Sense of Contradiction

In private law, modern legal thought begins with the rejection of Classical individualism. Its premise is that Classical theory failed to show either that the genius of our institutions is individualist or that it is possible to deduce concrete legal rules from concepts like liberty, property or bodily security. For this reason, morality and policy reappear in modern discussions, in place of first principles and logic. The problem is that morality is no longer unequivocally altruist – there is a conflict of moralities. Nor is policy any longer unequivocally individualist – there are arguments for collectivism, regulation, the welfare state, along with the theory of economic development through laissez-faire. This conflict of morality with morality and of policy with policy pervades every important issue of private law.

1. *The Critique of Classical Individualism.*— This is not the place for a description of the argumentative strategies by which more or less altruist thinkers, working in many different fields,[107] disintegrated the Classical individualist structure. I will make do with some flat assertions. First, modern legal thought and especially modern legal education are committed to the position that no issue of substance can be resolved merely by reference to one of the Classical concepts. This applies to liberty, free will, property, fault, proximate cause, the "subject matter of the contract," title, cause of action, privity, necessary party, "literal mean-

ing," "strictly private activity," and a host of others.

Second, the problem with the concepts is that they assert the possibility of making clear and convincing on-off distinctions among fact situations, along the lines of free vs. coerced; proximate vs. remote cause; private vs. affected with a public interest. In modern legal thought, it is a premise that any real fact situation will contain elements from both sides of the conceptual polarity. The problem of classification is therefore that of locating the situation on a continuum. This process is not self-executing: people are certain to disagree strongly about how to classify, according to their purposes in making the distinction in the first place, and there is no "objective" or "absolute" standard of correctness for resolving these disagreements.[108]

Third, given the indeterminacy of the concepts, their inherent ambiguity as criteria of decision, it is implausible to describe the total body of legal rules as implicit in general principles like "protection of property" or "freedom of contract." Since it is not possible to move in a deductive fashion from concept to implications, we need some other way to account for the process of judicial lawmaking. That explanation will be found in the judge's moral, political and economic views and in the idiosyncrasies of his understanding of the character of the fact situation.[109]

Fourth, there are numerous issues on which there exists a judicial and also a societal consensus, so that the judge's use of his views on policy will be noncontroversial. But there are also situations in which there is great conflict. The judge is then faced with a dilemma: to impose his personal views may bring on accusations that he is acting "politically" rather than "judicially." He can respond to this with legalistic mumbo jumbo, that is, by appealing to the concepts and pretending that they have decided the case for him. Or he can take the risks inherent in acknowledging the full extent of his discretion.[110]

2. The Sense of Contradiction.—The death of conceptualism has brought on a new phase of the conflict of individualism and altruism. To begin with it has reduced them to the same argumentative level. While he still believed in the Classical system, the individualist had no problem in defining and justifying his position on any given issue. He could derive everything from the concepts. The altruist, on the other hand, had no deductive system that explained where she would stop short of total collectivism. She was obliged to argue in an ad hoc manner from the injustice, immorality or irrationality of particular individualist outcomes.

But modern individualism presents itself not as a deductive system, but as a pole, or tendency or vector or bias, in the debate with altruism over the legitimacy of the system of rules that emerged in the late nineteenth century. As a consequence, altruists can argue for the establishment of legal institutions like zoning, workmen's compensation, social security, compulsory collective bargaining, products liability and no-fault automobile insurance without being vulnerable to the charge of subverting a logical structure. They admit that such institutions are anti-individualist, and also that they have no principles capable of logically determining where, short of total collectivism, they would stop the expansion of legally enforceable altruistic duty. But given the death of the concepts, the individualists no longer have any principles that determine where, short of the state of nature, *they* would stop the *contraction* of altruistic duty. They are open to the charge of dissolving society, or of stacking the rules in favor of particular blackguards.

This parity in argumentative positions is the starting point of the modern debate about what to do with the rule structure Classical individualism created through deduction from first principles. The new scepticism destroyed the presumptive legitimacy of the old system, creating a vast number of difficult legal problems, but solving none of them. Rules that referred directly to the discredited concepts (duress equals overbearing of the will) were recognized as indeterminate, and had to be replaced or reconceived as vague standards. More concrete rules that had been derived from the abstract premises (silence cannot be acceptance) had to be justified in their own right or rejected. The new, more altruistic institutions like labor law, consumer protection, social insurance and securities regulation immediately became a battleground. Their boundaries and internal structure had to be defined by the courts. A thoroughgoing individualist interpretation of altruist statutes might have constricted them to the point of de facto nullification.

In private law, this modern phase of conflict occurs over three main issues, which I will call, somewhat arbitrarily, community vs. autonomy, regulation vs. facilitation, and paternalism vs. self-determination.[111] Each particular debate has a stalemated quality that reflects the inability of either individualism or altruism to generate a new set of principles or metaprinciples to replace the late lamented concepts.

(*a*) *Community vs. Autonomy.*—The issue here is the extent to which one person should have to share or make sacrifices in the interest of another in the absence of agreement or other manifestation of intention. At first sight this issue may seem largely confined to torts and quasi-contract, but it arises in identical form in many other areas as well. The law must define the reciprocal rights of neighboring land holders through the law of easements, and the rights of third party beneficiaries and assignees against obligors. Within consensual arrangements, it must decide how to dispose of the multitude of possible controversies not covered or ambiguously covered by the parties themselves. There is the issue of the scope and intensity of the duties of fiduciaries to beneficiaries, including duties of directors and officers of corporations to shareholders. There is the whole apparatus of interpretation, excuses and damage measures in the law of contracts. And there is the borderline area of pre- or extra-contractual liability represented by the doctrine of promissory estoppel.

The conflict of community and autonomy is the modern form of the early nineteenth century debate about the impact on economic growth of extending or contracting nonconsensual altruistic duties. The legal institutions involved are those that I characterized in Section I as intermediate between pure formalities (where the law is indifferent as to which of a number of courses of action the parties undertake) and rules designed to deter wrongdoing. We noted there that this category could be regarded either as designed to deter tort and breach of contract as wrongful in themselves, or, in the more common mode, as designed to offer a choice between no injury and injury *cum* compensation.

The adoption of the second view represents a decision to place *general* limits on the ability of the legal system to enforce altruistic duty. If damages are a tariff, the "wrongdoer" is authorized to consult his own interest exclusively, so long as he is willing to make the payment that secures the other party's rights. This may well involve two distinct breaches of altruistic duty.

First, even if compensation is perfect, the injuring party is forcing the injured party to take compensation, rather than specific performance or freedom from tortious interference. Second, the injuring party is under no obligation to share the excess over the compensation payment that he may derive from inflicting the injury. Once I have paid the expectation damage measure, *all* the windfall profits from breach of contract go to me.[112]

Given the decision to regard contract and tort law as compensatory rather than punitive, the altruist and individualist have disagreements at three levels:

> *Scope of obligation*: Given a particular relationship or situation, is there any duty at all to look out for the interests of the other?

> *Intensity of obligation*: Given duty, how great is the duty on the scale from mere abstention from violence to the highest fiduciary obligation?

> *Extent of liability for consequences*: Given breach of duty, how far down the chain of causation should we extend liability?

The individualist position is the restriction of obligations of sharing and sacrifice. This means being opposed to the broadening, intensifying and extension of liability *and* opposed to the liberalization of excuses once duty is established. This position is only superficially paradoxical. The contraction of initial liability leaves greater areas for people to behave in a self-interested fashion. Liberal rules of excuse have the opposite effect: they oblige the beneficiary of a duty to share the losses of the obligor when for some reason he is unable to perform. The altruist position is the expansion of the network of liability and also the liberalization of excuses.

(*b*) *Regulation vs. Facilitation.*—The issue here is the use of bargaining power as the determinant of the distribution of desired objects and the allocation of resources to different uses. It arises whenever two parties with conflicting claims or interests reach an accommodation through bargaining, and the stronger party attempts to enforce it through the legal system. The judge must then decide whether the stronger party has pressed her advantage further in her own interests than is acceptable to the legal system. If she has not, then the agreement will be enforced; if she has, a sanction will be applied, ranging from the voiding of the agreement to criminal punishment of the abuse of bargaining power.[113]

There are many approaches to the control of bargaining power, including:

Incapacitation of classes of people deemed particularly likely to lack adequate bargaining power (children, lunatics, etc.) with the effect that they can void their contracts if they want to.

Outlawing particular tactics, such as the use of physical violence, duress of goods, threats to inflict malicious harm, fraudulent statements, "bargaining in bad faith," etc.

Outlawing particular transactions that are thought to involve great dangers of overreaching, such as the settlement of debts for less than the full amount or the making of unilaterally beneficial modifications in the course of performance of contracts.

Control of the competitive structure of markets, either by atomizing concentrated economic power or by creating countervailing centers strong enough to bargain equally.

Direct policing of the substantive fairness of bargains, whether by direct price fixing or quality specification, by setting maxima or minima, or by announcing a standard such as "reasonableness" or "unconscionability."

The individualist position is that judges ought not to conceive of themselves as regulators of the use of economic power. This means conceiving of the legal system as a limited set of existing restraints imposed on

the state of nature, and then refusing to extend those constraints to new situations. The altruist position is that existing restraints represent an attempt to achieve distributive justice which the judges should carry forward rather than impede.

(*c*) *Paternalism vs. Self-Determination.*—This issue is distinct from that of regulation vs. facilitation because it arises in situations not of conflict but of error. A party to an agreement or one who has unilaterally incurred a legal obligation seeks to void it on the grounds that they acted against their "real" interests. The beneficiary of the agreement or duty refuses to let the obligor back out. An issue of altruistic duty arises because the obligee ought to take the asserted "real" interests into account, both at the bargaining stage, if he is aware of them, and at the enforcement stage, if he only becomes aware of them then. On the other hand, he may have innocently relied on the obligor's own definition of his objectives, so that he will have to sacrifice something of his own if he behaves mercifully.

No issue of bargaining power is necessarily involved in such situations. For example:

Liquidated damage clauses freely agreed to by both parties are often voided on grounds of unreasonableness.

Express conditions unequivocal on their face are excused on grounds of forfeiture or interpreted out of existence.

Merger clauses that would waive liability for fraudulent misrepresentations are struck down or reinterpreted.

No oral modification clauses are held to be waived by actions of the beneficiary or disallowed altogether.

Modifications of contract remedy such as disclaimers of warranty or of liability for negligence, limitations of venue, waiver of defenses, and limitations on time for complaints are policed under various standards, even where they apparently result from conscious risk allocation rather than from mere superior power.

Persons lacking in capacity are allowed to void contracts that are uncoerced and substantively fair.

Consideration doctrine sometimes renders promises unenforceable because there was no "real" exchange, as in the cases of the promissory note of a widow given in exchange for a discharge of her husband's worthless debts, or that of a contract for "conjuring."

Fraud and Unconscionability doctrine protect against "unfair surprise" in situations where a party is a victim of his own foolishness rather than of the exercise of power.

The individualist position is that the parties themselves are the best and only legitimate judges of their own interests, subject to a limited number of exceptions, such as incapacity. People should be allowed to behave foolishly, do themselves harm, and otherwise refuse to accept any other person's view of what is best for them. Other people should respect this freedom; they should also be able to rely on those who exercise it to accept the consequences of their folly. The altruist response is that the paternalist rules are not exceptions, but the representatives of a developed counterpolicy of forcing people to look to the "real" interests of those they deal with. This policy is as legitimate as that of self-determination and should be extended as circumstances permit or require.

One way of conceiving of the transition from Classical to modern legal thought is through the imagery of core and periphery. Classical individualism dealt with the issues of community vs. autonomy, regulation vs. facilitation and paternalism vs. self-determination by affirming the existence of a core of legal freedom which was equated with firm adherence to autonomy, facilitation and self-determination. The existence of countertendencies was acknowledged, but in a backhanded way. By its "very nature," freedom must have limits; these could be derived as implications *from* that nature; and they would then constitute a periphery of exceptions to the core doctrines.

What distinguishes the modern situation is the breakdown of the conceptual boundary between the core and the periphery, so that all the conflicting positions are at least potentially relevant to all issues. The Classical concepts oriented us to one ethos or the other – to core or periphery – and then permitted consistent argument within that point of view, with a few hard cases occurring at the borderline. Now, each of the conflicting visions claims universal relevance, but is unable to establish hegemony anywhere.

V   The Correspondence Between Formal and Substantive Moral Arguments

This and the two following sections develop the connection between the formal dimension of rules and standards and the substantive dimension of individualism and altruism. This section deals with the issue at the level of moral discourse; those that follow deal with the economic and political issues. The three sections also have a second purpose: to trace the larger dispute between individualism/rules and altruism/standards through the series of stages that lead to the modern confrontation of contradictory premises that is the subject of Section VIII. We began this intellectual historical task in the last section, in the course of explicating the substantive conflict. The historical discussions in the next two sections are likewise designed both to illustrate the analytic arguments linking form and substance, and to fill in the background of the current situation.

One might attempt to link the substantive and formal dimensions at the level of social reality. This would involve investigating, from the points of view of individualism and altruism, the actual influence of private law decisions on economic, social, and political life. One could then ask how the form in which the judge chooses to cast his decision contributes to these effects, being careful to determine the *actual* degree of formal realizability and generality of the rule or standard in question.[114] This method is hopelessly difficult, given the current limited state of the art of assessing either actual effects of decisions or their actual formal properties. *Theories* of the practical importance of deciding private law disputes in one way or another abound, but ways to test those theories do not. This gives most legal argument a distinctly unreal, even fantastic quality that this essay will do nothing to dispel. Rather, my subject is that often unreal and fantastic rhetoric itself. This is no more than a first step, but it may be an important one.

There is a strong analogy between the arguments that lawyers make when they are defending a "strict" interpretation of a rule and those they put forward when they are asking a judge to make a rule that is substantively individualist. Likewise, there is a rhetorical analogy between the arguments lawyers make for "relaxing the rigor" of a regime of rules and those they offer in support of substantively altruist lawmaking. The simplest of these analogies is at the level of moral argument. Individualist rhetoric in general emphasizes self-reliance as a cardinal virtue. In the substantive debate with altruism, this means claiming that people *ought* to be willing to accept the consequences of their own actions. They ought not to rely on their fellows or on government when things turn out badly for them. They should recognize that they must look to their own efforts to attain their objectives. It is implicit in this idea that they are entitled to put others at arms length – to refuse to participate in their losses or make sacrifices for them.

In the formal dispute about rules and standards, this argument has a prominent role in assessing the seriousness of the over- and underinclusiveness of rules. Everyone agrees that this imprecision is a liability, but the proponent of rules is likely to argue that we should not feel too badly about it, because those who suffer have no one to blame but themselves. Formally realizable general rules are, by definition, knowable in advance. A person who finds that he is included in liability to a sanction that was designed for someone else has little basis for complaint. Conversely, a person who gains by the victim's miscalculation is under no obligation to forego those gains.

This argument is strongest with respect to formalities. Here the meaning of underinclusion is that because of a failure to follow the prescribed form, the law refuses to carry out a party's intention to create some special set of legal relationships (e.g. voiding a will for failure to sign it). Overinclusion means that a party is

treated as having an intention (e.g. to enter a contract) when he actually intended the opposite. The advocate of rules is likely to present each of these adverse results as in some sense deserved, since there is no good reason why the victim should not have engaged in competent advance planning to avoid what has happened to him.[115]

The same argument applies to rules that are designed to enforce substantive policies rather than merely to facilitate choice between equally acceptable alternatives. Like formalities, these rules are concerned with intentional behavior in situations defined in advance. When one enters a perfectly fair contract with an infant, one has no right to complain when the infant voids it for reasons having nothing to do with the law's desire to protect him from his own folly or from overreaching.

The position of the advocate of rule enforcement is unmistakably individualist. It is the sibling if not the twin of the general argument that those who fare ill in the struggle for economic or any other kind of success should shoulder the responsibility, recognize that they deserved what they got, and refrain from demanding state intervention to bail them out. The difference is that the formal argument is interstitial. It presupposes that the state has already intervened to some extent (*e.g.*, by enforcing contracts rather than leaving them to business honor and nonlegal sanctions). It asserts that *within* this context, it is up to the parties to look out for themselves. The fact of altruistic substantive state intervention does not ipso facto wipe out the individual's duty to take care of herself.

The argument of the advocate of "relaxation," of converting the rigid rule into a standard, will include an enumeration of all the particular factors in the situation that mitigate the failure to avoid over- or underinclusion. There will be reference to the substantive purpose of the rule in order to show the arbitrariness of the result. But the ultimate point will be that there is a moral duty on the part of the private beneficiary of the over- or underinclusion to forego an advantage that is a result of the other's harmless folly. Those who take an inheritance by course of law because the testator failed to sign his will should hand the property over to those the testator wanted to receive it. A contracting party *ought not* to employ the statute of frauds to void a contract honestly made but become onerous because of a price break.

This argument smacks as unmistakably of altruism as the argument for rules smacks of individualism. The essential idea is that of mercy, here concretized as sharing or sacrifice. The ethic of self-reliance is rejected in both its branches: the altruist will neither punish the incompetent nor respect the "right" of the other party to cleave to her own interests. Again, the difference between the substantive and the formal arguments is the area of their application. It may well be that the structure of rules falls far short of requiring the level of altruistic behavior that the altruist would prefer. But within that structure, whatever it may be, there are still duties of sharing and sacrifice evoked by the very operation of the rules.

It is important to note that the altruist demand for mercy will be equally strong whether we are dealing with formalities, or with rules designed to deter substantively undesirable behavior (crimes, unconscionable contracts). The party who tries to get out of a losing contract because of failure to comply with a formality is betraying a contractual partner, someone toward whom he has assumed special duties. The infant who voids the same contract although it was neither foolish nor coerced is behaving equally reprehensibly.

VI The Correspondence Between Formal and Substantive Economic Arguments

The correspondence between the formal and substantive economic arguments is more intricate and harder to grasp than the moral debate. I have divided the discussion into two parts: an abstract statement of the structural analogy of the formal and substantive positions, and an historical synopsis of how the positions got to their present state.

A. An Abstract Statement of the Analogy

1. Nonintervention vs. Result-Orientation.— Suppose a situation in which the people who are the objects of the lawmaking process can do any one of three things: X, Y and Z. The lawmaker wants them to do X, and he wants them to refrain from Y and Z. If he does not intervene at all, they will do some X, some Y and some Z. As an individualist, the lawmaker believes that it would be wrong to try to force everyone to do X all the time. He may see freedom to do Y as a natural right, or believe that if he forbids Z, most people will find themselves choosing X over Y as often as if it were legally compelled. Or he may take the view that the bad side effects of state intervention to prohibit Y outweigh the benefits.

There is still the problem of the *form* of the injunction against Z. There may be a number of tactical considerations that push in the direction either of a rule or of a standard. For example, if the law appliers are very strongly in favor of compelling X, then they may use the discretion inherent in a standard to ban both Z *and* Y, thus smuggling in the substantive policy the lawmaker had rejected. On the other hand, it may be that the nature of the Y-Z distinction defies precise formulation except in terms of rules that will lead to the arbitrary inclusion of a very large amount of Y in the Z category, so that a standard seems the only workable formal mechanism.

In spite of these contextual factors, there is a close analogy between the substantive individualist position and the argument for rules. The individualist claims that we must achieve X through a strategy that permits Y. The rule advocate claims that we can best achieve the prohibition of Z through a rule that not only permits some Z (underinclusion) but also arbitrarily punishes some Y (overinclusion).

What ties the two arguments together is that they both reject result orientation in the particular case in favor of an indirect strategy. They both claim that the attempt to achieve a total ordering in accord with the lawmaker's purpose will be counterproductive. More success will be achieved by limited interventions creating a structure that influences the pattern of private activity without pretensions to full realization of the underlying purpose. In short, the arguments for rules over standards is inherently noninterventionist, and it is for that reason inherently individualist.

The main difficulty with seeing rules as noninterventionist is that they presuppose state intervention. In other words, the issue of rules vs. standards only arises after the lawmaker has decided against the state of nature and in favor of the imposition of some level of duty, however minimal. The point is that *within this structure*, whatever it may be, rules are less result oriented than standards. As with the moral argument, the economic individualism of rules is interstitial and relative rather than absolute.

2. Tolerance of Breach of Altruistic Duty: The Sanction of Abandonment.—In the economic area, the analogy between the arguments for rules and those for substantive individualism goes beyond their common noninterventionism. Both strategies rely on the sanctioning effect of nonintervention to stimulate private activity that will remedy the evils that the state refuses to attack directly.

The fundamental premise of economic individualism is that people will create and share out among themselves more wealth if the state refuses either to direct them to work or to force them to share. Given human nature and the limited effectiveness of legal intervention, the attempt to guarantee everyone a high level of welfare, regardless of their productivity, would require massive state interference in every aspect of human activity, and still could not prevent a precipitous drop in output. On the other hand, a regime which convincingly demonstrates that it will let people starve (or fall to very low levels of welfare) before forcing others to help them will create the most powerful of incentives to production and exchange.

The self-conscious use of the sanction of abandonment as an incentive to production expresses itself on two different levels of the legal system. In private law, it means that people are authorized to refuse to share their superfluous wealth with those who need it more than they do. The most elementary doctrines of property law carry out this idea: trespass and conversion are not excused by need, short of *actual*

starvation, and even then subject to a duty of restitution. In public law, the individualist opposes welfare programs financed through the tax system as a form of compulsory collective altruism that endangers the wealth of society.

The advocate of rules as the proper form for private law proposes a strategy that is exactly analogous to that of substantive individualism. The sanction of abandonment consists of not adjusting legal intervention to take account of the particularities of the case. The enforcement of the rule in situations where it is plainly over- or underinclusive involves condoning a violation of altruistic duty by the beneficiary. The motive for this passivity in the face of a miscarriage of the lawmaker's goal is to stimulate those subject to the rules to invest in formal proficiency, and thereby indirectly reduce the evil tolerated in the particular case.

In the area of formalities, the sanction of nullity works in the same fashion as the sanction of starvation in the substantive debate. The parties are told that unless they use the proper language in expressing their intentions, they will fail of legal effect. The result will be that a party who thought he had a legally enforceable agreement turns out to be vulnerable to betrayal by his partner. The law will tolerate this betrayal, although the whole purpose of instituting a regime of enforceable promises was to prevent it. In the area of rules designed to deter wrongdoing, the analogue of the sanction of abandonment is reliance on a rule to alert the potential victims to their danger. Caveat emptor and the rule of full legal capacity at 21 years are supposed to reduce wrongdoing, in spite of their radical underinclusiveness, because they induce vigilance where a standard would foster a false sense of security. Again, the theory is that permitting A to injure B may be the best way to save B from injury.

For the intermediate category consisting of suppletory directives (interpretation, excuses) and directives defining liability (fault, breach, damages), the decision to use rules rather than standards has a similar justification. Here the sanction is the imposition of liability on the actor who is not morally blameworthy, as for example for a breach of contract that is involuntary, but not within the doctrine of impossibility, or for a violation of an objective rule of tort liability. The result is a gain to the other party that he has an altruistic duty to disgorge. The motive for condoning the refusal to perform this duty, for enforcing the rule, is to stimulate people to make accurate advance calculations of those impacts of their activities on others that the law regards as justifying compensation. The thesis of the advocate of rules is that people will learn to make rational choices between abstention from injury and injury *cum* compensation only under a regime that tolerates occasional over- and under-compensation.

The basic notion behind these arguments for rules is that ability to manipulate formalities, vigilance in one's interests and awareness of the legally protected rights of others are all economic goods, components of the wealth of a society. The same considerations apply to them as apply to wealth in general. The best way to stimulate their production is to sanction those who fail to acquire them, by exposing them to breach of altruistic duty by those who are more provident. The rule advocate may affirm that "this hurts me more than it does you" as she administers the sanction. But the refusal to tolerate present inequity would make everyone worse off in the long run.

3. Transaction in General.—There is a third element to the abstract parallel between substantive and formal dimensions. The argument is that both rules and the substantive reduction of altruistic duty will encourage transaction in general.[116] The classic statement of the substantive position is that of Holmes:[117]

> A man need not, it is true, do this or that act, – the term act implies a choice, – but he must act somehow. Furthermore, the public generally profits by individual activity. As action cannot be avoided, and tends to the public good, there is obviously no policy in throwing the hazard of what is at once desirable and inevitable upon the actor.
>
> The state might conceivably make itself a mutual insurance company against accidents, and distribute the burden of its citizens' mishaps among all its members. There might be a pension for paralytics, and state aid for those who suffered in person or estate from tempest or wild beasts. As between individuals it might adopt the mutual insurance principle pro tanto, and divide damages

when both were in fault, as in the rusticum judicium of the admiralty, or it might throw all loss upon the actor irrespective of fault. The state does none of these things, however, and the prevailing view is that its cumbrous and expensive machinery ought not to be set in motion unless some clear benefit is to be derived from disturbing the status quo. State interference is an evil, where it cannot be shown to be a good. Universal insurance, if desired, can be better and more cheaply accomplished by private enterprise.

This is not a simple argument. Holmes does not explain why the activity encouraged by permitting breach of altruistic duty should lead to a public good. Presumably he would not have generalized his position to cover all such duties, although a return to the state of nature would certainly stimulate a vast amount of activity now deterred by fear of legal intervention. Further, the limitation of duty should have an inhibiting effect on the activity of those subjected to uncompensated injury. Holmes simply assumes that these inhibiting effects on desirable activity (or stimulating effects on undesirable activity) do not cancel out the gains from the "liberation of energy."

The implicit premise seems to be that the aggressive action of the injurers, looked at as a class, has greater social value than the activity of the injured inhibited by the removal of protection. In Holmes's thought, this premise is linked to Social Darwinism and the belief in the desirability of conflict in general.[118] As he saw it, the outcome of bargaining under individualist background rules would be to place control of productive resources, and therefore of investment, in the hands of those most likely to use them for the long-run good of the community. Regulatory, paternalism and communitarian objectives are all less important than secular economic growth. The management of growth requires exactly those capacities for aggressive self-reliance that are rewarded under an individualist regime of contract and fault. Regulation, paternalism and communitarian obligation shift economic power from those who know how to use it to those who do not.[119]

The parallel argument about rules is that "security" encourages transaction in general.

The minimization of "judicial risk" (the risk that the judge will upset a transaction and defeat the intentions of the parties) leads to a higher level of activity than would occur under a regime of standards. Of course, some people will be *deterred* from transacting by fear of the mechanical arbitrariness of a system of formally realizable general rules. But their activity is less important, less socially desirable than that of the self-reliant class of actors who will master and then rely on the rule system.

The formal argument rests on the same implicit Social Darwinism as the substantive. Security of transaction is purchased at the expense of tolerating breach of altruistic duty on the part of the beneficiary of mechanical arbitrariness. The liberation of that actor's energy is achieved through a kind of subsidy based on a long term judgment that society gains through the actions of the aggressive and competent even when those actions are directly at the expense of the weak.

B.   *Rules as an Aspect of Classical Laissez-Faire*

The conclusion of the abstract consideration of the relationship of form and substance is that there is a sound analytical basis for the intuition of a connection between individualism and rules. The connection is structural rather than contextual. It is *not* a connection that is necessary in practice, or even verifiable empirically. It consists in the exact correspondence between the structures of the two arguments.

For all one can tell from the discussion so far, this structural similarity is an interesting historical accident. On the basis of the analogy we might hazard a guess that particular values or premises that make substantive nonintervention attractive will tend to make formal nonintervention attractive as well. But this would be no more than a psychological speculation (of a type which I will undertake at some length in the last section of this essay).

But there is also an historical dimension to the problem. Economic individualism was once much more tightly linked to advocacy of rules than it is today, because they were both parts of a larger intellectual entity: the Classical theory of

laissez-faire. That theory asserted that economics could discover general laws about the welfare consequences of particular legal regimes looked at as wholes. The scientific study of such regimes suggested that the best was that in which the state systematically refused to intervene ad hoc to achieve particular economic results.

The study of the theory of laissez-faire has intrinsic interest, but it is also useful for our particular purposes. Modern altruism is in large part a critique of the premises on which it was based, rather than a developed countertheory. As a result of the altruist critique, the modern individualist will admit that *sometimes* rules don't work, and standards do. But because the critique is *only* a critique, the altruist will concede that rules are sometimes necessary. This pragmatic reasonableness on both sides conceals the fact that the disputants reached their similar positions by different routes.

The individualist has reached the pragmatic position after abandoning a general theory of why rules are rationally required by the laws of economic science. The altruist has arrived in the same place after abandoning a more tentative and (among legal thinkers) much less widely shared vision of a social harmony so complete as to obviate the need for any rules at all. We can ignore the existence of these divergent historical paths so long as we ourselves are interested in a purely instrumental understanding of the issue of form. But if we are interested in the values intrinsic *to* form, in the fundamental conflict of visions of the universe that underlies instrumental discussion, then it is dangerous to make a sharp distinction between where we are and how we got here.

1. Laissez-Faire.—It is not easy to reconstruct the Classical individualist economic vision, especially if we want to understand it from the inside as plausible, rather than absurd or obviously evil. While there were several strands of argumentation, the most important seems to have been the idea that the outcome of economic activity within a common law framework of contract and tort rules mechanically applied would be a natural allocation of resources and distribution of income.

The outcome was natural because it was a reflection of the real bargaining power of the parties, given the supply and demand conditions in the market in question. No legal intervention could change it except in the direction of making everyone worse off, unless the reformer was willing to establish full collectivism. It was simply an implication of the immutable laws of economics that piecemeal reform must be self-defeating or counterproductive.

The refusal to enforce contracts or contract terms because of disapproval of the abuse of bargaining power is a case in point. Each party was willing to exchange on the designated terms; each therefore thought he would profit. Refusal to enforce deprives each of that profit. It does *not*, however, modify their bargaining power. If we refuse to enforce a particular term, they will readjust the rest of the bargain, and the stronger will exact in the form of a higher price, or whatever, the advantage that can no longer express itself in an allocation of a risk. The net result will be to drive some of the buyers out of the market, because they cannot afford to pay the higher price imposed by regulation. The victims of exclusion from the market are likely to be precisely those poorer buyers the regulator was trying to help.

If we respond by trying to fix the price directly, the result will be an imbalance of supply and demand, since the prices we are trying to change were those necessary to clear the market. If we want to prevent the disappointment of sellers or buyers, we will have to establish rationing or compulsory contracts. These cannot be enforced without a degree of supervision of individual businesses that amounts to socialism de facto, if not de jure.[120]

The assertion of the "naturalness" of economic interaction under property and contract rules is not plausible for us. Its plausibility in 1900 was based on the combination of the belief that the substantive content of the common law rules was an embodiment of the idea of freedom with the belief that official intervention to enforce the rules was nondiscretionary. The basis of the first belief, as we have seen, was conceptualism. The second notion expressed itself through a complex of doctrines, including stare decisis, the nondelegation doctrine, the void for vagueness doctrine, objectivism in contracts, the reasonable person standard in torts,

the distinction between questions of law and questions of fact, and the general idea that law tended to develop toward formally realizable general rules.

If one could believe that the common law rules were logically derived from the idea of freedom and that there was no discretionary element in their application, it made sense to describe the legal order itself as at least neutral, nonpolitical if not really "natural." The economy was regulated, if one compared it to the state of nature, but it was regulated in the interests of its own freedom. What happened to economic actors when they exercised that freedom had almost as much claim to being natural as what would have happened if there was no state at all.

2. The Altruist Attack on Laissez-Faire.— The altruist attack on laissez-faire denied the neutrality of the outcomes of bargaining within the background rules. The altruists began from the proposition that outcomes are heavily conditioned by the legal order in effect at any given moment. Those who enforce that legal order must accept responsibility for the allocation of resources and distribution of income it produces. In particular, bargaining power is a function of the legal order. All the individualist rules restrain or liberate that power. Changes in the rules alter its pattern. The outcome of bargaining will therefore be radically different according to whether we allow a state of nature, enforce a much more regulatory individualist regime, or a still more regulatory altruist one. All the outcomes are equally "natural." The question is which one is best.

The persuasiveness of the altruist attack depended heavily on discrediting both conceptualism and the claim that the legal order is composed of rules judges merely apply. As long as one believed in these two ideas, one could distinguish easily enough between an individualist regime and either the state of nature or a more altruist welfare state. Only the individualist regime was based on freedom. Under that regime, economic actors were never subjected to political restraints or to interference based on altruism. The rules that governed conduct depended neither on legislative consensus nor on a utopian morality, but on deduction from first principles acceptable to everyone. They were applied without the exercise of discretion by judges who had no power to inject their own politics or morals into the process.

The altruists attempted to show that neither conceptualism nor the idea of law as rules had any reality at all as a basis for defining a truly individualist legal order. As we have seen, the charge against conceptualism was that it was a mystification: there simply was no deductive process by which one could derive the "right" legal answer from abstractions like freedom or property.[121] The attack on the claimed objectivity of the law-applying process covered the whole complex of doctrines that supposedly eliminated the discretionary element from official intervention.[122] The aim was to show that as a matter of fact most rules were standards. The legal order, in this view, was shot through with discretion masquerading as the rule of law.

If the judges had neither derived the common law rules from the concepts nor applied them mechanically to the facts, then what *had* they been doing? The altruist answer was that they had been legislating and then enforcing their economic *biases*. The legal order represented not a coherent individualist philosophy, but concrete individualist economic interests dressed up in gibberish.[123] This once recognized, the next target was the argument that interference with the "free market" (market regulated by conceptually derived groundrules mechanically applied) would necessarily make everyone worse off.

The altruists demonstrated that no single general analysis could predict the effects of legal intervention in the economy. Everything depended on the structure of the particular market, which in turn depended on the legal system. It was quite true that attempts to regulate the exercise of economic power by interfering with particular terms of bargains *might* be self-defeating, if the market was perfectly competitive (so that price was equal to cost), or if the stronger party could shift his exactions from one term to another. But this was not *always* the case. Compulsory standardized terms in insurance policies might reduce the bargaining power of the sellers by increasing the buyers' understanding of the transaction.

Even supposing that the result of intervention is to force most people to transact on the new set of terms at a higher price while driving the rest out of the market, this might be justified on paternalist grounds. According to the new, post-conceptual mode of analysis, the common law was already full of paternalism, that is, of rules like those of capacity, which could no longer be rationalized through the will theory. The extension of the protective policy to, say, disclaimer of warranties to consumers would not represent any radical break with common law tradition.

It was also possible to relativize the argument about direct price regulation: its impact was a function of the whole situation, rather than of any general maxim about supply and demand. For example, where sellers cannot easily withdraw from the market, a compulsory price reduction may not reduce supply, except over the long, long run. A monopolist who is forced to reduce his price may *increase* supply in order to maintain the highest possible level of profit.

Finally, there were many ways to influence economic outcomes in an altruist direction without directly regulating outcomes, and there was no reason at all to believe that these would reduce welfare. The optimizing tendencies of the market will work, within the leeways we choose to leave for them, no matter how we make the initial definition and allocation of property rights. For example, we can limit the tactics employers can use in bargaining with employees. This changes the balance of power that existed under the old rules about what people could do with their property. But it does not "impede the functioning of the market" any more or less than we impeded it by imposing the rules of property and contract in the first place.[124]

This line of altruist argument applies with exactly equal force to changes in form and to changes in substance. For example, a working class automobile buyer may be highly skilled at price bargaining but have neither the time nor the education to argue successfully about warranties. Competition may not force the seller to translate his self-interested warranty terms into a lower price, because there may be no competition.

The normal rule that parties are bound to their contracts whether or not they read and understand them has obvious advantages in many situations, but here it will allow the seller to dictate to the buyer. The judge may reduce the seller's bargaining power if he adopts a more flexible approach based on a "reasonable understanding of a prudent lay buyer in all the circumstances." The result may be that there is a net increase in protection for buyers, a change whose cost is absorbed by the seller out of his monopoly profits.

It *may* be that the judge can counteract the ill effects of the normal rule about intent through substantive doctrines about duress, fraud, unconscionability or whatever. But there will be formal problems with these doctrines as well. They may be underinclusive in ways that are desirable in general but deprive them of efficacy in this situation (*e.g.*, failure to explain the boilerplate is not fraud because there has been no false statement of fact). A series of highly particularized applications of a general standard of "reasonable understanding" may be the only effective way to deal with the problem, short of the more intrusive approach of judicially constructed compulsory terms.

The choice between the old "strict" rule, a standard of "reasonable understanding," and compulsory terms cannot be made in a neutral fashion. Each choice affects the balance of economic power, to the advantage of one side and the disadvantage of the other. Since these effects are directly attributable to the legal order, the judge must take responsibility for choosing among them. He is an "interventionist" no matter what he does.[125]

Stripped to essentials, the altruist substantive and formal arguments are identical. Legislative, administrative and judicial action based on a detailed knowledge of particular situations can achieve paternalist and regulatory objectives without paralyzing private economic energies. The state should move directly to implement "the public interest" rather than relying on the combination of property and contract rules with private activity to produce a social maximum. At the substantive level of lawmaking, the altruist rejects the individualist position that it is necessary to tolerate inequality of bargaining

power and other abuses of altruistic duty as between large social groups. The economic argument for standards is the formal version of the same proposition. It is that we can sometimes enforce our substantive values in particular cases, as well as in general, without the disastrous consequences the individualist predicts.

VII   The Political Arguments About Judicial Result Orientation

Thus far, we have dealt with a moral confrontation between the ethic of self-reliance and that of sacrifice and sharing. We then took up an economic dispute that opposed equity in adjudication (defined in terms of the lawmaker's purposes) to the achievement of the general welfare through non-intervention. Here we take up the political confrontation, in which the opposed slogans are rights and powers. The advocate of rules argues that the casting of law as standards is inconsistent with the fundamental rights of a citizen of a democratic state.

There are two branches to the argument. I will call them the institutional competence and the political question gambits. The premise of the institutional competence argument is that judges do not have the equipment they would need if they were to try to determine the likely consequences of their decisions for the total pattern of social activity. In other words, rational result orientation requires factual inquiries that are at once particularized and wide-ranging. Only the legislature is competent to carry out such investigations. Judges should therefore restrict themselves to *general* prescriptions.

The premise of the political question gambit is that there is a radical distinction between the activity of following rules and that of applying standards. Standards refer directly to the substantive values or purposes of the community. They involve "value judgments." Since value judgments are inherently arbitrary and subjective, they should be made only according to majority vote. By contrast, formally realizable rules involve the finding of facts. Factfinding poses objective questions susceptible to rational discussion. So long as the rulemaking process is democratically legitimate, there is no political objection to the delegation of rule application to judges.[126]

Of course, so long as the judge has the power to formulate a new rule rather than applying an old one, it is clear that he has a measure of political or legislative power. The argument for rules, in the form in which we will consider it, is therefore a matter of degree. But rulemaking followed by rule application should be *less* political than proceeding according to standards. Both rule-making and rule application limit discretion, by publicizing it at the legislative stage and by providing criteria for criticizing it at the stage of application.

Together, the institutional competence and political question arguments would produce a regime in which judges did nothing but formulate and apply formally realizable general rules. This procedure would minimize both the institutionally inappropriate investigation of the likely results of decision and the inherently legislative activity of making value judgments. A regime of standards would have the opposite effect. Every case would require a detailed, open-ended factual investigation *and* a direct appeal to values or purposes.

It seems intuitively obvious that both of these gambits are prototypically individualist. Each is an argument for nonintervention, for judicial passivity in the face of breach of altruistic duty. It would therefore seem reasonable to expect that we would find an exactly parallel substantive claim that the judge should not attempt to impose a high standard of altruistic duty because he has neither the knowledge nor the democratic legitimacy required for the enterprise. Such an argument does in fact exist. It is the central thesis of the modern conservative attack on judicial activism in both public and private law.[127] Indeed, in this area the formal and substantive arguments are so close to identical that I will treat them as a unit.

Because the institutional competence and political question gambits apply so clearly both to form and to substance, they pose more sharply than the economic arguments the underlying question of the relationship of individualism and altruism in modern legal thought.

But before we can take up this issue, we must deal with a difficult historical problem.

The modern forms of the institutional competence and political question gambits are the inventions of pre-World War II altruism, rather than of individualism. Their first application was to the U.S. Supreme Court's activist use of the due process clause to strike down social legislation. Men who devoted most of their lives to furthering communitarian, paternalist and regulatory goals within the legal system are responsible for the most powerful statement of the political case for judicial nonintervention in public *and* private law. One purpose of this section is to show that in private law the gambits are nonetheless "essentially" individualist. Their adoption by the altruists in the constitutional context of 1936 was an unfortunate, if perhaps necessary tactic. The long-run result has been that modern altruists spend much of their rhetorical energy defending themselves against their own analysis of forty years ago.

A. The Origins of the Institutional Competence and Political Question Gambits

1. The Classical Individualist Position on Judicial Review.—We have seen already that a particular definition of the judicial role was an important component of the Classical individualist vision of the nature and function of the legal order. We might call it the "rule of law" model.[128] The two operations that defined it were the deduction of legal rules from first principles, and the mechanical application of the rules to fact situations. Each operation was strictly rational or objective; the judge could and should exclude his own political or economic values from the process of judgment. Other doctrines (nondelegation, vagueness, law vs. fact, stare decisis, etc.)[129] fleshed out the model so that it could be used to describe virtually all acts of officials impinging on the rights of citizens.

This theory of the judicial role played an especially important part in the Classical theory of judicial review. In that theory, the Constitution was law like any other law, except higher. Judicial review consisted of the deductive elaboration of its principles and their application to particular statutes. As such, the task was wholly rational and objective. It made no sense to accuse the judges of usurping the political powers or functions of the legislature, because there was nothing political (prudential, discretionary) about what the judges were doing.[130]

While this much went back to Marshall,[131] the Classical individualist thinkers added a new dimension. They were possessed of the post-Civil War theory of *private* law as a set of deductions from the concept of free will, whereas in Marshall's time the dominant jurisprudence presented private law rules either as given through the forms of action or as the outcome of the conflict between morality and policy. What the Classical thinkers did was to equate the "liberty" secured by the due process clause of the federal and state constitutions with the "free will" from which they believed they could deduce the common law rules.

This bold stroke integrated public and private law. It provided a set of tests of the constitutionality of legislation that had the assumed neutrality of private law to back them up against the charge that the courts were overstepping themselves. For example, the "liberty" of the constitutions meant liberty of contract. It followed that the state *must* enforce the set of legal rules that were implicit in the very idea of contract. In particular, an injunctive remedy against union attempts to organize workers bound by "yellow dog contracts" was constitutionally required.[132] Conversely, an attempt by the legislature to expand the law of duress to ban contracts that "really" represented free will was unconstitutional and void.[133]

Applied to the hilt, this approach would have meant freezing into the legal system the whole structure of laissez-faire that the Classical individualists claimed to be able to derive deductively from the concepts. But even in the 1920's, the heyday of activist judicial review, no court attempted anything so radical. In practice, the individualist argument was as much historical and pragmatic as purely conceptual, drawing on the idea that American law had always been committed to free enterprise, which was the only policy short of socialism that accorded with the "laws of economic science."

We can take Justice Sutherland's dissenting opinion in *West Coast Hotel Co. v. Parrish*[134] as an example. The issue was the constitutionality of a statute establishing a commission with power to fix minimum wages for different categories of women workers in the District of Columbia. Sutherland argued that the due process clause made freedom of contract a constitutional right. Its enforcement against attempts at legislative abridgment was the duty of the judiciary, indistinguishable from the duty to enforce private law rules in contests between the lowliest private parties.

The right was subject to legislative control, but a control strictly limited to paternalist interventions, such as specification of the mode of payment or maximum hours. Here, by contrast, the object was regulatory: to eliminate the actual bargaining power of worker and employer as the determinant of the wage rate. Unlike earlier legislation that let the parties adjust the wage rate to reflect state imposed conditions of labor, this law threw state power into the contest on the side of the worker. It therefore amounted to forcing the employer to donate a part of his income to support the worker at a minimum level of welfare. The measure of the subsidy was the difference between the minimum wage and what the worker could have earned in the "free market."

The goal, according to Sutherland, might be laudable, but the means adopted amounted to a taking of the employer's property without compensation, combined with a violation of the employee's freedom of contract, all to the detriment of everyone involved. First, the plaintiff employee had lost her job because she was not allowed to make a contract that was satisfactory to her. She had been denied her constitutional rights with no compensating gain whatever, since the statute had impoverished her rather than guaranteeing her a minimum level of welfare. Second, where the statute succeeded in making workers better off, it did so through an arbitrary redistribution of income between particular employers and workers, allocating the burden of maintaining welfare in such a way as to have a maximum negative impact on the incentive to create wealth and employment.

2. The Altruists Accept the Individualist Theory of the Judicial Role.—In retrospect, there appear to have been two plausible lines of altruist attack on the individualist attempt to constitutionalize the groundrules of laissez-faire. The road not taken was the more radical. It involved accepting the analogy of private and public law, and then arguing that *both* were inherently "political," in the sense of requiring the judge to make choices between the rival social visions of individualism and altruism. The altruists could then have argued for judicial deference to altruist social legislation either on the ground that judges are the constitutional inferiors of the legislature, or on the ground that the particular legislation in question was affirmatively just and desirable, retaining the option of striking down any future legislation that infringed fundamental human rights.

In fact, the altruist response was fragmented and evasive. There are hints of the more radical argument in some opinions,[135] and in the *Carolene Products*[136] footnote about the role of the judiciary in protecting minorities. But the dominant strain was different. It consisted of an attempt to distinguish the inescapably "political" role of the judges in reviewing legislation from more conventional aspects of the judicial function, such as private law adjudication. Nonetheless, it drew inconsistently on altruist arguments developed in the private law context.

First, the altruists pointed out that the individualist public law position was conceptualist. Individualism claimed to deduce a theory of judicial review from the mere fact that the Constitution was "law," and that the court was "judicial." It asserted that "liberty" had a single meaning from which it was possible to deduce rules of review that would distinguish in a nonpolitical fashion between regulatory statutes. In the background was the claim that common law rules could serve as a benchmark of constitutionality because they represented deductions from free will.

The altruists attacked this position on both historical and analytic grounds. Paternalist and regulatory intervention had been common throughout the antebellum period,[137] and no one had ever supposed that it violated the due process clause.[138] The conceptual arguments about the logical implications of the words "law," "judge" and "liberty" were meaningless. Any state intervention, however minimal, represented a step along the path toward altruism and away from the state of nature. Once one recognized this, it was clear that the courts had upheld dozens and dozens of regulatory and paternalist statutes (*e.g.*, regulation of the mode of payment) on the basis of conceptualist quibbles whose only real meaning was that the Constitution validates *both* individualist and altruist ideals.[139]

In the case of the minimum wage, for example, the altruists made the by now familiar argument that there was no way to deduce the effects of the law from first principles. There was no such thing as "natural" bargaining power or worth of labor in the "free market," since the market was already heavily regulated through private law institutions. The impact of this particular statute could be determined only through a complex, specific factual inquiry into the supply and demand conditions and competitive structure of the market for unskilled women workers in the District of Columbia in the mid-1930's.[140]

The crucial step in the altruist argument was the next one: Since the Constitution embodied both altruist and individualist ideals, and the impact of the statute on those ideals was obscure, the question of its validity was political and therefore inappropriate for judicial determination. It was not that the altruist position was correct in this case that made the statute valid. Rather, the issue of validity was inherently legislative. Judicial attempts to define rightness and wrongness in areas of legislative intervention to achieve communitarian, paternalist or regulatory objectives were inappropriate, because *any* decision required one to choose between conflicting values.[141]

The altruists thus accepted the individualist dichotomy between legislative and judicial functions. Although their purpose was to defend altruistic intervention in the economy, they cast their position in the form of an argument against intervention by the judiciary in cases that involved the conflict of individualism and altruism. The basis for the position was that judicial review of social legislation was sui generis in terms of the judicial role. The reformers were implicitly contrasting it with the unequivocally judicial task of private law adjudication when they spoke of "inquiries for which the judiciary is ill equipped," and the "necessity for choice between rival political philosophies."[142]

3. The Inconsistency of the Altruist Distinction Between Public and Private Law.—Hindsight suggests that this formulation of the distinction between public and private law was a misrepresentation of the real positions of the altruist reformers. It may have been essential in the political task of mobilizing opposition to the Nine Old Men. It permitted an appeal to the ideal of legality in defense of legislative supremacy, thereby avoiding a polarized confrontation between those who believed in the total politicization of everything and those who believed in rights as well as in democracy. But it was intellectually dishonest.

The problem was that the altruist *private law* theorists had been busy for years in showing that common law adjudication was not one whit less "political" or "value laden" than judicial review. Moreover, they had confronted the institutional competence and political question gambits as they apply to private law, and concluded that they led to a theory of the judicial role that was both false in itself and intrinsically biased toward individualist outcomes. At the very same time that their public law allies were stressing the neutrality of private law adjudication by way of contrast to the political character of judicial review, the private law theorists were undermining the basis for such a distinction and attacking its implications. It is their arguments, rather than those developed in the public law context, that are important for our purposes here.

First, Classical individualist private law was no less dependent on conceptualism than public law for its claim to neutrality and legitimacy. It was equally open to the charge that the judges had used the ambiguity of the concepts to smuggle in their biases.[143] Second, a major strand in the public law argument was precisely that common law rules of property, tort and contract represented a massive state interven-

tion in the economy. These private law rules, rather than "natural" or "real" strength, were the basis of the bargaining power the altruists were trying to regulate. Exactly the same "choice between rival philosophies" as in public law was necessary, after the death of the concepts, in deciding how state force should be used to structure economic conflict. And the institutional competence gambit was, if anything, stronger for private than for public law.[144]

Take the case of the judge asked to declare disclaimers of power lawnmower warranties void as against public policy. To begin with, there is the question of how his action will affect the price of mowers and of how a change in price will affect demand. Then there are the "inherently political" questions: (a) should we overrule the choices of those who prefer a cheaper mower without a warranty; (b) should we drive those who can't afford the mower with a warranty out of the market; (c) supposing that we can eliminate disclaimers without causing a fully compensating price hike, is it either ethically or economically *desirable* thus to shift the balance of economic power toward the consumer at the expense of the manufacturer? Finally, can the court successfully impose its decision on the market in question, given consumer ignorance, the limited impact of the sanction of nullity, the court's inability either to publicize its view or to enforce it through continuing supervision, the decentralization of the decision process, and so forth.

It is possible to argue that the warranty case is an exception, because it involves judicial interference with freedom of contract, and that most of contract and tort law is at least relatively nonpolitical. This is true in the sense that it is not generally *perceived* as political, but it is plainly false if the assertion is that it does not involve "value judgments" of the kind that are supposed to be inherently legislative. Much of the altruist scholarly tradition in contracts, for example, is devoted precisely to politicizing the most apparently mundane doctrinal issues, as the quotation in the Introduction to this Article sweepingly illustrates.

To take one of a series of examples that could be extended indefinitely, it is not possible to decide when a breach of contract is "substantial," and therefore justifies recission by the non-breaching party, without taking a position on a basic individualist–altruist conflict. The judge who is not mechanically applying a rule must look to the degree of risk that the victim will undergo if forced to perform and then sue for damages, and weigh it against the reliance loss or unjust impoverishment that will befall the breaching party if the other takes his marbles and goes home. Fault will be inescapably relevant, as will the degree of involvement or intimacy of the parties prior to the mishap. The underlying issue is that of the degree of altruistic duty we want to impose on the non-breaching party, and this can be determined "rationally" only on the basis of a detailed factual inquiry, followed by a "choice between rival philosophies."[145]

Thus there is really a single altruist critique of constitutional *and* common law judicial lawmaking. The institutional competence and political question gambits apply to both or to neither. The altruist argument can not be that some law is political while other law is neutral. If the gambits are valid in public but not in private law, it must be because we should draw different conclusions from the discovery of the political element according to whether we are dealing with the Constitution or with common law institutions.

B.   The Individualist Character of the Gambits in Private Law

This is not the place to try to develop an altruist theory of judicial review. It is enough for our purposes to show that in private law, the institutional competence and political question gambits have a distinctively individualist character.

Judicial private lawmaking takes place precisely in those marginal and interstitial areas of the legal system where there is no unequivocal, or even extremely suggestive indication of legislative will. The judge is asked to add to the corpus of common law rules and standards by deciding how to fill a gap, resolve a contradiction, or harmonize an old doctrine with new perceptions. It follows that the institutional

competence and political question doctrines have a special meaning. They do *not* demand deference to legislative will because there is none in the premises. Rather, they enjoin the judge to perform his lawmaking in such a way as not to usurp legislative power by *performing legislative functions.*[146]

This is a good deal more than an injunction to avoid nullifying the decisions of the elected representatives of the people. The argument is the general one that the judge will be acting both ineffectively and illegitimately if he attempts, at the margin or in the interstices, to implement the community's substantive purposes with respect to individualism and altruism. The formal corollary, that he should cast his resolution of marginal and interstitial disputes as formally realizable general rules, follows directly from the premise that he should not behave politically.

In this individualist argument, the judge has a legitimate function as a marginal and interstitial lawmaker, and as a law applier, so long as he eschews result orientation. The problem for the individualist is to describe to him exactly how he is to decide without taking results into account. The Classical answer was that the common law is a gapless, closed system of Classical individualist principles. According to this view, it is possible to distinguish between two kinds of common law adjudication, one involving the application of these existing principles to a new situation, and the other the introduction of new principles. The activity of applying existing principles to new situations is the non-controversial core of the judicial role. But the creation of new principles is political and therefore legislative. For example, it would be inappropriate for a judge to outlaw disclaimers of warranties on power lawnmowers, because that would require him to create a new exception to the existing common law principle of freedom of contract. Since the only basis for doing this is the political one of furthering altruism, the judge has no basis for acting.

It is implicit in this view that the judge does have a basis for enforcing the disclaimer by throwing out an injured user's suit for damages. Likewise, he would have a basis for applying the general rules of offer and acceptance to power lawnmower contracts whenever a case of first impression should arise. But he would be usurping legislative power if he were to create, on particularistic altruist grounds, special lawnmower contract doctrines. In other words, there are three tiers of activity. First, the private parties interact, and someone acquires a grievance. Second, the judge applies the system of Classical individualist common law rules, and either grants or denies a remedy. Third, the legislature, if it wishes, but not the judge, imposes altruistic duties that go beyond the common law system of remedies.[147]

The altruist response is that the three tiered system leads to deference to *private power*, rather than to the legislature. The judge is not deferring to the legislature because the legislature has said nothing. The will that the judge is enforcing when he refuses to interfere with freedom of contract is the will of the parties, or of the dominant party, if the relationship is an unequal one. Such a program is quintessentially individualist. Unless he is willing with Austin, to embrace the fiction that no sparrow falls without the legislature's tacit consent, the judge cannot claim that he has no responsibility for this "political" outcome.

Furthermore, the individualist proposal assumes that the common law system, defined in terms of some point in the past, has the qualities of internal consistency necessary to allow the judge to distinguish between usurpation and the simple extension of existing principles. The whole altruist analytic assault on conceptualism was designed to show that the real, historical common law lacked these qualities. First, the concepts that were supposedly the basis for the rules were useless as grounds of decision. Second, the actual pattern of outcomes reflected an unstable compromise somewhere in between pure egotism and total collectivism.

Once one accepts such a conception, the three tiered structure collapses. The judge, by hypothesis, cannot appeal to a legislative command, and the common law with which she is to harmonize her result points in both directions at the same time. Certainly it falls far short of imposing the altruist's vision of social duties of sharing and sacrifice. Yet it is possible to argue

that *all* of its doctrines point in that direction, *i.e.*, toward collectivization and away from the state of nature. The trouble is that the glass may be half empty rather than half full. It is just as plausible to see the common law, as we have inherited it, as the manifesto of individualism against feudal and mercantilist attempts to create an organic relationship between state and society. There is nothing left of the three tiers but a field of forces. In order to decide cases, the judge will have to align herself one way or the other. But there can be no justification for her choice – other than a circular statement of commitment to one or the other of the conflicting visions.

C.   Two Proposed Solutions to the Political Dilemma

While in 1940 one might reasonably have asserted that the net effect of individualist-altruist conflict in private law had been to deprive the judge of any basis for deciding cases beyond personal orientation to results, there have since been two major attempts to help him out of this embarrassing situation, and to restore the prestige of law by vindicating its claim to autonomy from politics. The first of these is based on the assertion of immanent, nonpolitical rationality in the social order, or of immanent moral consensus among the citizenry. The second is based on the premise that if the judge leaves all issues of distributive justice to the legislature there will remain a rational science of resource allocation that can serve as a clear guide to marginal and interstitial lawmaking.

It is impossible to sum up these two movements in a paragraph or two, but that is what I will try to do, beginning with the more recent. The law and economics movement,[148] insomuch as it purports to offer a theory of what judges should do, is an attempt to formalize the three-tiered system while at the same time substituting the authority of economic science for that of the historical common law. The distinction between legislative and judicial questions rests squarely on the institutional competence and political question gambits, here cast in the economist's language of allocation and distribution. The point that the common law is in fact distributive is answered by the assertion that it ought not to be.

The problem with this position, even supposing that one accepts its revolutionary rejection of the common law tradition, is that efficient resource allocation cannot provide a determinate answer for the judge's dilemma as to what law to make. The theory tells him only that the outcomes of free bargaining – efficient by definition – are preferable to state-directed outcomes, because they generate gains which could make everyone better off if redistributed.

But free bargaining presupposes an existing definition and distribution of property rights. The basic insight of the critics of classical individualism was that *all* legal rules go into the definition of initial bargaining positions – *all* rules are property rules in that sense. By hypothesis, the judge is trying to decide a marginal or interstitial question concerning those rules. Whatever he decides, subsequent bargaining will produce an efficient outcome. It is therefore circular to suggest that he can decide on the basis of efficiency. Another way to put the same point is to say that the outcome of bargaining would be efficient even in the state of nature. All interventions are distributively motivated.[149]

It follows that the elimination of the effects of transaction costs on the allocation of resources cannot provide an independent objective criterion for judicial lawmaking. It is only possible to decide that these effects are bad if we can establish that the outcome under some initial regime of legal rules, without transaction costs, would be good. But this cannot be done through criteria of efficiency, since *all* initial regimes meet that test. Before he starts applying the transaction cost analysis, the judge must therefore decide just how altruistic the background regime ought to be. Even supposing that he has done this, the steps required before the analysis can yield a determinate result involve a whole series of "value judgments."[150]

The alternative proposal, that the judge engage in "reasoned elaboration" of the immanent social purposes of the legal order, or that he decide on the basis of a "moral discourse," rejects the dichotomy of factual judgments and value judgments.[151] But it also creates a three-tiered structure. There is the outcome of private activity. There is judicial intervention *via* reasoned elaboration. And there is legislative intervention in pursuit of goals that the judge must ignore. As with the Classical individualist and law and economics solutions, the judge must define his jurisdiction through the institutional competence and political question gambits to avoid usurpation. As with the other solutions, usurpation means result orientation, here defined as going beyond the immanent rationality or immanent social morality of the legal order.

This proposal represents the recognition that the altruist analysis of the economic and political content of common law rules led into a dilemma. If the judge could not escape a role as an autonomous lawmaker, there seemed to be only two alternatives. He might retreat into passivity, and thereby behave in an objectively individualist way by facilitating the exercise of private power. Or he might take responsibility for imposing his "subjective value judgments" on the populace.

The proposed way out is a *partial* rejection of both the institutional competence and political question gambits. *Some* kinds of complex factual questions are appropriate for the judiciary; others are not. *Some* social values or purposes are capable of reasoned elaboration by judges; others are not, and must be left to the legislature. On the formal level, there is eclecticism about when we should use rules and when standards. *Sometimes* it will be true that we can trust the judge to apply the purposes of the legal order directly to the particular facts, without worrying either about arbitrariness or about the inefficiencies generated by uncertainty. Sometimes, on the other hand, we will want him to distinguish clearly between his lawmaking and law-applying roles.

This attempted compromise is a coherently incoherent response to the individualist's last ditch insistence on the institutional competence and political question gambits. The individualist can counter only with a reassertion of the ontological first principle that facts and values are radically distinct. It is simply *true* of all values that they are subjective and arbitrary. Immanent rationality, according to the individualist, is an illusion or a contingency based on an accidental and unstable social consensus, and the judge's role is therefore inevitably discretionary in the fullest sense.[152] The postulate of democracy then requires the judge to restrict his lawmaking to the narrowest possible compass by adopting a regime of formally realizable general rules.

But a compromise of this kind is as hostile to the altruist program of result orientation as it is to individualism. Like the other three tiered structures, it asserts that there are some effects of decision that the judge cannot take into account. To relativize the distinction between legislative and judicial questions is a very different thing from abolishing it altogether. The reasoned elaborator is the ally of the individualist in asserting that there are some values that can be enforced only through legislation.

The essence of the immanent rationality approach is that it attempts to finesse the confrontation of opposing philosophies by developing a middle ground. The strategy is predicated on the belief that individualism and altruism lead to conflict only on a fringe of disputed questions, leaving a fully judicial core within which there is consensus. Marginal and interstitial lawmaking within the core favors neither of the competing ideologies. It is only if the judge makes the mistake of moving into the "political" periphery that he will find himself obliged to make a choice between them.

There is no logical problem with this way of looking at the legal order. The question is whether it is more or less plausible than the vision, shared by individualist and altruist alike, of a battleground on which no foot of ground is undisputed. The reasoned elaborator can protest to the individualist that he has gained the principle of judicial restraint in exchange for admitting a limited number of altruist principles into the legal core. To the altruist he will point out that the sacrifice of full result orientation is well worth it, given that some altruist principles have been legitimated as a source of judicial lawmaking.

My own view is that the ideologists offer a convincing description of reality when they answer that there is no core. Every occasion for lawmaking will raise the fundamental conflict of individualism and altruism, on both a substantive and a formal level. It would be convenient, indeed providential, if there really were a core, but if one ever existed it has long since been devoured by the encroaching periphery.

If this is the case, then there is simply no way for the judge to be neutral. It is not that the concepts, liberty, equality, justice, welfare, that are supposed to motivate him are utterly without meaning or possible influence on his behavior. They are deeply ingrained in culture and for most of us it is impossible to make sense of the world without them. The problem is that they make two senses of the world, one altruist and the other individualist. This is true alike for issues of form and issues of substance. Indeed, I hope I have shown that the dimension of rules vs. standards is no more than a fourth instance of the altruist-individualist conflict of community vs. autonomy, regulation vs. facilitation and paternalism vs. self-determination. What remains is to explore the level of contradiction that lies below the conflict as it manifests itself in debates about the form and substance of legal rules.

VIII   Fundamental Premises of Individualism and Altruism

Whatever their status may have been at different points over the last hundred years, individualism and altruism are now strikingly parallel in their conflicting claims. The individualist attempt at a comprehensive rational theory of the form and content of private law was a failure. But altruism has not emerged as a comprehensive rational counter theory able to accomplish the task which has defeated its adversary.

Nonetheless, the two positions live on and even flourish. The individualist who accepts the (at least temporary) impossibility of constructing a truly neutral judicial role still insists that there is a rational basis for a presumption of non-intervention or judicial passivity. The altruist, who can do no better with the problem of neutrality, is an activist all the same, arguing that the judge should accept the responsibility of enforcing communitarian, paternalist and regulatory standards wherever possible.

In this section, I will argue that the persistence of these attitudes as organizing principles of legal discourse is derived from the fact that they reflect not only practical and moral dispute, but also conflict about the nature of humanity, economy and society. There are two sets of conflicting fundamental premises that are available when we attempt to reason abstractly about the world, and these are linked with the positions that are available to us on the more mundane level of substantive and formal issues in the legal system.

Individualism is associated with the body of thought about man and society sometimes very generally described as liberalism. It is not necessary (in a logical or any other sense of necessity) for an individualist to hold to the liberal theory.[153] It is possible to believe passionately in the intrinsic moral rightness of self-reliance and in the obvious validity of the practical arguments for an individualist bias in law, and yet reject the liberal premises. It is a fact, however, that liberal theory has been an important component of individualism in our political culture at least since Hobbes. The whole enterprise of Classical individualist conceptualism was to show that a determinate legal regime could be deduced from liberal premises, as well as derived from individualist morality and practicality.

The same is true on the altruist side. The organicist premises with which the altruist responds to the liberal political argument are on another level altogether from the moral and practical assertions we have dealt with up to now. Yet, as is the case with individualism, there is both an historical connection and a powerful modern resonation between the levels of argument.

The importance of adding this theoretical dimension to the moral and practical is that it leads to a new kind of understanding of the conflict of individualism and altruism. In particular, it helps to explain what I called earlier the sticking points of the two sides – the moments at which the individualist, in his movement towards the state of nature, suddenly reverses himself and becomes an altruist, and the symmetrical moment at which the altruist becomes an advocate of rules and self-reliance rather than slide all the way to total collectivism or anarchism.

A. *Fundamental Premises of Individualism*

The characteristic structure of individualist social order consists of two elements.[154] First, there are areas within which actors (groups or individuals) have total arbitrary discretion (often referred to as total freedom) to pursue their ends (purposes, values, desires, goals, interests) without regard to the impact of their actions on others. Second, there are rules, of two kinds: those defining the spheres of freedom or arbitrary discretion, and those governing the cooperative activities of actors – that is, their activity outside their spheres of arbitrariness. A full individualist order is the combination of (a) property rules that establish, with respect to everything valued, a legal owner with arbitrary control within fixed limits, and (b) contract rules – part supplied by the parties acting privately and part by the group as a whole acting legislatively – determining how the parties shall interact when they choose to do so.[155]

The most important characteristic of an order with this structure is that individuals encounter one another in only three situations.

(a) *A* is permitted to ignore *B* and carry on within the sphere of his discretion as though *B* did not exist. *A* can let *B* starve, or, indeed, kill him, so long as this can be accomplished without running afoul of one of the limits of discretion.

(b) *A* and *B* are negotiating, either as private contracting parties or as public legislators, the establishment of some rules to govern their future relations. These rules will be binding whether or not based on agreement between *A* and *B* about what ends they should pursue or even about what ends the rules are designed to serve. *A* and *B* are working only toward binding directives that will benefit each *according to his own view of desirable outcomes.*

(c) *A* and *B* are once again permitted to ignore one another, so long as each follows the rules that govern their cooperative behavior. Although they are working together, neither need have the slightest concern for the other's ends, or indeed for the other's person, so long as he executes the plan.

Thus an individualist social order eliminates any necessity for A and B to engage in a discussion of ends or values. They can achieve the most complex imaginable interdependence in the domains of production and consumption, without acknowledging any interdependence whatever as moral beings. If we define freedom as the ability to choose for oneself the ends one will pursue, then an individualist order maximizes freedom, within the constraints of whatever substantive regime is in force.

The creation of an order within which there are no occasions on which it is necessary for group members to achieve a consensus about the ends they are to pursue, or indeed for group members to make the slightest effort toward the achievement of other ends than their own, makes perfect sense if one operates on the premise that values, as opposed to facts, are inherently arbitrary and subjective. Like the relationship between the other components of individualism (or of Romanticism, Classicism, etc.), the link between the two sets of ideas is more complicated than one of logical implication. But it is enough for our purposes to mention briefly some of the ways in which the idea of the subjectivity and arbitrariness of values reinforces or resonates the rule/discretion structure.

The *subjectivity* of values means that it is, by postulate, impossible to verify directly another person's statement about his experience of ends. That is, when A asserts that for him a particular state of affairs involves particular values in particular ways, B must choose between accepting the statement or challenging the good faith of the report. B knows about the actual state of affairs only through the medium of A's words and actions. She cannot engage A in an argument about A's values except on the basis of that information.[156]

The postulate of the *arbitrariness* of values means that there is little basis for discussing them. Even supposing that values were objective, so that we could all agree which ones were involved in a particular situation, and how they were involved, it would still be impossible to show by any rational process how one ought to change that objective situation. Our understanding of the existence of values, according

to the postulate, is not founded on rational deductive or inductive processes. Values are simply *there* in the psyche as the springs of all action. And since we cannot explain – except by appeal to behavioristic notions like those of learning theory – why or how they *are* there, we cannot expect to converse intelligently about what they ought to be or become.

Given these conditions, it seems likely that mechanisms of social order dependent on consensus about ends will run into terrible trouble. If, by providential arrangement (or perhaps by conditioning) everyone's values turn out to be identical (or to produce identical effects), then all is well; if there is disagreement, chaos ensues. This expectation is reinforced by the other major postulate of liberal theory: that people enter groups in order to achieve ends that pre-exist the group, so that the group is a means or instrument of its members considered as individuals.

Once again, this idea is *logically* connected neither with the postulate of the arbitrariness of values nor with the characteristic rule/discretion structure of an individualist social order. It merely "resonates" these allied conceptions. Thus, if the state is only an instrument each party adopts to achieve his individual purposes, it is hard to see how it would ever make sense to set up state processes founded on the notions of changing or developing values. If the state is truly only a means to values, and all values are inherently arbitrary and subjective, the only legitimate state institutions are *facilitative*. The instant the state adopts change or development of values as a purpose, we will suspect that it does so in opposition to certain members whose values other members desire to change. The state then becomes not a means to the ends of all, but an instrument of some in their struggle with others, supposing that those others desire to retain and pursue their disfavored purposes.

The individualist theory of the judicial role follows directly from these premises. In its pure form, that theory makes the judge a simple rule applier, and rules are defined as directives whose predicates are always facts and never values. So long as the judge refers only to facts in deciding the question of liability, and the remedial consequences, he is in the realm of the objective. Since facts are objective rather than subjective, they can be determined, and one can assert that the judge is right or wrong in what he does. The result is both the certainty necessary for private maximization and the exclusion of arbitrary use of state power to further some ends (values) at the expense of others.

Classical late nineteenth century individualism had to deal with the argument that it was impossible to formulate a code of laws that would deal with all situations in advance through formally realizable rules. The response was that the truly common, though minimal, ends that led to the creation of the state could be formulated as concepts from which formally realizable rules could be deduced. The judge could then deal with gaps in the legal order – with new situations – by deductively elaborating new rules. The process of elaboration would be objective, because rational, just as the application of rules was objective because referring only to facts.

Modern individualism accepts that this enterprise was a failure, but it does not follow that the judge is totally at large. There is still a rational presumption in favor of nonintervention, based on the fundamental liberal premises. These have been strengthened rather than weakened by the failure of the Classical enterprise, which asserted that there was at least enough consensus about values to found an aggressive theory of the "right," if not of the good.

Nonintervention is consistent with the liberal premises because it means the refusal of the group to use the state to enforce its vision of altruistic duty against the conflicting visions of individuals pursuing their self-interest. The judge should be intensely aware of the subjectivity and arbitrariness of values, and of the instrumental character of the state he represents. He may not be able to frame a coherent theory of what it means to be neutral, and in this sense the legitimacy of everything he does is problematic. All reason can offer him in this dilemma is the injunction to respect autonomy, to facilitate rather than to regulate, to avoid paternalism, and to favor formal realizability and generality in his decisions. If nothing else, his action should be relatively predictable, and

subject to democratic review through the alteration or prospective legislative overruling of his decisions.

B.   *Fundamental Premises of Altruism*

The utopian counter-program of altruist justice is collectivism.[157] It asserts that justice consists of order according to shared ends. Everything else is rampant or residual injustice. The state, and with it the judge, are destined to disappear as people come to feel their brotherhood; it will be unnecessary to make them act "as if." The direct application of moral norms through judicial standards is therefore far preferable to a regime of rules based on moral agnosticism. But it still leaves us far from anything worthy of the name of altruistic order. The judge, after all, is there because we feel that force is necessary. Arbitrators are an improvement; mediators even better. But we attain the goal only when we surmount our alienation from one another and share ends to such an extent that contingency provides occasions for ingenuity but never for dispute.

Altruism denies the arbitrariness of values. It asserts that we understand our own goals and purposes and those of others to be at all times in a state of evolution, progress or retrogression, in terms of a universal ideal of human brotherhood. The laws of this evolution are reducible neither to rules of cause and effect, nor to a logic, nor to arbitrary impulses of the actor. We do not control our own moral development in the sense that the mechanic controls his machine or legal rules control the citizen, but we do participate in it rather than simply undergoing it. It follows that we can speak meaningfully about values, perhaps even that this is the highest form of discourse.

Altruism also denies the subjectivity of values. My neighbor's experience is anything but a closed book to me. Economists make the simplifying assumption of the "independence of utility functions," by which they suppose that *A*'s welfare is unaffected by *B*'s welfare. This notion is at *two* removes from reality: *A*'s utility function is not only dependent on *B*'s, it cannot truthfully be distinguished from *B*'s. Quite true that we suffer *for* the suffering of others; more important that we suffer directly the suffering of others.

For the altruist, it is simply wrong to imagine the state as a means to the pre-existing ends of the citizens. Ends are collective and in process of development. It follows that the purposes that form a basis for moral decision are those of man-in-society rather than those of individuals. The administration of justice is more than a means to the ends of this whole. It is a part of it. In other words, judging is not something we have to *tolerate*; it is not a *cost* unavoidable if we are to achieve the various individual benefits of living together in groups.

Good judging, in this view, means the creation and development of values, not just the more efficient attainment of whatever we may already want. The parties and the judge are bound together, because their disputes derive an integral part of their meaning from his participation, first imagined, later real. It is desirable rather than not that they should see their negotiations as part of a collective social activity from which they cannot, short of utopia, exclude a representative of the group. A theory that presents the judge as an instrument denies this. Recognizing it means accepting that private citizens do or do not practice justice. It is an illusion to think that they only submit to or evade it.

Perhaps as important, an instrumental theory of judging lies to the judge himself, telling him that he has two kinds of existence. He is a private citizen, a *subject*, a cluster of ends "consuming" the world. And he is an official, an *object*, a service consumed by private parties. As an instrument, the judge is not implicated in the legislature's exercise of force through him. Only when he chooses to make his own rules, rather than blindly apply those given him, must he take moral responsibility. And then, that responsibility is asserted to be altogether individual, his alone, and therefore fatally close to tyranny. The judge must choose alienation from his judgment (rule application) or the role of God (rule making).

By contrast, altruism denies the judge the right to apply rules without looking over his shoulder at the results. Altruism also denies that the only alternative to the passive stance is the claim of total discretion as creator of the legal universe. It asserts that we can gain an understanding of the values people have woven into their particular relationships, and of the moral tendency of their acts. These sometimes permit the judge to reach a decision, after the fact, on the basis of all the circumstances, as a person-in-society rather than as an individual.[158] Though these faculties do not permit him to make rules for the future, that they permit him to decide is enough to make decision his duty. He must accept that his official life is personal, just as his private life, as manipulator of the legal order and as litigant, is social. The dichotomy of the private and the official is untenable, and the judge must undertake to practice justice, rather than merely transmit or invent it.

Altruism offers its own definitions of legal certainty, efficiency, and freedom. The certainty of individualism is perfectly embodied in the calculations of Holmes' "bad man," who is concerned with law only as a means or an obstacle to the accomplishment of his antisocial ends. The essence of individualist certainty-through-rules is that because it identifies for the bad man the precise limits of toleration for his badness, it authorizes him to hew as close as he can to those limits. To the altruist this is a kind of collective insanity by which we traduce our values while pretending to define them. Of what possible benefit can it be that the bad man calculates with certainty the contours within which vice is unrestrained? Altruism proposes an altogether different standard: the law is certain when not the bad but the *good* man is secure in the expectation that if he goes forward in good faith, with due regard for his neighbor's interest as well as his own, and a suspicious eye to the temptations of greed, then the law will not turn up as a dagger in his back. As for the bad man, let him beware; the good man's security and his own are incompatible.

"Efficiency" in the resolution of disputes is a pernicious objective unless it includes in the calculus of benefits set against the costs of administering justice the moral development of society through deliberation on the problem of our apparently disparate ends. Indeed, attempts to achieve the efficiency celebrated by individualism are likely to make these true benefits of judging unattainable, and end in a cheaper and cheaper production of injustice and social disintegration.

The "freedom" of individualism is negative, alienated and arbitrary. It consists in the absence of restraint on the individual's choice of ends, and has no moral content whatever. When the group creates an order consisting of spheres of autonomy separated by (property) and linked by (contract) rules, each member declares her indifference to her neighbor's salvation – washes her hands of him the better to "deal" with him. The altruist asserts that the staccato alternation of mechanical control and obliviousness is destructive of every value that makes freedom a thing to be desired. We can achieve real freedom only collectively, through *group* self-determination. We are simply too weak to realize ourselves in isolation. True, collective self-determination, short of utopia, implies the use of force against the individual. But we experience and accept the use of physical and psychic coercion every day, in family life, education and culture. We experience it indirectly, often unconsciously, in political and economic life. The problem is the conversion of force into moral force, in the fact of the experience of moral indeterminacy. A definition of freedom that ignores this problem is no more than a rationalization of indifference, or the velvet glove for the hand of domination through rules.

C. *The Implications of Contradictions Within Consciousness*

The explanation of the sticking points of the modern individualist and altruist is that both believe quite firmly in both of these sets of premises, in spite of the fact that they are radically contradictory. The altruist critique of liberalism rings true for the individualist who no longer believes in the possibility of generating concepts that will in turn generate rules defining a just social order. The liberal critique of anarchy or collectivism rings true for the altruist, who acknowledges that after all we have not overcome the fundamental dichotomy of subject and object. So long as others are, to some degree, independent and unknowable beings,

the slogan of shared values carries a real threat of a tyranny more oppressive than alienation in an at least somewhat altruistic liberal state.

The acknowledgment of contradiction does not abate the moral and practical conflict, but it does permit us to make some progress in characterizing it. At an elementary level, it makes it clear that it is futile to imagine that moral and practical conflict will yield to analysis in terms of higher level concepts. The meaning of contradiction at the level of abstraction is that there is no metasystem that would, if only we could find it, key us into one mode or the other as circumstances "required."

Second, the acknowledgment of contradiction means that we cannot "balance" individualist and altruist values or rules against equitable standards, except in the tautological sense that we can, as a matter of fact, decide if we have to. The imagery of balancing presupposes exactly the kind of more abstract unit of measurement that the sense of contradiction excludes. The only kind of imagery that conveys the process by which we act and act and act in one direction, but then reach the sticking point, is that of existentialist philosophy. We make commitments, and pursue them. The moment of abandonment is no more rational than that of beginning, and equally a moment of terror.

Third, the recognition that both participants in the rhetorical struggle of individualism and altruism operate from premises that they accept only in this problematic fashion weakens the individualist argument that result orientation is dynamically unstable. Given contradiction at the level of pure theory, the open recognition of the altruist element in the legal system does not mean an irrevocable slide down the slope to totalitarianism, any more that it would lead to the definitive establishment of substantive justice in the teeth of the individualist rule structure.

Individualism, whether in the social form of private property or in that of rules, is *not* an heroically won, always precariously held symbol of man's fingernail grip on civilized behavior. That is a liberal myth. In any developed legal system, individualist attitudes, and especially the advocacy of rules, respond to a host of concrete interests having everything to lose by their erosion. Lawyers are necessary because of rules; the prestige of the judge is professional and technical, as well as charismatic and arcane, because of them; litigants who have mastered the language of form can dominate and oppress others, or perhaps simply prosper because of it; academics without number hitch their wagon-loads of words to the star of technicality. Individualism is the structure of the status quo.

But there is more to it even than that. In elites, it responds to fear of the masses. In the masses, it responds to fear of the caprice of rulers. In small groups, it responds to fear of intimacy. In the psyche, it responds to the ego's primordial fear of being overwhelmed by the id. Its roots are deep enough so that one suspects an element of the paranoid in the refusal to recognize its contradictory sibling within consciousness.

Finally, the acknowledgment of contradiction makes it easier to understand judicial behavior that offends the ideal of the judge as a supremely rational being. The judge cannot, any more than the analyst, avoid the moment of truth in which one simply shifts modes. In place of the apparatus of rule making and rule application, with its attendant premises and attitudes, we come suddenly on a gap, a balancing test, a good faith standard, a fake or incoherent rule, or the enthusiastic adoption of a train of reasoning all know will be ignored in the next case. In terms of individualism, the judge has suddenly begun to act in bad faith. In terms of altruism *she has found herself*. The only thing that counts is this change in attitude, but it is hard to imagine anything more elusive of analysis.

IX   Conclusion

There *is* a connection, in the rhetoric of private law, between individualism and a preference for rules, and between altruism and a preference for standards. The substantive and formal dimensions are related because the same moral, economic and political arguments appear in each. For most of the areas of conflict, the two sides emerge as biases or tendencies whose proponents have much in common and a large basis for adjustment through the analysis of the particularities of fact situations. But there is a

deeper level, at which the individualist/formalist and the altruist/informalist operate from flatly contradictory visions of the universe. Fortunately or unfortunately, the contradiction is as much internal as external, since there are few participants in modern legal culture who avoid the sense of believing in both sides simultaneously.

Even this conclusion applies only so long as it is possible to abstract from the context of compromises within the mixed economy and the bureaucratic welfare state. In practice, the choice between rules and standards is often instrumental to the pursuit of substantive objectives. We cannot assess the moral or economic or political significance of standards in a real administration of justice independently of our assessment of the substantive structure within which they operate.

It follows that the political tendency of the resort to standards, as it occurs in the real world, cannot be determined a priori. The most barbarous body of law may be rendered "human," and therefore tolerable, by their operation. Indeed, the "corruption" of formality by informality may be the greatest source of strength for an oppressive social order. Or equally plausibly, standards may be a vehicle for opposition to the dominant ideology (opposition *within* a particular judge as well as opposition among judges), keeping alive resistance in spite of the capture of the substantive order by the enemy. These currents of resistance may be reactionary or revolutionary, reformist or mildly conservative.[159] Standards may even be accepted into the predominant conception of how a rule system works, treated as an area of "inchoacy" or of "emerging rules," as though altruist justice were inevitably the prelude to a higher stage of individualism.

How should a person committed to altruism in the contradictory fashion I have been describing assess the significance of informality in our actual law of contracts, for example? I have only a little confidence in my own answer, which is that the case for standards is problematic but worth making. There is a strong argument that the altruist judges who have created the modern law of unconscionability and promissory estoppel have diverted resources available for the reform of the overall substantive structure into a dead end. There is an argument that individualist judges are restrained from working social horrors only by a mistaken faith in judicial neutrality that it would be folly to upset. It might be better to ignore contract law, or to treat it in an aggressively formal way, in order to heighten the level of political and economic conflict within our society.

Nonetheless, I believe that there is value as well as an element of real nobility in the judicial decision to throw out, every time the opportunity arises, consumer contracts designed to perpetuate the exploitation of the poorest class of buyers on credit. Real people are involved, even if there are not very many whose lives the decision can affect. The altruist judge can view himself as a resource whose effectiveness in the cause of substantive justice is to be maximized, but to adopt this attitude is to abandon the crucial proposition that altruistic duty is owed by one individual to another, without the interposition of the general category of humanity.

Further, judges like Skelly Wright are important actors in a symbolic representation of the conflict of commitments.[160] Given the present inability of altruism to transform society, it is only a dramatic production, ancillary to a hypothetical conflict that would be revolutionary. As such, the judge is a cultural figure engaged in the task of persuading adversaries, in spite of the arbitrariness of values. More, he is at work on the indispensable task of imagining an altruistic order. Contract law may be an ideal context for this labor, precisely because it presents problems of daily life, immediate and inescapable, yet deeply resistant to political understanding. It seems to me that we should be grateful for this much, and wish the enterprise what success is possible short of the overcoming of its contradictions.

Notes

1   H. HART & A. SACKS, THE LEGAL PROCESS 113 (tent. ed. 1958).

2   Macaulay, *Private Legislation and the Duty to Read – Business Run by IBM Machine, The Law of*

Contracts and Credit Cards, 19 VAND. L. REV. 1051, 1056–69 (1966).

3   F. KESSLER & G. GILMORE, CONTRACTS, CASES AND MATERIALS 1118 (2d ed. 1970) [hereinafter cited as KESSLER & GILMORE].

4   The principal sources on the jurisprudence of form with which I am acquainted are: 6 J. BENTHAM, THE WORKS OF JEREMY BENTHAM 60–86, 508–85 (Bowring ed. 1839); 2 AUSTIN, LECTURES ON JURISPRUDENCE 939–44 (4th ed. 1873); 3 R. VON IHERING, DER GEIST DES ROMSICHEN RECHT § 4, at 50–55 (1883) [available in French translation as R. VON IHERING, L'ESPRIT DU DROIT ROMAIN (Meulenaere trans. 1877); future citations are to French ed.]; 2 M. WEBER, ECONOMY AND SOCIETY 656–67, 880–88 (Ross & Wittich eds. 1969); Pound, *The Theory of Judicial Decision, III*, 36 HARV. L. REV. 940 (1923); Fuller, *Consideration and Form*, 41 COLUM. L. REV. 799 (1941); von Mehren, *Civil Law Analogues to Consideration: An Exercise in Comparative Analysis*, 72 HARV. L. REV. 1009 (1959); Macaulay, *Justice Traynor and the Law of Contracts*, 13 STAN. L. REV. 812 (1961); Fried, *Two Concepts of Interests: Some Reflections on the Supreme Court's Balancing Test*, 76 HARV. L. REV. 755 (1963); Friedman, *Law, Rules and the Interpretation of Written Documents*, 59 NW. U.L. REV. 751 (1965); Macaulay, *supra* note 2; Dworkin, *The Model of Rules*, 35 U. CHI. L. REV. 14 (1967); K. DAVIS, DISCRETIONARY JUSTICE: A PRELIMINARY INQUIRY (1969); P. SELZNICK, LAW, SOCIETY AND INDUSTRIAL JUSTICE 11–18 (1969); Kennedy, *Legal Formality*, 2 J. LEG. STUD. 351 (1973); R. UNGER, LAW IN MODERN SOCIETY 203–16 (1976); A. KATZ, *Vagueness and Legal Control of Children in Need of Supervision*, in STUDIES IN BOUNDARY THEORY (unpublished manuscript on file at Harvard Law Review, 1976).

5   *See* 1 R. VON IHERING, *supra* note 4, at 51–56.

6   *See* H. HART & A. SACKS, *supra* note 1, at 126–29; Friedman, *supra* note 4, at 753–54; Dawson, *Unconscionable Coercion: The German Version*, 89 HARV. L. REV. 1041, 1042–47 (1976). The extent to which particular words or categories are regarded as sufficiently "factual" to serve as the basis of formally realizable rules changes through time, is subject to dispute at any particular time, and is a matter of degree. For example, the idea of competition may appear to one writer to be capable of generating precise and predictable answers to particu-

lar questions of antitrust law, while another may regard it as no more than a standard, unadministrable except though a further body of per se rules. *Compare* Bork, *The Rule of Reason and the Per Se Concept: Price Fixing and the Market Division*, 74 YALE L.J. 775 (1965), *with* Turner, *The Principles of American Antitrust Law*, in COMPARATIVE ASPECTS OF ANTITRUST LAW IN THE UNITED STATES, THE UNITED KINGDOM AND THE EUROPEAN ECONOMIC COMMUNITY 9–12 (Int'l & Comp. L. Q. Supp. Vol. 6, 1963). "Best interests of the child" has been subject to a similar dispute. *See* Mnookin, *Child Custody Adjudication: Judicial Functions in the Face of Indeterminacy*, 1975 LAW & CONTEMP. PROB. 226. The grandfather of such controversies in Anglo-American law is the "objectivism" issue. Late nineteenth century legal thought claimed that "subjective intent" was no more than a standard, and that legal directives dependent on its determination should be recast as rules referring to "external" aspects of the situation. *See* Kennedy, *supra* note 4, at 364 n.22.

7   While certainty is now praised through the formal language of efficiency, the idea has been familiar for centuries. Montesquieu put it as follows, speaking of the peasants of the Ottoman Empire in the eighteenth century: "Ownership of land is uncertain, and the incentive for agricultural development is consequently weakened: there is neither title nor possession that is good against the caprice of the rulers." C. DE MONTESQUIEU, LETTRES PERSANES 64 (1721). *See* Kennedy, *supra* note 4, at 365–77.

8   R. VON IHERING, *supra* note 4, at 54–55.

9   *See generally* Friedman, *Legal Rules and the Process of Social Change*, 19 STAN. L. REV. 786, 832–35 (1967); Leff, *Contract as Thing*, 19 AMER. U.L. REV. 131, 131–37 (1970). For an illustration of how the issue arises in legal argument, see Meinhard v. Salmon, 249 N.Y. 458, 472, 164 N.E. 545, 549 (1928) (Andrews, J., dissenting). *See also* note 10 *infra*.

10 This phenomenon is discussed in Surrey, *Complexity and the Internal Revenue Code: The Problem of the Management of Tax Detail*, 1969 LAW & CONTEMP. PROB. 673, 695–702; Amsterdam, *Perspectives on the Fourth Amendment*, 58 MINN. L. REV. 349, 374–77, 388–95 (1974).

11 On the obligation to formulate rules as a check on discretionary power, see K. DAVIS, *supra* note 4, at 52–96; Amsterdam, *supra* note 10, at 416–28.

12 Chief Justice Shaw gave classic expression to this view in Norway Plains Co. v. Boston & Maine R.R. Co., 67 Mass. (1 Gray) 263, 267 (1854):

> It is one of the great merits and advantages of the common law, that, instead of a series of detailed practical rules, established by positive provisions, and adapted to the precise circumstances of particular cases, which would become obsolete and fail, when the practice and course of business, to which they apply, should cease or change, the common law consists of a few broad and comprehensive principles founded on reason, natural justice, and enlightened public policy modified and adapted to the circumstances of all the particular cases which fall within it.

13 *See generally* Fuller, *supra* note 4; von Mehren, *supra* note 4.

14 The limitation of the functions of formalities to the cautionary and evidentiary defies the modern trend, begun by Fuller, to multiply functions almost indefinitely. The cautionary function, as I use it, includes both making the parties think twice about what they are doing and making them think twice about the legal consequences. The evidentiary function includes both providing good evidence of the existence of a transaction and providing good evidence of the legal consequences the parties intended should follow. For our purposes, it is unnecessary to subdivide further. *See* Kennedy, *supra* note 4, at 374–76. More detailed treatment of functions of form can be found in Fuller, *supra* note 4, at 800–04; von Mehren, *supra* note 4, at 1016–17; I. MACNEIL, CASES AND MATERIALS ON CONTRACTS, EXCHANGE TRANSACTIONS AND RELATIONSHIPS 1314–19 (1971); Perillo, *The Statute of Frauds in the Light of the Functions and Dysfunctions of Form*, 43 FORD. L. REV. 39, 43–69 (1974).

15 *See* Perillo, *supra* note 14, at 70–77.

16 *See* note 33 *infra*.

17 *See, e.g.*, United States v. Braunstein, 75 F. Supp. 137 (S.D.N.Y. 1947); Friedman, *supra* note 4, at 775–76.

18 *See, e.g.*, B. CARDOZO, THE GROWTH OF THE LAW 110–11 (1924).

19 *See* von Mehren, *supra* note 4, at 1016–17.

20 *See generally* Calabresi & Melamed, *Property Rules, Liability Rules and Inalienability: One View of the Cathedral*, 85 HARV. L. REV. 1089 (1972); R. NOZICK, ANARCHY, STATE AND UTOPIA 54–87 (1974); E. DURKHEIM, THE DIVISION OF LABOR IN SOCIETY 68–69, 127–29 (Simpson trans. 1933); Wellington,

Common Law Rules and Constitutional Double Standards: Some Notes on Adjudication, 83 YALE L.J. 221, 229–35 (1973). *See also* notes 22, 112 *infra*.

21 *See* 3 A. CORBIN, CONTRACTS § 534 (1960); 3A *id.* §§ 632, 653; E. DURKHEIM, *supra* note 20, at 123–25; H. HART & A. SACKS, *supra* note 1, at 251–56; Holmes, *The Path of the Law*, 10 HARV. L. REV. 457, 466 (1897). On impossibility, see KESSLER & GILMORE, *supra* note 3, at 742–44; Berman, *Excuse for Nonperformance in the Light of Contract Practices in International Trade*, 63 COLUM. L. REV. 1413 (1963); Note, *The Economic Implications of the Doctrine of Impossibility*, 26 HAST. L.J. 1251 (1975).

22 *See* O. HOLMES, THE COMMON LAW 233–39 (Howe ed. 1963); 2 M. HOWE, JUSTICE OLIVER WENDELL HOLMES 76–80 (1963); Calabresi & Melamed, *supra* note 20; Posner, *A Theory of Negligence*, 1 J. LEG. STUD. 29 (1972).

23 *See, e.g.*, Note, *Once More Into the Breach: Promissory Estoppel and Traditional Damage Doctrine*, 37 U. CHI. L. REV. 559 (1970).

24 *See* S. WILLISTON, CONTRACTS § 37 (2d ed. 1937).

25 UNIFORM COMMERCIAL CODE [U.C.C.] § 2–204. For Williston's criticism, see Williston, *The Law of Sales in the Proposed Uniform Commercial Code*, 63 HARV. L. REV. 561, 576 (1950).

26 For another example, see Professor Perillo's proposed revision of the Statute of Frauds in Perillo, *supra* note 14, at 71–77.

27 For a comprehensive discussion of this general subject in the context of administrative law, see Gifford, *Communication of Legal Standards, Policy Development, and Effective Conduct Regulation*, 56 CORNELL L. REV. 409 (1971).

28 *See* Note, *The Void for Vagueness Doctrine in the Supreme Court*, 109 U. PA. L. REV. 67 (1960).

29 *See* Hay, *Property, Authority and Criminal Law*, in ALBION´S FATAL TREE 17–26 (1975).

30 *See* Kessler, *The Protection of the Consumer under Modern Sales Law, Part I*, 74 YALE L.J. 262, 266–67 (1964); Hamilton, *The Ancient Maxim Caveat Emptor*, 40 YALE L.J. 1133, 1178–82 (1931).

31 *See* Fuller & Perdue, *The Reliance Interest in Contract Damages*, I, 46 YALE L.J. 52, 60–63 (1936).

32 This is the consequence of adopting an "objective" theory of contract to deal with problems like mistake and parol evidence. *Compare* Williston, *Mutual Assent in the Formation of Contracts*, 14 ILL. L. REV. 85 (1919), *with* Whittier,

The Restatement of Contracts and Mutual Assent, 17 CALIF. L. REV. 441 (1929).

33 *See* S. WILLISTON, CONTRACTS §§ 631–47 (2d ed. 1937); Calamari & Perillo, *A Plea for a Uniform Parol Evidence Rule and Principles of Contract Interpretation*, 42 IND. L.J. 333 (1967).

34 *See* Fuller & Perdue, *supra* note 31, at 60–63; Kennedy, *supra* note 4, at 365–77.

35 See the literature on contracts of adhesion collected in Leff, *supra* note 9, at 140–44; Friedman, *supra* note 4, at 759–61, 771–72, 779.

36 *See* Macaulay, *The Use and Non-Use of Contracts in the Manufacturing Industry*, 9 PRACTICAL LAWYER 13 (1963).

37 *See generally* Galanter, *Why the "Haves" Come Out Ahead: Speculations on the Limits of Legal Change*, 9 LAW & SOC. REV. 95 (1974); Perillo, *supra* note 14, at 70–71.

38 *See generally* Llewellyn, *A Realistic Jurisprudence – The Next Step*, 30 COLUM. L. REV. 431 (1930); Llewellyn, *On Reading and Using the Newer Jurisprudence*, 40 COLUM. L. REV. 581 (1940).

39 *See* Thayer, *Unilateral Mistake and Unjust Enrichment as a Ground for the Avoidance of Legal Transactions*, in HARVARD LEGAL ESSAYS 467 (1934).

40 See the cases and notes collected in KESSLER & GILMORE, *supra* note 3, at 478–508; U.C.C. § 2–209; RESTATEMENT (SECOND) OF CONTRACTS § 89D.

41 *See, e.g.*, Gellhorn, *Contracts and Public Policy*, 35 COLUM. L. REV. 679, 683–84 (1935); C. KAYSEN & D. TURNER, ANTITRUST POLICY: AN ECONOMIC AND LEGAL ANALYSIS 235 (1959); Perillo, *Restitution in a Contractual Context*, 73 COLUM. L. REV. 1208 (1973). On the development of promissory estoppel as an alternative contract cause of action through which damages can be recovered without compliance with formal requirements, see G. GILMORE, THE DEATH OF CONTRACT 66, 90 (1974).

42 Pound, *supra* note 4, at 951.

43 *Id.* at 954.

44 *Id.* at 952. The following is his most complete statement:

Social engineering may not expect to meet all its problems with the same machinery. Its tasks are as varied as life and the complicated problems of a complex social order call for a complicated mechanism and a variety of legal implements. This is too large a subject for discussion in the present connection. Suffice it to say that conveyance of land, inheritance and succession, and commercial law have always proved susceptible of legislative statement, while no codification of the law of torts and no juristic or judicial defining of fraud or of fiduciary duties has ever maintained itself. In other words, the social interests in security of acquisitions and security of transactions – the economic side of human activity in civilized society – call for rule or conception authoritatively prescribed in advance and mechanically applied. These interests also call peculiarly for judicial justice. Titles to land and the effects of promissory notes or commercial contracts cannot be suffered to depend in any degree on the unique circumstances of the controversies in which they come in question. It is one of the grave faults of our present theory of judicial decision that, covering up all individualization, it sometimes allows individualized application to creep into those situations where it is anything but a wise social engineering. On the other hand, where we have to do with the social interest in the individual human life and with individual claims to free self-assertion subsumed thereunder, free judicial finding of the grounds of decision for the case in hand is the most effective way of bringing about a practicable compromise and has always gone on in fact no matter how rigidly in theory the tribunals have been tied down by the texts of codes or statutes.

Id. at 956–57.

45 *See* Mnookin, *supra* note 6; Katz, *supra* note 4.

46 *See* Shulman, *Reason, Contract and Law in Labor Relations*, 68 HARV. L. REV. 999, 1016 (1955). The administration of the NLRA requirement of bargaining in good faith has also been the subject of debate. *See, e.g.*, H. K. Porter v. NLRB, 397 U.S. 99 (1970); NLRB v. General Electric, 418 F. 2d 736 (2d Cir. 1969), *cert. denied*, 398 U.S. 965 (1970); H. WELLINGTON, LABOR & THE LEGAL PROCESS 52–63 (1968).

47 *See* C. KAYSEN & D. TURNER, *supra* note 41, at 234–45; Bork, *supra* note 6; Bok, *Section 7 of the Clayton Act and the Merging of Law and Economics*, 74 HARV. L. REV. 226, 295–98 (1960); Turner, *supra* note 6, at 9–12.

48 It has been argued that the judicial use of a general standard of "prevention of tax avoidance" in interpreting the Tax Code has rendered the Code more certain. *See* Surrey, *supra* note 10, at 694–95; 2 S. SURREY, W. WARREN, P. MCDANIEL & H. AULT, FEDERAL INCOME TAXATION 633–34 (1973).

49 *See In re* Gault, 387 U.S. 1 (1967); McKeiver v. Pennsylvania, 403 U.S. 528 (1971); Griffiths, *Ideology in Criminal Procedure, or A Third "Model" of the Criminal Process*, 79 YALE L.J. 359, 399–404 (1970).

50 *See* Dershowitz, *Background Paper*, in FAIR AND CERTAIN PUNISHMENT 67–100 (Report of the Twentieth Century Fund Task Force on Criminal Sentencing, 1976).

51 *See generally* Gifford, *supra* note 27; K. DAVIS, *supra* note 4.

52 *See* 2 F. POLLOCK & F. MAITLAND, THE HISTORY OF ENGLISH LAW BEFORE THE TIME OF EDWARD I 562–64 (Milsom ed. 1968); Chayes, *The Role of the Judge in Public Law Litigation*, 89 HARV. L. REV. 1281 (1976).

53 *See* Friedman, *supra* note 4, at 777–79; L. FRIEDMAN, CONTRACT LAW IN AMERICA (1965); Perillo, *supra* note 14, at 41–42.

54 Tribe, *Structural Due Process*, 10 HARV. CIV. RIGHTS – CIV. LIB. L. REV. 269, 307 (1975).

55 Heymann & Holtz, *The Severely Defective Newborn: The Dilemma and the Decision Process*, 23 PUBLIC POLICY 381, 410–16 (1975).

56 2 M. WEBER, *supra* note 4; Macaulay, *supra* note 4; Friedman, *supra* note 4, at 764–77; Macaulay, *supra* note 2 at 1056–69; Friedman, *supra* note 53; Friedman, *supra* note 9.

57 *See* W. TWINING, KARL LLEWELLYN AND THE REALIST MOVEMENT, ch. 12 (1973); Danzig, *A Comment on The Jurisprudence of the Uniform Commercial Code*, 27 STAN. L. REV. 621 (1975).

58 *See* McCloskey, *Economic Due Process and the Supreme Court: An Exhumation and Reburial*, 1962 SUP. CT. REV. 34, 36–40. On vagueness in contracts as the outcome of compromise, see Macaulay, *supra* note 36, at 14–17. On legislative standards, see Friedman, *supra* note 9, at 835–36.

59 *See* Miranda v. Arizona, 384 U.S. 436, 455–70 (1966); Amsterdam, *supra* note 10, at 429–39. On the use of detailed rules by the legislature as a means to curb judicial discretion, *see* Friedman, *supra* note 4, at 752 n.4.

60 *See* KESSLER & GILMORE, *supra* note 3, at 1016–21; Friedman, *supra* note 4, at 778; Horwitz, *The Emergence of an Instrumental Conception of American Law*, in 5 PERSPECTIVES IN AMERICAN HISTORY 287, 323 (1971).

61 *See* Albemarle Paper Co. v. Moody, 422 U.S. 405 (1975). For a discussion of the impact of the choice of form in out-of-court settlement, see Macaulay, *supra* note 2, at 1065. On reapportionment, see Friedman, *supra* note 9, at 815–20.

62 See the discussion of the "non-directive functions of rules" in A. GOULDNER, PATTERNS OF INDUSTRIAL BUREAUCRACY 157–81 (1955). Even the highly qualified generalization in the text is open to serious question. For example, Gifford, *supra* note 27, argues that the use of standards may be characteristic of under-

funded administrative agencies that know that an accurate description of what they intend to do would reveal their weakness and encourage violators.

The idea that rules guarantee private actors an area of "autonomy" from judicial control is developed in Friedman, *supra* note 4, at 754–55, 764–74, and in Kennedy, *supra* note 4, at 366–77. Weber argues that the trend to standards in modern law reflects the desire of judges and lawyers to reassert their power and prestige relative to legislatures and private parties grown independent under the protection of a regime of rules. 2 M. WEBER, *supra* note 4, at 886.

63   *See* Note, *Civil Disabilities and the First Amendment*, 78 YALE L.J. 842, 851–52 (1969).

64   The literature on balancing is collected in Note, *supra* note 63, at 842–52. *See, e.g.*, Dennis v. United States, 342 U.S. 494, 524–25, 542–43 (1951) (Frankfurter, J., concurring); P. FREUND, THE SUPREME COURT OF THE UNITED STATES 44 (1949).

65   *See, e.g.*, Frantz, *Is the First Amendment Law? A Reply To Professor Mendelson*, 51 CALIF. L. REV. 729 (1963).

66   M. SHAPIRO, FREEDOM OF SPEECH: THE SUPREME COURT AND JUDICIAL REVIEW 103 (1966).

67   Reynolds v. Sims, 377 U.S. 533 (1964).

68   Roe v. Wade, 410 U.S. 113 (1973).

69   *See generally* Friedman, *supra* note 9, at 820–25. On abortion, see Tribe, *Supreme Court, 1972 Term – Foreword: Toward A Model of Roles in the Due Process of Life & Law*, 87 HARV. L. REV. 1, 4, 26–29 (1973); Ely, *The Wages of Crying Wolf: A Comment on Roe v. Wade*, 82 YALE L. J. 920, 924–26 (1973). On reapportionment, see A. BICKEL, THE SUPREME COURT AND THE IDEA OF PROGRESS 151–73 (1970).

70   The associations and contradictions in my two lists pose no special problem for the contextualizer. First, it is sometimes possible simply to ignore the values that seem implicit in the choice of form on the ground that the people involved don't care about them, or that the substantive values at stake are vastly more important. The opponent of mechanical rules in family life may think it absurd to worry about mechanicalness when the issue is enforcing a minimum wage law. Second, and more important, we can incorporate the values that inhere in different formal arrangements into the substantive decision process. Instead of deciding first what we want and then how to get it, we can treat the

"how" as an aspect of the "what." The decision-maker formulates his objectives "subject to the constraint" that he will be able to use only acceptable means to achieve them. Or he engages in a back-and-forth process of investigating goals, then means, then returning to reformulate goals in light of the new information. Or he integrates the whole process, treating processual or formal values as indistinguishable from those relating to outcomes. *See* Tribe, *Policy Science: Analysis or Ideology*, 2 PHIL. & PUB. AFF. 66 (1972); Tribe, *Ways Not to Think About Plastic Trees: New Foundations for Environmental Law*, 83 YALE L.J. 1315, 1317–25 (1974).

71   Two introductions to the American literature are M. WHITE, SOCIAL THOUGHT IN AMERICA: THE REVOLT AGAINST FORMALISM (2d ed. 1957), and E. PURCELL, THE CRISIS OF DEMOCRATIC THEORY: SCIENTIFIC NATURALISM AND THE PROBLEM OF VALUE (1973). For law, see Hart, *Positivism and Separation of Law and Morals*, 71 HARV. L. REV. 593, 620–29 (1958); HART & SACKS, *supra* note 1, at 126–29.

72   *See* P. SELZNICK, *supra* note 4.

73   Some important works in the tradition I am referring to are G. HEGEL, PHILOSOPHY OF RIGHT (Knox trans. 1952); K. MARX, *On the Jewish Question*, in EARLY WRITINGS (Benton trans. 1975); R. VON IHERING, *supra* note 4; F. POLLOCK & D. MAITLAND, *supra* note 52; Lukacs, *Reification and the Consciousness of the Proletariat*, in HISTORY AND CLASS-CONSCIOUSNESS: STUDIES IN MARXIST DIALECTICS (Livingstone trans. 1971); K. MANNHEIM, IDEOLOGY AND UTOPIA: AN INTRODUCTION TO THE SOCIOLOGY OF KNOWLEDGE (1936); H. MARCUSE, REASON AND REVOLUTION: HEGEL AND THE RISE OF SOCIAL THEORY (1941); C. LÉVI-STRAUSS, THE SAVAGE MIND (1966); R. UNGER, KNOWLEDGE AND POLITICS (1975); A. KATZ, *supra* note 4. Not all of these works, or even most of them, are based on the premises about the permanence of contradictions in consciousness that are described in the text following this note. My position is closest to that of Mannheim and Lévi-Strauss. It is also close to that of Griffiths, *supra* note 49, and Katz, *supra* note 4.

74   Some interesting nineteenth century treatments of self-reliance are R. EMERSON, *Self-Reliance*, in ESSAYS, FIRST SERIES 37 (1847) and H. SPENCER, JUSTICE (1891). A judicial classic

in the individualist vein is Smith v. Brady, 17 N.Y. 173 (1858).

My definition of individualism owes much to A. Dicey, Lectures on the Relation Between Law and Public Opinion in England During the Nineteenth Century (1905). The American legal realists used the term extensively to describe the "spirit" of 19th century private and public law. *See, e.g.,* Hamilton, *Property – According to Locke,* 41 Yale L. J. 864 (1932). This usage is still current; *see* Dawson, *supra* note 6, at 1047.

On the intellectual history of individualism, see R. McCloskey, American Conservatism in the Age of Enterprise (1951); R. Hofstadter, Social Darwinism in American Thought, 1860–1915 (1944); E. Kirkland, Dream and Thought in the Business Community, 1860–1900 (1956); S. Fine, Laissez-Faire and the General-Welfare State, A Study of Conflict in American Thought, 1865–1901 (1956); R. Wiebe, The Search for Order, 1877–1920 (1967).

The rhetoric of self-reliance is a permanent theme of American public discourse: " 'We must strike a better balance in our society,' [said President Ford.] 'We must introduce a new balance in the relationship between the individual and the Government, a balance that favors a greater individual freedom and self-reliance.' " N.Y. Times, July 18, 1976, at 24, col. 2.

The individualist ethic is reflected in a perennial strain of economic theorizing that emphasizes the natural and beneficial character of economic conflict and competition. According to this view, social welfare, *over the long run*, will be maximized only if we preserve a powerful set of incentives to individual activity. The argument is that the wealth and happiness of a people depend less on natural advantages or the wisdom of rulers than on the moral fiber of the citizenry, that is, on their self-reliance. If they are self-reliant, they will overcome obstacles, adjust easily to changes in fortune, and, above all, they will generate progress through the continual quest for personal advantage within the existing structure of rights.

The classic statement of this position is J. Bentham, The Theory of Legislation 119–22 (Ogden ed. 1931). On the nineteenth century United States, see J. Hurst, Law and the Conditions of Freedom in the Nineteenth Century United States (1956). *See also* the works of intellectual history cited in this note. A representative modern statement is A.

Okun, Equality and Efficiency, The Big Tradeoff (1975). Economic individualism, as I am using the term, is not synonymous with nineteenth century laissez-faire. It appeals to the beneficial effects of competition and self-reliance within whatever structure of rights and regulations the state may have set up. *See* C.B. Macpherson, The Political Theory of Possessive Individualism: Hobbes to Locke 57–58 (1962); E. Rostow, Planning for Freedom 10–45 (1959).

The political expression of individualism is the concept of a regime that secures liberty within a structure of legal rights. Liberty or freedom or autonomy is conceived as a good in itself, because it is synonymous with the ability to pursue one's own conception of the good to the best of one's ability. The function of the state (its only primary and intrinsically legitimate function) is to enforce the like rights of all members of the body politic. The state guarantees that so long as one remains within the area of autonomy for the individual free will, one will receive the benefits and suffer the ill consequences of one's chosen course of action. Thus rights simultaneously protect us in the possession of the fruits of our activities and prevent us from demanding that others participate in our misfortunes.

The progenitor of American theories of this kind is J. Locke, Two Treatises of Government (Laslett ed. 1960). An example of the nineteenth century version is H. Spencer, Justice 176 (1891). The modern conservative version is best represented by F. Hayek, The Constitution of Liberty (1960). The modern civil libertarian version is all around us but has no master expositors. *See* Black, *The Bill of Rights,* 35 N.Y.U.L. Rev. 865 (1960).

75 On the problem and the conventional solutions, see J. Rawls, A Theory of Justice 3–43 (1971). *See also* Kennedy, *supra* note 4, at 361–62.

76 T. Hobbes, Leviathan 109–13 (Oxford ed. 1957).

77 J. Locke, *supra* note 74, at § 13, §§ 123–26.

78 *See* R. Nozick, Anarchy, State and Utopia 149–82 (1974).

79 There is a large literature about altruism, much of it concerned with the question of whether the concept can have any meaning at all. If I sacrifice or share, can I be said to behave altruistically, given that presumably I preferred sacrifice or sharing to the alternatives? Wouldn't it be better to speak of "internalizing another person's utility function"? For my purposes, it makes no difference how one answers these questions. In the

cases that I deal with, there is no problem in distinguishing self-interested from altruistic behavior in the rough way suggested in the text. On the "larger" issue, see T. NAGEL, THE POSSIBILITY OF ALTRUISM (1970).

For an example of a typically altruistic but decidedly non-socialistic program of legal reform, see Pound, *The New Feudalism*, 35 COMMERCIAL L. J. 397 (1930). For more typical examples of altruist thinking about economic and social life, see, *e.g.*, A. GORZ, STRATEGY FOR LABOR: A RADICAL PROPOSAL (Nicolaus & Ortiz trans. 1964); Hamilton, *Competition*, in 4 ENCYCLOPEDIA SOC. SCI. 141 (1931); H. GEORGE, PROGRESS AND POVERTY (1879). *See also* M. RICHTER, THE POLITICS OF CONSCIENCE, T.H. GREEN AND HIS AGE 267–91 (1964). On the conservative element in nineteenth century altruism, see Dicey, *supra* note 74, at 220–40; J. RUSKIN, UNTO THIS LAST: FOUR ESSAYS ON THE FIRST PRINCIPLES OF POLITICAL ECONOMY (1862). On the conservative aspects of modern reform, see G. KOLKO, THE TRIUMPH OF CONSERVATISM (1963); J. WEINSTEIN, THE CORPORATE IDEAL IN THE LIBERAL STATE: 1900–1918 (1968); E. HAWLEY, THE NEW DEAL AND THE PROBLEM OF MONOPOLY (1966).

80 *See* the discussions in I. MACNEIL, *supra* note 14, at 68–79; Macneil, *The Many Futures of Contract*, 47 S. CAL. L. REV. 691, 797–800 (1974).

81 *See* Cohen, *The Ethical Basis of Legal Criticism*, 41 YALE L.J. 201 (1931). *See also* E. DURKHEIM, *supra* note 20, at 121–22:

It is customary to distinguish carefully justice from charity; that is, simple respect for the rights of another from every act which goes beyond this purely negative virtue. We see in the two sorts of activity two independent layers of morality: justice, in itself, would only consist of fundamental postulates; charity would be the perfection of justice. The distinction is so radical that, according to partisans of a certain type of morality, justice alone would serve to make the functioning of social life good; generous self-denial would be a private virtue, worthy of pursuit by a particular individual, but dispensable to society. Many even look askance at its intrusion into public life. We can see from what has preceded how little in accord with the facts this conception is. In reality, for men to recognize and mutually guarantee rights, they must, first of all, love each other, they must, for some reason, depend upon each other and on the same society of which they are a part. Justice is full of charity, or, to employ our expressions, negative solidarity is only an emanation from some other solidarity whose nature is positive. It is the repercus-

sion in the sphere of real rights of social sentiments which come from another source. There is nothing specific about it, but it is the necessary accompaniment of every type of solidarity. It is met with forcefully wherever men live a common life, and that comes from the division of social labor or from the attraction of like for like.

82 The master of the social function approach is Max Weber. For an introduction, see Trubek, *Max Weber on Law and the Rise of Capitalism*, 1972 WIS. L. REV. 720; A. GOULDNER, THE COMING CRISIS OF WESTERN SOCIOLOGY 341–70 (1970). An example of the typical modern combination of the social function and class interest ideas is L. FRIEDMAN, A HISTORY OF AMERICAN LAW 14–15 (1973). *See generally* Gordon, *Introduction: J. Willard Hurst and the Common Law Tradition in American Historiography*, 10 LAW & SOC. REV. 9 (1975). The criticism offered in the text following this note is similar to that of E. THOMPSON, WHIGS AND HUNTERS: THE ORIGIN OF THE BLACK ACT 258–69 (1975).

83 See the cases collected in KESSLER & GILMORE, *supra* note 3, at 337–62.

84 Weber himself was forced to recognize this difficulty by the "case of England," which attained a high level of economic development under a legal regime which, as he saw it, was profoundly irrational. *See* 2 M. WEBER, *supra* note 4, at 890–92. *See also* Trubek, *supra* note 82, at 746–48.

85 *See* R. UNGER, *supra* note 4, at 214–16.

86 *See* K. LLEWELLYN, THE COMMON LAW TRADITION: DECIDING APPEALS 521–35 (1960).

87 *See* R. UNGER, *supra* note 73, at 12–16, 106–19; A. GOULDNER, *supra* note 73, at 20–60. For an early nineteenth century attempt to deal with the problem, see Coleridge, *Essays on the Principles of Method*, I THE FRIEND 448–524 (Rooke ed. 1969).

88 For a useful summary, see Christie, *Objectivity in Law*, 78 YALE L.J. 1311, 1312–26 (1969). The most striking recent formulation of the problem is Deutsch, *Neutrality, Legitimacy and the Supreme Court: Some Intersections Between Law and Political Science*, 20 STAN. L. REV. 169 (1968). *See also* Gordon, *supra* note 82.

89 *See* 1 W. BLACKSTONE, COMMENTARIES *38–*61. An English judge could write the following even in 1828: "It has been argued that the law does not compel every line of conduct which humanity or religion may require; but there is no act which Christianity forbids, that

the law will not reach: if it were otherwise, Christianity would not be, as it has always been held to be, part of the law of England." Bird v. Holbrook, 29 Rev. R., 657, 667 (Ct. Com. Pleas 1828).

90 The discussion in this section is a compressed version of a larger work tentatively called *The Rise and Fall of Classical Legal Thought: 1850–1940.* Copies of the completed chapters are on file at the office of the Harvard Law Review.

91 Laidlaw v. Organ, 15 U.S. (2 Wheat.) 178, 193 (1817).

92 *See generally* M. Horwitz, The Transformation of American Law: 1780–1860, ch. 3 (forthcoming in 1977).

93 T. Parsons, The Law of Contracts *767–78 (1855).

94 *See* M. Horwitz, *supra* note 92, ch. 7, § I.

95 *See* J. Hurst, The Legitimacy of the Business Corporation in the Law of the United States: 1780–1970, at 31–32 (1970).

96 *See, e.g.,* Mills v. Wyman, 20 Mass. (3 Pick.) 207 (1825).

97 *Compare* Britton v. Turner, 6 N.H. 481 (1834), *with* Smith v. Brady, 17 N.Y. 173 (1858).

98 2 J. Kent, Commentaries on American Law *391 n.(a), *394 n.(a) (1826).

99 The legal thought of this period is generally referred to as formal or formalist. *See* K. Llewellyn, The Common Law Tradition: Deciding Appeals 38–40 (1960); G. Gilmore, *supra* note 41; Horwitz, *The Rise of Legal Formalism,* 19 Am. J. Leg. Hist, 251 (1975); Nelson, *The Impact of the Antislavery Movement Upon Styles of Judicial Reasoning in Nineteenth Century America,* 87 Harv. L. Rev. 513, 547 (1974).

100 For an illustration, see M. Fuller, Chief Justice of the United States, *Address in Commemoration of the Inauguration of George Washington,* Dec. II, 1889 (G.P.O. 1890).

101 For an illustration, see Ames, *Undisclosed Principal – His Rights and Liabilities,* 18 Yale L.J. 443 (1909).

102 For an illustration, see J. Bradley, *Law, Its Nature and Office as the Bond and Basis of Civil Society,* in Miscellaneous Writings 226–66 (1901).

103 *See* Horwitz, *Historical Foundations of Modern Contract Law,* 87 Harv. L. Rev. 917 (1974).

104 For an illustration, see S. Amos, A Systematic View of the Science of Jurisprudence 85–92, 176–213 (London 1872).

105 For an illustration, see F. Pollock, The Law of Torts 1–15 (1887).

106 The classic illustration is the majority opinion in Coppage v. Kansas, 236 U.S. 1 (1915).

107 For useful treatments of American thought during the period in question, see E. Purcell, The Crisis of Democratic Theory: Scientific Naturalism and the Problem of Value (1973); White, *From Sociological Jurisprudence to Realism: Jurisprudence and Social Change in Twentieth Century America,* 58 Va. L. Rev. 999 (1972).

108 *See* Dewey, *Logical Method and Law,* 10 Cornell L.Q. 17 (1924); Cohen, *Transcendental Nonsense and the Functional Approach,* 35 Colum. L. Rev. 809 (1935); Cohen, *On Absolutisms in Legal Thought,* 84 U. Pa. L. Rev. 681 (1936); R. Unger, *supra* note 73, at 29–144; A. Katz, *supra* note 4.

109 *See* Cohen, *The Basis of Contract,* 46 Harv. L. Rev. 553 (1933); Cohen, *Property and Sovereignty,* 13 Cornell L.Q. 8 (1927); Cohen, *The Ethical Basis of Legal Criticism,* 41 Yale L. J. 201 (1931).

110 *See* Deutsch, *supra* note 88; A. Bickel, *supra* note 69.

111 The general idea of categorizing legal doctrines in the way suggested here owes much to I. Macneil, *supra* note 14; Macaulay, *supra* note 2; Gardner, *An Inquiry into the Principles of the Law of Contracts,* 46 Harv. L. Rev. 1 (1932).

112 *See* R. Nozick, *supra* note 78, at 63–71; Ames, *Law and Morals,* 22 Harv. L. Rev. 97, 106 (1909); Wellington, *supra* note 20, at 229–33.

113 The classic treatment is Dawson, *Economic Duress – An Essay In Perspective,* 45 Mich. L. Rev. 253 (1947).

114 The closest thing we have to such a study is L. Friedman, *supra* note 51.

115 *See* Macaulay, *supra* note 2, at 1067.

116 *See* pp. 1725–27 *supra*; M. Horwitz, *supra* note 92, ch. 3. For a typical application of the theory to the case of Hadley v. Baxendale, 156 Eng. Rep. 145 (1854), see Patterson, *The Apportionment of Business Risks Though Legal Devices,* 24 Colum. L. Rev. 335, 342 (1924); Danzig, *Hadley v. Baxendale: A Study in the Industrialization of the Law,* 4 J. Leg. Stud. 249 (1975).

117 O. Holmes, *supra* note 22, at 77.

118 See the discussion of Holmes' overall position in R. Faulkner, The Jurisprudence of John Marshall 227–68 (1968).

119　O. HOLMES, *Economic Elements*, in COLLECTED LEGAL PAPERS 279–83 (1920).

120　*See generally* the works on laissez-faire cited in note 90 *supra*, and L. ROBBINS, THE THEORY OF ECONOMIC POLICY IN ENGLISH CLASSICAL POLITICAL ECONOMY (1952); W. SAMUELS, THE CLASSICAL THEORY OF POLITICAL ECONOMY (1966); Coppage v. Kansas, 236 U.S. 1 (1915); West Coast Hotel v. Parrish, 300 U.S. 379, 400–14 (1937) (Sutherland, J., dissenting).

121　*See* p. 1732 *supra*.

122　On stare decisis, *see* Dewey, *supra* note 108, and the sources cited in Christie, *supra* note 88, at 1317 n. 27. On nondelegation, *see* Jaffe, *Law Making By Private Groups*, 51 HARV. L. REV. 201 (1937); K. DAVIS, *supra* note 4, ch. 2. On law and fact, *see* H. HART & A. SACKS, *supra* note 1, at 366–85. On objectivism, see Costigan, *Implied-in-Fact Contracts and Mutual Assent*, 33 HARV. L. REV. 376 (1920). *See also* pp. 1700–01 *supra*.

123　The single greatest statement of this position is the first: Marx's theory of the fetishism of commodities. K. MARX, CAPITAL 81–96 (Moore & Aveling transl. 1906). For a modern Marxist statement, *see* Perlman, *The Reproduction of Daily Life* in "ALL WE ARE SAYING . . .," THE PHILOSOPHY OF THE NEW LEFT 133 (Lothstein, ed. 1970). The major works in the American, non-Marxist critique of the Classical theory of economic policy as applied to law are R. ELY, PROPERTY AND CONTRACT IN THEIR RELATIONS TO THE DISTRIBUTION OF WEALTH (1914); J. COMMONS, LEGAL FOUNDATIONS OF CAPITALISM (1924). The clearest statement of the general position is Hale, *Bargaining, Duress and Economic Liberty*, 43 COLUM. L. REV. 603 (1943).

124　The critique of the Classical welfare propositions has two strands. One of these is institutional economics, an American outgrowth of the German rejection of *Classical* economics. On institutionalism, see B. SELIGMAN, MAIN CURRENTS IN MODERN ECONOMICS, PT. 1 (1962) and 3 J. DORFMAN, THE ECONOMIC MIND IN AMERICAN CIVILIZATION, 1865–1918 (1949). The second strand was the neo-classical formalization and positivization of Classical economic theory, which aimed to rob categories like value, equilibrium, competition, efficiency, and the free market of their ethical overtones. Useful discussions will be found in J. SCHUMPETER, HISTORY OF

ECONOMIC ANALYSIS (1954) and E. ROLL, A HISTORY OF ECONOMIC THOUGHT (3d ed. 1954). The starting point for modern discussion is L. ROBBINS, AN ESSAY ON THE NATURE AND SIGNIFICANCE OF ECONOMIC SCIENCE (2d ed. 1935).

125　*See* p. 1700 & note 37 *supra*.

126　*See* Macaulay, *supra* note 2, at 1065–69.

127　*See, e.g.*, Wechsler, *Toward Neutral Principles of Constitutional Law*, 73 HARV. L. REV. 1 (1959); Left, *Unconscionability and the Code—The Emperor's New Clause*, 115 U. PA. L. REV. 485 (1967). The connection between public and private law is made explicitly in Wellington, *supra* note 20, *passim*.

128　On the "rule of law" see A. DICEY, LECTURES INTRODUCTORY TO THE STUDY OF THE LAW OF THE CONSTITUTION 179–201 (8th ed. 1915); F. HAYEK, THE CONSTITUTION OF LIBERTY 162–233 (1960); Kennedy, *supra* note 4.

129　*See* pp. 1748–49 & note 122 *supra*.

130　This was the position of *both* liberals and conservatives in the conflict about the constitutionality of social legislation. *Compare* the dissent of Harlan, J., *with* the majority opinion in Lochner v. New York, 198 U.S. 45, 52–65 (Peckham, J.), 65–74 (Harlan, J., dissenting) (1905).

131　*See* Marbury v. Madison, 5 U.S. (I Cranch) 137 (1803).

132　*See* Hitchman Coal & Coke Co. v. Mitchell, 245 U.S. 229 (1917).

133　*See* Coppage v. Kansas, 236 U.S. 1 (1915).

134　300 U.S. 379, 400–14 (1937).

135　*See, e.g.*, Home Building & Loan Ass'n v. Blaisdell, 290 U.S. 398 (1934).

136　United States v. Carolene Prods., 304 U.S. 144, 152–53 n.4 (1938).

137　*See, e.g.*, O. & M. HANDLIN, COMMONWEALTH – A STUDY OF THE ROLE OF GOVERNMENT IN THE AMERICAN ECONOMY: MASSACHUSETTS, 1774–1861 (rev. ed. 1969).

138　*See* Corwin, *The Doctrine of Due Process of Law Before the Civil War*, 24 HARV. L. REV. 366, 460 (1911).

139　*See* pp. 1731–37 *supra*; R. MCCLOSKEY, THE AMERICAN SUPREME COURT 101–79 (1960).

140　*See* pp. 1745–51 *supra*.

141　*See* Nebbia v. New York, 291 U.S. 502 (1934); Powell, *The Judiciality of Minimum Wage Legislation*, 37 HARV. L. REV. 545 (1924).

142　United States v. Trenton Potteries Co., 273 U.S. 392 (1927) (Stone, J.).

143   *See* pp. 200–1, 216–20 *supra*.

144   *See* Hale, *supra* note 123.

145   *See* Jacob & Youngs, Inc. v. Kent, 230 N.Y. 239, 129, N.E. 889 (1921).

146   *See* International News Serv. v. Associated Press, 248 U.S. 215, 248–67 (1918) (Brandeis, J., dissenting).

147   *See, e.g.,* Roberson v. Rochester Folding Box Co., 171 N.Y. 538, 64 N.E. 442 (1902).

148   R. POSNER, ECONOMIC ANALYSIS OF LAW (1972); G. CALABRESI, THE COSTS OF AC-CIDENTS (1970).

149   *See* Calabresi, *Transaction Costs, Resource Allocation and Liability Rules*, 11 J. LAW & ECON. 67 (1968); Baker, *The Ideology of the Economic Analysis of Law*, 5 PHIL. & PUB. AFF. 3, 32 n.56 (1975).

150   This formulation owes much to a conversation with Tom Heller of the University of Wisconsin Law School. *See generally* Polinsky, *Economic Analysis as a Potentially Defective Product: A Buyer's Guide to Posner's Economic Analysis of Law*, 87 HARV. L. REV. 1655 (1974); Leff, *Economic Analysis of Law: Some Realism About Nominalism*, 60 VA. L. REV. 451 (1974); Baker, *supra* note 149; Mishan, *Pangloss on Pollution*, 73 SWED. J. ECON. 113 (1971).

151   *See* H. HART & A. SACKS, *supra* note 1, at 116–20; Dworkin, *supra* note 4; L. FULLER, THE MORALITY OF LAW (1964); Fuller, *Positivism and Fidelity to Law – A Reply to Professor Hart*, 71 HARV. L. REV. 630 (1958); Hart, *The Supreme Court, 1958 Term, Foreword: The Time Chart of the Justices*, 73 HARV. L. REV. 84 (1959); K. LLEWELLYN, *supra* note 99; P. SELZNICK, *supra* note 4; Wellington, *supra* note 20. For a recent piece of analysis in this mode, see Dawson, *supra* note 6. For criticisms of this approach, see Clark & Trubek, *The Creative Role of the Judge: Restraint and Freedom in the Common Law Tradition*, 71 YALE L.J. 255 (1961); Arnold, *Professor Hart's Theology*, 73 HARV. L. REV. 1298 (1960); Kennedy, *supra* note 4, at 395–98.

152   *See* Arnold, *supra* note 151; Clark & Trubek, *supra* note 151; Hart, *Positivism and the Separation of Law and Morals*, 71 HARV. L. REV. 593 (1958); Nagel, *Fact, Value and Human Purpose*, 4 NATURAL LAW FORUM 26 (1959).

153   On the methodological problem, see p. 229 & note 87 *supra*.

154   *See* K. MARX, *supra* note 73; R. UNGER, *supra* note 73; A. KATZ, *supra* note 4 for analysis of a similar kind.

155   For a similar conception, see E. DURKHEIM, *supra* note 20, at 115–32.

156   On this basis alone it may be easy to show that *A*'s statement of his experience of values is self-contradictory, and this may cause *A* such discomfort that he will actually undertake to rectify the orderliness of his values. *B*'s conduct still resolves itself into (a) rational, objective discourse about facts (showing *A*'s self-contradiction) and (b) a-rational, subjective exhortation about values (urging *A* to attain consistency on the ground that consistency is "good").

157   *See* K. MARX, *Economic and Philosophical Manuscripts* (1844), in EARLY WORKS 322–34, 345–58 (Benton trans. 1975); S. AVINERI, THE SOCIAL AND POLITICAL THOUGHT OF KARL MARX 65–95 (1968); E. DURKHEIM, *supra* note 20 at 193–99. For a recent attempt to develop similar notions in the context of American constitutional law, *see* Tribe, *supra* note 54, at 310–14.

158   Of course there must be a selection among "all the circumstances," or the judge would never get beyond the collection of his facts. And of course the selection is intimately guided by *criteria* (or concepts) of some kind. And of course those criteria in turn are closely linked to the criteria of justice to be applied (why gather facts irrelevant to the issue at hand). But it does *not* follow that because we can select *a mass* of relevant facts from among the larger mass available, we can determine how *particular* facts, capable of founding per se rules, will define the circumstances of justice in the future. I am here asserting the existence of a grey area, a slippage, a no-man's land, between two quite clearly defined aspects of the situation. Yes, it *is* true that there are criteria of justice well enough defined to orient the search for relevant facts. No, it is *not* true that these are now or seem to have any tendency to become the kind of criteria that constitute a formal system. The world is intelligible, *but not intelligible enough*.

159   *See* Hay, *supra* note 29.

160   *See, e.g.,* Williams v. Walker-Thomas Furniture Co., 350 F.2d 445 (D.C. Cir. 1965).

11

Legal
Indeterminacy

Ken Kress

> Our discussion will be adequate if it has as much clearness as the subject matter admits of, for precision is not to be sought for alike in all discussions . . .
>
> *Aristotle*[1]

> The practical reason is concerned with practical matters, which are singular and contingent: but not with necessary things, with which speculative reason is concerned. Wherefore human laws cannot have that inerrancy that belongs to the demonstrated conclusions of sciences.
>
> *Aquinas*[2]

Critical legal scholars, building on the work of legal realists, have developed an extensive array of arguments concluding that law is radically indeterminate, incoherent, and contradictory. Law is indeterminate to the extent that legal questions lack single right answers. In adjudication, law is indeterminate to the extent that authoritive legal materials and methods permit multiple outcomes to lawsuits. If arguments for radical indeterminacy are valid, they may raise serious doubts about the possibility of legitimate, nonarbitrary legal systems and adjudicative procedures.

In this Article, I defend the claim that the indeterminacy of the law is no more than moderate and reject critical legal scholars' arguments for radical indeterminacy. In addition, I argue that indeterminacy is a much less serious defect in the law than it is often thought to be. In particular, I maintain that moderate indeterminacy does not undermine the law's legitimacy.

My main argument contains two major strands. Part I argues that moderate indeterminacy, even if true, has at most modest and not devastating consequences for political legit-imacy and kindred concepts, contrary to the conclusions of Kennedy, Singer, and other critical legal scholars. Part II urges that critical legal scholars' arguments for radical indeterminacy fail, and that indeterminacy is at most moderate.

The argument in Part II that there is at most moderate indeterminacy proceeds in stages. Section A employs the pervasiveness of easy cases to challenge the alleged existence of radical indeterminacy and support the claim that indeterminacy is at most moderate. The burden of proof then shifts to advocates of radical indeterminacy to rebut this claim. Section B examines legal realists' arguments for indeterminacy from precedent, and critical legal scholars' arguments for indeterminacy from ideological struggle and internal contradictory attitudes. Section C looks specifically at four allegedly contradictory dichotomies. Section D describes three mistaken assumptions about legal reasoning that critical scholars make in their arguments for indeterminacy. These mistaken assumptions substantially exaggerate critical legal scholars' assessment of the extent of legal indeterminacy. After consideration of the various arguments for indeterminacy, Part II concludes that critical legal scholars have failed to prove that indeterminacy is radical, and that to the extent that indeterminacy exists, it is moderate.

Before proceeding with the argument, I want to exclude from consideration two ways in which critical legal scholars deploy the indeterminacy thesis.[3] First, some critical legal scholars treat the indeterminacy thesis solely as instrumental to their political agenda. Critical legal scholars note that judicial opinions and legal briefs are frequently written as though the law "necessitated"[4] the outcome. Critical legal scholars believe that the use of this rhetoric creates a false social consciousness which unduly restricts imaginative thought and solutions to legal problems. These scholars employ the indeterminacy thesis to unfreeze this false sense of necessity, allowing consideration of alternative forms of social life more congenial to their political vision.[5] Second, the indeterminacy thesis is sometimes intended simply as an attack ("immanent critique") on popular culture and not as an attempt to describe accurately the underlying phenomena.[6]

Neither of these uses of the indeterminacy thesis has substantial consequences for the *actual*, as opposed to the *perceived*, legitimacy of the state, and each is therefore foreign to my main purpose here. This Article challenges the truth of the indeterminacy thesis, and thus, such instrumental functions are irrelevant to my inquiries.

I   Indeterminacy and Legitimacy

With these considerations set aside, we can ask "Why do and should we care about indeterminacy?" Indeterminacy matters because legitimacy matters. Many legal scholars hold that the legitimacy of judicial decisionmaking depends upon judges applying the law and not creating their own. They claim that judicial decisions are legitimate only if judges are constrained either completely or within narrow bounds.[7] The term "legitimate" is used here as it is used in classical political philosophy: If a judicial decision is legitimate, it provides a prima facie moral obligation for citizens to obey the decision.[8] This use of "legitimate"

should be sharply differentiated from the sociological, Weberian notion of legitimation, or perceived legitimacy. The sociological notion of legitimation asks a causal question about how the legal system induces belief in its authority and compliance with its laws.[9]

The claim that courts' legitimacy requires constraining the judiciary is not limited to legal academics. The debate about judicial activism within the nonlegal academy, the political community, and popular culture[10] rests upon a similar presupposition that a judicial decision is legitimate if it accurately applies the law, but it is open to question, if not downright immoral, if it reflects nonlegal factors such as the judge's personal preferences or political ideology. The indeterminacy thesis asserts that law does not constrain judges sufficiently, raising the specter that judicial decisionmaking is often or always illegitimate.

I do not claim that the *only* reason indeterminacy matters is its consequences for legitimacy. But the consequences for legitimacy are prima facie the main reason why legal scholars do and should care about indeterminacy. Few are interested in indeterminacy purely as a metaphysical or epistemological issue. If critical legal scholars could show that the legal system is indeterminate and therefore illegitimate, they would have a powerful critique. Liberal[11] theorists would be obligated to acknowledge that critique and revise their theories to accommodate it, or if that is not possible, to relinquish belief in conventional theories of law and justice.[12]

Many critical legal scholars do urge that law is illegitimate because it is indeterminate. Joseph Singer claims that liberal legal theory requires substantial determinacy to satisfy the requirements of the rule of law.[13] Determinacy is desirable because it restrains "arbitrary judicial power."[14] Although complete determinacy it attainable in a legal system (Singer considers the rule: The plaintiff always loses), any completely determinate system would fail to be "just or legitimate" because it would insufficiently protect "security, privacy, reputation, freedom of movement" and other competing values.[15] On Singer's reading, liberal legal theory therefore attempts to provide the right mix of determinacy and indeterminacy. But, Singer argues, no existing legal system or legal theory provides anywhere near the amount of determinacy that is required:

> Legal doctrine is far more indeterminate than traditional theorists realize it is. If traditional legal theorists are correct about the importance of determinacy to the rule of law, then – by their own criteria – the rule of law has never existed anywhere. This is the real bite of the critique.[16]

In an especially clear discussion of indeterminacy, Andrew Altman argues that the indeterminacy which flows from inconsistencies that reflect ideological struggle among lawmakers demonstrates that Dworkin's legal philosophy fails to legitimate judicial decisionmaking because it fails to put practical constraints upon judges.[17] Perhaps Duncan Kennedy, in his first published attack upon liberal legal theory, best described the connection between indeterminacy and legitimacy inherent in critical legal theory:

> My . . . purpose in this essay is to clarify that version of the liberal theory of justice which asserts that justice consists in the impartial application of rules deriving their legitimacy from the prior consent of those subject to them . . . [and] to contribute to the critique of [that theory]. . . . My argument is that a distinction between rule making and rule applying cannot be made to legitimate the coercive power of judges. . . . [T]his version of liberal thought has been unsuccessful in the attempt to use a theory of rules to transfer the postulated legitimacy of decision based on consent to the judicial administrators of a body of legal rules.[18]

The core connection between indeterminacy and legitimacy explicit or implicit in this critical legal scholarship can be understood as follows. Critical scholars assume (either for purposes of internal critique or without reflection) that legislative enactments are legitimated by consent.[19] Insofar as judges are merely applying rules created by the legislature, their actions are legitimate and enforcement of their decisions is justified. On some accounts, judges enjoy a carefully limited discretion to "legislate interstitially" to smooth out the rough edges in statutes and to correct minor legislative oversights.[20] Thus, judges may legitimately legislate in what H. L. A. Hart calls the "penumbra of uncertainty."[21] According to Hart, the penumbra of uncertainty derives from the vagueness and open texture of the language of enactments.[22] But any more extensive lawmaking by the judiciary would be a usurpation of the authority of the people's representatives.

Radical versions of indeterminacy threaten this formalistic model by claiming that there are very few or no clear cases where law is strictly applied. The penumbra of uncertain cases swallows up the core of formalistic rule application. Every case of adjudication requires judicial legislation. In consequence, adjudication is illegitimate.

But the problem with this argument is twofold. First, the assumption that consent legitimates the state is dubious, because almost no one actually or tacitly consents to the state except perhaps immigrants or foreign visitors. Second, and more importantly, the argument implicitly assumes that the *only* way judicial decisions could be legitimate is if they rigidly follow ("strictly interpret or construe") statutory or constitutional provisions, themselves legitimated by consent. This implicit assumption – indeed, fixation – of many legal scholars is a serious mistake.[23] I cannot overemphasize how much mischief has been caused by this failure to acknowledge the possibility of other ways of legitimating adjudication. The existence of other ways of legitimating adjudication is as telling against conventional scholars who advocate strict construction or neutral principles as it is against critical scholars who employ the conventional framework for legitimating judicial review in the service of more radical ends. Thus, the argument which follows, if successful, has broad implications extending beyond the critique of critical legal studies scholarship.

I will clarify my objections to the argument that the pervasiveness of judicial legislation entails that adjudication is illegitimate by analyzing the logical structure of the assumptions and claims of both liberal legal theory (as articulated by critical legal scholarship) and the critical legal response. For simplicity of exposition I restrict the analysis to statutory law.

Critical scholarship reads liberal legal theory to assert:[24]

(1) Citizens have consented to rules duly enacted by the legislature and are therefore obligated to obey them.
(2) When judges apply legislative rules (or, in some versions, interstitially legislate) citizens are obligated to obey those decisions in consequence of (1).
(3) All judicial decisions are applications of duly enacted statutes (or interstitial legislation thereof).
(4) Therefore, citizens are obligated to obey judicial decisions.

Critical legal scholars accept arguendo (1) and (2), but urge that the indeterminacy thesis shows (3) to be false. Thus, they urge that (4) has not been demonstrated.[25] But note that the order of these premises is not arbitrary. Each premise's relevance depends upon the truth of the prior premise. It is because (1) proclaims the legitimacy of legislative rules that (2), the claim that adjudication is legitimate when the judge applies legislative rules, is plausible. The logical form of (2) "if judges apply rules, then judicial decisions are legitimate" makes its antecedent, (3) "judges always apply rules," relevant to legitimacy. And it is because (3) is relevant to legitimacy that the critical legal scholars' denial of (3), in consequence of the indeterminacy thesis, is relevant to legitimacy.

But because (1) is false, and patently so,[26] (2) is irrelevant. In consequence, (3) also is irrelevant, as is the critical scholars' denial of (3). Indeterminacy *may* be a red herring.

I took care to not yet claim that indeterminacy is a red herring, that it is irrelevant to legitimacy. This is because, as should have been obvious, there are many potential grounds for legitimizing judicial decisionmaking, and those grounds may turn out to be affected by the truth of the indeterminacy thesis. Although the above argument from consent fails, that does not end the matter. Some other potential ground for legitimacy may succeed. Thus, contrary to the desires of many critical legal

scholars and strict constructionists, indeterminacy, even if true, does not, for all we have seen so far, entail that adjudication is illegitimate. At most, indeterminacy shows that one route to legitimacy has been blocked. We must still examine the other routes. For the same reason, the rejection of consent as legitimating the legislature does not show that indeterminacy is irrelevant to legitimacy. It merely shows that one argument connecting the two fails. To ascertain whether indeterminacy is relevant to legitimacy, we must consider each of the potential grounds for legitimacy that liberal theory invokes, and see if indeterminacy of the law is relevant, or decisive, to any such ground.

On what basis does liberal theory claim that political decisionmaking is legitimate? It is now a commonplace assertion of liberal political theory that not one of the most prominent and plausible grounds of political obligation alone is sufficient to establish a general obligation to obey the law.[27] Not consent, tacit consent, fair play, the duty to uphold just institutions, legitimate authority, fraternity, utility, nor gratitude succeeds, by itself, in generating political obligations applicable to all or most citizens. While no potential ground of legitimacy succeeds in establishing a general obligation for *all* citizens to obey the law, some grounds may nonetheless, under certain circumstances, obligate some citizens to obey some, or all, laws.

For example, consent does not create a general obligation for all citizens to obey law because most citizens have not consented to the state. But some naturalized citizens may have consented to the state, and government officials may have agreed to follow the law in their official capacities. Thus, consent may obligate some citizens to obey all laws and others to obey some or all laws in their official capacities. Similarly, the other theories of political obligation, such as the principle of fair play, may be seen to generate grounds which, under particular circumstances, obligate some citizens to obey some or all laws. Thus, the situations where there are obligations to obey, and the range of laws which are obligatory, may vary among citizens, depending upon which, if any, grounds apply to each citizen. For some, there may be no obligation to obey, or only obligations over limited areas.

Summing the obligations arising from each of the particular grounds yields the full scope of citizens' obligations to obey law. This is the new orthodoxy.[28] Indeterminacy will be relevant to legitimacy only to the extent of the sum of its relevance to each of these particular grounds of obligation. If indeterminacy turns out to have little relevance to each ground on an individual basis then its overall relevance will be modest at best.

My argument proceeds as follows: There is no general moral obligation to obey the law just because it is the law. But there may be particular local and context-dependent grounds that obligate particular individuals over some portion, or over the entirety of the law. For nearly every such alleged ground, with only occasional exceptions, either (1) the ground fails to generate a true moral obligation to obey, or if it does obligate, then (2) it obligates even where the law is indeterminate.[29]

Consider, for example, consent. Since most citizens have not freely consented to the state (perhaps some naturalized citizens are the exception), consent does not generate a general obligation for all citizens to obey the law.[30] Moreover, for those who have consented, the scope and content of the obligation will depend upon the particulars of the act that constitutes undertaking a voluntary, deliberate obligation to obey. Did they consent to obey all judicial decisions? Or only those decisions that are grounded in determinate authoritative sources? It is thus in part an empirical matter how often indeterminacy is relevant to consent-generated legitimacy. Thus, although it is possible that some might consent to government only if law is not too indeterminate, or only over the range where law is determinate, it seems unlikely that this is frequently the case. Most who consent will have consented to the government or some institution in toto, indeterminacy (if any) and all.

Tacit consent arguments fare no better. The most common version of tacit consent as a general ground of obligation is residence. Rousseau, for example, contends: "After the State is instituted, residence implies consent: To inhabit the territory is to submit to the sovereign."[31] But residence cannot constitute tacit consent to government because it is unreasonable to suppose that resident revolutionaries, anarchists, and outlaws consent to a government which they actively oppose.[32] Moreover, as Hume argues, the costs of emigration vitiate the voluntariness of a decision not to emigrate:

> Can we seriously say, that a poor peasant or artizan has a free choice to leave his country, when he knows no foreign language or manners, and lives from day to day, by the small wages which he acquires? We may as well assert, that a man, by remaining in a vessel, freely consents to the dominion of the master; though he was carried on board while asleep, and must leap into the ocean, and perish, the moment he leaves her.[33]

Perhaps a foreign visitor tacitly consents to the state's laws when his passport is stamped upon entering the jurisdiction. But even if that is so, would not that tacit consent extend to areas where the law is indeterminate?

Indeterminacy is even less likely to be relevant to obligations stemming from the principle of fair play than it is to be relevant to obligations based on consent or tacit consent. Speaking very roughly, the principle of fair play holds that those who voluntarily accept the benefits of a scheme of social cooperation must accept the burdens of that scheme.[34] This ground of political obligation differs from consent in that one need not voluntarily commit to undertake the burdens of the scheme to be obligated; one need only voluntarily accept the benefits. (Indeed, this is its advantage over consent as a ground of political obligation.) Thus, the scope of the obligation depends not on the content of some voluntary undertaking by the citizen, but rather upon the terms of the scheme of social cooperation. The scheme can (though it need not) obligate a participant to the outcome of an adjudicatory process even if the outcome is indeterminate, provided that the outcome is not excessively unjust. Indeed, as part of the overall cooperative scheme, individuals accepting a fair share of governmental benefits may well be obligated to comply with unfavorable outcomes of both determinate and indeterminate adjudicatory processes.

The relevance of the duty to uphold just institutions to indeterminacy and legitimacy requires more extended discussion.[35] The standard criticism of the duty to uphold just institutions is that it fails to capture the intimate nature of a citizen's obligation to his country;[36] it cannot explain, for example, why Americans have a special duty to the United States government that they do not have to other equally just governments. Thus, it could be argued that the duty to uphold just institutions, even if it exists, does not explain political obligation.

This conclusion, however, is premature. The argument only shows that current expositions of the duty to uphold just institutions are incomplete. It is not implausible to suppose that one has a duty to uphold all just institutions, but that what that duty requires may be highly context-dependent. Thus, assuming that the British, French, and American governments are just, an American's duty to uphold just institutions may require only that she not hinder the just actions of the French government. Yet her obligations to Britain, which she frequently visits, may be far greater, and might include obeying British law while visiting, but would not extend to supporting or fighting in its armed forces. Certainly, her obligations to her country of citizenship would be greater still. That she has little opportunity to uphold French institutions, modest opportunities to aid British institutions, and frequent opportunities to aid British institutions, and frequent opportunities to support American institutions does not explain these varying obligations.[37] After all, she could as easily send a check to the French government as to the Internal Revenue Service, and if she can travel to Britain, surely France is within her means. So advocates of the duty to uphold just institutions still owe us an explanation for why what the duty requires varies in the ways we have just seen. If that explanation is sound and does not smuggle in some other ground of political obligation, the traditional objection will be tamed. Hence, rejection of the duty as a ground of political obligation is premature.

We must therefore ask whether indeterminacy is relevant to obligation under the duty to support just institutions. Critical legal scholars will undoubtedly argue that an institution plagued by indeterminacy is less just and therefore less legitimate than a determinate one, all

else being equal. This is so, they argue, because in practice indeterminacy is a cloak for partial and arbitrary actions in the interest of the ruling elite. But then it is the partiality and arbitrariness of the institution, and not its indeterminacy, that makes it unjust. Moreover, it is arguable that justice not only permits, but indeed requires moderate indeterminacy. Although justice demands that most things be settled in advance, there must be room for flexibility in marginal and exceptional cases in order that equity be done.

Under Raz's normal justification thesis for legitimate authority, an authority is legitimate for an individual over a particular subject matter if (among other conditions) the individual is more likely to do the act required by the reasons that apply to him if he attempts to follow the directives of the authority than if he makes his own independent calculation of what right reason requires.[38] Where indeterminacy prevails, courts, owing to their impartiality, training, and experience, are especially likely to be better guides to what right reason requires than citizens who have only untutored judgments to guide them. Under the normal justification thesis, far from delegitimating courts, indeterminacy may well enhance courts' legitimacy and citizens' obligations to obey.

It must be conceded, however, that for a small class of individuals in certain areas, indeterminacy may be relevant to courts' authority over them. Indeterminacy will delegitimate courts' authority respecting particular areas for those individuals who are better than courts at calculating what reason requires where legal reasoning is indeterminate yet worse than courts where legal reasoning is determinate.

Moderate indeterminacy is no bar to legitimacy under Dworkin's recent revival of the ideal of fraternity or associational obligation.[39] Rather, it is the occasion for dialogue, and necessary for the flourishing of the interpretive attitude which plays a central role in his political and legal theory.[40] Indeterminacy would bar legitimacy for Dworkin only if it reflected a substantial breakdown in community that ensured that dialogue about the best interpretation of our legal practices could not succeed.

Utilitarianism is in such disrepute these days that one might be excused from discussing utilitarian grounds for legitimacy. Although I am sympathetic to many of the standard objections to utilitarian thinking, it would nevertheless be a mistake not to consider utilitarian grounds for legitimacy. For under some utilitarian and coordination of behavior arguments, indeterminacy may well be relevant to legitimacy. Bentham, for example, thought that the purpose of law was to settle people's expectations. If a government failed in this task, it would, for Bentham, lack legitimacy.[41] Yet even here complete determinacy and predictability must be weighed against the need for flexibility. Flexibility is needed to permit experimentation with and investigation of alternative normative structures, to assure fairness, and to promote other substantive values in situations not anticipated or fully appreciated in advance. Additionally, the inefficiency of indeterminacy can be mitigated insofar as areas of indeterminacy can be identified. We may be certain that here the law is uncertain.

Moreover, even if law were fully determinate and predictable, public expectations would not be perfectly settled, because public knowledge would not reflect that determinacy. Even attorneys would be likely to give mistaken advice on occasion. It is possible, therefore, that moderate indeterminacy will have only minimal consequences for public expectations, and that minimal loss in settled expectations will be outweighed in a utilitarian calculus by the substantive values the indeterminacy promotes. Thus, as I concluded in my discussion of the duty to uphold just institutions, indeterminacy that cloaks unjust and arbitrary decisions undercuts legitimacy, but indeterminacy that promotes the doing of equity enhances legitimacy.[42]

The duty of gratitude may be dealt with summarily. The duty of gratitude is insufficient on its own to generate political obligations, although it may enhance the force of other potential grounds of obligation.[43]

In summary, indeterminacy appears to have limited relevance to legitimacy because only infrequently does any valid ground of obligation require determinacy to succeed. For each potential ground of political obligation, either the specified ground fails to obligate, or if it does obligate where law is determinate, it also obligates (with respect to judicial decisions) where law is indeterminate. In essence, determinacy is neither necessary nor sufficient for legitimacy at the global level, and only rarely necessary or sufficient at the local or individual level.

Much more than these primitive thoughts must be ventured before it can be conclusively concluded that indeterminacy is in fact largely irrelevant to legitimacy. But suppose that large claim could be defended. Where would we be? Critical legal scholarship often aims at exposing liberal reform as at best a palliative for patriarchal, hegemonic, and oppressive social structures. Radical surgery is required if we are to have even a hope of achieving a moderately just and egalitarian society. The indeterminacy thesis plays a crucial role in the critique of the rule of law and liberal claims of the legitimacy of adjudication and the legitimacy of the law. But, if one may critique the critics, their attack on judicial decisionmaking itself appears superficial, the removal of a minor and perhaps irrelevant blemish on a liberal doctrine with a decayed foundation. Insofar as critical legal scholarship accepts the postulate that the state is legitimated by the consent of the governed, it fails to go for the jugular and enfeebles its critique. In this way, it is insufficiently radical. It should regroup and address the legitimacy of the state and of adjudication at its foundation.

II Moderate Indeterminacy

Assuming the argument that moderate indeterminacy presents only minimal legitimacy problems succeeds, my argument that indeterminacy has not undermined legitimacy is still incomplete until I have shown that at most only moderate indeterminacy exists. My argument that indeterminacy is at most moderate proceeds in stages. Section A advances the pervasiveness of easy cases as strong support for the thesis that at most there is moderate indeterminacy and shifts the burden of proof to advocates of radical indeterminacy to demonstrate law's radical, and not merely moderate, indeterminacy.

But advocates of radical indeterminacy fail to carry this burden. Section B considers traditional arguments for indeterminacy from the doctrine of precedent and concludes that they do not establish the existence of radical indeterminacy. Section C considers critical legal scholars' arguments that law and conventional legal theory contain pervasive contradictory principles which give rise to radical indeterminacy. Two explanations for pervasive inconsistency – the patchwork quilt argument and the fundamental contradiction argument – are examined and found wanting. The patchwork quilt argument assumes that the forces and motivations which produce law become law, contrary to plausible holistic positivist and natural law theories. Because critical legal scholars fail to refute these theories, the patchwork quilt argument is unpersuasive. The fundamental contradiction argument supposes that psychological conflict gives rise to doctrinal inconsistency. Yet the theory neither convincingly establishes the connection between psychology and doctrine, nor sets forth why the conflict gives rise to contradiction rather than reconcilable tension.

Section C also considers four allegedly contradictory structures believed to inhere in conventional legal doctrine and theory: rules vs. standards; altruism vs. individualism; objectivism vs. subjectivism; and free will vs. determinism. I conclude that each of these alleged contradictions either reflects only tension or uncertainty, not contradiction, or else is set up only to attack a straw position.

Section D shifts gears and argues that critical scholars' arguments for indeterminacy make three mistaken assumptions about legal reasoning. Critical legal scholars unnecessarily impoverish the premises available to judges. They also incorrectly limit the inferential techniques that judges may deploy. Finally, critical scholars assume that conflict between standards leads to indeterminacy unless there are explicit metaprinciples, stated in advance, to resolve the conflict. Each of these mistakes leads critical legal scholars to exaggerate the indeterminacy in adjudication.

A.   Easy Cases

The pervasiveness of easy cases undercuts critical scholars' claim of radical indeterminacy. Preoccupation with controversial appellate and Supreme Court cases engenders the illusion of pervasive indeterminacy. Focusing instead on everyday acts governed by law reveals the pervasiveness of determinate and correct legal outcomes. For instance, in writing the first paragraph of this Article, I did not commit assault and battery on George Bush. Nor did I slander Gore Vidal.[44] If I drove eighty miles per hour on the way home from work, however, I clearly would have violated laws prohibiting speeding.

Think of the tens, if not hundreds, of actions you perform everyday. You shut off the alarm clock, arise from bed, walk to the bathroom, brush your teeth, shower, dress, make coffee, prepare breakfast, eat breakfast, wash the dishes, put on a warm coat, exit your house, lock the front door, walk to work, enter your place of business, unlock your office door, enter your office, take off your coat, hang it up, sit down at your desk, open your mail. The overwhelming majority of individuals' actions give rise to determinate legal consequences.

I will not belabor this argument as it has been developed at great length by others.[45] The pervasiveness of easy cases with determinate legal consequences generates near certainty that the amount of indeterminacy which exists is not radical but at most moderate. The burden is therefore on advocates of radical indeterminacy to overcome the implausibility of their thesis. The remainder of this Article argues that this burden has not been met.[46]

B.   Indeterminacy and Precedent

Perhaps the most famous argument for indeterminacy is Llewellyn's argument in *The Bramble Bush* (and elsewhere) that the common law is indeterminate because there are two different, contradictory doctrines of precedent, each of which is available to the judge.[47] Llewellyn claims that our legal system countenances both a strict and a loose doctrine of precedent.[48] In its most extreme version, the loose view of precedent accepts as law any language found in past opinions. It is "loose" because it cuts judicial language loose from the facts of the case that spawned it, and thus legitimizes even the most outrageous dicta.[49] It is loose also because it accepts so much language as legally authoritative. More moderate versions of the loose view may accept as authoritative not all judicial language, but only those "points on which [the court] chose to rest a case, or on which it chose, after due argument, to pass."[50] Regardless of the version, the loose view of precedent is a technique for capitalizing on welcome precedents.[51]

By contrast, the strict, or orthodox, view of precedent is used to whittle away or eliminate unwelcome precedents. It is the technique of distinguishing cases.[52] Instead of embracing all language in the opinion as legitimate, it employs a strict version of the doctrine of obiter dicta as a weapon to minimize the scope of judicial pronouncements.[53] This strict doctrine of dicta maintains that the judge has authority to pronounce only on issues that are properly raised by the particular facts of the case before her. Any rationale or rule in an opinion not strictly necessary to reach the judgment is considered excess verbiage, mere obiter dictum, and not binding on later courts.[54] Carried to the extreme, this strict view of precedent limits the rule's applicability to only the precise facts of the decided case.

This orthodox view of precedent can be stated formally. Assuming that judicially created rules of law can be formulated as "If A and B, then Z," where A and B are facts and Z is a legal consequence, Llewellyn's strict theory of precedent is a technique for generating ever narrower rules of law as follows.

1. Start with the rule of the case as stated in the opinion.[55]
2. Suppose it has the form "if A, then Z." Then for each fact B,[56] true of the decided case, the court's failure to limit the scope of its opinion to that fact constitutes an overreaching of its authority. Thus, the proper rule should be "if A and B, then Z."

3. By successive iterations of this technique, the rule can be narrowed until it has the form "if A and B and C and D and ..., then Z," where A, B, C, D, ... are facts whose conjunction is uniquely true of the decided case and holds of no other factual situation. This is confining a case strictly to its facts.
4. Without confining a case to its facts, a clever advocate can nonetheless always distinguish an unwelcome precedent by finding a particular fact F true of the decided case yet false of his client's situation, thus making the unwelcome rule inapplicable to his client's case. "If A, then Z" yields the legal consequence Z (assuming A is true). But, by hypothesis, F is false of the client's case and therefore the revised rule "if A and F, then Z" is inapplicable and does not result in Z in the client's situation.

In this way, Llewellyn argues that in each factual situation, a judge, by invoking the loose and the strict doctrines of precedent, can interpret any relevant precedent in at least two differing ways ("if A, then Z" and "if A and F, then Z"), one of which recommends a particular outcome and the other of which does not. This result is sometimes described as a consequence of the problem of determining the appropriate level of generality of the ratio decidendi.[57]

Interestingly, Llewellyn actually understates the apparent power of precedential techniques to generate inconsistent rules and outcomes. Perhaps because he concentrates on individual precedents rather than lines of precedent, Llewellyn fails to note the powerful precedential technique of reconstruction. This technique permits an entirely novel statement of the rule or rationale of a line of precedents on the condition that the new rule justifies the outcomes in all of the precedent cases. Various versions of this technique have been championed by Justice Cardozo, Felix Cohen, Edward Levi, and Ronald Dworkin.[58] This reconstructive doctrine of precedent enriches Llewellyn's argument. It substantially increases the potential for contradiction since it generates many more possible rules than are allowed under the orthodox, strict doctrine of precedent. These potential interpretations include some which exceed the scope of application of the ratio decidendi stated in the opinion. Indeed, the orthodox theory is a special case of the reconstructive technique, since the orthodox method ensures that each rule generated coincides in outcome with the prior case or line of cases.[59] This is because the orthodox doctrine allows the addition of a fact F to the antecedent of the rule "if A, then Z" yielding if "A and F, then Z" only when F is true in the factual settings of each of the precedent cases which state the original rule "if A, then Z". Thus, any rule generated by the orthodox theory could also be generated by the reconstructive technique. But the converse is not true. The reconstructive technique can generate rules that do not follow from the orthodox technique.

Discussion of the reconstructive technique might be thought to be overkill because the contradictions emanating from Llewellyn's loose and strict doctrines of precedent are enough to demonstrate pervasive indeterminacy. This objection is premature. It is engendered by the uncritical reception I have so far afforded Llewellyn's orthodox and loose techniques. Even Llewellyn has acknowledged that not every rule or ratio decidendi generated by the orthodox and loose techniques is defensible.[60] This is especially true of the orthodox technique.

For example, Llewellyn states that the strict doctrine can be used in an extreme application to restrict a rule to "redheaded Walpoles in pale magenta Buick cars."[61] Yet it is clear, and no doubt Llewellyn would agree, that distinguishing a precedent in this way when your client happily is not a redhead or else prefers green Pontiacs should not persuade a judge. This is because most of us consider hair color and preference in automobiles irrelevant to the application of any legal rule (except under very bizarre circumstances). Thus, the precedential techniques must be restricted to ensure that only relevant facts appear in the rules they generate or that the rules are defensible or justified.[62] In effect, a theory of which facts are relevant would be a theory of common law adjudication. It will generate amended strict and loose doctrines of precedent which may not lead to contradictory rules for every factual situation. Thus, the reconstructive technique might be

thought necessary to sustain the claim of pervasive inconsistency.

But it is unclear that the reconstructive technique, properly construed, will lead to pervasive inconsistency. Notice that the reconstructive technique can lead to legal categories that are every bit as arbitrary as those that result from application of the strict, or orthodox, doctrine of precedent. This must be so because the reconstructive technique is a generalization of the orthodox doctrine. As noted earlier, every rule or ratio decidendi that can be generated by the orthodox theory is also a consequence of the reconstructive technique. It follows that not every output of the reconstructive technique is defensible. Thus, the reconstructive technique must also be restricted to relevant or morally justifiable legal categories.

For example, Dworkin's version of the reconstructive technique chooses from among all those rules that coincide in outcome with most prior precedents the one that is preferred on moral grounds.[63] So construed, the reconstructive technique will lead to indeterminacy only when there are contradictory legal standards that fit most precedents and tie as morally best. Given a dense and discriminating moral metric, such ties will be sufficiently "rare as to be exotic."[64] On this interpretation, the reconstructive technique will lead to little, if any, indeterminacy.[65] It will fall far short of generating radical indeterminacy. In the absence of a convincing refutation of this interpretation of the reconstructive technique, or of a plausible interpretation of the technique that leads to radical indeterminacy, realist and reconstructive arguments from precedent do not demonstrate the existence of radical indeterminacy.[66]

C. Critical Legal Scholars and Radical Indeterminacy

Critical legal scholars accept many realist arguments for indeterminacy. They also greatly enrich the theoretical grounds for indeterminacy, arguing that there are deeper and more pervasive forms of indeterminacy than the realists recognized. Many critical legal scholars claim that the law is radically and pervasively incoherent and contradictory.[67]

Critical legal scholars maintain that each area of law embodies conflicting principles and counterprinciples that cannot be reconciled, balanced, or harmonized.[68] Nor can the applications of these principles and counterprinciples be confined by metaprinciples to mutually exclusive spheres of social activity.[69] The principles and counterprinciples are manifestations of broader social visions or "prescriptive conceptions of society" which are themselves inconsistent.[70] Some critical legal scholarship claims that unresolvable conflicts arise in every or nearly every case.[71] More moderate positions make less extreme claims. According to one such position, there are matched stereotyped pairs of pro and con arguments resulting in "opposing positions seem[ing] to cancel each other out. Yet this is not *always* the case in practice."[72] In some factual situations, one side appears more plausible than the other.[73] There are, however, no available metaprinciples that explain why the apparently more plausible side is preferable and frequently it turns out not to be preferable.[74]

Two major explanations have been advanced by critical legal scholars for the existence of pervasive conflicting principles: the patchwork quilt argument and the fundamental contradiction argument.[75]

1. Patchwork Quilt Argument

Doctrinal materials, critical legal scholars urge, are the contingent and unstable compromise of ideological struggle among competing social groups and visions.[76] Since this compromise allegedly corrupts, impairs, adjusts, and pollutes the inherent rationality and coherence of these various social visions, it would be surprising if those doctrinal materials embodied a coherent rationality or an intelligible social vision.[77] Thus, Unger states:

> It would be strange if the results of a coherent, richly developed normative theory were to coincide with a major portion of any extended branch of law. The many conflicts of interest and vision that lawmaking involves, fought out by countless minds and wills working at cross-purposes, would have to be the vehicle of an immanent moral

rationality whose message could be articulated by a single cohesive theory.[78]

Unger adds that it would be a "miracle" for there to be a "preestablished harmony between the content of the laws and the teachings of a coherent theory of right."[79] Law is as incoherent as a patchwork quilt.

In this way, Unger links a causal thesis about the genesis of doctrine to a logical thesis about the possibility of a consistent and coherent rational reconstruction of law.[80] But this causal argument for incoherence is vulnerable if the forces that produce law are not themselves law. It may well be true that authoritative legal actors have widely varying political motivations and that right-wing motivations play a significant causal role in some official acts and left-wing motivations play the same role in others; still other acts may reflect a compromise of competing motivations. But unless the motivations as well as the official acts become law, it is not clear why law should be inconsistent simply because some of its motivations are. Of course, conflict among different legal officials' motivations reminds us that nothing about law's creation guarantees us that it will be coherent. But legal theory attempts to "impose order over doctrine, not to discover order in the forces that created it."[81] Viewed somewhat differently, the legal principles, if any, that are created by a legitimate official act may well diverge from the justification employed by the actor. For example, the principles employed in an opinion may be considered dicta, the real rationale involving quite different principles. Reconstructing in this manner, the rationale is the ambition, however successful, of much legal argument. Consider, for example, Brandeis and Warren's argument for a right of privacy.[82] Warren and Brandeis explain cases the courts justified with property and contract doctrine as following instead from principles of privacy. They claim that the courts' rationales failed to account for the outcomes in all the precedents and that the cases were better justified by a general right to privacy.[83]

For most official acts of legislation and adjudication, left-wing, centrist, and right-wing justifications are devisable. Thus, a theory of law that contemplates that official acts generate underlying legal principles may allow construction of a coherent scheme of legal principles which justify official acts if the actual justifications, or motivations of, the legal actors may be disregarded. This is particularly plausible if the theory need not explain every institutional act and contemplates discounting some (but not too many) decisions as institutional mistakes.[84]

Theorists have developed both positivist and natural law theories that need not accept the justifications given in judicial opinions. Sartorius advocates a positivist theory of binding law consisting, in the first instance, of constitutional provisions, legislative enactments, and judicial decisions (conceived as the judgments given the facts, but not including the rules or principles stated in opinions).[85] In addition, law would include those principles and policies that imply the above authoritative sources.[86] On this view, the principles and policies that imply the authoritative sources need not be those articulated in judicial decisions. For one thing, the principles and policies judges employ may in fact fail to imply the decisions they make. Second, even where the outcome does follow from the principles and policies employed in an opinion, a holistic account of all judicial decisions may find alternative principles and policies preferable. Suppose that opinion A employs principles A' while opinion B employs principles B', yet principles B' imply the decisions in both case A and case B. In that event, considerations of theoretical simplicity may recommend accepting principles B' yet rejecting principles A' as otiose. Or it may be that principles B' lack internal theoretical fit with principles D', which are required to explain decisions D, E, and F. In that case, principles B' may be rejected in favor of principles C' which explain decisions A and B, and fit well with principles D'.

Natural law theories can even more easily reject the principles appearing in judicial opinions. In *Taking Rights Seriously* Dworkin endorses as legal principles those principles that form part of the best explanation and justification of settled law.[87] Thus, Dworkin, like Sartorius, rejects the principles judges use when these principles do not explain the settled law as well as alternative principles. In addition,

Dworkin may even reject judicial principles that fit the settled law well if they do not satisfactorily justify it. Dworkin's justification requirement permits rejection of principles on substantive moral grounds. Thus, both positivist and natural law theories of law and adjudication may resist the force of the patchwork quilt argument for indeterminacy by driving a wedge between judicial justifications and legal principles. In the absence of a convincing refutation of these plausible theories, the patchwork quilt argument does not prove that law is radically indeterminate.

2. Fundamental Contradiction Argument

Some critical legal scholars, rather than emphasizing inconsistency arising out of struggle among ideologically opposed factions, emphasize inconsistency within individual lawmakers and within each one of us: "[W]e are divided, among ourselves and also within ourselves, between irreconcilable visions of humanity and society, and between radically different aspirations for our common future."[88]

This contradiction consists in a psychological ambivalence or simultaneous commitment in each of us to contradictory visions, such as altruism and individualism. This ambivalence, however, is deeper than abstract theoretical political commitment. It reflects a "fundamental contradiction" between the deeply felt desire to fuse with others and the desire to retain one's separateness, between the need to express individuality and to recognize that one's self is largely socially constructed, between society's nuturing and its demand for conformity.[89] Put briefly, individual freedom is both dependent upon and incompatible with community.[90] This fundamental contradiction is alleged to be at the core of every legal problem.[91]

But it is unclear what is meant by contradiction in this context, as well as in the patchwork quilt argument. Our need for others and fear of them is surely not "contradictory" in the strict sense in which logicians use the word: that is, P and not-P.[92] Advocates of the fundamental contradiction are not saying that we need others yet it is not the case that we need others.[93] Rather, it appears that the fundamental contradiction consists in our having opposed though not formally contradictory feelings. For example, we may have both contempt and admiration for the same individual. ("He's a consummate villain.")[94] Yet it is unclear why these opposed feelings should be thought to result in irresolvable conflict. We need water to survive, yet we fear that large quantities of it can drown us.[95] We need others, yet we fear pervasive interaction can suffocate us. Advocates of the fundamental contradiction need to explain why we cannot achieve a balance of human interaction and solitude, community and autonomy, just as we can quench our thirst without drowning ourselves. Even where we experience conflict between our desire for ice cream and desire to avoid cholesterol and calories, it appears that we can best satisfy our overall desires by eating some but not too much ice cream, or by eating more of a low calorie, cholesterol reduced ice cream, or by eating frozen yogurt. Admittedly, achieving maximally satisfying relations with others is a more complicated task; nevertheless, advocates of the fundamental contradiction argument have not convincingly demonstrated that it differs in principle.

Advocates of the fundamental contradiction argument must explain the sense in which the principles and counterprinciples of legal doctrine are contradictory. Insofar as the principles and counterprinciples of legal doctrine reflect psychological tension rather than a strict contradiction, it would appear that only competition, not contradiction, in principle should emerge.[96]

Advocates of the fundamental contradiction argument must also clarify the connection between the psychological conflicts they allege and legal doctrine and moral theory. Is the connection conceptual? If so, must an accurate moral and legal theory reflect the structure of psychological facts? Or is the connection causal? If causal, does legal doctrine result from a conscious attempt to cover up the psychological conflict?[97] Or does legal doctrine result from an unconscious manipulation of that psychological conflict?[98] Or does legal doctrine reproduce the conflict without, or despite, any conscious or unconscious attempt to hide it?

The sense of contradiction in the fundamental contradiction argument and its relation to legal doctrine and moral theory are too vague to be part of a persuasive argument for radical indeterminacy. Construed in its most plausible light, the fundamental contradiction argument reflects opposed feelings that appear prima facie in tension. Advocates of the fundamental contradiction argument have not shown that the tension cannot be resolved, or how the tension is reflected in legal doctrine, or that the tension leads to contradiction rather than competition in legal principles. The fundamental contradiction argument does not establish that there is radical indeterminacy.

3. Particular Contradictions

Critical scholars have elaborated and supported their claim that law is radically contradictory by arguing that particular contradictory structures permeate large areas or the entirety of the law. This Section discusses four of the major dichotomies that are alleged to underlie legal doctrine: rules vs. standards; altruism vs. individualism; objectivism vs. subjectivism; and free will vs. determinism. After examining these four dichotomies, this Section concludes that none of these contradictions demonstrates the existence of radical indeterminacy. The first two, like the claim of fundamental contradiction discussed above, employ exaggerated rhetoric and only demonstrate tension and competition among principles. The third misrepresents and distorts liberal political and legal theory. And the fourth makes both errors; it misrepresents and distorts liberal law and it demonstrates only tension and uncertainty, not contradiction.

Critical scholars argue that in private law adjudication there is a conflict in the purely formal dimension concerning whether to employ rules or standards[99] in formulating legal directives.[100] There are many arguments for and against employing each form, and many methodologies for choosing among them, most of which Duncan Kennedy deftly summarizes in a widely cited article, *Form and Substance in Private Law Adjudication*.[101] Generally, rules are considered relatively determinate because they require only "hard" factual findings for their application. Standards, by contrast, are vague and require discretionary policy judgments in their application.[102] Rules provide certainty and restrain official arbitrariness but they exact a high price. Because rules do not directly express their underlying purposes, those objectives may not be achieved. Thus rules are both over- and underinclusive; a rule that is designed to punish immoral acts may proscribe some innocent behavior and fail to sanction some immoral behavior.[103] Conversely, the advantage of standards is that they directly set forth their purposes. Thus, those applying standards may be able to comply with the underlying purposes. Because standards cannot be as rigidly applied as rules and because they give only broad guidance, however, they require greater discretion in their application. As a consequence, this discretion often results in uncertainty and arbitrariness.

Kennedy believes that liberal legal thought arbitrarily privileges rules over standards, overemphasizing the virtues of rules and the vices of standards. He therefore takes special care to discuss rules' defects. Kennedy notes that rules may be particular or general. Particularity in rules leads to their multiplication, which in turn leads to the increased possibility of conflict between rules.[104] The exercise of discretion necessary to resolve these conflicts undermines the certainty and restraint of arbitrariness allegedly characteristic of rules. Additionally, to the extent that the structure of rules becomes unwieldy, sophisticated legal actors may employ their greater familiarity with its intricacies, and thus take advantage of others and magnify the problem of over- and underinclusiveness. The more general the rules are, the fewer opportunities there are for conflict.[105] But with greater generality comes increased over- and underinclusiveness. Moreover, the more general a rule, the more likely it is to chill desirable voluntary activity.

In those situations where rules are formalities intended to facilitate private transactions, it is not clear that individuals will in fact respond to the threat of the sanction that the transaction will be nullified by learning to operate the system, or that a stable, highly formal regime of rules is possible. Therefore, rules cannot

bring about the objectives that they purport to ensure.

In these ways, Kennedy argues that the assumptions underlying arguments for the superiority of the "mechanical" arbitrariness of rules over the "biased" arbitrariness of standards are implausible. Yet Kennedy does not argue that standards can be rationally demonstrated to be superior. Rather, he maintains that we are simultaneously committed to both rules and standards and that there is no way to "'balance' ... rules against equitable standards."[106]

Clearly the arguments for employing rules and for using standards compete with one another, and we may have great difficulty deciding which arguments are more powerful in particular contexts, or how to reach the best compromise between them. But this tension falls far short of strict contradiction. Kennedy's arguments do not show that this conflict is as problematic as strict contradiction. Thus, it is does not appear that the "contradiction" between rules and standards yields radical indeterminacy.

Nevertheless, Kennedy maintains that there is a *formal*[107] contradiction between rules and standards, which in turn reflects a deeper *substantive* contradiction between individualist and altruist visions of human interaction. Kennedy's paradigm of individualism is two self-interested, self-reliant strangers meeting at high noon to conduct a one-time arm's length transaction. But because this individualism invokes mutual respect for the rights of others, it falls short of pure egoism.[108] In contrast, altruism conjures up images of community, sacrifice, sharing, and mercy, yet it does not require saintliness.[109]

Kennedy, Unger, and other critical legal scholars have developed the contradiction between altruist and individualist social visions largely, but not exclusively, in contract law. In Unger's variation, the role played by altruism in Kennedy's version is played by an area of family, friendship, and community with "reciprocal loyalty and support," which neither "need[s] much law nor [is] capable of tolerating it."[110] This vision conflicts with an ideal of "contractual freedom" in a "world of self-interested commerce."[111] Each vision of social life "both denies the other and depends on it. Each is at once the other's partner and its enemy."[112] The contradiction between altruist and individualist social visions is an earlier and more concrete version of the fundamental contradiction discussed above.[113] The difficulties noted with the fundamental contradiction argument apply, mutatis mutandis, to this earlier incarnation.

A third contradiction announced by critical scholars is Kelman's contention that liberalism is simultaneously committed to value subjectivity and value objectivity.[114] The discussion is marred by Kelman's biased reading of liberalism, and by his failure to distinguish different senses of value subjectivity. Kelman interprets liberalism as committed to extreme individualism and to the subjectivity of values. He views libertarianism and utilitarianism as the major traditional liberal movements.[115] Among modern theories, he considers Posner's law and economics the quintessential liberal doctrine, presumably because it more completely embodies and privileges individualism and value subjectivity.[116] In consequence, Kelman employs a biased interpretation which identifies liberalism with its most conservative, right-wing strains.[117]

Kelman claims that despite its "somewhat ... extreme" "right-wing" "bias," the version of liberalism he attacks is not a straw man.[118] He produces two arguments, neither of which justifies this startling claim. First, Kelman argues that liberals are more "culturally and intellectually self-confident" with a libertarian stance than with left-wing positions.[119] In particular, they can argue more articulately and coherently for "right-wing libertarian[ism]" than for their more left-wing beliefs.[120] But how does this allegation aid Kelman's defense to the straw man charge? If it followed from left-wing liberals' articulateness in defending libertarianism either that left-wing liberals are really committed to libertarianism or else that libertarianism is a more worthy opponent because it is supported by stronger arguments, then Kelman would be justified in taking libertarianism as his liberal opponent. But this is not an inference Kelman can sanction. He admits that:

> CLS adherents find themselves in roughly the same relationship to their actual political beliefs as left liberals are [in] to theirs. That is, they have all learned to argue confidently for a position one step to the right of their actual position. CLS proponents have, in a sense, developed a coherent and self-confident left-liberal discourse that the left liberals have not yet devised.... [CLS a]rguments for their *actual* vision seem far vaguer and more unfocused.... [121]

If Kelman argues that left liberals are really libertarians, then he must concede that critical legal scholars are really left liberals. If Kelman claims that libertarianism is a more worthy opponent than left liberalism because it is more coherently articulated, then he must concede that left liberalism is superior to critical legal scholars' radicalism because it is more coherently articulated. Moreover, if Kelman is correct that critical scholars have devised a coherent defense of left liberalism, then the claim that libertarianism is superior to left liberalism because it is more coherent is undermined. Thus, this defense of Kelman's libertarian interpretation of liberalism is unpersuasive.

Kelman's second defense is more direct, but no more successful. He claims that all liberals

> *must* adopt ... the social theory of the Chicago school adherents, even if they genuinely bristle at any summary statement of the theory, because it really *is* the social theory ... of a coherent liberal individualism that sees society as fundamentally successful when it *responds* to the will of individuals, and mediates the conflicts between individuals simply by making everyone pay his way.[122]

This defense begs the question against liberals such as Rawls who do not view government's primary role as responding to the will of individuals.[123] This defense also unnecessarily constrains the options of left liberals who accept that facilitative role for government. Even if Kelman were correct that Chicago law and economics follows from this facilitative vision of government's role, such liberals have two options, not just one. They can accept Chicago law and economics, or they can reconsider their acceptance of the facilitative view of government. Kelman provides no argument why the second option would not be preferable. Thus, Kelman's second defense, like his first, fails to demonstrate that all liberals are committed to right-wing liberalism. The charge that Kelman's interpretation of liberalism is a straw man stands.

More importantly, Kelman's discussion of liberalism's contradictory commitments to value subjectivity and value objectivity is unsuccessful because he neglects to distinguish differing senses of value subjectivity, and various senses of value objectivity.[124] Economists contend that values are subjective in the sense that the value of a commodity, or the value of satisfying a consumer's preference, is measured by the price that the consumer will pay, which in turn reflects the intensity of the consumer's subjective desire. A related utilitarian position would urge that in summing utilities, the utilities depend upon the actual satisfaction or happiness derived by individuals. Utility is subjective because different individuals may derive varying levels of satisfaction from the same experience. At the same time, the utilitarian can consistently maintain that the determination of which actions are morally preferable is objective, because it results from an objective summing of the subjective utilities of all who are affected by the considered actions. All of these positions should be sharply distinguished from the liberal principle that government should be strictly neutral among citizens' visions of the good. Finally, none of the above positions is inconsistent with the claim that some political arrangements are objectively superior to others. Liberals endorse this claim by advocating liberalism over alternative schemes of government. These distinguishable meanings of value subjectivity and distinguishable meanings of value objectivity are confused in critical legal scholars' assertion of liberalism's contradictory commitment to subjectivity and objectivity, as the following summary discloses.

Critical legal scholars assert numerous respects in which liberalism is committed to value subjectivity. Thus it has been urged that "[f]rom the start, liberal political thought has been in revolt against the conception of objective value."[125] Liberals, it is said, must treat each person's "values" (desires) as having equal weight. Beliefs about what to pursue or what is worth pursuing are mere "tastes, the purely

arbitrary assertions of individuals."[126] The job of the state is merely to facilitate the satisfaction of as many of these "values" as possible.[127]

Critical scholars claim that this commitment to value subjectivity is forced upon liberal theorists by the denial of the doctrine of intelligible essences. Intelligible essences are humanly perceivable properties which form the basis for classifying objects into separate categories.[128] The denial of the existence of intelligible essences, it is alleged, means that there are no predetermined ways of cutting up the world into discrete categories. There are numberless equally justified (or equally unjustified) ways in which objects and events may be classified.[129]

The world does not determine our system of names, rather our system of names determines the world. Critical scholars claim that in the absence of intelligible essences classification can be justified only by reference to human purposes and desires. This includes classification of moral, political, and legal terms. But desires, being psychic events, cannot ground the objectivity of moral, legal, political, or other values. Psychic events, like all events, are not objective because objectivity requires the doctrine of intelligible essences.[130]

This argument is fallacious. Objectivity could be a consequence of essences that were not humanly perceivable, but which nevertheless exist. They might be inferrable, even if not directly perceivable. Even if essences could not be humanly determined, even by inference, that would not cast doubt on the world's objectivity, but merely speak to our knowledge of that objectivity. More importantly, objectivity could derive from agreement in concrete judgments among language users regardless of what grounded that agreement. Critical scholars appear to acknowledge this possibility but ultimately reject it on the ground that agreement would have to be a matter of shared group values and not mere convergence of interests to ground objectivity.[131] It is unclear why this should be so, or why shared social practices irrespective of shared values would not suffice.

Critical scholars claim that liberal legal thought is simultaneously committed to value objectivity on several grounds. First, liberal theorists must believe that objective moral reasons require the state to satisfy as much individual subjective desire as possible.[132] Put differently, utilitarianism is an objective moral theory, and not merely the subjective preference of its advocates. Second, subjective desires will take shape only in the context of a preexisting arrangement of entitlements. That preexisting arrangement of entitlements cannot then be justified by its ability to maximize preference satisfaction on pain of vicious regress.[133] Preexisting entitlements therefore require objective moral justification. Third, rule-following behavior cannot be fully justified in terms of rational self-interest because on at least some occasions there will be a low likelihood that one's lawbreaking will be detected, or if detected that one will be caught, or that knowledge of one's lawbreaking will induce others to noncompliance. Thus, the justification for compliance requires substantive moral principles.[134]

This description of liberal legal theory lies somewhere between grossly unsympathetic and fraudulent. Although Hobbes maintained that values were subjective,[135] his liberal credentials are surely suspect since he believed in absolute sovereignty. Locke, Mill, Rawls, and Dworkin all deny that values are subjective.[136] It does not demonstrate that liberalism is inconsistent to show that one liberal thinker held that values were subjective, while another rejected that claim.[137] More important, critical scholars confuse the liberal principle that government should be neutral respecting visions of the good life with value subjectivity. The duty of government to treat each person's desires as being of equal weight is not value subjectivity in a sense which contradicts the claim that moral and political theory are objective. Liberals may embrace equal treatment of individuals' desires on objective moral grounds, for example, a principle of human equality.[138] Finally, modern liberals are hardly committed to utilitarianism despite the fact that many historical liberals were. Rawls, for example, explicitly denies that the only purpose of the state is to satisfy individuals' desires.[139]

The contradiction between subjective and objective theories of values that critical legal scholars claim inheres in liberal theory, in fact inheres only in a strawperson's version of liberal theory, and not in modern liberal political theory. Moreover, critical scholars confuse different senses in which values may be subjective. Therefore, they have not demonstrated the existence of radical indeterminacy as a product of contradiction between objectivity and subjectivity.

A fourth major substantive contradiction is Kelman's claim that the law, particularly criminal law, is simultaneously committed to free will (intentionalism) and to determinism. In consequence of this commitment to apparently polar values, Kelman claims law is contradictory and attempts to provide moral justifications for law are unstable.[140] He asserts that liberalism makes use of two distinct discourses to describe human action: intentionalist discourse, which involves free will and therefore the possibility of moral responsibility; and determinist discourse, which pictures human action as resulting from a predetermined chain of events and therefore as amoral. He contends that we are "actually *simultaneously* drawn" to both discourses, so that "our relationship with the discourses is ... *contradictory*."[141] The potential of conduct to be characterized under either discourse yields indeterminacy in the justifications underlying legal rules and decisions. The heart of Kelman's argument consists of a discussion of criminal law cases intended to demonstrate the indeterminacy resulting from this contradiction.

As my discussion of the other alleged contradictions in liberal theory has made apparent, critical scholars maintain that liberal discourse privileges one side of each dichotomy. It prefers rules over standards, individualism over altruism, subjectivism over objectivism. Likewise, Kelman claims, liberal theory privileges intentionalism over determinism. Liberalism privileges intentionalism either by ignoring the difficulty in choosing between intentionalistic and deterministic descriptions of action or by "purportedly *confining* determinist discourse."[142] This privileging, according to Kelman, takes the form of claims that we can distinguish between domains of freedom and domains of determinism, and that social life is improved to the extent that it is increasingly occupied by domains of freedom.[143]

Kelman's treatment of this contradiction and its privileged pole is seriously confused. This confusion is demonstrated by Kelman's alternating use of two different levels of discourse relevant to the notion of free action.[144]

On the first level is the opposition between free will and determinism as fundamental ways to describe the nature of human action. At this level, we raise such questions as: Are all human actions causally determined? Are any human actions free? Are any human actions free in a sense that permits moral agency and responsibility? Is the exercise of free will compatible or incompatible with the claim that human actions are causally determined? Kelman appears to accept the popular notion that determinism is incompatible with free will[145] in spite of most current philosophers' preference for the compatibilist thesis that human actions can be free even if they have antecedent, external causes.[146]

If the possibility of free action giving rise to moral responsibility is accepted at this first level, a second level discourse and set of inquiries arises. At this second level, which presupposes the discourse of intentionistic action and free will, we distinguish acts that are voluntary for purposes of assigning responsibility, from those that are involuntary. It must be emphasized, however, that the doctrine of free will does not include the claim that all human actions are voluntary, but only the claim that some are. Even an advocate of both free will and incompatibilism can maintain that some human actions are determined, while others are free. Contrary to Kelman's apparent suggestion, one can find an action involuntary, and thus not subject to moral or legal sanction, without giving up intentionalist discourse, and returning to a deterministic world view that rejects the doctrine of free will. Rather, involuntariness is an issue arising entirely within intentionalist discourse. Confusion arises because we sometimes express our belief in free will by saying that an action is free while other times we express the idea that a particular action is voluntary by saying it is free. To avoid this confusion, it is useful to restrict use of the terms "free", "intentional", and "determined" to discussions at the first level and to employ the terms "voluntary" and "involuntary" at the second level.

The central problem with Kelman's argument is that he needs to show liberal theory's commitment to both terms of the intentionalism–determinism dichotomy to establish his contradiction claim, but his examples deal only with the voluntary-involuntary dichotomy.[147] The examples, therefore, support only the view that intentionalism is a presupposition of our legal system and of liberal thought. Kelman certainly does not show that liberalism is also committed to determinism.

But perhaps there is more to Kelman's argument. It might be that our legal system is simultaneously committed to calling actions both voluntary and involuntary (if not intentional and predetermined) and it is therefore contradictory and results in indeterminacy. Kelman does show how in some criminal cases action may be characterized as voluntary (blameworthy) and *also* as involuntary (blameless). From these cases, he concludes that we are drawn to both discourses and possess no metaprinciple that allows us to choose between them. Thus, perhaps the contradiction does exist after all, but Kelman is simply mistaken about the level at which it is found.

The first response to be made to this approach is to deny that there is "simultaneous commitment" to both poles in the voluntary–involuntary dichotomy. Rather, the legal system distinguishes between voluntariness and involuntariness and mandates that we determine whether a given action is voluntary or involuntary. Of course this is no easy task. As Kelman's examples illustrate, factors are often present that mitigate the voluntariness of actions; the conditions for a voluntary act can be present in varying degrees, creating a spectrum of voluntariness.[148] At what point, then, are we to call an action voluntary for the purpose of assigning blame? Although the answer to this question will be easy in many cases, there will be cases, as Kelman demonstrates, in which it is difficult to determine whether an action is voluntary or involuntary. The point is that this amounts to some uncertainty in understanding the psychological and ethical requirements for moral and legal responsibility. It does not show that liberalism is committed to contradictory discourses.

In order for Kelman to demonstrate indeterminacy, he must show that this uncertainty in how we should classify actions on the borderline between being voluntary and involuntary reflects a pervasive incoherence in the proper classification of actions. He must show that any attempt to distinguish voluntary from involuntary actions would be unsuccessful or arbitrary. Yet even if the precise location of the line is not clear, it does not follow that the drawing of this line is necessarily an arbitrary matter.

It will be useful here to examine how Kelman takes himself to have established the impossibility of a coherent classification of actions as voluntary and involuntary. He argues, for example, that "[i]n many cases a more covert battle between intentionalistic and deterministic discourses goes on in the criminal area precisely because each discourse is so available to us."[149] Here he supplies sample cases and illustrates how they can be described equally well in both voluntaristic and involuntaristic terms. For example, he notes that in a case like *Martin v. State*,[150] in which the defendant is apprehended at home while drunk, brought to a public place by police officers, and arrested for public drunkenness, the common interpretation is that the public appearance is involuntary. Even though the defendant voluntarily got drunk, his actions are characterized as involuntary because he did not choose to go out in public, and it was not "reasonably foreseeable" that he would end up there. By contrast, in a case like *People v. Decina*,[151] where the defendant was convicted of negligent homicide even though he was unconscious when he hit the victim with his automobile, the common interpretation is that the defendant's actions were voluntary and, hence, blameworthy. His actions were voluntary because he chose to drive, fully realizing the possibility that he might have an epileptic seizure and kill someone. In each case the defendant voluntarily performed some action that contributed to his arrest, yet involuntarily brought about some consequence that he did not specifically intend. Kelman claims that in each case we can use either description since both are readily available.

But what does Kelman mean by "available?" If he means that either description can be used without a formal contradiction, then he is correct. But in the context of justificatory schemes, if one description is more appropriate or the arguments for it are better than those for the other, then it is the only description "available" in the relevant sense. Even in each of Kelman's examples it appears that one description is more appropriate than the other. In *Martin*, the voluntary act, getting drunk at home, is done with no reasonable expectation of making a public appearance, and the public appearance results from the intervening voluntary act of the police. Thus, the overall occurrence of public drunkenness is best characterized as involuntary. In *Decina*, the voluntary act of driving is performed with awareness of both the possibility of an epileptic attack and the risks of such an attack. For this reason, the killing of the victim is more appropriately characterized as a voluntary act. A similar analysis applies to Kelman's examples of status crimes, strict liability, and provocation and duress.[152]

In all these cases Kelman contends that we are simultaneously drawn to two different "discourses." In fact, in each case we are working completely within the discourse of intentionalism. Furthermore, we are not "drawn" to both a voluntaristic and an involuntaristic description; rather we are convinced that these are borderline cases in which we experience some uncertainty in characterizing the actions as either voluntary or involuntary. This is because the cases: (1) exhibit a certain degree of voluntariness; or (2) involve more than one act to be tested for voluntariness; or (3) involve an action with two aspects, one of which is voluntary and one of which is involuntary. Despite this lack of clarity, we may still find that one description is more appropriate than the other. Thus we do have a kind of "metaprinciple" or method that guides us in choosing between descriptions: our rationality, moral sensitivity, and ability to use words meaningfully. This "metaprinciple" cannot be made completely explicit nor captured mechanically, but this reflects the limits of our knowledge, not the ineliminable incoherence of law.[153]

Kelman does not deny that the outcome in *Martin* was predictable, but he does assert that it was not the characterization of the act as involuntary that determined the outcome. Rather, Martin's behavior was either justified because we consider public drunkenness a lesser evil than resisting the police, or excused because the police involvement amounted to entrapment.[154] If Kelman is correct, then in fact the case is not indeterminate. The case generates confusion because its true rationale differs from that stated in the opinion. If Kelman is correct, the true justification for Martin's acquittal rests not on Martin's act being involuntary, but rather on its being justified or excused. Thus, Kelman's critique, stripped of its philosophical cloak, is just a normative criticism of the court's analysis, the stock-in-trade of traditional scholarship. Nevertheless, Kelman succeeds in establishing that there are tensions, difficulties, and some mistaken decisions in criminal law cases as well as inadequacies in the criminal theories he considers. This, however, falls far short of demonstrating that we are simultaneously committed to contradictory principles.

Kelman's work evokes an additional comment. Just as Kelman discovers inadequacies in criminal law and theory, so other critical scholars make useful critiques of other areas of the law and legal theory. But critique is not enough. All legal systems and all legal theories are flawed. We are, after all, humans, not gods. Legal argument is comparative, and so is theory. We decide which theory to believe by provisionally accepting that theory which has the best overall combination of virtues and vices. It is therefore incumbent on critical scholars to present not only critiques, but also alternatives preferable to the doctrine and theories they critique. (Some critical scholars are now vigorously making that attempt.)[155] Otherwise, critical scholars give us no cause to change our beliefs or our actions.

D. *Errant Legal Reasoning and Indeterminacy*

This Section focuses on three mistakes advocates of indeterminacy make in their accounts of law and legal reasoning.[156] Each of these mistakes generates the illusion of greater indeterminacy than actually exists. I do not claim that all advocates of radical indeterminacy make all three mistakes. But one can find each mistake in the literature, and some authors make more than one.

The close conceptual connection between indeterminacy and legal reasoning explains why critical scholars' incorrect views about legal reasoning can have consequences for indeterminacy. Indeed, legal indeterminacy may properly be defined in terms of legal reasoning, as follows: Law is indeterminate where the correct theory of legal reasoning fails to yield a right answer or permits multiple answers to legal questions. Insofar as the theories of legal reasoning employed by critical scholars do not produce right answers while more accurate theories of legal reasoning yield right answers, critical scholars' mistakes about legal reasoning inflate their assessment of the extent of indeterminacy.

Before summarizing the three respects in which critical scholars' mistakes about legal reasoning lead to exaggerated indeterminacy claims, it is necessary to mention some basic features of legal reasoning. First, any theory of legal reasoning must have a method for determining which general propositions of law are permissible premises in legal argument and in adjudication. Specifically, the theory of legal reasoning must determine whether such propositions encompass only rules, or include principles, policies, and other standards. Additionally, the theory must provide criteria with which to determine which specific propositions within the categories it permits are legitimate and which are illegitimate, in legal argument. Second, a theory of legal reasoning must determine which inferences from the legitimate premises are authorized. Are only deductive inferences allowed, or are arguments by analogy, or to standards which cohere with accepted standards also permitted? Third, a theory of legal reasoning must provide for the prospect of conflicting legal standards. This may be accomplished by delegitimating one of the conflicting standards, by accommodating the conflicting standards in a concrete compromise, or by generating revised, compatible standards.[157] These three features fall considerably short of constituting a complete theory of legal reasoning, but these aspects will suffice for the argument that follows.

I argue that critical legal scholars' arguments for radical indeterminacy explicitly or implicitly presuppose claims about these three aspects of legal reasoning each of which is rejected by numerous plausible theories of adjudication accepted or advocated in recent conventional legal scholarship. The positions taken by critical scholars respecting each of these aspects impoverish legal reasoning in a manner that increases prospects for indeterminacy. The critical scholars' arguments for indeterminacy, however, do not purport to demonstrate, and therefore do not demonstrate, that the claims of conventional scholars about these three aspects of legal reasoning are incorrect. The critical arguments for radical indeterminacy are thus inadequate because they do not refute plausible conventional accounts of legal reasoning which are significantly more determinate.

Before more fully developing this argument, I will summarize the three respects in which critical scholars hold mistaken assumptions about legal reasoning. First, critical scholars unnecessarily limit and impoverish the premises that may be employed in legal argument. Some critical scholars' arguments presuppose that only rules are law, while standards, such as principles, policies, legal culture, and social context are not law. If it were true that law encompassed only black-letter rules, there might well be radical indeterminacy. The use, however, of nonrule standards in legal argument substantially reduces indeterminacy.

Second, critical scholars frequently presuppose that only deductive inferences are permitted in legal argument. They therefore deny legitimacy to inference to standards that cohere with accepted principles and to argument by analogy. Nondeductive inferences to standards that cohere with settled principles, and to analogous outcomes, substantially reduce the indeterminacy which might emerge if legal reasoning permitted only deductive inferences.

Third, critical scholars assume that the existence of conflicting principles yields indeterminacy in the absence of explicit metaprinciples that resolve those conflicts. Even without such metaprinciples, however, conflicts may be re-

solved by concrete compromises reflecting the contribution of each of the conflicting principles. Moreover, even where legal principles are truly contradictory, they can be reconstructed into a revised and consistent set. Such a method of reconstruction is valid even if it cannot be accomplished mechanically and even if the reconstructed principles could not have been explicitly stated in advance.

1. Impoverished Premises

In this Section, I argue that many critical scholars' arguments for radical indeterminacy are flawed because they too strictly limit the premises that may be deployed in legal arguments. Subsequent sections examine critical scholars' mistakes about the inferences permitted in legal argument, and the methods necessary to resolve prima facie inconsistency in legal standards.

I argue in this Section that the predictability of legal practice embarrasses advocates of radical indeterminacy. Critical legal scholars reject the plausible claim that law is reasonably predictable because law is reasonably determinate. Instead, critical legal scholars urge that law's predictability is a consequence of judges illegitimately deciding cases in accordance with their hidden ideologies. I claim, in contrast, that the predictability of legal practice is better explained by sophisticated theories of legal reasoning that yield at most moderate indeterminacy.

Arguments for radical indeterminacy artificially limit the types of legal standards judges may employ as premises in reaching legal conclusions. Some arguments assume that only black-letter rules are authorized, others countenance as well policies, principles, and standards derived from institutional roles. However, arguments for radical indeterminacy almost invariably assume that standards derived from social context, legal culture, and morality are extra-legal standards which judges may not consider in reaching legal decisions.

Critical scholars urge that judicial use of these extra-legal standards explains how legal practice can be predictable despite law's radical indeterminacy. By contrast, recent liberal legal scholarship denies that these standards are extra-legal. Numerous recent theories describe them as legally authoritative standards. Theories that permit use of such standards in adjudication are descriptively and normatively superior to theories that do not.

One theme running through this Section as well as the next Section is that arguments from stringent theories of legal reasoning to radical indeterminacy are best reconceived as demonstrating the invalidity of the stringent theory of legal reasoning. Such stringent theories should be replaced by richer theories of legal reasoning which result in less indeterminacy. After a brief section describing the logical basis for reconceiving an argument to an implausible conclusion as demonstrating the falsity of the argument's premise, the method is applied to arguments for radical indeterminacy.

The argument will be similar to critiques of skepticism which claim that skeptics employ an excessively demanding criterion of knowledge. For example, one modern response to skeptical arguments that conclude that we cannot have knowledge of the material world has been to steadfastly deny their conclusions. The response contends that we are much more convinced that material objects exist than we are of the validity of any sophisticated philosophical argument concluding that we cannot know if the material world exists. The interesting philosophical challenge, therefore, is to find the fallacy in the sophisticated argument.[158] This requires examination of the premises and inferences of the argument.

If the conclusion is false and the inferences from premises to conclusion valid, it follows that one, or more, of the premises is false. The argument may be turned on its head so that the negation of the false premise becomes the conclusion and the negation of the conclusion becomes a premise.[159] An argument from a false premise by valid inferences to a false conclusion is reconceived as a sound argument from the negation of the original conclusion to the negation of the original premise. In essence, this is merely an application of the classic rule of inference *modus tollens*.

Consider the skeptical argument from the premise that knowledge requires absolute cer-

tainty to the implausible conclusion that we know little, if anything.[160] This argument can be turned on its head, as follows. The argument can be reconceived as from the plausible premise that we know many things to the conclusion that knowledge does not reqire absolute certainty. Consider, as a second example, a slight variation on the classic syllogism:

Premise	(1)	All people are immortal.
Premise	(2)	Socrates is a person.
Conclusion	(3)	Therefore, Socrates is immortal.

Clearly this inference is logically valid.[161] Necessarily, if the premises were true, the conclusion would be. Yet the conclusion is surely false. It follows that (at least) one of the premises is false. Since (2) is true, the troublemaker must be (1) All people are immortal.

Thus, we can turn the above valid (but not sound) argument to a false conclusion on its head so that it yields a true conclusion.

Premise	(a)	Socrates is not immortal.
Premise	(b)	Socrates is a person.
Conclusion	(c)	Therefore, not all people are immortal. I.e., some people are mortal.

The predictability of legal practice may serve a role in rejecting radical versions of indeterminacy analogous to the role our belief in the existence of material objects plays in rejecting skepticism about the external world.[162] Those who claim that the law is radically indeterminate must account for the fact that most legal results are not open to serious doubt and are highly predictable. Justice Cardozo once claimed that in no more than ten percent of the cases that courts decide was there any indeterminacy or doubt about the correct outcome.[163] Recent empirical studies confirm Cardozo's intuition. For example, in his Berkeley Centenary Lecture Judge Jon O. Newman stated that in the year ended June 30, 1983 dissents were filed in federal courts of appeals in less than four percent of the cases.[164] Judge Alvin Rubin similarly reported that from 1981 to 1985 dissents were filed in less than four percent of all Fifth Circuit cases.[165] These reports confirm J. Woodford Howard's 1965–67 study which found mean dissent rates for individual appellate judges to be under four percent.[166]

Of course, dissent rates are not precise measurements of judicial disagreement. No doubt many judges reject the majority opinion but do not write a dissent because they do not think the issue is sufficiently important or simply because they are overworked.[167] Howard, for one, considered a number of explanations for the low dissent rate and concluded that "the magnitude of routine litigation in the circuits was undoubtedly a major factor in depressing dissents."[168] Nonetheless, studies of appelate decisionmaking certainly provide at least modest support for Cardozo's estimate. It would be surprising to find that the dissent rate was four percent yet judges disagreed in forty percent of all cases. Moreover, if we look at trial courts, or disputes not leading to formal legal action, or merely at events governed by law, the levels of agreement and thus the predictability of outcome may be even higher. Academic attention to appellate decisionmaking should not blind us to the bulk of social activity where law plays a role. Belief in indeterminacy results in part from a bad diet.

The existence of widespread predictability is a potential embarrassment to claims of radical indeterminacy and suggests that their supporting argument must be flawed. One place to look is in the theory of legal reasoning implicit in the indeterminacy thesis. Characterizations of indeterminacy and theories of legal reasoning can be matched up via the following definition. The legal system is indeterminate to the extent that, according to theory of legal reasoning LR, multiple outcomes are possible. Thus, each new theory of legal reasoning LR may generate a different conclusion respecting the extent of indeterminacy. One way to turn an argument for radical indeterminacy on its head in light of predictability is to attack its associated theory of legal reasoning as unnecessarily impoverished.

The recent history of legal theory confirms this hypothesis. The legal realists attacked the formalist theory that legal reasoning consists solely in deductive argument from legally authoritative rules. The realists argued that since those doctrinal materials fail to determine the outcomes of lawsuits, something else must determine the outcome. Some realists claimed that this something else was what the judge ate for breakfast, or judicial personality,[169] or

hunch.[170] More thoughtful realists, or some realists in their more thoughtful moments, said that the something else was social policy.[171] If, however, social policy is legally authoritative, then law is not indeterminate. Rather, the correct theory of legal reasoning is richer than mechanical jurisprudence contemplates. In a sense, the legal realists anticipated this position with their demand that judges reveal the true grounds of legal decisions so that those grounds would be open to public scrutiny.[172]

Thus, we find that in addition to rules, theories of legal reasoning came to countenance social policy. In more recent theories of legal reasoning, principles and other standards are added to the judge's stock of authoritative materials.[173] Of course, besides filling gaps, adding materials can create conflicts between authoritative materials. Thus, the addition of nonrule standards does not necessarily eliminate indeterminacy.[174] Indeed, the critical legal scholars' arguments for indeterminacy, such as the patchwork quilt argument and the fundamental contradiction argument, enrich realist skepticism by invoking deeper forms of conflict.

But these arguments for the existence of more radical forms of indeterminacy are therefore more deeply embarrassed by the reasonable predictability of legal outcomes. Naturally, the critics are aware of the need to reconcile indeterminacy with predictability.[175] Like the legal realists before them, critical scholars explain predictability as a consequence of "something else," something beyond the elements of legal reasoning. That something else may include social context, legal culture, institutional roles, convention, or the ideology of the decisionmaker.[176] But traditional legal theorists can counter the critical scholars' explanation of predictability by developing an even richer theory of legal reasoning that includes social context, legal culture, and many of the other elements which critical legal scholars employ to explain predictability. If the richer theory of legal reasoning provides a better explanation of predictability than that supplied by the critical scholars, the plausibility of indeterminacy is eroded.

Each of the elements in the critical scholars' explanation of predictability has been employed in a richer theory of legal reasoning than formalist doctrinal deduction. For instance, institutional role is the bedrock of the legal process school developed by Hart, Sacks, and Fuller.[177] Social context, convention, and legal culture are legitimate sources of law in some conventional theories of adjudication. Some such theories authorize judges to employ conventional morality, others view the legal profession or the judiciary as an interpretive culture whose practices and dispositions determine legal truth.[178] Even political ideology, interpreted as the judge's sincerely held political convictions, is authoritative in some recent legal theories, such as Dworkin's.[179]

Advocates of naturalist or natural law theories are not alone in legitimizing "political ideology" in adjudication. Some positivists, while denying that moral principles are legally authoritative based upon their substantive merits, argue that substantive moral principles are incorporated into the law by conventional practices among judges to employ them in legal argument.[180]

Other positivists, such as Raz, reject this incorporation thesis,[181] but are free to develop a theory of adjudication in hard cases that requires judges to employ moral principles. The difference is that such a positivist will not label those moral principles "law" (until after the decisions).[182]

These enriched theories of legal reasoning provide a better explanation for law's predictability than critical scholars' claim of a hidden political ideology. These theories explain judges' frequent references to social and public policy, moral principles, and institutional competence. Such judicial references would be a mystery under the critical scholars' claim that such standards are not authoritative. Moreover, were judicial opinions mere pretense, hiding decisions reached on other grounds, it would be astonishing that the pretense could be successful for so long. Besides, many judges and legal theorists do not hide their political visions, but rather celebrate them.

In addition to these descriptive arguments, normative considerations support interpreting our legal institutional history as embracing arguments from ethics, policy, and political theory, rather than hiding them. If moral and political argument is a legitimate tool of judicial decision-making (at least in hard cases), then it is appropriate for legal actors and citizens to engage in a dialogue about what constitutes a good society, or the best conditions for human flourishing, or the best understanding of our common culture. Public officials would be held accountable in the public arena for the moral decisions they make. The vision of officials and citizens engaging in this enterprise is far nobler than the image of public officials oppressing the populace in the interest of a dominant elite while falsely invoking the name of justice. For these and like reasons, predictability is better explained by enriched theories of adjudication than by hidden ideology.

Critical scholars' explanation of predictability as a consequence of hidden and tilted political ideology is, thus, best reconstrued as a normative attack on the moral principles judges employ. So conceived, it is simply good legal analysis, not qualitatively different from traditional legal scholarship.

In summary, the law's predictability is better explained by rich theories of adjudication than by radical indeterminacy and judges' hidden ideology. Critical scholars unnecessarily impoverish the premises judges may deploy in adjudicating conflicts. Institutional role, legal conventions, conventional morality, critical morality, and political theory enrich legal reasoning and reduce indeterminacy.

2. *Inferential Techniques*

A second respect in which critical legal scholars set incorrect standards for adjudication relates not to the premises they find legitimate but to the inferential techniques that they find legitimate. Critical scholars assume that legal right answers must flow from legally authorized premises by deductive or similarly watertight inferential techniques to avoid indeterminacy. When formalist methods prove unworkable, they infer that law is arbitrary, incoherent, or indeterminate. They fail to contemplate less stingy inferential techniques such as argument by analogy and those deployed in coherence theories.

The critics' arguments go awry, like those of skeptics, in setting unrealistic and unattainable standards for the law and then failing to envision a middle ground between formalism and radical indeterminacy. Critical legal scholars are, in Hart's fine phrase, "disappointed absolutist[s]."[183] Critical scholars implicitly, and often explicitly, assume that law is satisfactory only if legal reasoning is deductive or demonstrable. For example, some critical scholars may have thought or hoped that a formalist, deductive approach to adjudication was workable.[184] Disabused of that notion, they have gone to the other extreme and have claimed that law is arbitrary and completely indeterminate. This is a form of the irrationalist fallacy.[185] It is a myopic view which fails to envision a middle ground between formalism and radical indeterminacy. It also fails to recognize the common ground between formalism and radical indeterminacy. Both views presuppose an exceedingly strict standard for adjudication, legal truth, or legal knowledge. The difference is that only the formalist believes that the strict test can be met.[186] Critical scholars demand that for something to be law it must meet an impossibly high standard. The consequence of critical scholars' unrealistic requirement for law is that there can be no law. But this is too high a price to pay. For the most part, critical legal scholars themselves refuse to accept this consequence of their deductive standard for legal truth.[187]

As disappointed absolutists, the critical scholars embrace the same extremist position as the caricature of right-wing theorists and strict constructionists, who are allegedly committed to the unattainable watertight standard for law and adjudication.[188] Some critics' error appears to be the acceptance of this conservative criterion as the standard of adequacy for law. Other critics claim that their attack on legal theory is intended only as internal ("immanent") critique, a means of criticizing liberal legal theory according to its own criteria of adequacy.[189] So viewed, these critics' error is to attribute to all of traditional legal theory the criteria of adequacy currently embraced, if at all, only by a few right-wing scholars and politicians.[190] Thus, the attack on legal reasoning is against a straw man, not traditional legal theory.[191]

Critical scholars' assumption that legal reasoning is deductive manifests itself in their claim that even limited or occasional inconsistency demonstrates the inadequacy of law and legal theory.[192] Yet coherence theories of legal reasoning[193] can handle minor inconsistencies by classifying them as mistakes to be eliminated from the scheme of principles that they recognize as authoritative.[194] Coherence theories of law maintain that a proposition of law is true if it fits well, or coheres, with other legal propositions held to be true.[195] More precisely, a proposition is true if it is part of the best coherent justification and explanation of legal institutional history. A judge following coherence methodology would collect the constitution, statutes, regulations, precedents, and administrative writings in her jurisdiction. She would then attempt to develop a coherent scheme of principles that would explain and justify the institutional facts she had collected. In a mature and complex legal system, it is unlikely that any scheme of principles would explain all of the institutional facts. Some statutes and precedents will not cohere with the rest of the settled law. This is the kernal of truth in the patchwork quilt argument.[196] The judge then would adjust the principles she had developed and reject some precedents and other parts of the institutional history as mistakes. Adjustment of general principles and institutional facts continues until the overall scheme fits together without inconsistency. At this point the judge will have reached what Rawls has described as "reflective equilibrium,"[197] where the final scheme of principles explains and justifies the institutional history remaining after institutional mistakes are deleted. Coherence theories of legal reasoning are thus a generalization of moderate versions of the reconstructive doctrine of precedent to accommodate statutes and constitutions.[198] Thus, minor inconsistencies in institutional materials are unproblematic for coherence methodology.

3. *Explicit Metaprinciples and Conflicting Standards*

Critical scholars' assumption that legal reasoning is formalist and deductive is revealed again in their demand for explicit metaprinciples to resolve conflicts between rules, principles, and other authoritative materials. The critics enrich legal realist arguments for indeterminacy by claiming that law embodies conflicting principles and counterprinciples which cannot be reconciled, balanced, or harmonized. For example, critical scholars assert that in contract law, a principle of altruism and community conflicts with the perspective of self-interested autonomous individualism. Because of these commitments to seemingly conflicting principles, critical scholars invoke the need for – and criticize the lack of – guiding metaprinciples specifiable in advance. They argue that these metaprinciples are necessary for determinate outcomes because without them decisionmakers cannot justify their choice between opposing alternatives. In consequence, there is rampant indeterminacy. Kennedy, for example, claims that there is no available metaprinciple to explain in particular concrete contexts which principle should prevail.[199] Altman faults Dworkin's theory of adjudication for its failure to provide such metaprinciples.[200] Singer reiterates these claims:

> [W]e require a metatheory that can tell us *precisely* how we are to choose between the available alternatives. In the absence of such a metatheory, we are left free to choose between the contradictory principles. The arguments therefore do not determine the result.[201]

This demand for an explicit, mechanically applicable, metatheory is unrealistic and unnecessary. That law lacks the mechanical decision procedure for determining theorems of simple logical systems like the logic of propositions is neither surprising nor cause for concern.[202] Law may be determinate without there being a mechanical method for deciding legal questions. Indeed, standard first-order logic lacks a mechanical decision procedure for determining its theorems (although of course it has a proof procedure).[203]

It is hardly a fault that law is not more determinable in this respect than standard first-order logic! Of course, given an alleged argument (i.e., proof) in first-order logic, we can mechanically check its correctness. But nothing in logic, arithmetic, or geometry, for that matter, guarantees us a proof of any debated proposition. It

may require nonmechanical creativity and insight, as Fermat's Last Theorem demonstrates.[204]

Like classical mathematics, law may be ontologically determinate, even if there is no explicit metatheory that "tells us precisely"[205] what the law is. Unlike mathematical arguments, however, legal arguments do require judgment in the assessment of their validity. (Why else do they call those people in the black robes "judges"?) The exercise of judgment, as Aristotle, Kant, and Wittgenstein clearly saw, cannot be fully characterized in an explicit metatheory. Kant, for example, argued that concepts, including legal concepts, are best understood as rules for classifying objects.[206] Thus, the concept "offer" is a rule we use to determine whether particular manifestations of intent are offers. Kant argues that understanding how to apply a rule cannot consist solely in mastering some additional secondary rule or rules, because we would also need to understand how to apply the secondary rules, and they would then require tertiary rules, and we would be stuck in an infinite regress. At some point, the ability to apply rules must rest on some capacity other than mastering rules. This ability, which Kant called judgment (*mutterwitz* – literally, "motherwit" or "native smarts"), is a knack for determining whether something falls within the scope of a rule.[207] Once one recognizes the necessity of this separate faculty of judgment, principles of theoretical simplicity and elegance provide strong reasons for not positing any rules beyond this first level. However, this notion of judgment, for Kant, is unstable. A fortiori it is unstable in a "metatheory that can tell us precisely" which things fall within the scope of the rule or under the concept, as the vicious regress argument shows.

Wittgenstein makes a slightly different argument but arrives at a similar conclusion.

> [T]here is a way of grasping a rule which is *not* an *interpretation*, but which is exhibited in what we call "obeying the rule" and "going against it" in actual cases.
>
> Hence there is an inclination to say: every action according to the rule is an interpretation. But we ought to restrict the term "interpretation"

to the substitution of one expression of the rule for another.[208]

For Wittgenstein, understanding a rule simply consists of the ability to apply it.

Unlike Kant, Wittgenstein did not think that this ability required a separate faculty of judgment. He would deny that the acquisition of a metarule for applying a rule in controversial cases would itself constitute understanding the rule. Only correct application of the rule could demonstrate understanding. Thus, Wittgenstein would stop the regress one step earlier than Kant.

The law cannot be fully spelled out in advance since each explanation for how to apply a rule, principle, or concept will itself require explanation in novel situations or where conflict arises.[209] Thus critical scholars' claim that we cannot provide, in advance, fully explicit metaprinciples to resolve all conflicts accurately describes a limitation of all rules of behavior, not just legal theory. The question is what attitude we should take towards this fact. Since the request for mechanically applicable metaprinciples to resolve conflicts and vagueness cannot be satisfied, we should accept our lot and give up the demand. To retain the demand would set an impossibly high standard whose acceptance in turn would invite disappointment and skepticism. To give up the demand is to be realistic.

We should accept the richness and complexity of the moral decisionmaking and interpretive methods which inform law. We may not be able to deduce legal outcomes in advance, but nonetheless we have a rational, nonarbitrary process by which we can implement the abstract demands of justice.

While this process can never be fully articulated, it can be more completely elaborated and understood. We can construct deeper and more fundamental justificatory schemes through experience, insight, inspiration, and just plain hard work. The unarticulated aspects of legal systems need not be irrational or arbitrary. Resolving conflicting principles in concrete settings or deciding cases of first impression requires judgment which may be more akin to art than to science. It is a skill requiring sensitivity from its practitioners. Judgments can be better or worse, even when we cannot yet articulate why. It is no flaw in a legal theory that it employs terms and concepts whose meanings are only fully manifest in their use and application by the appropriate linguistic community. Nor is it a flaw that judges do not write infinitely long opinions, but rather eventually act, and reach a decision.[210] It is unrealistic to demand more. The finitude of theory and practice are not tantamount to their inconsistency and illegitimacy.

Critical scholars correctly perceive that law cannot be made fully explicit and deductive, yet misconstrue the significance of this fact. The issue of conflicting principles and the lack of explicit metaprinciples which resolve the conflict has been discussed at some length because beneath it lies critical scholars' most powerful argument for indeterminacy. The critics' attack would be more powerful if they deemphasized the demand for explicit metaprinciples and argued – not merely asserted – that the conflicting principles are either equally balanced or incommensurable.[211] This would, of course, be difficult to prove because it would have to be shown, not that some particular attempt to balance, reconcile, or combine the principles fails, but that no attempt could succeed.

A normative argument suggests that it would be difficult to establish that conflicting principles are frequently of equal weight, so that they balance to a tie, leading to indeterminacy between the outcomes urged by the respective conflicting principles. Notice that the more fine-grained one's measure of weight of principles, the fewer ties one is likely to find. Assume that there were only three measures of weight of principles: weak, moderate, and powerful. Consider cases where one principle is pitted against a single counterprinciple. If principles were randomly distributed among the three categories of weight, then we would expect ties between conflicting principles and counterprinciples one-third of the time, whenever the principle and counterprinciple were in the same category. But if there were twenty categories of strength of principles, not three, then under the assumption of random distribution we would expect ties in only one-twentieth of the conflicts.[212]

Since the law's function is to settle disputes, a litigant has a right to a decision in her favor if the principles that can be adduced in support of her claim are the tiniest bit more powerful than the principles against it.[213] It follows that judges should employ the subtlest, most fine-grained measure of weight possible. The complexity of mature legal systems and density of their precedents and statutes have been urged in support of the claim that the measure of weight in those systems is very fine grained indeed.[214]

Descriptive and normative considerations suggest that critics cannot establish that conflicting principles are incommensurate or that incommensurability would lead to illegitimacy. The descriptive consideration is that we combine principles all the time. The normative consideration, which returns us to the issue of legitimacy, is that if conflicting principles were truly incommensurable or were of precisely equal weight, there would, in the end, be no reason for choosing among a number of alternative outcomes. If, however, there is no ultimate reason for preferring one possible outcome over a number of alternatives, then there can be no ground for criticizing the judge no matter which outcome she chooses. She fulfills her duty and her decision is legitimate as long as she chooses from among the set of equally good outcomes.[215]

Before concluding, a few brief comments are in order concerning the instrumental use of the indeterminacy thesis to unfreeze the legal mind and encourage creative legal solutions. First, if the argument of this Article is valid and the indeterminacy thesis is false, its strategic employment will involve deception and manipulation of the audience. Even if the end is valuable, its instrumental use may not justify the disrespectful means employed. Second, if the indeterminacy thesis is perceived as false, its strategic employment will be rhetorically ineffective. Third, if believed, the thesis might enervate rather than mobilize political action. Finally, and most importantly, if judges and other legal actors accept the indeterminacy thesis, they may read this as license to decide cases in accordance with their political convictions. Given the current composition of the judiciary, this is likely to engender a more conservative legal doctrine,

hardly a result in which critical scholars would delight.

Conclusion

I have argued that the plausibility of extensive indeterminacy derives from attention to controversial appellate and Supreme Court cases. When focus is shifted to garden variety actions governed by law, determinacy predominates. The pervasiveness of easy cases makes it implausible that there is radical indeterminacy. I have further urged that critical scholars' arguments fail to satisfy the burden of dispelling this appearance of at most moderate indeterminacy. The patchwork quilt and fundamental contradiction arguments for pervasive contradiction do not yield radical indeterminacy for two main reasons. First, the arguments do not refute plausible holistic theories which reject the claim that judicial and legislative rationales and motivations are necessarily law. Second, they fail to demonstrate the existence of strict contradiction rather than reconcilable tension. This last reason explains, in large part, why the particular contradictions between rules and standards, altruism and individualism, and free will and determinism fail to yield radical indeterminacy. The alleged contradictions between free will and determinism and between subjective and objective views of value in liberal theory are flawed because they misdescribe modern liberal theory. In short, neither the abstract explanations for pervasive contradiction nor particular alleged contradictory structures demonstrate radical indeterminacy.

This conclusion is further supported by exposing three errors about legal reasoning commonly made by critical scholars. Critical arguments impoverish the premises and limit the inferential techniques available in legal argument. Moreover, they mistakenly suppose that conflicting standards can be reconciled only by explicit mechanical metaprinciples, stated in advance. This requirement of explicit metaprinciples is too demanding. Law is not mathematics, and cannot deploy only deductive, watertight methods. Law is not contradictory because its "life . . . has not been logic."[216]

I have urged also that moderate indeterminacy, even if true, has little or no consequences for political legitimacy because only rarely will anyone's obligations depend upon whether law is determinate. This conclusion emerges from a systematic consideration of the relevance of determinacy for each of the commonly alleged grounds of political obligation. For each such ground, with only occasional exceptions, I have claimed that either the ground fails to obligate or else it obligates even where law is indeterminate.

But where does this leave the issue of indeterminacy itself? Is it simply irrelevant? Not at all. Radical indeterminacy may vitiate legality, as Fuller argues.[217] It may betoken that in fact no legal system exists. Moderate indeterminacy, in contrast, is compatible with legality. But it serves to put us on inquiry. Why is this rule, area of law, or entire legal system indeterminate? It may be to allow flexibility in application, given our inability to determine the ramifications of unforeseen circumstances, as the due care standard in negligence law is said to do.[218] Or it may be because the requirements of justice are inherently abstract, or simply because no authority has had the need or the occasion to resolve the indeterminacy. On the other hand, indeterminacy may be a cloak for partial or arbitrary action. In short, indeterminacy may exist for any one of a myriad of reasons. It may, on occasion, be the visible manifestation of serious trouble at a deeper level. But we must engage in a contextually sensitive inquiry into the reasons for the indeterminacy before reaching that grave charge. No blanket condemnation – or celebration – of indeterminacy is possible, or desirable.

Notes

1   NICOMACHEAN ETHICS, bk. I, ch. 3. at 1094b, 13–14 (W. Ross trans. 1940).

2   SUMMA THEOLOGICA II (Part I), question 91, article 3, reply objection 3.

3   I return to the first aspect at the conclusion of the Article.

4   It is sometimes difficult to determine which sense of "necessitated" critical legal scholars intend. *See*

Solum, *On the Indeterminacy Crisis: Critiquing Critical Dogma*, 54 U. CHI. L. REV. 462, 491–95 (1987).

5   Gordon, *Law and Ideology*, 3 TIKKUN 14, 16–17, 85, 86 (1988); Gordon, *New Developments in Legal Theory*, in THE POLITICS OF LAW: A PROGRESSIVE CRITIQUE 281, 286–92 (D. Kairys ed. 1982) [hereinafter Gordon, *New Developments*]; Gordon, *Unfreezing Legal Reality: Critical Approaches to Law*, 15 FLA. ST. U.L. REV. 145, 197–201, 217, 220 (1987).

6   Informal conversation with Mark Tushnet (June 9, 1988).

7   *See, e.g.*, Fiss, *Objectivity and Interpretation*, 34 STAN L. REV. 739, 749 (1982); Griswold, *The Judicial Process*, 31 FED. B. J. 309, 314 (1972).

8   *See* J. RAZ, THE MORALITY OF FREEDOM 100–01 (1986); *see also* A. SIMMONS, MORAL PRINCIPLES AND POLITICAL OBLIGATIONS 6–7, 12, 195–96 (1979).

9   *See* Hyde, *The Concept of Legitimation in The Sociology of Law*, 1983 WIS. L. REV. 379.

10 Tushnet, *Following the Rules Laid Down: A Critique of Interpretivism and Neutral Principles*, 96 HARV. L. REV. 781, 781–82 (1983).

11 "Liberal" is used throughout this Article to refer to the tradition of political philosophy that is based upon the moral authority of the individual, a tradition exemplified by Locke, Hume, Kant, Bentham, Mill, and Rawls. In this usage, Reagan, Bush, Bork, and Posner, as well as Dworkin, Dukakis, Carter, and the Kennedys are liberals.

12 Actually, there are two separable questions here. First, why would conventional, liberal legal theorists care if the indeterminacy thesis were true? Second, what do critical legal scholars claim that the indeterminacy thesis shows to be wrong with conventional legal theory? My suggestion is that both conventional legal theorists and some influential critical legal scholars accept the view that significant indeterminacy undercuts the legitimacy of courts, although the attribution of that view to liberal legal theorists is more certain than the attribution to critical legal scholars.

   Even if some critical scholars would not locate the significance of the indeterminacy thesis in its consequences for political legitimacy, there is certainly a significant strain within critical legal scholarship that would. It will therefore repay our patience if we examine the connection between these critical legal scholars' claims of indeterminacy and legitimacy by brief consideration of the texts of Singer, Altman, and Kennedy.

It should be acknowledged that there is a third view in critical legal scholarship regarding the significance of the indeterminacy thesis in addition to its consequences for legitimacy, and its instrumental value in unfreezing legal consciousness and effectuating critical scholars' political agenda. If law is indeterminate, then judges are political actors wielding great power. Law is politics. Indeterminacy thus raises issues concerning the proper and best exercise of that power by judges, and of which institutional frameworks are most conducive to the wise exercise of that power. But these inquiries raise, albeit indirectly, much the same questions as would be raised by inquiring directly about the legitimacy of adjudication under conditions of indeterminacy. This is especially so if the conditions for wise exercise of judicial power and the legitimacy of adjudication are, as this Article suggests, largely dependent on the substantive virtues of the decisions judges make.

13 Singer, *The Player and The Cards: Nihilism and Legal Theory*, 94 YALE L.J. 1, 12–13 (1984).

14 *Id.* at 12.

15 *Id.* at 11.

16 *Id.* at 14.

17 Altman, *Legal Realism, Critical Legal Studies, and Dworkin*, 15 PHIL. & PUB. AFF. 205, 227–35 (1986).

18 Kennedy, *Legal Formality*, 2 J. LEGAL STUD. 351, 351–54 (1973).

19 The requisite consent could be to the entire constitutional framework. Alternatively, it might be thought that voting for legislative representatives is a form of tacit consent.

20 B. CARDOZO, THE NATURE OF THE JUDICIAL PROCESS 102–05, 113–15 (1921); *see* Southern Pacific. Co. v. Jensen, 244 U.S. 205, 221 (1917) (Holmes, J., dissenting) ("I recognize without hesitation that judges do and must legislate, but they can do so only interstitially; they are confined from molar to molecular motions.").

21 Hart, *Positivism and the Separation of Law and Morals*, 71 HARV. L. REV. 593, 606–07 (1958).

22 *Id.*

23 S. BURTON, AN INTRODUCTION TO LAW AND LEGAL REASONING 176–84, 199–214 (1985) (suggesting contextual grounds for legitimacy in place of criteria requiring rigid formalist construction).

24 *See, e.g.,* Kennedy, *supra* note 18, at 351–54.

25 For an analogous reconstruction of the formalists' argument that adjudication is illegitimate

because judges do not always apply law, see S. BURTON, *supra* note 23, at 183–84.

26 *See infra* note 30.

27 A. SIMMONS, *supra* note 8, at 191.

28 *See* L. GREEN, THE AUTHORITY OF THE STATE (1988); J. RAZ, THE AUTHORITY OF LAW 233–49 (1979); A. SIMMONS, *supra* note 8, at 191–95; Burton, *Law, Obligation, and a Good Faith Claim of Justice* (Book Review), 73 CALIF. L. REV. 1956, 1980–82 (1985).

29 This may appear incoherent because where law is indeterminate, there is no action which must be performed or avoided. Where law is indeterminate, there is no norm to obey. But the point is that citizens are obligated to obey official acts that *specify* or *concretize* the law, thus making it determinate where it was formerly indeterminate.

30 The claim that most or all citizens have consented to the law is considered a fantasy by most contemporary political theorists. *See, e.g.,* R. DWORKIN, LAW'S EMPIRE 194 (1986) [hereinafter, LAW'S EMPIRE]; D. LYONS, ETHICS AND THE RULE OF LAW 211 (1984); Smith, *Is There a Prima Facie Obligation to Obey the Law?*, 82 YALE L.J. 950, 960–64 (1973).

31 J. ROUSSEAU, THE SOCIAL CONTRACT 153 (M. Cranston trans. 1968) (footnote omitted).

32 *See* Hume, *On the Original Contract*, in DAVID HUME, ESSAYS: MORAL, POLITICAL, AND LITERARY 475 (E. Miller ed. 1985); J. PLAMENATZ, CONSENT, FREEDOM, AND POLITICAL OBLIGATION 7 (2d ed. 1968).

33 Hume, *supra* note 32, at 475; *see* LAW'S EMPIRE, *supra* note 30, at 192–93.

34 J. RAWLS, A THEORY OF JUSTICE 342–50 (1971) [hereinafter A THEORY OF JUSTICE]; A SIMMONS, *supra* note 8, at 101–08; Hart, *Are There Any Natural Rights?* 64 PHIL. REV. 175, 185 (1955); Rawls, *Legal Obligation and The Duty of Fair Play*, in LAW AND PHILOSOPHY 3, 9–10 (S. Hook ed. 1964).

35 For discussion of the duty to uphold just institutions, see A THEORY OF JUSTICE, *supra* note 34, at 333–42; A. SIMMONS, *supra* note 8, at 143–56; *see also* Rawls, *The Justification of Civil Disobedience*, in CIVIL DISOBEDIENCE: THEORY AND PRACTICE 240, 241 (H. Bedau ed. 1969).

36 LAW'S EMPIRE, *supra* note 30, at 193.

37 These practical distinctions still "fail[] to capture the intimacy of the special duty." *Id.*

38 J. RAZ, *supra* note 8, at 53.

39 LAW'S EMPIRE, *supra* note 30, at 195–216.

40 *Id.* at 88–89, 136–39; Kress, *The Interpretive Turn*, 97 ETHICS 834, 836 (1987) ("Law, Dworkin contends, requires disagreement at the appropriate golden mean to flourish. Too little and law stagnates; too much and law founders." (page reference omitted)).

41 G. POSTEMA, BENTHAM AND THE COMMON LAW TRADITION 160–62, 168–82 (1986). *See generally id.* at 147–90.

42 This is an appropriate place to note an oversimplification in the analysis. I have at various points moved freely between the legitimacy of government, or the institution of adjudication, and the citizen's obligation to obey. In fact, there are other legitimacy values besides the obligation to obey law, including rule of law and democratic values. While a more extensive examination would need to consider them, the conclusion of the analysis would remain unchanged.

Another complication worth noting but insufficient to affect the argument concerns the relationship between governmental legitimacy and citizens' obligations to obey. Although these two notions are usually coextensive, they are analytically separable and on occasion will come apart. *See* Waldron, *Theoretical Foundations of Liberalism*, 37 PHIL. Q. 127, 136–39 (1987) (arguing that consent, especially hypothetical consent, arguments for legitimacy are sometimes more powerful than consent arguments for obligation). For example, under the Benthamite settled expectations rationale for government legitimacy, sufficient indeterminacy which fails to promote utilitarian values exceeding that of the expectations it unsettles will block legitimacy. But given *de facto* adjudicatory institutions, it may nonetheless promote utility to obey their decisions, to avoid interminable disputes, and to promote coordination of behavior. Thus, a legal system which is illegitimate on Benthamite grounds because significantly more deterministic legal systems are available may nonetheless generate an obligation that citizens obey its commands. Similarly, a particular judicial order which is illegitimate and should not have been given because it fails to maximize utility may nonetheless once given generate an obligation to obey deriving from the disutilities arising from disobedience.

43 *But see* Walker, *Political Obligation and the Argument from Gratitude*, 17 PHIL. & PUB. AFF. 191 (1988) (defending the argument from gratitude).

44 *See* Solum, *supra* note 4, at 471.

45 *See, e.g.*, S. BURTON, *supra* note 23, at 95–96; Hegland, *Goodbye to Deconstruction*, 58 S. CAL. L. REV. 1203 (1985); Schauer, *Easy Cases*, 58 S. CAL. L. REV. 399 (1985); Solum, *supra* note 4.

46 Some readers may object that the legitimacy of adjudication and law depends not on the legal outcomes of everyday acts, but on how the legal system handles those controversial cases which matter most to citizens. This objection is mistaken. The legitimacy of the legal system depends on its overall performance in both everyday situations and controversial cases. Since everyday situations predominate, government legitimacy depends largely on how they are handled. Moreover, the importance to citizens of the legal system's performance in everyday situations should not be taken for granted or held against the system. Were the legal system less successful in everyday situations that mattered greatly, those cases might well become controversial.

Other readers may advance a different objection. They may find radical indeterminacy sufficiently plausible, despite the easy cases argument, that they would resist placing the burden of proof on advocates of radical indeterminacy. Rather than understanding Part II as showing that at most indeterminacy is moderate, such readers may reinterpret Part II as demonstrating the inadequacy of the arguments urged in support of radical indeterminacy.

My own reasons for denying the plausibility of radical indeterminacy are elaborated throughout the rest of this Article.

47 K. LLEWELLYN, THE BRAMBLE BUSH 66–69 (1951).

48 *Id.*

49 *Id.* at 67–68.

50 *Id.* at 68.

51 *Id.*

52 *Id.* at 67.

53 *Id.*

54 *See* J. GRAY, THE NATURE AND SOURCES OF THE LAW 261 (2d ed. 1921). This doctrine of dicta may not be coherent. In a case with two or more alternative rationales, each sufficient to support the outcome, neither rationale is necessary to the outcome. Arguably such cases would have no ratio decidendi, and therefore would stand for nothing. (The formal structure of this argument presents a difficulty which parallels the problem that multiple causes, each sufficient for the plaintiff's injury, pose for the traditional *sine qua non*, or "but for," test of causation.)

To circumvent this difficulty one could claim that such cases stand for the proposition that at least one of the alternative rationales is correct. While this solution provides a rule of the case, its ad hoc quality and employment of disjunctive rules makes it unattractive.

55 Llewellyn does not indicate how to proceed if there is no rule stated in the opinion.

56 Nothing in this procedure is limited to positive facts. In addition to *B*, for example, *not-C* could be a fact true of the decided case.

57 Oliphant, *A Return to Stare Decisis*, 6 AM. L. SCH. REV. 215 (1928); Goodhart, *Determining the Ratio Decidendi of a Case*, 40 YALE L.J. 161 (1930); F. COHEN, ETHICAL SYSTEMS AND LEGAL IDEALS 34–35 n.47 (1933); Montrose, *Ratio Decidendi and the House of Lords*, 20 MOD. L. REV. 124 (1957); Simpson, *The Ratio Decidendi of a Case*, 20 MOD. L. REV. 413 (1957); Montrose, *The Ratio Decidendi of a Case*, 20 MOD. L. REV. 587 (1957); Simpson, *The Ratio Decidendi of a Case*, 21 MOD. L. REV. 155 (1958); Goodhart, *The Ratio Decidendi of a Case*, 22 MOD. L. REV. 117 (1959); *see* K. LLEWELLYN, *supra* note 47, at 45–47.

58 B. CARDOZO, THE NATURE OF THE JUDICIAL PROCESS (1921); F. COHEN, *supra* note 57, at 33–40 (especially at 33–37); LAW'S EMPIRE, *supra* note 30, at 247–48; R. DWORKIN, TAKING RIGHTS SERIOUSLY 118–19 (1978) (describing Brandeis and Warren's argument for a right to privacy as an attempt to reconstruct precedent) [hereinafter TAKING RIGHTS SERIOUSLY]; E. LEVI, AN INTRODUCTION TO LEGAL REASONING 1–27 (in particular, at 3) (1949). *But see* Kress, *The Interpretive Turn*, 97 ETHICS 834, 847–48 (1987) (noting a criticism of Dworkin's reconstructive technique).

The technique described in the text might be labelled the strong reconstructive technique. Under more moderate versions, justifying all or most prior cases is a necessary, but not a sufficient, condition for a successful reconstruction. Dworkin, for example, requires that the reconstruction be more morally attractive than any alternative that explains the past decisions reasonably well. For elaboration, see Kress, *Legal Reasoning and Coherence Theories: Dworkin's Rights Thesis, Retroactivity, and the Linear Order of Decisions*, 72 CALIF. L. REV. 369, 377–78 & n.53 (1984) [hereinafter Kress, *Legal Reasoning*].

59 The above discussion of the orthodox technique assumes that only one case is under discussion. With minor changes, the technique can be generalized to apply to lines of precedent.

60 K. LLEWELLYN, *supra* note 47, at 73.

61 *Id.* at 67.

62 Felix Cohen argues that the orthodox doctrine of precedent should create narrower rules only when the distinction from the wider rule which is urged is morally relevant. F. COHEN, *supra* note 57, at 37; *see also* S. BURTON, *supra* note 23, at 31–39, 50–56, 81–107; E. LEVI, *supra* note 58, at 6.

63 TAKING RIGHTS SERIOUSLY, *supra* note 58, at 340–42, 360; LAW'S EMPIRE, *supra* note 30, at 231, 246–47, 254–58.

64 R. DWORKIN, A MATTER OF PRINCIPLE 143 (1985) [hereinafter A MATTER OF PRINCIPLE].

65 This interpretation of the reconstructive technique therefore assumes that there are right answers to moral questions and that legal standards can be compared in terms of moral value. But the argument may remain neutral among various particular justifications for that claim. For arguments that there are right answers to legal and moral questions, see *Id.* at 119–45; LAW'S EMPIRE, *supra* note 30, at 76–85; Moore, *Moral Reality*, 1982 WIS. L. REV. 1061; Moore, *Metaphysics, Epistemology and Legal Theory* (Book Review), 60 S. CAL. L. REV. 453 (1987).

66 The realists' claim of indeterminacy did not rest solely on the vagueness, ambiguity, or contradictory character of precedent. Although many realists did view (the two doctrines of) precedent as the richest source of indeterminacy, they also argued for indeterminacy in constitutional and statutory interpretation, and in ascertaining the facts. *See* J. FRANK, COURTS ON TRIAL 14–36, 168–69 (1949); J. FRANK, LAW AND THE MODERN MIND 125, 144–45 (1963); K. LLEWELLYN, *supra* note 47, at 88–90; K. LLEWELLYN, THE COMMON LAW TRADITION: DECIDING APPEALS 521–35 (1960); Braden, *The Search for Objectivity in Constitutional Law*, 57 YALE L.J. 571 (1948). They claimed that in most cases, not just one precedent, but many lines of precedent or authoritative provisions might be relevant. This creates the possibility of inconsistency, or that vagueness in more than one of the relevant rules will combine to generate an indeterminate result. Interesting as these ar-

guments are, they show at most modest amounts of indeterminacy.

67 M. KELMAN, A GUIDE TO CRITICAL LEGAL STUDIES 3–4, 13 (1987) [hereinafter M. KELMAN, GUIDE]; Dalton, *An Essay in The Deconstruction of Contract Doctrine*, 94 YALE L.J. 997, 1006–07 (1985); Frug, *The Ideology of Bureaucracy in American Law*, 97 HARV. L. REV. 1276, 1292 (1984); Gordon, *Critical Legal Histories*, 36 STAN. L. REV. 57, 114–16 (1984); Gordon, NEW DEVELOPMENTS, *supra* note 5, at 290; Kairys, *Legal Reasoning*, in THE POLITICS OF LAW, *supra* note 5, at 11, 13–14; Kennedy, *Form and Substance in Private Law Adjudication*, 89 HARV. L. REV. 1685, 1723 (1976) [hereinafter Kennedy, *Form and Substance*]; Kennedy, *Legal Education as Training for Hierarchy*, in THE POLITICS OF LAW, *supra* note 5, at 48–49 [hereinafter Kennedy, *Legal Education*]; Peller, *The Metaphysics of American Law*, 73 CALIF. L. REV. 1151, 1169 (1985); Singer, *supra* note 13, at 6–7, 14, 20; Spann, *Deconstructing the Legislative Veto*, 68 MINN. L. REV. 473, 528 (1984); Trubek, *Where the Action Is: Critical Legal Studies and Empiricism*, 36 STAN. L. REV. 575, 595–96 (1985); Unger, *The Critical Legal Studies Movement*, 96 HARV. L. REV. 561, 578, 619 (1983) [hereinafter Unger, *CLS*]; Yablon, *The Indeterminacy of The Law: Critical Legal Studies and The Problem of Legal Explanation*, 6 CARDOZO L. REV. 917, 917–18 (1985).

68 Unger, *CLS*, *supra* note 67, at 578.

69 *Id.* For example, Unger claims that no metaprinciple can distinguish circumstances where the courts will not review the substantive fairness of bargains from situations where bargains will be unenforcable because unconscionable. *See id.* at 625.

70 *Id.* at 578, 619.

71 Kairys, *Legal Reasoning, supra* note 67, at 11, 14; Kennedy, *Legal Education, supra* note 67, at 40, 47–48; Singer, *supra* note 13, at 6, 20.

72 Kennedy, *Form and Substance, supra* note 67, at 1723 (emphasis in original).

73 *Id.* at 1724; *see also id.* at 1773 & n.158.

74 *Id.* at 1724; *see also id.* at 1773 & n.158.

75 This Article focuses on critical scholars' patchwork quilt and fundamental contradiction arguments for radical indeterminacy and not on the linguistic or post-modern arguments because the former are more plausible and have received greater attention.

76 Unger, *CLS*, *supra* note 67, at 571.

77 *Id.; see also* Altman, *Legal Realism, Critical Legal Studies, and Dworkin*, 15 PHIL. & PUB. AFF. 205, 221 (1986).

78 Unger, *CLS*, *supra* note 67, at 571.

79 *Id.; see also id.* at 566.

80 Altman, *supra* note 77, at 221.

81 LAW'S EMPIRE, *supra* note 30, at 273 (1986).

82 Warren & Brandeis, *The Right of Privacy*, 4 HARV. L. REV. 193 (1890).

83 Respecting property cases, Warren and Brandeis argue, "Although the courts have asserted that they rested their decisions on the narrow grounds of protection to property . . . [t]he principle which protects personal writings . . . against publication in any form, is in reality not the principle of private property, but that of an inviolate personality." *Id.* at 204–05. Respecting contract cases, they assert, "We must therefore conclude that the rights, so protected, whatever their exact nature, are not rights arising from contract or from special trust . . . the principle which protects [them] . . . is the right to privacy." *Id.* at 213. Brandeis and Warren's argument is an application of the reconstructive doctrine of precedent, discussed above. *See supra* text accompanying notes 58–66.

84 *See* TAKING RIGHTS SERIOUSLY, *supra* note 58, at 118–23.

85 R. SARTORIUS, INDIVIDUAL CONDUCT AND SOCIAL NORMS 192 (1975).

86 *Id.* Sartorius actually states that the additional principles and policies are those implied by or incorporated into law, directly or indirectly, by constitutions, statutes, and particular judicial decisions, and not that the principles and policies imply the constitutions, statutes, and decisions. This misstatement may be the result of confusion on Sartorius' part. Or it may be that he intends the phrase "implies indirectly" to encompass the situation where the principle or policy is necessary to explain deductively the constitutional provision, statutory enactment, or judicial decision. The principle or policy explains, by implying, the provision, enactment, or decision, and thus provides a deductive justification for it.

87 TAKING RIGHTS SERIOUSLY, *supra* note 58, at 81–130; Kress, *supra* note 58, at 377–79 & n.53. Dworkin minimizes the influence of policies in his theory of adjudication. TAKING RIGHTS SERIOUSLY, *supra* note 58, at 81–130.

88 Kennedy, *Form and Substance, supra* note 67, at 1685; *see also id.* at 1774, 1776.

89   Kennedy, *The Structure of Blackstone's Commentaries*, 28 Buffalo L. Rev. 205, 211–12, (1979) [hereinafter Kennedy, *Structure*]; *see* M. Kelman, Guide, *supra* note 67, at 17.

90   Kennedy, *Structure*, *supra* note 89, at 211–12.

91   *Id.* at 213; Kennedy, *Form and Substance*, *supra* note 67, at 1776. In later writings, Kennedy renounces the fundamental contradiction and the abstract concepts of individualism and altruism. Gabel & Kennedy, *Roll Over Beethoven*, 36 Stan. L. Rev. 1, 15–16 (1986). Kennedy's most recent writing on the subject interprets indeterminacy as the experience one has when one is unsure how the law comes out in a particular concrete context. Kennedy, *Freedom and Constraint in Adjudication: A Critical Phenomenology*, 36 J.L. Educ. 518 (1986). This phenomenological or psychological account of indeterminacy, in contrast to an ontological account, has no troublesome implications for the legitimacy of adjudication.

92   As logicians use the word, two propositions are contradictory if some proposition and its external negation are derivable from the original two propositions within standard first-order logic. The external negation of "John is six feet tall," for example, is "It is not the case that John is six feet tall." For a discussion of first-order logic, *see* 1 A. Church, Introduction to Mathematical Logic (1956).

93   Nor are critical legal scholars claiming that there is an internal contradiction: we need fusion with others and we need that there not be fusion with others.

94   *See, e.g.*, Kennedy, *Structure*, *supra* note 89 at 257.

95   Herzog, *As Many as Six Impossible Things Before Breakfast*, 75 Calif. L. Rev. 609, 610 (1987).

96   This terminology derives from Dworkin, Law's Empire, *supra* note 30, at 241, 268, 269, 274–75.

97   Kennedy, *Structure*, *supra* note 89, at 210, 218, 219, 279, 294.

98   *Id.* at 220.

99   The distinction is described in H. Hart & A. Sacks, The Legal Process: Basic Problems in the Making and Application of Law 155–60 (tent. ed. 1958); Kennedy, *Form and Substance*, *supra* note 67, at 1687–88.

100 Kennedy, *Form and Substance*, *supra* note 67, at 1685.

101 *Id.* at 1687–90, 1697–1701. For further discussion, *see* M. Kelman, Guide, *supra* note 67, at 15–63.

102 *See* sources cited *supra* note 99; Kennedy, *Form and Substance*, *supra* note 67, at 1770.

103 Kennedy, *Form and Substance*, *supra* note 67, at 1695.

104 *Id.* at 1690. Increased conflict, however, will not arise if the rules are confined to mutually exclusive areas.

105 *Id.* at 1699–1700. This argument assumes that because there are fewer rules, there will be fewer conflicts between them. Yet their enlarged scope might lead to more frequent conflicts.

106 *Id.* at 1775.

107 "Formal" invokes here whether to use the rule or standard form. The logician's sense of strict, formal contradiction is not intended.

108 Kennedy, *Form and Substance*, *supra* note 67, at 1713–16.

109 *Id.* at 1717–22 (esp. 1717–18).

110 Unger, *CLS*, *supra* note 67, at 622. *But see* Waldron, *When Justice Replaces Affection: The Need for Rights*, 11 Harv. J. L. & Pub. Pol. 625 (1988) (arguing that rights are necessary as a safety net when affectional relationships go awry).

111 Unger, *CLS*, *supra* note 67, at 622. It should be noted that Unger also provides a "more subtle and justifiable" account of the dichotomy. The details of this more subtle account are unnecessary for present purposes.

112 *Id.* at 623.

113 *See supra* text accompanying notes 88–98.

114 M. Kelman, Guide, *supra* note 67, at 65. *See generally id.* at 64–87.

115 *Id.* at 118.

116 *Id.* at 4, 5.

117 Kelman's right-wing interpretation of liberalism reveals a formalist strain in his thought. Right-wing libertarian and economic versions of liberalism are more truly liberal because they are purer and more coherent. *Id.* at 5. That is, they exemplify an immanent rationality, and thus a formal purity, which Kelman does not perceive in more complex, left-wing, deontological and egalitarian strains of liberalism. For an intriguing discussion of formalism and conceptual coherence, see Weinrib, *Legal Formalism: On the Immanent Rationality of Law*, 97 Yale L.J. 949 (1988).

118 M. Kelman, Guide, *supra* note 67, at 4, 5.

119 *Id.* at 5.

120 *Id.*

121 *Id.* (emphasis in original).

122 *Id.* at 118 (emphasis in original).

123 A THEORY OF JUSTICE, *supra* note 34, at 520–29.

124 Stick, *Charting the Development of Critical Legal Studies* (Book Review), 88 COLUM L. REV. 407, 416–17 (1988); *accord* LAW'S EMPIRE, *supra* note 30, at 440 n.19 & 441 n.20.

125 R. UNGER, KNOWLEDGE AND POLITICS 76 (1975) [hereinafter KNOWLEDGE AND POLITICS]. The contradiction between value subjectivity and value objectivity has been elaborated more in the realm of political theory than in legal doctrine.

126 M. KELMAN, GUIDE, *supra* note 67, at 64; *see* KNOWLEDGE AND POLITICS, *supra* note 125, at 76; Hutchison, *Of Kings and Dirty Rascals: The Struggle for Democracy*, 1984 QUEENS L.J. 273, 282; Tushnet, *Following The Rules Laid Down: A Critique of Interpretivism and Neutral Principles*, 96 HARV, L. REV. 781 (1983).

127 M. KELMAN, GUIDE, *supra* note 67, at 66.

128 KNOWLEDGE AND POLITICS, *supra* note 125, at 31. While philosophers have frequently discussed essences and essential properties, the notion of "intelligible essences" is not in current philosophical usage. Unger claims that the doctrine of intelligible essences has a long philosophical pedigree, but the attributions he makes of his definition to various philosophers are dubious. Ewald, *Unger's Philosophy: A Critical Legal Study*, 97 YALE L.J. 665, 693–95 & n.120 (1988).

129 KNOWLEDGE AND POLITICS, *supra* note 125, at 32.

130 *Id.* at 79.

131 *Id.* at 101–02.

132 M. KELMAN, GUIDE, *supra* note 67, at 64, 66.

133 *Id.* at 75 (stating an analogous dilemma in the context of Posner's doctrine that legal rules should mimic the market); *see also* Kelman, *Trashing*, 36 STAN. L. REV. 293, 294 (1984).

134 M. KELMAN, GUIDE, *supra* note 67, at 69–70.

135 T. HOBBES, LEVIATHAN ch. 6 (Liberal Arts Press ed. 1958) (1651).

136 *See, e.g.*, J. LOCKE, AN ESSAY CONCERNING HUMAN UNDERSTANDING bk. IV, ch.3, paras. 18–20 (Fraser ed., Dover Press ed. 1959) (v.2 at 207–12); J. MILL, UTILITARIANISM ch. 2 (Liberal Arts Press ed. 1957) (1863); A THEORY OF JUSTICE, *supra* note 34; TAKING RIGHTS SERIOUSLY, *supra* note 58.

137 *See* Ewald, *supra* note 128, at 673–91, for a powerful criticism of Unger's attempt to describe and critique the core of liberalism in order to avoid consideration of differences among liberal theories.

138 A MATTER OF PRINCIPLE, *supra* note 64, 191–92, 203.

139 A THEORY OF JUSTICE, *supra* note 34, at 520–29.

140 M. KELMAN, GUIDE, *supra* note 67, at 86–113.

141 *Id.* at 87 (emphasis in original). There are at least two separable notions of free will. One is understood as the absence of material causation, or the absence of externally determined action. Human agents are "uncaused causers." The other appears to require causation, as it is defined either in terms of the agent's ability to have done otherwise, or as an act which flows from some aspect of the agent's personality. Most current theorists opt for some version of the second notion.

142 *Id.* at 91 (emphasis in original).

143 *Id.* at 86–87.

144 Stick, *supra* note 124, at 414.

145 M. KELMAN, GUIDE, *supra* note 67, at 87.

146 Foot, *Free Will as Involving Determinism*, 66 THE PHILOSOPHICAL REVIEW 439, 439 (1957) ("The idea that free will can be reconciled with determinism is now very widely accepted."); *see also* A. J. Ayer, *Freedom and Necessity* in PHILOSOPHICAL ESSAYS 278–84 (1954); D. HUME, AN INQUIRY CONCERNING HUMAN UNDERSTANDING 90–91, 105–11 (C. Hendel ed. 1955) (§ 8); 2 J. S. MILL, AN EXAMINATION OF SIR WILLIAM HAMILTON'S PHILOSOPHY 265–304 (1873); M. MOORE, LAW AND PSYCHIATRY: RETHINKING THE RELATIONSHIP 360–65 (1984); Hobart, *Free Will as Involving Determinism and Inconceivable Without It*, 63 MIND 1 (1934); Smith, *Free Will and Moral Responsibility*, 57 MIND 45, 45–46 (1948).

147 Showing liberal theory's commitment to both free will and determinism is necessary, but not sufficient, to establish a contradictory commitment. Kelman must also establish incompatibilism. *See supra* text accompanying notes 145–146.

148 *See* M. KELMAN, GUIDE, *supra* note 67, at 95–99.

149 *Id.* at 87.

150 31 Ala. App. 334, 17 So. 2d 427 (1944).

151 2 N. Y. 2d 133, 2 N. Y. S. 2d 558, 138 N. E. 2d 799 (1956).

152 M. KELMAN, GUIDE, *supra* note 67, at 93–96.

153 For additional discussion of our inability to provide complete and explicit metaprinciples in advance, see *infra* text accompanying notes 202–215.

154 *See* M. KELMAN, GUIDE, *supra* note 67, at 93.

155 Kelman, *Trashing, supra* note 133, at 299–304 (reciting constructive proposals by critical scholars).

156 S. BURTON, *supra* note 23, at 167–204; Langille, *Revolution Without Foundation: The Grammar of Skepticism and Law*, 33 MCGILL L. REV. 451, 486 n. 162 (1988); Stick, *Can Nihilism Be Pragmatic*, 100 HARV. L. REV. 332, 345–48 (1986).

157 Developed in this way, the provision for conflicting standards may be seen as part of a complex method for determining the legitimate premises. The conflicting standards were only the result of an initial stage in determining the legitimate premises. Standards which pass this initial test may nevertheless ultimately not be legitimate because they do not survive when the first stage standards are reconstructed to eliminate inconsistency and conflict. Only those propositions which form part of the reconstructed set are truly legitimate.

   Alternatively, each of the conflicting or inconsistent standards may be seen as legitimate, but the methods of inference permitted by the theory of legal reasoning cannot then be standard deduction, but must be considerably more sophisticated. In first-order logic, any proposition at all follows from two inconsistent premises. Under a theory of legal reasoning which legitimizes inconsistent standards, rules of legal inference must be designed to avoid the consequence that every proposition is legally true. Consequently, such theories of legal reasoning cannot deploy the standard axioms and rules of inference of first-order deductive logic.

158 This argument is sometimes attributed to G. E. Moore. *See* G. MOORE, PHILOSOPHICAL PAPERS chs. 2, 7 and 9 (1959); G. HARMAN, THOUGHT 3, 7 (1972).

159 The negation of the proposition p is "It is not the case that p."

160 The argument requires a second plausible premise that we are absolutely certain of very few things.

161 Logicians distinguish logical validity from soundness. An argument is logically valid if the truth of its premises necessitates the truth of its conclusion. An argument is sound if the argument is logically valid, and all of its prem-

ises are true. The conclusion of a logically valid argument may (but need not) be false, if one or more premises is false. The conclusion of a sound argument must be true. *See* I. COPI, INTRODUCTION TO LOGIC 24–25 (3d ed. 1968).

162 To be precise, the analogy is between our belief that the best explanation of legal predictability is determinacy and our belief that the best explanation of our perceptions is the existence of middle-sized material objects.

163 B. CARDOZO, THE GROWTH OF THE LAW 60 (1924).

164 Newman, *Between Legal Realism and Neutral Principles: The Legitimacy of Institutional Values*, 72 CALIF. L. REV. 200, 204 (1984).

165 Rubin, *Doctrine in Decision-Making: Rationale or Rationalization*, 1987 UTAH L. REV. 357, 367.

166 J. HOWARD, COURTS OF APPEALS IN THE FEDERAL JUDICIAL SYSTEM 193 (1981).

167 Heavy caseloads do not always suppress dissents. Judge Posner reports growth in the number of "nonreasoned" separate opinions – concurrences as well as dissents – consisting of a conclusion and a few lines hinting at the reasoning. R. POSNER, THE FEDERAL COURTS: CRISIS AND REFORM 128–29 (1985).

168 J. HOWARD, *supra* note 166, at 193.

169 J. FRANK, COURTS ON TRIAL: MYTH AND REALITY IN AMERICAN JUSTICE 162–64 (1949).

170 Hutcheson, *The Judgment Intuitive: The Function of the "Hunch" in Judicial Decision*, 14 CORNELL L. Q. 274, 274–77 (1929); Hutcheson, *Lawyer's Law, and the Little, Small Dice*, 7 TUL. L. REV. 1, 3–12 (1932).

171 *E.g.*, F. COHEN, ETHICAL SYSTEMS AND LEGAL IDEALS 3–7 (1933); Cohen, *The Problems of Functional Jurisprudence*, in THE LEGAL CONSCIENCE: SELECTED PAPERS OF FELIX S. COHEN 76, 93–94 (1960) [hereinafter THE LEGAL CONSCIENCE]; Llewellyn, *Some Realism About Realism*, in JURISPRUDENCE: REALISM IN THEORY AND PRACTICE 70–71 (1962).

172 *E.g.*, Cohen, *Field Theory and Judicial Logic*, in THE LEGAL CONSCIENCE, *supra* note 171, at 146.

173 *E.g.*, H. HART & A. SACKS, *supra* note 99, at 158–60; TAKING RIGHTS SERIOUSLY, *supra* note 58 at 22, 84 (1978) (principles and rules only).

174 Dworkin appears to fall victim to this fallacy in TAKING RIGHTS SERIOUSLY, *supra* note 58, at 29–30.

The strongest realist arguments are based on conflict, not gaps. Yet conflict can be conceived as a form of gap: namely, no metaprinciple to resolve the conflict.

175 Dalton, *supra* note 67, at 1009–10; Singer, *supra* note 13, at 10, 19. The consequences of conflict for legal indeterminacy are discussed in detail *infra* at text accompanying notes 199–215.

176 Singer, *supra* note 13, at 21–25. Singer also mentions "existing structure of legal argumentation" and existing "orientation of (legal) thought." *Id.* at 21. These also seem to be authoritative.

177 *See, e.g.*, H. HART & A. SACKS, *supra* note 99; Fuller, *The Forms and Limits of Adjudication*, 92 HARV. L. REV. 353 (1978).

178 *See, e.g.*, S. BURTON, *supra* note 23, at 94–98, 111–23; M. EISENBERG, THE NATURE OF THE COMMON LAW (1988); Fiss, *supra* note 7.

179 LAW'S EMPIRE, *supra* note 30. *Law's Empire* may be read as requiring each judge to act on her sincerely held political convictions. Alternatively, it may be read as requiring each judge to act on what true political morality would require. Dworkin leans toward this latter interpretation when he claims that there are right answers to legal issues. When he wishes to emphasize how legal reasoning looks from the judge's point of view, Dworkin employs the first version. Of course, in attempting to follow true political morality, the judge must rely on her own convictions about political morality, so in practice the two recommendations yield indistinguishable outcomes. The difference between the two versions is reflected in whether a judge who sincerely holds incorrect political views and acts on them is to be described as violating her judicial duties, or as satisfying them, but poorly.

180 Coleman, *Negative and Positive Positivism*, 11 J. LEGAL STUD. 139, 156–64 (1982); Lyons, *Moral Aspects of Legal Theory*, in 7 MIDWEST STUDIES IN PHILOSOPHY 223, 237 (P. French, T. Vehling, Jr., H. Wettstein eds. 1982); Lyons, *Principles, Positivism and Legal Theory* (Book Review), 87 YALE. L.J. 415, 425 (1977); Soper, *Legal Theory and the Obligation of the Judge: The Hart-Dworkin Dispute*, 75 MICH. L. REV. 473, 511–12 (1977).

181 Raz, *Authority, Law and Morality*, 68 THE MONIST 295, 311–15 (1985).

182 Notably, this response shifts the issue from whether law is indeterminate to whether proper outcomes of adjudication are. But this shift seems appropriate. It is proper outcomes of lawsuits and legal issues, and not the correct usage of the word "law" or the concept of a legal system about which critical legal scholars are concerned.

183 H. L. A. HART, THE CONCEPT OF LAW 135 (1961) (referring to the legal realists' skepticism about the bindingness of legal rules).

184 For arguments demonstrating that legal reasoning is not deductive, see S. BURTON, *supra* note 23, at 41–59 (1985); Moore, *The Semantics of Judging*, 54 S. CAL. L. REV. 151 (1981).

185 R. WASSERSTROM, THE JUDICIAL DECISION 23–24 (1961).

186 S. BURTON, *supra* note 23, at 191.

187 *See, e.g.*, Kennedy, *Form and Substance, supra* note 67, at 1724, 1773 n.158.

188 Stick, *supra* note 156, at 346, 363–65. The attribution of deductive standards to strict constructionists and right-wing theorists is a caricature and does not survive a careful reading of their texts. *See, e.g.*, Bork, *The Constitution, Original Intent, and Economic Rights*, 23 SAN DIEGO L. REV. 823 (1986); Bork, *Neutral Principles and Some First Amendment Problems*, 47 IND. L. REV. 1 (1971); Meese, *The Supreme Court of the United States: Bulwark of a Limited Constitution*, 27 S. TEX. L. REV. 455 (1986).

189 Singer, *supra* note 13, at 10.

190 Stick, *supra* note 156, at 346, 350–51; KNOWLEDGE AND POLITICS, *supra* note 125, at 15. *But see* Unger, *CLS, supra* note 67, at 564 (denying that his attack conceives of formalism as a deductive or quasi-deductive method capable of producing determinate results).

191 For example, Ronald Dworkin is a favorite target of critical scholars' attacks. Unger, *CLS, supra* note 67, at 575–76 (describing the rights and principles school). Yet, from the beginning he has denied that his theory of legal reasoning is deductive or mechanically applicable. TAKING RIGHTS SERIOUSLY, *supra* note 58, at 81. Steven Burton, David Lyons, and Michael Moore similarly deny that adjudication employs only deductive, watertight reasoning. S. BURTON, *supra* note 23, at 165–85; Lyons, *Justification and Judicial Responsibility*, 72 CALIF. L. REV. 178 (1984); Lyons, *Derivability, Defensibility and the Justification of Judicial Decisions*, 68 THE MONIST 325 (1985); Moore, *supra* note 184, at 151.

192 Singer, *supra* note 13, at 15–16; Stick, *supra* note 156, at 347.

193 S. Burton, *supra* note 23, at 132–45; Taking Rights Seriously, *supra* note 58, at 81–130.

194 For a discussion of coherence theories, *see* Feinberg, *Justice, Fairness and Rationality*, 81 Yale L.J. 1004, 1018–21 (1972); Haven, *Justification as Coherence*, in Law, Morality and Rights 67 (M.A. Stewart ed. 1983). The goal of coherentist methods is to reach a state of reflective equilibrium. For discussion of reflective equilibrium, see A Theory of Justice, *supra* note 34, at 46–53; Rawls, *Outline of a Decision Procedure for Ethics*, 60 Phil. Rev. 177 (1951).

195 Taking Rights Seriously, *supra* note 58, at 283. *See generally* Kress, *supra* note 58, at 369. The exposition of coherence theories in the text follows Dworkin in Taking Rights Seriously, *supra* note 58, at 81–130, 159–68 and Law's Empire, *supra* note 30, at 46–73, 225–58, 264–65.

196 *See supra* text accompanying notes 76–87.

197 A Theory of Justice, *supra* note 34, at 46–53; Taking Rights Seriously, *supra* note 58, at 118–23, 159–68.

198 *See supra* note 58.

199 Kennedy, *Form and Substance, supra* note 67, at 1723–24.

200 Altman, *supra* note 17, at 218–19. Altman also claims that Dworkin's theory requires these metaprinciples because it rejects intuitionism. *Id.*

201 Singer, *supra* note 13, at 16 (1984) (emphasis added); *see also id.* at 15–18.

202 The logic of propositions, or propositional calculus, covers the logic of the sentential connectives (operators that take sentences as objects to form other sentences). The standard sentential connectives are: negation – it is not the case that *P*; disjunction – *P* or *Q*; conjunction – *P* and *Q*; implication – if *P*, then *Q*; equivalence – *P* if and only if *Q*. *See, e.g.*, A Church, *supra* note 92, at 69–166.

    A decision procedure is an effective procedure or algorithm (i.e., a mechanically applicable means) by which to determine for any arbitrary sentence of a logical system whether or not it is a theorem, and if so, to provide a proof of it. (Some writers omit the requirement that a proof be provided.) *Id.* at 99 & n.183.

203 This result was first proven by Alonzo Church. *See* Church, *A Note on the Entscheidungs Problem*, 1 J. Symbolic Logic 40 (1936);

Church, *Correction*, 1 J. Symbolic Logic 101 (1936). For more accessible proofs, see G. Boolos & R. Jeffrey, Computability and Logic 115–24 (1974) and S. Kleene, Introduction to Metamathematics 432–35 (1950). Standard first-order logic contains, in addition to the propositional calculus, means to express the quantifiers, all and some. A. Church, *supra* note 92, at 168–76.

204 Fermat was a famous mathematican who wrote a "theorem" on the margin of a book with the remark that the margin was too small to contain the proof. Generations of mathematicians have been unable to verify Fermat's claim.

205 Singer, *supra* note 13, at 16.

206 The interpretation of Kant in the text follows C. Larmore, Patterns of Moral Complexity 1–3 (1987); *see* I. Kant, Critique of Pure Reason A132/B171 – A134/B174 (N.K. Smith trans. 1929).

207 C. Larmore, *supra* note 206, at 2–3.

208 L. Wittgenstein, Philosophical Investigations § 201 (G. Anscombe trans. 3d ed. 1958) (italics in original); *see also id.* § 1 ("Well, I assume he *acts* as I have described. Explanations come to an end somewhere.") (italics in original); S. Kripke, Wittgenstein on Rules and Private Language (1982). *But cf.* C. McGinn, Wittgenstein on Meaning (1984) (criticizing Kripke's interpretation).

209 Thus, either an infinite regress ensues, or the explanations fold back onto themselves resulting in vicious circularity.

210 Burton, *Law as Practical Reason*, 62 S. Cal. L. Rev.—(1989).

211 Stick, *supra* note 156, at 362 n. 130, 364 n.141.

212 Of course, the assumptions of equal distribution among the categories of weight, and the artificial restriction of one principle to each side are false. The lesson remains valid nevertheless under realistic conditions.

213 Taking Rights Seriously, *supra* note 58, at 44.

214 *Id.* at 286–87.

215 One could argue that the existence of judicial choice among equally acceptable outcomes or incommensurate principles shows that judicial decisions may not represent determinate compromises between conflicting principles. Thus, the claim that judges resolve conflicts all the time is suspect. While the logical possibility of principles being equally balanced or incommensurate must be conceded, the pervasiveness

of the practice need not be. If courts frequently choose between equally good outcomes or incommensurate principles, one would expect judicial opinions to occasionally acknowledge such decisions. Yet I know of no opinion which does so.

For an argument that even if outcomes are equally good, judges should not act as if they are, but should rather strive to find a best answer, see Sartorius, *Bayes' Theorem, Hard Cases, and Judicial Discretion*, 11 Ga. L. Rev. 1269 (1977).

216   O. Holmes, The Common Law 1 (1923).

217   L. Fuller, The Morality of Law 39 (rev. ed. 1969).

218   H. L. A. Hart, *supra* note 183, at 129.

Part V

Rights and Other Legal Concepts

12

Some Fundamental Legal Conceptions as Applied in Judicial Reasoning

Wesley N. Hohfeld

From very early days down to the present time the essential nature of trusts and other equitable interests has formed a favorite subject for analysis and disputation. The classical discussions of Bacon[1] and Coke are familiar to all students of equity, and the famous definition of the great chief justice (however inadequate it may really be) is quoted even in the latest textbooks on trusts.[2] That the subject has had a peculiar fascination for modern legal thinkers is abundantly evidenced by the well known articles of Langdell[3] and Ames,[4] by the oft-repeated observations of Maitland in his Lectures on Equity,[5] by the very divergent treatment of Austin in his Lectures on Jurisprudence,[6] by the still bolder thesis of Salmond in his volume on Jurisprudence,[7] and by the discordant utterances of Mr. Hart[8] and Mr. Whitlock[9] in their very recent contributions to our periodical literature.

It is believed that all of the discussions and analyses referred to are inadequate. Perhaps, however, it would have to be admitted that even the great intrinsic interest of the subject itself and the noteworthy divergence of opinion existing among thoughtful lawyers of all times would fail to afford more than a comparatively slight excuse for any further discussion considered as a mere end in itself. But, quite apart from the presumably practical consideration of endeavoring to "think straight" in relation to all legal problems, it is apparent that the true analysis of trusts and other equitable interests is a matter that should appeal to even the most extreme pragmatists of the law. It may well be that one's view as to the correct analysis of such interests would control the decision of a number of specific questions. This is obviously true as regards the solution of many difficult and delicate problems in constitutional law and in the conflict of laws.[10] So, too, in certain questions in the law of perpetuities, the intrinsic nature of equitable interests is of great significance, as attested by the well-known *Gomm* case[11] and others more or less similar. The same thing is apt to be true of a number of special questions relating to the subject of *bona fide* purchase for value. So on indefinitely.[12]

But all this may seem like misplaced emphasis; for the suggestions last made are not peculiarly applicable to equitable interests: the same points and the same examples seem valid in relation to all possible kinds of jural interests, legal as well as equitable, – and that too, whether we are concerned with "property," "contracts," "torts," or any other title of the law. Special reference has therefore been made to the subject of trusts and other equitable interests only for the reason that the striking divergence of opinion relating thereto conspicuously exemplifies the need for dealing somewhat more intensively and systematically than is usual with the nature and analysis of all types of jural interests. Indeed, it would be virtually impossible to consider the subject of trusts at all adequately without, at the very threshold analyzing and discriminating the various fundamental conceptions that are involved in practically every legal problem. In this connection the suggestion may be ventured that the usual discussions of trusts and other jural interests seem inadequate (and at times misleading) for the very reason that they are not founded on a sufficiently comprehensive and discriminating analysis of jural relations in general. Putting the matter in another way, the tendency – and the fallacy – has been to treat the specific problem as if it were far less complex than it really is; and this commendable effort to treat as simple that which is really complex has, it is believed, furnished a serious obstacle to the clear understanding, the orderly statement, and the correct solution of legal problems. In short, it is submitted that the right kind of simplicity can result only from more searching and more discriminating analysis.

If, therefore, the title of this article suggests a merely philosophical inquiry as to the nature of law and legal relations, – a discussion regarded more or less as an end in itself, – the writer may be pardoned for repudiating such a connotation in advance. On the contrary, in response to the invitation of the editor of this journal, the main purpose of the writer is to emphasize certain oft-neglected matters that may aid in the understanding and in the solution of practical, everyday problems of the law. With this end in view, the present article and another soon to follow will discuss, as of chief concern, the basic conceptions of the law, – the legal elements that

enter into all types of jural interests. A later article will deal specially with the analysis of certain typical and important interests of a complex character, – more particularly trusts and other equitable interests. In passing, it seems necessary to state that both of these articles are intended more for law school students than for any other class of readers. For that reason, it is hoped that the more learned reader may pardon certain parts of the discussion that might otherwise seem unnecessarily elementary and detailed. On the other hand, the limits of space inherent in a periodical article must furnish the excuse for as great a brevity of treatment as is consistent with clearness, and for a comparatively meager discussion – or even a total neglect – of certain matters the intrinsic importance of which might otherwise merit greater attention. In short, the emphasis is to be placed on those points believed to have the greatest practical value.

Legal Conceptions Contrasted with Non-Legal Conceptions

At the very outset it seems necessary to emphasize the importance of differentiating purely legal relations from the physical and mental facts that call such relations into being. Obvious as this initial suggestion may seem to be, the arguments that one may hear in court almost any day and likewise a considerable number of judicial opinions afford ample evidence of the inveterate and unfortunate tendency to confuse and blend the legal and the non-legal quantities in a given problem. There are at least two special reasons for this.

For one thing, the association of ideas involved in the two sets of relations – the physical and the mental on the one hand, and the purely legal on the other – is in the very nature of the case, extremely close. This fact has necessarily had a marked influence upon the general doctrines and the specific rules of early systems of law. Thus, we are told by Pollock and Maitland:

> Ancient German law, like ancient Roman law, sees great difficulties in the way of an assignment

of a debt or other benefit of a contract ... men do not see how there can be a transfer of a right unless that right is embodied in some corporeal thing. The history of the incorporeal things has shown us this; they are not completely transferred until the transferee has obtained seisin, has turned his beasts onto the pasture, presented a clerk to the church or hanged a thief upon the gallows. A covenant or a warranty of title may be so bound up with land that the assignee of the land will be able to sue the covenantor or warrantor.[13]

In another connection, the same learned authors observe:

The realm of mediæval law is rich with incorporeal things. Any permanant right which is of a transferable nature, at all events if it has what we may call a territorial ambit, is thought of as a thing that is very like a piece of land. Just because it is a thing it is transferable. This is no fiction invented by the speculative jurists. For the popular mind these things are things. The lawyer's business is not to make them things but to point out that they are incorporeal. The layman who wishes to convey the advowson of a church will say that he conveys the church; it is for Bracton to explain to him that what he means to transfer is not that structure of wood and stone which belongs to God and the saints but a thing incorporeal, as incorporeal as his own soul or the *anima mundi*.[14]

A second reason for the tendency to confuse or blend non-legal and legal conceptions consists in the ambiguity and looseness of our legal terminology. The word "property" furnishes a striking example. Both with lawyers and with laymen this term has no definite or stable connotation. Sometimes it is employed to indicate the physical object to which various legal rights, privileges, etc., relate; then again – with far greater discrimination and accuracy – the word is used to denote the legal interest (or aggregate of legal relations) appertaining to such physical object. Frequently there is a rapid and fallacious shift from the one meaning to the other. At times, also, the term is used in such a "blended" sense as to convey no definite meaning whatever.

For the purpose of exemplifying the looser usage just referred to, we may quote from *Wilson v. Ward Lumber Co.*:[15]

The term 'property', as commonly used denotes any external object *over which* the *right* of property is exercised. In this sense it is a very wide term, and includes every class of acquisitions which a man can own or have an interest in.

Perhaps the ablest statement to exemplify the opposite and more accurate usage is that of Professor Jeremiah Smith (then Mr. Justice Smith) in the leading case of *Eaton v. B. C. & M. R. R. Co.*:[16]

In a strict legal sense, land is not 'property', but the subject of property. The term 'property', although in common parlance frequently applied to a tract of land or a chattel, in its legal signification 'means only the rights of the owner in relation to it'. 'It denotes a right over a determinate thing'. 'Property is the right of any person to possess, use, enjoy, and dispose of a thing'. Selden, J., in *Wynehamer v. People*, 13 N. Y., 378, p. 433; 1 Blackstone's com., 138; 2 Austin's *Jurisprudence*, 3rd ed., 817, 818. ... The right of indefinite user (or of using indefinitely) is an essential quality of absolute property, without which absolute property can have no existence. ... This right of user necessarily includes the right and power of excluding others from using the land. See 2 *Austin on Jurisprudence*, 3rd ed., 836; Wells, J., in *Walker v. O. C. W. R. R.*, 103 Mass., 10, p. 14.

Another useful passage is to be found in the opinion of Sherwood, J., in *St. Louis v. Hall*:[17]

Sometimes the term is applied to the thing itself, as a horse, or a tract of land; these things, however, though the subjects of property, are, when coupled with possession, but the *indicia*, the visible manifestation of invisible rights, 'the evidence of things not seen.'

Property, then, in a determinate object, is composed of certain constituent elements, to wit: The unrestricted right of use, enjoyment, and disposal, of that object.

In connection with the ambiguities latent in the term "property", it seems well to observe that similar looseness of thought and expression lurks in the supposed (but false) contrast between "corporeal" and "incorporeal" property. The second passage above quoted from Pollock and Maitland exhibits one phase of this matter. For further striking illustration, reference may be made to Blackstone's well-known discussion of corporeal and incorporeal hereditaments. Thus, the great commentator tells us:

> But an hereditament, says Sir Edward Coke, is by much the largest and most comprehensive expression; for it includes not only lands and tenements, but whatsoever *may be inherited*, be it corporeal or incorporeal, real, personal, or mixed.[18]

It is clear that only *legal interests* as such can be inherited; yet in the foregoing quotation there is inextricable confusion between the physical or "corporeal" objects and the corresponding legal interests, all of which latter must necessarily be "incorporeal," or "invisible," to use the expression of Mr. Justice Sherwood. This ambiguity of thought and language continues throughout Blackstone's discussion; for a little later he says:

> Hereditaments, then, to use the largest expression, are of two kinds, corporeal and incorporeal. Corporeal consist of such as affect the senses, such as may be seen and handled by the body; incorporeal are not the objects of sensation, can neither be seen nor handled; are creatures of the mind, and exist only in contemplation.

Still further on he says:

> An incorporeal hereditament is a right issuing out of a thing corporate (whether real or personal), or concerning, or annexed to, or exercisable within, the same....
>
> Incorporeal hereditaments are principally of ten sorts: advowsons, tithes, commons, ways, offices, dignities, franchises, corodies or pensions, annuities, and rents.

Since all legal interests are "incorporeal" – consisting, as they do, of more or less limited aggregates of *abstract* legal relations – such a supposed contrast as that sought to be drawn by Blackstone can but serve to mislead the unwary. The legal interest of the fee

simple owner of land and the comparatively limited interest of the owner of a "right of way" over such land are alike so far as "incorporeality" is concerned; the true contrast consists, of course, primarily in the fact that the fee simple owner's aggregate of legal relations is far more extensive than the aggregate of the easement owner.

Much of the difficulty, as regards legal terminology, arises from the fact that many of our words were originally applicable only to physical things;[19] so that their use in connection with legal relations is, strictly speaking, figurative or fictional. The term, "transfer," is a good example. If X says that he has transferred his watch to Y, he may conceivably mean, quite literally, that he has physically handed over the watch to Y; or, more likely, that he has "transferred" his *legal interest*, without any delivery of possession, – the latter, of course, being a relatively figurative use of the term. This point will be reached again, when we come to treat of the "transfer" of legal interests. As another instance of this essentially metaphorical use of a term borrowed from the physical world, the word "power" may be mentioned. In legal discourse, as in daily life, it may frequently be used in the sense of physical or mental capacity to do a thing; but, more usually and aptly, it is used to indicate a "*legal* power", the connotation of which latter term is fundamentally different. The same observations apply, *mutatis mutandis*, to the term "liberty".

Passing to the field of contracts, we soon discover a similar inveterate tendency to confuse and blur legal discussions by failing to discriminate between the mental and physical facts involved in the so-called "agreement" of the parties, and the legal "contractual obligation" to which those facts give rise. Such ambiguity and confusion are peculiarly incident to the use of the term "contract." One moment the word may mean *the agreement* of the parties; and then, with a rapid and unexpected shift, the writer or speaker may use the term to indicate the *contractual obligation* created by law as a result of the agreement. Further instances of this sort of ambiguity will be noticed as the discussion proceeds.

Operative Facts Contrasted With Evidential Facts

For the purpose of subsequent convenient reference, it seems necessary at this point to lay emphasis upon another important distinction inherent in the very nature of things. The facts important in relation to a given jural transaction may be either *operative* facts or *evidential* facts. Operative, constitutive, causal, or "dispositive" facts are those which, under the general legal rules that are applicable, suffice to change legal relations, that is, either to create a new relation, or to extinguish an old one, or to perform both of these functions simultaneously.[20] For example, in the creation of a contractual obligation between A and B, the *affirmative* operative facts are, *inter alia*, that each of the parties is a human being, that each of them has lived for not less than a certain period of time, (is not "under age"), that A has made an "offer," that B has "accepted" it, etc. It is sometimes necessary to consider, also, what may, from the particular point of view, be regarded as *negative* operative facts. Thus, *e.g.*, the fact that A did not wilfully misrepresent an important matter to B, and the fact that A had not "revoked" his offer, must really be included as parts of the totality of operative facts in the case already put.

Taking another example, – this time from the general field of torts – if X commits an assault on Y by putting the latter in fear of bodily harm, this particular group of facts immediately create in Y the privilege of self-defense, – that is, the privilege of using sufficient force to repel X's attack; or, correlatively, the otherwise existing duty of Y to refrain from the application of force to the person of X is, by virtue of the special operative facts, immediately terminated or extinguished.

In passing, it may not be amiss to notice that the term, "facts in issue," is sometimes used in the present connection. If, as is usual, the term means "facts put in issue by the *pleadings*," the expression is an unfortunate one. The operative facts alleged by the pleadings are more or less *generic* in character; and if the pleadings be sufficient, only such *generic* operative facts are

"put in issue." The operative facts of real life are, on the other hand, very specific. That being so, it is clear that the *real* and *specific* facts finally relied on are comparatively seldom put in issue by the pleadings. Thus, if, in an action of tort, the declaration of A alleges that he was, through the carelessness, etc., of B, bitten by the latter's dog, the fact alleged is generic in character, and it matters not whether it was dog Jim or dog Dick that did the biting. Even assuming, therefore, that the biting was done by Jim, (rather than by Dick), it could not be said that this specific fact was put in issue by the pleadings. Similarly, and more obviously, the pleading in an ordinary action involving so-called negligence, is usually very generic in character,[21] so that any one of various possible groups of specific operative facts would suffice, so far as the defendant's obligation *ex delicto* is concerned. It therefore could not be said that any one of such groups had been put in issue by the pleadings. A common fallacy in this connection is to regard the *specific* operative facts established in a given case as being but "evidence" of the *generic* (or "ultimate") operative facts alleged in the pleadings.[22]

An evidential fact is one which, on being ascertained, affords some logical basis – not conclusive – for inferring some other fact. The latter may be either a constitutive fact or an intermediate evidential fact. Of all the facts to be ascertained by the tribunal, the operative are, of course, of primary importance; the evidential are subsidiary in their functions.[23] As a rule there is little danger of confusing evidential facts with operative facts. But there is one type of case that not infrequently gives rise to this sort of error. Suppose that in January last a contractual obligation was created by written agreement passing between A and B. In an action now pending between these parties, the physical *instrument* is offered for inspection by the tribunal. If one were thoughtless, he would be apt to say that this is a case where part of the operative facts creating the original obligation are directly presented to the senses of the tribunal. Yet a moment's reflection will show that such is not the case. The document, in its then existing shape, had, as regards its operative effect, spent its force as soon as it was delivered in January last. If, therefore, the unaltered document is produced for inspection, the facts thus ascertained must, as regards the alleged contractual agreement, be purely evidential in character. That is to say, the present existence of the piece of paper, its specific tenor, etc., may, along with other evidential facts (relating to absence of change) tend to prove the various operative facts of last January, – to wit, that such paper existed at that time; that its tenor was then the same as it now is; that it was delivered by A to B, and so forth.

It now remains to observe that in many situations a single convenient term is employed to designate (generically) certain miscellaneous groups of operative facts which, though differing widely as to their individual "ingredients," have, as regards a given matter, the same *net* force and effect. When employed with discrimination, the term "possession" is a word of this character; so also the term "capacity," the term "domicile," etc. But the general tendency to confuse legal and non-legal quantities is manifest here as elsewhere; so that only too frequently these words are used rather nebulously to indicate legal relations as such.[24]

Fundamental Jural Relations Contrasted With One Another

One of the greatest hindrances to the clear understanding, the incisive statement, and the true solution of legal problems frequently arises from the express or tacit assumption that all legal relations may be reduced to "rights" and "duties," and that these latter categories are therefore adequate for the purpose of analyzing even the most complex legal interests, such as trusts, options, escrows, "future" interests, corporate interests, etc. Even if the difficulty related merely to inadequacy and ambiguity of terminology, its seriousness would nevertheless be worthy of definite recognition and persistent effort toward improvement; for in any closely reasoned problem, whether legal or non-legal, chameleon-hued words are a peril both to clear thought and to lucid expression.[25] As a matter of fact, however, the above mentioned inadequacy and ambiguity of terms unfortunately

reflect, all too often, corresponding paucity and confusion as regards actual legal conceptions. That this is so may appear in some measure from the discussion to follow.

The strictly fundamental legal relations are, after all, *sui generis;* and thus it is that attempts at formal definition are always unsatisfactory, if not altogether useless. Accordingly, the most promising line of procedure seems to consist in exhibiting all of the various relations in a scheme of "opposites" and "correlatives," and then proceeding to exemplify their individual scope and application in concrete cases. An effort will be made to pursue this method:

$$
\left\{\begin{array}{l} \text{Jural} \\ \text{Opposites} \end{array}\right. \begin{array}{llll} \text{rights} & \text{privilege} & \text{power} & \text{immunity} \\ \text{no-rights} & \text{duty} & \text{disability} & \text{liability} \end{array}
$$

$$
\left\{\begin{array}{l} \text{Jural} \\ \text{Correlatives} \end{array}\right. \begin{array}{llll} \text{right} & \text{privilege} & \text{power} & \text{immunity} \\ \text{duty} & \text{no-right} & \text{liability} & \text{disability} \end{array}
$$

Rights and Duties. As already intimated, the term "rights" tends to be used indiscriminately to cover what in a given case may be a privilege, a power, or an immunity, rather than a right in the strictest sense; and this looseness of usage is occasionally recognized by the authorities. As said by Mr. Justice Strong in *People v. Dikeman:*[26]

> The word 'right' is defined by lexicographers to denote, among other things, *property, interest, power, prerogative, immunity, privilege* (Walker's Dict. word 'Right'). In law it is most frequently applied to property in its restricted sense, but it is often used to designate *power, prerogative*, and *privilege*, ...

Recognition of this ambiguity is also found in the language of Mr. Justice Jackson, in *United States v. Patrick:*[27]

> The words 'right' or 'privilege' have, of course, a variety of meanings, according to the connection or context in which they are used. Their definition, as given by standard lexicographers, include 'that which one has a *legal claim to do,*' 'legal power,' 'authority,' 'immunity granted by authority,' 'the investiture with special or peculiar rights.'

And, similarly, in the language of Mr. Justice Sneed, in *Lonas v. State:*[28]

The state, then, is forbidden from making and enforcing any law which shall abridge the *privileges* and *immunities* of citizens of the United States. It is said that the words *rights, privileges* and *immunities*, are abusively used, as if they were synonymous. The word *rights* is generic, common, embracing whatever may be lawfully claimed.[29]

It is interesting to observe, also, that a tendency toward discrimination may be found in a number of important constitutional and statutory provisions. Just how accurate the distinctions in the mind of the draftsman may have been it is, of course, impossible to say.[30]

Recognizing, as we must, the very broad and indiscriminate use of the term, "right," what clue do we find, in ordinary legal discourse, toward limiting the word in question to a definite and appropriate meaning. That clue lies in the correlative "duty," for it is certain that even those who use the word and the conception "right" in the broadest possible way are accustomed to thinking of "duty" as the invariable correlative. As said in *Lake Shore & M. S. R. Co. v. Kurtz*:[31]

> A duty or a legal obligation is that which one ought or ought not to do. 'Duty' and 'right' are correlative terms. When a right is invaded, a duty is violated.[32]

In other words, if X has a right against Y that he shall stay off the former's land, the correlative (and equivalent) is that Y is under a duty toward X to stay off the place. If, as seems desirable, we should seek a synonym for the term "right" in this limited and proper meaning, perhaps the word "claim" would prove the best. The latter has the advantage of being a monosyllable. In this connection, the language of Lord Watson in *Studd v. Cook*[33] is instructive:

> Any words which in a settlement of moveables would be recognized by the law of Scotland as sufficient to create a right *or claim* in favor of an executor ... must receive effect if used with reference to lands in Scotland.

Privileges and "No-Rights." As indicated in the above scheme of jural relations, a privilege is the opposite of a duty, and the correlative of a "no-right." In the example last put, whereas X has a *right* or *claim* that Y, the other man, should stay off the land, he himself has the *privilege* of entering on the land; or, in equivalent words, X does not have a duty to stay off. The privilege of entering is the negation of a duty to stay off. As indicated by this case, some caution is necessary at this point, for, always, when it is said that a given privilege is the mere negation of a *duty*, what is meant, of course, is a duty having a content or tenor precisely *opposite* to that of the privilege in question. Thus, if, for some special reason, X has contracted with Y to go on the former's own land, it is obvious that X has, as regards Y, both the privilege of entering and the *duty of entering*. The privilege is perfectly consistent with this sort of duty, – for the latter is of the *same* content or tenor as the privilege; – but it still holds good that, as regards Y, X's privilege of entering is the precise negation of a duty *to stay off*. Similarly, if A has not contracted with B to perform certain work for the latter, A's privilege of *not* doing so is the very negation of a duty of *doing* so. Here again the duty contrasted is of a content or tenor exactly opposite to that of the privilege.

Passing now to the question of "correlatives," it will be remembered, of course, that a duty is the invariable correlative of that legal relation which is most properly called a right or claim. That being so, if further evidence be needed as to the fundamental and important difference between a right (or claim) and a privilege, surely it is found in the fact that the correlative of the latter relation is a "no-right," there being no single term available to express the latter conception. Thus, the correlative of X's right that Y shall not enter on the land is Y's duty not to enter; but the correlative of X's privilege of entering himself is manifestly Y's "no-right" that X shall not enter.

In view of the considerations thus far emphasized, the importance of keeping the conception of a right (or claim) and the conception of a privilege quite distinct from each other seems evident; and more than that, it is equally clear that there should be a separate term to represent the latter relation. No doubt, as already indicated, it is very common to use the term "right" indiscriminately, even when the relation designated is really that of privilege;[34] and only too often this identity of terms has involved for the particular speaker or writer a confusion or blurring of ideas. Good instances of this may be found even in unexpected places. Thus Professor Holland, in his work on Jurisprudence, referring to a different and well known sort of ambiguity inherent in the Latin "*Ius*," the German "*Recht*," the Italian "*Diritto*," and the French "*Droit*," – terms used to express "not only 'a right,' but also 'Law' in the abstract," – very aptly observes:

> If the expression of widely different ideas by one and the same term resulted only in the necessity for ... clumsy paraphrases, or obviously inaccurate paraphrases, no great harm would be done; but unfortunately the identity of terms seems irresistibly to suggest an identity between the ideas expressed by them.[35]

Curiously enough, however, in the very chapter where this appears, – the chapter on "Rights," – the notions of right, privilege and power seem to be blended, and that, too, although the learned author states that "the correlative of ... legal right is legal duty," and that "these pairs of terms express ... in each case the same state of facts viewed from opposite sides." While the whole chapter must be read in order to appreciate the seriousness of this lack of discrimination a single passage must suffice by way of example:

> If ... the power of the State will protect him in so carrying out his wishes, and will compel such acts or forbearances on the part of other people as may be necessary in order that his wishes may be so carried out, then he has a 'legal right' so to carry out his wishes.[36]

The first part of this passage suggests privileges, the middle part rights (or claims), and the last part privileges.

Similar difficulties seem to exist in Professor Gray's able and entertaining work on The Nature and Sources of Law. In his chapter on "Legal Rights and Duties" the distinguished author takes the position that a right always has a duty as its correlative;[37] and he seems to define the former relation substantially according to the more limited meaning of "claim." Legal privileges, powers, and immunities are *prima facie* ignored, and the impression conveyed that all legal relations can be comprehended under the conceptions, "right" and "duty." But, with the greatest hesitation and deference, the suggestion may be ventured that a number of his examples seem to show the inadequacy of such mode of treatment. Thus, *e.g.*, he says:

> The eating of shrimp salad is an interest of mine, and, if I can pay for it, the law will protect that interest, and it is therefore a right of mine to eat shrimp salad which I have paid for, although I know that shrimp salad always gives me the colic.[38]

This passage seems to suggest primarily two classes of relations: *first*, the party's respective privileges, as against A, B, C, D and others in relation to eating the salad, or, correlatively, the respective "no-rights" of A. B. C. D and others that the party should not eat the salad; *second*, the party's respective rights (or claims) as against A. B. C. D and others that they should not interfere with the physical act of eating the salad, or, correlatively, the respective duties of A, B, C, D and others that they should not interfere.

These two groups of relations seem perfectly distinct; and the privileges could, in a given case exist even though the rights mentioned did not. A. B. C. and D, being the owners of the salad, might say to X: "Eat the salad, if you can; you have our license to do so, but we don't agree not to interfere with you." In such a case the privileges exist, so that if X succeeds in eating the salad, he has violated no rights of any of the parties. But it is equally clear that if A had succeeded in holding so fast to the dish that X couldn't eat the contents, no right of X would have been violated.[39]

Perhaps the essential character and importance of the distinction can be shown by a slight variation of the facts. Suppose that X, being already the legal owner of the salad, contracts with Y that he (X) will never eat this particular food. With A, B, C, D and others no such contract has been made. One of the relations now existing between X and Y is, as a consequence, fundamentally different from the relation between X and A. As regards Y, X has no privilege of eating the salad; but as regards either A or any of the others, X has such a privilege. It is to be observed incidentally that X's right that Y should not eat the food persists even though X's own privilege of doing so has been extinguished.[40]

On grounds already emphasized, it would seem that the line of reasoning pursued by Lord Lindley in the great case of *Quinn v. Leathem*[41] is deserving of comment:

> The plaintiff had the ordinary *rights* of the British subject. He was *at liberty* to earn his living in his own way, provided he did not violate some special law prohibiting him from so doing, and provided he did not infringe the rights of other people. This *liberty* involved *the liberty* to deal with other persons who were willing to deal with him. *This liberty* is *a right* recognized by law; its *correlative* is the general *duty* of every one not to prevent the free exercise of this *liberty* except so far as his own liberty of action may justify him in so doing. But a person's *liberty* or *right* to deal with others is nugatory unless they are at liberty to deal with him if they choose to do so. Any interference with their liberty to deal with him affects him.

A "liberty" considered as a legal relation (or "right" in the loose and generic sense of that term) must mean, if it have any definite content at all, precisely the same thing as *privilege*,[42] and certainly that is the fair connotation of the term as used the first three times in the passage quoted. It is equally clear, as already indicated, that such a privilege or liberty to deal with others at will might very conceivably exist without any peculiar concomitant rights against "third parties" as regards certain kinds of interference.[43] Whether there should be such concomitant rights (or claims) is ultimately a question of justice and policy; and it should be considered, as such, on its merits. The only correlative logically implied by the privileges or liberties in question are the "no-rights" of "third parties." It would therefore be a *non sequitur* to conclude from the mere existence of

such liberties that "third parties." are under a *duty* not to interfere, etc. Yet in the middle of the above passage from Lord Lindley's opinion there is a sudden and question-begging shift in the use of terms. First, the "liberty" in question is transmuted into a "right," and then, possibly under the seductive influence of the latter word, it is assumed that the "correlative" must be "the general duty of every one not to prevent," etc.

Another interesting and instructive example may be taken from Lord Bowen's oft-quoted opinion in *Mogul Steamship Co. v. McGregor.*[44]

> We are presented in this case with an apparent conflict or antinomy between two rights that are equally regarded by the law – the right of the plaintiffs to be protected in the legitimate exercise of their trade, and the right of the defendants to carry on their business as seems best to them, provided they commit no wrong to others.

As the learned judge states, the conflict or antinomy is only apparent; but this fact seems to be obscured by the very indefinite and rapidly shifting meanings with which the term "right" is used in the above quoted language. Construing the passage as a whole, it seems plain enough that by "the right of the plaintiffs" in relation to the defendants a legal right or claim in the strict sense must be meant; whereas by "the right of the defendants" in relation to the plaintiffs a legal privilege must be intended. That being so, the "two rights" mentioned in the beginning of the passage, being respectively claim and privilege, could not be in conflict with each other. To the extent that the defendants have privileges the plaintiffs have no rights; and conversely, to the extent that the plaintiffs have rights the defendants have no privileges ("no-privilege" equals duty of opposite tenor).[45]

Thus far it has been assumed that the term "privilege" is the most appropriate and satisfactory to designate the mere negation of duty. Is there good warrant for this?

In Mackeldey's Roman Law[46] it is said:

> Positive laws either contain general principles embodied in the rules of law ... or for especial reasons they establish something that differs from those general principles. In the first case they

contain a common law (*jus commune*), in the second a special law (*jus singulare s. exorbitans*). The latter is either favorable or unfavorable ... according as it enlarges or restricts, in opposition to the common rule, the rights of those for whom it is established. The favorable special law (*jus singulare*) as also the right created by it ... in the Roman law is termed benefit of the law (*beneficium juris*) or privilege (*privilegium*) ...[47]

First a special law, and then by association of ideas, a special advantage conferred by such a law. With such antecedents, it is not surprising that the English word "privilege" is not infrequently used, even at the present time, in the sense of a special or peculiar legal advantage (whether right, privilege, power or immunity) belonging either to some individual or to some particular class of persons.[48] There are, indeed, a number of judicial opinions recognizing this as one of the meanings of the term in question.[49] That the word has a wider signification even in ordinary non-technical usage is sufficiently indicated, however, by the fact that the term "*special* privileges" is so often used to indicate a contrast to ordinary or general privileges. More than this, the dominant specific connotation of the term as used in popular speech seems to be more *negation of duty*. This is manifest in the terse and oft-repeated expression, "That is your privilege," – meaning, of course, "You are under no duty to do otherwise."

Such being the case, it is not surprising to find, from a wide survey of judicial precedents, that the *dominant* technical meaning of the term is, similarly, negation of *legal duty*.[50] There are two very common examples of this, relating respectively to "privileged communications" in the law of libel and to "privileges against self-crimination" in the law of evidence. As regards the first case, it is elementary that if a certain group of operative facts are present, a privilege exists, which, without such facts, would not be recognized.[51] It is, of course, equally clear that even though all such facts be present as last supposed, the superadded fact of malice will, in cases of so-called "conditional privilege," extinguish the privilege that otherwise would exist. It must be evident also, that whenever the privilege does exist, it is not special in the

sense of arising from a special law, or of being conferred as a special favor on a particular individual. The same privilege would exist, by virtue of general rules, for any person whatever under similar circumstances. So, also, in the law of evidence, the privilege against self-crimination signifies the mere negation of a duty, to testify, – a duty which rests upon a witness in relation to all ordinary matters; and, quite obviously, such privilege arises, if at all, only by virtue of general laws.[52]

As already intimated, while both the conception and the term "privilege" find conspicuous exemplification under the law of libel and the law of evidence, they nevertheless have a much wider significance and utility as a matter of judicial usage. To make this clear, a few miscellaneous judicial precedents will now be noticed. In Dowman's Case,[53] decided in the year 1583, and reported by Coke, the court applied the term to the subject of waste:

> And as to the objection which was made, that the said privilege to be without impeachment of waste cannot be without deed, etc. To that it was answered and resolved, that if it was admitted that a deed in such case should be requisite, yet without question all the estates limited would be good, although it is admitted, that the clause concerning the said privilege would be void.

In the great case of *Allen v. Flood*[54] the opinion of Mr. Justice Hawkins furnishes a useful passage for the purpose now in view:

> Every person has a privilege ... in the interests of public justice to put the criminal law in motion against another whom be *bona fide*, and upon reasonable and probable cause, believes to have been guilty of a crime. ... It must not, however, be supposed that hatred and ill-will existing in the mind of a prosecutor must of necessity *destroy* the *privilege*, for it is not impossible that such hatred and ill-will may have very natural and pardonable reasons for existing....

Applying the term in relation to the subject of property, Mr. Justice Foster, of the Supreme Court of Maine, said in the case of *Pulitzer v. Lumgston:*[55]

It is contrary to the policy of the law that there should be any outstanding titles, estates, or powers, by the existence, operation or exercise of which, at a period of time beyond lives in being and twenty-one years and a fraction thereafter, the complete and unfettered enjoyment of an estate, *with all the rights, privileges and powers incident to ownership*, should be qualified or impeded.

As a final example in the present connection, the language of Baron Alderson in *Hilton v. Eckerley*[56] may be noticed:

> *Prima facie* it is the privilege of a trader in a free country, in all matters not contrary to law, to regulate his own mode of carrying them on according to his discretion and choice.[57]

The closest synonym of legal "privilege" seems to be legal "liberty." This is sufficiently indicated by an unusually discriminating and instructive passage in Mr. Justice Cave's opinion in *Allen v. Flood:*[58]

> The personal rights with which we are most familiar are: 1. Rights of reputation; 2. Rights of bodily safety and freedom; 3. Rights of property; or, in other words, rights relating to mind, body and estate, ...

> In my subsequent remarks the word 'right' will, as far as possible, always be used in the above sense; and it is the more necessary to insist on this as during the argument at your Lordship's bar it was frequently used in a much wider and more indefinite sense. Thus it was said that a man has a perfect right to fire off a gun, when all that was meant, apparently, was that a man has a *freedom* or *liberty* to fire off a gun, so long as he does not violate or infringe any one's rights in doing so, which is a very different thing from a right, the violation or disturbance of which can be remedied or prevented by legal process.[59]

While there are numerous other instances of the apt use of the term "liberty," both in judicial opinions[60] and in conveyancing documents,[61] it is by no means so common or definite a word as "privilege." The former term is far more likely to be used in the sense of physical or personal freedom (*i.e.*, absence of physical restraint), as distinguished from a legal relation; and very frequently there is the connotation of *general* political liberty, as distinguished from a particular relation between two definite individuals. Besides all this, the term "privilege" has the advantage of giving us, as a variable, the adjective "privileged". Thus, it is frequently convenient to speak of a privileged act, a privileged transaction, a privileged conveyance, etc.

The term "license", sometimes used as if it were synonymous with "privilege," is not strictly appropriate. This is simply another of those innumerable cases in which the mental and physical facts are so frequently confused with the legal relation which they create. Accurately used, "license" is a generic term to indicate a group of *operative* facts required to create a particular privilege, – this being especially evident when the word is used in the common phrase "leave and license." This point is brought out by a passage from Mr. Justice Adams' opinion in *Clifford v. O'Neill:*[62]

> A license is merely a *permission* to do an act which, *without such permission*, would amount to a trespass ... nor will the continuous enjoyment of the privilege *conferred*, for any period of time cause it to ripen into a tangible interest in the land affected.[63]

Powers and Liabilities. As indicated in the preliminary scheme of jural relations, a legal power (as distinguished, of course, from a mental or physical power) is the opposite of legal disability, and the correlative of legal liability. But what is the intrinsic nature of a legal power as such? Is it possible to analyze the conception represented by this constantly employed and very important term of legal discourse? Too close an analysis might seem metaphysical rather than useful; so that what is here presented is intended only as an approximate explanation sufficient for all practical purposes.

A change in a given legal relation may result (1) from some superadded fact or group of facts not under the volitional control of a human being (or human beings); or (2) from some superadded fact or group of facts which are under the volitional control of one or more human beings. As regards the second class of cases, the person (or persons) whose volitional control is paramount may be said to have the (legal) power to effect the particular change of legal relations that is involved in the problem.

The second class of cases – powers in the technical sense – must now be further considered. The nearest synonym for any ordinary case seems to be (legal) "ability,"[64] – the latter being obviously the opposite of "inability," or "disability." The term "right," so frequently and loosely used in the present connection, is an unfortunate term for the purpose, – a not unusual result being confusion of thought as well as ambiguity of expression.[65] The term "capacity" is equally unfortunate; for, as we have already seen, when used with discrimination, this word denotes a particular group of operative facts, and not a legal relation of any kind.

Many examples of legal powers may readily be given. Thus, X, the owner of ordinary personal property "in a tangible object" has the power to extinguish his own legal interest (rights, powers, immunities, etc.) through that totality of operative facts known as abandonment; and – simultaneously and correlatively – to create in other persons privileges and powers relating to the abandoned object, – e.g., the power to acquire title to the later by appropriating it.[66] *Similarly*, X has the power to transfer his interest to Y, – that is, to extinguish his own interest and concomitantly create in Y a new and corresponding interest.[67] So also X has the power to create contractual obligations of various kinds. Agency cases are likewise instructive. By the use of some *metaphorical* expression such as the Latin, *qui facit per alium, facit per se*, the true nature of agency relations is only too frequently obscured. The creation of an agency relation involves, *inter alia*, the grant of legal powers to the so-called agent, and the creation of correlative liabilities in the principal.[68] That is to say, one party P has the power to create agency powers in another party A, – for example, the power to convey X's property, the power to impose (so-called) contractual obligations on P, the power to discharge a debt, owing to P, the power to "receive" title to property so that it shall vest in P, and so forth. In passing, it may be well to observe that the

term "authority," so frequently used in agency cases, is very ambiguous and slippery in its connotation. Properly employed in the present connection, the word seems to be an abstract or qualitative term corresponding to the concrete "authorization," – the latter consisting of a particular group of operative facts taking place between the principal and the agent. All too often, however, the term in question is so used as to blend and confuse these operative facts with the powers and privileges thereby created in the agent.[69] A careful discrimination in these particulars would, it is submitted, go far toward clearing up certain problems in the law of agency.[70]

Essentially similar to the powers of agents are powers of appointment in relation to property interests. So, too, the powers of public officers are, intrinsically considered, comparable to those of agents, – for example, the power of a sheriff to sell property under a writ of execution. The power of a donor, in a gift *causa mortis*, to revoke the gift and divest the title of the donee is another clear example of the legal quantities now being considered;[71] also a pledgee's statutory power of sale.[72]

There are, on the other hand, cases where the true nature of the relations involved has not, perhaps, been so clearly recognized. Thus, in the case of a conditional sale of personality, assuming the vendee's agreement has been fully performed except as to the payment of the last installment and the time for the latter has arrived, what is the interest of such vendee as regards the property? Has he, as so often assumed, merely a contractual *right* to have title passed to him by consent of the vendor, on final payment being made; or has he, irrespective of the consent of the vendor the power to divest the title of the latter and to acquire a perfect title for himself? Though the language of the cases is not always so clear as it might be, the vendee seems to have precisely that sort of power.[73] Fundamentally considered, the typical escrow transaction in which the performance of conditions is within the volitional control of the grantee, is somewhat similar to the conditional sale of personalty; and, when reduced to its lowest terms, the problem seems easily to be solved in terms of legal powers. Once the "escrow" is formed, the grantor still has the legal title; but the grantee has an irrevocable power to divest that title by performance of certain conditions (*i.e.*, the addition of various operative facts), and concomitantly to vest title in himself. While such power is outstanding, the grantor is, of course, subject to a correlative liability to have his title divested.[74] Similarly, in the case of a conveyance of land in fee simple subject to condition subsequent, after the condition has been performed, the original grantor is commonly said to have a "*right*" of entry." If, however, the problem is analyzed, it will be seen that, as of primary importance, the grantor has two legal quantities, (1) the privilege of entering, and (2) the power, by means of such entry, to divest the estate of the grantee.[75] The latter's estate endures, subject to the correlative liability of being divested, until such power is acutally exercised.[76]

Passing now to the field of contracts, suppose A mails a letter to B offering to sell the former's land, Whiteacre, to the latter for ten thousand dollars, such letter being duly received. The operative facts thus far mentioned have created a power as regards B and a correlative liability as regards A. B, by dropping a letter of acceptance in the box, has the power to impose potential or inchoate[77] obligation *ex contractu* on A and himself; and, assuming that the land is worth fifteen thousand dollars, that particular legal quantity – the "power *plus* liability" relation between A and B – seems to be worth about five thousand dollars to B. The liability of A will continue for a reasonable time unless, in exercise of his power to do so, A previously extinguishes it by that series of operative facts known as "revocation." These last matters are usually described by saying that A's "offer" will "continue" or "remain open" for a reasonable time, or for the definite time actually specified, unless A previously "withdraws" or "revokes" such offer.[78] While no doubt, in the great majority of cases no harm results from the use of such expressions, yet these forms of statement seem to represent a blending of non-legal and legal quantities which, in any problem requiring careful reasoning, should preferably be kept distinct. An offer, considered as a series of physical and mental operative facts, has spent its force as soon

as such series has been completed by the "offeree's receipt." The real question is therefore as to the *legal effect*, if any, at that moment of time. If the latter consist of B's power and A's correlative liability, manifestly it is those *legal relations* that "continue" or "remain open" until modified by revocation or other operative facts. What has thus far been said concerning contracts completed by mail would seem to apply, *mutatis mutandis*, to every type of contract. Even where the parties are in the presence of each other, the offer creates a liability against the offerer, together with a correlative power in favor of the offeree. The only distinction for present purposes would be in the fact that such power and such liability would expire within a very short period of time.

Perhaps the practical justification for this method of analysis is somewhat greater in relation to the subject of options. In his able work on Contracts,[79] Langdell says:

> If the offerer stipulates that his offer shall remain open for a specified time, the first question is whether such stipulation constitutes a binding contract. ... When such a stipulation is binding, the further question arises, whether it makes the offer irrevocable. It has been a common opinion that it does, but that is clearly a mistake.... An offer is merely one of the elements of a contract; and it is indispensable to the making of a contract that the wills of the contracting parties do, in legal contemplation, concur at the moment of making it. An offer, therefore, which the party making it has no power to revoke, is a legal impossibility. Moreover, if the stipulation should make the offer irrevocable, it would be a contract incapable of being broken; which is also a legal impossibility. The only effect, therefore, of such a stipulation is to give the offeree a claim for damages if the stipulation be broken by revoking the offer.[80]

The foregoing reasoning ignores the fact that an ordinary offer *ipso facto* creates a legal relation – a legal power and a legal liability, – and that it is this relation (rather than the physical and mental facts constituting the offer) that "remains open." If these points be conceded, there seems no difficulty in recognizing an unilateral option agreement supported by consideration or embodied in a sealed instrument as creating in the optionee an irrevocable power to create, at any time within the period specified, a bilateral obligation as between himself and the giver of the option. Correlatively to that power, there would, of course, be a liability against the option-giver which he himself would have no power to extinguish. The courts seem to have no difficulty in reaching precisely this result as a matter of substance; though their explanations are always in terms of "withdrawal of offer," and similar expressions savoring of physical and mental quantities.[81]

In connection with the powers and liabilities created respectively by an ordinary offer and by an option, it is interesting to consider the liabilities of a person engaged in a "public calling;" for, as it seems, such a party's characteristic position is, one might almost say, intermediate between that of an ordinary contractual offerer and that of an option-giver. It has indeed been usual to assert that such a party is (generally speaking) under a present *duty* to all other parties; but this is believed to be erroneous. Thus, Professor Wyman, in his work on Public Service Companies,[82] says:

> The duty placed upon every one exercising a public calling is primarily a duty to serve every man who is a member of the public. . . . It is somewhat difficult to place this exceptional duty in our legal system. . . . The truth of the matter is that the obligation resting upon one who has undertaken the performance of public duty is *sui generis*.[83]

It is submitted that the learned writer's difficulties arise primarily from a failure to see that the innkeeper, the common carrier and others similarly "holding out" are under present *liabilities* rather than present *duties*. Correlatively to those liabilities are the respective powers of the various members of the public. Thus, for example, a travelling member of the public has the legal power, by making proper application and sufficient tender, to impose a duty on the innkeeper to receive him as a guest. For breach of the duty *thus* created an action would of course lie. It would therefore seem that the innkeeper is, to some extent, like one who had given an option to every travelling member of the public. He differs, as regards net legal effect, only because he can extinguish his present li-

abilities and the correlative powers of the travelling members of the public *by going out of business*. Yet, on the other hand, his liabilities are more onerous than that of an ordinary contractual offerer, for he cannot extinguish his liabilities by any simple performance akin to revocation of offer.

As regards all the "legal powers" thus far considered, possibly some caution is necessary. If, for example, we consider the ordinary property owner's power of alienation, it is necessary to distinguish carefully between the *legal* power, the *physical* power to do the things necessary for the "exercise" of the legal power, and, finally, the *privilege* of doing these things – that is, if such privilege does really exist. It may or may not. Thus, if X, a landowner, has contracted with Y that the former will not alienate to Z, the acts of X necessary to exercise the power of alienating to Z are privileged as between X and every party other than Y; but, obviously, as between X and Y, the former has no privilege of doing the necessary acts; or conversely, he is under a duty to Y not to do what is necessary to exercise the power.

In view of what has already been said, very little may suffice concerning a *liability* as such. The latter, as we have seen, is the correlative of power, and the opposite of immunity (or exemption). While no doubt the term "liability" is often loosely used as a synonym for "duty," or "obligation," it is believed, from an extensive survey of judicial precedents, that the connotation already adopted as most appropriate to the word in question is fully justified. A few cases tending to indicate this will now be noticed. In *McNeer v. McNeer*,[84] Mr. Justice Magruder balanced the conceptions of power and liability as follows:

> So long as she lived, however, his interest in her land lacked those *elements of property*, such as *power of disposition* and *liability to sale on* execution which had formerly given it the character of a vested estate.

In *Booth v. Commonwealth*,[85] the court had to construe a Virginia statute providing "that all free white male persons who are twenty-one years of age and not over sixty, shall be *liable* to serve as jurors, except as hereinafter provided." It is plain that this enactment imposed only a *liability* and not a *duty*. It is a liability to have a duty created. The latter would arise only when, in exercise of their powers, the parties litigant and the court officers, had done what was necessary to impose a specific duty to perform the functions of a juror. The language of the court, by Moncure, J., is particularly apposite as indicating that liability is the opposite, or negative, of immunity (or exemption):

> The word both expressed and implied is 'liable,' which has a very different meaning from 'qualified' .... It's meaning is 'bound' or 'obliged' .... A person exempt from serving on juries is not liable to serve, and a person not liable to serve is exempt from serving. The terms seem to be convertible.

A further good example of judicial usage is to be found in *Emery v. Clough*.[86] Referring to a gift *causa mortis* and the donee's liability to have his already vested interest divested by the donor's exercise of his power of revocation, Mr. Justice Smith said:

> The title to the gift *causa mortis* passed by the delivery, defeasible only in the lifetime of the donor, and his death perfects the title in the donee by terminating the donor's right or *power of defeasance*. The property passes from the donor to the donee directly ... and after his death it is *liable* to be divested only in favor of the donor's creditors. ... His right and power ceased with his death.

Perhaps the nearest synonym of "liability" is "subjection" or "responsibility." As regards the latter word, a passage from Mr. Justice Day's opinion in *McElfresh v. Kirkendall*[87] is interesting:

> The words 'debt' and 'liability' are not synonymous, and they are not commonly so understood. As applied to the pecuniary relations of the parties, liability is a term of broader significance than debt. ... Liability is responsibility.

While the term in question has the broad generic connotation already indicated, no doubt it very frequently indicates that specific form of liability (or complex of liabilities) that is correlative to a power (or complex of powers)[88] vested in a party litigant and the various court officers. Such was held to be the meaning of a certain California statute involved in the case of *Lattin v. Gillette*.[89] Said Mr. Justice Harrison:

> The word 'liability' is the condition in which an individual is placed after a breach of his contract, or a violation of any obligation resting upon him. It is defined by Bouvier to be responsibility.[90]

Immunities and Disabilities. As already brought out, immunity is the correlative of disability ("no-power"), and the opposite, or negation, of liability. Perhaps it will also be plain, from the preliminary outline and from the discussion down to this point, that a power bears the same general contrast to an immunity that a right does to a privilege. A right is one's affirmative claim against another, and a privilege is one's freedom from the right or claim of another. Similarly, a power is one's affirmative "control" over a given legal relation as against another; whereas an immunity is one's freedom from the legal power or "control" of another as regards some legal relation.

A few examples may serve to make this clear. X, a landowner, has, as we have seen, power to alienate to Y or to any other ordinary party. On the other hand, X has also various immunities as against Y, and all other ordinary parties. For Y is under a disability (*i.e.*, has no power) so far as shifting the legal interest either to himself or to a third party is concerned; and what is true of Y applies similarly to every one else who has not by virtue of special operative facts acquired a power to alienate X's property. If, indeed, a sheriff has been duly empowered by a writ of execution to sell X's interest, that is a very different matter: correlative to such sheriff's power would be the *liability* of X, – the very opposite of immunity (or exemption). It is elementary, too, that as against the sheriff, X might be immune or exempt in relation to certain parcels of property, and be liable as to others. Similarly, if an agent has been duly appointed by X to sell a given piece of property, then, as to the latter, X has, in relation to such agent, a liability rather than an immunity.

For over a century there has been, in this country, a great deal of important litigation involving immunities from powers of taxation. If there be any lingering misgivings as to the "practical" importance of accuracy and discrimination in legal conceptions and legal terms, perhaps some of such doubts would be dispelled by considering the numerous cases on valuable taxation exemptions coming before the United States Supreme Court. Thus, in *Phoenix Ins. Co. v. Tennessee*,[91] Mr. Justice Peckham expressed the views of the court as follows:

> In granting to the De Sota Company 'all the rights, privileges, and immunities' of the Bluff City Company, all words are used which could be regarded as necessary to carry the exemption from taxation possessed by the Bluff City Company; while in the next following grant, that of the charter of the plaintiff in error, the word 'immunity' is omitted. Is there any meaning to be attached to that omission, and if so, what? We think some meaning is to be attached to it. The word 'immunity' expresses more clearly and definitely an intention to include therein an exemption from taxation than does either of the other words. Exemption from taxation is more accurately described as an 'immunity' than as a privilege, although it is not to be denied that the latter word may sometimes and under some circumstances include such exemptions.

In *Morgan v. Louisiana*,[92] there is an instructive discussion from the pen of Mr. Justice Field. In holding that on a foreclosure sale of the franchise and property of a railroad corporation an immunity from taxation did not pass to the purchaser, the learned Judge said:

> As has been often said by this court, the whole community is interested in retaining the power of taxation undiminished .... The exemption of the property of the company from taxation, and the exemption of its officers and servants from jury and military duty, were both intended for the benefit of the company, and its benefit alone. In their personal character they are analogous to exemptions from execution of certain property of debtors, made by laws of several of the states.[93]

So far as immunities are concerned, the two judicial discussions last quoted concern respect-ively problems of interpretation and problems of alienability. In many other cases difficult constitutional questions have arisen as the result of statutes impairing or extending various kinds of immunities. Litigants have, from time to time, had occasion to appeal both to the clause against impairment of the obligation of contracts and to the provision against depriving a person of property without due process of law. This has been especially true as regards exemptions from taxation[94] and exemptions from execution.[95]

If a word may now be permitted with respect to mere terms as such, the first thing to note is that the word "right" is overworked in the field of immunities as elsewhere.[96] As indicated, however, by the judicial expressions already quoted, the best synonym is, of course, the term "exemption."[97] It is instructive to note, also, that the word "impunity" has a very similar connotation. This is made evident by the interesting discriminations of Lord Chancellor Finch in *Skelton v. Skelton*,[98] a case decided in 1677:

> But this I would by no means allow, that equity should enlarge the restraints of the disabilities introduced by act of parliament; and as to the granting of injunctions to stay waste, I took a distinction where the tenant hath only *impunita-tem*, and where he hath *jus in arboribus*. If the tenant have only a bare indemnity or *exemption* from an action (at law), if he committed waste, there it is fit he should be restrained by injunction from committing it.[99]

In the latter part of the preceding discussion, eight conceptions of the law have been analyzed and compared in some detail, the purpose having been to exhibit not only their intrinsic meaning and scope, but also their relations to one another and the methods by which they are applied, in judicial reasoning, to the solution of concrete problems of litigation. Before concluding this branch of the discussion a general suggestion may be ventured as to the great practical importance of a clear appreciation of the distinctions and discriminations set forth. If a homely metaphor be permitted, these eight conceptions, – rights and duties, privileges and no-rights, powers and liabilities, immunities and disabilities, – seem to be what may be called "the lowest common denominators of the law." Ten fractions (1–3, 2–5, etc.) may, *superficially*, seem so different from one another as to defy comparison. If, however, they are expressed in terms of their lowest common denominators (5–15, 6–15, etc.), comparison becomes easy, and fundamental similarity may be discovered. The same thing is of course true as regards the lowest generic conceptions to which any and all "legal quantities" may be reduced.

Reverting, for example, to the subject powers, it might be difficult at first glance to discover any essential and fundamental similarity between conditional sales of personality, escrow transactions, option agreements, agency relations, powers of appointment, etc. But if all these relations are reduced to their lowest generic terms, the conceptions of legal power and legal liability are seen to be dominantly, though not exclusively, applicable throughout the series. By such a process it becomes possible not only to discover essential similarities and illuminating analogies in the midst of what appears superficially to be infinite and hopeless variety, but also to discern common principles of justice and policy underlying the various jural problems involved. An indirect, yet very practical, consequence is that it frequently becomes feasible, by virtue of such analysis, to use as persuasive authorities judicial precedents that might otherwise seem altogether irrelevant. If this point be valid with respect to powers, it would seem to be equally so as regards all of the other basic conceptions of the law. In short, the deeper the analysis, the greater becomes one's perception of fundamental unity and harmony in the law.[100]

Notes

1 Bacon on Uses (Circa 1602; Rowe's ed. 1806), pp. 5–6: "The nature of an use is best discerned by considering what it is not, and then what it is. . . . First, an use is no right, title, or interest in law; and therefore master attorney, who read upon this statute, said well, that there are but two rights: *Jus in re: Jus ad rem*."

"The one is an estate, which is *jus in re*: the other a demand, which is *jus ad rems* but an use is neither. . . . So as now we are come by negatives to the affirmative, what an use is. . . . *Usus est dominium fiduciarium*: Use is an ownership in trust.

"So that *usus & status, sive possessio, potius differunt secundum rationem fori, quam secundum raturam rei*, for that one of them is in court of law, the other in court of conscience. . . ."

2 Co. Lit. (1628) 272 b: "*Nota*, an use is a trust or confidence reposed in some other, which is not issuing out of the land, but as a thing collaterall, annexed in privitie to the estate of the land, and to the person touching the land, *scilicet*, that *cesty que use* shall take the profit, and that the terre-tenant shall make an estate according to his direction. So as *cesty que use* had neither *jus in re*, nor *jus ad rem*, but only a confidence and trust for which he had no remedie by the common law, but for the breach of trust, his remedie was only by *subpoena* in chancerie. . . ."

This definition is quoted and discussed approvingly in Lewin, Trusts (12th ed., 1911), p. 11. It is also noticed in Maitland, Lectures on Equity (1909), pp. 43, 116.

3 See Langdell, Classification of Rights and Wrongs (1900), 13 Harv. L. Rev., 659, 673: "Can equity then create such rights as it finds to be necessary for the purposes of justice? As equity wields only physical power, it seems to be impossible that it should actually create anything. . . . It seems, therefore, that equitable rights exist only in contemplation of equity, i.e., that they are a *fiction* invented by equity for the promotion of justice. . . ."

"Shutting our eyes, then, to the fact that equitable rights are a fiction, and assuming them to have an actual existence, what is their nature, what their extent, and what is the field which they occupy? . . . They must not violate the law . . . Legal and equitable rights must, therefore, exist side by side, and the latter cannot interfere with, or in any manner affect, the former."

See also (1887) 1 Harv. L. Rev., 55, 60: "Upon the whole, it may be said that equity could not create rights *in rem* if it would, and that it would not if it could." Compare *Ibid*. 58; and Summary of Eq. Plead. (2nd ed., 1883) secs. 45, 182–184.

4 See Ames, "Purchase for Value Without Notice" (1887), 1 Harv. L. Rev., 1, 9: "The trustee is the owner of the land, and, of course, two persons with adverse interests cannot be owners of the same thing. What the *costui que trust* really owns

is the obligation of the trustee; for an obligation is as truly the subject matter of property as any physical *res*. The most striking difference between property in a thing and property in an obligation is in the mode of enjoyment. The owner of a house or a horse enjoys the fruits of ownership without the aid of any other person. The only way in which the owner of an obligation can realize his ownership is by compelling its performance by the obliger. Hence, in the one case, the owner is said to have a right *in rem*, and in the other, a right *in personam*. In other respects the common rules of property apply equally to ownership of things and ownership of obligations. For example, what may be called the passive rights of ownership are the same in both cases. The general duty resting on all mankind not to destroy the property of another, is as cogent in favor of an obligee as it is in favor of the owner of a horse. And the violation of this duty is as pure a tort in the one case as in the other."

5 Lect. on Eq. (1909), 17, 18, 112: "The thesis that I have to maintain is this, that equitable estates and interests are not *jura in rem*. For reasons that we shall perceive by and by, they have come to look very like *jura in rem*; but just for this very reason it is the more necessary for us to observe that they are essentially *jura in personam*, not rights against the world at large, but rights against certain persons."

See also Maitland, Trust and Corporation (1904), reprinted in 3 Collected Papers, 321, 325.

6 (5th ed.) Vol. I, p. 378: "By the provisions of that part of the English law which is called equity, a contract to sell at once vests *jus in rem* or ownership in buyer, and the seller has only *jus in re aliena*. ... To complete the transaction the legal interest of the seller must be passed to the buyer, in legal form. To this purpose the buyer has only *jus in personam*: a right to compel the seller to pass his legal interest; but speaking generally, he has *dominium* or *jus in rem*, and the instrument is a conveyance."

7 (2nd ed., 1907) p. 230: "If we have regard to the essence of the matter rather than to the form of it, a trustee is not an owner at all, but a mere agent, upon whom the law has conferred the power and imposed the duty of administering the property of another person. In legal theory, however, he is not a mere agent, but an owner. He is a person to whom the property of someone else is fictitiously attributed by the law, to the intent that the rights and powers thus rested in a *nominal* owner shall be used by him on behalf of the real owner."

8 See Walter G. Hart (author of "Digest of Law of Trusts"), The Place of Trust in Jurisprudence (1912), 28 Law Quart. Rev., 290, 296. His position is substantially that of Ames and Maitland.

At the end of this article Sir Frederick Pollock, the editor, puts the query: "Why is Trust not entitled to rank as a head *sui generis?*"

9 See A. N. Whitlock, Classification of the Law of Trusts (1913), I Calif, Law Rev., 215, 218: "It is submitted," says the writer, "that the *cestui* has in fact something more than a right *in personam*, that such a right might be more properly described as a right *in personam ad rem*, or, possibly, a right *in rem per personam*."

Surely such nebulous and cumbrous expressions as these could hardly fail to make "confusion worse confounded."

10 See Beale, Equitable Interests in Foreign Property, 20 Harv. L. Rev. (1907), 382; and compare the important cases, *Fall v. Eastin* (1905), 75 Neb., 104; S. C. (1909), 215 U. S., 1, 14–15 (especially concurring opinion of Holmes. J.); *Selover, Bates & Co. v. Walsh* (1912), 226 U. S., 112; *Bank of Africa Limited v. Cohen* (1909), 2 Ch. 129, 143.

11 (1882) 20 Ch. D. 562, 580, per Sir George Jessel, M. R.: "If then the rule as to remoteness applies to a covenant of this nature, this covenant clearly is bad as extending beyond the period allowed by the rule. Whether the rule applies or not depends upon this, as it appears to me, does or does not the covenant give *an interest in the land?* ... If it is a mere personal contract it cannot be enforced against the assignee. Therefore the company must admit that somehow it *binds the land*. But if it binds the land, it creates *an equitable interest in the land*."

12 Compare *Ball v. Milliken* (1910), 31 R. I., 36; 76 Atl., 789, 793, involving a point other than perpetuities, but quoting in support of the decision reached Sir George Jessel's language as to "equitable interests in land." See preceding note.

13 2 Hist. Eng. Law (2nd ed., 1905), 226.

14 *Ibid.*, 124.

15 (1895) 67 Fed. Rep., 674, 677. For a somewhat similar, and even more confusing, form of statement, see *In re Fixen* (1900), 102 Fed. Rep., 295, 296.

16 51 N. H., 504, 511. Se also the excellent similar statements of Comstock, J., in *Wynehamer v. People* (1856), 13 N. Y., 378, 396; Selden J., S. C., 13 N. Y., 378, 433–434; Ryan, C., in *Law v. Rees Printing Co.* (1894), 41 Neb., 127,

146; Magruder, J., in *Dixon v. People* (1897), 168 Ill., 179, 190.

17 (1893) 116 Mo., 527, 533–534. That the last sentence quoted is not altogether adequate as an analysis of property will appear, it is hoped, from the latter part of the present discussion.

See also, as regards the term, "property," the opinion of Doe, C. J.: in *Smith v. Fairloh* (1894), 68 N. H. 123, 144–145. ("By considering the property *dissolved* into the *legal rights* of which it consists" etc.)

18 2 Black. Com. (1765), 16–43.

19 Compare Poll. & Maitl. Hist. Eng. Law (2nd ed., 1905), Vol. II, p. 31: "Few, if any, of the terms in our legal vocabulary have always been technical terms. The license that the man of science can allow himself of coining new words is one which by the nature of the case is denied to lawyers. They have to take their terms out of the popular speech; gradually the words so taken are defined; sometimes a word continues to have both a technical meaning for lawyers and a different and vaguer meaning for laymen; sometimes the word that lawyers have adopted is abandoned by the laity." Compare also *Ibid.*, p. 33.

20 Compare Waldo, C. J., in *White v. Multonomah Co.* (1886), 13 Ore., 317, 323: "A 'right' has been defined by Mr. Justice Holmes to be the legal consequence which attaches to certain facts. (The Common Law, 214). Every fact which forms one of the group of facts of which the right is the legal consequence appertains to the substance of the right."

The present writer's choice of the term "operative" has been suggested by the following passage from Thayer, Prelim. Treat. Evid. (1893), p. 393: "Another discrimination to be observed is that between documents which constitute a contract, fact, or transaction, and those which merely certify and evidence something outside of themselves, – a something valid and *operative*, independent of the writing."

Compare also Holland, Jurisp. (10th ed, 1906), 151: "A fact giving rise to a right has long been described as a 'title'; but no such well-worn equivalent can be found for a fact through which a right is transferred, or for one by which a right is extinguished. A new nomenclature was accordingly invented by Bentham, which is convenient for scientific use, although it has not found its way into ordinary language. He describes this whole class of facts as 'Dispositive'; distinguishing as 'Investitive' those by means of which a right comes into existence, as

'Divestitive' those through which it terminates, and as 'Translative' those through which it passes from one person to another."

The word "ultimate," sometimes used in this connection, does not seem to be so pointed and useful a term as either "operative" or "constitutive."

21 Compare, however, *Illinois Steel Co. v. Ostrowski* (1902), 194 Ill., 376, 384, correctly sustaining a declaration alleging the operative facts *specifically* instead of *generically*, as required by the more approved forms of pleading.

The rules of pleading determining whether allegations must be generic or specific – and if the latter, to what degree – are, like other rules of law, based on considerations of policy and convenience. Thus the facts constituting *fraud* are frequently required to be alleged in comparatively specific form; and similarly as regards *cruelty* in an action for divorce based on that ground. The reasons of policy are obvious in each case.

22 Compare *McCaughey v. Schuette* (1897), 117 Cal., 223. While the decision in this case can be supported, the statement that the specific facts pleaded were "evidentiary" seems inaccurate and misleading.

There are, of course, genuine instances of the fatally erroneous pleading of strictly evidential facts instead of either generic or specific operative facts. See *Rogers v. Milwaukee*, 13 Wis., 610; and contrast *Illinois Steel Co. v. Ostrowski, supra*, note 21.

23 Both operative and evidential facts must, under the law, be *ascertained* in some one or more of four possible modes: 1. By judicial admissions (what is not disputed); 2. By judicial notice, or knowledge (what is known or easily knowable); 3. By judicial perception (what is ascertained directly through the senses; cf. "real evidence"); 4. By judicial inference (what is ascertained by reasoning from facts already ascertained by one or more of the four methods here outlined).

24 As an example of this, compare Lord Westbury, in *Bell v. Kennedy* (1868), L. R. 1 H. L. (Sc.), 307: "Domicile, therefore, is an idea of the law. It is the *relation* which the *law creates* between an individual and a particular locality or country."

Contrast the far more accurate language of Chief Justice Shaw, in *Abington v. Bridgewater* (1840), 23 Pick., 170: "The *fact* of domicile is often one of the highest importance to a person; it *determines* his civil and political rights and privileges, duties and obligations...."

25   In this connection, the words of one of the great masters of the common law are significant. In his notable Preliminary Treatise on Evidence (1898), p. 190, Professor James Bradley Thayer said:

"As our law develops it becomes more and more important to give definiteness to its phraseology; discriminations multiply, new situations and complications of fact arise, and the old outfit of ideas, discriminations, and phrases has to be carefully revised. Law is not so unlike all other subjects of human contemplation that clearness of thought will not help us powerfully in grasping it. If terms in common legal use are used exactly, it is well to know it; if they are used inexactly, it is well to know that, and to remark just how they are used."

Perhaps the most characteristic feature of this author's great constructive contribution to the law of evidence is his constant insistence on the need for clarifying our legal terminology, and making careful "discriminations" between conceptions and terms that are constantly being treated as if they were one and the same. See, *e.g., Ibid.*, pp. vii, 183, 189–190, 278, 306, 351, 355, 390–393. How great the influence of those discriminations has been is well known to all students of the law of evidence.

The comparatively recent remarks of Professor John Chipman Gray, in his Nature and Sources of the Law (1909), Pref. p. viii, are also to the point:

"The student of Jurisprudence is at times troubled by the thought that he is dealing not with things, but with words, that he is busy with the shape and size of counters in a game of logomachy, but when he fully realizes how these words have been passed and are still being passed as money, not only by fools and on fools, but by and on some of the acutest minds, he feels that there is work worthy of being done, if only it can be done worthily."

No less significant and suggestive is the recent and characteristic utterance of one of the greatest jurists of our time, Mr. Justice Holmes. In *Hyde v. United States* (1911), 225 U. S., 347, 391, the learned judge very aptly remarked: "It is one of the misfortunes of the law that ideas become encysted in phrases and thereafter for a long time cease to provoke further analysis."

See also, Field, J., in *Morgan v. Louisiana* (1876), 93 U. S., 217, 223, and Peckham, J. in *Phoenix Ins. Co. v. Tennessee* (1895), 161 U. S., 174, 177, 178.

26   (1852) 7 How. Pr., 124, 130.

27   (1893) 54 Fed. Rep., 338, 348.

28   (1871) 3 Heisk. (Tenn.), 287, 306–307.

29   See also, for similar judicial observations, *Atchison & Neb. R. Co. v. Baty* (1877), 6 Neb., 37, 40. (The term *right* in civil society is defined to mean that which a man is entitled *to have*, or *to do*, or *to receive* from others within the limits prescribed by law."); *San Francisco v. S. V. Water Co.* (   ), 48 Cal., 531 ("We are to ascertain the *rights, privileges, powers, duties* and *obligations* of the Spring Valley Water Co., by reference to the general law.").

Compare also Gilbert, Evid. (4th ed., 1777), 126: "The men of one county, city, hundred, town, corporation, or parish are evidence in relation to the *rights, privileges, immunities* and affairs of such town, city, etc."

30   See *Kearns v. Cordwainers' Co.* (1859), 6 C. B. N. S., 388, 409 (construing The Thames Conservancy Act, 1857, 20 and 21 Vict. c. cxlvii., s. 179: "None of the powers by this act conferred ... shall extend to, take away, alter or abridge any right, claim, privilege, franchise, exemption, or immunity to which any owners ... of any lands ... are now by law entitled."); *Fearon v. Mitchell* (1872), L. R. 7 Q. B., 690, 695 ("The other question remains to be disposed of, as to whether the case comes within the proviso of s. 50 of 21 and 22 Vict. c. 98, that 'no market shall be established in pursuance of this section so as to interfere with any rights, powers, or privileges enjoyed within the district by any person without his consent.' "); Cal. Civ. Code, sec. 648a: "Building and loan associations may be formed under this title with or without guarantee or other capital stock, with all the rights, powers, and privileges, and subject to all the restrictions and liabilities set forth in this title."); Tenn. Const. of 1834, Art. 9, sec. 7: "The legislature shall have no power to pass any law granting to any individual or individuals, rights, privileges and immunities or exemptions, other than ... ").

31   (1894) 10 Ind. App., 60; 37 N. E., 303, 304.

32   See also *Howley Park Coal, etc., Co. v. L. & N. W. Ry.* (1913), A. C. 11, 25, 27 (per Viscount Haldane, L. C.: "There is an obligation (of lateral support) on the neighbor, and in that sense there is a correlative right on the part of the owner of the first piece of land;" per Lord Shaw: "There is a reciprocal right to lateral support for their respective lands and a reciprocal obligation upon the part of each owner.... No diminution of the right on the one hand or of

the obligation on the other can be effected except as the result of a plain contract.... ").

Compare, to similar effect, *Galveston, etc. Ry. Co. v. Harrigan* (1903), 76 S. W., 452, 453 (Tex. Civ. App.).

33 (1883) 8 App. Cas., at p. 597.

34 For merely a few out of numberless judicial instances of this loose usage, see *Pearce v. Scotcher* (1882), L. R. 9 Q. B.; 162, 167; *Quinn v. Leathem* (1901), A. C. 495 (*passim*); *Allen v. Flood* (1898), A. C. 1 (*passim*); *Lindley v. Nat. Carbonic Acid Gas Co.* (1910), 220 U. S., 61, 75; *Smith v. Cornell Univ.* (1894), 45 N. Y. Supp., 640, 643; *Farnum v. Kern Valley Bk.* (1910), 107 Pac., 568. See also *post*, n. 38.

35 El. Jurisp. (10th ed.), 83.

36 *Ibid.*, 82.

37 See Nat. and Sources of Law (1909), secs. 45, 184.

38 *Ibid.*, sec. 48.

39 Other instances in Professor Gray's work may be noted. In sec. 53, he says: "So again, a householder has the right to eject by force a trespasser from his 'castle.' That is, if sued by the trespasser for an assault, he can call upon the court to refuse the plaintiff its help. In other words, a man's legal rights include not only the power effectually to call for aid from an organized society against another, but also the power to call effectually upon the society to abstain from aiding others."

This, it is respectfully submitted, seems to confuse the householder's privilege of ejecting the trespasser (and the "no-right" of the latter) with a complex of *potential* rights, privileges, powers and immunities relating to the supposed action at law.

In sec. 102, the same learned author says: "If there is an ordinance that the town constable may kill all dogs without collars, the constable may have a legal right to kill such dogs, but the dogs are not under a legal duty to wear collars."

It would seem, however, that what the ordinance did was to create a privilege – the absence of the duty not to kill which otherwise would have existed in favor of the owner of the dog. Moreover, that appears to be the most natural connotation of the passage. The latter doesn't except very remotely, call up the idea of the constable's accompanying rights against all others that they shouldn't interfere with his actual killing of the dog.

See, also, secs. 145, 186.

40 It may be noted incidentally that a statute depriving a party of privileges as such may raise serious constitutional questions under the Fourteenth Amendment. Compare, *e.g.*, *Lindley v. Nat. Carbonic Gas Co.* (1910), 220 U. S., 61.

41 (1901) A. C., 495, 534.

42 See *post*, pp. 38–44.

43 Compare *Allen v. Flood* (1898), A. C., 1.

44 (1889) 23 Q. B. D., 59.

45 Cases almost without number might be cited to exemplify similar blending of fundamental conceptions and rapid shifting in the use of terms; – and that, too, even when the problems involved have been such as to invite close and careful reasoning. For a few important cases of this character, see *Allen v. Flood* (1898), A. C, 1, (Hawkins, J., p. 16: "I know it may be asked, 'What is the legal right of the plaintiffs which is said to have been invaded?' My answer is, that right which should never be lost sight of, and which I have already stated – the right freely to pursue their lawful calling;" Lord Halsbury, p. 84: "To dig into one's own land under the circumstances stated requires no cause or excuse. He may act from mere caprice, but his right on his own land is absolute, so long as he does not interfere with the rights of others;" Lord Ashbourne, p. 112: "The plaintiff had, in my opinion, a clear right to pursue their lawful calling.... It would be, I think, an unsatisfactory state of the law that allowed the wilful invader of such a right without lawful leave or justification to escape from the consequences of his action."); *Quinn v. Leathem* (1901), A. C., 495, 533; *Lindsley v. Natural Carbonic Gas Co* (1910), 220 U. S., 61, 74; *Robertson v. Rochester Folding Box Co.* (1902), 171 N. Y., 538 (Parker, C. J., p. 544: "The so-called right of privacy is, as the phrase suggests, founded upon the claim that a man has the right to pass through this world, if he wills, without having his picture published."); *Wabash, St. L. & P. R. Co. v. Shacklet* (1883), 105 Ill., 364, 389.

In *Purdy v. State* (1901), 43 Fla., 538, 540, the anomalous expression "right of privilege" is employed.

46 (Dropsie Tr.) secs. 196–197.

47 The same matter is put somewhat less clearly in Sohm's Institutes (Ledlies Tr., 3rd ed.), 28.

See also *Rector, etc. of Christ Church v. Philadelphia* (1860), 24 How., 300, 301, 302.

48 According to an older usage, the term "privilege" was frequently employed to indicate a "franchise," the latter being really a

miscellaneous complex of special rights, privileges, powers, or immunities, etc. Thus, in an early book, *Termes de la Ley*, there is the following definition: " 'Privileges' are liberties and franchises granted to an office, place, towne, or manor by the King's great charter, letters patent, or Act of Parliament, as toll, sake, socke, infangstheefe, outfangstheefe, turne, or delfe, and divers such like."

Compare *Blades v Higgs* (1865), 11 H. L. Cas., 621, 631, per Lord Westbury: "Property *ratione privilegii* is the right which by a peculiar franchise anciently granted by the Crown, by virtue of prerogative, one may have of taking animals *ferae naturae* on the land of another; and in like manner the game when taken by virtue of the privilege becomes the absolute property of the owner of the franchise."

49 See *Humphrey v. Pegues* (1872), 16 Wall., 244, 247, per Hunt, J.: "All the 'privileges' as well as powers and rights of the prior company, were granted to the latter. A more important or more comprehensive privilege than a perpetual immunity from taxation can scarcely be imagined. It contains the essential idea of a peculiar benefit or advantage, of a special exemption from a burden falling upon others."

See also *Smith v. Floyd* (1893), 140 N. Y., 337, 342; *Lonas v. State* (1871). 3 Heisk., 287, 306, 307; *Territory v Stokes* (1881), 2 N. M., 161, 169, 170; *Ripley v. Knight* (1878), 123 Mass., 515, 519; *Dike v. State* (1888), 38 Minn., 366; *Re Miller* (1893), 1 Q. B., 327.

Compare *Wisener v. Burrell* (1911), 28 Okla., 546.

50 Compare *Louisville & N. R Co. v. Gaines* (1880), 3 Fed. Rep., 266, 278, per Baxter, Asso. J.: "Paschal says (the term privilege) is a special right belonging to an individual or class; *properly*, an *exemption* from some *duty*."

51 For apt use of the terms, "privilege" and "privileged" in relation to libel, see Hawkins, J., in *Allen v. Flood* (1898), A. C. 1, 20–21.

52 As regards the general duty to testify, specific performance may usually be had under duress of potential or actual contempt proceedings; and, apart from that, failure to testify might subject the wrongdoer either to a statutory liability for a penalty in favor of the injured party litigant or, in case of actual damage, to a common law action on the case.

The subject of witnesses is usually thought of as a branch of the so-called *adjective* law, as distinguished, from the so-called *substantive* law. But, as the writer has had occasion to emphasize on another occasion (The Relations between Equity and Law, 11 Mich. L. Rev., 537, 554, 556, 569), there seems to be no intrinsic or essential difference between those jural relations that relate to the "substantive" law and those that relate to the "adjective" law. This matter will be considered more fully in a later part of the discussion.

53 (1583) 9 Coke, 1.

54 (1898) A. C., 1, 19.

55 (1896) 89 Me., 359.

56 (1856) 6 E. & B., 47. 74.

57 For other examples of apt use of the term in question, see *Borland v Boston* (1882), 132 Mass., 89 ("municipal rights, privileges, powers or duties"); *Hamilton v. Graham* (1871), L. R. 2 H. L. (Sc.), 167, 169, per Hatherley, L. C.; *Jones v. De Moss* (1911), 151 Ia., 112, 117; *Kripp v. Curtis* (1886), 71 Cal., 62, 63; *Lamer v. Booth* (1874), 50 Miss., 411, 413; *Weller v. Brown* (1911), Cal.,; 117 Pac., 517; *Mathews v. People* (1903), 202 Ill., 389, 401; *Abington v. North Bridgewater* (1840), 23 Pick., 170.

58 (1898) A. C., 1, 29.

59 For the reference to Mr. Justice Cave's opinion, the present writer is indebted to Salmond's work on Jurisprudence. Citing this case and one other, *Starey v. Graham* (1899), 1 Q. B., 406, 411, the learned author adopts and uses exclusively the term "liberty" to indicate the opposite of "duty," and apparently overlooks the importance of *privilege* in the present connection. Curiously enough, moreover, in his separate Treatise on Torts, his discussion of the law of defamation gives no explicit intimation that *privilege* in relation to that subject represents merely *liberty*, or "*no-duty*."

Sir Frederick Pollock, in his volume on Jurisprudence (2nd ed., 1904), 62, seems in effect to deny that legal liberty represents any true legal relation as such. Thus, he says, *inter alia*: "The act may be right in the popular and rudimentary sense of not being forbidden, but freedom has not the character of legal right until we consider the risk of unauthorized interference. It is the duty of all of us not to interfere with our neighbors' lawful freedom. This brings the so-called primitive rights into the sphere of legal rule and protection. *Sometimes it is thought that lawful power or liberty is different from the right not to be interfered with; but for the reason just given this opinion, though plausible, does not seem correct*." Compare also Pollock, Essays in Jurisp. & Ethics (1882), Ch. I.

It is difficult to see, however, why, as between X and Y, the "privilege + no-right" situation is not just as real a jural relation as the precisely opposite "duty + right" relation between any two parties. Perhaps the habit of recognizing exclusively the latter as a jural relation springs more or less from the traditional tendency to think of the law as consisting of "commands," or imperative rules. This, however, seems fallacious. A rule of law that *permits* is just as real as a rule of law that *forbids*; and, similarly, saying that the law *permits* a given act to X as between himself and Y predicates just as genuine a legal relation as saying that the law *forbids* a certain act to X as between himself and Y. That this is so seems, in some measure, to be confirmed by the fact that the first sort of act would ordinarily be pronounced "lawful," and the second "unlawful." Compare *Thomas v. Sorrel* (1673), Vaughan, 331, 351.

60 Compare *Dow v. Newborough* (1728), Comyns, 242 ("For the use is only a liberty to take the profits, but two cannot severally take the profits of the same land, therefore there cannot be an use upon a use." It should be observed that in this and the next case to be cited, along with the liberty or privilege there are associated powers and rights, etc.: for instance, the *power* to acquire a title to the things severed from the realty); *Bourne v. Taylor* (1808), 10 East., 189 (Ellenborough, C. J.): "The second question is whether the replication ought to have traversed the liberty of working the mines. ... The word *liberty*, too, implies the same thing. It imports, *ex vi termini*, that it is a *privilege* to be exercised over another man's estates"); *Wickham v. Hawkes* (1840), 7 M. & W., 63, 78–79; *Quinn v. Leathem* (1901), A. C. 495, 534 (per Lord Lindley: see quotation *aent*, p.   ); *Pollock v. Farmers' Loan & Trust Co.* (1895), 157 U. S., 429, 652 (per White, J., "rights and liberties"); *Mathews v. People* (1903), 202 Ill., 389, 401 (Magruder, C. J.: "It is now settled that the privilege of contracting is both a liberty, and a property right.").

For *legislative* use of the term in question, see the Copyright Act. 8 Anne (1709) c. 19 ("Shall have the sole right and liberty of printing each book and books for the term of ... ").

Like the word "privilege" (see *ante* p. 38, n. 48), the term "liberty" is occasionally used, especially in the older books, to indicate a franchise, or complex of special rights, privileges, powers, or immunities. Thus in Noy's Maxims (1641) there is this definition: "Liberty is a royal privilege in the hands of a subject;" and, similarly, Blackstone (2 Com. 37) says: "Franchise and liberty are used as synonymous terms; and their definition is, a royal privilege, or branch of the king's prerogative, subsisting in the hands of a subject."

This definition is quoted in *S. F. Waterworks v. Schottler* (1882), 62 Cal. 69, 106, and *Central R. & Banking Co. v. State* (1875), 54 Ga., 401, 409. Compare also *Rex v. Halifax & Co.* (1891), 2 Q. B., 263.

61 Compare *Pond v. Bates*, 34 L. J. (N. S.), 406 ("With full power and free liberty to sink for, win and work the same, with all liberties, privileges, etc., necessary and convenient," etc.); *Hamilton v. Graham* (1871), L. R. 2 H. L. (Sc.), 166, 167; *Attersoll v. Stevens* (1808), 1 Taunt., 183; *Wickham v. Hawker* (1840), 7 M. & W., 63, 78–79.

62 (1896) 12 App. Div., 17; 42 N. Y. Sup., 607, 609.

63 See, in accord, the oft-quoted passage from *Thomas v. Sorrell* (1673), Vaughan, 331, 351 ("A dispensation or license properly passes no interest, nor alters or transfers property in anything, but only makes an action lawful, which without it had been unlawful. As a license to go beyond the seas, to hunt in a man's park, to come into his house, are only actions, which without license, had been unlawful.").

Compare also *Taylor v. Waters* (1817), 7 Taunt., 374, 384 ("Those cases abundantly prove that a license to enjoy a beneficial privilege in land may be granted, and, notwithstanding the statue of frauds, without writing." In this case the license (operative facts) is more or less confused with privileges (the legal relation created); *Heap v. Hartley* (1889), 42 Ch. D., 461, 470.

64 Compare *Remington v. Parkins* (1873), 10 R. I., 550, 553, per Durfee, J.: "A power is an ability to do."

65 See *People v. Dikeman* (1852), 7 Howard Pr., 124, 130; and *Lonas v. State* (1871), 3 Heisk. (Tenn.), 287, 306–307, quoted *ante*.

See also *Mabre v. Whittaker* (1906), 10 Wash., 656, 663 (Washington Laws of 1871 provided in relation to community property: "The husband shall have the management of all the common property, but shall not have the *right* to sell or encumber real estate except he shall be joined in the sale or encumbrance by the wife. ... " Per Scott, J.: " 'Right' in the sense used there means power").

Compare also *St. Joseph Fire & Marine Ins. Co. v. Hanck* (1876), 63 Mo., 112, 118.

Numberless additional instances might be given of the use of the term "right," where the legal quantity involved is really a power rather than a right in the sense of claim.

66   It is to be noted that abandonment would leave X himself with precisely the same sort of privileges and powers as any other person.

67   Compare *Wynehamer v. People* (1856), 13 N. Y., 378, 396 (Comstock, J.: "I can form no notion of property which does not include the essential characteristics and attributes with which it is clothed by the laws of society ... among which are, fundamentally the right of the occupant or owner to use and enjoy (the objects) exclusively, and his *absolute power to sell and dispose of them*"); *Bartemeyer v. Iowa* (1873), 18 Wall., 129, 137 (Field, J.: "The right of property in an article involves the *power to sell and dispose* of such articles as well as to use and enjoy it"); *Low v. Rees Printing Co.* (1894), 41 Neb., 127, 146 (Ryan, C.: "Property, in its broad sense, is not the physical thing which may be the subject of ownership, but is the right of dominion, possession, and *power of disposition* which may be acquired over it.").

Since the power of alienation is frequently one of the fundamental elements of a complex legal interest (or property aggregate), it is obvious that a statute extinguishing such power may, in a given case be unconstitutional as depriving the owner of property without due process of law. See the cases just cited.

68   For a leading case exhibiting the nature of agency powers, especially powers "coupled with an interest," see *Hunt v. Rousmanier* (1883), 8 Wheat., 173, 201.

It is interesting to note that in the German Civil Code the provisions relating to agency are expressed in terms of powers, – *e.g.*, sec. 168: "The expiration of the power is determined by the legal relations upon which the giving of the power is founded. The power is also revocable in the event of the continuance of the legal relation, unless something different results from the latter."

Incidentally, it may be noticed also, that as a matter of English usage, the term "power of attorney" has, by association of ideas, come to be used to designate the mere operative *instrument* creating the powers of an agent.

69   For examples of the loose and confusing employment of the term "authority" in agency cases, –

and that too, in problems of the conflict of laws requiring the closest reason, – see *Pope v. Nickerson* (1844), 3 Story, 465, 473, 476, 481, 483; *Lloyd v Guibert* (1865), 6 B. & S., 100, 117; *King v. Sarria* (1877), 69 N. Y., 24, 28, 30–32; *Risdon, etc., Works v. Furness* (1905), 1 K. B. 304; (1906) 1 K. B. 49.

For a criticism of these cases in relation to the present matter, see the writer's article The Individual Liability of Stockholders and the Conflict of Laws (1909). 9 Columb. L. Rev., 492, 512, n. 46, 521, n. 71; 10 Columb. L. Rev., 542–544.

70   The clear understanding and recognition of the agency relation as involving the creation of legal powers may be of crucial importance in many cases, – especially, as already intimated, in regard to problems in the conflict of laws. Besides the cases in the preceding note, two others may be referred to, *Milliken v. Pratt* (1878), 125 Mass., 374, presenting no analysis of the agency problem; and, on the other hand, *Freeman's Appeal* (1897), 68 Conn., 533, involving a careful analysis of the agency relation by Baldwin, J. Led by this analysis to reach a decision essentially opposite to that of the Massachusetts case, the learned judge said, *inter alia*:

"Such was, in effect, the act by which Mrs. Mitchell undertook to do what she had no legal capacity to do, by making her husband her agent to deliver the guaranty to the bank. He had no more power to make it operative by delivery in Chicago to one of his creditors in Illinois, than he would have had to make it operative by delivery here, had it been drawn in favor of one of his creditors in Connecticut. It is not the place of delivery that controls, but the power of delivery."

71   See *Emery v. Clough* (1885), 63 N. H., 552 ("right or power of defeasance").

72   See *Hudgens v. Chamberlain* (1911), 161 Cal., 710, 713, 715. For another instance of statutory powers, see *Capital, etc., Bk. v. Rhodes* (1903), 1 Ch. 631, 655 (powers under registry acts.).

73   Though the nebulous term "rights" is used by the courts, it is evident that powers are the actual quantities involved.

Thus, in the instructive case of *Carpenter v. Scott* (1881), 13 R. I., 477, 479, the court said, by Matteson, J.: "Under it (the conditional sale) the vendee acquires not only the right of possession and use, but the right to become the absolute owner upon complying with the terms of the contract. These are rights of which no act of the vendor can divest him, and which, in the absence of any stipulation in the contract restraining him, he can transfer by sale or mortgage. Upon performance of the conditions of the sale, the title to the property vests in the vendee, or in the event that he has sold, or mortgaged it, in his vendee, or mortgagee, without further bill of sale. . . . These rights constitute an actual, present interest in the property, which, as we have seen above, is capable of transfer by sale or mortage."

It is interesting to notice that in the foregoing passage, the term "right" is first used to indicate *privileges* of possession and use; next the term is employed primarily in the sense of legal power, though possibly there is a partial blending of this idea with that of legal claim, or right (in the narrowest connotation); then the term (in plural form) is used for the third time so as to lump together the vendee's privileges, powers and claims.

For another case indicating in substance the true nature of the vendee's interest, see *Christensen v. Nelson* (1901), 38 Or. 473, 477, 479, indicating, in effect, that the vendee's powers as well as privileges may be transferred to another, and that a proper tender constitutes "the equivalen of payment."

74 See Davis v. Clark (1897), 58 Kan. 100; 48 Pac., 563, 565; Leiter v. Pike (1889), 127 Ill., 287, 326; Welstur v. Trust Co. (1895), 145 N. Y., 275, 283; Furley v. Palmer (1870), 20 Oh. St., 223, 225.

The proposition that the grantee's power is irrevocable is subject to the qualification that it might possibly be extinguished (or modified *pro tanto*) as the result of a transaction between the grantor and one having the position of *bona fide purchaser*, or the equivalent.

It is hardly necessary to add that the courts, instead of analyzing the problem of the escrow in terms of powers, as here indicated, are accustomed to stating the question and deciding it in terms of "delivery," "relation back," "performance of conditions," etc.

75 In this connection it is worthy of note that Sugden, in his work on Powers (8th ed., 1861) 4, uses, contrary to general practice, the expression, "*power* of entry for condition broken."

76 For miscellaneous instances of powers, see the good opinions in *Bk. of S. Australia v. Abrahams*, L. R. P. C., 265; *Barlow v. Ross* (1890), 24 Q. B. D., 381, 384.

77 As to "inchoate" obligations, see *Frost v. Knight* (1872) L. R. 7 Ex. 111, per Cockburn, C. J. This

matter will receive further attention in a later part of the discussion.

78 Compare *Boston R. Co. v. Bartlett* (1849), 3 Cush., 225: "Though the writing signed by the defendant was but an offer, and an offer which might be revoked, yet while it remained in force and unrevoked, it was a continuing offer, during the time limited for acceptance, and during the whole of the rest of the time it was an offer every instant; but as soon as it was accepted, it ceased to be an offer merely."

Compare also the forms of statement in Ashley, Contr. (1911), 16 *et. seq.*

79 Langdell, Sum. Contr. (2nd ed., 1880), sec. 178.

80 Langdell's *a priori* premises and specific conclusions have been adopted by a number of other writers on the subject. See, for example, Ashley, Contr. (1911), 25 *et seq.*, R. L. McWilliams, Enforcement of Option Agreements (1913), 1 Calif. Law Rev., 122.

81 For a recent judicial expression on the subject, see *W. G. Reese Co. v. House* (1912), 162 Cal., 740, 745 per Sloss J.: "Where there is a consideration, the option cannot be withdrawn during the time agreed upon for its duration, while, if there be no consideration the party who has given the option may revoke it at any time before acceptance, even though the time limited has not expired . . . such offer, duly accepted, constitutes a contract binding upon both parties and enforceable by either."

See, to the same effect, *Linn v. McLean* (1885), 80 Ala., 360, 364; *O'Brien v. Boland* (1896), 166 Mass., 481, 483 (sealed offer).

Most of the cases recognizing the irrevocable power of the optionee have arisen in equitable suits for specific performance; but there seems to be no reason for doubting that the same doctrine should be applied in a common law action for damages. See, in accord, *Baker v. Shaw* (1912), 68 Wash., 99 103 (*dicta* in an action for damages).

82 Secs. 330–333.

83 Compare, to the same effect, Keener, Quasi-Contr. (1893), p. 18.

84 (1892) 142 Ill., 388, 397.

85 (1861) 16 Grat., 519, 525.

86 (1885) 63 N. H., 552.

87 (1873) 36 Ia., 224, 226.

88 Compare *Attorney General v. Sudeley* (1896), 1 Q. B., 354, 359 (per Lord Esher: "What is called a 'right of action' is not the *power* of bringing an action. Anybody can bring an action though he has no right at all."); *Kroessin v. Keller* (1895), 60

Minn., 372 (per Collins, J.: "The power to bring such actions").

89   (1892) 95 Cal., 317, 319.

90   We are apt to think of liability as exclusively an onerous relation of one party to another. But, in its broad technical significance, this is not necessarily so. Thus X, the owner of a watch, has the power to abandon his property – that is, to extinguish his existing rights, powers, and immunities relating thereto (not, however, his privileges, for until someone else has acquired title to the abandoned watch, X would have the same privileges as before); and correlatively to X's power of abandonment there is a liability in every other person. But such a liability instead of being onerous or unwelcome, is quite the opposite. As regards another person M, for example, it is a *liability to have created in his favor (though against his will) a privilege and a power* relating to the watch, – that is, the privilege of taking possession and the power, by doing so, to vest a title in himself. See *Dougherty v. Creary* (1866), 30 Cal., 290, 298. Contrast with this agreeable form of liability the *liability to have a duty created* – for example the liability of one who has made or given an option in a case where the value of the property has greatly risen.

91   (1895) 161 U. S., 174, 177.

92   (1876) 93 U. S., 217, 222.

93   See, in accord, *Picard v. Tennessee, etc., R. Co.* (1888), 130 U. S., 637, 642, (Field, J.); *Rochester Railway Co. v. Rochester* (1906) 205 U. S., 236, 252 (Moody, J., reviewing the many other cases on the subject).

In *Internat. & G. N. Ry. Co. v. State* (1899), 75 Tex., 356, a different view was taken as to the *alienability* of an immunity from taxation. Speaking by Stayton, C. J., the court said:

"Looking at the provisions of the Act of March 10, 1875, we think there can be no doubt the exemption from taxation given by it, instead of being a right vesting only in appellant, is a right which inheres in the property to which it applies, and follows it into the hands of whosover becomes the owner.... The existence of this right enhances the value of the property to which it applies. Shareholders and creditors must be presumed to have dealt with the corporation on the faith of the contract which gave the exemption, and it cannot be taken away by legislation, by dissolution of the corporation, or in any other manner not sufficient to pass title to any other property from one person to another. The right to exemption from taxation is

secured by the same guaranty which secures titles to those owning lands granted under the act, and though the corporation may be dissolved, will continue to exist in favor of persons owning the property to which the immunity applies. Lawful dissolution of a corporation will destroy all its corporate franchises or privileges vested the act of incorporation; but if it holds rights, privileges, and franchises in the nature of property, secured by contract based on valuable consideration, these will survive the dissolution of the corporation, for the benefit of those who may have a right to or just claim upon its assets."

Compare, as regard homestead exemptions, Sloss, J., in *Smith v. Bougham* (1909), 156 Cal., 359, 365: "A declaration of homestead... attaches certain privileges and immunities to such title as may at the time be held."

94   See *Choate v. Trapp* (1912), 224 U. S., 665.

95   See *Brearly School, Limited v. Ward* (1911), 201 N. Y., 358; 94 N. E., 1001 (an interesting decision, with three judges dissenting). The other cases on the subject are collected in Ann. Cas., 1912 B, 259.

96   See *Brearly School, Limited v. Ward*, cited in preceding note; also *Internat. & G. N. Ry. Co. v. State* (1899), 75 Tex., 356, quoted from, *ante*, n. 91.

97   Compare also *Wilson v. Gaines* (1877), 9 Baxt. (Tenn.), 546, 550–551, Turney, J.: "The use in the statutes of two only of the words of the constitution, *i. e.*, 'rights' and 'privileges,' and the omission to employ either of the other two following in immediate succession, viz., 'immunities' and 'exemptions,' either of which would have made clear the construction claimed by complainant, evidence a purposed intention on the part of the legislature not to grant the benefit claimed by the b:11."

Only very rarely is a court found seeking to draw a subtle distinction between an immunity and an exemption. Thus, in a recent case, *Strahan v. Wayne Co.* (June, 1913), 142 N. W., 678, 680 (Neb.), Mr. Justice Barnes said: "It has been held by the great weight of authority that dower is not immune (from the inheritance tax) because it is dower, but because it... belonged to her unchoately during (the husband's) life.... Strictly speaking, the widow's share should be considered as immune, rather than exempt, from an inheritance tax. It is free, rather than freed, from such tax."

98   (1677) 2 Swanst., 170.

99　In *Skelton v. Skelton*, it will be observed, the word "*impunity*" and the word "*exemption*" are used as the opposite of *liability* to the powers of a plaintiff in an action at law.

For similar recent instances, see *Vacher & Sons, Limited v. London Society of Compositors* (1913), A. C. 107, 118, 125 (per Lord Macnaghten: "Now there is nothing absurd in the notion of an association or body enjoying immunity from actions at law;" per Lord Atkinson: "Conferring on the trustees immunity as absolute," etc.).

Compare also *Baylies v. Bishop of London* (1913), 1 Ch., 127, 139, 140, per Hamilton, L. J.

For instances of the apt use of the term "disability" as equivalent to the negation of legal power, see *Poury v. Hordern* (1900), 1 Ch., 492, 495; *Sheridan v. Elden* (1862), 24 N. Y., 281, 384.

100　The next article in the present series will discuss the distinctions between legal and equitable jural relations; also the contrast between rights, etc., *in rem*, and rights, etc., *in personam*. The supposed distinctions between substantive and adjective jural relations will also be considered, – chiefly with the purpose of showing that, so far as the intrinsic and essential nature of those relations is concerned, the distinctions commonly assumed to exist are imaginary rather than real. Finally, some attention will be given to the nature and analysis of complex legal interests, or aggregates of jural relations.

Part VI

The Autonomy of Law and Legal Reasoning

13

Legal Formalism: On the Immanent Rationality of Law

Ernest J. Weinrib

I Introduction

A. *The Disrepute of Formalism*

This essay elucidates and defends legal formalism. In current academic discussion, the avowed formalist is the missing interlocutor. Formalism is like a heresy driven underground, whose tenets must be surmised from the derogatory comments of its detractors. Everyone knows that legal formalism asserts the distinction of law and politics. The curiosity of this distinction makes formalism seem at best a pathetic escape from the functionalism of law, and at worst a vicious camouflage of the realities of power. One would not guess that formalism, properly understood and stripped of the encrustations of hostile polemics, embodies a profound and inescapable truth about law's inner coherence. My purpose here is to lay bare this truth.

The most explicit criticism of formalism is to be found in the scholarship of the Critical Legal Studies movement.[1] On the fundamental issue of whether law can in any significant sense be differentiated from politics, however, the Critical Legal Studies denunciation of formalism is merely a provocative statement of a commonly held academic belief. Rarely does one find today

an espousal of what the anti-formalists labor to undermine. Most of the sophisticated writing in the United States assumes that law is a manifestation of political purposes; dispute centers on the questions of what those purposes should properly be and how they should be woven into the fabric of law.[2]

My defense of formalism is an exploration of the sense in which law can, after all, be differentiated from politics. This differentation is tied here to a complex of broader issues: How is law intelligible? In what does the coherence of juridical relationships consist? Is a non-instrumental conception of law possible? The distinction between law and politics is thus the precipitate of an endeavor to vindicate the law's autonomy. For current legal scholarship this autonomy is, of course, as much a delusion as the distinction between law and politics.[3] My treatment of legal formalism, therefore, calls contemporary assumptions into question across a wide front.

This attempt to resurrect formalism is not merely a perverse theoretical indulgence. Although legal scholars may deny the distinctiveness or autonomy of law, lawyers engaged in the practice of law have always sensed that their intellectual world is not fully reflected in these academic conclusions. Legal activity invariably takes place within some structure, however lax. No matter how often the impossibility of such structure is announced by academics, murmurs of disbelief are heard in the trenches below. Legal formalism is the effort to make sense of the lawyer's perception of an intelligible order. This is why in the last two centuries formalism has been killed again and again, but has always refused to stay dead.

Formalism postulates that law is intelligible as an internally coherent phenomenon. The implications of the formalist claim extend to every aspect of reflection about law. It affects one's view of the nature of legal justification, the limits of the judicial role and judicial competence, the meaning of legal mistake, the relevance of instrumentalism, the relation of law and society, the viability of contemporary legal scholarship, and the place of law among the intellectual disciplines. The scope and importance of these issues attest to the inescapably fundamental nature of the formalist claim.

Although its rigorous separation of the juridical and the political sets formalism apart from the main body of contemporary writing, formalism stands most opposed to Critical Legal Studies. Yet this very opposition also, paradoxically, brings the two together, for they do at least place the same issue at the heart of jurisprudence. For the formalist, the law's inner rationality reflects the possibility of its coherence, and this possibility is what Critical Legal Studies scholarship emphatically denies. The assumption common to both opposing views is that the law's moral legitimacy hangs on the outcome of their dispute. Mainstream scholarship, in contrast, allows itself to see the law as a plurality of competing or unintegrated purposes.[4] It implicitly concedes the point made by its radical critics but refuses to be embarrassed by it, claiming that the law's incoherence is manageable or even productive of good.[5] Both formalism and Critical Legal Studies reject this confession and avoidance, and insist on the importance of coherence for law.[6]

Formalism's theme – the internal intelligibility of law – is indispensable to any serious effort of legal philosophy. Juristic activity includes reflection on its own self-understandings and aspirations. This internal stand point cannot be ignored: Only by reference to it is legal philosophy assured of having made contact with its subject matter. Nothing is more senseless than to attempt to understand law from a vantage point entirely extrinsic to it.[7] Formalism takes the internal standpoint to its extreme and makes it decisive for the understanding of juridical relationships. It thereby offers the most uncompromising construal of the law's inner intelligibility.

B.   What Formalism Is

My starting point is the formalism described in Roberto Unger's influential critique.[8] Unger regards formalism as fundamental to the legal thought that he opposes and considers to have been conclusively discredited. His description is, nevertheless, a valuable statement of formalism's principal themes and identifies the matter at issue. Indeed, in the litany of recent criticism of formalism, Unger is almost unique in providing an unsuperficial delineation of a position worth opposing. His description combines lack of sympathy with insight.

In Unger's account formalism brings together three features. First, formalism asserts the possibility of "a method of legal justification that can be clearly contrasted to open-ended disputes about the basic terms of social life."[9] In this conception law features a mode of rationality that is different in kind from the less determinate rationality of political and ideological contest. Legal doctrine is possible only through "a restrained, relatively apolitical method of analysis."[10] Second, the distinctive rationality of law is immanent to the legal material on which it operates. Formalist doctrine is characterized by the working out of the implications of law from a standpoint internal to law. Unger accordingly defines legal analysis as

a form of conceptual practice that combines . . . the willingness to work from the institutionally defined materials of a given collective tradition and the claim to speak authoritatively within this tradition, to elaborate it from within in a way that is meant, at least ultimately, to affect the application of state power.[11]

Finally, formalism presupposes that the ensemble of authoritative legal materials "display, though always imperfectly, an intelligible moral order."[12] Formalism relies on some guiding vision about human association that supplies the normative theory sanctifying the tradition as a whole and yet allows some of the received understandings and decisions in it to be rejected as mistaken.

Formalism can accordingly be summed up as proffering the possibility of an "immanent moral rationality."[13] Each term in this phrase corresponds to one of the three features in Unger's description. The first feature, that law has a distinctive rationality, expresses the formalist conception of law negatively through a contrast with political justification. The second, the immanent operation of legal rationality, characterizes law's distinctiveness affirmatively through the claim that the content of law is elaborated from within. The third asserts the moral dimension of this rationality, ascribing normative force to its application.

Unger's description gives a satisfactory preliminary sketch.[14] All that needs to be added is that formalism, at least as I shall present it here, is an integrative notion. The rationality, immanence, and normativity that characterize it are not disjointed attributes contingently combined, but mutually connected aspects of a single complex. For the formalist, law is not merely rational *and* immanent *and* normative; rather, it has each of these qualities only because it also has the other two.[15] Formalism postulates not merely the compresence of the features that Unger perceptively notices, but their mutual dependence and interrelationship in a single approach to legal understanding.

The most mysterious of the three formalist attributes is that of immanence.[16] By suggesting that the rationality of law lies in a moral order immanent to legal material, formalism postulates that juridical content can somehow sustain itself from within. The internalist dimension of formalism is at odds with current assumptions about law in several ways.

The dominant tendency today is to look upon the content of law from the standpoint of some external ideal that the law is to enforce or make authoritative. Implicit in contemporary scholarship is the idea that the law embodies or should embody some goal (e.g., wealth maximization,[17] market deterrence,[18] liberty,[19] utility,[20] solidarity[21]) that can be specified apart from law and can serve as the standard by which law is to be assessed. Thus law is regarded as an instrument for forwarding some independently desirable purpose given to it from the outside.

The external relation that these scholars believe exists between law and the content it comes to have reflects their positivist understanding of law. In the positivist conception, a legal reality is brought into existence by an act of will that transforms into law that which is otherwise not law.[22] The content of law as such is only the product of some law–creating act. Because the power to create law can work for good or for evil, a legal system is not a phenomenon that in itself immanently embodies a moral rationality.[23] Whether any particular law is moral is a matter to be settled by an argument outside rather than inside the law, through reference to the independent desirability of the ideals that the particular law reflects.

In this conception the legislative process is the distinctive vehicle of legality. Through this process, something that is otherwise without legal significance gets inscribed into the schedule of collectively approved and authoritative aims. Legislation is the mechanism through which the legal system imports from the outside the material that it makes its own. It is not merely that the expressly legislative organs of governance are regarded as paradigmatic, but that public authority generally is conceived as being fundamentally legislative: Positivists consider even adjudication to be a species of legislative activity. All legal norms, even those elaborated by judges, depend on the metamorphosis into law of material that is orginally non-legal.

This conception ascribes to law a primarily political nature. It is preoccupied with the notions of coercion, authority, and validity and with the identification of the external purposes that are to be transformed into legal norms. Law is regarded as wafting down from the publicly recognized organs of power, and legal relations are in the first instance relations between the holders of authority and the subjects of authority.[24]

In construing law as an immanent moral rationality, formalism directly challenges these assumptions about law's provenance, nature, and characteristic process. In the formalist conception, law has a content that is not imported from without but elaborated from within. Law is not so much an instrument in the service of foreign ideals as an end in itself constituting, as it were, its own ideal. Rather than being an exclusively positivist transformation of the non-legal into the juridical, law can involve the recognition of that which already has an inchoate juridical significance. The paradigmatic legal function is not the manufacturing of legal norms but the understanding of what is intimated by juridical arrangements and relationships. Legal creativity here is essentially cognitive, and it is most naturally expressed in adjudication conceived more as the discovery than as the making of law.

Legal formalism's postulation of an immanent rationality ties it to the rationalist tradition in Western philosophy, which grappled with the question of how something could be understood in and through itself.[25] To understand something in this way is to understand it unconditionally in the literal sense, i.e., as something whose intelligibility is not conditioned by or dependent upon anything extrinsic. The legal formalist asserts that whatever else can or cannot be understood in this way, law at least can.

In particular, legal formalism endeavors to make the notion of form central to the understanding of juridical relationships. This notion has a distinguished and venerable history that stretches back from the present century to the great thinkers of classical antiquity. Yet contemporary writing on law rarely attends to its significance. My elucidation of formalism will attempt to make good this defect by first outlining what form is and then tracking its implications for legal philosophy. Form is the bedrock on which formalism rests. The general inattention to the significance of form renders the conclusion that formalism has been discredited the merest dogma. I wish to call this dogma into question, to expose it as such by focusing on what it ignores, and to suggest that formalism, properly understood, is indispensable to our understanding of law.

II   The Nature of Form

Legal formalism claims that juridical relationships can be understood as embodying, in Unger's phrase, an "immanent moral rationality." The function of law for the formalist is to express this immanent rationality in the doctrines, institutions, and decisions of the positive law.[26] Juridical relationships so conceived are intelligible by reference to themselves and not solely as the translation into law of an independently desirable political purpose.

Legal form is concerned with the understanding of juridical relationships.[27] Since the point of my entire exposition of formalism is to present an affirmative conception of the juridical, I can indicate the significance of the term at this preliminary only negatively. One example is the relationship that obtains between the victim and the person who intentionally inflicts a blow. While this is a physical event, its juridical significance cannot be grasped solely through the investigation of the mechanics of the impact. Nor can its juridical significance be understood solely by reference to the positive law of a particular jurisdiction. It is true that a sophisticated system of positive law aims at an intelligible connection between the existence and the resolution of controversy and that its holdings are therefore relevant to the understanding of the juridical nature of the relationship. The holdings that govern this incident, however, may be mistaken even from a legal standpoint. The positive law may provide only a defective rendering of the juridical significance of what happened.[28] Similarly, a juridical relationship is not defined historically or sociologically in terms of the development of this positive law or of the societal considerations that sustain it. The juridical nature of a relationship refers, in a sense still to be defined, to a paradigmatically legal mode of intelligibility that goes beyond the physical, the positive, the historical, or the sociological.

Our first task, then, is to clarify the formalist conception of understanding. What is it for something to be intelligible? And how do juridical relationships fit into this conception of intelligibility?

A. Form and Content

The intelligibility of any matter refers to a relationship between the matter's content and its form. When we seek the intelligibility of something, we want to know *what* the something is. This search for "whatness" presupposes that the something is a *this* and not a *that*, that it has, in other words, a determinate content. This content is determinate because it sets the matter apart from other matters and prevents it from falling back into the chaos of unintelligible indeterminacy that its identification as a something denies. The content has thus both a positive and a negative significance: It makes the matter in question what it is, and it differentiates it from what it is not.

The set of properties that renders a content determinate[29] is, when considered in itself, the matter's form.[30] Form is the ensemble of characteristics that constitute the matter in question as a unity identical to that of other matters of the same kind and distinguishable from matters of a different kind. Form is not separate from content but is the ensemble of characteristics that marks the content as determinate, and therefore marks the content as a content.

The interrelationship between form and content can be illustrated by considering the form of a table. Those characteristics that mark the content of a table as determinate may include elevation, flatness, hardness, typical function, and so on. By reference to the ensemble of the characteristics of "tableness" that make up the form of a table, we can understand all the embodiments of this form as being the same sort of thing and each table as being a single thing. The ensemble of characteristics that constitute its form makes this thing intelligible as a table, and it has the determinate content of a table inasmuch as it is the embodiment of this intelligible form.

Form and content are correlative and interpenetrating. If any content were formless, it would lack the very determinateness which makes it possible for us to experience it as a something, and it would therefore be, so far as we are concerned, an indeterminate something or other that is nothing in particular. If a form, on the other hand, were without content, it would not be a form *of* anything and therefore not a form at all. Form therefore *is* content and content form, with the distinction between them being notional, not ontological. A thing's form is not a new thing existing separately from that of which it is the form. Rather, form discloses the intelligibility of the thing's content, so that the form is the content qua intelligible and, conversely, the content is the form qua determinate. We understand something when form and content are congruent, that is, when the ensemble of characteristics that we consider to be the form represents what the content really is and, equivalently, when what we consider to be the content adequately expresses the thing's form. Whatever is thought to be in the gap between content and form (for example, a characteristic ascribed to the content that is not a component of its form or a characteristic considered part of the form but not present in the content) is either error or ignorance.[31]

The notion of form has three interrelated aspects. First, to see the form of something is to regard that thing as having a certain character. This character is the ensemble of characteristics that allows us to define something as the sort of thing it is. The specification of the characteristics that go to a thing's form is not an exhaustive recapitulation of all of a thing's individuating attributes; that would be as unilluminating as a detailed map drawn to actual scale that reproduced the topography it was supposed to outline. Rather, the exercise demands a selection of the attributes so decisive of the thing's character that they can truly be said to *characterize* it, and this entails a differentiation between the attributes that are definitive of the thing and those that are merely incidental.[32] Accordingly, in inquiring after form we can ask, "[W]hat elements of a conception are for other constituents of the same conception logically determining, in the sense that they cannot be left out of account, if one is not to lose the entire mental representation which is directly under discussion ...?"[33] Through reference to the ensemble of characteristics that give a thing its character, we comprehend the thing in question as what it is; in classical terminology, we grasp its nature or essence. And conversely, if its character eludes us, we cannot be said to have understood it at all.

Second, form is a principle of structure or unity. The thing that has a form is a single entity, characterized by the ensemble of attributes that make it what it is. In comprehending a thing's form, we understand the thing neither as an aggregate of independently intelligible properties nor as a homogeneous unit consisting of an extended single property. Rather, the thing is a single entity comprised of the set of characteristics that defines it, and it has the unity of an articulated whole that is not reducible to – is therefore greater than – the sum of all of its parts. The component characteristics that partake of any form are accordingly understood as mutually related through the oneness of what they inform.

Third, form signifies the genericity of the thing's character. Genericity is that which allows us to regard all the instances of the matter in question as having the same character and as being other than whatever has a different character. Because specifying an ensemble of characteristics involves distinguishing the essential from the inessential qualities, form refers not to the thing's fully individuated particularity, but to the general class under which it falls. The set of properties that makes something a table, for instance, is found in all tables and constitutes the genericity of what it is to be a table. Form is thus the principle that allows a thing to be grouped with others of the same sort.

Thus form exhibits character, unity and genericity as the three essential aspects of intelligibility. Together the characteristics comprise the thing's character, the grasp of which is indispensable to the understanding of what the thing is. The character is not the aggregate of these characteristics wherever any of them is located, but a set that achieves its distinctive unity by constituting the thing in question as a single thing classifiable with other things of the same sort. Such characteristics are not significant in isolation but only inasmuch as they make up the character of the whole that they constitute: To modify an essential characteristic is to modify the whole, and to modify the whole is to alter the significance of its constitutive characteristics.

B.   *The Relevance of Immanent Intelligibility*

The point of referring to something's form is to grasp the thing's nature or intelligible essence, and thus to understand that thing as what it is. One might object that this enterprise is doomed to failure, because in setting out what purports to be a thing's form, we are not exhibiting anything about the thing but only about ourselves. The way in which we divide and classify the world and associate certain objects with certain qualities is a reflection, it might be said, of the circumstances and requirements of our own life rather than of the world on to which our conclusions are projected. Form varies according to vocabulary, linguistic practices, and particular needs and purposes: Such variability belies the permanence and universality that is sought in the notion of form. As Locke put it, "those *Forms*, which there hath been so much noise made about, are only *Chimaera's*; which give us no light into the specifick Natures of Things . . . . [T]hese Boundaries of *Species*, are as Men, and not as Nature makes them. . . . "[34]

This objection alleges that the characteristics going to the form of something do not assume their significance from the internal nature of the thing but from our external requirements as users, observers, and inquirers. The inquirer approaches the object from the outside and subjects it to the demands of his or her enterprise, while the object itself lies shapeless and is available to whatever form the cognizing mind reads into it. For example, the peculiarly shaped wood before us is a table because we can make it serviceable for a function that we ascribe to it or that dominated the mind of its manufacturer. Form thus bespeaks an intelligibility introduced from the outside.

The crucial presupposition of this criticism is that a qualitative disjunction exists between the inquirer's thought and the object of the enquiry. According to this view, the object is the target, but need not be the embodiment, of thought. In specifying the attributes through which it characterizes the object, thought has no access to whatever might illuminate the thing's intelligibility from within and therefore imposes a foreign occupation that serves its own interests.

Whatever the validity of this presupposition with regard to natural or artifactual objects, the legal formalist denies that this is the entire truth with respect to law. Legal formalism postulates that the law's content can be understood in and through itself by reference to the mode of thinking that shapes it from inside. For the formalist, law is *constituted* by thought: Its content is made up of the concepts (e.g., cause, remoteness, duty, consideration, offer and acceptance) that inform juridical relationships. Law is identical to the ideas of which it is comprised, and the intelligibility of law lies in grasping the order and connection of these ideas.[35] Because law is, at least in the formalist understanding, essentially conceptual, it does not present itself as alien to the enquirer's efforts to comprehend it. Thus the formalist assumption is that law is, however inchoately, an exhibition of intelligence.[36] For this reason our understanding can, without sacrifice or diminution, assume the perspective that animates the juridical enterprise from within. Accordingly, in the formalist view there is in law an integration of the activity of understanding with the matter to be understood. Since law is assumed to be intelligible from within, the content of law is regarded as being homogeneous with, and therefore accessible to, thought.

By eliminating the disjunction between the understanding and the object one is endeavoring to understand, the formalist assumption, if it can be sustained, opens the path to the elucidation of juridical content in terms of its underlying form. If law is constituted by thought and therefore accessible from within to the operation of our intelligence, the sting is drawn – at least with respect to law – from Locke's observation that the boundaries of form are as men and not as nature makes them. Inasmuch as law's nature is to be immanently intelligible, one can grasp this nature without distortion. Just as one can understand geometry by working through a geometrical perplexity from the inside, so one can understand law by an effort of mind that penetrates to, and participates in, the structure of thought that law embodies.

The elucidation of law through the notion of form is a way of exhibiting the immanent intel-ligibility of the law's content. One might suppose that formalism's dependence on immanent intelligibility is self-defeating: If law is already immanently intelligible, nothing remains to be accomplished through the elucidation of legal form. This, however, is not so. Although the law is capable of being understood from within, such an understanding is not necessarily fully explicit in the legal materials. Moreover, because sophisticated legal systems admit the possibility that a given juridical determination may be erroneous from an internal perspective, the law's immanent intelligibility may be defect-ively expressed in any given case. The task for the formalist is to make explicit the intelligibil-ity latent in the legal materials and thereby to indicate that from which legal error is a devi-ation. Form represents the interplay of charac-ter, unity, and genericity. Thus the formalist will attempt to discern the essential characteris-tics of a legal relationship and to disclose how these characteristics cohere to make this rela-tionship irreducible and hence classifiable with other relationships of the same sort. The func-tion of form is to draw out the law's immanent intelligibility by making salient the nature of unity and coherence both within and among legal relationships.

C. Some Implications of Immanent Intelligibility

The following parts of this Article clarify how the formalist elucidation of law proceeds and the assumption of law's immanent intelligibility is substantiated. It is appropriate at this point, however, to signal several general implications of this conception of intelligibility.

Immanent intelligibility is not a subclass but a paradigm of intelligibility. Its virtue is that whatever is immanently intelligible can be understood self-sufficiently without recourse to something external that would pose the problem of intelligibility afresh. If something is not intelligible in and through itself, it must, if it is intelligible at all, be intelligible through something else. But unless that other thing is in its turn intelligible through itself, it will merely point to something else on which its own under-standing depends. This regression continues until the understanding alights upon something that is immanently intelligible. Therefore, intelligibility that is immanent to its subject matter is the most satisfactory notion of understanding, and not merely one among many.

Moreover, something that is immanently intelligible must be understood by reference to this quality. If the immanence of a thing's intelligibility is disregarded in favor of an external mode of comprehension, we simply fail to understand the most understandable aspect of the thing in question. Just as the profoundest understanding of the Pythagorean theorem comes from working through its geometric proof rather than by examining the economic conditions of Magna Graecia that may have influenced Pythagoras in his day, so any immanently intelligible matter must be grasped by reference to its immanent intelligibility.

Two consequences of conceiving law in terms of the immanent intelligibility of form merit particular notice. First, the scientific explanation of natural phenomena is not exemplary for matters that are immanently intelligible. The scientist is not an omnisciently pantheistic god who knows nature from inside. Scientific explanation is based on observation combined with the hypothesis that natural phenomena conform to pervasive regularities. Since the content of science is, as Hegel put it, "not known as moulded from within through the thoughts which lie at the ground of it,"[37] this understanding is categorically different from, and inferior to, an intelligibility that has an internal dimension.[38]

The relationship of immanent intelligibility to scientific explanation bears directly on a very common anti-formalist argument. Through the notion of form the formalist draws attention to the rationality inherent in legal relationships and thereby denies law's radical contingency. The objection points to the contention of philosophers of science that even the supposedly objective enterprise of scientific inquiry is conducted on the shifting sands of historical contingency, and concludes that this contingency applies to law *a fortiori*.[39] From the formalist perspective, however, this argument does not get off the ground. Even if the controversy about scientific objectivity is resolved in the

manner most favorable to the objector,[40] formalism rejects the premise that our notion of legal understanding must follow in the ruts of scientific explanation. For the legal formalist, legal phenomena are assumed to differ from natural phenomena because they are immanently understandable. Since on this assumption law is more perspicuous than nature, it is a mistake to burden law with conclusions drawn from the scientist's external – and therefore less secure – mode of cognition.

The second consequence of the connection between law and the immanent intelligibility of form is that legal form is inherently non-instrumental. An instrument can be understood only by reference to the purpose it serves. The instrument's intelligibility lies outside itself in the end toward which the instrument is a means. Therefore, to the extent that juridical relationships can be seen in the light of their underlying forms and thus by reference to themselves, there is no need to grasp them instrumentally. For formalism, legal ordering is not the collective pursuit of a desirable purpose. Instead, it is the specification of the norms and principles immanent to juridically intelligible relationships. Formalism repudiates analysis that conceives of legal justification in terms of some goal that is independent of the conceptual structure of the legal arrangement in question.

The formalist separation of law from politics reflects this distinction between immanent and instrumental understandings. Politics is differentiated from law to the extent that politics is the domain of collective instrumentalist purposes. What Unger noted was the more determinate rationality of law is the set of values which can be located within the immanently intelligible enterprise of juridical elaboration, as contrasted with the state's ranging at large among the possible ends to which it might orient its efforts.

The formalist asserts the possibility of a non-instrumental understanding of juridical relations. This assertion, however, contains the following insidious implication: The mere possibility of a non-instrumental understanding renders instrumental understandings of the same legal material superfluous, but not vice versa. This follows from the paradigmatic quality of immanent intelligibility. Instrumental understandings are by their nature imperfect. They first transfer the burden of intelligibility from the subject of the inquiry to the external end this subject serves and then, in turn, require that end to be grasped somehow, presumably by reference to some further external end. Unless this endless shifting of ends can be arrested at a point of non-instrumental stability, the understanding is caught in a game of musical chairs, in which it seems to know everything only because it knows nothing.[41] Perhaps the melancholy truth is that instrumentalism is the most that legal analysis can achieve. But the possibility of a non-instrumental understanding, once established, reveals the inferiority of the instrumentalist alternative. Therefore instrumental and non-instrumental understandings do not have an equal footing. The latter is independent and fundamental; the former comes into play only by default, as a second-best. Instrumentalism cannot remain in the competition once non-instrumentalism enters the field.

D. *Summary*

Form, then, is the ensemble of characteristics that determines the content as a content, as a *this* and not a *that*, and thus differentiates content from the indeterminacy of featureless existence. By exhibiting the essential characteristics of some matter, form allows the matter to be conceived of as something possessing the unity of singleness and to be grouped with other things of the same sort. Form and content are not separate. Rather, they stand in a reciprocal relationship, with form being the intelligibility of determinate content and content being the realization of intelligible form. No extrinsic standpoint is brought to bear upon this relationship between form and content. Form signifies the immanence of intelligibility to that which is being understood. If this approach can be sustained for law, the intelligibility it yields will be one which is internal to juridical relations: These relations will be understood by reference to themselves, and not by reference to something else. An instrumental understanding, in contrast, posits a dependence of the instrument on an end that is beyond it. The extent to which juridical relations can be understood in terms of themselves, therefore, is also the extent to which the political understanding of law – as a means to some ulterior end – is excluded.

III Moving From Content Toward Form

A. *The Two-Stage Movement*

To understand law as the manifestation of form is to discern an internal dimension of intelligibility in law's content. The shape of this intelligibility emerges in two stages. One must first discern the essential characteristics of juridical relationships in a sophisticated legal system. Because the sophistication of such a system consists in its tendency toward coherence,[42] one can then inquire into the extent to which these initially-identified characteristics can be understood as a unified set. In this way, an appreciation of the nature of coherence for juridical relationships arises out of reflection on the content of law. Because form is the intelligibility of a determinate content, the traces of juridical form should be visible in and through the most significant features of the law's content. In this section I wish to outline this movement from content toward form.

1. *Identifying Essential Characteristics*

In the first stage we distill from the law's content the features that might plausibly be considered the essential characteristics of juridical intelligibility.[43] These features will be those that are so central that they must be understood if there is to be any understanding at all of the legal phenomena in question. At this stage these features seem to emerge spontaneously as Archimedean points in legal consciousness; even in the absence of a theoretical account of their ground or interrelation, their centrality is provisionally certified because any intuitively plausible discussion of law either invokes them or presupposes them. At the level of theory, these are the features which must be explained or explained away: Any exposition that ignores them or does them violence runs the risk of being regarded as contrived or artificial or somehow amiss. And at the level of practice, legal discourse will incorporate or presuppose these features and will explicitly or implicitly recognize them as inescapably basic to the continuing elaboration of legal doctrine.

Consider, for example, an action for negligence. One thinks through a problem in negligence not only by reference to the corpus of specific holdings directed toward very specific questions (for example, whether there is liability for nervous shock[44] or whether the landlord is under a duty to protect tenants against criminals[45]), but by seeing these holdings as representing broader legal concepts (for instance, duty, cause, and fault). These concepts, in turn, eddy out into more fundamental and comprehensive notions. Causation, for instance, applies only in a situation of misfeasance and not non-feasance. This presupposes the distinction between the duty to abstain from inflicting harm and the freedom to withhold a benefit, and this distinction, in turn, points to a wide correlativity of plaintiff's right and defendant's duty. These features of legal doctrine figure in a litigational format that grants standing to two parties who appear before a disinterested and impartial adjudicator and that culminates, if the plaintiff is successful, in the transfer of a sum from one party to the other.

These doctrinal, conceptual, and institutional features, and others like them, are fixed points of tort law. When we refer to tort law, such features characterize the object of our attention. These features form the stuff of lawyers' talk. Their relevance is not due merely to the statistical regularity of their appearance or invocation in the ever-expanding corpus of legal materials. Rather, this regularity is itself a consequence of our funneling our thinking through them as we engage in the enterprise of understanding and elaborating the law.

The apparent centrality of these features does not mean that they escape controversy. Court decisions or legal scholarship may call any of them into question. For instance, a court can disregard the convention of retroactive judgment by restricting its holding to its prospective effect,[46] or the economic analysis of tort law can, through its use of Coase's theorem,[47] ignore the distinction between non-feasance and misfeasance, or the scholarship of Critical Legal Studies can attempt to extirpate root and branch the sense of significance that attaches to all of these features. These developments, however, often attest to the felt significance of these characteristics of law. Doctrinal innovations, such as prospective overruling, are reserved for special occasions and require special justifications. And the eclat of economic analysis or Critical Legal Studies can be explained by the exhilaration they produce precisely because they float free of the moorings generally accepted for legal understanding.

These challenges gain their plausibility from the fact that the initial singling out of the essential features of juridical intelligibility is at an intuitive level.[48] In the absence of an account of the significance of these features, their centrality can be denied by the mere assertion of a different intuition. Taken by itself, the process sketched so far is exposed to the charge that the inarticulate legal experience on which it rests camouflages an ideological or subjective selection for which no valid criteria exist.

2.   *The Coherence of the Characteristics*

Identifying elements of the content of a sophisticated legal system as apparently fixed points of intelligibility, however, is only the first step toward understanding law. Confirming that these elements are truly essential depends on the answer to a further question: Do they constitute a coherent ensemble? If these elements are unconnected or pull in different directions, the initial illumination that they offer would, for the formalist, be fraudulent. The formalist assumes that a juridically intelligible relationship cannot consist in an aggregate of conceptually disjunct or inconsistent elements that, like a pile of pebbles, happen to be juxtaposed. If an initially identified feature is to serve as a fixed point of legal understanding, it must participate in the unity that renders a legal relationship intelligible as what it is. It must, in short, signify an underlying form.

As we have seen, form is a principle of structure. To the extent that the law governing a relationship is more than a succession of ad hoc resolutions of particular controversies, the law's doctrines and institutions will bear some imprint of form. Through this form the features that characterize the relationship can be understood as making up a unified whole. Because for the formalist a relationship is intelligible only insofar as its features are coherent, their coherence is a way of determining whether the features initially identified truly have the significance that legal experience ascribes to them.

Many components of negligence law, for instance, seem to exemplify a single theme, that the relationship between tortfeasor and victim is bipolar. Factual causation does this by connecting the tortfeasor and the victim through the transitivity of cause and effect. The issues of duty and proximity are similarly bipolar: Through them the riskiness of the defendant's act is viewed from the standpoint of its reasonably foreseeable effects on the plaintiff. The adjudicative framework of tort law institutionally matches the bipolar nature of negligence doctrine. The award of damages is the remedial expression of bipolarity. This convergence suggests that bipolarity is the key to the coherence of negligence law. The formalist attempts to see whether these doctrinal and institutional elements can indeed be understood as the articulations of a coherent justificatory structure of bipolar interaction. If they can, the centrality of the bipolar characteristics that were initially identified as essential is confirmed. At its most inclusive, such a coherent justificatory structure is the form that renders intelligible the relationships to which it applies. Conversely, any feature incapable of integration into a coherent structure cannot be truly constitutive of the intelligibility of a juridical relationship.

For the formalist, a juridical relationship is a conceptual organism, in which each component is meaningful as part of a whole. The functioning of any constituent of this unity can be fully understood only in the light of the functioning of all the others. If, for example, fault and causation are as essential as tort doctrine assumes, each will compliment the other, and the relationship of tortfeasor and victim will be

unintelligible without both.[49] A conception of tort liability in which the plaintiff can recover from the defendant for injury in the absence of wrongdoing, or in which the defendant is liable to the plaintiff for a wrong that does not materialize in injury, would be a "conceptual monstrosity" produced by the hacking apart of aspects that for this relationship have – so it is assumed – significance only in combination.[50] These essential doctrinal aspects and the adjudicative framework in which they are elaborated must be similarly integrated. The tort relationship is thus constituted by an ensemble of conceptual and institutional characteristics. If the intelligibility of a tort relationship could withstand the omission or amputation of any aspect of this ensemble, that very fact would show that the initial inclusion of that aspect among the relationship's essential characteristics was mistaken. Conversely, the reciprocal interconnection of all the truly essential aspects of a tort relation would mean that the omission of one of them would undermine the intelligibility of all the others.

B.   *Justificatory Coherence*

The unity revealed by the notion of legal form represents, accordingly, an extremely ambitious conception of coherence. A legal form is a single justificatory structure that embraces the conceptual and institutional aspects essential to the understanding of a juridical relationship. Although this structure can be articulated into parts, these parts have no vitality independent of the structure that unifies them. It is, of course, possible to examine one part without explicitly referring to another, as tort casebooks and treatises do when they examine *seriatim* the various ingredients of the negligence action. If these ingredients are truly essential to the intelligibility of negligence law by being aspects of its form, however, all of them implicitly remain present when the spotlight is directed onto one. Because they are cognizable only through the unity that they comprise, the intelligibility of each simultaneously conditions, and is conditioned by, the intelligibility of all the others.

The formalist conception of coherence can be illustrated by consideration of the loss-spreading justification for tort liability. Under this justification, a court regards liability as a mechanism for distributing the accident loss among the largest number of persons. It has long been recognized that the principle of the diminishing marginal utility of money on which this justification rests should lead to social insurance of accident losses and, more generally, to a redistribution of wealth through progressive taxation.[51] Nevertheless, loss-spreading has been defended as consistent with the general ideology tort law on two grounds: First, the judicial enforcement of loss-spreading preserves the decentralized decision-making that is traditional to tort law, and, second, loss-spreading does not aim at a new pattern of wealth, but at re-establishing the distribution that was disturbed by the perpetration of an injury.[52]

For the formalist these defenses are unsatisfactory because of their incoherent joinder of the doctrinal and the institutional. They turn on using the adjudicative format of tort law to restrict the reach of the justificatory force of the principle that animates loss-spreading. Because loss-spreading is triggered by the plaintiff's suit against the defendant, it can be mandated only in a sporadic and decentralized way. Since a successful tort action undoes only the effects of an injury caused by another, the distributional impetus of loss-spreading is controlled by the impossibility of holding the defendant liable for the injuries he or she has not caused. Nothing about loss-spreading as a principle, however, is coterminous with the scope or occasion provided by tort law. The idea that money should be exacted from some for the benefit of others in order to spread the burden of a catastrophic loss as lightly and as widely as possible is as pertinent to a non-tortious, as to a tortious, injury. The levies loss-spreading justifies are not confined to tortfeasors. Accordingly, the appropriate institutional setting for loss-spreading is not the bipolarity of litigation, but a general scheme of social insurance or taxation that would spread accidental loss as thinly and broadly as possible. The restrictions arising out of the adjudicative format do not, therefore, correspond to any feature internal to the idea of loss-spreading. Rather, they are imposed on this idea from outside it, so that it is not operationalized to the full extent of its normative reach.

Adjudication and the principle underlying loss-spreading are not part of each other's justificatory structure. The incoherence of their combination demonstrates that they are not aspects of the same legal form. To attempt loss-spreading through tort adjudication is to fail to give full faith and credit to the justificatory dimension of either loss-spreading or adjudication, the former because it is channelled into an institutional framework that does not give effect to its normative force, the latter because it is placed in the service of an ideal that exceeds its competence. Each is compromised by its artificial juxtaposition with the other.

Formalism insists on the integrity of law's justification. It arranges the various doctrinal and institutional considerations into internally coherent justificatory structures, so that the components of any single such structure partake of whatever normative force gives life to the structure in its entirety. Since all the aspects of any justificatory structure comprise a single whole whose parts are interdependent, the structure's normative force is as present in one part as it is in any other. Justification, therefore, cannot properly be truncated. It must be allowed to expand completely into the space that it naturally fills.

C.   *Implications and Objections*

Coherence is the criterion of truth for the formalist understanding of a juridical relationship.[53] As the loss-spreading example demonstrated, the coherence of an ensemble of justificatory aspects can confirm or negate the essentiality of a given legal feature. The formalist elucidation of legal phenomena is devoted to making explicit the unity possible in juridical relationships, and the disclosure of this unity is the yardstick of its success. The point is not that the positive law of a given jurisdiction necessarily embodies justificatory coherence, but that such coherence is possible, and that positive law is intelligible to the extent that it is achieved and defective to the extent that it is not.

Coherence is inherently expansive: It resists compartmentalization and seeks to encompass as much as possible. The illumination that formalism yields is proportional to the possible unity that its analysis can disclose. Just as formalism resists treating every tortious incident as a particular that is conceptually unconnected with the understanding of any other tortious incident, so it resists considering tort law, taken in its entirety, to be conceptually unconnected to other branches of law. Formalism thus seeks to confirm the possibility that tort law, for example, is not only coherent on its own, but that the underlying contours of this coherence can be found throughout private law (and perhaps beyond). In this way, private law as a whole might be understood as a massive expression of legal form. Accordingly, the unity of form is operative among – as well as within – juridical relationships. Or rather, to put it more accurately, the most inclusive conception of the unity of a relationship is also the most general conception of the justificatory structure that the relationship exemplifies. Unity and genericity are thus mutually intertwined in the coherence of the features that make up the legal form. The greater the reach of that coherence, the more profound the understanding of the juridical relationship.

The reason coherence functions as the criterion of truth is that legal form is concerned with immanent intelligibility. Such an intelligibility cannot be validated by anything outside itself, for then it would no longer be immanent. Formalism thus denies that juridical coherence can properly be compromised for the sake of some extrinsic end, however desirable. The sole criterion is an internal one. Form is the principle of the unity immanent to an ensemble of legal features, and judgment about intelligibility can flow only from this unity. Because the intelligibility of form is immanent to its content, no other criterion is available; and if immanent intelligibility is (as claimed in Part II of this essay) the most satisfactory mode of understanding, no other is needed.

Not only can no point outside the form indicate the truth of formalism, but no point or points, atomistically viewed, located inside the form can do so either. Because form constitutes the unity of a set of legal phenomena, no single element has a significance that is independent of its interplay with the others. Therefore, it is not the presence or absence of this or that desirable feature that is decisive for judgment about a juridical relationship, but the extent to which all of its features cohere.

Thus, to return to our illustration, the adverse judgment that formalism passes on the loss-spreading justification in tort law is not due to an antipathy to loss-spreading considered on its own. Loss-spreading in this context is shunned for the company that it keeps, not for what it is. The objection is to the linkage of loss-spreading and adjudication, and to the consequent failure of this doctrinal and institutional conglomerate to express a coherent justificatory structure. If loss-spreading appeared in conjunction with the other elements of its own form, the demands of formalism would be fully met. The formalist is not, therefore, a libertarian who, by opposing loss-spreading through tort law, stands against the use of state machinery to transfer wealth from those who have it to those whose need for it is more pressing. Nor is the formalist's insistence on the possibility of a coherent tort law an argument that tort law should be preferred to a general social insurance scheme that embodies loss-spreading or any other compensatory principle. What is paramount to the formalist is not the desirability of loss-spreading as a substantive policy, but the coherence with which it is integrated into a justificatory ensemble.

The same considerations that make coherence formalism's criterion of truth also allow formalism to float clear of politics. The formalist's concern is not with whether a given exercise of state power is desirable, either in its own terms or in terms of the larger ends that it serves, but with whether it is intelligible as part of a coherent structure of justification. Formalism abstracts from any substantive goal to the coherent ensemble of features into which that goal might adequately fit. In decrying the tension in our example between loss-spreading and the adjudication of tort claims, the formalist stakes out no position about the merits either of loss spreading or of adjudication as techniques for dealing with accidents. Although the formalist might have political opinions, he is, *qua* formalist, interested solely in whether the components of any legal relationship express an integrated justificatory structure. Without disputing the legitimacy of politics, the formalist insists that the product of politics live up to the conception of justificatory coherence that is immanent to it.

The postulate that juridical relationships bear the stamp of an immanently unifying form allows the internal understanding of law to progress beyond the unsupported assertion of the intuitively central features upon which it initially seizes. Because the notion of form provides an internal standpoint of intelligibility, the features for which juristic experience claims an immediate internal significance may implicitly be articulations of the relevant form. Once the form is itself made explicit, the features originally identified can be scrutinized to determine their adequacy as articulations of this form. The selection of these features can now be seen as the first stage in the search for the form of the legal arrangements in which they figure. Inasmuch as these features are elements in an internal understanding, form is implicit in them. The dynamic of internal intelligibility can be carried through from the initial identification of these features to the explicitness of form, which can in turn serve as a touchstone for the initial identification. The movement is a circle of thought that feeds upon its own unfolding explicitness: from the content of law to the immediate juristic understanding of this content, to the form implicit in this understanding, to the explicit elucidation of the form, to the testing of the content for its adequacy to the now explicit form.

Intelligibility involves the interpenetration of content and its immanent form. One achieves a complete understanding when the form is exhibited and the content is seen as adequate to it. If the elements initially identified have the truly fundamental significance that legal experience claims for them, they will be constituents in the distinctive unity that makes the juridical relationship what it is. The immediate understanding of legal experience is only provisional until form becomes explicit. Then juridical intelligibility emerges from a mutually reinforcing movement between form and content: Form is the organizing idea latent in the content of a

sophisticated legal culture, and the ultimate test for legal content is its adequacy to the form it expresses. In this movement the understanding of law is completely internal to what it understands.

Now it might be objected that legal philosophy thus conceived is both circular and apologetic: Inasmuch as its account of law does not strive for any standpoint beyond law, the most that it can do is plough over the same ground in ever deeper furrows, with the implication that the law as given is suffused with positive value. But of these two criticisms, circularity and apology, the first is true but not a vice, and the second is not true.

Circularity is a consequence of the self-contained nature of intelligibility. Because form is the distinct principle of unity that renders intelligible the content that realizes it, no criterion of understanding can exist outside form's encompassing embrace. Provided that the circle is inclusive enough, circularity is here, as elsewhere in philosophical explanation, a strength and not a weakness.[54] For if the matter at hand were to be non-circularly explained by some point outside it, the matter's intelligibility would hang on something that was not itself intelligible until it was, in its turn, integrated into a wider unity. Criticism on the grounds of circularity implies the superiority of the defective mode of explanation that leaves outside the range of intelligibility the very starting point upon which the whole enterprise depends.[55]

As for the objection that an account in terms of form is inherently apologetic, this misses the radically critical lever that an internal understanding makes available. The sophisticated legal system is taken as the focus of attention because such a system makes an implicit claim to an inner rationality that bears on the formalist's interest in what such a claim might amount to. Holding the legal content to its immanent form allows an assessment, in its own terms, of the legal system's congratulatory self-understanding. The determinations of the legal system can be adjudged confused or mistaken to the extent that they are inadequate expressions of the underlying form. Thus arises a standpoint for criticism that is decisive precisely because it is internal. Whereas criticism from the outside can be sloughed off with the argument that the critic's favored position is simply irrelevant to the law's immanent rationality, criticism from the inside engages law ineluctably on its home ground.[56]

IV   The Forms of Justice

A.   *The Quest for Comprehensiveness*

Let us now look more closely at the notion of legal form. The previous section traced the movement of thought that works toward the idea of form from reflection on the law's content. There it was pointed out that coherence is the formalist's criterion of truth, and that the more encompassing the coherence the greater the illumination. A juridical relationship's most inclusive unity is, therefore, also the most generalized justificatory structure that the relationship instantiates. These generalized justificatory structures, which are the most adequate conceptions of legal form, are the focus of this section.

In this context, inclusiveness is achieved not by adding another item to an aggregation, but by subsuming the item under a higher level of abstraction. Form is a unity, all the component characteristics of which comprise an ensemble whose intelligibility is greater than that of the sum of its parts. The components of a legal form thus collectively express a single idea. A form is accordingly not a manifold that can incorporate new elements without their being integrated into its organizing unity. If a form is to encompass the widest possible variety of juridical relationships, these relationships cannot be pluralistically tacked on to one another, but must exemplify the unifying idea of the form to which they belong. This requires abstracting to clarify the common structure that various relationships instantiate through their participation in a single form.

In its quest for the most comprehensive unities, formalism gives extreme expression to the tendency to abstraction that marks legal thinking. Although the events that give rise to a juridical relationship are particular – John Doe did such and such to Richard Roe – these events are understood by the lawyer in terms of cat-

egories (such as tort law's notions of cause, duty of care, and fault) that abstract from the particularity of the occurrence. Particulars are legally relevant only inasmuch as they can be brought within juridical categories. Accordingly, a datum is legally significant not as a particular added to an aggregate of particulars, but as the instantiation of a category that can coherently combine with other legal categories. Now just as legal thinking sees the particularities within its ken as the embodiments of abstractions, so legal formalism abstracts further from these abstractions in its quest for the most abstract conceptions of juridical relationships. These conceptions will be the barest and most inclusive representations of the unities that can characterize juridical relationships, and the law's content will be intelligible only to the extent that it conforms to one of these most abstract forms.

B.   *The Two Forms*

The task of formulating the most inclusive juridical abstractions is not a new one. The first description of these abstractions can be found in Aristotle's discussion of justice.[57] Aristotle observed that juridical relationships are paradigmatically those that obtain between parties regarded as external to each other, each with separate interests of mine and thine.[58] Aristotle's decisive contribution was to notice the conceptual patterns that inhere in juridical relationships. Substantive legal rules are intelligible to the extent that they embody the rationality exhibited by these patterns. In Aristotle's terminology, these patterns are the forms of justice.[59]

The value of Aristotle's account is that he definitively identified the forms that are most consistent with the process I have sketched so far. Aristotle achieved this through reflection on the law of his own day.[60] So inclusive and abstract are the forms he set out, however, that his conclusions apply to any legal ordering of external interaction. Aristotle provides the most formal account possible of the structures that could be latent in external dealings among persons. Since these abstractions are immanent in (and therefore not severable from) the content of law, they could not be discovered except through reflection on particular legal systems. But once elucidated, their very abstractness makes them the ultimate categories for the coherence of juridical relationships generally. Not only are these forms immanent in any sophisticated legal system, but the adequacy of the law's content to these immanent forms is the measure of that system's sophistication.

Aristotle observed that what we would now call private law has a special structure of its own. Justice is effected by an award of damages and the consequent transfer of a certain amount of money from one party to another.[61] An award of damages simultaneously quantifies the wrong suffered by plaintiff and the wrongfulness inflicted by the defendant. It thus expresses the integration of action and injury in the wrong that one litigant has done to the other. This wrong, and the damage award that undoes it, represents a single nexus of activity and passivity where actor and victim are defined in relation to each other.

This special structure is the most abstract mode of coherence for the bipolar relationships of private law. It captures the correlativity within a single transaction, of wrongful doing and suffering – and with it the correlativity in private law of the defendant's duty to avoid inflicting such suffering and the plaintiff's right to immunity from it. All the bilateral aspects of private law, from the adjudicative format of the plaintiff–defendant lawsuit to the doctrines that link doer and sufferer, are encompassed by this structure. The doctrine of factual causation, for instance, is an expression of the relation of one party to another through their doing and suffering of the same harm. In the same vein, no tort liability arises in a situation of nonfeasance, because the failure of one party to extend a benefit to another is categorically different from a harm done and suffered. Moreover, the treatment of the doing and suffering as a single unit underlies the requirement that the plaintiff's injury be within the ambit of the risk that the defendant's act wrongfully creates.[62] Similarly, the contract doctrines defining the formation and consequences of exchange (e.g., consideration, offer and acceptance, and expectation damages) embrace both parties.[63] The bilateral nature of the contractual relationship means that the promised performance is not largess unilaterally proffered and unilaterally revocable, but rather the content of an entitlement. Accordingly, the promisor's breach is the doing of a harm to (and, correlatively, the suffering of a harm by) the promisee.

This two-party structure underlies not only relationships that exemplify the doing and suffering of a single harm, such as those of contract and tort law, but also relationships whose intelligibility presupposes the special significance of doing and suffering. Form signals the *conceptual* coherence of legal doctrine and institutions, and its inclusiveness refers to all the legal relationships that must be understood in its light. Because the inclusiveness of form is for the formalist a conceptual matter, the implications of the special nature of doing and suffering can render intelligible relationships that might not themselves be regarded as relationships of doing and suffering. Consider, for example, the law of restitution. One can hardly say that the recipient of a mistaken payment, who is under a legal obligation to disgorge the benefit,[64] has done the payor a harm. The activity was on the side of the plaintiff who made the payment; the defendant was merely the passive beneficiary of the plaintiff's error. Nevertheless, the intelligibility of their relationship and of the defendant's obligation to return the unjust enrichment is conceptually dependent on the significance of doing and suffering. Since under this form one must avoid inflicting an unjust harm, there is no legal obligation to confer a gratuitous benefit. Therefore, for benefits to have a legal standing, their conferral must conform to specific conditions concerning the transferor's intent and the mechanics of transfer. In the common law these conditions are laid down in the law of gifts, trusts, and seals. Other unilateral transfers, including payments made under mistake, are invalid. Thus, the relationship consequent on a mistaken payment presupposes the special juridical significance of doing and suffering. In other words, the form instantiated in contract and tort law allows us to think of the payee's retention of a mistaken payment as a harm inflicted on the payor.[65]

The second structure underlying law is one in which parties are related, not as doer and sufferer, but as persons subject to a common benefit or burden. In this relationship, the law's task is to divide the benefit or the burden according to some criterion. The interaction between the parties is defined not in terms of what one person has done to another but in terms of the common nature of the benefit or the burden, and the consequent entitlement or liability under the criterion that distributes it.

These two understandings of interaction Aristotle called corrective justice and distributive justice. They correspond to the two ways of conceiving of the external relations upon which law fastens. For Aristotle, these two kinds of justice were not particular substantive ideals.[66] Rather, they were the most general conceptual patterns to which any substantive ideal of legal ordering would have to conform if it was to have inner coherence. In corrective justice the relationship between the parties is that of the immediacy of doing and suffering in a transaction, whether that transaction be a contract, a tort, or the retention of an undue benefit. In distributive justice the relationship between the parties is mediated by a scheme of distribution; particular entitlements are a function not of a direct relationship between the beneficiaries to the distribution but of the criterion according to which the distribution is organized. Distributions embody what Nozick has more recently termed "patterning,"[67] and justifications under distributions can typically be formulated in terms of "to [from] each according to...."[68] Corrective and distributive justice represent the intelligibility of unmediated and mediated interaction respectively.

These two forms of justice are categorically different and this difference can be expressed in terms of the distinct notions of equality that each employs.[69] Corrective justice abstracts from the particular attributes of the parties that are not essential to the intelligibility of doing and suffering. Accordingly, whatever their social status or wealth or character, the parties are considered equal at the outset of the transaction. This notional equality represents the implicit rationality of the transaction. A wrong is conceptualized as one party's disturbance of this equality at the expense of the other. Corrective justice does not, therefore, refer merely to an official act of dispute settlement; rather, the court's intervention is intelligible as specifying what is implicit in the relationship that already exists between the parties.[70] In reflecting this relationship through the interpretation and enforcement of its normative implications, the court is itself part of the justificatory structure applicable to the transaction that it judges. The function of the court is to preserve the initial equality by transferring from one party to the other the fixed quantity that marks the deviation from the transaction's implicit rationality. This sum represents either the plaintiff's loss or the defendant's gain, and in paradigmatic instances of restitution, gain and loss will be identical. Because it restores the notional antecedent equality between the parties by making one of them transfer a fixed quantity to the other, corrective justice construes the interaction as immediately pertaining to no more than two parties. In encompassing both the wrong that one party has done to the other and the juridical reflex rectifying the wrong, corrective justice represents the structure of adjudication between plaintiff and defendant in private law.[71]

In contrast, a distribution embodies not the transference of a quantity but the fixing of a proportion. Distributive justice integrates three elements: the benefit or burden that is the subject of the distribution, the recipients among whom the benefit or burden is to be distributed, and the criterion according to which the distribution is to take place. The class of participants and the subject matter of the distribution are notionally separate. The entitlement of each member in the class to his share in the subject matter is determined by the application of the distributive criteria so that, relative to this criterion, the entitlement of each is equal. Because the integration of the three elements takes the form of a proportion, there is no internal restriction on the number of participants: the more there are, the smaller the portions, and the fewer there are, the greater the portions. This can be contrasted with corrective justice, where the determination of the quantity that restores the initial equality requires two parties, no more (because the transfer of a quantity cannot re-store equality as between more than two) and no less (because if there were only one there would be no transaction and nothing to correct).

C. The Formalism of the Forms

In this account justice does not in the first instance refer to substantive principles; instead, it points to the different structures according to which external interaction can be construed. Corrective justice discloses the form of a transaction as the immediate inter-action of two parties. The proportional equality of distributive justice captures the structure of a distribution by indicating what distinguishes a distribution from a merely haphazard dispersion among persons and goods. The notions of equality employed by the forms of justice are, like the forms themselves, formal and not sub-stantive. Equality is a term of relation appropri-ate to justice as the ordering of external relationships, and it makes interaction intelli-gible by operating with reference either to a quantity or to a proportion.[72]

Corrective and distributive justice are the forms that are immanent to the understanding of transactions and distributions. As patterns of interpersonal ordering they exhibit the nature of rationality *in* their respective types of arrange-ment and do not refer to some external purpose towards which these arrangements ought to be oriented. Each pattern represents a different mode of coherence for external relationships. Corrective justice treats the transaction between the doer and sufferer as a unity that can find juridical expression in the sum that the defend-ant must transfer to the successful plaintiff. Distributive justice treats the distribution as a unity that integrates the benefit or burden to be distributed, the persons who might be subject to it, and the criterion according to which the distribution takes place. Since law, as an ordering of external relationships, is directive of transactions and distributions in accordance with their immanent intelligibility, the content of law is required to be an adequate realization of these forms of justice.

A specific legal content is intelligible to the extent of its adequacy to a form of justice.

Adjudication of private disputes can be under-stood as the actualization of corrective justice, and the legislative and administrative direction of the community as the pursuit of distributive justice.[73] This is not to say that the positive law of these domains is substantively just; only that it is internally intelligible in terms of the con-ceptual structure of categories of external inter-action. The very point of the forms of justice, and what gives them their critical bite, is that they are forms: Inasmuch as they set out the implicit patterns of interaction that illuminate juridical relationships from within, they also provide an internal standpoint of criticism that is decisive for law because it cannot be deflected or escaped by a change of standpoint.

Corrective and distributive justice are the most abstract forms that render juridical rela-tionships intelligible. Indeed so abstract are they that Aristotle was able to represent them math-ematically as different functions of equality, the one quantitative and the other proportional. Each refers to an inclusive notion of interaction and to a corresponding conception of juridical coherence. Corrective justice is the ordering principle of transactions, whether these be delictual, restitutionary, or contractual:[74] It abstracts from the particular contours of a given transaction to its most general quality as an episode of doing and suffering. Coherence here lies in the singleness of the relationship of doing and suffering. Similarly, distributive just-ice abstracts from all particular distributions to the shape they share as distributions. Coherence here is a harmony of criterion, benefit (or burden), and beneficiaries (or burden-bearers).

These forms of justice are structurally differ-ent and mutually irreducible. Just as restoring the equality of two quantities is a categorically different mathematical operation from continu-ing a proportion, so the two forms of justice cannot be assimilated to each other. The math-ematical terms in which Aristotle explains the different functionings of equality in corrective and distributive justice certify that these two forms are conceptually distinct. They constitute the most abstractly comprehensive structures of justification and thus cannot be combined into a single overarching justificatory structure. Each form is its own distinctive and self-contained unity.[75] They both pertain to the ordering of external relations among persons, but they order these relations in different ways.

Because the forms of justice represent mutually irreducible conceptions of coherence for juridical relationships, no single juridical relationship can coherently combine the two forms. If a corrective element is mixed with a distributive one, each necessarily undermines the justificatory force of the other, and the relationship cannot manifest either unifying structure. Such mixing was the root of the problem in our loss-spreading example. The principle that accident losses should be distributed so as to minimize their felt impact has the proportional structure of distributive justice; it mandates the sharing of burdens in accordance with a criterion. Its use in tort law, however, fails to achieve distributive justice, since continuing the proportion by applying the principle to everyone within its reach is inconsistent with its being channelled through the doer and sufferer of a single harm. Conversely, since the issue of how the loss is ultimately spread is not part of the intelligibility of the relationship of doing and suffering as such (indeed the best conduit for loss-spreading might be some third party), the orienting of tort law toward loss-spreading cannot adequately actualize corrective justice. The combination of elements from both forms of justice ensures that neither form is achieved. And since coherence depends on the adequacy of the law's content to some form or other, loss-spreading as a tort doctrine is incoherent.

The forms of justice are justificatory structures. They furnish the morphology to which the justification of a juridical relationship must conform. A relationship can be construed as one of corrective justice if the justification applicable to it is an explication of the equality applicable to doing and suffering. Conversely, a relationship instantiates distributive justice if the argument that supports it has the patterning of a proportion. What matters is that a justification be coherent in terms of one or the other of the forms that constitute the broadest and most abstract conceptions of justificatory coherence. A relationship whose justification is not adequate to either of these structures is

unintelligible; in creating such a relationship, positive law commits a juridical mistake.

Because the forms of justice are justificatory structures, their concern is with the coherence of the justifications for legal arrangements, not with subject matter of these arrangements as brute facts. Accordingly, the effects that one person might have on another cannot be pre-classified as belonging to one or the other form. For the formalist the crucial consideration is not what happened but how one is to understand the justificatory structure that is latent in the legal arrangements that might deal with what happened.[76] My injuring you is in itself neither a transaction that calls for corrective justice nor a distribution that falls under distributive justice. It will be handled correctively if you sue me in tort so that the issue becomes whether the relationship of my doing and your suffering justifies my paying you damages. Alternatively, it will be handled distributively if you have recourse to a fund that, for example, compensates injured persons in proportion to the seriousness of their injuries.

Formalism, accordingly, is not a kind of jurisprudential federalism with different incidents assigned to the jurisdiction of either corrective or distributive authority. Nor does formalism provide a basis for preferring to treat the facts of the world in accordance with one form rather than the other; such preference can come neither from within either form nor from any overarching form. Formalism's concern is entirely with the coherence of legal arrangements and with the way that the doctrinal and institutional components of law manifest that coherence. The forms of justice are the most abstract and inclusive representations of the kinds of unity that can be expressed in juridical relationships. Coherence is, therefore, a matter of the adequacy of the law's content to one or the other of these forms.

V   Politics and Formalism

With these forms in hand, we can now consider the relationship between law and politics. As we saw at the outset of this essay, legal formalism is notorious for distinguishing between the two.

The purpose of this section is to sustain and illuminate the distinction by reference to the forms of juridical interaction outlined in Part IV.

A.   *Politics and the Judicial Role*

The distinction between law and politics manifests itself in scholarship as a controversy about the judicial role. Adherents of the distinction have seen the judge as the guardian and expositor of whatever is non-politically legal, the nature of which emerges from a consideration of the limits appropriate to judicial, as opposed to legislative, lawmaking. Private law raises this issue in connection with the propriety of reforming legal doctrine through the courts.[77] In constitutional and administrative law, the dispute concerns the status of the values underlying judicial review of legislative and administrative action.[78]

Pointing to the courts' relative lack of institutional competence and democratic accountability, proponents of a distinct judicial role have demarcated legitimate court activity by reference to two considerations. First, the courts' role is anchored by the preexisting body of rules, standards, policies, and principles from which courts move by a process of "reasoned elaboration."[79] Second, the courts are expected to distance themselves from the realm of "current political controversy," so that they are restricted to the area left unclaimed by the political agenda of the day.[80]

These formulations render the judicial role a contingent matter. While implicitly asserting a crucial difference in principle between the juridical and the political, they would have this difference hinge on whatever happens to receive the attention of courts and legislatures respectively. Whether a particular factor, such as loss-spreading, is legitimately within judicial competence would not depend on its nature as a justification but on whether it (or something from which it can be elaborated) has already ensconced itself in the legal doctrine, or on whether it has, or can be expected to, become a matter of political controversy.[81]

For the formalist these considerations are insufficiently grounded and are thus, at best,

shadows of the truth. The formalist seeks to connect this controversy about judicial role and the insight on which it is based – that "[t]o call a court 'political' is merely to deny it the character of a court of law"[82] – to the features of form that characterize and give coherence to the understanding of juridical relationships. These features are conceptual rather than contingent. They refer not to what may have come within the purview of judicial or legislative treatment in a given jurisdiction, but to the elements of structure that mark the intelligibility of external interaction among persons generally.

Formalism is especially relevant to the controversy over the judicial role. Proponents of a limited judicial role do not – or at least need not – dispute the desirability of the doctrinal innovations that the judiciary may introduce. Their contention would be unaffected by the concession that the specific new doctrine urged on the court is meritorious. At issue is not what is to be done but who is to do it. The claim is that although certain arguments may justify a specific policy, they are not the sort of justification that is pertinent to the adjudicative process. At issue is not the soundness of certain justifications but their coherence with the justificatory structure appropriate to adjudication.

The formalist understanding of the juridical, as opposed to the political, centers on the immanence of the legal forms to the intelligibility of the interactions that they order. Corrective and distributive justice are not extrinsic impositions on transactions and distributions. They are appropriate to transactions and distributions because they are the justificatory structures that inhere in these two understandings of interaction. An interaction is intelligible as a transaction only inasmuch as it is capable of being ordered by corrective justice; its conformity to this ordering is the perfection of living up to its own intelligible nature as a transaction. The same applies, *mutatis mutandis*, to distributions.

The juridical can be defined as that which is contained within the intelligibility of external interaction. The forms of justice represent the modes of understanding that pertain to interaction from within; the expression of these forms in a specific legal system is the province of the juridical. The forms' immanence to the understanding of the interactions they govern means that officials charged with explicating the juridical – in our legal culture, pre-eminently judges – can treat the ordering of an interaction as an interpretive function in which they draw out the juridical significance of the features that unify the interaction from within. Adjudication involves holding the particular transaction or distribution to its coherence as a transaction or a distribution. The judge is prohibited from orienting the juridical relationship to some external goal of the judge's choosing. The justificatory structures of corrective and distributive justice set the conceptual limits of the judge's jurisdiction, and the judge's role is to apply, in the context of a particular episode of adjudication, the form of justice appropriate to it.

Corrective or distributive justice need not be expressly considered by the judges or mentioned in their judgments. These forms of justice are categories of legal philosophy, not ingredients of positive law. They exhibit the structures of justification latent in a sophisticated legal system, and thus underlie its discourse without being themselves necessarily parts of it. The forms of justice are, as we have seen, the most abstract conceptions of juridical relations. Even if these abstractions are not explicit in positive law, they must be implicit in positive law if its content is coherent, because they represent the ways in which a juridical relationship can be conceived as a unity. The discourse of a sophisticated legal system, i.e., one that values coherence, will for particular controversies and sets of controversies tend to actualize one or the other of these implicit abstractions. The common law of negligence, for example, does not explicitly refer to corrective justice. Its categories of wrongdoing and causation, however, can be read as capturing in the context of delictual transactions the abstract equality of doing and suffering that is at the heart of corrective justice.[83] The same can be said for contract law's doctrines of consideration, offer and acceptance, expectation damages, and unconscionability.[84] Accordingly, the judge gives voice to the specifically juridical when he or she elaborates and applies elements

of positive law that express or specify aspects of these forms of justice.

The political, in contrast to the juridical, refers to considerations whose intelligibility stands outside the interconnecting aspects of juridical form. Political determinations are extrinsic to juridical form in the sense that, although expressible *through* form, they do not derive justificatory force entirely *from* form. They are expressible through form because otherwise they could not be intelligible as part of a coherent ordering. However, they must be justified by more than their participation in an internally coherent structure of justification. Any particular political determination must have a desirability that is independent of the elucidation or specification of form.

B.   Politics and Distributive Justice

The home of the political is distributive justice. In corrective justice, all that is present is the immediate relationship of person to person; nothing extrinsic is relevant to this relationship. In distributive justice, by contrast, the relation between persons is mediated by the criterion that assigns things to them in accordance with a proportional equality. The whole complex of persons, things, and criterion is an expression of a particular mediating purpose. Because it mediates, this purpose is not immediate to the relationship of person to person but is brought to bear upon them from outside. The intelligibility of this purpose is thus extrinsic to the relationship of person to person as such.

In the case of distributions, an external orientation is both possible and required. Distributive justice, it is true, is the internal integration of persons and things according to some criterion, so that the formal adequacy of a given distribution is a matter of integrating the elements constituting distributive justice's distinctive unity. But this internal aspect must be supplemented from the outside. Although the elements of distributive justice are internally structured, the fixing of a *particular* distribution involves selection from among many possible different distributions. Distributive justice goes to the inner coherence of a distribution, not to the choice of one distribution over another.

Assume, for instance, that one wanted to replace or supplement tort law by introducing a distributive scheme of compensation for personal injuries. A decision must be made as to the class of injuries for which compensation will be paid, the persons who will be burdened by the levies necessary to finance the scheme, the criteria by which recovery will be limited if the need for compensation exceeds the available financing, and so on.[85] For any such particular distribution one can require that its various elements fit with one another, but the notion of internal ordering is not sufficiently powerful to establish the boundaries or the criterion of the scheme. Whatever distribution is chosen must live up to the coherence of distributive justice. Distributive justice, however, understood as the coherent ordering of persons, things, and criterion, cannot single out which of the available distributions is to be preferred.

A particular distribution is the product of political institutions that have the capacity and authority to evaluate the full range of possible distributions, and that are accountable for their choices from among those possibilities. Hence, considerations of institutional competence and electoral responsibility figure prominently in discussions of the legal process.[86] Since no particular distribution can be excluded *ab initio*, competence and accountability must be of a global character. The authorization of some distributions and the rejection of others involve decisions about the interests of all members of the community. Those responsible for these decisions should correspondingly be answerable to all. Judges, who have limited control over their own agendas, who see controversy through the prism of bipolar argument, who must funnel the effects of their judgments through litigants, and who are relatively insulated from accountability to the community, are not appropriately situated to select from among possible distributions.[87]

A political element is therefore present in distributions. A distribution must distribute something and it must distribute it to particular persons according to a criterion that embodies a particular purpose, to be chosen from the many available purposes. Distributive justice implies that a political authority must define and particularize the scope or criterion of any scheme of distribution. This selection cannot be completely insulated from the interplay of power, persuasion, sympathy, and interest that characterizes the political process. The purpose of a specific distribution is not elaborated from within distributive justice, but must be authoritatively incorporated into the schedule of collective aims. Until then, this distribution is merely one of any number of possible distributions.

Although distributive justice requires politics, it is not reducible to politics. What is common to all possible distributions is precisely that they are *distributions*, not just haphazard dispersions; they are therefore coherent only insofar as they are expressions of distributive justice. Since distributive justice is the form generic to all distributions, no matter what their particular purposes, its justificatory structure is implicit in them all without exception. Political authority cannot make its extrinsic purposes part of an intelligible order unless its prescriptions conform to distributive justice. Consequently, any distribution must respect the relationship among the conceptual elements out of which distributive justice is constituted.

Distributive justice, as the integration of persons and things in accordance with a criterion, incorporates two related presuppositions. First, distributive justice postulates a distinction between things and persons. If a distribution is to observe the ordering characteristic of its form, it cannot treat persons as things. The difference between a person and a thing is that a thing can be a means to any end for which it is useful, whereas the nature of a person is to be an end and never only a means to an end.[88] The implicitness of this Kantian idea in distributive justice means that the instrumentalism of extrinsic purpose is constrained by the non-instrumental notion of personhood. The immanent intelligibility of distributive ordering presupposes that the recipient of the distributive benefit or burden can be immanently – and thus non-instrumentally – conceived in terms of being one's own end.

Second, distributive justice presupposes that the criterion of distribution applies equally to all who fall under its justificatory force, without underinclusion or overinclusion. Implicit in distributive justice as a justificatory structure is the notion that equality is conceptually necessary to this mode of understanding juridical relations. Equality, as used here, is not a substantive ideal that stands outside distribution, nor does it refer to any particular subject matter (such as welfare or resources[89]) whose equal distribution is independently desirable. Rather, it is applicable to whatever is being distributed because it is immanent to the understanding of a distribution as an internally intelligible arrangement. Accordingly, a distribution decreed by positive law that does not observe equality is defective from the standpoint of its own intelligibility.

Because personhood and equality are conceptual components in the form of distributive justice, and because distributive justice, being a form, is a principle of unity, personhood and equality are themselves interdependent. Those who share in the distribution are entitled to demand equality only because they are persons and thus not available for use according to the distributor's pleasure. Similarly, a mark of their personhood is the claim they have to equal standing in the distribution. A distribution that did not embody the equality of persons – a checkerboard scheme, for instance[90] – would fail to manifest an intelligible integration of persons and things with a distributive criterion. Instead of harmonizing the components of distributive justice, it would throw them together. Such a distribution would make inclusion or exclusion a matter of sport; the persons affected would implicitly be not ends in themselves but playthings for the distributing authority.

Personhood and equality are the presuppositions that make distributive justice conceivable. In their absence, distributive justice as a form would disappear. Bereft of the principle that gives them order from within, distributions would be internally indistinguishable from haphazard dispersions. Only the operation of extrinsic purpose on a juridically unintelligible world would remain. Distributions would be whatever political authority makes them. An assertion that the pattern of distribution was unintelligible or random could be decisively met by pointing to its being an expression of

political purpose validly enacted into positive law. Distributive justice thus preserves distributions as juridical relationships among the persons who are to share in them rather than as instances of largess bestowed by political authority on whatsoever terms it pleases.

Legislative and administrative action can legitimately be made to respect the conceptual contours of personhood and equality that underlie the ordering of distributions. The positive law may give effect to the fundamental values of personhood and equality in a variety of ways: by incorporating them into the techniques for construing statutes, by elaborating notions of natural justice or fairness for administrative procedures, or by enshrining specifications of personhood and equality into constitutional documents. The manifestation of these values represents the realization in positive law of the conceptual elements that constitute distributive justice and that are accordingly necessary for the juridical ordering of the extrinsic goals pursued by political authority.

As the expositors of the juridical, judges have a legitimate role in developing the notions of personhood and equality. Although judicial review does not allow the substitution of the court's preferred distribution for the one laid down by the authoritative political organ, a court can insist that, in setting up and executing a scheme of distributive justice, political authority not treat persons as things or violate the equality of persons under the distributional criterion. Juridical activity of this sort does not encroach on the prerogatives of the political organ; it only insists that the favored distributions conform to their own intelligible structure.

In requiring respect for the values of personhood and equality, courts are not engaging in a new distribution. Personhood and equality are not things that lie stored up somewhere waiting to be dispensed by a political authority according to a certain distributive criterion. They are not themselves distributed, but are the conceptual grounds for the possibility of distributing anything. Judicial review can therefore legitimately give specificity to the concept of the person and to the norm of equality that distributive justice postulates.

Distributions have a two-fold intelligibility, facing outward to the extrinsic purposes that they serve and inward to the form they embody. Accordingly, a distribution must be understood both from the instrumental standpoint of its particular extrinsic purpose and from the conceptual standpoint of its universally immanent structure. The former dimension of distribution is political, the latter juridical. The different institutional competences and spheres of legitimacy for legislative and for judicial action reflect these two dimensions of distribution, both of which must be encompassed in the understanding of distributive justice.

C. *Politics and Corrective Justice*

The situation in corrective justice is categorically different because politics is absent. Since the bilateral interaction between the parties is understood as immediate, no extrinsic purpose can intrude itself. Private law may have political consequences and may be the result of a political decision to establish the appropriate institutions of adjudication, but *qua* realization of corrective justice, it has no political aspect.[91] The parties to a transaction are active and passive with respect to a single harm; the significance of their interaction lies not in the specification by political authority of a collective external goal but in the interpretation of the immediate intersection of doing and suffering as each party pursues his or her own goal.

Corrective justice is therefore immune to the external ends that characterize distributions. This immunity manifests itself in the different ways in which corrective and distributive justice are particularized. In distributive justice, the specification of a distribution involves a choice from among many different possibilities. A workers' compensation scheme, a crime – victim compensation program, and a more general accident compensation plan are different distributions each of which exemplifies the category of distributive justice in personal injury compensation, just as apples and oranges are different examples of the category of fruit. Every distribution has its own separate integrity as the actualization of its own specific purpose and scope; together they constitute the inven-

tory of distributions from which the political authority may or may not select. In contrast, when construing a transaction in accordance with corrective justice, the adjudicator does not choose one scheme of correction over another but rather specifies the meaning of corrective justice with respect to the transaction in question. The varieties of distribution are the several relationships that can be mediated through different distributive purposes, but as between doer and sufferer, a single relationship of corrective justice gets worked out in accordance with its particular facts and history. Whereas the category of distributive justice encompasses different instantiating distributions from which the distributor may choose, the category of corrective justice is a single noninstrumental conception whose meaning is judicially elaborated in the different circumstances of its application.

In illuminating from within the juridical relationships that exemplify it, corrective justice excludes their being oriented toward any extrinsic goal. Corrective justice is intelligible solely in non-instrumental terms. An understanding of corrective justice by reference to something beyond itself transforms it into what it is not and thus fails to grasp it as it is.

The ascription of an external purpose to a transaction is incompatible with the structure of corrective justice in at least two ways. First, corrective justice holds the parties to the equality inherent in their immediate interaction. An extrinsic purpose, however, cannot be true to the unmediated relationship of doer and sufferer; it must favor one of the interacting parties and thereby contradict the initial equality that marks corrective justice as a distinctive form. For instance, the analysis of tort law in terms of possible aims such as compensation or deterrence[92] is incompatible with the understanding of tort law as the operation of corrective justice. The first of these aims is intelligible with reference to the plaintiff only; the second with reference to the defendant only. Yet the form of corrective justice postulates that each party has an equal standing and that neither is subordinate to the other or superfluous to their relationship.

The second way in which the projection of an external purpose onto a transaction is incompatible with corrective justice is that the purpose in question cannot be necessarily limited to the interaction of the two parties to the transaction. The purpose must embrace all those who fall under it; the immediate link between plaintiff and defendant is irrelevant. Since a transaction does not realize a collective goal, there is no necessary reason that the scope of the transaction should be coextensive with the operation of any purpose. Take tort law again as an example. If the purpose of tort law is considered to be the provision of financial support to those who suffer from personal injuries, the claim of a plaintiff can be no stronger than the claim of any person who is injured even non-tortiously and who therefore falls within the ambit of the purpose. Similarly, if one conceives of the purpose of tort law as the deterrence of wrongful behavior, there is no warrant for restricting the deterring sanction to those instances of wrongful behavior which materialize in injury. The purpose as such is indifferent to the transactional context of the tortious injury.

These two incompatibilities between corrective justice and exogenously introduced goals are connected as follows. Corrective justice is the integrated unity of the doer and the sufferer of a single harm. The extrinsic goal disassembles this unity by isolating an aspect that would favor one or the other of the litigants and then bending the entire relationship to its promotion. But once the transaction is decomposed into competing aspects, the preferred goal has a vitality of its own that cannot rationally be confined to the bounds of the transaction's now disintegrated unity.[93] It must float free to cover all the instances that fall under its independent sway.[94]

In displaying the ordering that constitutes a transaction and that distinguishes it from a distribution, corrective justice reveals the inappropriateness of an instrumental interpretation of immediate interaction. The transactional equality between plaintiff and defendant, unlike the proportion that characterizes distributive justice, cannot be oriented towards an extrinsic objective. The exclusion of extrinsic purposes means that instrumentalism plays no role here.[95] Because corrective justice is therefore purely juridical, its elaboration can be assigned

to the judiciary. Private law is the detailed and concrete elaboration of corrective justice by the authoritative judicial institutions. Corrective justice yields a completely non-instrumental and non-political understanding of law.

D.   *The Normative Force of the Forms of Justice*

Formalism thus derives the distinction between the juridical and the political from the immanent rationality of the forms of justice. Corrective justice exhibits the form of rationality indigenous to transactions and presents a structure of interaction that is immune to an understanding in terms of extrinsic purpose. Distributive justice is the ordering immanent to distributions; it structures and constrains the operation of the extrinsic purposes that characterize particular distributions. Law is by its nature apolitical to the extent that it translates the conceptual contours of these forms into a legal reality.

Recall that Unger described formalism as postulating an "immanent moral rationality."[96] The immanence and the rationality (or intelligibility) of the forms of justice have perhaps now been sufficiently exhibited and related to the distinction between law and politics. What, however, is the moral force of these forms? For clearly they must have a moral dimension if the law is required to conform to their structure. Although they describe the nature of coherence in the content of sophisticated legal systems, the implicit demand that they issue to the positive law attests to a normative relevance that overrides any extrinsic political purpose. On what is this relevance based? How do the forms of justice secure a dimension of normativity that is independent of the justification of a particular extrinsic purpose or of the lawmaking process by which this purpose is brought into existence as a matter of positive law?

The answer to this cannot, of course, be derived from any good ulterior to these forms; if it were, their intelligibility as justificatory structures would be dependent on an extrinsic value. As a result, their normativity would be secured at the price of their immanence. Maintenance of the internal perspective requires that the normativity of juridical relationships be as immanent as their intelligibility. In other words, their moral force must come from the very integration of immanence and intelligibility in a juridical relationship. Because the justification of all immediate and mediated juridical relationships must – if there is to be such justification – conform to the shape of one or the other of these structures, the forms of justice carry with them the seeds of their own moral force. For the formalist, corrective and distributive justice are normative not because something else makes them normative, but because they constitute the essential nature of normativity with respect to the external relationships of persons.

The non-instrumental normativity that undergirds the forms of justice is to be found in Kantian legal philosophy. The forms of justice transpose into the intelligibility of external interaction the Kantian notion of obligatoriness. On the one hand, Kantian normativity is presupposed in the forms as a condition of their being justificatory. On the other, the structures of the two forms are themselves the juridical expressions of this presupposed Kantian normativity.

Because, as I shall argue, Kantian normativity is presupposed by the forms of justice, it does not supervene upon them from the outside as an optional or arbitrary postulate. Rather, it is implicit in them as justificatory structures. If we take the forms of justice as hitherto explicated and inquire into the preconditions of their justificatory function, we are ineluctably brought to their Kantian grounding. This is because the forms are so abstract that they do not incorporate a determinate notion of the good and therefore can be based only on a notion of Kantian right. The Aristotelian forms of justice and Kantian right provide dovetailing accounts of the non-instrumental intelligibility of juridical interaction. Kantian right traces this intelligibility back to the free acts that are necessitated by categorical imperatives of reason. Inasmuch as Kantian right is implicit in the forms of justice, they are grounded in a conception of normativity – indeed, in a particularly stringent conception of normativity.[97]

Consider first corrective justice, the presuppositions of which are all the clearer because it excludes the mediation of extrinsic purpose. Two features of corrective justice that are embedded in private law bear on the form's immanent normativity. First, corrective justice ignores such factors as the wealth, virtue, or merit of the interacting parties.[98] Second, the rectification worked by corrective justice is a restoration of an initial notional equality. The quantity transferred from defendant to plaintiff represents the amount by which this initial equality has been disturbed. This equality is itself formal and does not refer to the parties' particular attributes of need, merit, or status. In corrective justice the equality of the plaintiff and the defendant is neutral to all the particularities of condition or character that mark their difference and their possible inequality.

Corrective justice ignores the particular attributes of the litigants because these attributes are not relevant to the transaction as such. In corrective justice the interaction of the parties is immediate; there is no place for consideration of the varying degrees in which they partake of particular qualities and in accordance with which the mediating proportion of distributive justice might be constructed. In this respect corrective justice postulates an extreme version of interpersonal externality. All that matters is the interaction itself.

The parties may be conceived to be so completely external to one another because each is assumed to be internally constituted as a single person who acts and produces effects upon the circumambient world. The equality that corrective justice presumes is that which parties owe each other as persons with an equal capacity for acting.[99] Corrective justice conceives of the parties as freely active, purposive beings. As such, they are not determined to perform or pursue any given action or purpose; the essence of their activity and their purposiveness lies precisely in their being self-determined. This capacity for self-determination is an abstraction from all particularity; its very abstractness as a capacity is what allows it to be equally applicable to all actors. Corrective justice refers only to the person's formal capacity for free purposive action, while remaining indifferent to the background from which particular exercises of this capacity issue. In abstracting from the concrete richness of human particularity, corrective justice pays it the supreme compliment of seeing it as conceptually posterior to the operation of a self-determining will.

The presupposition of corrective justice outlined here will be familiar to readers of Kant and Rawls as moral personality.[100] Indeed, corrective justice can fairly be described in Kantian terms as the point of view from which noumenal selves see each other,[101] i.e., as the ordering of immediate interactions that Kantian moral persons would recognize as expressive of their natures. Kantian moral persons are duty bound to interact with each other on terms appropriate to their formally equal status: Their acts, as the acts of freely purposive beings, must be capable of co-existence with the freedom of everyone.[102] This normative requirement is not introduced from the outside but attaches at once as a conceptual consequence of their being moral persons.[103] Corrective justice's presupposition of moral personality therefore means that implicit in the intelligibility of immediate interaction are the obligations incumbent in Kantian legal theory on free beings under moral laws.

Distributive justice also presupposes moral personality. We have already seen that distributive justice postulates a distinction, explicable in Kantian terms, between persons and things. This distinction can be related to the abstractness of moral personality in the following way. Although particular distributions connect the subject matter of the distribution to the recipients of it, and are therefore not abstract, distributive justice as an ordering concept specifies no particular subject matter. A particular distribution concretizes the person by bestowing an entitlement to a particular benefit or an incumbency to a particular burden. Accordingly, the concreteness of personhood in a distribution is a consequence, not a presupposition, of that distribution. In particular distributions the person must be conceived as concretely attached to a share in the thing being distributed. Distributive justice, however, is the form underlying all possible distributions; in itself it is neutral to any particular ones. Therefore it presupposes abstract moral personality no less than does corrective justice.

Both corrective and distributive justice incorporate the normativity of externally interacting Kantian moral persons, but they express this normativity through distinct structures of quantitative and proportional equality. Hence the single normative presupposition that underlies immediate and mediated interactions has two different manifestations in positive law. In corrective justice, the relationship between the interacting parties is not mediated by the internal particularity of need or want. The relationship cannot, therefore, be understood in terms of an obligation on one to bestow a benefit on the other. What remain are the parties' reciprocal duties not to interfere wrongly with the embodiments (physical and proprietary) of each other's moral personality, and the rights that are correlative to these duties. The immediacy of their interaction yields in private law a set of negative rights and duties that immediately appertain to all interactors.[104] Distributive justice, on the other hand, mediates the relationship between persons through an extrinsic purpose determined by political authority and establishes no duties immediately owed by person to person. It operates on the mediation itself, requiring the exercise of political authority to respect moral personality by conforming to the justificatory structure immanent in all distributions. This normative constraint on collective purposes expresses itself legally in the possibility of invalidating legislative and administrative action through judicial review.

Positive law reflects the immanent normativity of corrective and distributive justice through the retrospective operation of legal remedies. When a court strikes down an administrative or legislative act or awards damages to a private law litigant, its judgment does not merely state what the law shall be from that moment on; it authoritatively defines the legal standards antecedently applicable to the very behavior at issue. This retrospectivity is problematic if the judgment is itself conceived as essentially legislative, since such legislation would give the parties affected no chance to guide their conduct by its prescriptions. The retrospectivity presumes that the standard had moral force at the time of the action at issue in the suit, and that the judgment is declaratory of this pre-existing moral force. Inasmuch as the judgment is itself a specification of the meaning of corrective or distributive justice in a particular context, the judgment's retrospective normativity presumably reflects the normativity that attaches at once to the juridically intelligible nature of a transaction or a distribution. The law assumes that the declared standard is notionally present to the interaction in advance of its being declared, thus implicitly attesting that the ordering of transactions and distributions through their respective forms of justice is an inherently normative exercise.[105]

VI   Conceptualism and Social Context

A.   *The Challenge to Conceptualism*

So far I have set out a version of legal formalism that construes juridical relationships in terms of the contrasting forms of corrective and distributive justice. Formalism, understood in this way, is avowedly and unabashedly conceptual in two respects. First, the components of form are conspicuously manifested in the concepts through which a coherent legal system is organized. Second, the forms are themselves the most abstract concepts that bear upon the intelligibility of juridical relations. These two points are related, in that the concepts of a coherent legal system are both the expression and the means of discovering the most abstract concepts of juridical coherence.[106]

At the heart of this conceptualism is the difference between the form of corrective justice and the form of distributive justice. Just as these two forms are the most abstract concepts underlying juridical relationships, so the difference between these forms is itself a conceptual one. The two forms of justice and the difference between them, although they are manifested in sophisticated legal systems that are socially and historically conditioned, are not themselves socially and historically conditioned. As patterns of intelligibility latent in the justification of all interactions regarded as external, they are not restricted to any particular episode of such interaction or to any particular set of such episodes. Their conceptual status guarantees for

them a significance that embraces external interaction whenever and wherever it occurs and that, accordingly, transcends society and historicity. As the categorically distinct abstractions underlying the particularity of external interaction, corrective and distributive justice are the stable substrata of intelligibility that persist through all the multifarious juridical relationships that realize them. In other words, the forms of justice are universals.

The current disfavor of formalism involves a rejection of such an essentially conceptual understanding of law. The contemporary assumption is that formalism is a necropolis of lifeless abstractions that repel meaningful contact with the movement and vitality of social life. Formalist conceptualism is thought to be incapable of comprehending the concrete legal reality that it wishes to illuminate. This assessment, however, is perhaps the most unfortunate consequence of the estrangement of contemporary legal thought from the tradition on which legal formalism draws.[107] In fact, formalism does not fall foul of the defect for which it is so routinely condemned. That, at least, is the theme of my argument in this Part.

The charge against formalism amounts to an accusation that it holds itself out to be a kind of moral geometry. These concepts are alleged to exist in a world of their own – they are, in Holmes' famous phrase, "a brooding omnipresence in the sky"[108] – and that world is categorically separate from the world of human activity. Formalism is dismissed as "the dogma that legal forms can be understood apart from their social context."[109] Further, critics claim, parallel to formalism's separation of concepts from social context is its separation of the self from connection with others. The Kantian notion of moral personality is said to ignore the way community is constitutive of the individual.[110] Thus the conceptual abstractness of formalism is equated by its critics with a withdrawal from social and historical situatedness.

This conception of formalism's separation from the world is matched by a conception of the way it impinges on the world. The formalist is alleged to construe legal analysis as the geometrical working out of the logical conclusions of a limited number of axioms. Its procedures are said to be deductive, and hence to ignore the inevitable indeterminacy inherent in the application of legal rules. Such indeterminacy purportedly can only be handled by reference to the political.[111]

These charges touch many profound issues: the relationship between the way law is and the theory of law; between the abstract and the concrete; between the universal and the particular. I wish to outline the misconceptions on which such criticism rests. My basic point is that this criticism does not take seriously the immanence of formal intelligibility.

B. The Detachment Issue

In the formalism I have been describing, the forms of justice do not inhabit a world detached from the juridical relationships they govern. They are not to be conceived as having an existence parallel to, but separate from, the existence of human interaction. The forms of justice go to the immanent coherence of juridical relationships. The formalism of these forms does not lie in their existing somewhere apart from the social world, but in their representing the different ways in which the juridical relationships of that world can be coherent.[112] Because they render interaction intelligible from within, they presuppose interaction and cannot be elucidated without it.

This point can also be made by reference to the concept of moral personality, which abstracts from particularity without dismissing it. One might think that, strictly speaking, moral persons as such cannot interact. The purposiveness characteristic of moral personality is a mere potentiality that, so long as it remains potential, does not issue into the world and therefore does not act upon or interact with anything or anyone. In abstracting from all particularity, moral personality, it might be said, withdraws from the world and cannot leave its mark upon it. Only through the realization of specific purposes does purposiveness radiate out from the actor and reach his surroundings: The faculty of will impinges upon others only insofar as it wills something. All this is true so far as it goes. But far from undermining the significance of moral personality, this merely indicates how moral personality

wins its way into the concreteness of interaction. Indeed, it confirms the essentiality of moral personality to freely purposive beings by acknowledging that the rich variety of specific purposes is but the actualization of the potentiality of purposiveness. The will, to be a will, must will something. The particularity of what it wills, however, does not confirm its status as a will; it merely completes its operation. From the standpoint of the forms of justice, purposiveness must issue into a particular purpose but into no purpose in particular. These forms, then, do not deny particularity; they treat it as a universal. They acknowledge that my purposiveness is complete only in *this* purpose; the content of the purpose, however, does not matter for them, because the "thisness" of this purpose refers to any and every purpose.[113]

Inasmuch as they admit the particularity of interaction, the forms of justice differ from the forms of geometry. The relationship of corrective and distributive justice to the transactions and the distributions that they respectively govern is not that of a triangle in Euclidian geometry to a triangle drawn on the blackboard. Whereas the geometer's triangle is completely intelligible apart from the blackboard representation – indeed the drawn triangle is always and necessarily a defective version of the idea that it supposedly renders – the forms of justice cannot be understood detached from the particularity of the external interactions that they govern and from the specific regimes of positive law that actualize them. As the ordering principles of interaction that become concrete in positive law, corrective and distributive justice are the structures of coherent meaning implicit in sophisticated legal systems.

The forms of justice are aspects of a mutually reinforcing movement between legal content and juridical form. The form, being the form *of* the content, does not exist separately from legal content. Indeed the notion of form, taken in itself and divorced from all inkling of what this form might be the form of, could never constitute a mode of intelligibility for anything. For a form that is not implicit in a determinate content whose form it is would be an abstraction from everything and thus, in itself, an absolute nullity. Even if we see corrective and distributive justice in terms of their different notions of equality, we must see these notions as devices that model different justificatory structures and that therefore refer to phenomena to which justifactory structures are pertinent. Otherwise the forms of justice would represent not modes of ordering interaction but merely the mathematical difference between a quantity and a proportion. This is why we first come to an appreciation of the forms of juridical relationship by working back from the content of legal systems that attach a value to coherence. This procedure ensures that the elucidation of form takes place in the context of a content whose forms they are.

The forms of justice are immanent and do not operate in detachment from society or from history. Their significance as forms is understood through the relationships they inform. These relationships are necessarily social and historical ones. They are social in that they feature the interaction of one person with another and thereby do not construe the person as living isolated on a desert island. They are historical in that they are the products of events in history, since these relationships come into being and fade away in a world of temporality, flux, and change.[114]

Juridical relationships, as comprehended by the formalist, not only take place in society, but have a public meaning. The formalist is concerned with the intelligibility of interactions in which the interacting parties are treated as external to one another.[115] The externality of interaction must be understood from a standpoint that is common to the parties to the interaction.[116] Accordingly, interpreting the interaction requires recourse to a shared public meaning. The forms of justice, as they apply to any specific juridical relationship, must draw upon this public meaning. Indeed, the justificatory structures themselves participate in this public realm, since justification with respect to external relationships involves the negation of purely private significances in favor of meanings that are accessible to all and that can be openly vindicated in the presence of all.

The external character of juridical relationships also means that the determination of the legal significance of a particular interaction must reside in an authority outside the parties.

Formalism is not satisfied merely by the correct elucidation of the adequacy of legal content to juridical form. In addition, an impartial and disinterested authority must be available who is recognized as expressing the public meaning of the interaction. In other words, for the forms of justice to be applied, the public significance of particular interactions must be expressible through mechanisms of positive law.[117]

In our legal culture, this function is performed by the judiciary. In determining whether a transaction or a distribution has lived up to its ordering form, the court declares the meaning of corrective or distributive justice in the context of the specific controversy at hand. It examines the particular transaction or distribution against the background of public understandings through which corrective and distributive justice can be expressed, and its judgment provides the publicly authoritative interpretation of how the appropriate form of justice is applied to the controversy at hand. This function is public, but it is not political. The court elucidates the public meaning of the transaction or the distribution at issue; it does not orient the juridical relationship to any extrinsic purpose.

One can, therefore, distinguish two public functions – one political, the other juridical – that formalism ascribes to the positivity of law. The first is the selection of the goal to be embodied in a particular distribution and thereby to be authoritatively inscribed into the schedule of the community's collective purposes.[118] The setting up of a particular distribution is an act of political authority that clothes its determinations with the attributes of positive law. Although the particular distribution must, if it is to actualize an intelligible order, conform to distributive justice, it embodies an extrinsic – and therefore political – purpose. The second function is juridical: to interpret particular transactions and distributions in accordance with the form of justice they instantiate. This function does not depend on a standpoint outside the forms of justice. Rather, it requires courts to specify, in a publicly authoritative way, the meaning of these forms in the context of particular interactions.

A recent case illustrates the distinction between these two functions. In *Lamb v. London Borough of Camden*,[119] the English Court of Appeal was confronted with a problem of proximate cause. The plaintiff homeowner was suing the defendant municipality for the damage resulting from the negligent repair of a sewer pipe. Contractors employed by the defendant had breached a water main and the resulting flood caused the plaintiff's house to subside. Because the house was then unsafe, the plaintiff used it only for storage as it awaited repair. While the house remained vacant squatters moved in. Subsequently, they were evicted, and the plaintiff boarded up the house. Nevertheless squatters moved in again, and this time damaged the house's interior. The question for the court was whether the municipality was liable for the damage done by the second set of squatters.

This case is typical of situations where several causes, including the actions of third parties, intervene between the plaintiff's damage and the tortfeasor's original negligence.[120] Given the number and variety of possible causes, courts have never been able – and doubtless never will be able – to come up with a definitive verbal formula for resolving these disputes. Confronted with this indeterminacy the members of the court took two different approaches. Lord Denning, declaring it "a question of policy for judges to decide,"[121] thought the decisive consideration was that damage to property, including damage caused by criminal acts, is usually covered by the owner's insurance, and that the insurers whose business it is to cover the risk should not be allowed by subrogation to pass the cost on to the defendant. Through insurance "the risk of loss is spread throughout the community. It does not fall too heavily on one pair of shoulders alone."[122] He accordingly ruled against liability.

In concurrence with Lord Denning in this result, Lord Justice Watkins made no reference to insurance or to loss-spreading. Instead, he drew attention to what is suggested by "the very features" of the act or event for which damages are claimed. This included such matters as the nature of the event, the time and place of its occurrence, the identity and

intentions of the perpetrator, and the responsibility for taking measures to avoid the occurrence.[123] These factors did not produce anything that could be a universal test, but Lord Justice Watkins found that they yielded "the instinctive feeling" that the squatters' damage was too remote for the defendant's liability.[124]

Both Lord Denning and Lord Justice Watkins issued public and authoritative declarations of positive law. There is, however, this difference between them. Lord Denning's approach was essentially political. It first required selecting the particular goal of loss-spreading from among the various goals (including general deterrence, specific deterrence and redistribution to the deepest pocket[125]) that his judgment might promote. It then necessitated electing to effect this goal through the homeowner's property insurance, not through the tortfeasor's liability insurance or through the municipality's self-insurance. Loss-spreading, however, like all external goals, is a matter for distributive justice and cannot be coherently achieved within the relationship of doer and sufferer. Nor is its positing the province of a judge, who is neither in a position to canvass the range of possible collective goals, nor accountable to the community for the particular goal chosen.

Lord Justice Watkins, in contrast, does not attempt to achieve any goal external to the relationship between plaintiff and defendant. His judgment is an exposition of the nature of that relationship through attention to the link between the defendant's wrongdoing and the plaintiff's damage. For him proximate cause is not an occasion for "policy", but is a juridical concept under which the court comprehends the nexus between the litigants by tracing the proximity of the wrongful act to the injurious effect. This concept does not have an existence independent of the interaction to which it is applied, and its features cannot be listed and weighted in a formula that yields a uniquely determinate conclusion. This explains Lord Justice Watkins' reference to intuition. The meaning of proximate cause in this situation is not a result of matching these facts to an independently conclusive formula; it is simply the most plausible construal of the relationship between the parties in light of the factors that are deemed relevant. For these facts, the conclusion constitutes the meaning of the concept they instantiate.

In concentrating on the features of the injurious act rather than on a mediating goal, Lord Justice Watkins treats proximate cause as a concept that bears on the immediate intelligibility of the parties' relationship. Proximate cause so treated is one of the set of concepts through which a delictual interaction is understandable as corrective justice. Because corrective justice is conceived as immanent to the transactions that it regulates, its operation is not intelligible independently of those transactions. The actualization of corrective justice through judicial decisions "is not the subsequent applying to a concrete case of a given universal that we understand first by itself, but it is the actual understanding of the universal itself that the given text constitutes for us."[126] The particular transactions and their intelligibility as corrective justice can be interpreted only from within a public realm of shared social meanings that judicial decision renders legally authoritative. The same process holds for the application to a particular distribution of the components of personhood and equality that are internal to distributive justice. This drawing out of the significance of the forms of justice for particular transactions and distributions is the juridical function of positive law. It is categorically different from the political role of determining the exogenous end that is to be embodied in a distribution.

C.   *The Determinacy Issue*

These remarks about the immanence of the forms of justice, and the consequent denial of the claim that they have a socially detached existence, also bear on the relevance of indeterminacy. As this account of Lord Justice Watkins' judgment in the *Lamb* case illustrates, formalism does not rely on the antecedent determinacy for particular cases of the concepts entrenched in positive law, even when those concepts reflect the appropriate form of justice. In *Lamb*, and cases like it, the organ of positive law has the function of determining an antecedently indeterminate controversy.

For formalism the crucial distinction is between the juridical, which is comprised of whatever expresses the internal coherence of the forms of justice, and the political, which is the domain of the collective goals extrinsic to those forms. Nothing about formalism precludes indeterminacy, as the critics understand it, within the juridical operation of either of the forms of justice. Formalism merely insists that such indeterminacy not be seen – as it was by Lord Denning in *Lamb* – as a reason for transforming a juridical exercise into a political one.

For formalism the possibility of indeterminacy neither can, nor need be, avoided. Indeterminacy follows from formalism's conception of the relationship between general and particular. Legal formalism deals with the particulars of external interaction by abstracting from them to a coherent set of juridical categories, and ultimately by abstracting further to corrective and distributive justice as the two concepts of juridical coherence. This approach to the intelligibility of the law's content aims at an illumination of the particular through the general: The particulars are the inexhaustible ways in which persons can externally affect one another, whereas the forms are the general patterns through which these particulars are understood as juridically coherent. The forms of justice, as the most abstract representations of a conceptual distinction within the structure of justification, are philosophical constructs that are not themselves variable. In contrast, the particulars of one person's impingement on another are unavoidably contingent. This difference between the enduring generality of the forms and the contingency of the particulars is precisely what, for the formalist, allows the former to be principles of ordering for the latter. It also prevents the law's treatment of all the possible particulars from being exhaustively specifiable by theory: Such exhaustiveness would mean that the particulars are theoretically as intelligible as the forms through which they are understood, and would render otiose the formalist's invocation of form. The predetermination of a uniquely correct result for every legal controversy, as the critics demand, would make formalism self-stultifying.

The critics deploy the charge of indeterminacy with respect to the results of particular legal controversies, and claim that for any case – or at least for any difficult case – no uniquely correct solution is available in advance. As directed against formalism, however, this criticism bites on air. Formalism does not require the determinacy of every particular case. The distinctive feature of formalism is that it denies the primacy of the particular by claiming that particulars are intelligible only through conceptual categories. Particulars, considered directly on their own as particulars, are regarded as unknowable. They can become objects of cognition only when their essential characteristics can be grasped as a unity that is classifiable with other unities of the same sort and distinguishable from unities of a different sort. For law this means that juridical relationships can be understood only through the nexus of concepts through which they attain their distinctive inner coherence as expressions of corrective or distributive justice. When these comprehensive abstractions are brought onto the stage, determinacy cannot be a matter of the uniquely correct solution to any particular case, since the particularity of interaction has an aspect of contingency with respect to the concepts under which it falls. A function of positive law is to resolve such unavoidable indeterminacy for particular cases.[127]

In another sense, however, formalist concepts do determine their particulars. To determine something is to set the boundaries that mark it off from something else. A concept can be determinative even though it does not exhaustively predetermine the particulars under it, if it intelligibly performs the determining function of marking something off from something else in a way appropriate to concepts. Corrective and distributive justice are determinative in the sense that they demarcate juridical relationships as ensembles of coherent justificatory significance. Form goes to the character, unity, and genericity of what it informs. The forms of justice determine juridical relationships by representing the justificatory structures through which those relationships can be understood as the sorts of thing that they are and to which they must conform if they are to be intelligible.

The forms of justice are thus determinative as the distinctive – not the exhaustive – modes for the understanding of law.[128]

These abstract forms determine juridical relationships in several ways. First, they set out the different structures of justification that legal phenomena can express and thus mark the boundaries within which coherent justifications subsist. Corrective justice and distributive justice are categorically distinct; as a result any given juridical relationship must maintain itself within the confines of its appropriate framework. Second, these two forms of justice are the most inclusive abstractions of juridical coherence; their conceptual components demarcate the limits of the juridical as opposed to the political. Third, the forms exhibit the different ways in which relations among persons can be understood as external; thus they demarcate a normativity that is distinguishable from the moral excellences, such as love and virtue, that are internal to the agent. Accordingly, the forms of justice are determinative in that they make salient the boundaries of juridical intelligibility. In light of these forms juridical relationships cannot be understood as a confusion either of the corrective and the distributive, or of the juridical and the political, or of the external and the internal. Since juridical relationships are formally determinable in these ways, legal phenomena are more than an indeterminate aggregate of particulars.

Determinacy, therefore, can refer both to the particularity of specific holdings and to the general abstractions under which they fall. In accordance with the meanings respectively appropriate to each, the particular and the general can be said to be mutually codetermining. The forms of justice determine particular holdings by supplying the structure immanent to the justification of those particular holdings. For any such holding the forms determine the kind of holding it is by representing the pattern of coherence that is exemplified in the reasoning that supports it. Conversely, the particular holding enunciated in positive law determines the form by exhibiting the particular shape that the form manifests in a particular social and historical context. The form marks out the conceptual genericity of the particular holding, and the holding marks out the contextual specificity of the form. Thus the form and the holding are locked in an embrace of reciprocal determination.

Both sides of this process are necessary for the understanding of a juridical relationship. A particular determination that is not adequate to any form of justice cannot be grasped as a coherent ordering of external interaction. Similarly, a form that is conceived independently of application to particular interactions is not a form that is immanent to the intelligibility of a legal content. On the one hand, a particular holding is intelligible only inasmuch as it instantiates a form of justice. Although, as *Lamb* illustrates, abstract concepts cannot predetermine the uniquely correct solution to every particular case, the character of the reasoning underlying a given judgment is limited to – and therefore determined by – what is permissible within the appropriate structure of justification. On the other hand, formalism requires that controversy about particular interaction be determinable through the distillation of social understandings in positive law, for otherwise the interaction could not achieve the full measure of external intelligibility toward which the forms of justice point.

Moreover, since the forms of justice are discovered by regression from the conceptual structure of a sophisticated legal system, they incorporate the recognition that in such systems of the inevitable insufficiency of concepts to predetermine the results of all the cases to which they might be applied. This recognition is institutionalized in the common law, for instance, in the allocation to the jury of deliberation, pursuant to the judge's instructions, regarding mixed questions of law and fact. Under this arrangement, the jury applies standards that are themselves specifications of more general legal categories, but the particularity of the jury function means that the force of its finding is restricted to the case at hand and lacks precedential status. Correspondingly, the conceptual nature of the forms of justice determines not the specificity of these decisions but the coherence of the ensemble of concepts on which the judge draws in formulating the relevant instruction.

Determinacy relates in different ways to the generality of the forms and to the particularity of external interaction. Formalism comprehends both these ways in their interrelation. The forms of justice are both determinate and indeterminate. They are indeterminate in that they do not predetermine exhaustively the particular results they govern. They are determinate in that they establish the bounds of coherence for the particulars that fall under them, thus making these particulars intelligible as the sorts of things that they are. In determining character, unity, and genericity for juridical relationships, the forms of justice determine all that they need to, or can, determine as forms.

As an ordering immanent to the intelligibility of external interaction, the forms of justice necessarily make contact with a social and historical world because they must be specified for particular cases. These specifications depend on the public meanings of such a world. Within the bounds of character, unity, and genericity, the forms are constituted by the shared understandings of society, and the forms' particular public shapes are authoritatively declared by the functionaries of positive law. Thus, although the forms as such, because they are conceptually distinguishable, have an ahistorical universality, their manifestations in a legal system are relative to a set of public meanings that obtain at a given time and place. In its governance of juridical relationships, formalism is universality with a variable content.

This variability has been recognized by formalists almost since the beginning. In his famous discussion of the relationship between what is just by nature and what is just by convention, Aristotle commented that "among us [as contrasted with what holds for gods] there are things which, though naturally just, are nevertheless changeable.... "[129] This sentence can now be interpreted as including the following understanding. The intelligibility of juridical relationships is not merely a conventional opinion, because corrective and distributive justice are the perduring justificatory structures through which the coherence of such relationships can be conceived. The way in which the forms of justice are realized in legal systems is, however, subject to the variations inherent in their public interpretation and application. Thus, the forms of justice coexist with indeterminacies whose resolution can vary from time to time and from culture to culture.

The version of formalism that I have been presenting is neither positivist nor historicist. Legal positivism and historicism construe the law's positivity and its history respectively as the exhaustive modes of understanding it. Formalism is not positivist, because corrective and distributive justice are conceptual categories that inform the content of law without themselves being posited by legal authority. It is not historicist because the forms of justice are not bound to a particular social and temporal context. But although formalism transcends positivity and history, it is not unconnected to them. Because formalism inquires into the intelligibility immanent to juridical relations, the object of its attention is the historical domain of social interaction and the public announcements by positive law of the terms of that interaction. In comprehending the social and historical arrangements established by positive law as the possible expressions of a coherent order, formalism does not ignore the history, positivity, and social reality of law. Rather, formalism claims to be their truth.

VII Formalism and Contemporary Legal Scholarship

My argument has been that the juridical, understood as the immanent intelligibility of the treatment of external interactions in a coherent legal system, is conceptually distinct from extrinsic political purpose. This argument has several steps. (i) Form is the integration of character, genericity, and unity that renders a determinate content intelligible. (ii) The content of a sophisticated legal system is intelligible from within. (iii) The presentation of legal intelligibility as the interpenetration of form and content stakes out a vantage point internal to law. (iv) Law authoritatively orders the external relations between persons, and justice is the intelligibility of this ordering. (v) The intelligibility of law therefore involves the disclosure of the relationship between the law's content

and the forms of justice that constitute the most inclusive justificatory structures applicable to external relations. (vi) Two different forms of justice can be discerned. Corrective justice constitutes the internal rationality of transactions. Distributive justice, which mediates the relations among persons, and between persons and things, according to some criterion, is the internal rationality of distributions. (vii) These two forms exhibit differing structures and are not reducible one to the other. (viii) Justifications that blend the components of these two different forms are necessarily incoherent. (ix) Only distributions are amenable to the extrinsic – and thus instrumental – operation of political purpose. (x) The juridical consists of the elucidation and specification, in the context of particular transactions and distributions, of a content that is adequate to the justificatory structures of these two forms. (xi) The two forms of justice have inherent normative force because they presuppose the Kantian notion of moral personality. (xii) The forms of justice, being immanent to the understanding of external interaction, are not divorced from the social and historical world. (xiii) They determine the juridical character, genericity and coherence of that world through the positive law that is their existence at the level of particular transactions and distributions.

This understanding of law makes salient the venerable notion of form. Legal formalism is the approach that tracks the implications of form through the doctrines, institutions, and conceptual structure of a sophisticated legal system. For such a system its own coherence is a regulative idea. Its determinations are not unconnected bits of particularity but draw their vitality from their participation in a community of concepts and justifications. The forms of justice represent these justifications at their most abstract and inclusive. Inasmuch as law is the ordering of external interaction, corrective and distributive justice provide the fundamental unities that inform such interaction.

Formalism stands for the possibility that the elaboration of law can be a coherent enterprise in justification. The formalist construes the doctrines, institutions and concepts of a sophisticated legal system as embodying the intelligible structures of external interaction and therefore as expressing in positive law the forms through which juridical coherence can be achieved. These forms are implicit in the content of law. The juridical function of legal ordering is to make transactions and distributions conform to their own latent unity. Correspondingly, the function of legal philosophy is to make these forms explicit as the justificatory structures through which the law's immanent intelligibility is grasped.

In relating law to the most abstract forms of interaction, formalism presents an uncompromising version of law's internal coherence and of the consequent possibility of distinguishing the juridical from the political. Its extremism can be seen from the contrast with the currently dominant modes of legal scholarship. Three approaches are particularly popular and significant: interpretation, economic analysis, and Critical Legal Studies. I wish to conclude with a criticism – suggestive rather than exhaustive – of each of these approaches.

First, in contemporary writing the internal intelligibility of law is dealt with under the rubric of interpretation.[130] The task of expounding the law's internal dimension is said to be subject to whatever constraints are felt to pervade any interpretive community or are inherent in the nature of interpretation. The phenomenon of interpretation is invoked both because it is familiar to lawyers and because its operation in law can be illuminated by reference to other intellectual domains, especially literary ones. The reference to non-legal interpretive enterprises, however, merely distances us from the task at hand. In the absence of an exposition of the specifically juridical nature of interpretation as applied to law, the appeal to the general phenomenon of interpretation is merely a restatement of the problem that profitlessly enlarges its scope. For it implies that interpretation in literature is a more lucid exercise than interpretation in law, so that the former can cast light on the latter. This ignores the possibility – prominent in hermeneutic writing[131] – that law is itself exemplary for the understanding of interpretation and that therefore one must grasp the nature of legal interpretation before one can grasp the nature of interpretation more

generally. Legal formalism supplies the compass points for the specifically juridical interpretation of interaction. From a perspective internal to the law's content, formalism draws out the implications of a sophisticated legal system's tendency to coherence by making explicit the justificatory patterns to which the content of such a system must conform. It thus carries the internal impetus of interpretation forward to its ultimate degree.[132]

In economic analysis the striving of legal doctrine for economic efficiency is what makes the law coherent. Economic efficiency, however, is a deeply flawed vehicle for the coherence of law. First of all, although efficiency is trumpeted as carrying the implicit logic of the common law,[133] it cannot account for the normative quality that attaches immediately to the holdings of private law.[134] Moreover, the hypothesis of the efficiency of law deals only with the law's specific determinations and not with the structure of thought internal to the law from which these determinations emerge as conclusions or specifications.[135] Consequently economic analysis treats legal results as understandable independent of their indigenous framework of justification. In this way economic analysis is detached from the most internally intelligible aspect of the law. Finally, efficiency is itself composed of a number of considerations – efficiency in incentives that minimize the risk of undesirable outcomes, efficiency in insurance incentives for bearing the risk, efficiency in the administration of legal rules[136] – that are not conceptually integrated and therefore exert competing pressures. Accordingly, in contrast to the notion of juridical form, the goal of efficiency stands to law as something that is neither moral, nor immanent, nor coherent.

Finally, the scholarship of Critical Legal Studies, provides the starkest contrast to the view presented here. Critical Legal Studies denies that law expresses or can express any notion of coherence, either immanent or extrinsic. In the absence of comprehensive frameworks through which the law can be understood, legal determination is dissolved into the particularity of choice. Pretending otherwise merely disguises the oppression of power under the specious vocabulary of right.

We can do no more than attend to the very bruteness of our choosings, all the while remaining conscious of the inevitably political nature of our collective decisions. To sanctify some choices as legal rather than political is to indulge in the vanity of myth.

Formalism asserts that this myth is true after all. For the formalist, the salutary contribution of Critical Legal Studies is to show that once we step outside the most rigorous notion of internal coherence, the slide to nihilism is swift and easy. In this sense, Critical Legal Studies captures the essence of contemporary scholarship by accentuating – and then exploding – its makeshift compromises. The significance of Critical Legal Studies is that it forces us to confront anew the problem of coherence in law. It raises the eternal question of legal philosophy, and presents us with its own skeptical answer.

In claiming that that answer is wrong, formalism gives voice to the most ancient aspirations of natural law theorizing by construing the law as permeated by reason. The forms of justice represent the conceptual structures applicable to the understanding of juridical phenomena, and the content of law is intelligible to the extent that its justifications express these structures. Because the forms are implicit in external interaction, they are present in everyday life, are accessible to the workaday jurists who take up the task of legal elaboration, and are reflected in whatever coherence sophisticated legal cultures attain. In the formalist understanding law is not the realization of a utopian project. It is, nonetheless, a supreme achievement of mind.

Notes

1   In his introduction to the symposium "Perspectives on Critical Legal Studies," Mark Tushnet identifies the attack on all types of formalism as one of the themes at the heart of the Critical Legal Studies approach. Tushnet, *Introduction*, 52 GEO. WASH. L. REV. 239 (1984). The Critical Legal Studies attack on liberal political theory is related to its attack on formalism, because liberal theory is considered to depend on formalism. Tushnet views formalism as claiming "that some type of analysis provides a solution to problems of legal choice, policy choice, or social analysis by limiting the range of pure choice within which the analyst – judge, policy-maker, social scientist – operates." *Id.* at 239.

2   Even when a distinction between legal and political justification is asserted, the distinction itself is justified in terms of a political vision. Accordingly, the Critical Legal Studies movement's trumpeting of the primacy of the political over the legal secures a position that is no longer contested. *See, e.g.,* R. DWORKIN, A MATTER OF PRINCIPLE (1985). (Part One of which is entitled "The Political Basis of Law"). Dworkin states that his conception of law is "deeply and thoroughly political." *Id.* at 146.

3   Posner, *The Decline of Law as an Autonomous Discipline: 1962–1987*, 100 HARV. L. REV. 761 (1987).

4   For an overview of this characteristic of contemporary scholarship see Weinrib, *Law as a Kantian Idea of Reason*, 87 COLUM. L. REV. 472, 474–78 (1987).

5   *See, e.g.,* Calabresi, *Concerning Cause and the Law of Torts: An Essay for Harry Kalven, Jr.*, 43 U. CHI. L. REV. 69, 100–08 (1975) (discussing functional advantages of seeing causation as interplay of different goals).

6   This commonality makes Critical Legal Studies dependent on formalism in two ways. First, the radical denial of legal coherence presupposes a grasp of what coherence might be and thus of what the formalist asserts. Without such a grasp, Critical Legal Studies risks misconceiving the target and thus firing to no effect. Second, the Critical Legal Studies practice of the immanent critique of legal doctrine presupposes a conception of the immanent, since one cannot properly criticize law from the inside without understanding the nature of the law's internality. However, although Critical Legal Studies depends on conceptions of the coherent and the immanent, no satisfactory account of these conceptions can be found either within its literature or (at least in contemporary scholarship) outside it. This essay, accordingly, attempts to supply the missing account of the law's immanent coherence.

7   For reliance on the law's internal point of view by philosophers of different persuasions see J. FINNIS, NATURAL LAW AND NATURAL RIGHTS 11–18 (1980); L. FULLER, THE MORALITY OF

LAW 33–94 (1964); H.L.A. HART, THE CON-
CEPT OF LAW 86–88 (1961); J. RAZ, PRAC-
TICAL REASON AND NORMS 170–77 (1975).

8   Unger, *The Critical Legal Studies Movement*,
96 HARV. L. REV. 561, 563–76 (1983). Reference to this well-known account guarantees
that my defense engages the anti-formalist con-
tentions to which it purports to respond. Moreover, the conception of formalism Unger
presents is (as he rightly points out, *see infra*
note 14) presupposed in the thinking of orthodox lawyers, so that it implicitly informs whatever assumptions are current concerning law's
internal order.

9   Unger, *supra* note 8, at 564.

10 *Id.* at 565.

11 *Id.*

12 *Id.* In Unger's terminology this feature is a
characteristic of objectivism rather than formalism. Unger seems to distinguish between formalism and objectivism only because "[t]he
modern lawyer may wish to keep his formalism
while avoiding objectivist assumptions." *Id.*
Since Unger himself considers (correctly in my
view) such a distinction to be untenable, we may
regard objectivism as an aspect of formalism.

13 *Id.* at 571.

14 The description reflects legal formalism both as
it has been understood in the philosophic tradition of natural law and natural right and as it is
presupposed in the ideal of coherence to which
sophisticated legal systems aspire. According to
the natural law tradition, law is a rational
ordering that cannot be understood apart from
the good which it functions to promote. The
classic account is by St. Thomas Aquinas, in
T. AQUINAS, *Treatise on Law*, in SUMMA
THEOLOGICA I–II, QQ. 90–105, and in THE
POLITICAL IDEAS OF ST. THOMAS AQUINAS
3–91 (D. Bigongiari ed. 1953). For recent expositions, see J. FINNIS, *supra* note 7; H. VEATCH,
HUMAN RIGHTS: FACTS OR FANCY (1985).
In the natural right tradition, law is the realization of the requirements of the rational will,
which is initially characterized by a capacity to
abstract from particular conceptions of the good.
See G. HEGEL, THE PHILOSOPHY OF RIGHT
(T. Knox trans. 1952); I. KANT, THE META-
PHYSICAL ELEMENTS OF JUSTICE (J. Ladd
trans. 1965). These traditions postulate a version
of formalism that has implications for the law's
content. This formalism is therefore distinguishable from the thinner formalism of positivism,
which contrasts the formal principle of legal

validity with the material content of law and
thus makes the notion of law as such indifferent
to the law's content. *See* H. KELSEN, GENERAL
THEORY OF LAW AND STATE (A. Wedberg
trans. 1945); *cf.* Hegel, *Prefatory Lectures on the
Philosophy of Law*, 8 CLIO 49 (A. Brudner trans.
1978):

> Positive jurisprudence has for its content authoritative
> law, all the laws that have validity in a state, and that
> have validity by virtue of being posited.... We
> are here concerned, first of all, with the form of law
> as the latter is an object for positive jurisprudence; the
> content will be given afterwards. The form is this:
> the law is valid whether the content is rational and
> intrinsically [*an und für sich*] just, or whether it is
> extremely irrational, unjust, completely arbitrary, and
> given by the authority of external force. The bare fact
> of being, of having authority, says nothing about
> worth.

Id. at 62. Since positivism does not construe law
as "an immanent moral rationality," its version
of formalism is implicitly excluded from Unger's
description, and it also falls outside the scope of
this essay.

A noteworthy feature of Unger's account of
formalism is that he now expressly refuses to
equate formalism with "the search for a method
of deduction from a gapless system of rules."
Unger, *supra* note 8, at 564. He thereby expands
the characterization of formalism that appeared
in his own earlier work, *see* R. UNGER, KNOW-
LEDGE AND POLITICS 92 (1975), and in the
work of others, *see, e.g.,* Kennedy, *Legal Formality*, 2 J. LEGAL STUD. 351 (1973); Schauer,
Formalism, 97 YALE L. J. 509 (1988). Unger's
account now includes the invocation of all
impersonal formulations of legal content, including principles that do not deductively yield determinate conclusions. The relation between
formalism and indeterminacy is discussed *infra*
Section VI.

The felicity of Unger's description undermines the only criticism he makes of formalism.
Unger's argument is one of probability. Formalism is

> unlikely to prove compatible with a broad range
> of the received understandings.... [Because] [t]he
> many conflicts of interest and vision that law-
> making involves, fought out by countless minds and
> wills working at cross-purposes, would have to be
> the vehicle of an immanent moral rationality whose
> message could be articulated by a single cohesive
> theory.

Unger, *supra* note 8, at 571. But Unger himself immediately points out that the compatibility of formalism and legal doctrine is "tacitly presupposed by the unreflective common sense of orthodox lawyers." *Id.* If the efforts of the legal profession (and of the judges drawn from its midst) are animated by this shared presupposition, the "countless minds and wills" that contribute to the elaboration of law may not in fact be "working at cross-purposes." At least, the tacit adherence to a common presupposition may cut down the odds of the incompatibility Unger postulates.

15 Its rationality, for instance, consists in its being immanent to the normative relationships that it orders. Similarly, the law's normativity is a function of its success in embodying in its doctrines and institutions the rationality inherent to them.

16 Although the significance of rationality and normativity is highly controversial, they are at least recognizable as terms of contemporary academic discourse.

17 *See, e.g.*, R. POSNER, ECONOMIC ANALYSIS OF LAW (3d ed. 1986); Posner, *Utilitarianism, Economics, and Legal Theory*, 8 J. LEGAL STUD. 103 (1979).

18 *See, e.g.*, G. CALABRESI, THE COSTS OF ACCIDENTS (1970).

19 *See, e.g.*, Epstein, *A Theory of Strict Liability*, 2 J. LEGAL STUD. 151 (1973).

20 *See, e.g.*, R. EPSTEIN, TAKINGS (1985).

21 *See, e.g.*, R. UNGER, PASSION: AN ESSAY ON PERSONALITY (1984).

22 *See* H. KELSEN, PURE THEORY OF LAW 2–10 (M. Knight trans. 1967).

23 In John Austin's famous formulation: "The existence of law is one thing; its merit or demerit is another." J. AUSTIN, THE PROVINCE OF JURISPRUDENCE DETERMINED 184 (1832). For a modern treatment, see Hart, *Positivism and the Separation of Law and Morals*, 71 HARV. L. REV. 593 (1958).

24 *See, e.g.*, Fiss, *The Supreme Court, 1978 Term – Foreword: The Forms of Justice*, 93 HARV. L. REV. 1, 41 (1979).

25 No doubt part of the unpopularity of legal formalism is based on the aversion of academic lawyers in the United States to this tradition. Rationalism has the reputation of being enmeshed in an arid conceptualism and encumbered with profitless metaphysical baggage. It is therefore regarded as incompatible with the pragmatic nature of legal analysis. The very fact that this tradition is now so remote should, however, make contemporary scholars leery of dismissing legal formalism as facilely as they do. Just as they are no longer familiar with what gives formalism its strength, so they perhaps ascribe unreal weaknesses to it. Having lost contact with the vocabulary, the philosophical literature and the conceptual apparatus that nourished legal formalism, can they be confident that their present rejection is based on anything more than an ignorant caricature?

26 The positive law is immanently rational to the extent that it captures and reflects the contours of rationality that are internal to the relationships that law governs.

27 I shall hereafter use the term "juridical" in its etymological sense to refer to that which is declaratory of *jus* and which thereby represents an essentially legal mode of intelligibility.

28 This essay is about law as a mode of ordering, not as a set of posited norms. Inasmuch as law is a mode of ordering, it has a capacity for coherence. My concern is with the nature of the coherence applicable to juridical relationships. Although I assume that there are legal systems that value coherence, *see infra* note 42, I make no claim about the extent to which the positive law of any jurisdiction (or set of jurisdictions) has achieved coherence.

29 Determinacy is discussed *infra* Section VI-C.

30 For a contemporary treatment of form, see A. BERNDTSON, POWER, FORM, AND MIND 105–24 (1981). Form has recently been discussed from the deconstructive standpoint. *See* H. STATEN, WITTGENSTEIN AND DERRIDA 4–19 (1984). For the classic modern treatment of form as an Aristotelian notion, see J. OWENS, THE DOCTRINE OF BEING IN THE ARISTOTELIAN 'METAPHYSICS' 307–99 (3d ed. 1978). Twentieth-century legal philosophers who have paid attention to the significance of form are G. DEL VECCHIO, THE FORMAL BASES OF LAW 68–80 (J. Lisle trans. 1921); M. OAKESHOTT, ON HUMAN CONDUCT 3–8 (1975) (understanding in terms of ideal character); and R. STAMMLER, THE THEORY OF JUSTICE 167–69 (I. Husik trans. 1925). Emilio Betti has defined form as "an homogeneous structure in which a number of perceptible elements are related to one another and which is suitable for preserving the character of the mind that created it or that is embodied in it." Betti, *Hermeneutics as the General Methodology of the* Geisteswissenschaften, in CONTEMPORARY HERMEN-

EUTICS 54 (J. Bleicher ed. 1980). For a recent treatment of related issues, see S. MEIKLE, ESSENTIALISM IN THE THOUGHT OF KARL MARX 153–74 (1985).

31 *See* G. HEGEL, THE PHILOSOPHY OF RIGHT, *supra* note 14, at 2 ("What we have to do with here is philosophical *science*, and in such science content is essentially bound up with form."); *cf.* G. HEGEL, THE PHILOSOPHY OF MIND (ENCYCLOPEDIA OF THE PHILOSOPHICAL SCIENCES) § 383, at 12 (W. Wallace trans. 1971) ("[F]or form in its most concrete signification is reason as speculative knowing, and content is reason as the substantial essence of actuality, whether ethical or natural. The known identity of these two is the philosophic idea.").

32 The differentiation is illustrated by Aquinas:

[T]he essence or nature includes only what falls within the definition of the species; as humanity includes all that falls within the definition of man, for it is by this that man is man, and it is this that humanity signifies, that, namely, whereby man is man. Now individual matter, with all the individuating accidents, does not fall within the definition of the species. For this particular flesh, these bones, this blackness or whiteness, etc., do not fall within the definition of a man. Therefore this flesh, these bones, and the accidental qualities designating this particular matter, are not included in humanity; and yet they are included in the reality which is a man. Hence, the reality which is a man has something in it that humanity does not have. Consequently, humanity and a man are not wholly identical, but humanity is taken to mean the formal part of a man, because the principles whereby a thing is defined function as the formal constituent in relation to individuating matter.

T. AQUINAS, SUMMA THEOLOGICA I., Q. 3, Art. 3, in INTRODUCTION TO ST. THOMAS AQUINAS 29 (A. Pegis ed. 1948).

33 Stammler, *Fundamental Tendencies in Modern Jurisprudence*, (pts. 1 & 2), 21 MICH. L. REV. 862, 883 (1922–1923).

34 J. LOCKE, AN ESSAY CONCERNING HUMAN UNDERSTANDING book III, ch. VI, § 30 (P. Nidditch ed. 1975).

35 The characteristics of a juridical relationship are not predicates ascribed it by outside observers, but are the concepts (and the corresponding doctrines and institutions) that make up its interior structure.

36 For an explication of the notion of an "exhibition of intelligence," see M. OAKESHOTT, *supra* note 30, at 13–15.

37 G. HEGEL, HEGEL´S LOGIC 190 (W. Wallace trans. 1975).

38 The point can be put in Kantian terms. Jurisprudence belongs to the realm of freedom, for which reason's principles are constitutive, whereas the principles for the interpretation of specific natural phenomena are merely regulative. *See, e.g.,* I. KANT, THE CRITIQUE OF JUDGEMENT 8 (J. Meredith trans. 1952). Kant suggests that the latter are thought of by analogy to the former. *Id.* at 20.

39 The canonical texts for this argument in epistemology and philosophy of science are T. KUHN, THE STRUCTURE OF SCIENTIFIC REVOLUTIONS (2d ed. 1970) and R. RORTY, PHILOSOPHY AND THE MIRROR OF NATURE (1979). For examples of the argument in legal theory, see Caudill, *Disclosing Tilt: A Partial Defence of Critical Legal Studies and a Comparative Introduction to the Philosophy of the Law-Idea,* 72 IOWA L. REV. 287, 305 (1987); Hutchinson & Monahan, *Law, Politics and the Critical Legal Scholars: The Unfolding Drama of American Legal Thought,* 36 STAN. L. REV. 199, 219–20 (1984); Singer, *The Player and the Cards: Nihilism and Legal Theory,* 94 YALE L. J. 1, 34 (1984).

40 For a recent defense of rationalism against the attacks of Kuhn and Feyerabend, see W. NEWTON-SMITH, THE RATIONALITY OF SCIENCE (1981).

41 Compare the following comments on Spinoza's rationalistic method:

[A] basic assumption of this method is that thought must find a resting place in a single first principle, which not only serves to explain everything else, but which is perfectly intelligible in its own right. Moreover, since a first principle cannot, by definition be explained in terms of anything prior, it must somehow be self-explicating or self-justifying. Anything less would fail to satisfy the demands of thought, for it would provide us with a principle of explanation that itself stands in need of explanation, and this would obviously lead to an infinite regress and be cause for hopeless skepticism.

H. ALLISON, BENEDICT DE SPINOZA: AN INTRODUCTION 60–61 (rev. ed. 1987).

42 In this essay, I often refer to a "sophisticated legal system," by which I mean a legal system that values coherence and, accordingly, has a tendency toward it. I assume that most readers of this essay will know of such systems from their own study or experience. In my opinion, the "great" legal systems (e.g., the common law,

Roman law and its civil law offspring, Talmudic law) are sophisticated in this sense. Reference to a sophisticated legal system is a way of making available insight drawn from the legal doctrines, concepts, and institutions with which we are familiar. Not every phenomenon that satisfies the positivist criteria of a legal system, *see, e.g.*, H. L. A. HART, THE CONCEPT OF LAW 77–96 (1961), is sophisticated in my sense, nor has every (or any) sophisticated legal system achieved the coherence toward which it tends. My concern here is with the nature of coherence, not with the mechanics through which the valuing of coherence is manifested or the tendency toward it is operative.

43 For an outstanding example of this kind of distillation, see H. HART & A. SACKS, THE LEGAL PROCESS: BASIC PROBLEMS IN THE MAKING AND APPLICATION OF LAW (tent. ed. 1958).

44 *See, e.g.*, McLoughlin v. O'Brian, [1983] 2 App. Cas. 410 (H.L.) (damages recoverable for nervous shock).

45 *See, e.g.*, Kline v. 1500 Massachusetts Ave. Apartment Corp., 439 F.2d 477 (D.C. Cir. 1970) (landlord has duty to protect tenants against criminals when landlord had notice).

46 *See, e.g.*, Li v. Yellow Cab Co. of Cal., 13 Cal. 3d 804, 532 P.2d 1226, 119 Cal. Rptr. 858 (1975) (adoption of comparative negligence rule made prospective).

47 *See, e.g.*, Coase, *The Problem of Social Cost*, 3 J.L. & ECON. 1 (1960).

48 Often, those who wish to defend the centrality of these features can do no more than baldly reiterate that what has been impugned is deeply embedded in our comprehension of the situation at hand. For example, Richard Epstein attempts to stave off the implications of the Coase theorem by (1) pointing to the transitive verbs used by Coase himself, and (2) distinguishing between causal reciprocity and the notion of redress for harm caused. R. EPSTEIN, *supra* note 19, at 164–65. Epstein does not explain (1) why linguistic structure overbears economic insight, or (2) how Coase can be refuted by rehashing the very distinction that Coase's analysis challenges. Epstein's assertion that a normative theory of torts must take into account common sense notions of individual responsibility is a conclusion that is consequent on the dismissal of economic analysis, not a reason for dismissing it. *Id.* at 151, 164.

49 For a detailed account, see Weinrib, *Causation and Wrongdoing*, 63 CHI.-KENT L. REV. 407 (1987).

50 Michael Oakeshott distinguishes two meanings of conceivability. The first refers to what can, as a merely psychological matter, be pictured or brought together in the mind. The second relates to what can be maintained as a coherent unity. A conceptual monstrosity is something that is conceivable in the first but not in the second of Oakeshott's two senses. *See* M. OAKESHOTT, EXPERIENCE AND ITS MODES 35–36 (1933).

51 G. CALABRESI, *supra* note 18, at 39–45.

52 *See* H. STEINER, MORAL ARGUMENT AND SOCIAL VISION IN THE COURTS 76–78 (1987). A specific example of loss-spreading is discussed *infra* note 119 and accompanying text.

53 Compare Kant's comments on the regulative employment of the ideas of reason:

If we consider in its whole range the knowledge obtained for us by the understanding, we find that what is peculiarly distinctive of reason in its attitude to this body of knowledge, is that it prescribes and seeks to achieve its *systematization*, that is, to exhibit the connection of its parts in conformity with a single principle. This unity of reason always presupposes an idea, namely, that of the form of a whole of knowledge – a whole which is prior to the determinate knowledge of the parts and which contains the conditions that determine *a priori* for every part its position and relation to the other parts.... The hypothetical employment of reason has, therefore, as its aim the systematic unity of the knowledge of understanding, and this unity is the *criterion of the truth* of its rules.

I. KANT, CRITIQUE OF PURE REASON 534–35 (N. Smith trans. 1929) (emphasis in original).

54 Recall Parmenides' claim at the dawn of philosophy that his thinking had penetrated to the "untrembling heart of well-circled truth." H. DIELS & W. KRANZ, DIE FRAGMENTE DER VORSOKRATIKER, Parmenides, fragment 1, line 29 (5th ed. 1952) (translated by author). Similarly, Hegel writes:

Philosophy forms a circle. It has a beginning, an immediate factor (for it must somehow make a start), something unproved which is not a result. But the *terminus a quo* of philosophy is simply relative, since it must appear in another terminus as a *terminus ad quem*. Philosophy is a sequence which does not hang in the air; it is not something which begins from nothing at all; on the contrary, it circles back into itself.

G. HEGEL., THE PHILOSOPHY OF RIGHT, *supra* note 14, at 225; *see also* G. HEGEL, HEGEL'S LOGIC, *supra* note 37, at 23. For instances of professed circularity in contemporary philosophy, see H. GADAMER, TRUTH AND METHOD 235–45 (1975) (discussing hermeneutic circle); N. GOODMAN, FACT, FICTION AND FORECAST 64 (4th ed. 1983) (discussing "virtuous circle").

55   For a conspicuous example of an ungrounded starting point, see J. BENTHAM, AN INTRODUCTION TO THE PRINCIPLES OF MORALS AND LEGISLATION 6 (London 1823) (renouncing the need to prove the principle of utility because "that which is used to prove every thing else, cannot itself be proved: a chain of proofs must have their commencement somewhere").

56   Compare Hegel's comments on refutation:

> [T]he refutation must not come from outside, that is, it must not proceed from assumptions lying outside the system in question and inconsistent with it. The system need only refuse to recognize those assumptions....The genuine refutation must penetrate the opponent's stronghold and meet him on his own ground; no advantage is gained by attacking him somewhere else and defeating him where he is not.

G. HEGEL, SCIENCE OF LOGIC 580–81 (A. Miller trans. 1969).

57   *See* ARISTOTLE, NICOMACHEAN ETHICS 115–23 (M. Ostwald trans. 1962). For a discussion of this text, see Weinrib, *Aristotle's Forms of Justice*, 2 RATIO JURIS 211 (1989).

58   By *external* dealings, *external* interaction, and *external* relations in this paragraph and hereinafter, I do not mean to point merely to a locus of physical impact outside the actor, but to a subject matter that is understood under the aspect of the parties' mutual externality, as when the separateness of their interests is conceived as the defining feature of their relationship. Thus, although in a loving relationship one person impacts externally on the other, it would not be a loving relationship unless each person identified the other's good with his or her own; such a relationship is not intelligible under the aspect of the lovers' mutual externality and is accordingly not external in the sense relevant here. Similarly, although virtuous actions affect others, the intelligibility of virtue lies in the character of the actor, not in the mutual externality of the actor and the party affected. As Aquinas put it:

> The virtues and vices...are concerned with the passions, for there we consider in what way a man may be internally influenced by reason of the passions; but we do not consider what is externally done, except as something secondary, inasmuch as external operations originate from internal passions. However, in treating justice and injustice we direct our principal attention to what a man does externally; how he is influenced internally we consider only as a byproduct, namely, according as he is helped or hindered in the [external] operation.

1   T. AQUINAS, COMMENTARY ON THE Nicomachean Ethics 384 (C. Litzinger trans. 1964). Thus virtue and justice can be "the same in substance but different in concept." *Id.* at 391 (commenting on ARISTOTLE, *supra* note 57, at 114–15). I neither claim nor imply that the external relationships are in any way superior to love or virtue. My focus throughout is on the intelligibility of external relationships, not on their desirability as compared to other kinds of relationship.

59   *See* ARISTOTLE, *supra* note 57, at 117–20.

60   *See* Lee, *The Legal Background of Two Passages in the* Nicomachean Ethics, 31 CLASSICAL Q. 129 (1937).

61   Aristotle is particularly interested in the structure of the relationship for which the award of damages (or the equivalent specific relief) is a rational response to the commission of the wrong. Since what matters is the conceptual structure of the relationship between the actor and the victim, his analysis does not require that a wrong actually have taken place or that damages actually have been awarded. His remarks are therefore as applicable to an injunction that prospectively restrains a wrong as to damages that retrospectively repair a wrong.

62   *See* Weinrib, *supra* note 49, at 429–32, 438–44.

63   A detailed formalist exposition of contract doctrine is contained in Benson, The Executory Contract in Natural Law (1986) (unpublished paper on file with author).

64   Kelly v. Solari, 152 Eng. Rep. 24 (Ex. Ch. 1841).

65   On the relationship between corrective justice and criminal law, see *infra* note 73.

66   These are substantive ideals in today's non-formalistic discourse, where Aristotle's terminology survives divorced from the mode of thought that gives it vitality. *See, e.g.*, R. NOZICK, ANARCHY, STATE, AND UTOPIA 150 (1974) (distributive justice as what justice requires concerning holdings); Coleman, *Moral Theories of Torts: Their Scope and Limits: Part II*, 2 LAW & PHIL. 5, 6

(1983) (corrective justice as the annulling of wrongful gains and losses); Epstein, *Nuisance Law: Corrective Justice and its Utilitarian Constraints*, 8 J. LEGAL STUD. 49, 50 (1979) (corrective justice as redress for plaintiff of any violation of his rights); Posner, *The Concept of Corrective Justice*, 10 J. LEGAL STUD. 187, 201 (1981) (corrective justice as wealth maximization).

67 *See* R. NOZICK, *supra* note 66, at 155–60.

68 *Id.* at 160.

69 The distinction which Aristotle draws in NICO-MACHEAN ETHICS, *supra* note 57, at 120, is made perspicuous by Aquinas:

He [Aristotle] says first that the just thing that exists in transactions agrees somewhat with the just thing directing distributions in this – that the just thing is equal, and the unjust thing, unequal. But they differ in the fact that the equal in commutative justice is not observed according to that proportionality, viz., geometrical, which was observed in distributive justice, but according to arithmetical proportionality which is observed according to equality of quantity, and not according to equality of proportion as in geometry. By arithmetical proportionality six is a mean between eight and four, because it is in excess of the one and exceeds the other by two. But there is not the same proportion on the one side and the other, for six is to four in a ratio of three to two while eight is to six in a ratio of four to three. On the contrary by geometrical proportionality the mean is exceeded and exceeds according to the same proportion but not according to the same quantity. In this way six is a mean between nine and four, since from both sides there is a three to two ratio. But there is not the same quantity, for nine exceeds six by three and six exceeds four by two.

T. AQUINAS, *supra* note 58, at 410; *cf.* ARISTOTLE, *supra* note 57, at 42–44 (discussing medians in emotions and actions).

70 On the difference between corrective justice and dispute resolution, see Weinrib, *Adjudications and Public Values: Fiss' Critique of Corrective Justice*, 39 U. TORONTO L.J. (1989).

71 In the tradition upon which I am drawing, the structure of bipolar correction is portrayed in a number of ways. Aristotle portrays it as the restoration of the antecedent equality of two lines. *See* ARISTOTLE, *supra* note 57, at 122–23. Kant explicates the idea as effect and counter-effect or action and reaction. *See* I. KANT, *supra* note 14, at 35–36; I. KANT, *On the Common Saying: 'This May Be True in Theory, But It Does Not Apply in Practice,'* in KANT'S POLITICAL WRITINGS 61, 76 (H. Reiss ed. 1970). Hegel describes it as negation

of a negation. G. HEGEL, THE PHILOSOPHY OF RIGHT, *supra* note 14, at 71–74.

72 Aristotle's discussion bears on a matter of recent controversy. Peter Westen argued that the rhetoric of equality should be abandoned because equality is a formal relationship derived from anterior substantive prescriptions and is therefore empty. *See* Westen, *The Empty Idea of Equality*, 95 HARV. L. REV. 537 (1982). For the ensuing debate, see Greenawalt, *How Empty is the Idea of Equality?*, 83 COLUM. L. REV. 1167 (1983); Westen, *To Lure the Tarantula from Its Hole: A Response*, 83 COLUM. L. REV. 1186 (1983); Burton, *Comment on "Empty Ideas": Logical Positivist Analyses of Equality and Rules*, 91 YALE L.J. 1136 (1982); Westen, *On "Confusing Ideas": Reply*, 91 YALE L.J. 1153 (1982); Chemerinsky, *In Defense of Equality: A Reply to Professor Westen*, 81 MICH. L. REV. 575 (1983). The entire debate seems to miss the following fundamental point that lies at the core of Aristotle's discussion. Even if equality is formal – indeed because equality is formal – it is situated in the two *different* formal structures of corrective and distributive justice. It therefore operates with respect to two different kinds of juridical relationship and with respect to two different kinds of normative prescription. Since the formalism of equality expresses difference, equality is formal without being empty: The formal equality of each form of justice has at least the negative content of excluding the formal equality appropriate to the other. Indeed (if my argument in this section is correct) this formal difference in the significance of equality marks the most basic division in juridical thought. Westen's work is an elaboration of an argument that Hans Kelsen directed against Aristotle. *See* Westen, *The Empty Idea of Equality*, *supra*, at 543; Westen, *On Confusing Ideas: Reply*, *supra*, at 1157. For Kelsen's argument, see H. KELSEN, *Aristotle's Doctrine of Justice*, in WHAT IS JUSTICE? 110, 128–36 (1957). For a discussion of Kelsen's error, see Weinrib, *supra* note 57.

73 Criminal law has a more complex relationship to these two forms. It is not distributive justice since the norms on which criminal law insists seem to crystallize conspicuous wrongs rather than to embody the proportionate distributions of benefits and burdens. (For a different view, see H. MORRIS, *Persons and Punishment*, in ON GUILT AND INNOCENCE 31 (1976), arguing that the criminal upsets the distribution of

benefits and burdens by taking an unfair advantage in a system of mutual constraints. This view has recently been effectively criticized by R. DUFF, TRIALS AND PUNISHMENTS 205–17 (1986).) Rather, criminal law falls under corrective justice, since it presupposes the special significance of doing and suffering. Criminal law diverges from tort law in two respects. First, a criminal wrong requires *mens rea*, whereas a tort can result from the defendant's failure to live up to an objectively reasonable standard. *See* Weinrib, *Toward a Moral Theory of Negligence Law*, 2 LAW & PHIL. 37 (1983). Second, the state rather than the private victim enforces the criminal norm. These differences between criminal law and tort law relate to corrective justice as follows. The negligent tortfeasor may violate the equality of corrective justice by implicitly mistaking what this equality requires (as where he acts to the best of his subjective capacity but falls short of the objectively reasonable standard, *see* Vaughan v. Menlove, 132 Eng. Rep. 490 (C.P. 1837)), but this mistake does not deny the applicability of such equality to his action. Tort is thus only a particular wrong to a particular victim, who can then reestablish his notionally equal position through an action for damages. In contrast, the criminal commits a willful harm, thus implicitly assigning to others the status of mere means to his own satisfaction. *Mens rea* is the expression in positive law of the criminal's setting his face against the very idea of the formal equality of corrective justice. This is not only a particular wrong to a particular victim, but an affront to the general equality of all potential doers and sufferers. Since the state is the representative of this general equality, state prosecution and punishment undoes the general wrong. For criminal law, the failure to conform to the equality of corrective justice takes the form of a wrong against the very notion of that equality. This explanation draws heavily on Hegel's *Philosophy of Right. See* G. HEGEL, THE PHILOSOPHY OF RIGHT, *supra* note 14, at 64–74. For an extended explication of Hegel's text, see Nicholson, *Hegel on Crime*, 3 HIST. POL. THOUGHT 103 (1982).

74   Some scholars see distributive justice as the general ordering principle in contract law. *See, e.g.,* Kronman, *Contract Law and Distributive Justice*, 89 YALE L.J. 472 (1980). Others see particular doctrines such as expectation damages as informed by distributive rather than corrective justice. *See, e.g.,* Fuller & Perdue, *The Reliance*

Interest in Contract Damages, 46 YALE L.J. 52, 56 (1936). This view, however, is mistaken, both on textual and on conceptual grounds. The relationship of promisor and promisee is as unmediated as the relationship of tortfeasor and victim. The immediacy of corrective justice refers not to the proximate physical sequence that is typical of tort law, but to the intelligibility of the plaintiff–defendant relationship as a bipolar one that precludes the continuous proportion of distributive justice. A contract expresses not a mediating criterion, but the terms resulting from the mutual recognition by the parties of each other as immediately interacting persons. For a detailed treatment of this, see Benson, *supra* note 63. *See also* ARISTOTLE, *supra* note 57, at 117.

75   It is sometimes said that corrective justice is derivative from distributive justice because corrective justice presupposes holdings, and holdings are a matter of distributive justice. *See, e.g.,* Radbruch, *Legal Philosophy*, in THE LEGAL PHILOSOPHIES OF LASK, RADBRUCH, AND DABIN 74 (K. Will trans. 1950). This is wrong on two accounts. First, it is not the case that the setting of holdings must necessarily be conceived as a matter of distributive justice. The Kantian and Hegelian theories of property are explicitly not theories of distributive justice. *See* I. KANT, THE PHILOSOPHY OF LAW 61–99 (W. Hastie trans. 1887); G. HEGEL, THE PHILOSOPHY OF RIGHT, *supra* note 14, at 40–57. Secondly, even if holdings were intelligible solely as distributive justice, the dependence of corrective justice on a previous distribution does not diminish the autonomy of the two forms of justice. These forms are the structures of justification applicable to external interaction. The fact that corrective justice must accept the distribution as given does not mean that the justification of the distribution is an aspect of justification in corrective justice. What matters for corrective justice is that the distribution exists, not that the distribution is justified. Corrective justice's mode of justification can operate against the background of a distribution without incorporating into its justificatory structure the justification of the distribution.

76   *See* T. AQUINAS, SUMMA THEOLOGICA II-II, Q. 61, Art. 3.

77   *See, e.g.,* Ursin, *Judicial Creativity and Tort Law*, 49 GEO. WASH. L. REV. 229 (1981).

78   For a survey of the problematic nature of these values, see J. ELY, DEMOCRACY AND DISTRUST 43–72 (1980).

79 H. HART & A. SACKS, *supra* note 43, at 162–68.

80 R. KEETON, VENTURING TO DO JUSTICE 92 (1969).

81 Moreover, since an issue can become politically controversial without its being definitively resolved, the second consideration gives those who can influence the political agenda a kind of heckler's veto over the direction of judicial activity.

82 Oakeshott, *The Vocabulary of a Modern European State* (Concluded), 23 POL. STUD. 409, 412 (1975).

83 *See* Weinrib, *supra* note 49.

84 *See* Benson, *supra* note 63.

85 For a discussion of the relevant considerations, see Blum & Kalven, *Ceilings, Costs, and Compulsion in Auto Compensation Legislation,* 1973 UTAH L. REV. 341.

86 *See, e.g.,* H. HART & A. SACKS, *supra* note 43, at 398, 662.

87 I am neither claiming nor denying that the accountability of political institutions is a *conceptual* correlate of distributive justice. This issue would require a careful consideration of the connection between political and legal theory that is beyond the scope of the present essay. It is sufficient for my purposes here that, given the existence of accountable political institutions, we can recognize that such institutions are adequate to the external orientation of distributive justice in a way that courts are not.

88 This idea has it roots in I. KANT, FOUNDATIONS OF THE METAPHYSICS OF MORALS 46 (L. Beck trans. 1959).

89 For an opposing view of equality, see Dworkin, *What is Equality? Part I: Equality of Welfare,* 10 PHIL. & PUB. AFF. 185 (1981); Dworkin, *Part II: Equality of Resources,* 10 PHIL. & PUB. AFF. 283 (1981).

90 *See* R. DWORKIN, LAW'S EMPIRE 178–84 (1986).

91 In classical terminology, the creation and the consequences of something pertains to efficient causation, not to form. *See* ARISTOTLE, PHYSICS II, § 3 (R. Hope trans. 1961).

92 *See* Williams, *The Aims of the Law of Tort,* 4 CURRENT LEGAL PROBS, 137, 144–72 (1951).

93 Private law is sheer mystery if it is considered to be solely the combination of independently valid goals. For instance, Marc Franklin's argument for a no-fault compensation scheme is animated by the irrationality of the respective plaintiffs' lottery and defendants' lottery that is set up when the independently conceived interest of each litigant is tied to his relationship with the other. *See* Franklin, *Replacing the Negligence Lottery: Compensation and Selective Reimbursement,* 53 VA. L. REV. 774 (1967). Whatever the strength of other arguments for a compensation scheme, this criticism of tort law is weak: Since its critical standpoint is external to the integrity of the delictual relationship, it is not a criticism of *tort* law but merely an ascribing to tort law of the defects of the critic's misunderstanding.

94 This conceptual dynamic is explained perfectly by Hegel in his critique of empiricism:

> In an organic relation to the manifold qualities into which the unity is divided (if they are not simply to be enumerated), one certain determinate aspect must be emphasized in order to reach a unity over this multiplicity; and that determinate aspect must be regarded as the essence of the relation. But the totality of the organic is precisely what cannot be thereby attained, and the remainder of the relation, excluded from the determinate aspect that was selected, falls under the dominion of this aspect which is elevated to be the essence and purpose of the relation. Thus, for example, to explain the relation of marriage, procreation, the holding of goods in common, or something else is proposed [as the determinant] and, from such a determinate aspect, is made prescriptive as the essence of the relation; the whole organic relation is delimited and contaminated. Or, in the case of punishment, one specific aspect is singled out – the criminal's moral reform, or the damage done, or the effect of his punishment on others, or the criminal's own notion of the punishment before he committed the crime, or the necessity of making this notion a reality by carrying out the threat, etc. And then some such single aspect is made the purpose and essence of the whole. The natural consequence is that, since such a specific aspect has no necessary connection with the other specific aspects which can be found and distinguished, there arises an endless struggle to find the necessary bearing and predominance of one over the others; and since inner necessity, non-existent in singularity, is missing, each aspect can perfectly well vindicate its independence of the other.

G. HEGEL, NATURAL LAW 60 (T. Knox trans. 1975).

95 For a specific account of the difficulties besetting instrumentalist considerations in the context of private law, see Trebilcock, *The Role of Insurance Considerations in the Choice of Efficient Liability Rules*; 4 J.L. ECON. & ORG – 243 (1988). With reference to a variety of legal situations, Trebilcock outlines the indeterminacies resulting from the attempt to achieve efficiency through judicial attention to insurance. He

classifies these indeterminacies under three headings: (i) the uncertainty generated in determining whether to confine the search for the best insurer to the immediate parties; (ii) the uncertainty over which of these two parties is the better insurer in view of the fact that the defendant can more readily estimate *ex ante* the likelihood of injury, whereas the plaintiff can more readily estimate the extent *ex ante* of the damage; and (iii) uncertainty as to trade-offs between insurance and other efficiency rationales. These three kinds of indeterminacy follow in the tracks of formalist objections to the application of extrinsic purposes to the immediate external interactions of corrective justice. The first arises from the indifference of extrinsic purpose to the immediacy of the transaction; the second from the decomposition of the unified normative relationship of doer and sufferer into aspects that are independently relevant to one or the other of them; the third from the fact that all extrinsic purposes are arbitrary with respect to the corrective justice relationship, and that therefore this arbitrariness generates uncertainties in the trade-offs possible among them. It should be noted that the difficulties Trebilcock discusses are not, as his formulations imply, mere uncertainties, similar in kind to the question of who will win the World Series fifteen years from now, for which we have at this moment too many possibilities and too little knowledge. Rather, these indeterminacies reflect the incoherence of applying to the bipolar relationships of corrective justice the extrinsic purposes available to distributive justice. This lack of fit between the normative considerations of economic analysis and the legal context is structural, not factual. Seen in this light, Trebilcock's powerful but straightforward exposition indicates why the normative economic analysis of private law can never, despite the intellectual virtuosity of its distinguished expositors, rise above unilluminating technicality.

96   *See* Unger, *supra* note 8, at 571.

97   I am not concerned here to describe or defend Kantian right (which I have done elsewhere, *see* Weinrib, *supra* note 4), but only to outline how the elements of Kant's legal philosophy are presupposed in the Aristotelian forms of justice.

98   The significance of this was first noted by Aristotle. *See* ARISTOTLE, *supra* note 57, at 120–21, 1132a2–7.

99   In this conception, no individual is synonymous with his particular determinations: Of no particular action can it be said that it could not have been otherwise.

100 *See* I. KANT, *supra* note 14, at 24; Rawls, *Kantian Constructivism and Moral Theory* 77 J. PHIL. 515, 525 (1980). It could also be termed (and its connection to my theme would be clearer if it were) "juridical personality," not only because this conception of the person is presupposed in juridical relationships, but also because law is the most primitive actualization of the freedom that exists in its potential state in the person so conceived. *See* Weinrib, *supra* note 4, at 481–85, 501–03.

     Of the two capacities that mark moral personality for Rawls, only the first, the capacity for a conception of the good, is involved here. As for the second (the capacity for a sense of justice), the coercion of law, in the Kantian view which distinguishes justice from virtue, is grounded precisely on the conceptual irrelevance of any person's having or not having this sense. *See* I. KANT, *supra* note 14, at 76. Even for Rawls, the two capacities of the moral person are not parallel. *See* Rawls, *The Basic Liberties and Their Priority*, in LIBERTY, EQUALITY AND LAW 27–30 (S. McMurrin ed. 1987).

101 Rawls characterizes the original position as "the point of view from which noumenal selves see the world." J. RAWLS, A THEORY OF JUSTICE 255 (1971).

102 *See* I. KANT, *supra* note 14, at 35.

103 For a fuller treatment of the inherent normativity of the components of Kant's legal theory, see Weinrib, *supra* note 4, at 485–87 (1987).

104 *See id.* at 489.

105 Because the forms of justice are inherently normative, the elucidation of the adequacy of a particular legal arrangement to one or the other of these is itself a normative argument. It therefore makes no sense, for instance, after the demonstration of the way in which a given private law doctrine conforms to corrective justice, to demand a separate enquiry into the normative basis of the private law doctrine. Such a demand would be the equivalent of asking "What is the color of the color green?" This fallacy has a distinguished intellectual history: Kant pointed out that Moses Mendelssohn's account of contractual obligation committed this very error. *See* I. KANT, THE PHILOSOPHY OF LAW

103–04 (W. Hastie trans. 1887); Benson, *External Freedom According to Kant*, 87 COLUM. L. REV. 559 (1987).

106   We discover the concept of corrective justice, for instance, by reflecting on the legal institutions we have and on the forms of order they presuppose. We see that particular legal holdings fit into a certain conceptual framework that makes salient the apparently fixed points of legal reasoning in a sophisticated legal culture (e.g., that a finding of negligence grows out of an adjudicated conglomerate of cause, standard of care, and causation). We can then examine the presuppositions about interaction evidenced in the components of this framework, all the while preserving the tendency toward coherence that characterizes both thought in general and sophisticated legal systems in particular. This process of regression on the conditions of private law leads to the category of corrective justice, which is, so to speak, the arch-concept in terms of which all other private law concepts must be conceptualized if they are to be coherent. And to see the forms of justice as presupposed in the concepts of a sophisticated legal system is also to see those concepts as expressive of the applicable form.

107   Compare the following response to the parallel criticism of Spinoza:

> Spinoza's method of exposition of his philosophical principles is particularly open to criticism in that he seems to begin from an abstract concept of being, which makes impossible his ever reaching the concrete reality whose nature and action it is his purpose to disclose. But what he wants to affirm is a reality that is not indeterminate but fully determinate and therefore the determinant of all lesser or derivative forms of existence. Such reality is not the negation of all characters and relations but their totality or correlation.

> Forsyth, *Spinoza's Doctrine of God in Relation to His Conception of Causality*, in STUDIES IN SPINOZA 4 (S. Kashap ed. 1972).

108   Southern Pac. Co. v. Jensen, 244 U.S. 205, 222 (1916).

109   Gordon, *Critical Legal Histories*, 36 STAN. L. REV. 57, 68 (1984).

110   *See, e.g.,* M. SANDEL, LIBERALISM AND THE LIMITS OF JUSTICE (1982); Sandel, *The Procedural Republic and the Unencumbered Self,* 12 POL. THEORY 81 (1984).

111   *See, e.g.,* Kennedy, *supra* note 14; Tushnet, *Following the Rules Laid Down: A Critique of Interpretivism and Neutral Principles,* 96 HARV. L. REV. 781 (1983).

112   The forms of justice are not forms in the Platonic sense, supposed to exist in a peculiar world of their own "on the other side of being." *See* PLATO, THE REPUBLIC 195–99 (R. Sterling & W. Scott trans. 1985) (on the form of the good). *But see* H. GADAMER, THE IDEA OF THE GOOD IN PLATONIC-ARISTOTELIAN PHILOSOPHY 27–31 (P. Smith trans. 1986) (Plato did not conceive of form of good as a trans-existent entity, but as the unity of what is unitary, i.e., as what is presupposed by anything ordered, enduring, and consistent).

113   *See* G. HEGEL, PHENOMENOLOGY OF SPIRIT 62 para. 102 (A. Miller trans. 1977).

114   A historicist critic of formalism might object that the formalist's pointing to the historical situatedness of juridical relations is beside the point because the real difficulty is with the historical intelligibility of those relations. The formalist postulates that though the forms govern historically situated relationships, the forms themselves are not *qua* abstractions historically situated. These forms are the ahistorical residue that is exposed to the historicist objection.

It is noteworthy, however, that contemporary critics of formalism do not always press their attacks so far. Even while proclaiming their historicism they recognize that the indeterminacies that reflect particular historical circumstances are embedded in an ahistorical framework of understanding. For example, Robert Gordon's justly celebrated account of historicism in legal scholarship begins with the statement that "law exists and must *to some extent* always be understood by reference to particular contexts of space and time. Gordon, *Historicism in Legal Scholarship*, 90 YALE L.J. 1017 (1981) (emphasis added); *see also id.* note 1. Gordon appears to regard this statement about law's contextual existence as antithetical to the attempt – which he stigmatizes as "rationalizing the real" – to show that "the law-making and law-applying activities that go on in our society make sense and may be rationally related to some coherent conceptual ordering scheme." *Id.* at 1018. However, Gordon's qualification of his thesis by the words "to some extent" indicates that he does not believe that law can exhaustively be understood by reference to particular contexts of space and time. His formulation implies that a residue of intelligibility survives all the particularity of historical context.

Perhaps there is good reason for such historicist self-abnegation. The attack on the ahistorical nature of formalist concepts would presumably have to be grounded in the assertion that all cognition is historically conditioned. But this would imply, paradoxically, that the assertion is itself historically conditioned. Some historicists indeed grasp this nettle boldly, if uncomfortably. *See, e.g.,* M. FOUCAULT, THE ARCHEOLOGY OF KNOWLEDGE 205 (A. Smith trans. 1972). For a discussion of the difficulties, see D. CARR, PHENOMENOLOGY AND THE PROBLEM OF HISTORY 237–59 (1974). The historicist may want to claim for his own assertions an immunity from historicism, but if so the question why the immunity extends only so far and does not include the formalist concepts remains unanswered. In this unravelling of historicism, the possibility that law "may be rationally related to some coherent conceptual ordering scheme" (in Gordon's words) cannot be categorically excluded. For this reason, the case for formalism has to be examined on its own merits, not on the basis of historicist preconceptions.

115   Their relationships are, therefore, not construed from a standpoint internal to the person by reference to virtues of character or private sentiments, however laudable, such as the loving identification by one person of the good of another with his or her own good. *See supra* note 58.

116   *See* T. AQUINAS, *supra* note 76, II-II, Q. 60, Art. 1, 3.

117   For a more extended treatment from a Kantian standpoint of the theme of externality summarized in the last two paragraphs, see Weinrib, *supra* note 4, at 491–500.

118   This function calls for a political body that is recognized as the locus of collective decision making, that can evaluate the full range of possible distributions, and that is accountable to the community as a whole for the particular ones that it selects.

119   2 All E.R. 408 (C.A.) (1981).

120   *See* W. PROSSER & W. KEETON, THE LAW OF TORTS § 44, at 301–19 (5th ed. 1984).

121   *Lamb*, 2 All E.R. at 414.

122   *Id.*

123   *Id.* at 421.

124   *Id.*

125   G. CALABRESI, *supra* note 18.

126   H. GADAMER, TRUTH AND METHOD 305 (1975). Gadamer speaks of "[t]he meaning of application that is involved in all forms of understanding...." *Id.* Although Gadamer considers legal interpretation to be paradigmatic of the hermeneutical approach to the relationship between the universal and the particular, he does not understand legal universals in terms of the formalist conceptions presented in this essay. His exposition of legal interpretation takes the form of a commentary on Aristotle's notion of equity. *See id.* at 278–89. In *Nicomachean Ethics*, Aristotle asserts that equity is:

a corrective of what is legally just. The reason is that all law is universal, but there are some things about which it is not possible to speak correctly in universal terms.... So in a situation in which the law speaks universally, but the case at issue happens to fall outside the universal formula, it is correct to rectify the shortcoming, in other words, the omission and mistake of the lawgiver due to the generality of his statement.

ARISTOTLE, *supra* note 57, at 141.

Gadamer does not relate this passage to Aristotle's discussion of the forms of justice which precedes it by several pages. There is, however, no tension between these passages. Under the rubric of equity, Aristotle analyzes a perennially difficult issue concerning positive law, when the forms of justice are made concrete through definitive statements of legal authorities. For Aristotle's discussion, it is these statements that attract the problem of infelicitous generalization, not the forms themselves.

Gadamer conceives of the universal not in terms of stable conceptual patterns (such as corrective and distributive justice), but – as Richard Bernstein summarizes his view – in terms of "those principles, norms, and laws that are founded in the life of a community and orient our particular decisions and actions." R. BERNSTEIN, PHILOSOPHICAL PROFILES 71 (1986). However, as Lord Justice Watkins' opinion in *Lamb* indicates, the significance of application is no different for the formalist's universals than it is for Gadamer's. The deep issue raised by the difference between Gadamer and the formalist is the following. Gadamer, as a representative of modernity, is situated between the "postmoderns" who postulate the utter contingency of social practices, *see id.* at 83–88, and the "premodern" conceptualists who claim that social practices can be understood through form. Is there room for such comfortable middle ground, or is his position intelligible only as a deformation of one or the other of the two extremes?

127 *See* ARISTOTLE, *supra* note 57, at 132, 1135a, 5–10 (while there are many specific acts, in each case only the universal is just); G. HEGEL, THE PHILOSOPHY OF RIGHT, *supra* note 14, at 137 (the concept merely lays down a general limit within which there is place for contingent decisions of positive law).

128 *Cf.* Radbruch, *supra* note 75, at 75 (justice is principle specific to law, not exhaustive of it).

129 ARISTOTLE, *supra* note 57, at 131.

130 Influential examples of such scholarship are Fiss, *Objectivity and Interpretation*, 34 STAN. L. REV. 739 (1982); R. DWORKIN, *supra* note 2, at 146–77.

131 *See* H. GADAMER, *supra* note 126, at 278; *see also* Hoy, *Interpreting the Law: Hermeneutical and Poststructuralist Perspectives*, 135 S. CAL. L. REV. 136, 150–51 (1985) (discussing whether law or art should be treated as the paradigm of interpretation).

132 Ronald Dworkin's Law's Empire is the most extensive attempt systematically to understand the relationship between law and interpretation. Dworkin's work is an exploration of law from the internal point of view. *See* R. DWORKIN, *supra* note 90, at 49. He characterizes interpretation as the striving to make an object the best it can be. *See id.* at 53. Dworkin's thesis is that the internal point of view necessitates, through interpretation, reference to "the best." Even if reference to "the best" is required by the internal point of view, however, is Dworkin's conception of the best itself internal to law? The matter can be put as follows: Is an interpretation best because it is internal or is it internal because it is best? Although Dworkin does not, to my knowledge, explicitly raise this issue, the answer he would give is crucial. If internality is controlling, Dworkin would be depending on an unarticulated notion of form. If on the other hand, goodness is controlling, Dworkin's theory would not be fully internal. Dworkin seems to want to have it both ways and to be simultaneously inside and outside. He takes legal interpretation to have two dimensions, fit with legal doctrine and attractiveness as an ideal of political morality, each of which influences the other. *See id.* at 231. While he does not tell us whether the second dimension is internal or external, he constantly analyzes it independently of the first, which seems unquestionably internal. Moreover, the ideal he proposes for the common law, an egalitarianism of resources, is defended as being superior to its competitor because "it fits our legal and moral practices no worse and is better in *abstract moral theory*." *Id.* at 301 (emphasis added) (footnote omitted). Since the determination of the second dimension is a matter of "abstract moral theory," its moral power is what (providing it satisfies a threshold of fit) qualifies it for admission to law. Perhaps his position can be summed up as follows: One understands law from the internal point of view, i.e., from the understanding of interpretation that this point of view contains. Interpretation, although itself an internal requirement, supplies the theorist with an import license to bring in "the best." This license is a limited one in that what the theorist can import depends on the products already circulating in the interpretive economy. The license is also limiting because the imports drive some of the domestic products out of the interpretive market. If this understanding of Dworkin is approximately correct, his view involves a jurisprudential renvoi, in which the internal notion of interpretation triggers the admission of external elements of political morality. Thus, Dworkin's standpoint is not as thoroughly internal as the formalist's.

133 *See, e.g.*, R. POSNER, ECONOMIC ANALYSIS OF LAW, *supra* note 17, at 21–22.

134 As the goal in an instrumentalist theory, efficiency does not attach immediately to private law but is independently posited on the basis of its desirability. Efficiency is also not immediate because it has no normative significance of its own and is at best a proxy for broader instrumentalist considerations. *See* Weinrib, *Utilitarianism, Economics, and Legal Theory*, 30 U. TORONTO L.J. 307 (1980).

135 *See, e.g.*, R. POSNER, ECONOMIC ANALYSIS OF LAW, *supra* note 17, at 21.

136 *See* M. POLINSKY, INTRODUCTION TO LAW AND ECONOMICS 116 (1983).

14

Law as Interpretation

Ronald Dworkin

I shall argue that legal practice is an exercise in interpretation not only when lawyers interpret particular documents or statutes but generally. Law so conceived is deeply and thoroughly political. Lawyers and judges cannot avoid politics in the broad sense of political theory. But law is not a matter of personal or partisan politics, and a critique of law that does not understand this difference will provide poor understanding and even poorer guidance. I propose that we can improve our understanding of law by comparing legal interpretation with interpretation in other fields of knowledge, particularly literature. I also expect that law, when better understood, will provide a better grasp of what interpretation is in general.

I Law

The central problem of analytical jurisprudence is this: What sense should be given to propositions of law? I mean the various statements lawyers make reporting what the law is on some question or other. Propositions of law can be very abstract and general, like the proposition that states of the United States may not discriminate on racial grounds in supplying basic services to citizens, or they can be relatively concrete, like the proposition that someone who accepts a check in the normal course of business without notice of any infirmities in its title is entitled to collect against the maker, or very concrete, like the proposition that Mrs. X

is liable in damages to Mr. Y in the amount of $1,150 because he slipped on her icy sidewalk and broke his hip. In each case a puzzle arises. What are propositions of law really about? What in the world could make them true or false?

The puzzle arises because propositions of law seem to be descriptive – they are about how things are in the law, not about how they should be – and yet it has proved extremely difficult to say exactly what it is that they describe. Legal positivists believe that propositions of law are indeed wholly descriptive: they are in fact pieces of history. A proposition of law, in their view, is true just in case some event of a designated law-making kind has taken place, and otherwise not. This seems to work reasonably well in very simple cases. If the Illinois legislature enacts the words "No will shall be valid without three witnesses," then the proposition of law, that an Illinois will needs three witnesses, seems to be true only in virtue of that historical event.

But in more difficult cases the analysis fails. Consider the proposition that a particular affirmative action scheme (not yet tested in the courts) is constitutionally valid. If that is true, it cannot be so just in virtue of the text of the Constitution and the fact of prior court decisions, because reasonable lawyers who know exactly what the Constitution says and what the courts have done may yet disagree whether it is true. (I am doubtful that the positivists' analysis holds even in the simple case of the will; but that is a different matter I shall not argue here.)

What are the other possibilities? One is to suppose that controversial propositions of law, like the affirmative action statement, are not descriptive at all but are rather expressions of what the speaker wants the law to be. Another is more ambitious: controversial statements are attempts to describe some pure objective or natural law, which exists in virtue of objective moral truth rather than historical decision. Both these projects take some legal statements, at least, to be purely evaluative as distinct from descriptive: they express either what the speaker prefers – his personal politics – or what he believes is objectively required by the principles of an ideal political morality. Neither of these projects is plausible, because someone who says that a particular untested affirmative action plan is constitutional does mean to describe the law as it is rather than as he wants it to be or thinks that, by the best moral theory, it should be. He might, indeed, say that he regrets that the plan is constitutional and thinks that, according to the best moral theory, it ought not to be.

There is a better alternative: propositions of law are not simply descriptive of legal history, in a straightforward way, nor are they simply evaluative in some way divorced from legal history. They are interpretive of legal history, which combines elements of both description and evaluation but is different from both. This suggestion will be congenial, at least at first blush, to many lawyers and legal philosophers. They are used to saying that law is a matter of interpretation; but only, perhaps, because they understand interpretation in a certain way. When a statute (or the Constitution) is unclear on some point, because some crucial term is vague or because a sentence is ambiguous, lawyers say that the statute must be interpreted, and they apply what they call "techniques of statutory construction." Most of the literature assumes that interpretation of a particular document is a matter of discovering what its authors (the legislators, or the delegates to the constitutional convention) meant to say in using the words they did. But lawyers recognize that on many issues the author had no intention either way and that on others his intention cannot be discovered. Some lawyers take a more skeptical position. They say that whenever judges pre-

tend they are discovering the intention behind some piece of legislation, this is simply a smoke screen behind which the judges impose their own view of what the statute should have been.

Interpretation as a technique of legal analysis is less familiar in the case of the common law, but not unfamiliar. Suppose the Supreme Court of Illinois decided, several years ago, that a negligent driver who ran down a child was liable for the emotional damage suffered by the child's mother, who was standing next to the child on the road. Now an aunt sues another careless driver for emotional damage suffered when she heard, on the telephone many miles from the accident, that her niece had been hit. Does the aunt have a right to recover for that damage? Lawyers often say that this is a matter of interpreting the earlier decision correctly. Does the legal theory on which the earlier judge actually relied, in making his decision about the mother on the road, cover the aunt on the telephone? Once again skeptics point out that it is unlikely that the earlier judge had in mind any theory sufficiently developed so as to decide the aunt's case either way, so that a judge "interpreting" the earlier decision is actually making new law in the way he or she thinks best.

The idea of interpretation cannot serve as a general account of the nature or truth value of propositions of law, however, unless it is cut loose from these associations with speaker's meaning or intention. Otherwise it becomes simply one version of the positivist's thesis that propositions of law describe decisions taken by people or institutions in the past. If interpretation is to form the basis of a different and more plausible theory about propositions of law, then we must develop a more inclusive account of what interpretation is. But that means that lawyers must not treat legal interpretation as an activity *sui generis*. We must study interpretation as a general activity, as a mode of knowledge, by attending to other contexts of that activity.

Lawyers would do well to study literary and other forms of artistic interpretation. That might seem bad advice (choosing the fire over the frying pan) because critics themselves are thoroughly divided about what literary interpretation is, and the situation is hardly better in the other arts. But that is exactly why lawyers should study these debates. Not all of the battles within literary criticism are edifying or even comprehensible, but many more theories of interpretation have been defended in literature than in law, and these include theories which challenge the flat distinction between description and evaluation that has enfeebled legal theory.

II   Literature

1.   *The Aesthetic Hypothesis*

If lawyers are to benefit from a comparison between legal and literary interpretation, however, they must see the latter in a certain light, and in this section I shall try to say what that is. (I would prefer the following remarks about literature to be uncontroversial among literary scholars, of course, but I am afraid they will not be.) Students of literature do many things under the titles of "interpretation" and "hermeneutics," and most of them are also called "discovering the meaning of a text." I shall not be interested, except incidentally, in one thing these students do, which is trying to discover the sense in which some author used a particular word or phrase. I am interested instead in arguments which offer some sort of interpretation of the meaning of a work as a whole. These sometimes take the form of assertions about characters: that Hamlet really loved his mother, for example, or that he really hated her, or that there really was no ghost but only Hamlet himself in a schizophrenic manifestation. Or about events in the story behind the story: that Hamlet and Ophelia were lovers before the play begins (or were not). More usually they offer hypotheses directly about the "point" or "theme" or "meaning" or "sense" or "tone" of the play as a whole: that *Hamlet* is a play about death, for example, or about generations, or about politics. These interpretive claims may have a practical point. They may guide a director staging a new performance of the play, for example. But they may also be of more general importance, helping us to an improved understanding of important

parts of our cultural environment. Of course, difficulties about the speaker's meaning of a particular word in the text (a "crux" of interpretation) may bear upon these larger matters. But the latter are about the point or meaning of the work as a whole, rather than the sense of a particular phrase.

Critics much disagree about how to answer such questions. I want, so far as is possible, not to take sides but to try to capture the disagreements in some sufficiently general description of what they are disagreeing about. My apparently banal suggestion (which I shall call the "aesthetic hypothesis") is this: an interpretation of a piece of literature attempts to show which way of reading (or speaking or directing or acting) the text reveals it as the best work of art. Different theories or schools or traditions of interpretation disagree, on this hypothesis, because they assume significantly different normative theories about what literature is and what it is for and about what makes one work of literature better than another.

I expect that this suggestion, in spite of its apparent weakness, will be rejected by many scholars as confusing interpretation with criticism or, in any case, as hopelessly relativistic, and therefore as a piece of skepticism that really denies the possibility of interpretation altogether. Indeed the aesthetic hypothesis might seem simply another formulation of a theory now popular, which is that since interpretation creates a work of art and represents only the fiat of a particular critical community, there are only interpretations and no best interpretation of any particular poem or novel or play. But the aesthetic hypothesis is neither so wild nor so weak nor so inevitably relativistic as might first appear.

Interpretation of a text attempts to show it as the best work of art it can be, and the pronoun insists on the difference between explaining a work of art and changing it into a different one. Perhaps Shakespeare could have written a better play based on the sources he used for *Hamlet* than he did, and in that better play the hero would have been a more forceful man of action. It does not follow that *Hamlet*, the play he wrote, really is like that after all. Of course, a theory of interpretation must contain a sub-theory about identity of a work of art in order to be able to tell the difference between interpreting and changing a work. (Any useful theory of identity will be controversial, so that this is one obvious way in which disagreements in interpretation will depend on more general disagreements in aesthetic theory.)

Contemporary theories of interpretation all seem to use, as part of their response to that requirement, the idea of a canonical text (or score, in the case of music, or unique physical object, in the case of most art). The text provides one severe constraint in the name of identity: all the words must be taken account of and none may be changed to make "it" a putatively better work of art. (This constraint, however familiar, is not inevitable. A joke, for example, may be the same joke though told in a variety of forms, none of them canonical; an interpretation of a joke will choose a particular way in which to put it, and this may be wholly original, in order to bring out its "real" point or why it is "really" funny.) So any literary critic's style of interpretation will be sensitive to his theoretical beliefs about the nature of and evidence for a canonical text.

An interpretive style will also be sensitive to the interpreter's opinions about coherence or integrity in art. An interpretation cannot make a work of art more distinguished if it makes a large part of the text irrelevant, or much of the incident accidental, or a great part of the trope or style unintegrated and answering only to independent standards of fine writing. So it does not follow, from the aesthetic hypothesis, that because a philosophical novel is aesthetically more valuable than a mystery story, an Agatha Christie novel is really a treatise on the meaning of death. This interpretation fails not only because an Agatha Christie, taken to be a tract on death, is a poor tract less valuable than a good mystery but because the interpretation makes the novel a shambles. All but one or two sentences would be irrelevant to the supposed theme; and the organization, style, and figures would be appropriate not to a philosophical novel but to an entirely different genre. Of course some books originally offered to the public as mysteries or thrillers (and perhaps thought of by their authors that way) have

indeed been "re-interpreted" as something more ambitious. The present critical interest in Raymond Chandler is an example. But the fact that this re-interpretation can be successful in the case of Chandler, but not Christie, illustrates the constraint of integrity.

There is nevertheless room for much disagreement among critics about what counts as integration, about which sort of unity is desirable and which irrelevant or undesirable. Is it really an advantage that the tongue of the reader, in reading a poem aloud, must "mime" motions or directions that figure in the tropes or narrative of the poem? Does this improve integrity by adding yet another dimension of coordination? Is it an advantage when conjunctions and line endings are arranged so that the reader "negotiating" a poem develops contradictory assumptions and readings as he goes on, so that his understanding at the end is very different from what it was at discrete points along the way? Does this add another dimension of complexity to unity, or does it rather compromise unity because a work of literature should be capable of having the same meaning or import when read a second time? Schools of interpretation will rise or fall in response to these questions of aesthetic theory, which is what the aesthetic hypothesis suggests.

The major differences among schools of interpretation are less subtle, however, because they touch not these quasi-formal aspects of art but the function or point of art more broadly conceived. Does literature have (primarily or substantially) a cognitive point? Is art better when it is in some way instructive, when we learn something from it about how people are or what the world is like? If so and if psychoanalysis is true (please forgive that crude way of putting it), then a psychoanalytic interpretation of a piece of literature will show why it is successful art. Is art good insofar as it is successful communication in the ordinary sense? If so, then a good interpretation will focus on what the author intended, because communication is not successful unless it expresses what a speaker wants it to express. Or is art good when it is expressive in a different sense, insofar as it has the capacity to stimulate or inform the lives of those who experience it? If so, then interpretation will place the reader (or listener or viewer) in the foreground. It will point out the reading of the work that makes it most valuable – best as a work of art – in that way.

Of course theories of art do not exist in isolation from philosophy, psychology, sociology, and cosmology. Someone who accepts a religious point of view will probably have a different theory of art from someone who does not, and recent critical theories have made us see how far interpretive style is sensitive to beliefs about meaning, reference, and other technical issues in the philosophy of language. But the aesthetic hypothesis does not assume that anyone who interprets literature will have a fully developed and self-conscious aesthetic theory. Nor that everyone who interprets must subscribe entirely to one or another of the schools I crudely described. The best critics, I think, deny that there is one unique function or point of literature. A novel or a play may be valuable in any number of ways, some of which we learn by reading or looking or listening, rather than by abstract reflection about what good art must be like or for.

Nevertheless anyone who interprets a work of art relies on beliefs of a theoretical character about identity and other formal properties of art, as well as on more explicitly normative beliefs about what is good in art. *Both* sorts of beliefs figure in the judgment that one way of reading a text makes it a better text than another way. These beliefs may be inarticulate (or "tacit"). They are still genuine beliefs (and not merely "reactions") because their force for any critic or reader can be seen at work not just on one isolated occasion of interpretation but in any number of other occasions, and because they figure in and are amenable to argument.[1] (These weak claims do not, of course, take sides in the running debate whether there are any necessary or sufficient "principles of value" in art or whether a theory of art could ever justify an interpretation in the absence of direct experience of the work being interpreted.)[2]

None of this touches the major complaint I anticipated against the aesthetic hypothesis: that it is trivial. Obviously (you might say) different interpretive styles are grounded in different theories of what art is and what it is for and what

makes art good art. The point is so banal that it might as well be put the other way around: different theories of art are generated by different theories of interpretation. If someone thinks stylistics are important to interpretation, he will think a work of art better because it integrates pronunciation and trope; if someone is attracted by deconstruction, he will dismiss reference in its familiar sense from any prominent place in an account of language. Nor does my elaboration of the hypothesis in any way help to adjudicate amongst theories of interpretation or to rebut the charge of nihilism or relativism. On the contrary, since people's views about what makes art good art are inherently subjective, the aesthetic hypothesis abandons hope of rescuing objectivity in interpretation except, perhaps, among those who hold very much the same theory of art, which is hardly very helpful.

No doubt the aesthetic hypothesis is in important ways banal – it must be abstract if it is to provide an account of what a wide variety of theories disagree about – but it is perhaps not so weak as all that. The hypothesis has the consequence that academic theories of interpretation are no longer seen as what they often claim to be – analyses of the very idea of interpretation – but rather as candidates for the best answer to the substantive question posed by interpretation. Interpretation becomes a concept of which different theories are competing conceptions. (It follows that there is no radical difference but only a difference in the level of abstraction between offering a theory of interpretation and offering an interpretation of a particular work of art.) The hypothesis denies, moreover, the sharp distinctions some scholars have cultivated. There is no longer a flat distinction between interpretation, conceived as discovering the real meaning of a work of art, and criticism, conceived as evaluating its success or importance. Of course some distinction remains because there is always a difference between saying how good a particular work can be made to be and saying how good that is. But evaluative beliefs about art figure in both these judgments.

Objectivity is another matter. It is an open question, I think, whether the main judgments we make about art can properly be said to be true or false, valid or invalid. This question is part of the more general philosophical issue of objectivity, presently much discussed in both ethics and the philosophy of language, and no one is entitled to a position who studies the case of aesthetic judgment alone. Of course no important aesthetic claim can be "demonstrated" to be true or false; no argument can be produced for any interpretation which we can be sure will commend itself to everyone, or even everyone with experience and training in the appropriate form of art. If this is what it means to say that aesthetic judgments are subjective – that they are not demonstrable – then of course they are subjective. But it does not follow that no normative theory about art is better than any other, nor that one theory cannot be the best that has so far been produced.

The aesthetic hypothesis reverses (I think to its credit) a familiar strategy. E. D. Hirsch, for example, argues that only a theory like his can make interpretation objective and particular interpretations valid.[3] This seems to me a mistake on two connected grounds. Interpretation is an enterprise, a public institution, and it is wrong to assume, a priori, that the propositions central to any public enterprise must be capable of validity. It is also wrong to assume much about what validity in such enterprises must be like – whether validity requires the possibility of demonstrability, for example. It seems better to proceed more empirically here. We should first study a variety of activities in which people assume that they have good reasons for what they say, which they assume hold generally and not just from one or another individual point of view. We can then judge what standards people accept in practice for thinking that they have reasons of that kind.

Nor is the point about reversibility – that a theory of art may depend upon a theory of interpretation as much as vice versa – an argument against the aesthetic hypothesis. I am not defending any particular explanation of how people come to have either theories of interpretation or theories of art but only a claim about the argumentative connections that hold between these theories however come by. Of course even at the level of argument these two kinds of theories are mutually reinforcing. It is

plainly a reason for doubting any theory of what an object of art is, for example, that that theory generates an obviously silly theory of interpretation. My point is exactly that the connection is reciprocal, so that anyone called upon to defend a particular approach to interpretation would be forced to rely on more general aspects of a theory of art, whether he realizes it or not. And this may be true even though the opposite is, to some extent, true as well. It would be a mistake, I should add, to count this fact of mutual dependence as offering, in itself, any reason for skepticism or relativism about interpretation. This seems to be the burden of slogans like "interpretation creates the text," but there is no more immediate skeptical consequence in the idea that what we take to be a work of art must comport with what we take interpreting a work of art to be than in the analogous idea that what we take a physical object to be must sit well with our theories of knowledge; so long as we add, in both cases, that the connection holds the other way around as well.

2. Author's Intention

The chief test of the aesthetic hypothesis lies, however, not in its resistance to these various charges but in its explanatory and particularly its critical power. If we accept that theories of interpretation are not independent analyses of what it means to interpret something but are rather based in and dependent upon normative theories of art, then we must accept that they are vulnerable to complaints against the normative theory in which they are based. It does seem to me, for example, that the more doctrinaire authors' intention theories are vulnerable in this way. These theories must suppose, on the present hypothesis, that what is valuable in a work of art, what should lead us to value one work of art more than another, is limited to what the author in some narrow and constrained sense intended to put there. This claim presupposes, as I suggested earlier, a more general thesis that art must be understood as a form of speaker-audience communication; but even that doubtful thesis turns out, on further inspection, not to support it.

Of course the intentionalists would object to these remarks. They would insist that their theory of interpretation is not an account of what is valuable in a book or poem or play but only an account of what any particular book or poem or play means and that we must understand what something means before we can decide whether it is valuable and where its value lies. And they would object that they do not say that only intentions of the author "in some narrow and constrained sense" count in fixing the meaning of his work.

In the first of these objections, the author's intention theory presents itself not as the upshot of the aesthetic hypothesis — not as the best theory of interpretation within the design stipulated by that hypothesis — but rather as a rival to it, a better theory about what kind of thing an interpretation is. But it is very difficult to understand the author's intention theory as any sort of rival to the present hypothesis. What question does it propose to answer better? Not, certainly, some question about the ordinary language or even technical meaning of the words "meaning" or "interpretation." An intentionalist cannot suppose that all his critics and those he criticizes mean, when they say "interpretation," the discovery of the author's intention. Nor can he think that his claims accurately describe what every member of the critical fraternity in fact does under the title "interpretation." If that were so, then his strictures and polemics would be unnecessary. But if his theory is not semantic or empirical in these ways, what sort of a theory is it?

Suppose an intentionalist replies: "It points out an important issue about works of literature, namely, What did the author of the work intend it to be? This is plainly an important question, even if its importance is preliminary to other equally or more important questions about significance or value. It is, in fact, what most people for a long time have called 'interpretation'. But the name does not matter, so long as the activity is recognized as important and so long as it is understood that scholars are in principle capable of supplying objectively correct answers to the question it poses."

This reply comes to this: we can discover what an author intended (or at least come to probabilistic conclusions about this), and it is important to do so for other literary purposes. But why is it important? What other purposes? Any answer will assume that value or significance in art attaches primarily to what the author intended, just because it is what the author intended. Otherwise, why should we evaluate what this style of interpretation declares to be the work of art? But then the claim that interpretation in this style is important depends on a highly controversial, normative theory of art, not a neutral observation preliminary to any coherent evaluation. Of course no plausible theory of interpretation holds that the intention of the author is always irrelevant. Sometimes it is plainly the heart of the matter, as when some issue turns on what Shakespeare meant by "hawk" as distinguished from "handsaw." But it is nevertheless controversial that we must know whether Shakespeare thought Hamlet was sane or a madman pretending to be mad in order to decide how good a play he wrote. The intentionalist thinks that we do, and that is exactly why his theory of interpretation is not a rival to the aesthetic hypothesis but rather a suitor for the crown that hypothesis holds out.

The second objection to my charge against author's intention theories may prove to be more interesting. Intentionalists make the author's state of mind central to interpretation. But they misunderstand, so far as I can tell, certain complexities in that state of mind; in particular they fail to appreciate how intentions *for* a work and beliefs *about* it interact. I have in mind an experience familiar to anyone who creates anything, of suddenly seeing something "in" it that he did not previously know was there. This is sometimes (though I think not very well) expressed in the author's cliché, that his characters seem to have minds of their own. John Fowles provides an example from popular fiction.

> When Charles left Sarah on her cliff edge, I ordered him to walk straight back to Lyme Regis. But he did not; he gratuitously turned and went down to the Dairy. Oh, but you say,

come on – what I really mean is that the idea crossed my mind as I wrote that it might be more clever to have him stop and drink milk... and meet Sarah again. That is certainly one explanation of what happened; but I can only report – and I am the most reliable witness – that the idea seemed to me to come clearly from Charles, not myself. It is not only that he has begun to gain an autonomy; I must respect it, and disrespect all my quasi-divine plans for him, if I wish him to be real.

Fowles changed his mind about how the story in *The French Lieutenant's Woman* "really" goes in the midst of writing it, if we are to credit this description. But he might also have changed his mind about some aspect of the novel's "point" years later, as he is rumored to have done after seeing the film made from his book. He might have come to see Sarah's motives very differently after reading Harold Pinter's screenplay or watching Meryl Streep play her; Pinter and Streep were interpreting the novel, and one or both of their interpretations might have led Fowles to change *his* interpretation once again. Perhaps I am wrong in supposing that this sort of thing happens often. But it happens often enough, and it is important to be clear about what it is that happens.

The intentionalist wants us to choose between two possibilities. Either the author suddenly realizes that he had a "subconscious intention" earlier, which he only now discovers, or he has simply changed his intention later. Neither of these explanations is at all satisfactory. The subconscious is in danger of becoming phlogiston here, unless we suppose some independent evidence, apart from the author's new view of his work, to suggest that he had an earlier subconscious intention. I do not mean that features of a work of art of which an author is unaware must be random accidents. On the contrary. If a novel is both more interesting and more coherent if we assume the characters have motives different from those the novelist thought of when he wrote (or if a poet's tropes and style tend to reinforce his theme in ways he did not appreciate at the time), the cause of this must in some way lie in the artist's talent. Of course there are unsolved mysteries in the psychology of creation, but the supposition of

subconscious *intentions*, unsupported by other evidence of the sort a psychoanalyst would insist on, solves no mysteries and provides no explanation. This is not crucial to the point, however, because whether or not Fowles had a subconscious intention to make Charles or Sarah different characters from the "quasi-divine plan" he thought he had, his later decisions and beliefs neither consist in nor are based on any discovery of that earlier intention. They are produced by confronting not his earlier self but the work he has produced.

Nor is any new belief Fowles forms about his characters properly called (as in the intentionalist's second suggestion) a new and discrete intention. It is not an intention about what sort of characters to create because it is a belief about what sort of characters he has created; and it is not an intention about how others should understand the book, though it may or may not include an expectation of that sort. Fowles changed his view in the course of writing his book, but he changed it, as he insists, by confronting the text he had already written, by treating its characters as real in the sense of detachable from his own antecedent designs, in short by interpreting it, and not by exploring the subconscious depths of some previous plan or finding that he had a new plan. If it is true that he changed his mind again, after seeing the film, then this was, once again, not a retrospective new intention or a rediscovered old one. It was another interpretation.

An author is capable of detaching what he has written from his earlier intentions and beliefs, of treating it as an object in itself. He is capable of reaching fresh conclusions about his work grounded in aesthetic judgments: that his book is both more coherent and a better analysis of more important themes read in a somewhat different way from what he thought when he was writing it. This is, I think, a very important fact for a number of reasons; but I want, for my present purpose, only to emphasize one. Any full description of what Fowles "intended" when he set out to write *The French Lieutenant's Woman* must include the intention to produce something capable of being treated that way, by himself and therefore by others, and so must include the intention to create something independent of his intentions. I quote Fowles once again, and again as a witness rather than for his metaphysics: "Only one reason is shared by all of us [novelists]: *we wish to create worlds as real as, but other than, the world that is.* Or was. That is why we cannot plan.... We also know that a genuinely created world must be independent of its creator."

I suspect that regarding something one has produced as a novel or poem or painting, rather than a set of propositions or marks, *depends* on regarding it as something that can be detached and interpreted in the sense I described. In any case this is characteristically how authors themselves regard what they have done. The intentions of authors are not simply conjunctive, like the intentions of someone who goes to market with a shopping list, but structured, so that the more concrete of these intentions, like intentions about the motives of a particular character in a novel, are contingent on interpretive beliefs whose soundness varies with what is produced and which might be radically altered from time to time.

We can, perhaps, isolate the full set of interpretive beliefs an author has at a particular moment (say at the moment he sends final galleys to the printer) and solemnly declare that these beliefs, in their full concreteness, fix what the novel is or means. (Of course, these beliefs would inevitably be incomplete, but that is another matter.) But even if we (wrongly) call this particular set of beliefs "intentions," we are, in choosing them, ignoring another kind or level of intention, which is the intention to create a work whose nature or meaning is not fixed in this way, because it is a work of art. That is why the author's intention school, as I understand it, makes the value of a work of art turn on a narrow and constrained view of the intentions of the author.

III. Law and Literature

1. *The Chain of Law*

These sketchy remarks about literary interpretation may have suggested too sharp a split between the role of the artist in creating a work of art and that of the critic in interpreting it later.

The artist can create nothing without interpreting as he creates; since he intends to produce art, he must have at least a tacit theory of why what he produces is art and why it is a better work of art through this stroke of the pen or the brush or the chisel rather than that. The critic, for his part, creates as he interprets; for though he is bound by the fact of the work, defined in the more formal and academic parts of his theory of art, his more practical artistic sense is engaged by his responsibility to decide which way of seeing or reading or understanding that work shows it as better art. Nevertheless there is a difference between interpreting while creating and creating while interpreting, and therefore a recognizable difference between the artist and the critic.

I want to use literary interpretation as a model for the central method of legal analysis, and I therefore need to show how even this distinction between artist and critic might be eroded in certain circumstances. Suppose that a group of novelists is engaged for a particular project and that they draw lots to determine the order of play. The lowest number writes the opening chapter of a novel, which he or she then sends to the next number who adds a chapter, with the understanding that he is adding a chapter to that novel rather than beginning a new one, and then sends the two chapters to the next number, and so on. Now every novelist but the first has the dual responsibilities of interpreting and creating because each must read all that has gone before in order to establish, in the interpretivist sense, what the novel so far created is.[4] He or she must decide what the characters are "really" like: what motives in fact guide them; what the point or theme of the developing novel is; how far some literary device or figure, consciously or unconsciously used, contributes to these, and whether it should be extended or refined or trimmed or dropped in order to send the novel further in one direction rather than another. This must be interpretation in a non-intention-bound style because, at least for all novelists after the second, there is no single author whose intentions any interpreter can, by the rules of the project, regard as decisive.

Some novels have in fact been written in this way (including the softcore pornographic novel *Naked Came the Stranger*), though for a debunking purpose; and certain parlor games, for rainy weekends in English country houses, have something of the same structure. But in my imaginary exercise the novelists are expected to take their responsibilities seriously and to recognize the duty to create, so far as they can, a single, unified novel rather than, for example, a series of independent short stories with characters bearing the same names. Perhaps this is an impossible assignment; perhaps the project is doomed to produce not simply a bad novel but no novel at all, because the best theory of art requires a single creator or, if more than one, that each have some control over the whole. But what about legends and jokes? I need not push that question further because I am interested only in the fact that the assignment makes sense, that each of the novelists in the chain can have some idea of what he or she is asked to do, whatever misgivings each might have about the value or character of what will then be produced.

Deciding hard cases at law is rather like this strange literary exercise. The similarity is most evident when judges consider and decide common-law cases; that is, when no statute figures centrally in the legal issue, and the argument turns on which rules or principles of law "underlie" the related decisions of other judges in the past. Each judge is then like a novelist in the chain. He or she must read through what other judges in the past have written not simply to discover what these judges have said, or their state of mind when they said it, but to reach an opinion about what these judges have collectively *done*, in the way that each of our novelists formed an opinion about the collective novel so far written. Any judge forced to decide a lawsuit will find, if he looks in the appropriate books, records of many arguably similar cases decided over decades or even centuries past by many other judges of different styles and judicial and political philosophies, in periods of different orthodoxies of procedure and judicial convention. Each judge must regard himself, in deciding the new case before him, as a partner in a complex chain enterprise of which these innu-

merable decisions, structures, conventions, and practices are the history; it is his job to continue that history into the future through what he does on the day. He *must* interpret what has gone before because he has a responsibility to advance the enterprise in hand rather than strike out in some new direction of his own. So he must determine, according to his own judgment, what the earlier decisions come to, what the point or theme of the practice so far, taken as a whole, really is.

The judge in the hypothetical case I mentioned earlier, about an aunt's emotional shock, must decide what the theme is not only of the particular precedent of the mother in the road but of accident cases, including that precedent, as a whole. He might be forced to choose, for example, between these two theories about the "meaning" of that chain of decisions. According to the first, negligent drivers are responsible to those whom their behavior is likely to cause physical harm, but they are responsible to these people for whatever injury – physical or emotional – they in fact cause. If this is the correct principle, then the decisive difference between that case and the aunt's case is just that the aunt was not within the physical risk, and therefore she cannot recover. On the second theory, however, negligent drivers are responsible for any damage they can reasonably be expected to foresee if they think about their behavior in advance. If that is the right principle, then the aunt may yet recover. Everything turns on whether it is sufficiently foreseeable that a child will have relatives, beyond his or her immediate parents, who may suffer emotional shock when they learn of the child's injury. The judge trying the aunt's case must decide which of these two principles represents the better "reading" of the chain of decisions he must continue.

Can we say, in some general way, what those who disagree about the best interpretation of legal precedent are disagreeing about? I said that a literary interpretation aims to show how the work in question can be seen as the most valuable work of art, and so must attend to formal features of identity, coherence, and integrity as well as more substantive considerations of artistic value. A plausible interpretation of legal practice must also, in a parallel way, satisfy a test of two dimensions: it must both fit that practice and show its point or value. But point or value here cannot mean artistic value because law, unlike literature, is not an artistic enterprise. Law is a political enterprise, whose general point, if it has one, lies in coordinating social and individual effort, or resolving social and individual disputes, or securing justice between citizens and between them and their government, or some combination of these. (This characterization is itself an interpretation, of course, but allowable now because relatively neutral.) So an interpretation of any body or division of law, like the law of accidents, must show the value of that body of law in political terms by demonstrating the best principle or policy it can be taken to serve.

We know from the parallel argument in literature that this general description of interpretation in law is not license for each judge to find in doctrinal history whatever he thinks should have been there. The same distinction holds between interpretation and ideal. A judge's duty is to interpret the legal history he finds, not to invent a better history. The dimensions of fit will provide some boundaries. There is, of course, no algorithm for deciding whether a particular interpretation sufficiently fits that history not to be ruled out. When a statute or constitution or other legal document is part of the doctrinal history, speaker's meaning will play a role. But the choice of which of several crucially different senses of speaker's or legislator's intention is the appropriate one cannot itself be referred to anyone's intention but must be decided, by whoever must make the decision, as a question of political theory.[5] In the common-law cases the question of fit is more complex. Any particular hypothesis about the point of a string of decisions ("these decisions establish the principle that no one can recover for emotional damage who did not lie within the area of physical danger himself") is likely to encounter if not flat counterexamples in some earlier case at least language or argument that seems to suggest the contrary. So any useful conception of interpretation must contain a doctrine of mistake – as must any novelist's theory of interpretation for the chain novel.

Sometimes a legal argument will explicitly recognize such mistakes: "Insofar as the cases of *A* v. *B* and *C* v. *D* may have held to the contrary, they were, we believe, wrongly decided and need not be followed here." Sometimes the doctrine of precedent forbids this crude approach and requires something like: "We held, in *E* v. *F*, that such-and-such, but that case raised special issues and must, we think, be confined to its own facts" (which is not quite so disingenuous as it might seem).

This flexibility may seem to erode the difference on which I insist, between interpretation and a fresh, clean-slate decision about what the law ought to be. But there is nevertheless this overriding constraint. Any judge's sense of the point or function of law, on which every aspect of his approach to interpretation will depend, will include or imply some conception of the integrity and coherence of law as an institution, and this conception will both tutor and constrain his working theory of fit – that is, his convictions about how much of the prior law an interpretation must fit, and which of it, and how. (The parallel with literary interpretation holds here as well.)

It should be apparent, however, that any particular judge's theory of fit will often fail to produce a unique interpretation. (The distinction between hard and easy cases at law is perhaps just the distinction between cases in which they do and do not.) Just as two readings of a poem may each find sufficient support in the text to show its unity and coherence, two principles may each find enough support in the various decisions of the past to satisfy any plausible theory of fit. In that case substantive political theory (like substantive considerations of artistic merit) will play a decisive role. Put bluntly, the interpretation of accident law, that a careless driver is liable to those whose damage is both substantial and foreseeable, is probably a better interpretation, if it is, only because it states a sounder principle of justice than any principle that distinguishes between physical and emotional damage or that makes recovery for emotional damage depend on whether the plaintiff was in danger of physical damage. (I should add that this issue, as an issue of political morality, is in fact very complex, and many distinguished judges and lawyers have taken each side.)

We might summarize these points this way. Judges develop a particular approach to legal interpretation by forming and refining a political theory sensitive to those issues on which interpretation in particular cases will depend; and they call this their legal philosophy. It will include both structural features, elaborating the general requirement that an interpretation must fit doctrinal history, and substantive claims about social goals and principles of justice. Any judge's opinion about the best interpretation will therefore be the consequence of beliefs other judges need not share. If a judge believes that the dominant purpose of a legal system, the main goal it ought to serve, is economic, then he will see in past accident decisions some strategy for reducing the economic costs of accidents overall. Other judges, who find any such picture of the law's function distasteful, will discover no such strategy in history but only, perhaps, an attempt to reinforce conventional morality of fault and responsibility. If we insist on a high order of neutrality in our description of legal interpretation, therefore, we cannot make our description of the nature of legal interpretation much more concrete than I have.

2. Author's Intention in Law

I want instead to consider various objections that might be made not to the detail of my argument but to the main thesis, that interpretation in law is essentially political. I shall not spend further time on the general objection already noticed: that this view of law makes it irreducibly and irredeemably subjective, just a matter of what particular judges think best or what they had for breakfast. Of course, for some lawyers and legal scholars this is not an objection at all, but only the beginnings of skeptical wisdom about law. But it is the nerve of my argument that the flat distinction between description and evaluation on which this skepticism relies – the distinction between finding the law just "there" in history and making it up wholesale – is misplaced here, because interpretation is something different from both.

I shall want, therefore, to repeat the various observations I made about subjectivity and objectivity in literary interpretation. There is no obvious reason in the account I gave of legal interpretation to doubt that one interpretation of law can be better than another and that one can be best of all. Whether this is so depends on general issues of philosophy not peculiar to law any more than to literature; and we would do well, in considering these general issues, not to begin with any fixed ideas about the necessary and sufficient conditions of objectivity (for example that no theory of law can be sound unless it is demonstrably sound, unless it would wring assent from a stone). In the meantime we can sensibly aim to develop various levels of a conception of law for ourselves, to find the interpretation of a complex and dramatically important practice which seems to us at once the right kind of interpretation for law and right as that kind of interpretation.

I shall consider one further, and rather different, objection in more detail: that my political hypothesis about legal interpretation, like the aesthetic hypothesis about artistic interpretation, fails to give an adequate place to author's intention. It fails to see that interpretation in law is simply a matter of discovering what various actors in the legal process – constitutional delegates, members of Congress and state legislatures, judges and executive officials – intended. Once again it is important to see what is at stake here. The political hypothesis makes room for the author's intention argument as a conception of interpretation, a conception which claims that the best political theory gives the intentions of legislators and past judges a decisive role in interpretation. Seen this way, the author's intention theory does not challenge the political hypothesis but contests for its authority. If the present objection is really an objection to the argument so far, therefore, its claim must be understood differently, as proposing, for example, that very "meaning" of interpretation in law requires that only these officials' intentions should count or that at least there is a firm consensus among lawyers to that effect. Both of these claims are as silly as the parallel claims about the idea or the practice of interpretation in art.

Suppose, therefore, that we do take the author's intention theory, more sensibly, as a conception rather than an explication of the concept of legal interpretation. The theory seems on firmest ground, as I suggested earlier, when interpretation is interpretation of a canonical legal text, like a clause of the Constitution, or a section of a statute, or a provision of a contract or will. But just as we noticed that a novelist's intention is complex and structured in ways that embarrass any simple author's intention theory in literature, we must now notice that a legislator's intention is complex in similar ways. Suppose a delegate to a constitutional convention votes for a clause guaranteeing equality of treatment, without regard to race, in matters touching people's fundamental interests; but he thinks that education is not a matter of fundamental interest and so does not believe that the clause makes racially segregated schools unconstitutional. We may sensibly distinguish an abstract and a concrete intention here: the delegate intends to prohibit discrimination in whatever in fact is of fundamental interest and also intends not to prohibit segregated schools. These are not isolated, discrete intentions; our descriptions, we might say, describe the same intention in different ways. But it matters very much which description a theory of legislative intention accepts as canonical. If we accept the first description, then a judge who wishes to follow the delegate's intentions, but who believes that education is a matter of fundamental interest, will hold segregation unconstitutional. If we accept the second, he will not. The choice between the two descriptions cannot be made by any further reflection about what an intention really is. It must be made by deciding that one rather than the other description is more appropriate in virtue of the best theory of representative democracy or on some other openly political grounds. (I might add that no compelling argument has yet been produced, so far as I am aware, in favor of deferring to a delegate's more concrete intentions, and that this is of major importance in arguments about whether the "original intention" of the framers requires abolishing, for example, racial discrimination or capital punishment.)

When we consider the common-law problems of interpretation, the author's intention theory shows in an even poorer light. The problems are not simply evidentiary. Perhaps we can discover what was "in the mind" of all the judges who decided cases about accidents at one time or another in our legal history. We might also discover (or speculate) about the psychodynamic or economic or social explanations of why each judge thought what he or she did. No doubt the result of all this research (or speculation) would be a mass of psychological data essentially different for each of the past judges included in the study, and order could be brought into the mass, if at all, only through statistical summaries about which proportion of judges in which historical period probably held which opinion and was more or less subject to which influence. But this mass, even tamed by statistical summary, would be of no more help to the judge trying to answer the question of what the prior decisions, taken as a whole, really come to than the parallel information would be to one of our chain novelists trying to decide what novel the novelists earlier in the chain had collectively written. That judgment, in each case, requires a fresh exercise of interpretation which is neither brute historical research nor a clean-slate expression of how things ideally ought to be.

A judge who believed in the importance of discerning an author's intention might try to escape these problems by selecting one particular judge or a small group of judges in the past (say, the judges who decided the most recent case something like his or the case he thinks closest to his) and asking what rule that judge or group intended to lay down for the future. This would treat the particular earlier judges as legislators and so invite all the problems of statutory interpretation including the very serious problem we just noticed. Even so it would not even escape the special problems of common-law adjudication after all, because the judge who applied this theory of interpretation would have to suppose himself entitled to look only to the intentions of the particular earlier judge or judges he had selected, and he could not suppose this unless he thought that it was the upshot of judicial practice as a whole (and not just the intentions of some *other* selected earlier judge) that this is what judges in his position should do.

IV Politics in Interpretation

If my claims about the role of politics in legal interpretation are sound, then we should expect to find distinctly liberal or radical or conservative opinions not only about what the Constitution and laws of our nation should be but also about what they are. And this is exactly what we do find. Interpretation of the Equal Protection Clause of the United States Constitution provides especially vivid examples. There can be no useful interpretation of what that clause means which is independent of some theory about what political equality is and how far equality is required by justice, and the history of the last half-century of constitutional law is largely an exploration of exactly these issues of political morality. Conservative lawyers argued steadily (though not consistently) in favor of an author's intentions style of interpreting this clause, and they accused others, who used a different style with more egalitarian results, of inventing rather than interpreting law. But this was bluster meant to hide the role their own political convictions played in their choice of interpretive style, and the great legal debates over the Equal Protection Clause would have been more illuminating if it had been more widely recognized that reliance on political theory is not a corruption of interpretation but part of what interpretation means.

Should politics play any comparable role in literary and other artistic interpretation? We have become used to the idea of the politics of interpretation. Stanley Fish, particularly, has promoted a theory of interpretation which supposes that contests between rival schools of literary interpretation are more political than argumentative: rival professoriates in search of dominion. And of course it is a truism of the sociology of literature, and not merely of the Marxist contribution to that discipline, that fashion in interpretation is sensitive to and

expresses more general political and economic structures. These important claims are external: they touch the causes of the rise of this or that approach to literature and interpretation.

Several of the essays for this conference discuss these issues. But we are now concerned with the internal question, about politics in rather than the politics of interpretation. How far can principles of political morality actually count as arguments for a particular interpretation of a particular work or for a general approach to artistic interpretation? There are many possibilities and many of them are parasitic on claims developed or mentioned in these essays. It was said that our commitment to feminism, or our fidelity to nation, or our dissatisfaction with the rise of the New Right ought to influence our evaluation and appreciation of literature. Indeed it was the general (though not unanimous) sense of the conference that professional criticism must be faulted for its inattention to such political issues. But if our convictions about these particular political issues count in deciding how good some novel or play or poem is, then they must also count in deciding, among particular interpretations of these works, which is the best interpretation. Or so they must if my argument is sound.

We might also explore a more indirect connection between aesthetic and political theory. Any comprehensive theory of art is likely to have, at its center, some epistemological thesis, some set of views about the relations that hold among experience, self-consciousness, and the perception or formation of values. If it assigns self-discovery any role in art, it will need a theory of personal identity adequate to mark off the boundaries of a person from his or her circumstances, and from other persons, or at least to deny the reality of any such boundaries. It seems likely that any comprehensive theory of social justice will also have roots in convictions about these or very closely related issues. Liberalism, for example, which assigns great importance to autonomy, may depend upon a particular picture of the role that judgments of value play in people's lives; it may depend on the thesis that people's convictions about value are beliefs, open to argument and review, rather than simply the givens of personality, fixed by genetic and social causes. And any political theory which gives an important place to equality also requires assumptions about the boundaries of persons, because it must distinguish between treating people as equals and changing them into different people.

It may be a sensible project, at least, to inquire whether there are not particular philosophical bases shared by particular aesthetic and particular political theories so that we can properly speak of a liberal or Marxist or perfectionist or totalitarian aesthetics, for example, in that sense. Common questions and problems hardly guarantee this, of course. It would be necessary to see, for example, whether liberalism can indeed be traced, as many philosophers have supposed, back into a discrete epistemological base, different from that of other political theories, and then ask whether that discrete base could be carried forward into aesthetic theory and there yield a distinctive interpretive style. I have no good idea that this project could be successful, and I end simply by acknowledging my sense that politics, art, and law are united, somehow, in philosophy.

Notes

1   See Gareth Evans, "Semantic Theory and Tacit Knowledge," in *Wittgenstein: To Follow a Rule*, ed. Steven H. Holtzman and Christopher M. Leich (London, 1981).
2   It may be one of the many important differences between interpretation in art and law, which I do not examine in this essay, that nothing in law corresponds to the direct experience of a work of art, though some lawyers of the romantic tradition do speak of a good judge's "sixth sense" which enables him to grasp which aspects of a chain of legal decisions reveal the "immanent" principle of law even though he cannot fully explain why.
3   See E. D. Hirsch, Jr., *Validity in Interpretation* (New Haven, Conn., 1967).
4   Even the first novelist has the responsibility of interpreting to the extent any writer must, which includes not only interpreting as he writes but interpreting the genre in which he sets out to write. Will novelists with higher numbers have less creative "freedom" than those with lower? In one sense, no novelist has any freedom at all,

because each is constrained to choose that interpretation which (he believes) makes the continuing work of art the best it can be. But we have already seen (and the discussion of law below will elaborate) two different dimensions along which any interpretation can be tested: the "formal" dimension, which asks how far the interpretation fits and integrates the text so far completed, and the "substantive" dimension, which considers the soundness of the view about what makes a novel good on which the interpretation relies. It seems reasonable to suppose that later novelists will normally – but certainly not inevitably – believe that fewer interpretations can survive the first of these tests than would have survived had they received fewer chapters. Most interpreters would think that a certain interpretation of *A Christmas Carol* – that Scrooge was inherently evil, for example – would pass the test of integrity just after the opening pages, but not toward the end of that novel. Our sense that later novelists are less free may reflect just that fact. This does not mean, of course, that there is more likely to be consensus about the correct interpretation later rather than earlier in the chain or that a later novelist is more likely to find an argument that "proves" his interpretation right beyond rational challenge. Reasonable disagreement is available on the formal as well as the substantive side, and even when most novelists would think only a particular interpretation could fit the novel to a certain point, some novelist of imagination might find some dramatic change in plot that (in his opinion) unexpectedly unifies what had seemed unnecessary and redeems what had seemed wrong or trivial. Once again, we should be careful not to confuse the fact that consensus would rarely be reached, at any point in the process, with the claim that any particular novelist's interpretation must be "merely subjective." No novelist, at any point, will be able simply to read the correct interpretation of the text he receives in a mechanical way, but it does not follow from that fact alone that one interpretation is not superior to others overall. In any case it will nevertheless be true, for all novelists beyond the first, that the assignment to find (what they believe to be) the correct interpretation of the text so far is a different assignment from the assignment to begin a new novel of their own. See, for a fuller discussion, my "Natural Law Revisited," 34 *U. Fla. L. Rev.* 165 (1982).
5   See my "The Forum of Principle," *New York University Law Review* 56 (1981).

15

The Problem of Social Cost

R. H. COASE

I   The Problem to be Examined[1]

This paper is concerned with those actions of
business firms which have harmful effects on
others. The standard example is that of a factory
the smoke from which has harmful effects on
those occupying neighbouring properties. The
economic analysis of such a situation has usually
proceeded in terms of a divergence between the
private and social product of the factory, in
which economists have largely followed the
treatment of Pigou in *The Economics of Welfare*.
The conclusions to which this kind of analysis
seems to have led most economists is that it
would be desirable to make the owner of
the factory liable for the damage caused to those
injured by the smoke, or alternatively, to place a
tax on the factory owner varying with the
amount of smoke produced and equivalent in
money terms to the damage it would cause, or
finally, to exclude the factory from residential
districts (and presumably from other areas in
which the emission of smoke would have harmful effects on others). It is my contention that
the suggested courses of action are inappropriate, in that they lead to results which are not
necessarily, or even usually, desirable.

II   The Reciprocal Nature of the Problem

The traditional approach has tended to obscure
the nature of the choice that has to be made.
The question is commonly thought of as one in
which A inflicts harm on B and what has to be
decided is: how should we restrain A? But this is
wrong. We are dealing with a problem of a
reciprocal nature. To avoid the harm to B
would inflict harm on A. The real question
that has to be decided is: should A be allowed
to harm B or should B be allowed to harm A?
The problem is to avoid the more serious harm.
I instanced in my previous article[2] the case of a
confectioner the noise and vibrations from
whose machinery disturbed a doctor in his
work. To avoid harming the doctor would
inflict harm on the confectioner. The problem
posed by this case was essentially whether it was
worth while, as a result of restricting the
methods of production which could be used by
the confectioner, to secure more doctoring at
the cost of a reduced supply of confectionary
products. Another example is afforded by the
problem of straying cattle which destroy crops
on neighbouring land. If it is inevitable that
some cattle will stray, an increase in the supply
of meat can only be obtained at the expense of a
decrease in the supply of crops. The nature of
the choice is clear: meat or crops. What answer
should be given is, of course, not clear unless we
know the value of what is obtained as well as the
value of what is sacrificed to obtain it. To give
another example, Professor George J. Stigler
instances the contamination of a stream.[3] If we
assume that the harmful effect of the pollution
is that it kills the fish, the question to be decided
is: is the value of the fish lost greater or less than
the value of the product which the contamination of the stream makes possible? It goes

almost without saying that this problem has to be looked at in total *and* at the margin.

III   The Pricing System with Liability for Damage

I propose to start my analysis by examining a case in which most economists would presumably agree that the problem would be solved in a completely satisfactory manner: when the damaging business has to pay for all damage caused *and* the pricing system works smoothly (strictly this means that the operation of a pricing system is without cost).

A good example of the problem under discussion is afforded by the case of straying cattle which destroy crops growing on neighbouring land. Let us suppose that a farmer and a cattle-raiser are operating on neighbouring properties. Let us further suppose that, without any fencing between the properties, an increase in the size of the cattle-raiser's herd increases the total damage to the farmer's crops. What happens to the marginal damage as the size of the herd increases is another matter. This depends on whether the cattle tend to follow one another or to roam side by side, on whether they tend to be more or less restless as the size of the herd increases and on other similar factors. For my immediate purpose, it is immaterial what assumption is made about marginal damage as the size of the herd increases.

To simplify the argument, I propose to use an arithmetical example. I shall assume that the annual cost of fencing the farmer's property is $9 and that the price of the crop is $1 per ton. Also, I assume that the relation between the number of cattle in the herd and the annual crop loss is as follows:

Number in Herd (Steers)	Annual Crop Loss (Tons)	Crop Loss per Additional Steer (Tons)
1	1	1
2	3	2
3	6	3
4	10	4

Given that the cattle-raiser is liable for the damage caused, the additional annual cost imposed on the cattle-raiser if he increased his herd from, say, 2 to 3 steers is $3 and in deciding on the size of the herd, he will take this into account along with his other costs. That is, he will not increase the size of the herd unless the value of the additional meat produced (assuming that the cattle-raiser slaughters the cattle), is greater than the additional costs that this will entail, including the value of the additional crops destroyed. Of course, if, by the employment of dogs, herdsmen, aeroplanes, mobile radio and other means, the amount of damage can be reduced, these means will be adopted when their cost is less than the value of the crop which they prevent being lost. Given that the annual cost of fencing is $9, the cattle-raiser who wished to have a herd with 4 steers or more would pay for fencing to be erected and maintained, assuming that other means of attaining the same end would not do so more cheaply. When the fence is erected, the marginal cost due to the liability for damage becomes zero, except to the extent that an increase in the size of the herd necessitates a stronger and therefore more expensive fence because more steers are liable to lean against it at the same time. But, of course, it may be cheaper for the cattle-raiser not to fence and to pay for the damaged crops, as in my arithmetical example, with 3 or fewer steers.

It might be thought that the fact that the cattle-raiser would pay for all crops damaged would lead the farmer to increase his planting if a cattle-raiser came to occupy the neighbouring property. But this is not so. If the crop was previously sold in conditions of perfect competition, marginal cost was equal to price for the amount of planting undertaken and any expansion would have reduced the profits of the farmer. In the new situation, the existence of crop damage would mean that the farmer would sell less on the open market but his receipts for a given production would remain the same, since the cattle-raiser would pay the market price for any crop damaged. Of course, if cattle-raising commonly involved the destruction of crops, the coming into existence of a cattle-raising industry might raise the price of the crops involved and farmers would then extend their planting. But I wish to confine my attention to the individual farmer.

I have said that the occupation of a neigh-bouring property by a cattle-raiser would not cause the amount of production, or perhaps more exactly the amount of planting, by the farmer to increase. In fact, if the cattle-raising has any effect, it will be to decrease the amount of planting. The reason for this is that, for any given tract of land, if the value of the crop damaged is so great that the receipts from the sale of the undamaged crop are less than the total costs of cultivating that tract of land, it will be profitable for the farmer and the cattle-raiser to make a bargain whereby that tract of land is left uncultivated. This can be made clear by means of an arithmetical example. Assume ini-tially that the value of the crop obtained from cultivating a given tract of land is $12 and that the cost incurred in cultivating this tract of land is $10, the net gain from cultivating the land being $2. I assume for purposes of simplicity that the farmer owns the land. Now assume that the cattle-raiser starts operations on the neighbouring property and that the value of the crops damaged is $1. In this case $11 is obtained by the farmer from sale on the market and $1 is obtained from the cattle-raiser for damage suffered and the net gain remains $2. Now suppose that the cattle-raiser finds it prof-itable to increase the size of his herd, even though the amount of damage rises to $3; which means that the value of the additional meat production is greater than the additional costs, including the additional $2 payment for damage. But the total payment for damage is now $3. The net gain to the farmer from culti-vating the land is still $2. The cattle-raiser would be better off if the farmer would agree not to cultivate his land for any payment less than $3. The farmer would be agreeable to not cultivating the land for any payment greater than $2. There is clearly room for a mutually satisfactory bargain which would lead to the abandonment of cultivation.[4] But the same argument applies not only to the whole tract cultivated by the farmer but also to any sub-division of it. Suppose, for example, that the cattle have a well-defined route, say, to a brook or to a shady area. In these circumstances, the amount of damage to the crop along the route may well be great and if so, it could

be that the farmer and the cattle-raiser would find it profitable to make a bargain whereby the farmer would agree not to cultivate this strip of land.

But this raises a further possibility. Suppose that there is such a well-defined route. Sup-pose further that the value of the crop that would be obtained by cultivating this strip of land is $10 but that the cost of cultivation is $11. In the absence of the cattle-raiser, the land would not be cultivated. However, given the presence of the cattle-raiser, it could well be that if the strip was cultivated, the whole crop would be destroyed by the cattle. In which case, the cattle-raiser would be forced to pay $10 to the farmer. It is true that the farmer would lose $1. But the cattle-raiser would lose $10. Clearly this is a situation which is not likely to last indefinitely since neither party would want this to happen. The aim of the farmer would be to induce the cattle-raiser to make a payment in return for an agreement to leave this land uncultivated. The farmer would not be able to obtain a payment greater than the cost of fen-cing off this piece of land nor so high as to lead the cattle-raiser to abandon the use of the neigh-bouring property. What payment would in fact be made would depend on the shrewdness of the farmer and the cattle-raiser as bargainers. But as the payment would not be so high as to cause the cattle-raiser to abandon this loca-tion and as it would not vary with the size of the herd, such an agreement would not affect the allocation of resources but would merely alter the distribution of income and wealth as between the cattle-raiser and the farmer.

I think it is clear that if the cattle-raiser is liable for damage caused and the pricing system works smoothly, the reduction in the value of production elsewhere will be taken into account in computing the additional cost involved in increasing the size of the herd. This cost will be weighed against the value of the additional meat production and, given perfect competition in the cattle industry, the allocation of resources in cattle-raising will be optimal. What needs to be emphasized is that the fall in the value of production elsewhere which would be taken into account in the costs of the cattle-raiser may well be less than the damage which the cattle would cause to the crops in the ordinary course of events. This is because it is possible, as a result of market transactions, to discontinue cultivation of the land. This is desirable in all cases in which the damage that the cattle would cause, and for which the cattle-raiser would be willing to pay, exceeds the amount which the farmer would pay for use of the land. In conditions of perfect competition, the amount which the farmer would pay for the use of the land is equal to the difference between the value of the total production when the factors are employed on this land and the value of the additional product yielded in their next best use (which would be what the farmer would have to pay for the factors). If damage exceeds the amount the farmer would pay for the use of the land, the value of the additional product of the factors employed elsewhere would exceed the value of the total product in this use after damage is taken into account. It follows that it would be desirable to abandon cultivation of the land and to release the factors employed for production elsewhere. A procedure which merely provided for payment for damage to the crop caused by the cattle but which did not allow for the possibility of cultivation being discontinued would result in too small an employment of factors of production in cattle-raising and too large an employment of factors in cultivation of the crop. But given the possibility of market transactions, a situation in which damage to crops exceeded the rent of the land would not endure. Whether the cattle-raiser pays the farmer to leave the land uncultivated or himself rents the land by paying the land-owner an amount slightly greater than the farmer would pay (if the farmer was himself renting the land), the final result would be the same and would maximise the value of production. Even when the farmer is induced to plant crops which it would not be profitable to cultivate for sale on the market, this will be a purely short-term phenomenon and may be expected to lead to an agreement under which the planting will cease. The cattle-raiser will remain in that location and the marginal cost of meat production will be the same as before, thus having no long-run effect on the allocation of resources.

IV   The Pricing System with No Liability for Damage

I now turn to the case in which, although the pricing system is assumed to work smoothly (that is, costlessly), the damaging business is not liable for any of the damage which it causes. This business does not have to make a payment to those damaged by its actions. I propose to show that the allocation of resources will be the same in this case as it was when the damaging business was liable for damage caused. As I showed in the previous case that the allocation of resources was optimal, it will not be necessary to repeat this part of the argument.

I return to the case of the farmer and the cattle-raiser. The farmer would suffer increased damage to his crop as the size of the herd increased. Suppose that the size of the cattle-raiser's herd is 3 steers (and that this is the size of the herd that would be maintained if crop damage was not taken into account). Then the farmer would be willing to pay up to $3 if the cattle-raiser would reduce his herd to 2 steers, up to $5 if the herd were reduced to 1 steer and would pay up to $6 if cattle-raising was abandoned. The cattle-raiser would therefore receive $3 from the farmer if he kept 2 steers instead of 3. This $3 foregone is therefore part of the cost incurred in keeping the third steer. Whether the $3 is a payment which the cattle-raiser has to make if he adds the third steer to his herd (which it would be if the cattle-raiser was liable to the farmer for damage caused to the crop) or whether it is a sum of money which he would have received if he did not keep a third steer (which it would be if the cattle-raiser was not liable to the farmer for damage caused to the crop) does not affect the final result. In both cases $3 is part of the cost of adding a third steer, to be included along with the other costs. If the increase in the value of production in cattle-raising through increasing the size of the herd from 2 to 3 is greater than the additional costs that have to be incurred (including the $3 damage to crops), the size of the herd will be increased. Otherwise, it will not. The size of the herd will be the same whether the cattle-raiser is liable for damage caused to the crop or not.

It may be argued that the assumed starting point – a herd of 3 steers – was arbitrary. And this is true. But the farmer would not wish to pay to avoid crop damage which the cattle-raiser would not be able to cause. For example, the maximum annual payment which the farmer could be induced to pay could not exceed $9, the annual cost of fencing. And the farmer would only be willing to pay this sum if it did not reduce his earnings to a level that would cause him to abandon cultivation of this particular tract of land. Furthermore, the farmer would only be willing to pay this amount if he believed that, in the absence of any payment by him, the size of the herd maintained by the cattle raiser would be 4 or more steers. Let us assume that this is the case. Then the farmer would be willing to pay up to $3 if the cattle raiser would reduce his herd to 3 steers, up to $6 if the herd were reduced to 2 steers, up to $8 if one steer only were kept and up to $9 if cattle-raising were abandoned. It will be noticed that the change in the starting point has not altered the amount which would accrue to the cattle-raiser if he reduced the size of his herd by any given amount. It is still true that the cattle-raiser could receive an additional $3 from the farmer if he agreed to reduce his herd from 3 steers to 2 and that the $3 represents the value of the crop that would be destroyed by adding the third steer to the herd. Although a different belief on the part of the farmer (whether justified or not) about the size of the herd that the cattle-raiser would maintain in the absence of payments from him may affect the total payment he can be induced to pay, it is not true that this different belief would have any effect on the size of the herd that the cattle-raiser will actually keep. This will be the same as it would be if the cattle-raiser had to pay for damage caused by his cattle, since a receipt foregone of a given amount is the equivalent of a payment of the same amount.

It might be thought that it would pay the cattle-raiser to increase his herd above the size that he would wish to maintain once a bargain had been made, in order to induce the farmer to make a larger total payment. And this may be true. It is similar in nature to the action of the farmer (when the cattle-raiser was liable for damage) in cultivating land on which, as a result of an agreement with the cattle-raiser, planting would subsequently be abandoned (including land which would not be cultivated at all in the absence of cattle-raising). But such manoeuvres are preliminaries to an agreement and do not affect the long-run equilibrium position, which is the same whether or not the cattle-raiser is held responsible for the crop damage brought about by his cattle.

It is necessary to know whether the damaging business is liable or not for damage caused since without the establishment of this initial delimitation of rights there can be no market transactions to transfer and recombine them. But the ultimate result (which maximises the value of production) is independent of the legal position if the pricing system is assumed to work without cost.

V   The Problem Illustrated Anew

The harmful effects of the activities of a business can assume a wide variety of forms. An early English case concerned a building which, by obstructing currents of air, hindered the operation of a windmill.[5] A recent case in Florida concerned a building which cast a shadow on the cabana, swimming pool and sunbathing areas of a neighbouring hotel.[6] The problem of straying cattle and the damaging of crops which was the subject of detailed examination in the two preceding sections, although it may have appeared to be rather a special case, is in fact but one example of a problem which arises in many different guises. To clarify the nature of my argument and to demonstrate its general applicability, I propose to illustrate it anew by reference to four actual cases.

Let us first reconsider the case of *Sturges v. Bridgman*[7] which I used as an illustration of the general problem in my article on "The Federal Communications Commission." In this case, a confectioner (in Wigmore Street) used two mortars and pestles in connection with his business (one had been in operation in the same position for more than 60 years and the other for more than 26 years). A doctor then came to occupy neighbouring premises (in Wimpole

Street). The confectioner's machinery caused the doctor no harm until, eight years after he had first occupied the premises, he built a consulting room at the end of his garden right against the confectioner's kitchen. It was then found that the noise and vibration caused by the confectioner's machinery made it difficult for the doctor to use his new consulting room. "In particular . . . the noise prevented him from examining his patients by auscultation[8] for diseases of the chest. He also found it impossible to engage with effect in any occupation which required thought and attention." The doctor therefore brought a legal action to force the confectioner to stop using his machinery. The courts had little difficulty in granting the doctor the injunction he sought. "Individual cases of hardship may occur in the strict carrying out of the principle upon which we found our judgment, but the negation of the principle would lead even more to individual hardship, and would at the same time produce a prejudicial effect upon the development of land for residential purposes."

The court's decision established that the doctor had the right to prevent the confectioner from using his machinery. But, of course, it would have been possible to modify the arrangements envisaged in the legal ruling by means of a bargain between the parties. The doctor would have been willing to waive his right and allow the machinery to continue in operation if the confectioner would have paid him a sum of money which was greater than the loss of income which he would suffer from having to move to a more costly or less convenient location or from having to curtail his activities at this location or, as was suggested as a possibility, from having to build a separate wall which would deaden the noise and vibration. The confectioner would have been willing to do this if the amount he would have to pay the doctor was less than the fall in income he would suffer if he had to change his mode of operation at this location, abandon his operation or move his confectionery business to some other location. The solution of the problem depends essentially on whether the continued use of the machinery adds more to the confectioner's income than it subtracts from the doctor's.[9] But now consider

the situation if the confectioner had won the case. The confectioner would then have had the right to continue operating his noise and vibration-generating machinery without having to pay anything to the doctor. The boot would have been on the other foot: the doctor would have had to pay the confectioner to induce him to stop using the machinery. If the doctor's income would have fallen more through continuance of the use of this machinery than it added to the income of the confectioner, there would clearly be room for a bargain whereby the doctor paid the confectioner to stop using the machinery. That is to say, the circumstances in which it would not pay the confectioner to continue to use the machinery and to compensate the doctor for the losses that this would bring (if the doctor had the right to prevent the confectioner's using his machinery) would be those in which it would be in the interest of the doctor to make a payment to the confectioner which would induce him to discontinue the use of the machinery (if the confectioner had the right to operate the machinery). The basic conditions are exactly the same in this case as they were in the example of the cattle which destroyed crops. With costless market transactions, the decision of the courts concerning liability for damage would be without effect on the allocation of resources. It was of course the view of the judges that they were affecting the working of the economic system – and in a desirable direction. Any other decision would have had "a prejudicial effect upon the development of land for residential purposes," an argument which was elaborated by examining the example of a forge operating on a barren moor, which was later developed for residual purposes. The judges' view that they were settling how the land was to be used would be true only in the case in which the costs of carrying out the necessary market transactions exceeded the gain which might be achieved by any rearrangement of rights. And it would be desirable to preserve the areas (Wimpole Street or the moor) for residential or professional use (by giving non-industrial users the right to stop the noise, vibration, smoke, etc., by injunction) only if the value of the additional residential facilities obtained was greater than the value of cakes or iron lost. But of this the judges seem to have been unaware.

Another example of the same problem is furnished by the case of *Cooke v. Forbes*.[10] One process in the weaving of cocoa-nut fibre matting was to immerse it in bleaching liquids after which it was hung out to dry. Fumes from a manufacturer of sulphate of ammonia had the effect of turning the matting from a bright to a dull and blackish colour. The reason for this was that the bleaching liquid contained chloride of tin, which, when affected by sulphuretted hydrogen, is turned to a darker colour. An injunction was sought to stop the manufacturer from emitting the fumes. The lawyers for the defendant argued that if the plaintiff "were not to use ... a particular bleaching liquid, their fibre would not be affected; that their process is unusual, not according to the custom of the trade, and even damaging to their own fabrics." The judge commented: " ... it appears to me quite plain that a person has a right to carry on upon his own property a manufacturing process in which he uses chloride of tin, or any sort of metallic dye, and that his neighbour is not at liberty to pour in gas which will interfere with his manufacture. If it can be traced to the neighbour, then, I apprehend, clearly he will have a right to come here and ask for relief." But in view of the fact that the damage was accidental and occasional, that careful precautions were taken and that there was no exceptional risk, an injunction was refused, leaving the plaintiff to bring an action for damages if he wished. What the subsequent developments were I do not know. But it is clear that the situation is essentially the same as that found in *Sturges v. Bridgman*, except that the cocoa-nut fibre matting manufacturer could not secure an injunction but would have to seek damages from the sulphate of ammonia manufacturer. The economic analysis of the situation is exactly the same as with the cattle which destroyed crops. To avoid the damage, the sulphate of ammonia manufacturer could increase his precautions or move to another location. Either course would presumably increase his costs. Alternatively he could pay for the damage. This he would do if the payments for damage were less than the additional costs that would

have to be incurred to avoid the damage. The payments for damage would then become part of the cost of production of sulphate of ammonia. Of course, if, as was suggested in the legal proceedings, the amount of damage could be eliminated by changing the bleaching agent (which would presumably increase the costs of the matting manufacturer) and if the additional cost was less than the damage that would otherwise occur, it should be possible for the two manufacturers to make a mutually satisfactory bargain whereby the new bleaching agent was used. Had the court decided against the matting manufacturer, as a consequence of which he would have had to suffer the damage without compensation, the allocation of resources would not have been affected. It would pay the matting manufacturer to change his bleaching agent if the additional cost involved was less than the reduction in damage. And since the matting manufacturer would be willing to pay the sulphate of ammonia manufacturer an amount up to his loss of income (the increase in costs or the damage suffered) if he would cease his activities, this loss of income would remain a cost of production for the manufacturer of sulphate of ammonia. This case is indeed analytically exactly the same as the cattle example.

Bryant v. Lefever[11] raised the problem of the smoke nuisance in a novel form. The plaintiff and the defendants were occupiers of adjoining houses, which were of about the same height.

> Before 1876 the plaintiff was able to light a fire in any room of his house without the chimneys smoking; the two houses had remained in the same condition some thirty or forty years. In 1876 the defendants took down their house, and began to rebuild it. They carried up a wall by the side of the plaintiff's chimneys much beyond its original height, and stacked timber on the roof of their house, and thereby caused the plaintiff's chimneys to smoke whenever he lighted fires.

The reason, of course, why the chimneys smoked was that the erection of the wall and the stacking of the timber prevented the free circulation of air. In a trial before a jury, the plaintiff was awarded damages of £40. The case then went to the Court of Appeals where the judgment was reversed. Bramwell, L.J., argued:

> ... it is said, and the jury have found, that the defendants have done that which caused a nuisance to the plaintiff's house. We think there is no evidence of this. No doubt there is a nuisance, but it is not of the defendant's causing. They have done nothing in causing the nuisance. Their house and their timber are harmless enough. It is the plaintiff who causes the nuisance by lighting a coal fire in a place the chimney of which is placed so near the defendants' wall, that the smoke does not escape, but comes into the house. Let the plaintiff cease to light his fire, let him move his chimney, let him carry it higher, and there would be no nuisance. Who then, causes it? It would be very clear that the plaintiff did, if he had built his house or chimney after the defendants had put up the timber on theirs, and it is really the same though he did so before the timber was there. But (what is in truth the same answer), if the defendants cause the nuisance, they have a right to do so. If the plaintiff has not the right to the passage of air, except subject to the defendants' right to build or put timber on their house, then his right is subject to their right, and though a nuisance follows from the exercise of their right, they are not liable.

And Cotton, L.J., said:

> Here it is found that the erection of the defendants' wall has sensibly and materially interfered with the comfort of human existence in the plaintiff's house, and it is said this is a nuisance for which the defendants are liable. Ordinarily this is so, but the defendants have done so, not by sending on to the plaintiff's property any smoke or noxious vapour, but by interrupting the egress of smoke from the plaintiff's house in a way to which ... the plaintiff has no legal right. The plaintiff creates the smoke, which interferes with his comfort. Unless he has ... a right to get rid of this in a particular way which has been interfered with by the defendants, he cannot sue the defendants, because the smoke made by himself, for which he has not provided any effectual means of escape, causes him annoyance. It is as if a man tried to get rid of liquid filth arising on his own land by a drain into his neighbour's land. Until a right had been acquired by user, the neighbour might stop the drain without incurring liability by so doing. No doubt great inconvenience would be caused to the owner of the property on which the liquid filth arises. But the act of his neighbour would be a lawful act, and he would not be liable for the consequences attributable to the fact that the man had accumulated filth without providing any effectual means of getting rid of it.

I do not propose to show that any subsequent modification of the situation, as a result of bargains between the parties (conditioned by the cost of stacking the timber elsewhere, the cost of extending the chimney higher, etc.), would have exactly the same result whatever decision the courts had come to since this point has already been adequately dealt with in the discussion of the cattle example and the two previous cases. What I shall discuss is the argument of the judges in the Court of Appeals that the smoke nuisance was not caused by the man who erected the wall but by the man who lit the fires. The novelty of the situation is that the smoke nuisance was suffered by the man who lit the fires and not by some third person. The question is not a trivial one since it lies at the heart of the problem under discussion. Who caused the smoke nuisance? The answer seems fairly clear. The smoke nuisance was caused both by the man who built the wall *and* by the man who lit the fires. Given the fires, there would have been no smoke nuisance without the wall; given the wall, there would have been no smoke nuisance without the fires. Eliminate the wall *or* the fires and the smoke nuisance would disappear. On the marginal principle it is clear that *both* were responsible and *both* should be forced to include the loss of amenity due to the smoke as a cost in deciding whether to continue the activity which gives rise to the smoke. And given the possibility of market transactions, this is what would in fact happen. Although the wall-builder was not liable legally for the nuisance, as the man with the smoking chimneys would presumably be willing to pay a sum equal to the monetary worth to him of eliminating the smoke, this sum would therefore become for the wall-builder, a cost of continuing to have the high wall with the timber stacked on the roof.

The judges' contention that it was the man who lit the fires who alone caused the smoke nuisance is true only if we assume that the wall is the given factor. This is what the judges did by deciding that the man who erected the higher wall had a legal right to do so. The case would have been even more interesting if the smoke from the chimneys had injured the timber. Then it would have been the wall-builder who suffered the damage. The case would then have closely paralleled *Sturges v. Bridgman* and there can be little doubt that the man who lit the fires would have been liable for the ensuing damage to the timber, in spite of the fact that no damage had occurred until the high wall was built by the man who owned the timber.

Judges have to decide on legal liability but this should not confuse economists about the nature of the economic problem involved. In the case of the cattle and the crops, it is true that there would be no crop damage without the cattle. It is equally true that there would be no crop damage without the crops. The doctor's work would not have been disturbed if the confectioner had not worked his machinery; but the machinery would have disturbed no one if the doctor had not set up his consulting room in that particular place. The matting was blackened by the fumes from the sulphate of ammonia manufacturer; but no damage would have occurred if the matting manufacturer had not chosen to hang out his matting in a particular place and to use a particular bleaching agent. If we are to discuss the problem in terms of causation, both parties cause the damage. If we are to attain an optimum allocation of resources, it is therefore desirable that both parties should take the harmful effect (the nuisance) into account in deciding on their course of action. It is one of the beauties of a smoothly operating pricing system that, as has already been explained, the fall in the value of production due to the harmful effect would be a cost for both parties.

Bass v. Gregory[12] will serve as an excellent final illustration of the problem. The plaintiffs were the owners and tenant of a public house called the Jolly Anglers. The defendant was the owner of some cottages and a yard adjoining the Jolly Anglers. Under the public house was a cellar excavated in the rock. From the cellar, a

hole or shaft had been cut into an old well situated in the defendant's yard. The well therefore became the ventilating shaft for the cellar. The cellar "had been used for a particular purpose in the process of brewing, which, without ventilation, could not be carried on." The cause of the action was that the defendant removed a grating from the mouth of the well, "so as to stop or prevent the free passage of air from [the] cellar upwards through the well . . . ." What caused the defendant to take this step is not clear from the report of the case. Perhaps "the air . . . impregnated by the brewing operations" which "passed up the well and out into the open air" was offensive to him. At any rate, he preferred to have the well in his yard stopped up. The court had first to determine whether the owners of the public house could have a legal right to a current of air. If they were to have such a right, this case would have to be distinguished from *Bryant v. Lefever* (already considered). This, however, presented no difficulty. In this case, the current of air was confined to "a strictly defined channel." In the case of *Bryant v. Lefever*, what was involved was "the general current of air common to all mankind." The judge therefore held that the owners of the public house could have the right to a current of air whereas the owner of the private house in *Bryant v. Lefever* could not. An economist might be tempted to add "but the air moved all the same." However, all that had been decided at this stage of the argument was that there could be a legal right, not that the owners of the public house possessed it. But evidence showed that the shaft from the cellar to the well had existed for over forty years and that the use of the well as a ventilating shaft must have been known to the owners of the yard since the air, when it emerged, smelt of the brewing operations. The judge therefore held that the public house had such a right by the "doctrine of lost grant." This doctrine states "that if a legal right is proved to have existed and been exercised for a number of years the law ought to presume that it had a legal origin."[13] So the owner of the cottages and yard had to unstop the well and endure the smell.

The reasoning employed by the courts in determining legal rights will often seem strange to an economist because many of the factors on which the decision turns are, to an economist, irrelevant. Because of this, situations which are, from an economic point of view, identical will be treated quite differently by the courts. The economic problem in all cases of harmful effects is how to maximise the value of production. In the case of *Bass v. Gregory* fresh air was drawn in through the well which facilitated the production of beer but foul air was expelled through the well which made life in the adjoining houses less pleasant. The economic problem was to decide which to choose: a lower cost of beer and worsened amenities in adjoining houses or a higher cost of beer and improved amenities. In deciding this question, the "doctrine of lost grant" is about as relevant as the colour of the judge's eyes. But it has to be remembered that the immediate question faced by the courts is *not* what shall be done by whom *but* who has the legal right to do what. It is always possible to modify by transactions on the market the initial legal delimitation of rights. And, of course, if such market transactions are costless, such a rearrangement of rights will always take place if it would lead to an increase in the value of production.

VI   The Cost of Market Transactions Taken into Account

The argument has proceeded up to this point on the assumption (explicit in Sections III and IV and tacit in Section V) that there were no costs involved in carrying out market transactions. This is, of course, a very unrealistic assumption. In order to carry out a market transaction it is necessary to discover who it is that one wishes to deal with, to inform people that one wishes to deal and on what terms, to conduct negotiations leading up to a bargain, to draw up the contract, to undertake the inspection needed to make sure that the terms of the contract are being observed, and so on. These operations are often extremely costly, sufficiently costly at any rate to prevent many transactions that would be carried out in a world in which the pricing system worked without cost.

In earlier sections, when dealing with the problem of the rearrangement of legal rights through the market, it was argued that such a rearrangement would be made through the market whenever this would lead to an increase in the value of production. But this assumed costless market transactions. Once the costs of carrying out market transactions are taken into account it is clear that such a rearrangement of rights will only be undertaken when the increase in the value of production consequent upon the rearrangement is greater than the costs which would be involved in bringing it about. When it is less, the granting of an injunction (or the knowledge that it would be granted) or the liability to pay damages may result in an activity being discontinued (or may prevent its being started) which would be undertaken if market transactions were costless. In these conditions the initial delimitation of legal rights does have an effect on the efficiency with which the economic system operates. One arrangement of rights may bring about a greater value of production than any other. But unless this is the arrangement of rights established by the legal system, the costs of reaching the same result by altering and combining rights through the market may be so great that this optimal arrangement of rights, and the greater value of production which it would bring, may never be achieved. The part played by economic considerations in the process of delimiting legal rights will be discussed in the next section. In this section, I will take the initial delimitation of rights and the costs of carrying out market transactions as given.

It is clear that an alternative form of economic organisation which could achieve the same result at less cost than would be incurred by using the market would enable the value of production to be raised. As I explained many years ago, the firm represents such an alternative to organising production through market transactions.[14] Within the firm individual bargains between the various cooperating factors of production are eliminated and for a market transaction is substituted an administrative decision. The rearrangement of production then takes place without the need for bargains between the owners of the factors of production. A landowner who has control of a large tract of land may devote his land to various uses taking into account the effect that the interrelations of the various activities will have on the net return of the land, thus rendering unnecessary bargains between those undertaking the various activities. Owners of a large building or of several adjoining properties in a given area may act in much the same way. In effect, using our earlier terminology, the firm would acquire the legal rights of all the parties and the rearrangement of activities would not follow on a rearrangement of rights by contract, but as a result of an administrative decision as to how the rights should be used.

It does not, of course, follow that the administrative costs of organising a transaction through a firm are inevitably less than the costs of the market transactions which are superseded. But where contracts are peculiarly difficult to draw up and an attempt to describe what the parties have agreed to do or not to do (e.g. the amount and kind of a smell or noise that they may make or will not make) would necessitate a lengthy and highly involved document, and, where, as is probable, a long-term contract would be desirable;[15] it would be hardly surprising if the emergence of a firm or the extension of the activities of an existing firm was not the solution adopted on many occasions to deal with the problem of harmful effects. This solution would be adopted whenever the administrative costs of the firm were less than the costs of the market transactions that it supersedes and the gains which would result from the rearrangement of activities greater than the firm's costs of organising them. I do not need to examine in great detail the character of this solution since I have explained what is involved in my earlier article.

But the firm is not the only possible answer to this problem. The administrative costs of organising transactions within the firm may also be high, and particularly so when many diverse activities are brought within the control of a single organisation. In the standard case of a smoke nuisance, which may affect a vast number of people engaged in a wide variety of activities, the administrative costs might well be so high as to make any attempt to deal with the problem within the confines of a single firm impossible. An alternative solution is direct Government regulation. Instead of instituting a legal system

of rights which can be modified by transactions on the market, the government may impose regulations which state what people must or must not do and which have to be obeyed. Thus, the government (by statute or perhaps more likely through an administrative agency) may, to deal with the problem of smoke nuisance, decree that certain methods of production should or should not be used (e.g. that smoke preventing devices should be installed or that coal or oil should not be burned) or may confine certain types of business to certain districts (zoning regulations).

The government is, in a sense, a super-firm (but of a very special kind) since it is able to influence the use of factors of production by administrative decision. But the ordinary firm is subject to checks in its operations because of the competition of other firms, which might administer the same activities at lower cost and also because there is always the alternative of market transactions as against organisation within the firm if the administrative costs become too great. The government is able, if it wishes, to avoid the market altogether, which a firm can never do. The firm has to make market agreements with the owners of the factors of production that it uses. Just as the government can conscript or seize property, so it can decree that factors of production should only be used in such-and-such a way. Such authoritarian methods save a lot of trouble (for those doing the organising). Furthermore, the government has at its disposal the police and the other law enforcement agencies to make sure that its regulations are carried out.

It is clear that the government has powers which might enable it to get some things done at a lower cost than could a private organisation (or at any rate one without special governmental powers). But the governmental administrative machine is not itself costless. It can, in fact, on occasion be extremely costly. Furthermore, there is no reason to suppose that the restrictive and zoning regulations, made by a fallible administration subject to political pressures and operating without any competitive check, will necessarily always be those which increase the efficiency with which the economic system operates. Furthermore, such general regulations which must apply to a wide variety of cases will be enforced in some cases in which they are clearly inappropriate. From these considerations it follows that direct governmental regulation will not necessarily give better results than leaving the problem to be solved by the market or the firm. But equally there is no reason why, on occasion, such governmental administrative regulation should not lead to an improvement in economic efficiency. This would seem particularly likely when, as is normally the case with the smoke nuisance, a large number of people are involved and in which therefore the costs of handling the problem through the market or the firm may be high.

There is, of course, a further alternative, which is to do nothing about the problem at all. And given that the costs involved in solving the problem by regulations issued by the governmental administrative machine will often be heavy (particularly if the costs are interpreted to include all the consequences which follow from the Government engaging in this kind of activity) it will no doubt be commonly the case that the gain which would come from regulating the actions which give rise to the harmful effects will be less than the costs involved in Government regulation.

The discussion of the problem of harmful effects in this section (when the costs of market transactions are taken into account) is extremely inadequate. But at least it has made clear that the problem is one of choosing the appropriate social arrangement for dealing with the harmful effects. All solutions have costs and there is no reason to suppose that government regulation is called for simply because the problem is not well handled by the market or the firm. Satisfactory views on policy can only come from a patient study of how, in practice, the market, firms and governments handle the problem of harmful effects. Economists need to study the work of the broker in bringing parties together, the effectiveness of restrictive covenants, the problems of the large-scale real-estate development company, the operation of Government zoning and other regulating activities. It is my belief that economists, and policy-makers generally, have tended to over-estimate the advantages which come from governmental regulation. But this belief, even if justified, does not do more than suggest that government regulation should be curtailed. It does not tell us where the boundary line should be drawn. This, it seems to me, has to come from a detailed investigation of the actual results of handling the problem in different ways. But it would be unfortunate if this investigation were undertaken with the aid of a faulty economic analysis. The aim of this article is to indicate what the economic approach to the problem should be.

VII The Legal Delimitation of Rights and the Economic Problem

The discussion in Section V not only served to illustrate the argument but also afforded a glimpse at the legal approach to the problem of harmful effects. The cases considered were all English but a similar selection of American cases could easily be made and the character of the reasoning would have been the same. Of course, if market transactions were costless, all that matters (questions of equity apart) is that the rights of the various parties should be well-defined and the results of legal actions easy to forecast. But as we have seen, the situation is quite different when market transactions are so costly as to make it difficult to change the arrangement of rights established by the law. In such cases, the courts directly influence economic activity. It would therefore seem desirable that the courts should understand the economic consequences of their decisions and should, insofar as this is possible without creating too much uncertainty about the legal position itself, take these consequences into account when making their decisions. Even when it is possible to change the legal delimitation of rights through market transactions, it is obviously desirable to reduce the need for such transactions and thus reduce the employment of resources in carrying them out.

A thorough examination of the presuppositions of the courts in trying such cases would be of great interest but I have not been able to attempt it. Nevertheless it is clear from a cursory study that the courts have often recognized the economic implications of their decisions and are aware (as many economists are not) of the reciprocal nature of the problem. Furthermore, from time to time, they take these economic implications into account, along with other factors, in arriving at their decisions. The American writers on this subject refer to the question in a more explicit fashion than do the British. Thus, to quote Prosser on Torts, a person may

> make use of his own property or . . . conduct his own affairs at the expense of some harm to his neighbors. He may operate a factory whose noise and smoke cause some discomfort to others, so long as he keeps within reasonable bounds. It is only when his conduct is unreasonable, *in the light of its utility and the harm which results* [italics added], that it becomes a nuisance . . . . As it was said in an ancient case in regard to candle-making in a town, "Le utility del chose excusera le noisomeness del stink."
>
> The world must have factories, smelters, oil refineries, noisy machinery and blasting, even at the expense of some inconvenience to those in the vicinity and the plaintiff may be required to accept some not unreasonable discomfort for the general good.[16]

The standard British writers do not state as explicitly as this that a comparison between the utility and harm produced is an element in deciding whether a harmful effect should be considered a nuisance. But similar views, if less strongly expressed, are to be found.[17] The doctrine that the harmful effect must be substantial before the court will act is, no doubt, in part a reflection of the fact that there will almost always be some gain to offset the harm. And in the reports of individual cases, it is clear that the judges have had in mind what would be lost as well as what would be gained in deciding whether to grant an injunction or award damages. Thus, in refusing to prevent the destruction of a prospect by a new building, the judge stated:

> I know no general rule of common law, which . . . says, that building so as to stop another's prospect is a nuisance. Was that the case, there could be no great towns; and I must grant injunctions to all the new buildings in this town . . . .[18]

In *Webb v. Bird*[19] it was decided that it was not a nuisance to build a schoolhouse so near a windmill as to obstruct currents of air and hinder the working of the mill. An early case seems to have been decided in an opposite direction. Gale commented:

> In old maps of London a row of windmills appears on the heights to the north of London. Probably in the time of King James it was thought an alarming circumstance, as affecting the supply of food to the city, that anyone should build so near them as to take the wind out from their sails.[20]

In one of the cases discussed in section V, *Sturges v. Bridgman*, it seems clear that the judges were thinking of the economic consequences of alternative decisions. To the argument that if the principle that they seemed to be following

> were carried out to its logical consequences, it would result in the most serious practical inconveniences, for a man might go – say into the midst of the tanneries of *Bermondsey*, or into any other locality devoted to any particular trade or manufacture of a noisy or unsavoury character, and by building a private residence upon a vacant piece of land put a stop to such trade or manufacture altogether,

the judges answered that

> whether anything is a nuisance or not is a question to be determined, not merely by an abstract consideration of the thing itself, but in reference to its circumstances; What would be a nuisance in *Belgrave Square* would not necessarily be so in *Bermondsey*; and where a locality is devoted to a particular trade or manufacture carried on by the traders or manufacturers in a particular and established manner not constituting a public nuisance, Judges and juries would be justified in finding, and may be trusted to find, that the trade or manufacture so carried on in that locality is not a private or actionable wrong.[21]

That the character of the neighborhood is relevant in deciding whether something is, or is not, a nuisance, is definitely established.

He who dislikes the noise of traffic must not set up his abode in the heart of a great city. He who loves peace and quiet must not live in a locality devoted to the business of making boilers or steamships.[22]

What has emerged has been described as "planning and zoning by the judiciary."[23] Of course there are sometimes considerable difficulties in applying the criteria.[24]

An interesting example of the problem is found in *Adams v. Ursell*[25] in which a fried fish shop in a predominantly working-class district was set up near houses of "a much better character." England without fish-and-chips is a contradiction in terms and the case was clearly one of high importance. The judge commented:

It was urged that an injunction would cause great hardship to the defendant and to the poor people who get food at his shop. The answer to that is that it does not follow that the defendant cannot carry on his business in another more suitable place somewhere in the neighbourhood. It by no means follows that because a fried fish shop is a nuisance in one place it is a nuisance in another.

In fact, the injunction which restrained Mr. Ursell from running his shop did not even extend to the whole street. So he was presumably able to move to other premises near houses of "a much worse character," the inhabitants of which would no doubt consider the availability of fish-and-chips to outweigh the pervading odour and "fog or mist" so graphically described by the plaintiff. Had there been no other "more suitable place in the neighbourhood," the case would have been more difficult and the decision might have been different. What would "the poor people" have had for food? No English judge would have said: "Let them eat cake."

The courts do not always refer very clearly to the economic problem posed by the cases brought before them but it seems probable that in the interpretation of words and phrases like "reasonable" or "common or ordinary use" there is some recognition, perhaps largely unconscious and certainly not very explicit, of the economic aspects of the questions at issue. A good example of this would seem to be the judgment in the Court of Appeals in *Andreae v. Selfridge and Company Ltd.*[26] In this case, a hotel (in Wigmore Street) was situated on part of an island site. The remainder of the site was acquired by Selfridges which demolished the existing buildings in order to erect another in their place. The hotel suffered a loss of custom in consequence of the noise and dust caused by the demolition. The owner of the hotel brought an action against Selfridges for damages. In the lower court, the hotel was awarded £4,500 damages. The case was then taken on appeal.

The judge who had found for the hotel proprietor in the lower court said:

I cannot regard what the defendants did on the site of the first operation as having been commonly done in the ordinary use and occupation of land or houses. It is neither usual nor common, in this country, for people to excavate a site to a depth of 60 feet and then to erect upon that site a steel framework and fasten the steel frames together with rivets.... Nor is it, I think, a common or ordinary use of land, in this country, to act as the defendants did when they were dealing with the site of their second operation – namely, to demolish all the houses that they had to demolish, five or six of them I think, if not more, and to use for the purpose of demolishing them pneumatic hammers.

Sir Wilfred Greene, M.R., speaking for the Court of Appeals, first noted

that when one is dealing with temporary operations, such as demolition and re-building, everybody has to put up with a certain amount of discomfort, because operations of that kind cannot be carried on at all without a certain amount of noise and a certain amount of dust. Therefore, the rule with regard to interference must be read subject to this qualification ....

He then referred to the previous judgment:

With great respect to the learned judge, I take the view that he has not approached this matter from the correct angle. It seems to me that it is not possible to say ... that the type of demolition, excavation and construction in which the defendant company was engaged in the course of these operations was of such an abnormal and unusual nature as to prevent the qualification to which I have referred coming into operation. It seems to me that, when the rule speaks of the common or ordinary use of land, it does not mean that the methods of using land and building on it are in some way to be stabilised for ever. As time goes on new inventions or new methods enable land to be more profitably used, either by digging down into the earth or by mounting up into the skies. Whether, from other points of view, that is a matter which is desirable for humanity is neither here nor there; but it is part of the normal use of land, to make use upon your land, in the matter of construction, of what particular type and what particular depth of foundations and particular height of building may be reasonable, in the circumstances, and in view of the developments of the day .... Guests at hotels are very easily upset. People coming to this hotel, who were accustomed to a quiet outlook at the back, coming back and finding demolition and building going on, may very well have taken the view that the particular merit of this hotel no longer existed. That would be a misfortune for the plaintiff; but assuming that there was nothing wrong in the defendant company's works, assuming the defendant company was carrying on the demolition and its building, productive of noise though it might be, with all reasonable skill, and taking all reasonable precautions not to cause annoyance to its neighbors, then the planitiff might lose all her clients in the hotel because they have lost the amenities of an open and quiet place behind, but she would have no cause of complaint .... [But those] who say that their interference with the comfort of their neighbors is justified because their operations are normal and usual and conducted with proper care and skill are under a specific duty ... to use that reasonable and proper care and skill. It is not a correct attitude to take to say: 'We will go on and do what we like until somebody complains!' .... Their duty is to take proper precautions and to see that the nuisance is reduced to a minimum. It is no answer for them to say: 'But this would mean that we should have to do the work more slowly than we would like to do it, or it would involve putting us to some extra expense.' All these questions are matters of common sense and degree, and quite clearly it would be unreasonable to expect people to conduct their work so slowly or so expensively, for the purpose of preventing a transient inconvenience, that the cost and trouble would be prohibitive .... In this case, the defendant company's attitude seems to have been to go on until somebody complained, and, further, that its desire to hurry its work and conduct it according to its own ideas and its own convenience was to prevail if there was a real conflict between it and the comfort of its neighbors. That ... is not carrying out the obligation of using reasonable care and skill .... The effect comes to this ... the plaintiff suffered an actionable nuisance; ... she is entitled, not to a nominal sum, but to a substantial sum, based upon those principles ... but in arriving at the sum ... I have discounted any loss of custom ... which might be due to the general loss of amenities owing to what was going on at the back ....

The upshot was that the damages awarded were reduced from £4,500 to £1,000.

The discussion in this section has, up to this point, been concerned with court decisions arising out of the common law relating to nuisance. Delimitation of rights in this area also comes about because of statutory enactments. Most economists would appear to assume that the aim of governmental action in this field is to extend the scope of the law of nuisance by designating as nuisances activities which would not be recognized as such by the common law. And there can be no doubt that some statutes, for example, the Public Health Acts, have had this effect. But not all Government enactments are of this kind. The effect of much of the legislation in this area is to protect businesses from the claims of those they have harmed by their actions. There is a long list of legalized nuisances.

The position has been summarized in *Halsbury's Laws of England* as follows:

Where the legislature directs that a thing shall in all events be done or authorises certain works at a particular place for a specific purposes or grants powers with the intention that they shall be exercised, although leaving some discretion as to the mode of exercise, no action will lie at common law for nuisance or damage which is the inevitable result of carrying out the statutory powers so conferred. This is so whether the act causing the damage is authorised for public purposes or private profit. Acts done under powers granted by persons to whom Parliament has delegated authority to grant such powers, for example, under provisional orders of the Board of Trade, are regarded as having been done under statutory authority. In the absence of negligence it seems that a body exercising statutory powers will not be liable to an action merely because it might, by acting in a different way, have minimised an injury.

Instances are next given of freedom from liability for acts authorized:

> An action has been held not to be against a body exercising its statutory powers without negligence in respect of the flooding of land by water escaping from watercourses, from water pipes, from drains, or from a canal; the escape of fumes from sewers; the escape of sewage: the subsidence of a road over a sewer; vibration or noise caused by a railway; fires caused by authorised acts; the pollution of a stream where statutory requirements to use the best known method of purifying before discharging the effluent have been satisfied; interference with a telephone or telegraph system by an electric tramway; the insertion of poles for tramways in the subsoil; annoyance caused by things reasonably necessary for the excavation of authorised works; accidental damage caused by the placing of a grating in a roadway; the escape of tar acid; or interference with the access of a frontager by a street shelter or safety railings on the edge of a pavement.[27]

The legal position in the United States would seem to be essentially the same as in England, except that the power of the legislatures to authorize what would otherwise be nuisances under the common law, at least without giving compensation to the person harmed, is somewhat more limited, as it is subject to constitutional restrictions.[28] Nonetheless, the power is there and cases more or less identical with the English cases can be found. The question has arisen in an acute form in connection with airports and the operation of aeroplanes. The case of *Delta Air Corporation v. Kersey, Kersey v. City of Atlanta*[29] is a good example. Mr. Kersey bought land and built a house on it. Some years later the City of Atlanta constructed an airport on land immediately adjoining that of Mr. Kersey. It was explained that his property was "a quiet, peaceful and proper location for a home before the airport was built, but dust, noises and low flying of airplanes caused by

the operation of the airport have rendered his property unsuitable as a home," a state of affairs which was described in the report of the case with a wealth of distressing detail. The judge first referred to an earlier case, *Thrasher v. City of Atlanta*[30] in which it was noted that the City of Atlanta had been expressly authorized to operate an airport.

> By this franchise aviation was recognised as a lawful business and also as an enterprise affected with a public interest...all persons using [the airport] in the manner contemplated by law are within the protection and immunity of the franchise granted by the municipality. An airport is not a nuisance per se, although it might become such from the manner of its construction or operation.

Since aviation was a lawful business affected with a public interest and the construction of the airport was autorized by statute, the judge next referred to *Georgia Railroad and Banking Co. v. Maddox*[31] in which it was said:

> Where a railroad terminal yard is located and its construction authorized, under statutory powers, if it be constructed and operated in a proper manner, it cannot be adjudged a nuisance. Accordingly, injuries and inconveniences to persons residing near such a yard, from noises of locomotives, rumbling of cars, vibrations produced thereby, and smoke, cinders, soot and the like, which result from the ordinary and necessary, therefore proper, use and operation of such a yard, are not nuisances, but are the necessary concomitants of the franchise granted.

In view of this, the judge decided that the noise and dust complained of by Mr. Kersey "may be deemed to be incidental to the proper operation of an airport, and as such they cannot be said to constitute a nuisance." But the complaint against low flying was different:

> ...can it be said that flights...at such a low height [25 to 50 feet above Mr. Kersey's house] as to be imminently dangerous to...life and health...are a necessary concomitant of an airport? We do not think this question can be answered in the affirmative. No reason appears

why the city could not obtain lands of an area [sufficiently large]... as not to require such low flights.... For the sake of public convenience adjoining-property owners must suffer such inconvenience from noise and dust as result from the usual and proper operation of an airport, but their private rights are entitled to preference in the eyes of the law where the inconvenience is not one demanded by a properly constructed and operated airport.

Of course this assumed that the City of Atlanta could prevent the low flying and continue to operate the airport. The judge therefore added:

From all that appears, the conditions causing the low flying may be remedied; but if on the trial it should appear that it is indispensable to the public interest that the airport should continue to be operated in its present condition, it may be said that the petitioner should be denied injunctive relief.

In the course of another aviation case, *Smith v. New England Aircraft Co.*,[32] the court surveyed the law in the United States regarding the legalizing of nuisances and it is apparent that, in the broad, it is very similar to that found in England:

It is the proper function of the legislative department of government in the exercise of the police power to consider the problems and risks that arise from the use of new inventions and endeavor to adjust private rights and harmonize conflicting interests by comprehensive statutes for the public welfare.... There are... analogies where the invasion of the airspace over underlying land by noise, smoke, vibration, dust and disagreeable odors, having been authorized by the legislative department of government and not being in effect a condemnation of the property although in some measure depreciating its market value, must be borne by the landowner without compensation or remedy. Legislative sanction makes that lawful which otherwise might be a nuisance. Examples of this are damages to adjacent land arising from smoke, vibration and noise in the operation of a railroad...; the noise of ringing factory bells...; the abatement of nuisances...; the erection of steam engines and furnaces...; unpleasant odors connected with sewers, oil refining and storage of naphtha....

Most economists seem to be unaware of all this. When they are prevented from sleeping at night by the roar of jet planes overhead (publicly authorized and perhaps publicly operated), are unable to think (or rest) in the day because of the noise and vibration from passing trains (publicly authorized and perhaps publicly operated), find it difficult to breathe because of the odour from a local sewage farm (publicly authorized and perhaps publicly operated) and are unable to escape because their driveways are blocked by a road obstruction (without any doubt, publicly devised), their nerves frayed and mental balance disturbed, they proceed to declaim about the disadvantages of private enterprise and the need for Government regulation.

While most economists seem to be under a misapprehension concerning the character of the situation with which they are dealing, it is also the case that the activities which they would like to see stopped or curtailed may well be socially justified. It is all a question of weighing up the gains that would accrue from eliminating these harmful effects against the gains that accrue from allowing them to continue. Of course, it is likely that an extension of Government economic activity will often lead to this protection against action for nuisance being pushed further than is desirable. For one thing, the Government is likely to look with a benevolent eye on enterprises which it is itself promoting. For another, it is possible to describe the committing of a nuisance by public enterprise in a much more pleasant way than when the same thing is done by private enterprise. In the words of Lord Justice Sir Alfred Denning:

...the significance of the social revolution of today is that, whereas in the past the balance was much too heavily in favor of the rights of property and freedom of contract, Parliament has repeatedly intervened so as to give the public good its proper place.[33]

There can be little doubt that the Welfare State is likely to bring an extension of that immunity from liability for damage, which economists have been in the habit of condemning (although they have tended to assume that this immunity was a sign of too little Government intervention in the economic system). For example, in Britain, the powers of local authorities are regarded as being either absolute or conditional. In the first category, the local authority has no discretion in exercising the power conferred on it. "The absolute power may be said to cover all the necessary consequences of its direct operation even if such consequences amount to nuisance." On the other hand, a conditional power may only be exercised in such a way that the consequences do not constitute a nuisance.

> It is the intention of the legislature which determines whether a power is absolute or conditional. ...[As] there is the possibility that the social policy of the legislature may change from time to time, a power which in one era would be construed as being conditional, might in another era be interpreted as being absolute in order to further the policy of the Welfare State. This point is one which should be borne in mind when considering some of the older cases upon this aspect of the law of nuisance.[34]

It would seem desirable to summarize the burden of this long section. The problem which we face in dealing with actions which have harmful effects is not simply one of restraining those responsible for them. What has to be decided is whether the gain from preventing the harm is greater than the loss which would be suffered elsewhere as a result of stopping the action which produces the harm. In a world in which there are costs of rearranging the rights established by the legal system, the courts, in cases relating to nuisance, are, in effect, making a decision on the economic problem and determining how resources are to be employed. It was argued that the courts are conscious of this and that they often make, although not always in a very explicit fashion, a comparison between what would be gained and what lost by preventing actions which have harmful effects. But the delimitation of rights is also the result of statutory enactments. Here we also find evidence of an appreciation of the reciprocal nature of the problem. While statutory enactments add to the list of nuisances, action is also taken to legalize what would otherwise be nuisances under the common

law. The kind of situation which economists are prone to consider as requiring corrective Government action is, in fact, often the result of Government action. Such action is not necessarily unwise. But there is a real danger that extensive Government intervention in the economic system may lead to the protection of those responsible for harmful effects being carried too far.

VIII Pigou's Treatment in "The Economics of Welfare"

The fountainhead for the modern economic analysis of the problem discussed in this article is Pigou's *Economics of Welfare* and, in particular, that section of Part II which deals with divergences between social and private net products which come about because

> one person A, in the course of rendering some service, for which payment is made, to a second person B, incidentally also renders services or disservices to other persons (not producers of like services), of such a sort that payment cannot be exacted from the benefited parties or compensation enforced on behalf of the injured parties.[35]

Pigou tells us that his aim in Part II of *The Economics of Welfare* is

> to ascertain how far the free play of self-interest, acting under the existing legal system, tends to distribute the country's resources in the way most favorable to the production of a large national dividend, and how far it is feasible for State action to improve upon 'natural' tendencies.[36]

To judge from the first part of this statement, Pigou's purpose is to discover whether any improvements could be made in the existing arrangements which determine the use of resources. Since Pigou's conclusion is that improvements could be made, one might have expected him to continue by saying that he proposed to set out the changes required to bring them about. Instead, Pigou adds a phrase which contrasts "natural" tendencies with State action, which seems in some sense to equate the present arrangements with "natural" tendencies and to imply that what is required to bring about these improvements is State action (if feasible). That this is more or less Pigou's position is evident from Chapter I of Part II.[37] Pigou starts by referring to "optimistic followers of the classical economists"[38] who have argued that the value of production would be maximised if the Government refrained from any interference in the economic system and the economic arrangements were those which came about "naturally." Pigou goes on to say that if self-interest does promote economic welfare, it is because human institutions have been devised to make it so. (This part of Pigou's argument, which he develops with the aid of a quotation from Cannan, seems to me to be essentially correct.) Pigou concludes:

> But even in the most advanced States there are failures and imperfections....there are many obstacles that prevent a community's resources from being distributed...in the most efficient way. The study of these constitutes our present problem....its purpose is essentially practical. It seeks to bring into clearer light some of the ways in which it now is, or eventually may become, feasible for governments to control the play of economic forces in such ways as to promote the economic welfare, and through that, the total welfare, of their citizens as a whole.[39]

Pigou's underlying thought would appear to be: some have argued that no State action is needed. But the system has performed as well as it has because of State action. Nonetheless, there are still imperfections. What additional State action is required?

If this is a correct summary of Pigou's position, its inadequacy can be demonstrated by examining the first example he gives of a divergence between private and social products.

> It might happen...that costs are thrown upon people not directly concerned, through, say, uncompensated damage done to surrounding woods by sparks from railway engines. All such effects must be included – some of them will be positive, others negative elements – in reckoning up the social net product of the marginal increment of any volume of resources turned into any use or place.[40]

The example used by Pigou refers to a real situation. In Britain, a railway does not normally have to compensate those who suffer damage by fire caused by sparks from an engine. Taken in conjunction with what he says in Chapter 9 of Part II [of *The Economics of Welfare*], I take Pigou's policy recommendations to be, first, that there should be State action to correct this "natural" situation and, second, that the railways should be forced to compensate those whose woods are burnt. If this is a correct interpretation of Pigou's position, I would argue that the first recommendation is based on a misapprehension of the facts and that the second is not necessarily desirable.

Let us consider the legal position. Under the heading "Sparks from engines," we find the following in Halsbury's Laws of England:

> If railway undertakers use steam engines on their railway without express statutory authority to do so, they are liable, irrespective of any negligence on their part, for fires caused by sparks from engines. Railway undertakers are, however, generally given statutory authority to use steam engines on their railway; accordingly, if an engine is constructed with the precautions which science suggests against fire and is used without negligence, they are not responsible at common law for any damage which may be done by sparks.... In the construction of an engine the undertaker is bound to use all the discoveries which science has put within its reach in order to avoid doing harm, provided they are such as it is reasonable to require the company to adopt, having proper regard to the likelihood of the damage and to the cost and convenience of the remedy; but it is not negligence on the part of an undertaker if it refuses to use an apparatus the efficiency of which is open to bona fide doubt.

To this general rule, there is a statutory exception arising from the Railway (Fires) Act, 1905, as amended in 1923. This concerns agricultural land or agricultural crops.

> In such a case the fact that the engine was used under statutory powers does not affect the liability of the company in an action for the damage.... These provisions, however, only apply where the claim for damage...does not exceed £ 200, [£ 100 in the 1905 Act] and where written notice

of the occurrence of the fire and the intention to claim has been sent to the company within seven days of the occurrence of the damage and particulars of the damage in writing showing the amount of the claim in money not exceeding £ 200 have been sent to the company within twenty-one days.

Agricultural land does not include moorland or buildings and agricultural crops do not include those led away or stacked.[41] I have not made a close study of the parliamentary history of this statutory exception, but to judge from debates in the House of Commons in 1922 and 1923, this exception was probably designed to help the smallholder.[42]

Let us return to Pigou's example of uncompensated damage to surrounding woods caused by sparks from railway engines. This is presumably intended to show how it is possible "for State action to improve on 'natural' tendencies." If we treat Pigou's example as referring to the position before 1905, or as being an arbitrary example (in that he might just as well have written "surrounding buildings" instead of "surrounding woods"), then it is clear that the reason why compensation was not paid must have been that the railway had statutory authority to run steam engines (which relieved it of liability for fires caused by sparks). That this was the legal position was established in 1860, in a case, oddly enough, which concerned the burning of surrounding woods by a railway,[43] and the law on this point has not been changed (apart from the one exception) by a century of railway legislation, including nationalisation. If we treat Pigou's example of "uncompensated damage done to surrounding woods by sparks from railway engines" literally, and assume that it refers to the period after 1905, then it is clear that the reason why compensation was not paid must have been that the damage was more than £100 (in the first edition of *The Economics of Welfare*) or more than £200 (in later editions) or that the owner of the wood failed to notify the railway in writing within seven days of the fire or did not send particulars of the damage, in writing, within twenty-one days. In the real world, Pigou's example could only exist as a result of a deliberate choice of the legislature. It is not, of course, easy to imagine the construction of a railway in a state of nature. The

nearest one can get to this is presumably a railway which uses steam engines "without express statutory authority." However, in this case the railway would be obliged to compensate those whose woods it burnt down. That is to say, compensation would be paid in the absence of Government action. The only circumstances in which compensation would not be paid would be those in which there had been Government action. It is strange that Pigou, who clearly thought it desirable that compensation should be paid, should have chosen this particular example to demonstrate how it is possible "for State action to improve on 'natural' tendencies."

Pigou seems to have had a faulty view of the facts of the situation. But it also seems likely that he was mistaken in his economic analysis. It is not necessarily desirable that the railway should be required to compensate those who suffer damage by fires caused by railway engines. I need not show here that, if the railway could make a bargain with everyone having property adjoining the railway line and there were no costs involved in making such bargains, it would not matter whether the railway was liable for damage caused by fires or not. This question has been treated at length in earlier sections. The problem is whether it would be desirable to make the railway liable in conditions in which it is too expensive for such bargains to be made. Pigou clearly thought it was desirable to force the railway to pay compensation and it is easy to see the kind of argument that would have led him to this conclusion. Suppose a railway is considering whether to run an additional train or to increase the speed of an existing train or to install spark-preventing devices on its engines. If the railway were not liable for fire damage, then, when making these decisions, it would not take into account as a cost the increase in damage resulting from the additional train or the faster train or the failure to install spark-preventing devices. This is the source of the divergence between private and social net products. It results in the railway performing acts which will lower the value of total production – and which it would not do if it were liable for the damage. This can be shown by means of an arithmetical example.

Consider a railway, which is *not* liable for damage by fires caused by sparks from its engines, which runs two trains per day on a certain line. Suppose that running one train per day would enable the railway to perform services worth $150 per annum and running two trains a day would enable the railway to perform services worth $250 per annum. Suppose further that the cost of running one train is $50 per annum and two trains $100 per annum. Assuming perfect competition, the cost equals the fall in the value of production elsewhere due to the employment of additional factors of production by the railway. Clearly the railway would find it profitable to run two trains per day. But suppose that running one train per day would destroy by fire crops worth (on an average over the year) $60 and two trains a day would result in the destruction of crops worth $120. In these circumstances running one train per day would raise the value of total production but the running of a second train would reduce the value of total production. The second train would enable additional railway services worth $100 per annum to be performed. But the fall in the value of production elsewhere would be $110 per annum; $50 as a result of the employment of additional factors of production and $60 as a result of the destruction of crops. Since it would be better if the second train were not run and since it would not run if the railway were liable for damage caused to crops, the conclusion that the railway should be made liable for the damage seems irresistible. Undoubtedly it is this kind of reasoning which underlies the Pigovian position.

The conclusion that it would be better if the second train did not run is correct. The conclusion that it is desirable that the railway should be made liable for the damage it causes is wrong. Let us change our assumption concerning the rule of liability. Suppose that the railway is liable for damage from fires caused by sparks from the engine. A farmer on lands adjoining the railway is then in the position that, if his crop is destroyed by fires caused by the railway, he will receive the market price from the railway; but if his crop is not damaged, he will receive the market price by sale. It therefore becomes a matter of indifference to him

whether his crop is damaged by fire or not. The position is very different when the railway is *not* liable. Any crop destruction through railway-caused fires would then reduce the receipts of the farmer. He would therefore take out of cultivation any land for which the damage is likely to be greater than the net return of the land (for reasons explained at length in Section III). A change from a regime in which the railway is *not* liable for damage to one in which it *is* liable is likely therefore to lead to an increase in the amount of cultivation on lands adjoining the railway. It will also, of course, lead to an increase in the amount of crop destruction due to railway-caused fires.

Let us return to our arithmetical example. Assume that, with the changed rule of liability, there is a doubling in the amount of crop destruction due to railway-caused fires. With one train per day, crops worth $120 would be destroyed each year and two trains per day would lead to the destruction of crops worth $240. We saw previously that it would not be profitable to run the second train if the railway had to pay $60 per annum as compensation for damage. With damage at $120 per annum the loss from running the second train would be $60 greater. But now let us consider the first train. The value of the transport services furnished by the first train is $150. The cost of running the train is $50. The amount that the railway would have to pay out as compensation for damage is $120. It follows that it would not be profitable to run any trains. With the figures in our example we reach the following result: if the railway is not liable for fire-damage, two trains per day would be run; if the railway is liable for fire-damage, it would cease operations altogether. Does this mean that it is better that there should be no railway? This question can be resolved by considering what would happen to the value of total production if it were decided to exempt the railway from liability for fire-damage, thus bringing it into operation (with two trains per day).

The operation of the railway would enable transport services worth $250 to be performed. It would also mean the employment of factors of production which would reduce the value of production elsewhere by $100. Furthermore it would mean the destruction of crops worth

$120. The coming of the railway will also have led to the abandonment of cultivation of some land. Since we know that, had this land been cultivated, the value of the crops destroyed by fire would have been $120, and since it is unlikely that the total crop on this land would have been destroyed, it seems reasonable to suppose that the value of the crop yield on this land would have been higher than this. Assume it would have been $160. But the abandonment of cultivation would have released factors of production for employment elsewhere. All we know is that the amount by which the value of production elsewhere will increase will be less than $160. Suppose that it is $150. Then the gain from operating the railway would be $250 (the value of the transport services) minus $100 (the cost of the factors of production) minus $120 (the value of crops destroyed by fire) minus $160 (the fall in the value of crop production due to the abandonment of cultivation) plus $150 (the value of production elsewhere of the released factors of production). Overall, operating the railway will increase the value of total production by $20. With these figures it is clear that it is better that the railway should not be liable for the damage it causes, thus enabling it to operate profitably. Of course, by altering the figures, it could be shown that there are other cases in which it would be desirable that the railway should be liable for the damage it causes. It is enough for my purpose to show that, from an economic point of view, a situation in which there is "uncompensated damage done to surrounding woods by sparks from railway engines" is not necessarily undesirable. Whether it is desirable or not depends on the particular circumstances.

How is it that the Pigovian analysis seems to give the wrong answer? The reason is that Pigou does not seem to have noticed that his analysis is dealing with an entirely different question. The analysis as such is correct. But it is quite illegitimate for Pigou to draw the particular conclusion he does. The question at issue is not whether it is desirable to run an additional train or a faster train or to install smoke-preventing devices; the question at issue is whether it is desirable to have a system in which the railway has to compensate those who suffer damage

from the fires which it causes or one in which the railway does not have to compensate them. When an economist is comparing alternative social arrangements, the proper procedure is to compare the total social product yielded by these different arrangements. The comparison of private and social products is neither here nor there. A simple example will demonstrate this. Imagine a town in which there are traffic lights. A motorist approaches an intersection and stops because the light is red. There are no cars approaching the intersection on the other street. If the motorist ignored the red signal, no accident would occur and the total product would increase because the motorist would arrive earlier at his destination. Why does he not do this? The reason is that if he ignored the light he would be fined. The private product from crossing the street is less than the social product. Should we conclude from this that the total product would be greater if there were no fines for failing to obey traffic signals? The Pigovian analysis shows us that it is possible to conceive of better worlds than the one in which we live. But the problem is to devise practical arrangements which will correct defects in one part of the system without causing more serious harm in other parts.

I have examined in considerable detail one example of a divergence between private and social products and I do not propose to make any further examination of Pigou's analytical system. But the main discussion of the problem considered in this article is to be found in that part of Chapter 9 in Part II which deals with Pigou's second class of divergence and it is of interest to see how Pigou develops his argument. Pigou's own description of this second class of divergence was quoted at the beginning of this section. Pigou distinguishes between the case in which a person renders services for which he receives no payment and the case in which a person renders disservices and compensation is not given to the injured parties. Our main attention has, of course, centred on this second case. It is therefore rather astonishing to find, as was pointed out to me by Professor Francesco Forte, that the problem of the smoking chimney – the "stock instance"[44] or "classroom example"[45] of the second case – is used by Pigou as an example of the first case (services rendered without payment) and is never mentioned, at any rate explicitly, in connection with the second case.[46] Pigou points out that factory owners who devote resources to preventing their chimneys from smoking render services for which they receive no payment. The implication, in the light of Pigou's discussion later in the chapter, is that a factory owner with a smokey chimney should be given a bounty to induce him to install smoke-preventing devices. Most modern economists would suggest that the owner of the factory with the smokey chimney should be taxed. It seems a pity that economists (apart from Professor Forte) do not seem to have noticed this feature of Pigou's treatment since a realisation that the problem could be tackled in either of these two ways would probably have led to an explicit recognition of its reciprocal nature.

In discussing the second case (disservices without compensation to those damaged), Pigou says that they are rendered "when the owner of a site in a residential quarter of a city builds a factory there and so destroys a great part of the amenities of neighbouring sites; or, in a less degree, when he uses his site in such a way as to spoil the lighting of the house opposite; or when he invests resources in erecting buildings in a crowded centre, which by contracting the air-space and the playing room of the neighbourhood, tend to injure the health and efficiency of the families living there."[47] Pigou is, of course, quite right to describe such actions as "uncharged disservices." But he is wrong when he describes these actions as "anti-social."[48] They may or may not be. It is necessary to weigh the harm against the good that will result. Nothing could be more "anti-social" than to oppose any action which causes any harm to anyone.

The example with which Pigou opens his discussion of "uncharged disservices" is not, as I have indicated, the case of the smokey chimney but the case of the overrunning rabbits: "... incidental uncharged disservices are rendered to third parties when the game-preserving activities of one occupier involve the overrunning of a neighbouring occupier's land

by rabbits. . . ." This example is of extraordinary interest, not so much because the economic analysis of the case is essentially any different from that of the other examples, but because of the peculiarities of the legal position and the light it throws on the part which economics can play in what is apparently the purely legal question of the delimitation of rights.

The problem of legal liability for the actions of rabbits is part of the general subject of liability for animals.[49] I will, although with reluctance, confine my discussion to rabbits. The early cases relating to rabbits concerned the relations between the lord of the manor and commoners, since, from the thirteenth century on, it became usual for the lord of the manor to stock the commons with conies (rabbits), both for the sake of the meat and the fur. But in 1597, in *Boulston*'s case, an action was brought by one landowner against a neighbouring landowner, alleging that the defendant had made coney-burrows and that the conies had increased and had destroyed the plaintiff's corn. The action failed for the reason that

> ... so soon as the coneys come on his neighbor's land he may kill them, for they are ferae naturae, and he who makes the coney-boroughs has no property in them, and he shall not be punished for the damage which the coneys do in which he has no property, and which the other may lawfully kill.[50]

As *Boulston*'s case has been treated as binding – Bray, J., in 1919, said that he was not aware that *Boulston*'s case has ever been overruled or questioned[51] – Pigou's rabbit example undoubtedly represented the legal position at the time *The Economics of Welfare* was written.[52] And in this case, it is not far from the truth to say that the state of affairs which Pigou describes came about because of an absence of Government action (at any rate in the form of statutory enactments) and was the result of "natural" tendencies.

Nonetheless, *Boulston's* case is something of a legal curiosity and Professor Williams makes no secret of his distaste for this decision:

> The conception of liability in nuisance as being based upon ownership is the result, apparently, of

a confusion with the action of cattle-trespass, and runs counter both to principle and to the medieval authorities on the escape of water, smoke and filth.... The prerequisite of any satisfactory treatment of the subject is the final abandonment of the pernicious doctrine in *Boulston*'s case.... Once *Boulston*'s case disappears, the way will be clear for a rational restatement of the whole subject, on lines that will harmonize with the principles prevailing in the rest of the law of nuisance.[53]

The judges in *Boulston*'s case were, of course, aware that their view of the matter depended on distinguishing this case from one involving nuisance:

> This cause is not like to the cases put, on the other side, of erecting a lime-kiln, dye-house, or the like; for there the annoyance is by the act of the parties who make them; but it is not so here, for the conies of themselves went into the plaintiff's land, and he might take them when they came upon his land, and make profit of them.[54]

Professor Williams comments:

> Once more the atavistic idea is emerging that the animals are guilty and not the landowner. It is not, of course, a satisfactory principle to introduce into a modern law of nuisance. If A. erects a house or plants a tree so that the rain runs or drips from it on to B.'s land, this is A.'s act for which he is liable; but if A. introduces rabbits into his land so that they escape from it into B.'s, this is the act of the rabbits for which A. is not liable – such is the specious distinction resulting from *Boulston*'s case.[55]

It has to be admitted that the decision in *Boulston*'s case seems a little odd. A man may be liable for damage caused by smoke or unpleasant smells, without it being necessary to determine whether he owns the smoke or the smell. And the rule in *Boulston*'s case has not always been followed in cases dealing with other animals. For example, in *Bland v. Yates*,[56] it was decided that an injunction could be granted to prevent someone from keeping an *unusual and excessive* collection of manure in which flies bred and which infested a neighbour's house. The question of who owned the flies was not raised. An economist would not

wish to object because legal reasoning sometimes appears a little odd. But there is a sound economic reason for supporting Professor Williams' view that the problem of liability for animals (and particularly rabbits) should be brought within the ordinary law of nuisance. The reason is not that the man who harbours rabbits is solely responsible for the damage; the man whose crops are eaten is equally responsible. And given that the costs of market transactions make a rearrangement of rights impossible, unless we know the particular circumstances, we cannot say whether it is desirable or not to make the man who harbours rabbits responsible for the damage committed by the rabbits on neighbouring properties. The objection to the rule in *Boulston*'s case is that, under it, the harbourer of rabbits can *never* be liable. It fixes the rule of liability at one pole: and this is as undesirable, from an economic point of view, as fixing the rule at the other pole and making the harbourer of rabbits always liable. But, as we saw in Section VII, the law of nuisance, as it is in fact handled by the courts, is flexible and allows for a comparison of the utility of an act with the harm it produces. As Professor Williams says: "The whole law of nuisance is an attempt to reconcile and compromise between conflicting interests...."[57] To bring the problem of rabbits within the ordinary law of nuisance would not mean *inevitably* making the harbourer of rabbits liable for damage committed by the rabbits. This is not to say that the sole task of the courts in such cases is to make a comparison between the harm and the utility of an act. Nor is it to be expected that the courts will always decide correctly after making such a comparison. But unless the courts act very foolishly, the ordinary law of nuisance would seem likely to give economically more satisfactory results than adopting a rigid rule. Pigou's case of the overrunning rabbits affords an excellent example of how problems of law and economics are interrelated, even though the correct policy to follow would seem to be different from that envisioned by Pigou.

Pigou allows one exception to his conclusion that there is a divergence between private and social products in the rabbit example. He adds:

"... unless ... the two occupiers stand in the relation of landlord and tenant, so that compensation is given in an adjustment of the rent."[58] This qualification is rather surprising since Pigou's first class of divergence is largely concerned with the difficulties of drawing up satisfactory contracts between landlords and tenants. In fact, all the recent cases on the problem of rabbits cited by Professor Williams involved disputes between landlords and tenants concerning sporting rights.[59] Pigou seems to make a distinction between the case in which no contract is possible (the second class) and that in which the contract is unsatisfactory (the first class). Thus he says that the second class of divergences between private and social net product

> cannot, like divergences due to tenancy laws, be mitigated by a modification of the contractual relation between any two contracting parties, because the divergence arises out of a service or disservice rendered to persons other than the contracting parties.[60]

But the reason why some activities are not the subject of contracts is exactly the same as the reason why some contracts are commonly unsatisfactory – it would cost too much to put the matter right. Indeed, the two cases are really the same since the contracts are unsatisfactory because they do not cover certain activities. The exact bearing of the discussion of the first class of divergence on Pigou's main argument is difficult to discover. He shows that in some circumstances contractual relations between landlord and tenant may result in a divergence between private and social products.[61] But he also goes on to show that Government-enforced compensation schemes and rent-controls will also produce divergences.[62] Furthermore, he shows that, when the Government is in a similar position to a private landlord, e.g. when granting a franchise to a public utility, exactly the same difficulties arise as when private individuals are involved.[63] The discussion is interesting but I have been unable to discover what general conclusions about economic policy, if any, Pigou expects us to draw from it.

Indeed, Pigou's treatment of the problems considered in this article is extremely elusive and the discussion of his views raises almost insuperable difficulties of interpretation. Consequently it is impossible to be sure that one has understood what Pigou really meant. Nevertheless, it is difficult to resist the conclusion, extraordinary though this may be in an economist of Pigou's stature, that the main source of this obscurity is that Pigou had not thought his position through.

IX The Pigovian Tradition

It is strange that a doctrine as faulty as that developed by Pigou should have been so influential, although part of its success has probably been due to the lack of clarity in the exposition. Not being clear, it was never clearly wrong. Curiously enough, this obscurity in the source has not prevented the emergence of a fairly well-defined oral tradition. What economists think they learn from Pigou, and what they tell their students, which I term the Pigovian tradition, is reasonably clear. I propose to show the inadequacy of this Pigovian tradition by demonstrating that both the analysis and the policy conclusions which it supports are incorrect.

I do not propose to justify my view as to the prevailing opinion by copious references to the literature. I do this partly because the treatment in the literature is usually so fragmentary, often involving little more than a reference to Pigou plus some explanatory comment, that detailed examination would be inappropriate. But the main reason for this lack of reference is that the doctrine, although based on Pigou, must have been largely the product of an oral tradition. Certainly economists with whom I have discussed these problems have shown a unanimity of opinion which is quite remarkable considering the meagre treatment accorded this subject in the literature. No doubt there are some economists who do not share the usual view but they must represent a small minority of the profession.

The approach to the problems under discussion is through an examination of the value of physical production. The private product is the value of the additional product resulting from a particular activity of a business. The social product equals the private product minus the fall in the value of production elsewhere for which no compensation is paid by the business. Thus, if 10 units of a factor (and no other factors) are used by a business to make a certain product with a value of $105; and the owner of this factor is not compensated for their use, which he is unable to prevent; and these 10 units of the factor would yield products in their best alternative use worth $100; then, the social product is $105 minus $100 or $5. If the business now pays for one unit of the factor and its price equals the value of its marginal product, then the social product rises to $15. If two units are paid for, the social product rises to $25 and so on until it reaches $105 when all units of the factor are paid for. It is not difficult to see why economists have so readily accepted this rather odd procedure. The analysis focusses on the individual business decision and since the use of certain resources is not allowed for in costs, receipts are reduced by the same amount. But, of course, this means that the value of the social product has no social significance whatsoever. It seems to me preferable to use the opportunity cost concept and to approach these problems by comparing the value of the product yielded by factors in alternative uses or by alternative arrangements. The main advantage of a pricing system is that it leads to the employment of factors in places where the value of the product yielded is greatest and does so at less cost than alternative systems (I leave aside that a pricing system also eases the problem of the redistribution of income). But if through some God-given natural harmony factors flowed to the places where the value of the product yielded was greatest without any use of the pricing system and consequently there was no compensation, I would find it a source of surprise rather than a cause for dismay.

The definition of the social product is queer but this does not mean that the conclusions for policy drawn from the analysis are necessarily wrong. However, there are bound to be dangers in an approach which diverts attention from the basic issues and there can be little doubt that it has been responsible for some of the errors in current doctrine. The belief that it is desirable that the business which causes harmful effects should be forced to compensate those who suffer damage (which was exhaustively discussed in section VIII in connection with Pigou's railway sparks example) is undoubtedly the result of not comparing the total product obtainable with alternative social arrangements.

The same fault is to be found in proposals for solving the problem of harmful effects by the use of taxes or bounties. Pigou lays considerable stress on this solution although he is, as usual, lacking in detail and qualified in his support.[64] Modern economists tend to think exclusively in terms of taxes and in a very precise way. The tax should be equal to the damage done and should therefore vary with the amount of the harmful effect. As it is not proposed that the proceeds of the tax should be paid to those suffering the damage, this solution is not the same as that which would force a business to pay compensation to those damaged by its actions, although economists generally do not seem to have noticed this and tend to treat the two solutions as being identical.

Assume that a factory which emits smoke is set up in a district previously free from smoke pollution, causing damage valued at $100 per annum. Assume that the taxation solution is adopted and that the factory owner is taxed $100 per annum as long as the factory emits the smoke. Assume further that a smoke-preventing device costing $90 per annum to run is available. In these circumstances, the smoke-preventing device would be installed. Damage of $100 would have been avoided at an expenditure of $90 and the factory-owner would be better off by $10 per annum. Yet the position achieved may not be optimal. Suppose that those who suffer the damage could avoid it by moving to other locations or by taking various precautions which would cost them, or be equivalent to a loss in income of, $40 per annum. Then there would be a gain in the value of production of $50 if the factory continued to emit its smoke and those now in the district moved elsewhere or made other adjustments to avoid the damage. If the factory owner is to be made to pay a tax equal to the damage caused, it would clearly be desirable to institute a double tax system and to make residents of the district pay an amount equal to the additional cost incurred by the factory owner (or the consumers of his products) in order to avoid the damage. In these conditions, people would not stay in the district or would take other measures to prevent the damage from occurring, when the costs of doing so were less than the costs that would be incurred by the producer to reduce the damage (the producer's object, of course, being not so much to reduce the damage as to reduce the tax payments). A tax system which was confined to a tax on the producer for damage caused would tend to lead to unduly high costs being incurred for the prevention of damage. Of course this could be avoided if it were possible to base the tax, not on the damage caused, but on the fall in the value of production (in its widest sense) resulting from the emission of smoke. But to do so would require a detailed knowledge of individual preferences and I am unable to imagine how the data needed for such a taxation system could be assembled. Indeed, the proposal to solve the smoke-pollution and similar problems by the use of taxes bristles with difficulties: the problem of calculation, the difference between average and marginal damage, the interrelations between the damage suffered on different properties, etc. But it is unnecessary to examine these problems here. It is enough for my purpose to show that, even if the tax is exactly adjusted to equal the damage that would be done to neighboring properties as a result of the emission of each additional puff of smoke, the tax would not necessarily bring about optimal conditions. An increase in the number of people living or of business operating in the vicinity of the smoke-emitting factory will increase the amount of harm produced by a given emission of smoke. The tax that would be imposed would therefore increase with an increase in the number of those in the vicinity. This will tend to lead to a decrease in the value of production of the factors employed by the factory, either because a reduction in production due to the tax will result in factors being used elsewhere in ways which are less valuable, or because factors will be diverted to produce means for reducing the amount of smoke emitted. But people deciding to establish themselves in the vicinity of the factory will not take into account this fall in the value of production which results from their presence. This failure to take into account costs imposed on others is comparable to the action of a factory-owner in not taking into account the harm resulting from his emission of smoke. Without the tax, there may be too much smoke and too few people in the vicinity of the factory; but with the tax there may be too little smoke and too many people in the vicinity of the factory. There is no reason to suppose that one of these results is necessarily preferable.

I need not devote much space to discussing the similar error involved in the suggestion that smoke producing factories should, by means of zoning regulations, be removed from the districts in which the smoke causes harmful effects. When the change in the location of the factory results in a reduction in production, this obviously needs to be taken into account and weighed against the harm which would result from the factory remaining in that location. The aim of such regulation should not be to eliminate smoke pollution but rather to secure the optimum amount of smoke pollution, this being the amount which will maximise the value of production.

X   A Change of Approach

It is my belief that the failure of economists to reach correct conclusions about the treatment of harmful effects cannot be ascribed simply to a few slips in analysis. It stems from basic defects in the current approach to problems of welfare economics. What is needed is a change of approach.

Analysis in terms of divergencies between private and social products concentrates attention on particular deficiencies in the system and tends to nourish the belief that any measure which will remove the deficiency is necessarily desirable. It diverts attention from those other changes in the system which are inevitably associated with the corrective measure, changes which may well produce more harm than the original deficiency. In the preceding sections of this article, we have seen many examples of this. But it is not necessary to approach the problem in this way. Economists who study problems of the firm habitually use an opportunity cost approach and compare the receipts obtained from a given combination of factors with alternative business arrangements. It would seem desirable to use a similar approach when dealing with questions of economic policy and to compare the total product yielded by alternative social arrangements. In this article, the analysis has been confined, as is usual in this part of economics, to comparisons of the value of production, as measured by the market. But it is, of course, desirable that the choice between different social arrangements for the solution of economic problems should be carried out in broader terms than this and that the total effect of these arrangements in all spheres of life should be taken into account. As Frank H. Knight has so often emphasized, problems of welfare economics must ultimately dissolve into a study of aesthetics and morals.

A second feature of the usual treatment of the problems discussed in this article is that the analysis proceeds in terms of a comparison between a state of laissez faire and some kind of ideal world. This approach inevitably leads to a looseness of thought since the nature of the alternatives being compared is never clear. In a state of laissez faire, is there a monetary, a legal or a political system and if so, what are they? In an ideal world, would there be a monetary, a legal or a political system and if so, what would they be? The answers to all these questions are shrouded in mystery and every man is free to draw whatever conclusions he likes. Actually very little analysis is required to show that an ideal world is better than a state of laissez faire, unless the definitions of a state of laissez faire and an ideal world happen to be the same. But the whole discussion is largely irrelevant for questions of economic policy since whatever we may have in mind as our ideal world, it is clear that we have not yet discovered how to get to it from where we are. A better approach would seem to be to start our analysis with a situation approximating that which actually exists, to examine the effects of a proposed

policy change and to attempt to decide whether the new situation would be, in total, better or worse than the original one. In this way, conclusions for policy would have some relevance to the actual situation.

A final reason for the failure to develop a theory adequate to handle the problem of harmful effects stems from a faulty concept of a factor of production. This is usually thought of as a physical entity which the businessman acquires and uses (an acre of land, a ton of fertiliser) instead of as a right to perform certain (physical) actions. We may speak of a person owning land and using it as a factor of production but what the land-owner in fact possesses is the right to carry out a circumscribed list of actions. The rights of a land-owner are not unlimited. It is not even always possible for him to remove the land to another place, for instance, by quarrying it. And although it may be possible for him to exclude some people from using "his" land, this may not be true of others. For example, some people may have the right to cross the land. Furthermore, it may or may not be possible to erect certain types of buildings or to grow certain crops or to use particular drainage systems on the land. This does not come about simply because of Government regulation. It would be equally true under the common law. In fact it would be true under any system of law. A system in which the rights of individuals were unlimited would be one in which there were no rights to acquire.

If factors of production are thought of as rights, it becomes easier to understand that the right to do something which has a harmful effect (such as the creation of smoke, noise, smells, etc.) is also a factor of production. Just as we may use a piece of land in such a way as to prevent someone else from crossing it, or parking his car, or building his house upon it, so we may use it in such a way as to deny him a view or quiet or unpolluted air. The cost of exercising a right (of using a factor of production) is always the loss which is suffered elsewhere in consequence of the exercise of that right – the inability to cross land, to park a car, to build a house, to enjoy a view, to have peace and quiet or to breathe clean air.

It would clearly be desirable if the only actions performed were those in which what was gained was worth more than what was lost. But in choosing between social arrangements within the context of which individual decisions are made, we have to bear in mind that a change in the existing system which will lead to an improvement in some decisions may well lead to a worsening of others. Furthermore we have to take into account the costs involved in operating the various social arrangements (whether it be the working of a market or of a government department), as well as the costs involved in moving to a new system. In devising and choosing between social arrangements we should have regard for the total effect. This, above all, is the change in approach which I am advocating.

Notes

1 This article, although concerned with a technical problem of economic analysis, arose out of the study of the Political Economy of Broadcasting which I am now conducting. The argument of the present article was implicit in a previous article dealing with the problem of allocating radio and television frequencies (The Federal Communications Commission, 2 J. Law & Econ. [1959]) but comments which I have received seemed to suggest that it would be desirable to deal with the question in a more explicit way and without reference to the original problem for the solution of which the analysis was developed.

2 Coase, The Federal Communications Commission, 2 J. Law & Econ. 26–27 (1959).

3 G. J. Stigler, The Theory of Price 105 (1952).

4 The argument in the text has proceeded on the assumption that the alternative to cultivation of the crop is abandonment of cultivation altogether. But this need not be so. There may be crops which are less liable to damage by cattle but which would not be as profitable as the crop grown in the absence of damage. Thus, if the cultivation of a new crop would yield a return to the farmer of $1 instead of $2, and the size of the herd which would cause $3 damage with the old crop would cause $1 damage with the new crop, it would be profitable to the cattle-raiser to pay any sum less than $2 to induce the farmer to change

his crop (since this would reduce damage liability from $3 to $1) and it would be profitable for the farmer to do so if the amount received was more than $1 (the reduction in his return caused by switching crops). In fact, there would be room for a mutually satisfactory bargain in all cases in which a change of crop would reduce the amount of damage by more than it reduces the value of the crop (excluding damage) – in all cases, that is, in which a change in the crop cultivated would lead to an increase in the value of production.

5 See Gale on Easements 237–39 (13th ed. M. Bowles 1959).

6 See Fontaineblue Hotel Corp. v. Forty-Five Twenty-Five, Inc., 114 So. 2d 357 (1959).

7 11 Ch. D. 852 (1879).

8 Auscultation is the act of listening by ear or stethoscope in order to judge by sound the condition of the body.

9 Note that what is taken into account is the change in income after allowing for alterations in methods of production, location, character of product, etc.

10 L. R. 5 Eq. 166 (1867–1868).

11 4 C.P.D. 172 (1878–1879).

12 25 Q.B.D. 481 (1890).

13 It may be asked why a lost grant could not also be presumed in the case of the confectioner who had operated one mortar for more than 60 years. The answer is that until the doctor built the consulting room at the end of his garden there was no nuisance. So the nuisance had not continued for many years. It is true that the confectioner in his affidavit referred to "an invalid lady who occupied the house upon one occasion, about thirty years before" who "requested him if possible to discontinue the use of the mortars before eight o'clock in the morning" and that there was some evidence that the garden wall had been subjected to vibration. But the court had little difficulty in disposing of this line of argument: ". . . this vibration, even if it existed at all, was so slight, and the complaint, if it can be called a complaint, of the invalid lady . . . was of so trifling a character, that . . . the Defendant's acts would not have given rise to any proceeding either at law or in equity" (11 Ch.D. 863). That is, the confectioner had not committed a nuisance until the doctor built his consulting room.

14 See Coase, The Nature of the Firm, 4 Economica, New Series, 386 (1937). Reprinted in Readings in Price Theory, 331 (1952).

15 For reasons explained in my earlier article, see Readings in Price Theory, n. 14 at 337.

16 See W. L. Prosser, The Law of Torts 398–99, 412 (2d ed. 1955). The quotation about the ancient case concerning candle-making is taken from Sir James Fitzjames Stephen, A General View of the Criminal Law of England 106 (1890). Sir James Stephen gives no reference. He perhaps had in mind *Rex. v. Ronkett*, included in Seavey, Keeton and Thurston, Cases on Torts 604 (1950). A similar view to that expressed by Prosser is to be found in F. V. Harper and F. James, The Law of Torts 67–74 (1956); Restatement, Torts § § 826, 827 and 828.

17 See Winfield on Torts 541–48 (6th ed. T. E. Lewis 1954); Salmond on the Law of Torts 181–90 (12th ed. R.F.V. Heuston 1957); H. Street, The Law of Torts 221–29 (1959).

18 Attorney General v. Doughty, 2 Ves. Sen. 453, 28 Eng. Rep. 290 (Ch. 1752). Compare in this connection the statement of an American judge, quoted in Prosser, op. cit. supra n. 16 at 413 n. 54: "Without smoke, Pittsburgh would have remained a very pretty village," Musmanno, J., in Versailles Borough v. McKeesport Coal & Coke Co., 1935, 83 Pitts. Leg. J. 379, 385.

19 10 C.B. (N.S.) 268, 142 Eng. Rep. 445 (1861); 13 C.B. (N.S.) 841, 143 Eng. Rep. 332 (1863).

20 See Gale on Easements 238, n. 6 (13th ed. M. Bowles 1959).

21 11 Ch.D. 865 (1879).

22 Salmond on the Law of Torts 182 (12th ed. R.F.V. Heuston 1957).

23 C.M. Haar, Land-Use Planning, A Casebook on the Use, Misuse, and Re-use of Urban Land 95 (1959).

24 See, for example, Rushmer v. Polsue and Alfieri, Ltd. [1906] 1 Ch. 234, which deals with the case of a house in a quiet situation in a noisy district.

25 [1913] 1 Ch. 269.

26 [1938] 1 Ch. 1.

27 See 30 Halsbury, Law of England 690–91 (3d ed. 1960), Article on Public Authorities and Public Officers.

28 See Prosser, op. cit. supra n. 16 at 421; Harper and James, op. cit. supra n. 16 at 86–87.

29 Supreme Court of Georgia. 193 Ga. 862, 20 S.E. 2d 245 (1942).

30 178 Ga. 514, 173 S.E. 817 (1934).

31 116 Ga. 64, 42 S.E. 315 (1902).

32 270 Mass. 511, 523, 170 N.E. 385, 390 (1930).

33 See Sir Alfred Denning, Freedom Under the Law 71 (1949).

34 M. B. Cairns, The Law of Tort in Local Government 28–32 (1954).

35 A. C. Pigou, The Economics of Welfare 183 (4th ed. 1932). My references will all be to the fourth edition but the argument and examples examined in this article remained substantially unchanged from the first edition in 1920 to the fourth in 1932. A large part (but not all) of this analysis had appeared previously in Wealth and Welfare (1912).

36 *Id.* at xii.

37 *Id.* at 127–30.

38 In Wealth and Welfare, Pigou attributes the "optimism" to Adam Smith himself and not to his followers. He there refers to the "highly optimistic theory of Adam Smith that the national dividend, in given circumstances of demand and supply, tends 'naturally' to a maximum" (p. 104).

39 Pigou, op. cit. supra n. 35 at 129–30.

40 *Id.* at 134.

41 See 31 Halsbury, Laws of England 474–75 (3d ed. 1960), Article on Railways and Canals, from which this summary of the legal position, and all quotations, are taken.

42 See 152 H.C. Deb. 2622–63 (1922); 161 H.C. Deb. 2935–55 (1923).

43 Vaughan v. Taff Vale Railway Co., 3 H. and N. 743 (Ex. 1858) and 5 H. and N. 679 (Ex. 1860).

44 Sir Dennis Robertson, I Lectures on Economic Principles 162 (1957).

45 E. J. Mishan, The Meaning of Efficiency in Economics, 189 The Bankers' Magazine 482 (June 1960).

46 Pigou, op. cit. supra n. 35 at 184.

47 *Id.* at 185–86.

48 *Id.* at 186 n. 1. For similar unqualified statements see Pigou's lecture "Some Aspects of the Housing Problem" in B. S. Rowntree and A. C. Pigou, Lectures on Housing, in 18 Manchester Univ. Lectures (1914).

49 See G. L. Williams, Liability for Animals—An Account of the Development and Present Law of Tortious Liability for Animals, Distress Damage Feasant and the Duty to Fence, in Great Britain, Northern Ireland and the Common Law Dominions (1939). Part Four, "The Action of Nuisance, in Relation to Liability for Animals," 236–62, is especially relevant to our discussion. The problem of liability for rabbits is discussed

in this part, 238–47. I do not know how far the common law in the United State regarding liability for animals has diverged from that in Britain. In some Western States of the United States, the English common law regarding the duty to fence has not been followed, in part because "the considerable amount of open, uncleared land made it a matter of public policy to allow cattle to run at large" (Williams, *op. cit. supra 227*). This affords a good example of how a different set of circumstances may make it economically desirable to change the legal rule regarding the delimitation of rights.

50 5 Coke (Vol. 3) 104 b. 77 Eng. Rep., 216, 217.

51 See Stearn v. Prentice Bros. Ltd., (1919) 1 K.B., 395, 397.

52 I have not looked into recent cases. The legal position has also been modified by statutory enactments.

53 Williams, op. cit. supra n. 49 at 242, 258.

54 Boulston v. Hardy, Cro. Eliz., 547, 548, 77 Eng. Rep. 216.

55 Williams, op. cit. supra n. 49 at 243.

56 58 Sol. J. 612 (1913–1914).

57 Williams, op. cit. supra n. 49 at 259.

58 Pigou, op. cit. supra n. 35 at 185.

59 Williams, op. cit. supra n. 49 at 244–47.

60 Pigou, op. cit. supra n. 35 at 192.

61 *Id.* 174–75.

62 *Id.* 177–83.

63 *Id.* 175–77.

64 *Id.* 192–4, 381 and Public Finance 94–100 (3d ed. 1947).

Index